A FIELD GUIDE TO
PLANTS OF COSTA RICA

A FIELD GUIDE to PLANTS of COSTA RICA

Margaret B. Gargiullo

With photographs by
Barbara L. Magnuson
& Larry D. Kimball

WITHDRAWN

OXFORD
UNIVERSITY PRESS
2008

OXFORD
UNIVERSITY PRESS

Oxford University Press, Inc., publishes works that further
Oxford University's objective of excellence
in research, scholarship, and education.

Oxford New York
Auckland Cape Town Dar es Salaam Hong Kong Karachi
Kuala Lumpur Madrid Melbourne Mexico City Nairobi
New Delhi Shanghai Taipei Toronto

With offices in
Argentina Austria Brazil Chile Czech Republic France Greece
Guatemala Hungary Italy Japan Poland Portugal Singapore
South Korea Switzerland Thailand Turkey Ukraine Vietnam

Published by Oxford University Press, Inc.
198 Madison Avenue, New York, New York 10016

www.oup.com

Oxford is a registered trademark of Oxford University Press

Library of Congress Cataloging-in-Publication Data
Gargiullo, Margaret B., 1942–
A field guide to plants of Costa Rica / Margaret B. Gargiullo ; with
photographs by Barbara L. Magnuson and Larry D. Kimball.
        p. cm.
    Includes bibliographical references and index.
    ISBN 978-0-19-518824-0; 978-0-19-518825-7 (pbk.)
    Identification.   2. Plants—Costa Rica—Pictorial works.   I. Magnuson,
    Barbara L., 1952–   II. Kimball, Larry D., 1946–   III. Title.
        QK217.G37   2007
        581.97286—dc22   2006035979

9 8 7 6 5 4 3 2 1

Printed in China
on acid-free paper

Dedicated to the memory of Dr. Ted Stiles
who saved so much land, and taught
so many people to love all that
blooms, burrows, creeps, and flies.

To my husband, Robert,
and my son, Michael,
and to all the people of Costa Rica
who are helping conserve the
diverse habitats and incredibly
rich flora of this lovely country.
—MBG

To all those who are in awe of
and appreciate the natural world.
—BLM and LDK

TROPICAL AMERICA (NEOTROPICS)

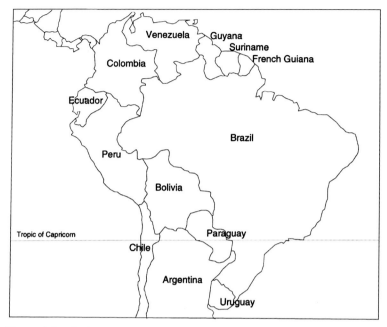

Tropical South America

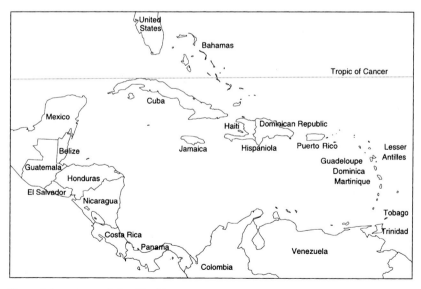

Central America and the Caribbean

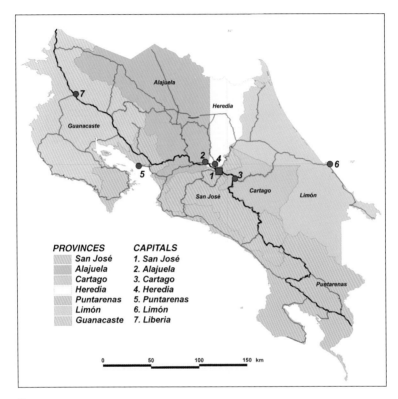

PROVINCES
San José
Alajuela
Cartago
Heredia
Puntarenas
Limón
Guanacaste

CAPITALS
1. San José
2. Alajuela
3. Cartago
4. Heredia
5. Puntarenas
6. Limón
7. Liberia

0   50   100   150 km

Provinces

CONTENTS

PREFACE

GENESIS AND MISSION

In 1990, I took a course in tropical ecology given by the Organization for Tropical Studies (OTS/OET). During that time I was continually frustrated by the lack of guidebooks to the wonderful plants surrounding us. Descriptions of these plants were generally scattered in technical papers and monographs, some from the late 1800s. When I returned to Costa Rica a couple of years later, it occurred to me that, since no one else was writing a guidebook to Costa Rican plants, I might take on such a project both to learn the flora for myself and to share it with other plant enthusiasts. The immense hubris of this plan concerned me, since I was a newly minted plant ecologist from North America, not a tropical botanist, nor a taxonomic expert, so many of whom have spent lifetimes studying these plants.

At the same time, wildlife photographers Barbara Magnuson and Larry Kimball were also frustrated by the lack of guidebooks to the plants they were encountering in Costa Rica. They asked Gail Hewson, then codirector of the Wilson Botanical Garden at Las Cruces Biological Station, to help them find a botanist with whom they could work on a guidebook to Costa Rican plants. Gail introduced us to one another in 1994, and so we began this project.

We have written this book for tourists, students, and urban dwelling Costa Ricans to offer a door into the "wall of green" that faces most visitors when they come to Costa Rican natural areas. We hope that giving the names, characters, and portraits of a few frequently encountered and conspicuous plants will help bring together the observer and the observed. It may be also that some who read this guide might go on to delve deeper into this flora.

—Margaret B. Gargiullo

ACKNOWLEDGMENTS

During the 14 years we have been developing this book, many experts helped us. Principle among these are Barry Hammel and Michael Grayum of the Missouri Botanical Garden, without whom the project could not have been done. They are two of the editors and authors completing *Manual de Plantas de Costa Rica*, a multivolume technical work that describes all 10,000 or so plants found in Costa Rica. Both Barry and Michael recommended lists of species to include in our guidebook and offered continued assistance over the years as a final species list took shape. Both have identified numerous plants and helped with technical descriptions of many species that we have included in the guidebook. Michael also was kind enough to look through hundreds of photographic slides and read my accompanying field notes to double-check and correct plant identities. William Burger, Curator Emeritus, Field Museum of Natural History in Chicago, and editor of *Flora Costaricensis*, was instrumental in editing and correcting technical errors in the taxonomy of the draft manuscript. He checked for errors in the matches between 1300 photos and text descriptions that will accompany them. He also filled in missing data for a number of my incomplete plant descriptions. For all this we are exceedingly grateful.

Numerous other people were instrumental in helping us find and identify plants in the field. Luis Diego Gómez, former Director, Wilson Botanical Garden, Las Cruces Biological Station, identified a number of ferns and other plant samples we brought to him. Orlando Vargas, former Scientific Director's Assistant at La Selva Biological Station, helped us locate and identify numerous plants at La Selva. Ulises Chavarria was our guide to plants in and around Palo Verde National Park, and Gerardo Herrera guided us to many places off the beaten track around Rio Macho Forest Reserve and Tapantí National Park. We would have missed many important plants without the help of these last three very able naturalists.

After the collecting and photographing of our selected plants, we had to identify each plant and secure valid expert confirmation of that identity. For their help with plant identifications we would like to thank the National Institute of Biodiversity (Instituto Nacional de Biodiversidad [INBio]) for use of its herbarium, both to process plant materials and for the use of their specimen collection to identify plants. Many of the taxonomists at INBio identified plants for us. We especially want to thank Nelson Zamora and Francisco Morales, who identified numerous species from many plant families both from specimens and from slides (a much more difficult task). Other INBio taxonomists who helped similarly include Reinaldo Aguilar, José González, Quirico Jiménez, Alexander Rodriguez, Alexander Rojas, and Armando Soto S., Herbarium Curator. We also thank Jorge Jiménez, former Director of Inventory, for his support and encouragement.

We have also been given generous help with these same processing and identification tasks at the Herbarium of the National Museum (Herbarío Nacional de Costa Rica, Museo Nacional). Members of the botanical staff whose assistance we especially appreciate include Armando Ruiz, Alfredo

Cascante, Armando Estrada Chevarría, Vanda Nilsson Laurito, Gerardo Rivera I., Silvia Lobo, Herbarium Curator, and, for her warm encouragement, Melania Ortiz Volio, former Director of the National Museum.

Although Michael Grayum identified the majority of specimens or confirmed their identities for us, there remained numerous plants whose identities were in doubt. This was partly because it is much more difficult to identify a plant from a photographic slide than from a pressed specimen, all of which we left in Costa Rica at the National Herbarium. Therefore, we thank a number of taxonomists at the Missouri Botanical Garden and other institutions who undertook this task. These include Charlotte Taylor, for her very generous help with many difficult species of Rubiaceae; Amy Pool, for species of Lamiaceae; Gerrit Davidse, for help with grasses; Jon Ricketson and Roger Sanders, for help with *Ardisia* and *Stachytarpheta*, respectively. Some very difficult orchids were identified from our photographs by Robert L. Dressler, Eric Hágsater, Calaway H. Dodson, and John Atwood, for which we thank them very much.

We also thank Lucinda McDade, Academy of Natural Sciences, Philadelphia, who helped us identify several Acanthaceae and was also one of the early and supportive reviewers of our guidebook proposal. We thank Lynn Bohs, University of Utah, for her identification of Solanaceae; Jorge Gómez Laurito, University of Costa Rica, for identification of species in the notoriously difficult family Cyperaceae; Paul A. Fryxell, University of Texas, for his identification of some difficult Malvaceae; Ricardo Callejas, Universidad de Antioquia, for his tireless work identifying a number of difficult Piperaceae; Robbin Moran, New York Botanical Garden, who identified numerous ferns and fern allies; Helen Kennedy, University of British Columbia, who helped us with several Marantaceae; Frank Almeda, California Academy of Science, who identified a number of Melastomataceae; and Lynn Clark, Iowa State University, who identified several bamboos.

Other taxonomists who identified plants for us include Alina Freire-Fierro, Missouri Botanical Garden; Marian Stafford, Department of Botany, Natural History Museum, London; Henricus Sipman, Berlin Herbarium, Germany; Alan Whittemore, U.S. National Arboretum, Washington, D.C.; Theodore Barkley, Botanical Research Institute of Texas; and James Zech, Herbarium, Department of Biology, Sul Ross State University, Alpine, Texas. We thank you all. Thanks also to Barbara Thiers, Director, New York Botanical Garden Herbarium, who assisted us with invaluable access to the garden's magnificent herbarium collection.

Over the 14 years we have worked on the guidebook, we have received support, encouragement, and guidance from numerous people. We are especially grateful to Peter Prescott, our editor at Oxford University Press, for his support, attention, patience, and diplomacy through the process of acquisition and publication.

We would like to thank Donald Stone, Professor Emeritus, Department of Botany, Duke University, former Director of the Organization for Tropical Studies (OTS), for his encouragement and assistance over a number of years. Thanks also to several anonymous reviewers who gave useful critiques of early drafts of the guidebook. Thanks to Kirk Jensen, formerly of Oxford University Press, an early enthusiast for publication of the guidebook; Peter H. Raven, Director of the Missouri Botanical Garden; and Fabio Rojas at INBio Press for their interest in publication of the guidebook. Thanks to

Annie Simpson de Gamboa and other staff members of OTS who helped me (M.B.G.) with obtaining and renewing my collecting permits and acting as intermediaries with the officials at the Ministry of the Environment and Energy (MINAE) and the National System of Conservation Areas (SINAC). We also received letters of support from Marco Tulio Picado, then of the Costarican Institute of Tourism; Mario A. Boza, then the Vice Minister of Natural Resources; Rolando Mendoza Hernándes, then of the Foundation for Environmental Education; and Virginia Rojas Arroyo, Ministry of Public Education.

For our "home away from home," in San José, a heartfelt *muchas gracias* to Elecxa and Edgar Zamora of Hotel Cacts for their material support of this project and for their warm friendship over the years. We would also like to thank Ricardo Alric of ATEC who guided us in and around Gandoca-Manzanillo Refuge; Ronald Muzman Mora, our guide near Puerto Jimenez on the OSA Peninsula; and last but not least, Chepo Hernandez Perez, who guided us around Mastatal and La Cangreja, and his wife, Odilie Perez Hidalgo, a most excellent cook.

INTRODUCTION

As you travel down a highway or hike a trail that parallels a river, notice the water. Is it flowing so clear and pure that you would like to drink from it? Can you see every color and detail of the pebbles lying on the river bed? Can you watch the fish swim lazily by as you dip your sockless feet into the water to cool them? Is it a little roily from a recent rain, or do you see only brown murky water flowing over that which you can just barely, if at all, make out? This is the difference between a river originating from and flowing through a pristine rainforest and one that originates from or flows through "developed" land or clear-cut forest.

Without the forest trees and all other ground-covering flora protecting the soils from washing into stream beds, the rivers turn dark, silty... undrinkable. Aside from this one simple example of the value of a forest, there are scores of other reasons to preserve our forests, no matter where they are.

Costa Rican rainforests are among the most accessible of the world's tropical forests in which we are currently discovering the vital nature of this ecosystem. They provide nesting or wintering habitats for many of the world's migrating bird species. In Costa Rica alone, 850 species of birds have been observed, more than are found on the entire North American continent. There are more forest types than occur in all of temperate North America. Of the 10,000 plant species existing here, many may have biological or medical properties and benefits yet to be discovered. The tropical forest serves as a storehouse for species diversity, producing foods, woods, medicines, fibers, resins, and other animal and vegetable products.

La Paz waterfall, near Braulio Carrillo N.P.

Our objective for compiling this guide is to fill a void. The study of this environment is still in relative infancy, and as a result, not much literature has been made available for the benefit of the general public. We hope you will find this book an indispensable reference to some of the most common plants you will see in Costa Rica while discovering the priceless nature of each, in its relationship to the entire ecosystem. Finally, it is our sincerest wish that you will be inspired to learn more and take an active role in the preservation of a fragile and diverse environment that could soon be lost forever.

Eroded hillside in deforested area. Courtesy of Margaret Gargiullo

GEOGRAPHY

Costa Rica lies 10 degrees north of the equator and is part of the bridge that links North America to South America. Because of this geographic placement and a favorable tropical climate, we find a tremendously diverse ecosystem containing endemic species as well as flora and fauna characteristic of both continents. It is situated between two oceans, the Atlantic and the Pacific, with the countries of Nicaragua to the north and Panama to the south. This 51,032 sq km (20,000 sq mi) territory is a mere 300 km (185 mi) across at its widest point and 125 km (75 mi) at its narrowest. Four mountain ranges divide the east from the west. The oldest and southernmost range is the Cordillera de Talamanca, where you will find Mount Chirripó, the highest in southern Central America at 3820 m (12,500 ft). Over half of Costa Rica's 2.9 million inhabitants live in the Central Valley and in the vicinity of the Central Volcanic Range. In various stages of activity, the volcanoes Turrialba, Irazú, Barva, and Poás make up this range and are responsible for the two-million-year accumulation of fertile soils that has supported indigenous people for thousands of years and drawn European settlers here for hundreds of years. Further to the northwest lies the nonvolcanic Tilarán Range, 1700 m (5500 ft) in elevation at its highest point. The Monteverde Cloud Forest Preserve is representative. Farthest northwest, the Guanacaste Range contains five active volcanoes including Rincón de la Vieja, 1806 m (5925 ft); Miravalles, 2028 m (6653 ft); and Volcán Arenal, 1633 m (5358 ft).

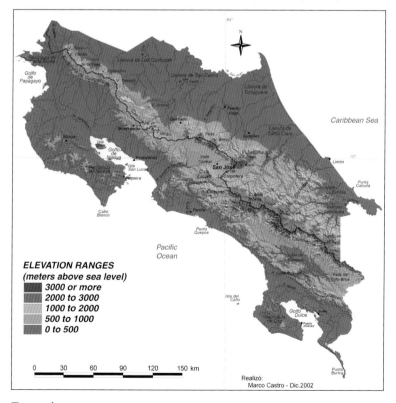

Topography

CLIMATE

The marked contrast in topography lends itself to a remarkable range of climate conditions. Take a day's drive and you can experience a crisp 10 to 13°C (50 to 55°F) in the misty highlands, a warm, humid 22°C (72°F) in the Central Valley, a hot, dry 26°C (80°F) tempered by sea breezes on the Guanacaste coast, and a hot, humid 26 to 32°C (80 to 90°F) at sea level in Limón or Puntarenas. Frost and temperatures below freezing have been recorded in the Talamanca Range, at Mount Chirripó. The wet and dry seasons are controlled largely by the northeast trade winds, the mountain chains running like a backbone down the length of Costa Rica, and the doldrums, a tropical zone of rising air that follows the sun north and south. The dry season, referred to as summer (verano, in Spanish), is usually December to April in San Jose and the west and until May in Guanacaste. It is during this period that the Guanacaste region may receive no moisture at all. The east coast is driest from February to April, although there is no definite dry season due to the moisture-laden trade winds coming from North America's northeastern, discharging moisture against the Cordilleras. The Osa Peninsula experiences a similar phenomenon when the southeastern trades come up against the mountains separating it from the rest of the country.

The rainy winter season (invierno) generally starts in May and continues through November. On the Pacific side, the wettest months are September and October. As you go farther south, the length of the wet season increases, and some areas, such as Golfo Dulce, may have virtually no dry season. Annual rainfall varies from 5 m (197 inches) in the south to less than 1.5 m (59 inches) in the central and northwest portions of the country. The Osa Peninsula may be the exception with up to 7 m (300 inches) of rainfall per year.

On the Atlantic (Caribbean) side, the rains begin in late April and end in January. The wettest time is November through January. The heaviest rainfall, exceeding 9 m (355 inches) per year, falls inland, while the coastal beaches may remain in sunshine. The remainder of the Caribbean lowlands average from 3 to 5 m (118 to 200 inches) annually.

NOTES FOR PHOTOGRAPHERS

The most obvious condition to be dealt with when photographing in the rain forest is . . . rain.

Keeping equipment dry when surrounded by foliage dripping from fog, mist, or rain is a challenge. When wading an estuary, waist-deep in saltwater during a downpour (as you might do at Manuel Antonio), keeping that same equipment dry becomes something more than a challenge.

Carrying camera equipment in a water-resistant case or pack, or at least under a waterproof garment, is a good start, but how do you keep the stuff dry when using it?

Rain covers, the kind that allow you to use the camera and still protect it, are a great investment. They can be custom made to fit each camera and lens combination that you might consistently use. An inexpensive alternative could be a plastic shower cap or garbage bag placed over the camera while moving about, and an umbrella to keep you and the camera dry for that one great shot. A simple towel or washcloth draped over camera and lens will protect nicely if there is a very light mist or a small amount of moisture dripping from the leaves, and either is handy to blot up droplets that will get on things no matter how careful we are. A lens hood is a good accessory for not only keeping stray light from the lens but preventing you from bumping the front element with a wet leaf.

Some recommend using lots of silica packets to protect equipment from excess moisture, but unless you have access to an oven in which to dry them, they become useless after a few days. Most people will spend just a week or two in and out of the wet and, with simple precautions, will have no problems with moisture building up in their equipment. We have found that avoiding some of the rain can be fairly easy, because in many areas, the mornings are dry, with the rain starting in the afternoon or evening. It becomes easier still during the dry season.

The lack of light is another hurdle, but like precipitation, it simply goes with the territory. Cloudy skies and dark foliage under the forest canopy can be a problem. Digital cameras allow greater flexibility with a simple change of the ISO settings and white balance. Fast 400 ISO film is an easy solution for film cameras but tends to be grainy, so we generally use 50 and 100 ISO slide films, using the slower speed on still subjects such as plant life. There are several solutions to slow film in low-light conditions. One is simply using a slow shutter speed and a tripod—indispensable for sharp photos. Another would be a reflector, commercial or home-made, with some aluminum foil adhered to a piece of cardboard or the backside of a 18 percent gray card, useful at times when metering is difficult. A white umbrella works nicely and does double duty as shelter from the rain. Fill flash is another very useful accessory and necessary at times, with or without a tripod. These suggestions, used in combination, will see you through most difficult low-light situations.

A circular polarizing filter for both digital and film cameras can be used to reduce leaf shine on many tropical plants with a very waxy surface, and a warming filter or the cloudy white balance setting will warm up cool shadows and enhance the quality of the photo.

Of course sometimes there is too much light, along forest edges or in light gaps under the canopy, causing extreme contrasts between light and shadow. For closeups, the shadow from a hat or white umbrella, making a less harsh shadow, will help moderate bright light. Other times you must simply meter for the subject and let some areas go light or dark.

Dust may not seem a problem in the rain forest, but during the dry season, unpaved roads get very dusty, and if you are near Volcán Arenal, volcanic ash will drift down over everything. Keep your equipment cased or covered whenever possible, and exercise care whenever changing film or lenses by gently brushing or blowing out the interior of your camera to prevent scratching film or spotting the digital sensor. Taping plastic bag material over camera joints can help to seal out dust and sand.

Another consideration is heat. Keep film out of the sun, and while traveling try to store equipment in the coolest area of the vehicle. That is not always possible if using public transportation, but a white towel (the one you used earlier to help keep things dry) used to cover a camera case will reflect a lot of direct sun coming through a window. A small inexpensive Styrofoam cooler works great for storing film, if you have the space.

When taking a picture of that incredible flower you have just come across, please remember that you are in a fragile environment. Avoid trampling other plants in order to get to the one you want to photograph. A telephoto lens can help get you into closer proximity without physically being there. A small clothespin or piece of string can be used to temporarily hold branches and leaves out of the way. Friends can be very helpful accessories for these awkward moments. Most importantly, visitors should avoid picking wildflowers or uprooting plants. They are vital elements to the health of an ecosystem and the wildlife that depends on them. Follow the camper's motto and leave only footprints, take only photographs.

The best advice, however, is to bring lots of film or memory cards, a sense of adventure, and enjoy the amazing diversity of this beautiful country!

—B. L. Magnuson and L. D. Kimball

A LITTLE TROPICAL PLANT ECOLOGY

Life Zones

Costa Rica's varied topography causes tremendous changes in rainfall, temperature, and vegetation from one part of the country to another. Ecologists divide Costa Rica into as many as 12 zones differing in climate and plant life, but we have combined several of the most similar to form just

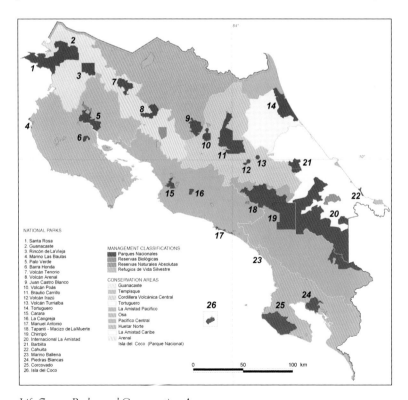

Life Zones, Parks, and Conservation Areas

Forest at Carara Biological Reserve

four major zones. The transitions between various life zones are gradual, and there are no hard dividing lines between each zone. A complete discussion of Costa Rican ecology can be found in D. H. Janzen's *Costa Rican Natural History* (1983).

Tropical Moist Forest is the most widespread zone and is found in many conservation areas (see map), including Pacífico Central (PAC), La Amistad Pacífico (LAP), La Amistad Caribe (LAC), Huetar Norte (HNO), Guanacaste (GUA), and Arenal (ARE). These areas receive roughly 2 to 4 m (80 to 160 inches) of rainfall a year, with a dry season from January through March. Moist forests are evergreen or partly deciduous. These are tall forests with trees up to 50 m (164 ft), many palms, vines, lianas, and very large herbs.

Ceiba pentandra at La Selva Biological Station

Tropical Wet Forest (including very wet rain forest) is the second most abundant life zone, concentrated mostly in the southwest and northeast lowlands of Osa and Tortuguero Conservation Areas, and parts of the Cordillera Volcánica Central around Tapantí National Park. These areas may receive 4–6 m (13–20 ft) of rain a year. There is a short dry season on the Pacific side but none on the Caribbean, although it rains less from January through March. Wet forests are evergreen with very tall trees reaching up to 55 m (180 ft). The understory has many palms, shrubs, and very large herbs. These wet, warm forests have more species than any other regions in the country.

Wet, lowland forest, Caño Palma waterway, Tortuguero N.P.

Tropical Dry Forest is found in the lowlands of northwest Costa Rica, mainly Guanacaste and Tempisque Conservation Areas, but extending eastward to San José and Cartago in the Central Valley. The driest lowlands of this region feature high temperatures and no rain for six months of the year. The forest is mostly leafless during that time. However, many trees bloom during the dry season. The trees are not as tall as those in moist and wet forests, up to 30 m (98 ft), and many small trees and shrubs are thorny. The forest canopy is also not as dense as those in wetter forests. The forest floor tends to be clear. During the dry season, streams dry up temporarily. Moisture loving plants are sometimes found along waterways. Pollinators and seed disseminators, such as butterflies, wasps, bats, and birds, increase their activity during this time and become more concentrated in areas where there is water.

Forest understory, Santa Rosa N.P.

Wet Mountain Forest, usually referred to as montane rain forest, extends in elevation from premontane rain forests, about 500 to 1500 m (1640 to 4920 ft) elevation, through higher-elevation montane oak forests, with a range of about 1200 to 3000 m (3936 to 9840 ft), and elfin forest, which is found at an elevation range of about 2000 to 3200 m (6560 to 10,496 ft). The trees in these rainy, misty forests are variable in height, becoming quite short near

Seasonally dry forest and marsh at Palo Verde N.P.

Tapantí N.P., forest interior

Elfin forest near Volcán Poás crater

the tree line, which occurs at roughly 3100 to 3300 m (10,168 to 10,824 ft).

The habitats referred to as *cloud forest* generally occur at about 1500 to 2000 m (1640 to 6560 ft) elevation. The trees are usually covered with mosses, lichens, fungi, ferns, orchids, and herbs. Tree ferns are abundant in mountain forests as temperatures grow cooler with increased elevation. Rincón de la Vieja National Park, Monteverde Cloud Forest Preserve, the adjacent Children's Rainforest Preserve, and Braulio Carrillo and Tapantí National Parks are fine examples of this cloud forest habitat.

At the highest elevations, 3200 to 3800 m (10,496 to 12,464 ft), nighttime temperatures often dip below freezing, greatly limiting the numbers of plant species. On high mountain peaks of the Cordillera de Talamanca, such as Cerro de la Muerte, and in Chirripó National Park, it can be cold, misty, and very windy

Montane oak forest, Rio Macho Forest Reserve

Cloud forest with Guzmania nicaraguensis, *Braulio Carrillo N.P.*

much of the time. The vegetation in this area, called *páramo*, is treeless, consisting of shrubs, dwarf bamboo, and herbs.

The Changing Forest

A tropical forest may look unchanging, dominated by huge canopy trees with an understory of palms and shrubs. Thick lianas wind upward into the tops of the trees reaching for the sun, while shade-tolerant ferns and other large herbs cover the forest floor. However, a tropical forest is full of plant activity in slow motion. The most fundamental activity is photosynthesis, the chemical reactions that combine carbon dioxide and water to make sugar, using the energy from sunlight. Chlorophyll, the green pigment in plants, captures sunlight to make photosynthesis possible. The abundant water and warmth of a wet tropical forest are vital to its prolific life, but sunlight is the foundation for all of this life. As animals must compete for available food, so too, plants in a forest must find ways to get enough light. Forest plants follow different strategies to ensure they get light to live and grow. Some need bright sun and must have open space. These are *gap colonizers* or *pioneer species* and shoot up quickly into open spaces left by large fallen trees. *Cecropia* species are typical pioneers. Other plants specialize in making the most of very dim light and can grow in the heavily shaded understory in which most other plants would starve. For-

Cerro de la Muerte, continental divide

Páramo on Cerro de la Muerte with Chusquea subtessellata, Diplostephium costaricense, *and* Myrrhidendron donnellsmithii

est floor dwellers jostle each other for the sun flecks that slant down through the canopy; saplings of shade-tolerant trees bide their time, hardly changing for years as they wait for a forest giant to fall and open up a space in the canopy. When a huge branch, laden with ferns, orchids, and bromeliads crashes to the ground, crushing palms, herbs, and saplings, it opens up space for others to take advantage of new light. The death of a large tree opens up a gap for trees and other plants that cannot grow in the dim light under a closed canopy. Seedlings often colonize the decaying trunks of fallen trees, escaping competition from plants on the forest floor. The forest is always a mixture of old stands and newer growth that helps perpetuate its tremendous diversity.

Partners in the Soil

One of the most active parts of the forest is in the soil, where insects, worms, and other small invertebrates start to decompose fallen leaves, branches, and animal

Forest layers, Monteverde

Roots of a fallen tree with seedling, La Selva Biological Station

Tree growing on a log, La Selva Biological Station

Cup fungus Cookeina speciosa
Ascomycota

remains. Fungi and bacteria complete the decay processes that return nitrogen, phosphorus, and trace minerals to the soil to be taken up by roots and once again incorporated into living plants. These nutrient cycles support all the plants and animals of the forests.

Fungi play another vital role in the forest as symbiotic (*sym* meaning *together*, and *bios* meaning *living*) partners of roots. Certain types of fungi are incorporated into the structure of roots and help them take up nutrients. In return, the host plant supplies the fungi with carbohydrates (sugars and starches). When large areas of forest are clear-cut, the most serious loss may be the soil fungi that support the trees and other plants. Without the shelter of the forest, the fungi die, and without the fungi the forest cannot reestablish itself even when the land is no longer cultivated or grazed. Erosion of soil, no longer held in place by roots, further degrades land and makes reestablishment of a forest more difficult.

While most plants must get their nitrogen from the soil, some plants can use nitrogen from the air to sustain themselves. These plants are legumes (families Fabaceae/Caesalpinioideae, Fabaceae/Faboideae, Fabaceae/Mimosoideae), recognizable by their fruit pods containing beanlike seeds. Legumes and a few other plant families (e.g., Gunneraceae and *Alnus*) have symbiotic bacteria that grow in small nodules in their roots. These bacteria take nitrogen gas from the air and chemically modify it into a form usable by the plant. With these bacterial partners, legumes can grow in low-nutrient, degraded, or eroded soils that cannot support most other plants.

Epiphytes

In forests with abundant moisture, many plants are able to grow on other plants, obtaining their water from rain and capturing nutrients from dust and debris that collect around their leaves and roots. *Epiphyte* means *upon plant*. Tree trunks and branches, especially those with rough bark, are host to mosses, ferns, bromeliads (relatives of pineapples), aroids (relatives of philodendrons), orchids, and many others. Aroids send out many thin aerial roots that hang down around a tree or adhere tightly to its trunk. The trunks of many trees may be totally covered by epiphytes, aerial roots, and vines. The older leaves of most plants also may have a covering of mosses and lichens. The leaves of most large

Nematoloma *sp.*, *Basidiomycota*   *Pentaclethra macroloba seedling, La Selva*

trees are obscured from view at ground level by intervening foliage of epiphytic shrubs and small trees growing on larger branches. Some epiphytic
plants, such as mistletoes, are parasites that derive nourishment directly from
the host tree. However, most epiphytes harm their host only indirectly by
overburdening branches that eventually break from the weight. There is an
ongoing controversy about whether epiphytes harm their hosts by compet-
ing for water and nutrients or whether they benefit their host by trapping
water and nutrient-rich debris. Some epiphytes, especially Bromeliaceae
with wide leaf bases, are home to frogs and other small animals.

Tree trunks with epiphytes, Braulio Carrillo N.P.

Stranglers are epiphytes that do harm their hosts. They start life as a seed in animal droppings on a tree limb. As the strangler grows it sends long roots down to the ground. As more and more roots encircle the host tree, it eventually dies and the strangler remains, often with a complex, interwoven trunk betraying its origin. These plants are either figs (*Ficus* spp., family Moraceae) or *Clusia* spp., (family Clusiaceae). Both *Costa Rican Natural History* (Janzen 1983) and *A Neotropical Companion* (Krichner 1989), have excellent discussions of epiphytes.

Reproduction

Because plants are not mobile, they cannot search for mates, nor can young plants set off from home to make their way in the world. So plants use the mobility of animals, wind, and water to help them with these tasks.

Several general categories of plant reproduction have evolved during evolutionary history. They form the basis for the classification systems used by plant biologists.

Ferns and other seedless plants (club mosses, spike mosses, quillworts, wisk ferns, and horse tails), called *pteridophytes*, meaning *fern plants*, evolved roughly 400 million years ago. They do not have flowers, fruits, or seeds but reproduce by spores.

Higher plants that produce seeds but not flowers or true fruits are called *gymnosperms*, meaning *naked seeds*. They include pines, cypresses, and cycads. Gymnosperms produce pollen, containing sperm cells, which is carried by wind to an egg within a female cone. A seed is an embryonic plant packaged in nutrient-rich tissues. Some gymnosperms produce seeds surrounded by a fleshy coating that is attractive to animals, but these are not true fruits. Gymnosperms were the dominant plant forms during the Jurassic period, about 190 million years ago.

The most abundant kind of plants are flowering plants, *angiosperms*, meaning *enclosed seed*. Angiosperms have flowers, in which pollen is contained within anthers, and seeds develop from fertilized eggs (ovules) within a protective ovary. A fruit is a mature ovary containing seeds. Some flowering plants are wind pollinated but very often animals such as insects, birds, or bats carry pollen. The animal is rewarded for coming to the flower by nectar or excess pollen. As the animal gathers nectar it gets dusted with pollen, which is carried to the next flower. The relationship between a plant and its pollinators can be a generalized one in which several different types of insects or other animals act as pollinators, or it may be quite specialized, with just one species of insect pollinating just one species of plant. For instance the flowers of *Didymopanax pittieri* are visited not only by bees but also by flies, beetles, and butterflies, whereas some orchids are pollinated only by one species of euglossine bee.

Some generalizations can be made about the types of animals that pollinate particular types of flowers. Flowers pollinated by bees are often blue or yellow but rarely red, since bees do not see red. Some genera of beetles are

Strangler on an oak, Rincón de la Vieja N.P.

specialist pollinators of *Dieffenbachia*, *Philodendron*, and other genera of the family Araceae (aroids). Flowers that are dark purplish red and have a foul odor are usually pollinated by carrion flies. Moths often pollinate whitish flowers that open at night and are sweetly scented, since moths are active at night. Butterflies, on the other hand, are active during the day and are attracted to bright yellow or red flowers with a nectar reward.

Hummingbirds pollinate many types of flowers. These flowers are tubular and usually bright red, orange, or yellow. They must also have abundant nectar to feed animals as large as hummingbirds. Some larger birds, such as

Heliconius pachinus visiting Asclepias curassavica

orioles, are known to pollinate the flowers of trees high in the forest canopy. Bats also pollinate many plants. Flowers adapted to bat pollination are large and sturdy. They sometimes grow directly from the trunk or branches of the tree and may have a musty or unpleasant odor.

Many plants keep out all animals except the best pollinators by having flowers that only certain insects or birds can enter. Probably the best example of this is the genus *Ficus* in the family Moraceae. *Ficus* flowers have highly specialized pollination relationships with various species of tiny wasp. The flowers line the inside of a rounded, fleshy, fruitlike structure, the fig, inside of which male and female flowers are separate.

A fig with mature female flowers has a small hole at its tip. Fertile female wasps, carrying fig pollen, enter this hole and lay eggs in some of the fig flowers, at the same time fertilizing them with pollen. The female wasps then die, and the wasp larvae develop in the flowers, destroying some seeds but leaving other seeds to mature. The wasps of both sexes and the male fig flowers mature at the same time. The wasps mate, and the fertile female wasps, now carrying fig pollen, crawl out of the hole in the fig and search for another fig in which to begin the cycle over again. The fig now matures and becomes attractive to birds and other animals that eat the figs, along with the dead wasps, and disperse the fig seeds (see *Costa Rican Natural History* [Janzen 1983] for more).

Another vital interaction between plants and animals is seed dispersal. Some seeds have wings or plumes that allow wind to carry them to new locations. Fruits of plants with wind-dispersed seeds are usually dry. A few fruits, such as coconuts, are dispersed by water. Plants in which the ovary becomes fleshy as the seeds mature are generally adapted to be eaten by birds or mammals. The seeds then pass through the animal and are distributed away from the parent plant. Some dry, hollow fruits split open and have seeds with a fleshy attachment that is probably adapted to animal dispersal. The vast majority of seeds die, but a few grow to become the next generation.

White nosed coati, Nasua narica *at La Selva*

Birds relish many fruits that are inedible by humans, although there are plenty of other fruits that attract both birds and mammals including humans. Most fleshy fruits are small and can be swallowed by small birds, but large fruits can be eaten by toucans and monkeys. Fruits that fall to the ground may be eaten by agoutis (a large rodent), which store food by burying seeds and often "forget" them, thereby acting as seed dispersers. Fruit-eating bats also disperse the seeds of many plants.

A number of "anachronistic," large, hard-skinned fruits, such as the pods of *Cassia grandis*, *Crescentia cujete*, and *Enterolobium cyclocarpum*, are adapted to dispersal by very large mammals, now long extinct (gomphotheres, giant ground sloths, and the horse, *Equus fraternus*). Modern horses (*E. cabalus*) and sometimes cattle are now their only dispersers (see *The Ghosts of Evolution* [Barlow 2000] for more).

Plant Defenses

Animals from howler monkeys to bruchid beetles and leaf-cutter ants attack leaves, flowers, fruits, and seeds of plants. Plants cannot avoid predators by running away, but they have evolved a wide array of defenses that work remarkably well. Every plant is essentially a chemical factory that can synthesize hundreds or thousands of compounds from a few abundant ingredients. From simple sugars, a little nitrogen, and trace minerals, a plant can make everything else it needs, including many toxins that discourage plant predators. To avoid these poisons, plant eaters must be very selective about the species they consume. Even the age of a leaf can make a difference in the level of toxins it contains.

Plants also use tough, indigestible fibers, thorns, stinging hairs, and other defenses to protect themselves. Some plants have recruited aggressive ants to act as bodyguards, such as those that live on ant acacias and in the stems of some cecropias. These ants attack anything that touches the plant, including unwary humans. They will even clip away vines that start to grow

Leafcutter ant, Atta cephalotes, *cutting leaf segment*

Acacia ant, Pseudomyrmex ferruginea, *emerging from an* Acacia collinsii *thorn*

on the plant. In return for defense, the plant supplies the ants with food, in the form of nectar exuded from special areas on stems, and shelter, in the form of hollow stems or large thorns (for more about ants and plants see the books by Kricher and Janzen mentioned above).

Humans have put plant toxins to work as medicines and mind-altering drugs for thousands of years. Caffeine in coffee, nicotine in tobacco, and the anticancer drug vincristine are all defensive chemicals produced by plants. There are endless useful products growing in tropical forests that still await discovery by us, but we must ensure the survival of these forests if we are to reap their benefits.

METHODS AND JUSTIFICATIONS

Choice of Plants

Our criteria for choosing which plants to collect and photograph included, first of all, the lists of common plants that Michael Grayum and Barry Hammel put together for us. Next, we used the frequency with which we saw a particular kind of plant, and at least one noticeable characteristic or visual "hook" that called attention to it. As visually sensitive photographers, and not botanists, Barbara's and Larry's reactions to particular plants were important elements in our choices, and we had many discussions about which species to describe. Costa Rica is, perhaps, the Neotropics's richest place for studying the great outdoors. With 10,000 or more plants to choose from, we had to narrow our selection to plants that tend to be common, eye-catching, and observable from the ground. Our general rule in choosing a plant was that we had to see it at least three times before we photographed and collected it. Some species have such outstanding features that we included them even though they are not particularly common. Many common plants, such as pasture and lawn weeds, do not appear here because they are not conspicuous enough to be noticed by most people. Some conspicuous plants are not included because they are tree canopy epiphytes, generally not observable from the ground, with the exception of some few fallen epiphytes. We also have included many common horticultural and agricultural plants as well as wild native plants, since people unfamiliar with tropical plants will want to know what these are, too, regardless of whether such plants are native to Costa Rica.

In a few cases photographs and descriptions of uncommon plants are here to serve as an example of a large genus, for example, *Digitaria costaricensis*. Upon seeing an early draft of our "target" plant list, Michael Grayum noted that some are "opportunistic," rather than carefully considered, or conveniently located common plants. We confess to the truth of this; however, our perspective must be compared to that of the nonspecialist visitor or student, with whom we identify, not to one who already knows well the extensive and complex local landscape and flora.

We have concentrated on describing the most easily observed characters of each plant, as well as those we saw at the time. In some cases, tropical plant taxonomists may disagree with our choice of characters or the way they are photographed, as for instance, when only fallen flowers of *Thunbergia grandiflora* or fruit of *Calatola costaricensis* is shown. In these cases we did make an opportunistic choice to photograph an interesting plant or plant part without being able to identify from which large tree, epiphyte, or canopy vine it came. Again, our point of view is that of the ecotourist or student who sees something of interest without being able to identify its ultimate source. That is one of the primary tasks of this guidebook, to start at the interesting object observed and describe the plant from which it comes.

Since I am a plant ecologist, this book tends to lean toward ecological information as opposed to human uses of plants. Also, I did not want to in any way encourage collecting of wild plants. Please collect only photographs and memories, not plants!

Plant Classification: Taxonomy

Living things are grouped together by how closely related they appear to be, based on anatomy, and more recently on similarities in their DNA. Taxonomy is the science that studies the evolutionary relationship among various types of organisms. The hierarchy generally used is kingdom, division, class. order. family, genus, species. The system is acknowledged to be rather artificial until one gets down to the level of species. A species is defined as a group of organisms that can interbreed freely and produce fertile offspring. A genus is a group of (presumably) closely related species, and a family is a group of (presumably) closely related genera.

Plant Variability

Botanists classify and categorize plants based on flower- or spore-producing (reproductive) structures. Reproductive structures are the most invariable, "conservative" plant parts, since random variation in these parts may prevent the plant from getting its genes into the next generation, which is the most important task for all living things. On the other hand, a plant can have variable leaf shape and size, or overall height without jeopardizing its ability to reproduce. The descriptions of leaf shape and size, hairiness, thorniness, and other "vegetative" traits given in this guide are, therefore, never absolute, and nonreproductive parts may vary considerably from what is shown in a given photograph of one individual plant. When trying to identify a plant, the most important structures that must match are the shape and size of flower, fruit, or spore-producing parts. Even flower color may vary, as long as the flower remains attractive to effective pollinators.

Scientific Names of Plants

The scientific name of a plant consists of two words, the *genus*, a proper noun, which is always capitalized, and the *species*, an adjective modifying the genus name. The species name is never capitalized even when it is derived from a proper noun. The words are latinized by long tradition. For instance, the name of coffee is *Coffea arabica*, which means *Arabian coffee*. This name is used worldwide and is unique. Many species names are descriptive, such as *latifolia* (wide-leaved), *angustifolia* (narrow-leaved), or *macrocarpa* (big fruit). Many plants are named for botanist who spent years studying Costa Rican flora *(Myrrhidendron donnellsmithii)*.

Pronunciation of Latin names is just as they are written. If you sound out each letter, you have the basics. Very often, the emphasis is on the second to the last syllable, although this may vary considerably. For instance, Melastomataceae is pronounced Mela stōma TĀcee ee (ā indicates that the pronounciation of the letter is long). The *eae* is pronounced *ē ē* (ae is pronounced as *ē* one syllable). For a more complete discussion see W. T. Stearn (1992).

The changing of scientific plant names used by botanists is a sore point for many plant enthusiasts (i.e., is it *Piper peltatum* or *Pothomorphe peltatum*). However, botany, like other sciences, is about discovery, and new information often dictates a change in the names used for a species. This is especially true now that DNA analysis is possible and relationships among plants can be determined at the genetic level.

Occasionally one may find a single plant with two or more scientific names, depending on the plant manual or guidebook listing the plant. This happens because at any given time, different taxonomic systems are used to classify plants. This is sometimes the result of new information being adopted by taxonomists over a period of time, or sometimes it is the result of disagreements among taxonomists about the status of a plant (to which genus or family it belongs or which is its legitimate species name). The system used to classify plants of a certain region is very often established by the botanical plant manual, or flora, written by the taxonomists who have studied these plants. The *Manual de Plantas de Costa Rica* is the new flora currently being written in a collaboration between the Instituto Nacional de Bioversidad (INBio) of Costa Rica, and the Missouri Botanical Garden. We have had a great deal of help from taxonomists from both these institutions and are using the classification system of this manual in our guidebook.

When a plant has more than one widely recognized name, or the name has been recently changed, we have included both the name of the plant as it appears in the *Manual de Plantas as de Costa Rica* and the commonly used synonym. Although we have included common names, we strongly urge use of scientific names.

Common Names of Plants

One plant may have several common names, and conversely, one common name may apply to a number of different plants. While this is true in most countries, the common names in Costa Rica are particularly varied, as they have widely diverse origins. First there are the names given by the indigenous people in Bribri, Güetar, or Nahua. Then there are the names of the same plant in Spanish, Afrocostaricenses, and English, and last all these names are mixed together as these various peoples speak to one another over time.

We have given up to three common names where they are available, but for many plants we must simply stick with the scientific name. We were unable to include many names due to lack of space.

Botanical Language and Plant Descriptions

Once we had obtained a reliable identification for a plant that we collected and photographed, it was necessary to find a botanically complete description of that plant. When a plant is described by a taxonomist, its characteristics are taken from numerous specimens of that species and cover the range of its variability. No two plants of the same species are exactly alike, as no two humans are exactly alike (excepting identical twins). Each taxonomist also describes plants with his or her own style and emphasis. Therefore, since we obtained these descriptions from numerous sources, the descriptions are not precisely parallel. Where one set of descriptions includes the range of sizes for leaves, another source gives only maximum dimensions for leaves. Some sources give little or no information on fruit or even flower color, while another includes these characters. We have emphasized characters that are the most highly visible, such as colorful bracts, or fruit, especially when the flowers of a given plant are very small or inconspicuous. We have omitted characters that are difficult to observe, generally if they are less than 0.1 cm long.

We have used as little technical botanical language as possible in this guidebook so that plant descriptions are accessible to a wide audience. Botany seems to have an inordinate number of terms, and although they provide a compact way to communicate plant descriptions to other botanists, they shut out those who have not studied this language. Basic terms of plant anatomy are defined both with drawings and in the glossary. In some cases, we have sacrificed precise botanical accuracy for the sake of descriptive clarity. For example, both the small, leaflike structures at the base of a leaf stalk and the bractlike structures that cover leaf buds in a number of plant families, such as Piperaceae, have all been lumped under the term *stipule*, although technically they may have several different names. We have also sacrificed the numerous technical terms for various types of plant hairs. Plant hairs can often be critical for classification, but observation usually requires the aid of a magnifying lens, which we assume most users of this guide will not have available.

DISTRIBUTION AND "COMMONNESS" OF PLANTS

Unlike the United States or Europe, Costa Rica has many plants that have not been described taxonomically. In addition, the range and abundance of many plants in the Neotropics are still being studied. In writing this guidebook, we have had to use the information available in previously published sources (including some herbarium lists published on-line). Due to lack of time and taxonomic expertise, we could not do primary research into the distribution of plant species. Because of this lack of information on the abundance and distribution of many plants, including agricultural crops and ornamentals, the information we present on these subjects is limited. Readers may find many plants in places that are not listed among the conservation areas in which these species have been collected for herbaria.

LIMITATIONS OF THIS GUIDE

Since 10,000 or more plants can be found growing in Costa Rica (counting agricultural and horticultural species), we have been able to include only about 8% of the country's flora in providing a truly portable guide. Our aim has been to provide an aid for field use in identifying as many as possible of the most common and conspicuous species. In order to keep the size of the book within "field guide" proportions, we also have had to limit the number of words to 200 or less in describing each plant. The other constraint on what we included has been our time. Like tourists, we do not live in Costa Rica, and despite several trips and a lot of research back home, were able to spend only a few weeks at a time traveling around the country seeking plants to photograph and describe. Clearly we missed a few spectacular species that have short blooming seasons and limited geographical ranges. Anyone visiting Tapantí in late October, for example, will wonder how we could have missed the forest floor herb *Besleria princeps* with its bright orange flowers, but we were just never lucky enough to be there at the right time. So it is with some other plants we would like to have included. We hope our readers will let us know, and possibly send photographs, for any future edition of this book.

HOW TO USE THIS BOOK

We have arranged this guidebook first of all by plant habit, that is, the type of plant structure, general size, growth pattern, and whether the main stem is woody (hard) or herbaceous (relatively soft, usually green). So all the palms and similar plants are grouped together, followed by large trees, then by smaller trees and shrubs. Next come woody vines (lianas) and soft-stemmed (herbaceous) vines. Then come herbs, grasses and grasslike plants, and finally, ferns and similar plants (club mosses etc.). Plant taxonomists organize flora differently, but because this book is for nonspecialists, we have used a more intuitively accessible organization showing the color of a key identifying feature of each plant. This feature might be a flower, fruit, leaf, bract, or in the case of *Bauhinia* vines, the shape of the stems.

Color can work well as a primary way to categorize herbs. Some might say this works less well for trees, shrubs, or climbers. A common way of organizing woody plants in field guides is by leaf arrangement; however, after careful consideration we decided to group large trees by family, genus, and species, because in wet tropical habitats, opposite and whorled leaf patterns and leaf placement on the stem are almost always impossible to see clearly from the ground, even with binoculars.

Within each chapter, plants are categorized by the color of the most conspicuous parts for which we have photographs (bracts, fruits, etc.). When both flowers and fruit are conspicuous, the plant is categorized by flower color (i.e., *Bixa orellana* is in the "white" section of the chapter on shrubs). On the other hand, a plant with large red bracts and small white flowers will be categorized as "red." Plants within each color category are listed alphabetically by family name, then by genus and species names. Plant types that do not have conspicuous or differing flower colors (palms, grasses, ferns) are listed alphabetically by plant family, genus, and species. This also includes large trees, the flowers of which are usually hidden in the canopy. Usually one sees only fallen flowers or fruit of canopy trees, and it is rarely possible to tell whether the flowers are from the tree itself or from an epiphyte or vine living on the tree. Some plants are rarely observed in bloom (e.g., *Yucca guatemalensis*). In a few plants the leaves are the most outstanding feature (e.g., *Elaeagia auriculata*). These plants are included in the section on green flowers and foliage plants.

A number of plant families and genera are too large to give our readers more than a hint of their diversity. In the case of families such as Rubiaceae, Poaceae, Orchidaceae, or Araceae the samples shown are not meant to provide a definitive means of identifying them in the field. Rather, we hope that the general features of the family will be illustrated by these examples. In other cases, such as *Wigandia urens*, *Cassia grandis*, or *Weinmannia pinnata*, the species are unique enough to be identified quite easily with the information we are able to provide.

Format of Descriptions

The format of the species descriptions differs from the one normally used by taxonomists. It puts flower and fruit color first, because color is what most people notice. The characteristics described include the following:

Type of plant (woody/herbaceous; tree, shrub, fern, etc.), size, stem characteristics. **Leaves** placement on stem (alternate/opposite; pinnate, etc.), size, shape, venation if known (pinnate, palmate, loop-connected), margin (lobed, toothed, smooth). **Flowers** color; symmetry (radial /bilateral, tubular), size, petals, sepals, stamens, if known; inflorescence type (branched, spike, solitary flower; size); bloom times; pollinators, if known. **Fruit** fleshy (color) or dry; size, seed number; fruiting time; disperser, if known. **Habitat:** description; elevation. Conservation areas: where the plant has been found in Costa Rica (identified by the abbreviations listed in the next section; see also the map of conservation areas and parks, page xxi). **Range:** countries in which the plant is found. **Notes:** number of species in this genus in Costa Rica; human use, if known or relevant.

The note "(photo)" is to indicate one of the accompanying images of a plant part that may not be completely obvious.

Key to Abbreviations

Conservation areas: ARE, Arenal; CVC, Cordillera Volcanica Central; GUA, Guanacaste; HNO, Huetar Norte; ICO, Isla del Coco; LAC, La Amistad Caribe; LAP, La Amistad Pacífico; OSA, Osa; PAC, Pacífico Central; TEM, Tempisque; TOR, Tortuguero.

Ranges: E, eastern; N, northern; S, southern; W, western; C, central; N Amer, North America; C Amer, Central America; Can, Canada; US, United States; AR, Arizona; CA, California; FL, Florida; LA, Louisiana; TX, Texas; Bel, Belize; CR, Costa Rica; El Salv, El Salvador; Gua, Guatemala; Hon, Honduras; Mex, Mexico; Nic, Nicaragua; Pan, Panama; Sur, Surinam; WI, West Indies; Ant, Antilles; Bh, Bahamas; DR, Dominican Republic; His, Hispaniola; Jam, Jamaica; LsAnt, Lesser Antilles; PtR, Puerto Rico; Tr, Trinidad; To, Tobago; VI, Virgin Islands; S Amer, South America; Arg, Argentina; Bol, Bolivia; Brz, Brazil; Col, Columbia; Ec, Ecuador; Guy, Guyanas; Par, Paraguay; Pr, Peru; Sur, Surinam; Ur, Uruguay; Ven, Venezuela.

ILLUSTRATED PLANT TERMS

FLOWER PARTS

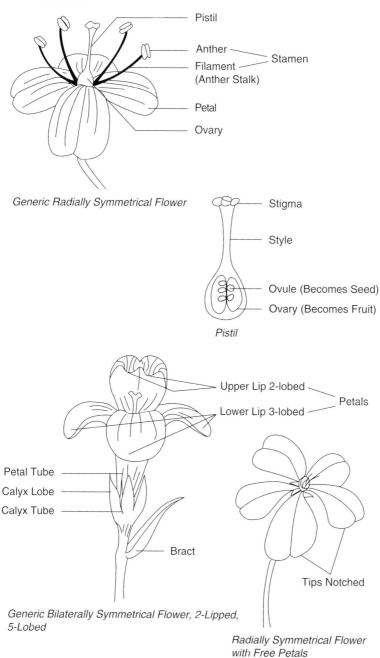

Pistil

Anther
Filament (Anther Stalk)
Stamen

Petal

Ovary

Generic Radially Symmetrical Flower

Stigma

Style

Ovule (Becomes Seed)
Ovary (Becomes Fruit)

Pistil

Upper Lip 2-lobed
Lower Lip 3-lobed
Petals

Petal Tube
Calyx Lobe
Calyx Tube

Bract

Tips Notched

*Generic Bilaterally Symmetrical Flower, 2-Lipped,
5-Lobed*

*Radially Symmetrical Flower
with Free Petals*

FLOWER VARIATION

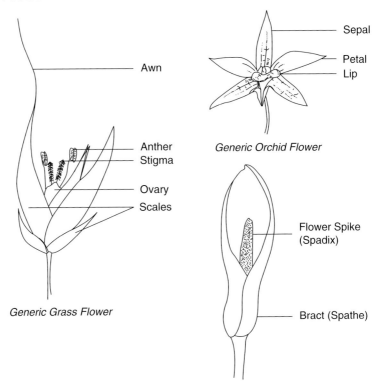

Awn

Sepal

Petal

Lip

Generic Orchid Flower

Anther
Stigma

Ovary

Scales

Flower Spike
(Spadix)

Generic Grass Flower

Bract (Spathe)

Generic Araceae (Aroid) Inflorescence

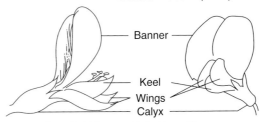

Banner

Keel
Wings
Calyx

Generic Fabaceae/Faboideae Flowers

Stigma
Anther
Disk Flowers
Ray Flower

Asteraceae Flower Head

INFLORESCENCES AND BRACTS

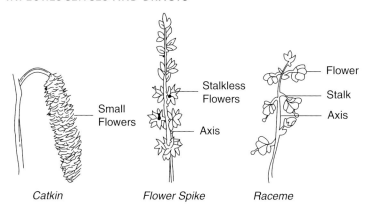

Catkin — Small Flowers

Flower Spike — Stalkless Flowers, Axis

Raceme — Flower, Stalk, Axis

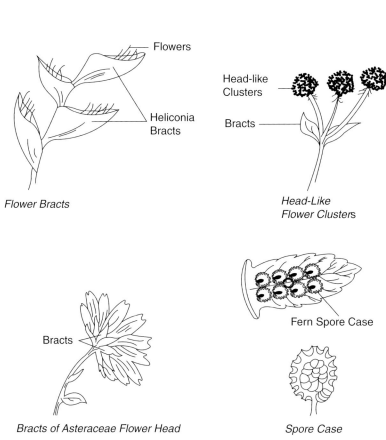

Flower Bracts — Flowers, Heliconia Bracts

Head-Like Flower Clusters — Head-like Clusters, Bracts

Bracts of Asteraceae Flower Head — Bracts

Spore Case — Fern Spore Case

FRUIT AND LEAVES

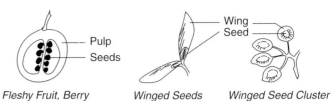

Pulp
Seeds

Fleshy Fruit, Berry

Wing
Seed

Winged Seeds

Winged Seed Cluster

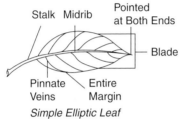

Aril

Seed

Fruit Section Showing Seeds with Arils

Open Fruit Husk

Stalk   Midrib   Pointed
at Both Ends

Blade

Pinnate
Veins

Entire
Margin

Simple Elliptic Leaf

Toothed Margin

Veins Palmate at Base

*Simple Egg-Shaped Leaf,
Slightly Lobed Base*

Marginal Vein
Tip Pointed

Base
Lobed

Simple Heart-Shaped Leaf

Tip Blunt

Veins
Loop-Connected

Simple Egg-Shaped Leaf

LEAF TYPES AND LEAF ARRANGEMENTS

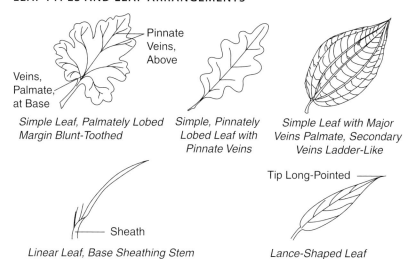

Pinnate Veins, Above

Veins, Palmate, at Base

Simple Leaf, Palmately Lobed Margin Blunt-Toothed

Simple, Pinnately Lobed Leaf with Pinnate Veins

Simple Leaf with Major Veins Palmate, Secondary Veins Ladder-Like

Sheath

Linear Leaf, Base Sheathing Stem

Tip Long-Pointed

Lance-Shaped Leaf

Base Tapered to Leaf Stelk

Tip Short-Pointed

Leaf with Blade Widest above Middle

Rachis (Axis)

Pinnae

Stem   Leaflets

Twice Pinnate Leaf

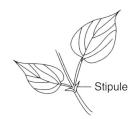

Axis (Rachis)   Leaflets

Odd Pinnate Leaf

Axillary Bud

Alternate Leaves with Axillary Buds

Stipule

Opposite Leaves with Stipules

LEAF AND STIPULE ARRANGEMENTS

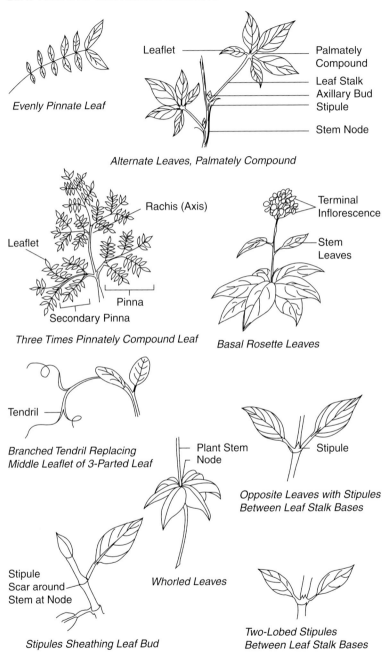

Evenly Pinnate Leaf

Leaflet

Palmately Compound

Leaf Stalk
Axillary Bud
Stipule

Stem Node

Alternate Leaves, Palmately Compound

Rachis (Axis)

Leaflet

Pinna

Secondary Pinna

Three Times Pinnately Compound Leaf

Terminal Inflorescence

Stem Leaves

Basal Rosette Leaves

Tendril

Branched Tendril Replacing Middle Leaflet of 3-Parted Leaf

Plant Stem Node

Stipule

Opposite Leaves with Stipules Between Leaf Stalk Bases

Stipule Scar around Stem at Node

Whorled Leaves

Stipules Sheathing Leaf Bud

Two-Lobed Stipules Between Leaf Stalk Bases

STEMS

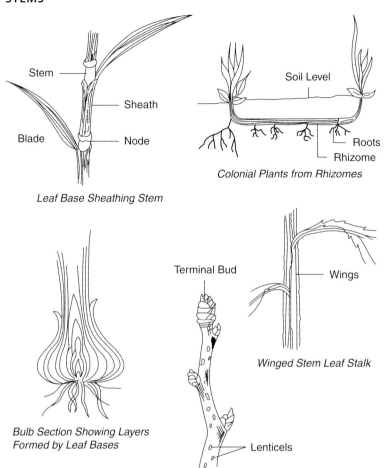

Leaf Base Sheathing Stem

Colonial Plants from Rhizomes

Bulb Section Showing Layers
Formed by Leaf Bases

Winged Stem Leaf Stalk

Twig with Lenticels and Buds

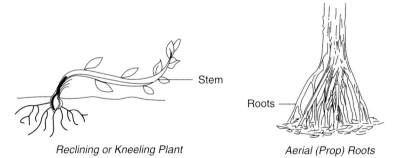

Reclining or Kneeling Plant

Aerial (Prop) Roots

SPECIALIZED TREE ROOTS AND BASES

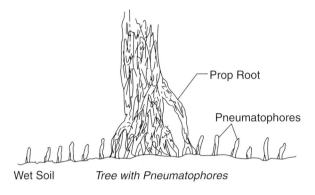

Prop Root

Pneumatophores

Wet Soil   *Tree with Pneumatophores*

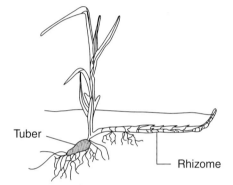

Tuber

Rhizome

Plant with Rhizome and a Tuberous Root

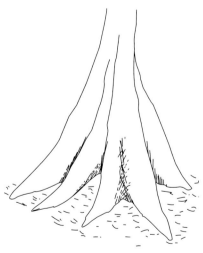

Tree Buttresses

PALMS AND PALMLIKE PLANTS

▨ FAMILY: *ARECACEAE* (PALMS)

Acrocomia aculeata
  (A. vinifera)
Asterogyne martiana
Astrocaryum alatum
Astrocaryum standleyanum
Attalea rostrata
  (A. butyracea,
  Scheelea r.)
Bactris gasipaes
Bactris guineensis
Bactris hondurensis
Bactris major
Calyptrogyne ghiesbreghtiana
  (C. sarapiquensis)
Chamaedorea costaricana
Chamaedorea pinnatifrons
Chamaedorea tepejilote
Cocos nucifera

Crysophila guagara
Desmoncus schippii
Elaeis guineensis
Euterpe precatoria
  (E. macrospadix)
Geonoma congesta
Geonoma cuneata
Geonoma interrupta
Iriartea deltoidea
Manicaria saccifera
Prestoea decurrens
Raphia taedigera
Reinhardtia gracilis
Socratea exorrhiza
  (S. durissima)
Synechanthus
  warscewiczianus
Welfia regia (W. georgii)

▨ FAMILY: *CYCLANTHACEAE*

Carludovica palmata
Cyclanthus bipartitus
Dicranopygium umbrophilum
Sphaeradenia praetermissa

▨ FAMILY: *ZAMIACEAE*
  (FORMERLY IN THE *CYCADACEAE*)

Zamia fairchildiana
Zamia neurophyllidia
  (Z. skinneri)

For tree ferns, see "Ferns and Other Seedless Plants" on page 435.

FAMILY: *ARECACEAE* (PALMS)

▨ *Acrocomia aculeata (A. vinifera)* (coyol)

Spiny palm 2–10 m tall, trunk 25–50 cm diameter, gray with patches of flat, flexible spines to 9 cm long, dead fronds persistent, covering upper trunk, base of trunk often swollen. **Leaves** alternate, stalk spiny and hairy, blade pinnate, 2–3.5 m long, leaflets narrow, off-white below, in several planes giving leaf a bottle-brush appearance, midrib densely spiny along underside, few spines on top. **Flowers** off-white to yellow, tiny; inflorescence from among leaves, large, drooping, with many thin, crimped branches, female flowers near stem bases; blooms Feb.–June. Pollinated by bees. **Fruit** hard, yellowish green, round, 3 cm long, 3–4.5 cm wide, numerous, at bases of crimped branches, seed solitary; ripens Mar.–June, Aug. **Habitat:** Wet to seasonally dry lowlands in disturbed habitats, pastures, roadsides. Altitude: Sea level to 500 m, Pacific slope. Conservation areas: GUA, OSA, PAC, TEM. **Range:** Mex–N Arg, Ant. **Notes:** This is the only species of *Acrocomia* in Costa Rica. Seeds once used by native people for food. Sap used to make a traditional drink known as *vino de coyol*.

▨ *Asterogyne martiana*

Small, solitary understory palm 1–2 m tall, trunk 3–5 cm diameter, usually reclining and rooting at nodes, top of trunk enclosed by leaf sheaths, bottom ringed with old leaf scars, appearing canelike but often hidden by old, persistent leaves. **Leaves** alternate, stalk 30–60 cm long, slender, blade simple, 0.5–1.3 m long, 15–28 cm wide, widest near apex, tip forked, sometimes splitting along margins with age, appearing pinnate. **Flowers** white, tiny; inflorescence from tip of main stalk, 40–90 cm long, with 5–8 stout, straight, spine-tipped branches each to 25 cm long, 0.8 cm wide, in a palmate arrangement; blooms most of the year. **Fruit** fleshy, reddish, becoming purple black, round, 1.2 cm long, 0.6 cm wide. **Habitat:** Wet forest understories. Altitude: Sea level to 1000 m, mostly below 500 m. Conservation areas: CVC, GUA, HNO, LAC, OSA, PAC, TOR. Especially OSA and TOR. **Range:** Bel–Ec. **Notes:** This is the only species of *Asterogyne* in Costa Rica. Much like *Geonoma congesta* and often found in same habitat; *G. congesta* has orange fruiting stems and a short leaf stalk.

▦ *Astrocaryum alatum* (coquillo, palma coquito, coyolillo)

Solitary, spiny palm 2–6 m tall, trunk 12–18 cm diameter, old leaves persistent, covering trunk near top, spines flat, black; trunk base often swollen, with low mound of dark, adventitious roots. **Leaves** alternate, stalk spiny, 1–3 m long, blade pinnate, 2.5–4.5 m long, arching, broad in outline, midrib spiny, leaflets 18–37 per side, of irregular widths, in one plane, often in groups, whitish below, often very close and leaf appearing undivided with toothed margins, tip forked. **Flowers** off-white, tiny; inflorescence of numerous spikes from a central axis, each roughly 10 cm long, 3 cm wide, below a pale, spiny, woody sheath about 50 cm long; blooms May, Sept., Nov. **Fruit** woody, yellow brown, 4–5 cm long, about 3.5 cm wide, spiny, looks like a small coconut, 1 at the base of each spike, densely crowded. **Habitat:** Wet lowland forests, sometimes in pastures. Altitude: Sea level to 800 m. Conservation areas: GUA, HNO, LAC, PAC. **Range:** Hon–Pan. **Notes:** There are three species of *Astrocaryum* in Costa Rica. They appear much like *Bactris* spp. but differ in having white leaf undersides.

▦ *Astrocaryum standleyanum* (chontadura, pejibaye de montaña, black palm)

Solitary, spiny palm 6–20 m tall, base often swollen, trunk 12–25 cm diameter (juveniles without trunk), internodes to 40 cm long, spines dense, to 15 cm, slender, flattened, about 0.3 cm wide, black, shiny, margins often thin, brown, leaf scars 4–5 cm wide, without spines. **Leaves** alternate, stalk 0.5–1.5 m long, spiny, blade pinnate, 2.5–4 m long, appearing shaggy, tip forked, midrib spiny, leaflets 100 per side, 75 cm long, 3 cm wide, whitish below, spaced irregularly at various angles (juvenile leaves not split into leaflets). **Flowers** white, tiny; inflorescence initially covered by a spiny, leaflike bract about 1 m long, flowering stem with many thin, crimped branches, more or less upright (becoming pedant in fruit); blooms and fruits most of the year. **Fruit** fleshy, orange, round, 3–6 cm long, to 3 cm wide, 1-seeded; numerous, on a stem to 1.2 m long. **Habitat:** Very wet lowland forests. Altitude: Sea level to 500 m, Pacific slope. Conservation areas. OSA, PAC. **Range:** CR–Col. **Notes:** Fruit eaten by many animals and used as food for domestic pigs.

3

▦ *Attalea rostrata (A. butyracea, Scheelea r.)*
(palma real, corozo, mamaca)

Palm 3–30 m tall, trunk 25–50 cm diameter, upper trunk broadened by persistent dead leaves. **Leaves** alternate, stalk 30–60 cm long, broad-based, blade pinnate, 3–9 m long, often arched, midrib stout, leaflets 180–235 per side, about 1 m long, 4 cm wide, held vertically above and below midrib in same plane, sometimes drooping on either side of midrib, regularly arranged. **Flowers** pale yellow, small, petals soon deciduous; inflorescence bract very large, 1–3 m long, woody, persistent, deeply grooved or pleated, inflorescence borne among leaves, 0.7–1 m long, of overlapping spikes, extending from a central axis, branches numerous; blooms May, June, Sept., Dec. **Fruit** woody, orange brown, 4.5–6 cm long, about 2.5 cm wide, smooth, oblong, 1–3 seeds, densely packed on

a massive stem; fruits Apr.–July; fruit eaten by many animals. **Habitat:** Moist to wet lowland forests. Altitude: Sea level to 800, mostly below 400 m. Conservation areas: LAC, LAP, PAC, TEM. **Range:** S Mex–Pan. **Notes:** This is the only species of *Attalea* in Costa Rica.

Flower sheath

▦ *Bactris gasipaes* (pejibaye, dikó)

Spiny palm 4–20 m tall, trunk 8–14 cm diameter, clustered or solitary, internodes about 20 cm long, usually densely spiny, spines to 10 cm long. **Leaves** alternate, sheath and stalk spiny, spines to 1 cm long, blade irregularly pinnate, 2–3 m long, midrib spiny, leaflets numerous, to 60 cm long, 3 cm wide, linear, tips forked, very unequal, margins often bristly, in clusters of 2–7, irregularly arranged, at various angles. **Flowers** yellow, to 1 cm; inflorescence to 30 cm long, with numerous branches, emerging from a spiny bract that becomes woody; blooms all year. **Fruit** fleshy, red orange, round, 5 cm long, 3 cm wide, edible; sold in markets about Apr.–Nov. **Habitat:** Cultivated, mostly in wet lowlands. Altitude: Sea level to 700 m, sometimes to 1200 m. Conservation areas: CVC. **Range:** Native from Ven to Brz but cultivated north to Gua. **Notes:** Possibly a selection from *B. macana*. Widely cultivated for fruit and heart of palm in kitchen gardens and plantations. Apparently not escaping from cultivation in Costa Rica. There are 17 species of *Bactris* in Costa Rica. They have multiple, erect, spiny trunks and spiny leaf stalks.

▥ *Bactris guineensis* (huiscoyol, uvita, viscoyol)

Small, spiny understory palm, stem 0.6–3.5 m tall, 3 cm diameter, colonial, spines to 9 cm long, yellowish with black tip and base. **Leaves** alternate, stalk very short or none, blade 20–50 cm long, pinnate, midrib spiny, that of new leaves white-woolly, leaflets 20–40 per side, often widely spaced, 12–30 cm long, 1–2 cm wide, sometimes spiny below and along margins, old leaves deciduous. **Flowers** whitish, about 0.4 cm wide; inflorescence with 9–30 branches 8–11 cm long along a main stalk 2–5 cm long; blooms Feb. **Fruit** fleshy, becoming purplish black 1–2 cm, wider than long, tip beaked; fruits Aug.–Jan. Ripe fruit is soaked in alcohol to make a bright red drink. **Habitat:** Seasonally dry to moist forests, and second growth. Altitude: Sea level to 60 m, sometimes to 150 m. Conservation areas: GUA, TEM. **Range:** Nic–Ven. **Notes:** *Bactris guineensis* and *B. major* are the only two *Bactris* species found in the seasonally dry region of northwestern Costa Rica.

▥ *Bactris hondurensis* (biscoyol)

Small, spiny understory palm, slender, stems 1–3 m tall, 0.5–1.5 cm diameter, most parts very spiny, spines mostly black, sometimes pale, to 16 cm long. **Leaves** alternate, spines to 7 cm long, stalk 16–27 cm long, blade 35–70 cm long, 26–39 cm wide, simple with forked tip, or irregularly pinnate with 2–9 leaflets per side, 18–23 cm long, 2–4 cm wide, softly white-hairy below, margins sparsely spiny. **Flowers** off-white; inflorescence about 20 cm long, 7 cm wide, with 3–7 branches, bract hairy-spiny, elliptic; blooms and fruits all year. **Fruit** fleshy, red orange when ripe, to 1.5 cm wide, round. **Habitat:** Very wet forest understories. Altitude: Sea level to 1200 m, most often in the Caribbean lowlands, below 500 m. Conservation areas: ARE, CVC, GUA, HNO, LAC, OSA, PAC, TOR. **Range:** Hon–Ec. **Notes:** Apparently the most common species of uncultivated *Bactris* in Costa Rica.

5

Bactris major (huiscoyol, viscoyol)

Small, spiny, colonial palm, often forming dense stands, stems 2–10 m tall, 2–6 cm diameter, spines to 11 cm long, black. **Leaves** alternate, stalk to 1.5 m long, blade pinnate 0.8–1.8 m long, about 50 cm wide, leaflets 25–48 per side, regularly arranged in one plane, 25–65 cm long, 1–3 cm wide, margins spiny-bristly, midrib often 4-sided, spines to 5 cm long, old leaves persistent; new leaves often white-woolly. **Flowers** whitish, small; inflorescence axis 1–5 cm long, with 5–15 stout branches 15–20 cm long, inflorescence bract 30–60 cm long with spines to 2 cm long. **Fruit** fleshy, juicy, purple black, 3–4 cm long, 2–3 cm wide, elliptical, in dense, egg-shaped cluster about 30 cm long, 20 cm wide; fruits most of the year. **Habitat:** Seasonally dry to very wet lowlands in sunny wet sites, brackish and freshwater marshes, wet pastures, swampy scrub. Altitude: Sea level to 400 m. Conservation areas: HNO, LAC, OSA, PAC, TEM, TOR. **Range:** S Mex–Brz, Tr.

Frond with spines

Calyptrogyne ghiesbreghtiana (C. sarapiquensis) (cola de gallo, coligallo, siuta, ukö)

Small, solitary palm 1–2.5 m tall, stem to 3 cm diameter, short or sometimes mostly underground. **Leaves** alternate, stalk 27–60 cm, blade about 1–1.5 m long, new blades simple, tips broadly forked, older blades splitting irregularly into 3–5 broad-based leaflets, tip forked, dead leaves persistent. **Flowers** white, tiny; inflorescence an unbranched spike 20–39 cm long on a stalk 1–2 m long, stiff, erect, held above leaves, bract falls before flowering, leaving a ring-shaped scar; blooms and fruits most of the year. **Fruit** fleshy, becoming dark blue to black, 1–2 cm long, egg-shaped, fruiting spike red. **Habitat:** Very wet forest understories. Altitude: Sea level to 1500 m. Conservation areas: ARE, CVC, GUA, LAC, OSA, TOR. **Range:** S Mex–W Pan. **Notes:** There are four species of *Calyptrogyne* in Costa Rica; *C. ghiesbreghtiana* is by far the most common. Leaves of *Calyptrogyne* are similar to those of *Geonoma* and *Asterogyne*.

Chamaedorea costaricana (pacaya, yawo)

Small tree 1–8 m tall, stems 1–5 cm diameter, clustered, erect or leaning, colonial from underground stems; leaf sheath with a flap on each side of the top. **Leaves** alternate, stalk about 20 cm long, blade regularly pinnate, leaflets 15–30 per side, in one plane, 20–40 cm long, 3–5 cm wide, narrowly lance-shaped. **Flowers** off-white, tiny, males and females on separate plants; inflorescence often drooping, branches 6–30, stalk with several papery bracts; blooms and fruits Aug.–May, mostly Oct.–Dec. **Fruit** fleshy, black, about 1.2 cm long, 0.9 cm wide, with persistent, thickened petals, fruiting stem orange. **Habitat:** Very wet forests, mostly at midelevations; also cultivated. Altitude: 500–2300 m, mostly on the Pacific slope. Conservation areas: ARE, CVC, GUA, LAC, LAP, OSA, PAC, TEM. **Range:** S Mex–W Pan.

Notes: There are 31 species of *Chamaedorea* in Costa Rica. They are all under 10 m tall, without spines, stems green, leaves regularly pinnate often with a much wider pair of leaflets at the leaf tip, or simple with a broadly forked tip, most are solitary.

Chamaedorea pinnatifrons (pacaya)

Solitary understory palm, stem 30 cm to 4 m tall, 0.5–3 cm diameter, erect, or reclining and rooting at nodes. **Leaves** alternate, 3–6, stalk 9–44 cm long, blade usually pinnate, leaflets 4–7 per side, S-shaped to broadly elliptic, 11–40 cm long, 2–9 cm wide, pointed at both ends, attachment to midrib rather narrow, leaflets at tip not much wider than those below, thin. **Flowers** off-white; inflorescence with 5–20 branches, male and female inflorescences separate, but sometimes on same plant, male branches elongate, drooping, females branches shorter, stiff. **Fruit** fleshy, to 1.5 cm long, 1 cm wide, becoming red orange then black, fruiting stems orange. **Habitat:** Wet to very wet forest understories. Altitude: Sea level to 2600 m, mostly above 1000 m. Conservation areas: ARE, CVC, GUA, HNO, LAC, LAP, PAC, TEM, TOR. **Range:** S Mex–Brz, Bol. **Notes:** The most common species of *Chamaedorea* in Costa Rica.

▦ *Chamaedorea tepejilote* (pacaya de danta, manita)

Understory palm, usually solitary, stems 0.5–5 m tall, 2–7 cm diameter, usually erect, base often with slender stilt roots. **Leaves** alternate, stalk 20–60 cm long, underside yellowish, blade 1–1.5 m long, pinnate, regular, leaflets 12–23 per side, S-shaped, 25–60 cm long, 2–10 cm wide, base only slightly narrowed, with broad attachment to leaf midrib. **Flowers** off-white, crowded; inflorescences from just below leaves, branched once, to 65 cm long, stems pale yellow in flower, bract almost vertical in bud, males and females on separate plants, males with drooping branches, females with stout branches; blooms and fruits all year. **Fruit** fleshy, to 1.5 cm long, 0.8 cm wide, elliptic, becoming black, almond-shaped; fruiting stems becoming red orange. **Habitat:** Wet forests. Also sometimes cultivated for edible unopened male inflorescences. Altitude: Sea level to 1600 m. Conservation areas: ARE, CVC, GUA, LAC, OSA, PAC, TEM, TOR. **Range:** S Mex–Col.

▦ *Cocos nucifera* (coco, coconut, cocotero, palo de pipa)

Tree 7–20 m tall, trunk 20–45 cm diameter, base of trunk often curved, tree leaning, leaf scars prominent, closely spaced, trunk gray brown, base bulging; leaf sheaths short, not extending down trunk. **Leaves** alternate, stalk to 2 m long, blade 2–6 m long, regularly pinnate, light green to yellow green, leaflets numerous, to 1.1 m long, 5 cm wide, all in one plane, shortest at either end of blade, midrib often yellow. **Flowers** dull white; inflorescence initially covered by a finely ribbed bract to 1 m long, flowering stems 1–2 m long, with 30–40 thin, branches to 40 cm long, female flowers at base of branches. **Fruit** woody-fibrous, to 30 cm long, 20 cm wide, in clusters, elliptical, green to brown, fibrous husk covering the woody nut; dispersed by ocean currents. **Habitat:** Along beaches throughout the tropics. Cultivated to 1000 m. Altitude: Sea level just above high-tide line. Conservation areas: GUA, LAC, OSA, PAC, TEM, TOR. **Range:** Pantropical. Possibly native to Polynesia, Australia, or the Philippines. **Notes:** This is the only species of *Cocos* worldwide. Important source of oil and fiber. Copra is the dried flesh, containing up to 70% oil.

Cocos nucifera

▓ **Crysophila guagara (quaquara, guágara, palmera de escoba, fan palm)**

Spiny tree 5–10 m tall, 8–13 cm diameter, solitary, trunk covered with branched spines, especially near base (photo), spines developing into aerial roots, juvenile plants without trunk. **Leaves** alternate, stalk 1–3 m long, blade palmately compound, 0.85–1.3 m long, 1.2–2 m wide, in fan-shaped sections, segments sharply, deeply toothed, pleated, or split into numerous leaflets (easily confused with *Carludovica palmata*, Cyclanthaceae), dark green above, white below, old leaves persistent. **Flowers** off-white; branched clusters from among leaves, elongate, drooping with many thin, yellowish bracts, falling before fruits mature. **Fruit** round, 1–2 cm wide, waxy white, clustered; blooms and fruits on and off most of the year. **Habitat:** Wet lowland forest understories, often many growing together. Altitude: Sea level to 500 m. Conservation areas: LAC, OSA, PAC. **Range:** CR–W Pan. **Notes:** There are four species of *Crysophila* in Costa Rica. The other fairly common species, *C. warscewiczii,* is very similar but is found up to 900 m elevation.

▨ *Desmoncus schippii* (matamba)

Spiny, vinelike palm, stems to 20 m long, 2–3 cm diameter, spines to 6 cm long. **Leaves** alternate, ranked along upper part of stem, stalk 2–5 cm, blade pinnate, 0.5–1 m long, 6 cm wide, leaflets 15–29 cm long, 2–5 cm wide, midrib elongated to 75 cm, with pairs of stiff, linear, back-slanted appendages replacing leaflets, acting as grappling hooks for climbing. **Flowers** off-white, small; inflorescence branched, bract spiny; blooms in July, Nov., Jan. **Fruit** fleshy, to 2 cm long, 1.5 cm wide, orange to red, eaten by birds and monkeys; fruits Oct.–June. **Habitat:** Wet regions, along edges and in second growth, climbing high into surrounding vegetation. Altitude: Sea level to 600 m, Caribbean lowlands. Conservation areas: CVC, GUA, LAC, TOR. Especially common in TOR. **Range:** Bel–CR. **Notes:** There are four species of *Desmoncus* in Costa Rica.

▨ *Elaeis guineensis* (palma africana, palma de aceite, African oil palm)

Stout palm to 20 m tall, trunk 20–75 cm diameter, leaf scars prominent on older trees, old leaf bases persistent, trunkless when young; leaf sheath short, not extending down trunk. **Leaves** alternate, stalk 1.5–2 m long, blade regularly pinnate, 3–5 m long, leaflets 1–1.2 m long, 3–4 cm wide, clustered in various planes, leaf appearing shaggy, midrib spiny near base. **Flowers** off-white; clusters initially enclosed by a large bract, inflorescence branched once, with 100–200 thin, crimped branches spiraled around floral axis, male and female flowers separate; blooms Dec. **Fruit** fleshy, orange, becoming black, oval, 2–5 cm, in crowded masses of 200–300 on inner parts of stems, ends of branches naked. **Habitat:** Cultivated in wet lowlands, apparently not escaping. Altitude: Sea level to 400 m. Seen in large plantations along the Pacific coast near Quepos. Conservation areas: LAC, OSA, PAC. **Range:** Native to Africa but cultivated pantropically. **Notes:** *Elaeis oleifera* is native to Costa Rica, found in wet lowlands habitats but not widely cultivated as its oil content is lower.

Euterpe precatoria (E. macrospadix) (palmito, palmito dulce)

Tall, solitary palm 3–25 m tall, trunk 4–23 cm diameter, graceful, slender, gray, without noticeable rings except near base of green leaf sheath (crown shaft) 1–2 m long, which covers upper part of trunk. Orange stilt roots at base of trunk, well-spaced, new stilt roots have rusty orange, scaly root cap with few short spines. **Leaves** alternate, stalk 10–30 cm long, blade 2.5–4 m long, regularly pinnate, leaflets 60–80 cm long, 2–4 cm wide, evenly spaced, in one plane, linear, close together, pendulous, old leaves immediately deciduous. **Flowers** pale yellow, tiny, buds pink; inflorescence at base of leaf sheath, 30–50 cm long, branched once, branches numerous, elongate, thin, densely white-hairy, widely spreading, facing upward at acute angle to trunk when in flower; blooms Mar.–Dec. **Fruit** fleshy, round, purple black, to 1.3 cm; fruits Aug.–Feb. **Habitat:** Very wet forests. Altitude: Sea level to 1100 m, most often below 500 m. Conservation areas: CVC, HNO, ICO, OSA, TOR. **Range:** Bel–Brz, Tr. **Notes:** This is the only species of *Euterpe* in Costa Rica. Euterpe is the goddess of song and poetry in Greek mythology.

Geonoma congesta (caña de danta, ukö)

Understory palm 1–6 m tall, stems 2–5 cm diameter, in clusters, often 10–20 together, pale brown or greenish. **Leaves** alternate, stalk 2–35 cm long, blade to 2 m long, irregularly pinnate, in one plane, divisions 25–86 cm long, of variable width, broad–based, leaf tip forked. **Flowers** white, very small; inflorescence stalk 5–10 cm long just below leaves, flowering axis branched once, branches 7–24 cm long, about 0.7 cm wide, irregularly sinuous; blooms on and off most of the year. **Fruit** fleshy, 1–1.4 cm long, elliptical, becoming black, rough–textured; inflorescence stems becoming bright orange in fruit;

fruits Sept.–May. **Habitat:** Very wet lowland forest understories. Altitude: Sea level to 850 m, most often below 400 m. Conservation areas: CVC, GUA, HNO, LAC, OSA, PAC, TOR. **Range:** Hon–NW Col. **Notes:** Much like *Asterogyne martiana*, which has longer leaf stalks. There are 15 species of *Geonoma* in Costa Rica. They comprise one of the most common genera of understory palms.

▨ *Geonoma cuneata* (suita)

Small understory palm, stems solitary, underground, or aboveground to 1.5 m tall, about 3 cm diameter. **Leaves** alternate, stalk about 15–60 cm long, much shorter than blade, blade to 1.2 m long, 17–36 cm wide, simple, or split in 2–15 irregular, broad-based segments, blade tip forked, base tapered to stalk. **Flowers** white, tiny; inflorescence a simple spike, slender, to 1 m long, 0.5 cm wide; blooms and fruits all year. **Fruit** fleshy, purple black, pealike, about 1 cm long; fruiting spike bright red to purplish. **Habitat:** Very wet forest understory. Altitude: Sea level to 1200 m, sometimes to 1900 m, but mostly below 600 m. Conservation areas: ARE, CVC, GUA, HNO, LAC, LAP, OSA, PAC, TOR. **Range:** SE Nic–Ec, Ven. **Notes:** Probably the most common species of *Geonoma* in Costa Rica.

▨ *Geonoma interrupta* (súrtuba)

Small to medium palm 1–10 m tall, stems solitary, 2–5 cm diameter, brown, canelike with prominent nodes; thin, prop roots growing from base of stems, sometimes red (photo); old leaves persistent; leaf sheath fibrous, short. **Leaves** alternate, stalk 2–90 cm long, blade to 2 m long, unevenly, pinnately divided, leaflets 33–68 cm long, broad-based, in one plane, of irregular widths. **Flowers** white, tiny; inflorescence among leaves 32–58 cm long, branched 1–3 times, branches 9–25 cm long, thin, to 0.3 cm wide; blooms and fruits on and off most of the year. **Fruit** fleshy, black, to 0.6 cm long; fruiting stems reddish. **Habitat:** Wet to very wet forest understories or disturbed second growth. Altitude: Sea level to 850 m, occasionally to 1700 m. Conservation areas: CVC, GUA, HNO, LAC, OSA, PAC, TOR. **Range:** S Mex–Pr.

Aerial roots

Iriartea deltoidea (maquenque, chonta, jira)

Solitary canopy palm 8–30 m tall, trunk 10–45 cm diameter, gray, ringed with leaf scars, columnar, or swollen with a bottlelike appearance, base with a dense cone of thick, black or orange, prickly, stilt roots to 1.5 m tall; leaf sheaths long, tubular, enclosing top of trunk in a crown shaft. **Leaves** alternate, stalk 0.5–1 m long, blade 2–3.5 m long, irregularly pinnate, leaflets asymmetrical, fish-tail-shaped, tip broad, rag\in all planes giving an "ostrich feather" appearance, terminal leaflet undivided. **Flowers** white, small; inflorescence below leaf sheath, bud to 2 m long, enclosed by a horn-shaped woody bract, inflorescence with 33–40 branches 0.5–1 m long; blooms Nov.–May; pollinated by bees. **Fruit** greenish yellow, round, 1–2.5 cm diameter, outer husk splitting open, 1-seeded; fruits on and off through the year; eaten by toucans, monkeys. **Habitat:** Very wet forests. Altitude: Sea level to 1300 m, mostly below 800 m. Conservation areas: ARE, GUA, CVC, LAC, OSA, TOR. **Range:** SE Nic–Ven, Bol, Brz. **Notes:** This is the only species of *Iriartea* worldwide. The leaves are much like those of *Socratea exorrhiza*.

Manicaria saccifera (sílico, palma real, yolillo)

Tree with 1 to several trunks, 2–8 m tall, trunk 15–30 cm diameter, covered by old leaves. **Leaves** alternate, stalk 1–2 m long, blade pinnate, 3–4 m long, 1–2 m wide, elliptic in outline, appearing paddle-shaped, tip blunt to split, surface usually pale, gray green compared to surrounding vegetation, leaflets numerous, in one plane, segments irregular 1–18 cm wide, closely spaced, margins toothed, irregular. **Flowers** off-white, clusters completely surrounded by a fibrous bract 1.1 m long, which stays closed; inflorescence stalk 35–50 cm long. **Fruit** brown, covered with short warty spines, 1–3 seeds rounded to 2- to 3-lobed, 4–5 cm long, 4–7 cm wide; fruits in Nov. **Habitat:** Very wet, low swampy, coastal forests. Apparently tolerant of brackish water. Altitude: Sea level to 100 m, Caribbean coast, rarely along southern Pacific coast. Conservation areas: OSA (rarely), very common in TOR. **Range:** Bel, Gua–Pr, Guy, Tr, Brz. **Notes:** This is the only species of *Manicaria* in Costa Rica, possibly the only species worldwide. Often seen with *Raphia taedigera*. Leaves used for thatching.

▦ *Prestoea decurrens* (caña lucia, palmito, palmitillo, mantequilla)

Tall slender palm, stems usually clustered, 3–8 m tall, 7–12 cm diameter, stems green, base with small reddish or yellowish aerial roots; old leaves often persistent. **Leaves** alternate, stalk 0.6–1.5 m long, blade 1.5–3 m long, regularly, finely pinnate, leaflets 25–80 cm long, 2–6 cm wide, linear, tip often rounded. **Flowers** off-white, small; inflorescence bract 0.6–1.3 m long, below leaves, branches 40–50, spikelike, thin, 27–60 cm long, at right angles to axis, becoming dark yellow; blooms and fruits most of the year. **Fruit** purple black, rounded, 0.6–0.9 cm long and wide, 1-seeded; fruiting stems often pinkish. **Habitat:** Very wet forests. Altitude: Sea level to 1000 m. Conservation areas: ARE, CVC, GUA, LAC, OSA, PAC, TOR. **Range:** Nic–Ec. **Notes:** There are five species of *Prestoea* in Costa Rica.

Raphia taedigera photo opposite

▦ *Raphia taedigera* (targuá, yolillo)

Palm 3–12 m tall, stems 25–60 cm diameter, usually in clusters, old leaves persistent, covering trunks; densely surrounded by small aerial roots (pneumatophores) that protrude from the surrounding mud when growing in frequently inundated sites. **Leaves** alternate, stalk 1.5–5 m long, 15 cm wide, base broad, spiny; blade pinnate, 5–15 m long, to 2.5 m wide, ends drooping, leaflets arranged in several planes, giving shaggy appearance, spiny along margins and veins. **Flowers** off-white, small; inflorescence of branched clusters 1–3 m long, drooping; blooms June–Aug. **Fruit** elliptic, 5–7 cm long, yellow, with reddish, overlapping scales like a small pineapple, 4 cm wide; fruit cluster to 3 m long, cone-shaped; eaten by peccaries and tapirs, seeds also dispersed by water. **Habitat:** Very wet regions in lowland, swampy areas, mostly coastal. Altitude: Sea level to 100 m. Conservation areas: OSA, TOR. **Range:** Nic–NW Col, NE Brz. **Notes:** This is the only species of *Raphia* in the Americas. It formerly covered large areas, but most large stands have been cleared for oil palm and banana plantations, An African species is the source of raffia fiber.

14

▨ *Reinhardtia gracilis* (window palm)

Small understory palm, stems usually in clusters, 40 cm to 2.5 m tall, 0.3–1 cm diameter, upper stem covered by old, brown, fibrous leaf sheaths. **Leaves** alternate, stalk 9–32 cm long; blade 12–45 cm long, simple with deeply split tip or pinnate with 2 leaflets per side, midrib very short, leaves may appear almost palmate, base of leaflets with holes, uppermost leaflets much larger than lower ones, tips broad, unequal, margins toothed, appearing rather ragged, bases wide, fused to midrib. **Flowers** off-white, small; inflorescence from among leaves, once-branched, stalk elongate; blooms and fruits most of the year. **Fruit** fleshy, purple black, egg-shaped, about 1.5 cm long, 1 seed; fruiting stems red. **Habitat:** Very wet forest understories. Altitude: Sea level to 850 m, mostly on the Caribbean slope. Conservation areas: ARE, CVC, GUA, LAC, TOR. **Range:** S Mex–NW Col. **Notes:** There are four species of *Reinhardtia* in Costa Rica. Several, including *R. gracilis*, are popular as garden or house plants.

Raphia taedigera

15

Socratea exorrhiza (S. durissima) (chonta, maquenque, palmito amargo)

Tree to 6–25 m tall, trunk 5–25 cm diameter, solitary, gray; prickly stilt roots forming an open cone, 1–3 m high, replacing trunk at base (photo); leaf sheaths bluish green, forming a long, tubular crown shaft 1–1.5 m long, extending down trunk, bulging at base. **Leaves** alternate, 4–7, stalk 10–40 cm long, blade pinnate, 2–4 m long, leaflets 8–25 per side, 30–60 cm long, in one plane, narrow at base, new leaflets fish-tail-shaped, deeply toothed or becoming divided, tips drooping; juvenile plants often with simple leaves. **Flowers** white, small; inflorescence below leaf sheath, branched once,

branches to 40 cm long, widely spreading; pollinated by small beetles. **Fruit** dull yellow, 2–3 cm long, elliptic, with a thin, woody husk; in drooping clusters; eaten by many birds and mammals. **Habitat:** Very wet forests. Altitude: Sea level to 750 m. Conservation areas: CVC, LAC, OSA, TOR. **Range:** SE Nic–Guy, Brz, Bol. **Notes:** The only species of Socratea in Costa Rica. Leaves much like those of Iriartea, but the open roots of Socratea are unique, thus the mnemonic "Socrates is not dense."

Synechanthus warscewiczianus

Understory palm, stems usually clustered, 0.6–5 m tall, 2–7 cm diameter, green, ringed by old leaf scars; leaf sheaths forming a short crown shaft. **Leaves** alternate, stalk 20–65 cm long, blade 0.7–1.2 m long, usually pinnate, sometimes simple with a forked tip; leaflets 20–60 cm long, 1–13 cm wide, in one plane, regular or irregular widths, tip forked. **Flowers** yellow, small; inflorescence to 1 m long, branches numerous, very slender, 8–48 cm long, stiffly spreading; blooms most of the year. **Fruit** fleshy, becoming bright yellow, orange, finally red (photo), 1–3 cm long, elliptic, like "jellybeans"; 1 seed, with brainlike grooves; fruits mostly July–Apr. **Habitat:** Very wet forest understories. Altitude: Sea level to 1450 m. Conservation areas: ARE CVC, GUA, LAC, OSA, PAC, TEM, TOR. **Range:** Nic–Ec. **Notes:** There are two species of Synechanthus in Costa Rica, S. fibrosus is not as common and is almost entirely on the Caribbean slope. Both are much like Chamaedorea, but fruits of Synechanthus are more fleshy with brainlike grooved seed.

▦ **Welfia regia (W. georgii)** (palma conga, palma real, maquenque)

Tree 5–25 m tall, trunk 10–30 cm diameter, solitary, erect, grayish, ringed by old leaf scars; crown large and dense, juvenile trees without trunk; leaf sheath short, brownish-hairy; old leaves not persistent. **Leaves** alternate, erect, stalk 0.3–1 m long, blade regularly pinnate, 3–6 m long, tip arching, leaflets 0.3–1.3 m long, 1–12 cm wide, narrowly lance-shaped, pointed at both ends, in one plane, drooping, new leaves red. **Flowers** off-white, small; inflorescence below leaves, large, becoming woody, main stalk 6–40 cm long with 4–10 stiff, 8-angled branches, 40–80 cm long, 1.5–2.5 cm diameter, each face has cavities that bear flowers; blooms Apr.–May. **Fruit** fleshy, reddish brown, elliptic, 2.5–4 cm long, 1–2 cm wide, fruit pulp sweet, 1 large seed, ripened fruits fall June–Oct., fruit eaten by birds and mammals, which disperse the seeds; old fruiting stalks are very recognizable, usually litter ground under the tree (photo). **Habitat:** Very wet, lowland primary forests. Altitude: Sea level to 750 m. Conservation areas: CVC, OSA, TOR. **Range:** Hon–Ec. **Notes:** This is the only species of *Welfia* in Costa Rica.

FAMILY *CYCLANTHACEAE*

▦ **Carludovica palmata** (chidra, estococa, tule, Panama hat plant)

Very large, stemless herb, 3–4 m tall. **Leaves** all from base of plant, stalk to 3.5 m tall, cylindrical, blade deeply, palmately lobed, to 1 m long, 1.9 m wide, surface pleated, lobes irregular, divided to past middle, lobe tips pointed, surface shiny on both sides, veins all parallel, extending to leaf tip. **Flowers** white, minute, crowded on a fleshy spike above several green, white and reddish purple bracts, each about 25 cm long, inflorescence stalk to 45 cm long, arising from ground, amid leaf stems; blooms and fruits Sept., Dec., Feb., May. **Fruit** spike green, about 12 cm long, 2.5 cm wide, with intricate geometric surface pattern; splits open bananalike, to reveal bright red orange fruit flesh and red, fleshy-coated seeds, about 1 cm, on a central core, May. **Habitat:** Wet to very wet lowland forest understories and disturbed sites; also cultivated. Altitude: Caribbean slope, sea level to 100 m. Conservation areas: LAC, LAP, TOR. **Range:** Mex–Bol. **Notes:** There are four species of *Carludovica* in Costa Rica.

Flower

*Dicranopygium umbrophilum
photos opposite*

Cyclanthus bipartitus (hoja de lapa, oreja de burro, tornillo)

Very large, stemless herb to 3.5 m tall, sap milky. **Leaves** all from base of plant, stalk to over 1 m, longer than blade, blade 0.6–1.2 m long, deeply 2-lobed, split almost completely in two, each lobe 8–21 cm wide, midribs on each half, near inner edge at base, becoming centered near tip, surface thin, shiny. **Flowers** off-white, very small, in disklike whorls, on a thick spike 9–14 cm long, 2.5–3.5 cm wide, initially covered by 4 inflorescence bracts, soon falling off; inflorescence stalk 40–90 cm long; blooms and fruits most of the year, especially July–Sept. Pollinated by small beetles. **Fruit** spike fleshy cylindrical, to 6 cm wide, ringed, yellowish, falling apart in short sections, each with numerous small seeds. **Habitat:** Very wet forest understories. Altitude: Sea level to 1600 m, mostly below 500 m. Conservation areas: ARE, CVC, GUA, HNO, LAC, LAP, OSA, PAC, TEM, TOR. **Range:** Bol, Ven, Trin, Guy, Brz, LsAnt. **Notes:** This is the only species of *Cyclanthus* in Costa Rica.

Fruit

Dicranopygium umbrophilum

Palmlike herb, terrestrial or vinelike at the base of trees, stem to about 50 cm tall. **Leaves** alternate, stalk about 30 cm long, base clasping stem, blade 16–47 cm long, 2-lobed, split 1/3–2/3 of its length, lobes 3–11 cm wide, tips long-pointed, base wedge-shaped, surface dark green, sharply pleated by impressed, parallel veins extending to lobe tips, margins entire. **Flowers** off-white, tiny, inconspicuous but forming a geometric pattern on the thick spike; initially enclosed by purplish, deciduous bracts; inflorescence often purplish, cylindrical, stalk much shorter than leaves; blooms and fruits most of the year. **Fruit** fleshy, green, a knoblike spike about 3.5 long, 1.5 cm wide, with a raised, tilelike pattern, splitting apart to release sticky, reddish, cylindrical seeds. **Habitat:** Very wet forest understories, sometimes on rocks or stream banks. Altitude: Sea level to 850 m, mostly below 500 m, Caribbean lowlands. Conservation areas: CVC, HNO, LAC, TOR. **Range:** Nic–Pan. **Notes:** There are six species of *Dicranopygium* in Costa Rica.

Sphaeradenia praetermissa

Epiphytic or occasionally terrestrial herb to about 1 m tall. **Leaves** alternate, stalk about 45 cm, base sheathing stem, blade 35–75 cm long, split 2/3–3/4 of its length, lobes 4–11 cm wide, surface leathery, pleated by impressed veins extending to lobe tips, margins smooth. **Flowers** white, small, individually inconspicuous but forming a geometric pattern on the thick spike; inflorescence reddish; blooms Sept.–Jan., June. **Fruit** fleshy, bright red, berrylike, 4–10 cm long, 2 cm wide, seeds white, embedded in a very sticky, gelatinous orange coating; fruits Apr.–May. **Habitat:** Very wet mountain forests. Altitude: 1000–2500 m. Conservation areas: CVC, LAC, LAP. **Range:** Endemic to CR. **Notes:** There are 12 species of *Sphaeradenia* in Costa Rica. They are all quite similar, with narrow, 2-lobed leaves. They are mostly epiphytic and are most often found on the Caribbean slope.

Dicranopygium umbrophilum

Fruit detail

19

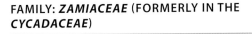

FAMILY: *ZAMIACEAE* (FORMERLY IN THE *CYCADACEAE*)

▨ *Zamia fairchildiana* (zamia)

Palmlike, woody, nonflowering plant to 2.5 m tall, trunk thin, fibrous, young plants trunkless. **Leaves** alternate, few, 0.65–2.0 m long including stalk; leaf stalks prickly near base, blade pinnate, leaflets 12–36 per side, 21–37 cm long, 3–5 cm wide, lance-shaped to elliptical, pointed at both ends, leathery, smooth, edges curled under, margins usually smooth. **Gymnosperm.** No flowers, no fruit, sexes on separate plants; female cones about 12–20 cm long, 5–7 cm wide, rust-colored, like thick ears of corn with coarse, angular seeds covered by red fleshy aril; male cones 8–16 cm long, 2–3 cm wide, bearing pollen; cones produced at top of stem amid leaf stems, present most of the year. **Habitat:** Understories of moist to very wet forests. Altitude: Sea level to 1700 m, mostly below 1000 m, on the Pacific slope. Conservation areas: LAC (infrequently), LAP, OSA (most often), PAC. **Range:** S Mex, CR, Pan. **Notes:** There are four species of *Zamia* listed for Costa Rica, this is the most common.

▨ *Zamia neurophyllidia* (*Z. skinneri*) (yuquilla, zamia)

Much like *Z. fairchildiana* but usually trunkless unless very old, often less than 1 m tall. **Leaves** alternate, few, to 1 m long including densely prickly leaf stalk; 1/3–1/2 length of leaf, blade pinnate, leaflets 5–10 per side, 22–30 cm long, 6–10 cm wide, elliptic, stiff, conspicuously corrugated from deeply impressed, parallel veins, margin spiny, young leaflets very shiny. **Gymnosperm.** No flowers, no fruit. Sexes on separate plants. Female cones brownish with seeds covered by red fleshy arils; male plants bear pollen-producing cones; cones present on and off June–Jan., mostly Aug.–Nov. **Habitat:** Understories of moist to very wet forests. Altitude: Sea level to 1100 m, mostly on the Caribbean slope. Conservation areas: ARE, CVC, GUA, LAC, TOR. Seen at La Selva Biological Station. **Range:** Gua–Pan.

TALL TREES

■ **LEAVES NEEDLE- OR SCALELIKE**

Casuarina cunninghamiana
Cupressus lusitanica
Pinus caribaea

■ **BROADLEAVED TREES**

Anacardium excelsum
Astronium graveolens
Mangifera indica
Spondias mombin
Cananga odorata
Rollinia mucosa
Plumeria rubra
Schefflera rodriguesiana
  (Didymopanax pittieri)
Alnus acuminata
Spathodea campanulata
Tabebuia ochracea subsp.
  neochrysantha
Tabebuia rosea
  (T. pentaphylla)
Bombacopsis quinata
Ceiba pentandra
Ochroma pyramidale
  (O. lagopus)
Pachira aquatica
Pseudobombax septenatum
Cordia alliodora
Brunellia costaricensis
Bursera simaruba
Caryocar costaricense
Cecropia peltata
Licania arborea
Calophyllum longifolium
Clusia rosea
Terminalia catappa
Terminalia oblonga
Diospyros digyna
Sloanea ampla
Hieronyma alchorneoides
Hura crepitans
Caesalpinia eriostachys
Cassia grandis

Hymenaea courbaril
Myrospermum frutescens
Prioria copaifera
Schizolobium parahyba
Dipteryx oleifera
  (D. panamensis)
Erythrina fusca
Erythrina poeppigiana
Lonchocarpus macrophyllus
Pterocarpus officinalis
Enterolobium cyclocarpum
Inga edulis
Inga multijuga
Inga punctata
Inga spectabilis
Inga vera
Pentaclethra macroloba
Samanea saman
  (Pithecellobium s.)
Quercus bumelioides
  (Q. copeyensis)
Quercus costaricensis
Quercus oleoides
Calatola costaricensis
Persea americana
Lecythis ampla
Magnolia poasana
Hampea appendiculata
Wercklea woodsonii
Cedrela odorata
Guarea rhopalocarpa
Swietenia humilis
Artocarpus altilis
Brosimum alicastrum
Brosimum utile
Castilla elastica
Ficus benjamina

Ficus costaricana
Ficus cotinifolia
Ficus insipida
Ficus maxima
Naucleopsis naga
Virola koschnyi
Eucalyptus deglupta
Myrcianthes fragrans
Cespedesia spathulata
    (C. macrophylla)
Triplaris melaenodendron
Rhizophora mangle
Alibertia patinoi
Calycophyllum candidissimum
Genipa americana
Guettarda crispiflora
Macrocnemum roseum
    (M. glabrescens)
Simira maxonii
    (Sickingia m.)
Salix humboldtiana
Billia hippocastanum

Blighia sapida
Nephelium lappaceum
Chrysophyllum cainito
Manilkara chicle
Pouteria fossicola
Pouteria sapota
    (P. mammosa)
Sideroxylon capiri
Guazuma ulmifolia
Pterygota excelsa
Sterculia apetala
Apeiba membranacea
Apeiba tibourbou
Goethalsia meiantha
Heliocarpus americanus
Luehea alternifolia
    (L. speciosa)
Luehea seemannii
Citharexylum
    donnell-smithii
Gmelina arborea
Tectona grandis

Woody plants growing to over 10 m (30 ft) tall, usually with a single trunk, are classed as tall trees. Many trees have a wide range of size and habit. Many may flower and fruit when quite small and shrublike. Trees with a maximum height of less than about 13 m (40 ft) that often bloom as shrubs or smaller trees are not included here.

LEAVES NEEDLE- OR SCALELIKE

■ *Casuarina cunninghamiana* (pino de Australia)
   Family Casuarinaceae

Evergreen tree to over 20 m tall, with a pine-tree-like appearance, bark dark, flaky, twigs slender, green with longitudinal ridges and thickened nodes. **Leaves** reduced to 7–10 minute scales, in whorls at each node, terminal branches look like long pine needles, gray green. **Flowers** inconspicuous; sexes separate; male flower clusters green, about 2 cm long, females reddish, conelike. **Fruit** dry, round, to 0.6–1 cm long, conelike, or like small pineapples, scales opening to release winged seeds. **Habitat:** Planted as windbreaks, rarely escaping from cultivation. Altitude: About 1000 to 2000 m. Conservation areas: ARE, CVC, PAC. **Range:** Native to Australia and New Guinea. Widely planted in many tropical regions, has become invasive in some places. **Notes:** The other species grown in Costa Rica is *Casuarina equisetifolia,* with 6–8 leaf-scales per whorl. It is very salt tolerant and grown along the shore in some places, has become invasive in southern Florida and other areas. Despite their appearance these are flowering plants, not conifers.

■ *Cupressus lusitanica (ciprés, ciprés mexicano)*
   Family Cupressaceae

Evergreen tree to 30 m tall, usually much shorter; more or less cylindrical or narrowly pyramid-shaped, trunk usually branching from near base, branches reaching upward, bark reddish brown, shredding, older bark fissured. **Leaves** opposite, tiny, scalelike, in 4 ranks, closely covering twigs (photo), blue green. **Gymnosperm.** No flowers or true fruit; female cones about 1 cm wide, irregularly berrylike, blue green to dark blue with a whitish bloom (photo), eventually turning brown, scales opening to release numerous tiny, winged seeds. Male cones small, producing pollen. **Habitat:** Open pastures, roadsides. Planted as windbreaks and groves, sometimes escaped from cultivation. Altitude: 1200–3000 m. Conservation areas: ARE, CVC, LAC. **Range:** Mex–Hon. **Notes:** Introduced to Lusitania, Portugal, in the 1600s, from which the name is derived. There may be up to four species of Cupressaceae in Costa Rica; none is native; *C. lusitanica* is the most common.

23

■ *Pinus caribaea* (pino Caribe)
Family Pinaceae
Tree to 45 m tall, trunk to 1 m diameter; crown conical, becoming irregular, young bark purple brown, thin, peeling, older bark dark brown to gray, fissured, shedding in wide, flat plates. **Leaves** needlelike, crowded at ends of twigs in tight clusters of 3 needles, each 15–30 cm long, 0.1 cm wide, tip sharply pointed, stiff, dark glossy green. **Gymnosperm.** No flowers or true fruit; female cones becoming reddish brown, 5–15 cm long, about 3 cm wide (when scales closed), egg-shaped, scales woody, eventually spreading, each tipped by a tiny spine; seeds winged, to 2.5 cm long, dispersed by wind. Pollen produced by small, herbaceous male cones 13 cm long, seasonally. **Habitat:** Planted in mountain regions as windbreaks and in plantations. Apparently not occurring in the wild. Altitude: Midelevation mountains. Conservation areas: ARE, CVC, LAC. **Range:** Mex–Nic. Widely cultivated in tropical and subtropical regions worldwide. Has become invasive in some Pacific islands. **Notes:** Costa Rica has up to seven species of *Pinus*, all nonnative; *P. caribaea* is probably the most common.

BROADLEAVED TREES

■ *Anacardium excelsum* (espavé, rabito, wild cashew)
Family Anacardiaceae
Large tree 15–60 m tall, trunk to 2 m diameter, base often somewhat buttressed, bark coarse, deeply fissured, sometimes flaking in patches, sap rust-colored. **Leaves** alternate, spiraled at ends of branches, stalks about 3 cm long, swollen at base, blade 9–40 cm long, 5–16 cm wide, widest near apex, tip rounded, notched, base tapered, veins pale, numerous, at nearly right angles to midrib, margin wavy. **Flowers** cream green to pinkish, radially symmetrical, small, petals about 0.6 cm long, linear, strong sweet scent, buds and calyx densely rusty-hairy, stamens 10; inflorescence of broad clusters at ends of branches; blooms Dec.–Apr. **Fruit** fleshy, kidney-shaped, 3–4 cm long, borne on a twisted, fleshy appendage to 3 cm long, Mar.–June; fruit eaten by many mammals and birds. **Habitat:** Wet forests, seasonally dry forests along rivers and streams. Altitude: Sea level to 1000 m, mostly on the Pacific slope. Conservation areas: ARE, GUA, OSA, PAC, TEM. **Range:** CR–N S Amer. **Notes:** Nuts contain a very toxic, caustic oil but are edible if roasted. *Anacardium excelsum* and *A. occidentalis* are the only species of Anacardium in Costa Rica.

■ *Astronium graveolens* (ron-ron, jovillo)
Family Anacardiaceae

Large tree to 35 m tall, trunk to 80 cm diameter, outer bark peeling off in small rounded patches leaving irregular, pale depressions. **Leaves** alternate, odd-pinnate, to 35 cm long including stalk, leaflets mostly opposite, on stalks to 0.6 cm long, blades 4–14 cm long, 2–7 cm wide, lance-shaped to elliptic-pointed at both ends, old leaves becoming yellow orange, briefly deciduous before flowering. **Flowers** yellowish green, radially symmetrical, sexes usually on separate plants, 5-parted, petals to 0.3 cm, sepals enlarging to 1.5 cm and persistent in fruit; inflorescence of broad clusters to 25 cm long; blooms Sept.–May. **Fruit** fleshy, oblong, to 1.5 cm long, 1-seeded. **Habitat:** Wet to seasonally dry forests. Altitude: Pacific slope, sea level to 1000 m. Conservation areas: GUA, OSA, PAC, TEM. **Range:** Mex–E Brz and Par. **Notes:** This is the only species of *Astronium* in Costa Rica.

■ *Mangifera indica* (mango, manga, manco de mecha)
Family Anacardiaceae

Tree to 40 m tall, trunk to 1 m diameter, bark dark gray, smooth or slightly flaky, sap milky. **Leaves** alternate, stalk to 6 cm long, blades 9–30 cm long, 2–7 cm wide oblong, pointed at both ends. **Flowers** white radially symmetrical, to 1 cm, 5-parted; inflorescence branched, of broad, clusters at ends of branches; blooms Sept.–Jan. **Fruit** fleshy, yellow to red, large, about 10 cm long or more, slightly kidney-shaped, flesh yellow, sweet, edible, sap of fruit rind irritating; ripening May–July. **Habitat:** Widely cultivated and escaped in open areas, roadsides, pastures, gardens. Altitude: Sea level to 1500 m. Conservation areas: Most parts of the country. **Range:** Native to southern Asia. Cultivated in tropical regions worldwide. **Notes:** This is the only species of *Mangifera* in Costa Rica.

■ *Spondias mombin* (jobo, jocote, wild plum)
Family Anacardiaceae

Tree to 35 m tall, trunk to 60 cm diameter, bark pale gray, deeply and coarsely fissured, the raised segments hard and rough, twigs tan, stout, leaf scars prominent. **Leaves** alternate, stalk about 8 cm, blade pinnate, to 60 cm long, leaflets opposite to subopposite, 5–20 cm long, 2–7 cm wide, oblong to egg-shaped, tips tapered, base asymmetrical, prominent vein around margin. **Flowers** white, radially symmetrical, to 0.7 cm wide, 5-parted petals curling inward, tips pointed, stamens 10; inflorescence of broad, branched clusters to 60 cm long; blooms Jan.–Apr., July, Sept. **Fruit** fleshy, yellow orange, to 3.5 cm long, oblong, sweet, edible, 1 large seed (photo); fruit present Feb.–Nov. **Habitat:** Wet to seasonally dry forests. Altitude: Sea level to 1000 m mostly on the Pacific slope, below 300 m. Conservation areas: GUA, OSA, PAC, TEM, TOR (infrequent). **Range:** Mex–SE Brz. Introduced in Africa and SE Asia. **Notes:** There are three other, less common species of *Spondias* in Costa Rica.

■ *Cananga odorata* (ilang-ilang)
Family Annonaceae

Tree to 15 m tall, trunk cylindrical, long branches arch down, tips upturned, bark whitish gray. **Leaves** alternate, in one plane along opposite sides of the stem, blade 10–15 cm long, 5–8 cm wide, oblong, tip tapered, base rounded. **Flowers** green, turning yellow, very fragrant, petals 6, elongate; you are likely to smell this tree before you see it; blooms Feb., Apr., June, Nov. **Fruit** fleshy, becoming black, small, in rounded clusters, radiating from the end of a stalk (photo). **Habitat:** Cultivated and naturalized in wet regions. Altitude: Sea level to 1200 m. Conservation areas: CVC, HNO, LAC, OSA, PAC, TOR. **Range:** Native to SE Asia, Australia, Indonesia. **Notes:** This is the only species of *Cananga* in Costa Rica. It has become an invasive tree in some tropical counties and many Pacific islands.

■ *Rollinia mucosa* (anonillo, anono)
Family Annonaceae

Tree 4–16 m tall. **Leaves** alternate, 10–24 cm long, 4–8.5 cm wide, oblong, ranked along branches, tip pointed, veins numerous, parallel. **Flowers** pale green to reddish green, 3-parted, 2 cm wide, petals like thick, fleshy wings, with a helical arrangement, not appearing flowerlike, surface finely rusty-hairy; inflorescence of 1–3, opposite a leaf; blooms Feb., July, Sept. **Fruit** hard-fleshy, becoming yellow, surface with thick, fleshy overlapping protuberances, rounded, 6–10 cm long, 1 seed 1 cm long; fruits Jan., June–Nov. **Habitat:** Wet to seasonally dry forests. Altitude: Sea level to 800 m, mostly on the Pacific slope. Conservation areas: CVC, GUA, PAC, TEM. **Range:** Mex–Pan. **Notes:** There are four species if *Rollinia* in Costa Rica, all have similar 3-parted, fleshy flowers and fruit with fleshy scales.

■ *Plumeria rubra* (flor blanca, frangipani, jiquiloche)
Family Apocynaceae

Tree or large shrub 5–15 m tall, bark gray, irregularly flaking, branches few, stout, reaching upward, ends of branches 3–4 cm diameter, tips rounded leaf scars large. **Leaves** alternate, 10–41 cm long, 4–14 cm wide, elliptic, pointed at both ends, thick, secondary veins with loop connections along margin, margins smooth, deciduous in dry season. **Flowers** white with yellow center, fragrant (flowers of cultivated shrubs red pink), petal lobes overlapping, appearing twisted; inflorescence of branched clusters; blooms and fruits most of the year. **Fruit** dry, elongate twin pods 17–38 cm long, 3–4 cm wide (bottom, right photo), splitting open to release winged seeds. **Habitat:** Mostly in seasonally dry forests, sometimes in wet forests. Altitude: Sea level to 1400 m, mostly below 300 m on the Pacific slope. Conservation areas: ARE, GUA, OSA (rarely), PAC, TEM. **Range:** Mex–Pan, WI. **Notes:** This is the only species of *Plumeria* in Costa Rica.

Courtesy of Margaret Gargiullo

■ *Schefflera rodriguesiana (Didymopanax pittieri)* (cacho de venado)
Family Araliaceae

Tree to 25 m tall, trunk to 40 cm diameter, bark flat, thin, mottled, with vertical rows of minute lenticels, sap with sweet, strong odor, old fruiting stems often sticking up above leaves, branches thick. **Leaves** alternate, clustered in spirals at ends of branches, stalk to 1 m long, swollen at base, blade palmately compound, leaflet stalks elongate, blades to 45 cm long, 19 cm wide, oblong, tip tapered, base blunt, densely rusty-hairy below. **Flowers** white to pale green, minute; inflorescence of dense, drooping, spikelike, bottle-brush-shaped clusters, to 50 cm long, at top of tree; blooms Feb.–Sept. **Fruit** fleshy, white, becoming red to purple (photo), 1 cm long, 0.4 cm wide, flattened, 2 seeds; fruit present Mar.–Sept. **Habitat:** Open sites, second growth. Altitude: 800–3200 m. Conservation areas: CVC, GUA, HNO, LAC, LAP, PAC. **Range:** CR, Pan. **Notes:** There are 12 species of *Schefflera* in Costa Rica.

Spathodea campanulata

■ *Alnus acuminata* (jaúl, aliso, alder)
Family Betulaceae

Tree 10–30 m tall, trunk to 40 cm diameter, slender, straight, bark pale, rather smooth, at least in smaller trees, usually mottled by lichen patches; sprouting from roots and often forming large stands. **Leaves** alternate, 5–17 cm long, 3–9 cm wide, egg-shaped, tip pointed, color gray green, secondary veins parallel, ascending, margins toothed. **Flowers** greenish brown, inconspicuous, minute, sexes separate, in dangling catkins made up of tiny bracts interspersed with flowers, male catkins 4–12 cm long, female catkins shorter; in small, branched clusters; probably wind pollinated; blooms Jan., Apr.–May. **Fruit** woody, cone-like, about 2 cm long with numerous small seeds enclosed by the woody bracts, wind dispersed; fruit present most of the year. **Habitat:** Common at higher elevations in open areas, primary or second forests, roadcuts. Altitude: 1100–3000 m. Conservation areas: ARE, CVC, LAC, LAP, PAC. **Range:** Mex–S Amer. **Notes:** Nodules in the roots associated with nitrogen-fixing bacteria explains their growth in poor soils. Used for timber and planted in reforestation projects. This is the only member of the Betulaceae in Costa Rica.

■ *Spathodea campanulata*
(llama del bosque, African tulip tree)
Family Bignoniaceae

Tree rarely taller than 20 m. **Leaves** opposite or in whorls of 3, blade pinnate, leaflets to 15 cm long, broadly elliptical, glossy, margins smooth. **Flowers** orange red often with yellow markings and dark lines, very showy, bilaterally symmetrical, broadly tubular, to 9 cm long, 5 cm wide across mouth of tube, flattened side to side, petal lobes 5, 2 cm long, calyx bractlike, tip pointed; inflorescence of dense, rounded clusters at ends of branches; blooms Feb.–Mar. **Fruit** dry, pods to 25 cm long, 6 cm wide, tapered at both ends, splitting into boat-shaped halves to release winged seeds, wind dispersed. **Habitat:** Widely cultivated, occasionally escaped into open sites in natural areas. Altitude: Sea level to 1100 m. Conservation areas: OSA, PAC. **Range:** Native to Africa. **Notes:** This is the only species of *Spathodea* in Costa Rica.

Alnus acuminata (all three above)

Spathodea campanulata photos opposite

■ *Tabebuia ochracea subsp. neochrysantha*
(guayacan, corteza amarilla, cortéz)
Family Bignoniaceae

Tree to 25 m tall, trunk to 50 cm diameter, outer bark with shallow vertical furrows between flat ridges, small branches 4-sided, hairy when young. **Leaves** opposite, palmately compound, leaflet blades 5–22 cm long, 2–4 cm wide, egg-shaped, tip pointed, base blunt, very thin, densely tan-hairy below, deciduous in dry season. **Flowers** yellow with red-tinged throat, showy, broadly tubular, bilaterally symmetrical, to 8 cm long, petal lobes 5; inflorescence of dense clusters at ends of branches; pollinated by bees; blooms when leafless, Jan.–Apr. **Fruit** dry, cylindrical with tapered ends, to 25 cm long, 1 cm wide, surface golden-woolly, splitting open to release winged seeds, about 2 cm wide. **Habitat:** Moist to seasonally dry forests, often in disturbed sites. Altitude: Pacific slope, sea level to 1000 m. Conservation areas: GUA, LAP, PAC, TEM. **Range:** El Salv and Hon–Ven, Tr. Other subspecies found in Brz, Par, Arg. **Notes:** Wood very dense and hard, sinks in water, used for furniture and utensils. There are six species of *Tabebuia* in Costa Rica. *Tabebuia chrysantha* and *T. guayacan* also have yellow flowers.

■ *Tabebuia rosea (T. pentaphylla)*
(roble de sabana, mayflower)
Family Bignoniaceae

Tree to 35 m tall, trunk to 1 m diameter, bark very thick, deeply fissured, twigs somewhat scaly. **Leaves** opposite, stalk 5–32 cm long, blade palmately compound, leaflet stalks 2–11 cm long, blade of center leaflet 8–35 cm long, 3–18 cm wide, the lateral leaflets smaller, broadly elliptic, tip abruptly pointed, base blunt, deciduous in dry season. **Flowers** lavender, magenta, or whitish, showy, bilaterally symmetrical, tubular, 5–10 cm long, 2–3 cm wide at top of tube, petal lobes 5, 2.5 cm long; inflorescence branched; blooms Feb.–Sept. **Fruit** dry, cylindrical, to 38 cm long, about 1 cm wide, pointed at both ends, densely scaly, splitting open to release winged seeds, to 4 cm wide. **Habitat:** Wet to seasonally dry forests. Also commonly cultivated, used as a street tree (Paseo Colón, in San José). Altitude: Sea level to 1000 m. Conservation areas: GUA, OSA, PAC, TEM, TOR. **Range:** Mex–Ven. **Notes:** Wood used to make furniture. *Tabebuia impetiginosa* also has red-purple flowers. *Tabebuia palustris* is a shrub of mangrove swamps with white flowers.

Tabebuia rosea

■ ***Bombacopsis quinata*** (pochote, cedro
espinoso, spiny cedar) Family Bombacaceae

Tree to 30 m tall, canopy wide, trunk to 1 m diameter, usually broadly buttressed, bark almost black, with short, stout
conical spines, very rough on older trees, fissured into rectangular plates, branches spiny, twigs stout, leafless during
dry season. **Leaves** alternate, stalk to 12 cm long, blade palmately compound, leaflets 4–17 cm long, 2–8 cm wide, widest near apex, tip rounded to pointed, base tapered. **Flowers**
white and dark purplish, radially symmetrical, petals 5, linear,
to 11 cm long, white inside, purple outside, stamens white,
numerous, as long as petals; blooms Jan.–Apr., Aug. **Fruit**
dry, 3- to 5-parted to 10 cm long, oblong, splitting open to
release seeds embedded in dense, woolly hairs (kapok); fruits
approximately Mar.–Aug. **Habitat:** Seasonally dry to moist
or, infrequently, wet forests. Altitude: Pacific slope, sea level
to 1300 m, mostly below 500 m. Conservation areas: GUA,
OSA, PAC, TEM. **Range:** Nic–Col and Ven. **Notes:** The
only other species of *Bombacopsis* in Costa Rica is *B. sessilis*,
which has greenish bark and no spines.

■ *Ceiba pentandra* (ceiba, pulí, kapok)
Family Bombacaceae

Tree to 40 m tall, trunk to 1.5 m diameter, crown broad, bark pale grayish brown, with horizontal lines, young trunks with warty, conical spines; older, buttressed trunks have rows of warty-flaky bumps about 1.5 cm diameter; buttresses large, thick, to 10 m tall, extending out to 10 m from base. **Leaves** alternate, crowded at branch tips, stalk 5–23 cm long, blade palmately compound, leaflets 10–21 cm long, 2–4 cm wide, lance-shaped, pointed at both ends; leafless during dry season. **Flowers** white, pale yellow, or pink, brown inside, showy, radially symmetrical, 5-parted, petals 3–4 cm long, 1 cm wide; pollinated by bats, visited by many insects; blooms Jan.–Feb. as leaves drop. **Fruit** dry, 5-parted, 10–26 cm long, to 4 cm wide, opening to expose grayish kapok fibers and seeds; fruits Mar.–Apr. **Habitat:** Wet to seasonally dry regions in open areas, secondary forests, pastures; also cultivated. Altitude: Sea level to 1000 m, mostly below 200 m. Conservation areas: CVC, GUA, HNO, OSA, PAC, TEM. **Range:** CR, Pan. **Notes:** The only other species of *Ceiba* in Costa Rica is *C. aesculifolia*, a tree with much larger flowers.

Ceiba pentandra (all three above)

■ *Ochroma pyramidale* (*O. lagopus*)
(balsa, enea, wlúklo)
Family Bombacaceae

Tree 12–30 m tall, trunk to 1.5 m diameter, buttresses small but elongate, trunk base irregular, bark dark, rough, twigs brown-hairy, wood very lightweight. **Leaves** alternate, clustered at ends of twigs, stalk 3–40 cm long, stout, blade simple, 9–40 cm long, 8–35 cm wide, usually with 3–5 lobes pointed at tips, base round-lobed, pale below, veins palmate at base, brown-hairy on blade underside. **Flowers** cream white, radially symmetrical, trumpet-shaped, petals to 15 cm long, 5 cm wide, widest near apex, fleshy, calyx dark green brown covering petal tube, stamens fused in a column to 12 cm long; blooms Nov.–Jan.; pollinated by bats. **Fruit** dry, black to 25 cm long, 2 cm wide, 5-parted, filled with hairs (kapok) and seeds; seeds wind dispersed. **Habitat:** Wet to seasonally dry forests, in open sites, edges, saplings common along roadsides and other open areas. Altitude: Sea level to 1000. Conservation areas: ARE, CVC, OSA, PAC, TEM, TOR. **Range:** Mex–Bol, Ant. **Notes:** Source of balsa wood. This is the only species of *Ochroma* in Costa Rica.

Ochroma pyramidale photos opposite

■ *Pachira aquatica* (lirio de montaña,
pluma, cacao de danta)
Family Bombacaceae

Tree to 23 m tall, trunk to 70 cm diameter, often buttressed,
bark hard, flat, thin, with small vertical fissures. **Leaves** alternate, stalk long, ribbed, swollen at both ends, blade palmately
compound, leaflets 5–29 cm long, 3–15 cm wide, elliptical,
pointed at both ends, whitish below. **Flowers** greenish white
to brown, radially symmetrical, fragrant, petals 5, 17–34 cm
long, about 1.5 cm wide, hairy outside, curling outward, stamens numerous, with red tips; blooms July–Feb. **Fruit** dry,
reddish brown to 30 cm long, 12 cm wide, with 5 grooves
(photo), seeds angular, large, edible, Jan.–Nov. **Habitat:** Wet
or swampy forests and shores. Altitude: Sea level to 2300 m,
mostly below 700 m. Conservation areas: ARE, CVC, GUA,
LAP, OSA, PAC, TOR. **Range:** Mex–Brz. **Notes:** This is the
only species of *Pachira* in Costa Rica.

Ochroma pyramidale

■ *Pseudobombax septenatum* (ceibo, ceibo barrigón, ceibo verde)
Family Bombacaceae

Tree to 25 m tall, trunk to 1.4 m diameter, bark thin, conspicuously striped with green, sometimes also yellow green and reddish brown areas, usually smooth, twigs whitish, stout, 1 cm thick at tips. **Leaves** alternate, stalks 10–60 cm long, blades palmately compound, leaflets 7–29 cm long, 4–14 cm wide, elliptic, pointed at both ends; deciduous in dry season. **Flowers** white to pink, radially symmetrical, petals 5, linear, 7–9 cm long, about 2 cm wide, curling backward, stamens long, very numerous, in a dense pufflike cluster to 9 cm wide, 6 cm long; blooms on and off most of the year. **Fruit** dry, green striped with purplish brown markings (photo), to 18 cm long, 9 cm wide, filled with seeds and kapok fibers. **Habitat:** Wet to seasonally dry lowland forests and open sites. Altitude: Sea level to 300 m, mostly on the Pacific slope, especially near the coast, less common in moist regions of Caribbean slope. Conservation areas: GUA, OSA, PAC, TEM. **Range:** Nic–N Brz and Pr. **Notes:** Resembles *Ceiba pentandra,* but the bark is conspicuously different. This is the only species of *Pseudobombax* in Costa Rica.

Pseudobombax septenatum
(all three above)

Cordia alliodora photos opposite

■ *Cordia alliodora* (molenito, laurel, onión)
Family Boraginaceae

Tree to 30 m tall, trunk to 90 cm diameter, trunk straight, cylindrical, bark gray, finely fissured, buttresses variable, young parts finely hairy, nodes of twigs swollen, often inhabited by ants. **Leaves** alternate, stalk to 3 cm, blade 7–18 cm long, 3–8 cm wide, elliptic, tip long-pointed, base blunt, rough-textured, whitish below, deciduous during early rainy season. **Flowers** white, small, to 1 cm, tubular, fragrant, in large branching clusters; blooms Nov.–Mar. Pollinated by insects. **Fruit** dry, tiny, wind dispersed; seeds shed in Apr. **Habitat:** Colonizes open sites in wet to seasonally dry regions. Altitude: Sea level to 1500 m. Conservation areas: CVC, GUA, LAC, OSA, TEM. **Range:** Mex–S Amer, Ant. **Notes:** Wood used for construction and furniture. There are 25 species of *Cordia* in Costa Rica.

■ *Brunellia costaricensis* (cedrillo, cedro macho, gallinazo)
Family Brunelliaceae

Tree to about 30 m tall, trunk over 50 cm diameter, bark pale tan, grainy, young parts yellowish, finely hairy, twigs thick. **Leaves** opposite, stalk to 4 cm, swollen at base, blade pinnate, about 35 cm long, leaflets stalks to 2 cm, blades to 22 cm long, 8 cm wide, smaller near base, oblong, tip abruptly pointed, base blunt, secondary veins parallel, conspicuous, old leaflets turn red before falling. **Flowers** greenish white, inconspicuous, about 0.3 cm, 5-parted, no petals, hairy, in clus-

ters to 20 cm long and wide; blooms Mar.–Oct. **Fruit** dry, small, hairy, asymmetrical, splitting to release bright orange or red seeds; Mar.–Oct. **Habitat:** Mountain forests. Altitude: 1100–3000 m. Conservation areas: ARE, CVC, LAC, LAP, PAC. **Range:** CR only. **Notes:** There are five species of *Brunellia* in Costa Rica.

Cordia alliodora

35

■ *Bursera simaruba* (caraño, jiñote, gumbo limbo)
Family Burseraceae

Tree 5–25 m tall, about 40 cm diameter, bark coppery red, shiny, thin, peeling to expose green layer beneath, sap aromatic with a turpentinelike odor. **Leaves** alternate, spirally arranged near ends of branches, stalk to 14 cm long, base swollen, blade pinnate, leaflet stalks swollen at top, blades 5–14 cm long, 3–8 cm wide, egg-shaped to lance-shaped, tip gradually tapered, base blunt, unequal, deciduous during dry season, young leaves densely woolly. **Flowers** greenish, minute, petals to 0.3 cm long; inflorescence of branched clusters, appearing with new leaves; blooms Mar.–May, pollinated by insects. **Fruit** dry, 3-sided, elliptical, reddish brown, to 1 cm, splitting open to reveal 1 white seed; sap very aromatic; fruit present June–Mar.; eaten by monkeys, squirrels, and birds. **Habitat:** Mostly in seasonally dry forests, also in wet regions, open sites, roadsides, pastures. Altitude: Sea level to 1900 m. Conservation areas: ARE, GUA, LAC, OSA, PAC, TEM, TOR. **Range:** FL, NE Mex–Pr and Brz, Ant. **Notes:** There are nine species of *Bursera* in Costa Rica.

■ *Caryocar costaricense* (ajo, manú, plátano, butternut)
Family Caryocaraceae

Tree to 50 m tall, trunk to 2 m diameter, straight, cylindrical, buttresses thick, short, bark dark gray, flaky, vertically fissured. **Leaves** opposite, stalk 5–12 cm, blade 3-parted, junction of main stalk and leaflet stalks with 2 rounded, curled stipules, 1 cm long; center leaflet to 13–16 cm long, 6–7 cm wide, elliptic, tip abruptly pointed, base rounded to abruptly tapered, margins coarsely toothed. **Flowers** bright yellow, about 3 cm wide, radially symmetrical, petals fused, 5-lobed, stamens numerous, strong garlic smell; inflorescence of unbranched clusters to 30 cm long at ends of branches; blooms Dec.–Apr.; pollinated by bats. Area under a tree in bloom is littered with bright, fallen flowers (photo). **Fruit** fleshy, yellow, 4 cm wide, flesh oily, yellow, stone woody, Mar.–Apr. **Habitat:** Wet lowland forests, Pacific slope. Altitude: Sea level to 600 m. Conservation areas: OSA, PAC. **Range:** CR–N S Amer. **Notes:** This is the only species of *Caryocar* in Costa Rica. The wood is valued for its rot resistance.

37

Male flowers

Cecropia polyphlebia *leaf growing pattern*

Female fruit and leaves

■ *Cecropia peltata* (guarumo, bitãk, ajköl)
Family Cecropiaceae

Tree 8–20 m tall, pale, trunks ringed by old leaf scars, leafy stems hollow, often occupied by biting ants. **Leaves** alternate, stalk 15–50 cm long, attached to underside of leaf blade, blade 25–90 cm long and wide, deeply 8- to 12-lobed, tips rounded, white-woolly below, margins pleated. **Flowers** off-white, minute, in short thick spikes, bract reddish; male spikes 3–7 cm long, thin, in clusters of 12–46; female spikes 4–10 cm long, to 1 cm wide, in clusters of 2–6; blooms most of the year. **Fruit** fleshy, greenish, spike becoming 1 cm wide. **Habitat:** Wet, moist, and seasonally dry forests, in second growth forests and disturbed sites. Altitude: Sea level to 1500 m, most often below 500 m, Pacific slope. Conservation areas: GUA, OSA, PAC, TEM. **Range:** Mex–Col, Ant. **Notes:** The only *Cecropia* found in seasonally dry forests. There are five species of *Cecropia* in Costa Rica. All very similar, recognized by their large, rounded, palmately divided leaves and ringed trunks. They are found nearly everywhere in the country, mostly in second growth or disturbed sites; *C. obtusifolia* and *C. insignis* are found in wet forests below 1500 m; *C. polyphlebia* is the only species in mountains 1200–2400 m.

■ *Licania arborea* (alcornoque, falso roble, aceituno)
Family Chrysobalanaceae

Tree to 25 m tall, wide spreading, bark dark gray, grainy, slightly flaky, trunk often twisted and grooved, branches thick, sinuous. **Leaves** alternate, stalk 0.3–1.5 cm long, swollen, with 2 small glands at top, blade 6–20 cm long, 2–11 cm wide, tip truncate to notched, base blunt or shallowly lobed, glossy above, pale below, leathery, veins pinnate, closely spaced. **Flowers** dull yellow, bilaterally symmetrical, to 0.3 cm wide, fragrant, anthers pink; inflorescence of branched clusters to 17 cm long; visited by very large, black wasps; blooms Jan.–Feb. **Fruit** fleshy, becoming black, 2–3 cm long, calyx persistent, 1 seed to 2 cm long, very oily; eaten by birds and monkeys; Mar.–Apr. **Habitat:** Wet to seasonally dry regions in open areas, forest edges, second growth, often near beaches. Altitude: Pacific lowlands, sea level to 700 m. Conservation areas: GUA, HNO, LAP, OSA, PAC, TEM. **Range:** Mex–Col and Pr. **Notes:** There are 18 species of *Licania* in Costa Rica.

■ *Calophyllum longifolium* (cedro María)
Family Clusiaceae

Tree 8–35 m tall, trunk to 1 m diameter, cylindrical, bark with deep, diamond-shaped fissures, sap yellow (greenish milky), odor of fresh pumpkin, twigs stout, 4-sided, young stems densely rusty-hairy. **Leaves** opposite, stalk thick, to 4 cm long, blade 11–30 cm long, 5–9 cm wide, oblong, tip rounded or notched, surface leathery, shiny, secondary veins perpendicular to midrib, very fine, numerous, closely spaced, extending to margin, midrib yellowish. **Flowers** white, sexes on separate trees, radially symmetrical, fleshy, about 1 cm wide, no petals, sepals 4, anthers yellow, 10–12, female flowers tipped by large, green pistil; inflorescence of branched clusters to 4 cm long, flower branches densely rusty-hairy; Nov.–Dec. **Fruit** thin-fleshy, blue green, 4–5 cm, round, leathery outside, 1 large seed (photo). **Habitat:** Wet and moist lowland forests. Altitude: Sea level to 500 m. Conservation areas: OSA, PAC. **Range:** CR–Col, Sur, Brz, and Pr. **Notes:** There are three species of *Calophyllum* in Costa Rica.

Leaves and flower buds. Developing fruit bottom left of center.

■ *Clusia rosea* (copey, azahar, balsam apple)
Family Clusiaceae

Tree 10–50 m tall, terrestrial or an epiphytic strangler with many aerial roots wrapped around host tree, branches horizontal, bark dark brown, sap yellow, sticky. **Leaves** opposite, stalk short, stout, blade 7–20 cm long, 5–13 cm wide, paddle-shaped, widest near apex, tip rounded, squared-off, or notched, base tapered then abruptly truncate, smooth, dull green, midrib pale, secondary veins inconspicuous. **Flowers** white, often marked with pink, to 10 cm wide, petals 7, thick, calyx pink, stamens in a dense ring around large, flat stigma; blooms Apr., Sept.–Nov. **Fruit** woody, 5–7 cm wide, green becoming brown, sepals and stigma persistent, fruit splitting open into 7 sections revealing dark red seeds with orange fleshy coat (aril), in a compartmented central structure, remains of fruit woody, star-shaped; fruit present Dec.–June. **Habitat:** Wet to seasonally dry regions, often growing near shore. Salt resistant. Often grown as an ornamental. Altitude: Sea level to 1200 m, mostly on the Pacific slope. Conservation areas: ARE, GUA, ICO, OSA. **Range:** Tropical America; widely planted in tropical regions. **Notes:** There are about 20 species of *Clusia* in Costa Rica; most are smaller epiphytes.

■ *Terminalia catappa* (almendro de playa, almendro de mar, Indian almond)
Family Combretaceae

Tree 3–25 m tall, pagoda-shaped, crown spreading, branches horizontal, bark gray, flaky. **Leaves** alternate, mostly in rosettes crowded at tips of branches, stalks short, blade to 25 cm long, 12 cm wide, widest near apex, tip rounded, base tapered, stiff, shiny; old leaves turn red before falling. **Flowers** white to greenish yellow, small (photo), sexes separate on same spike, radially symmetrical, no petals, calyx lobes 5, tips pointed, stamens conspicuous; inflorescence of spike-like clusters at ends of branches; blooms most of the

year. **Fruit** hard-fleshy, yellow or reddish, to 5 cm, flattened ovals, tip pointed, flesh fibrous, enclosing an edible nut; seeds dispersed by water. **Habitat:** Commonly planted and natural-ized along Pacific and Caribbean shores. Tolerates salt spray. Altitude: Sea level to 100 m. Conservation areas: GUA, ICO, LAC, OSA, PAC, TEM, TOR. **Range:** Pantropical. Native to SE Asia and parts of Oceania. Mex–Pr and Brz, WI, invasive in Hawai'i. **Notes:** Various parts used medicinally in Southeast Asia and tropical America. There are four species of *Terminalia* in Costa Rica; the others are large, native forest canopy trees.

■ *Terminalia oblonga* (surá, guayabón, guayabo de montaña)
Family Combretaceae

Tree 25–45 m tall, trunk to 1.3 m diameter, buttresses wide, to several m high, thin and flat; outer bark pale tan, smooth, thin, loose, falling off in large pieces, inner bark nearly white mottled, trunk above buttresses columnar, fluted irregu-larly. **Leaves** alternate, clustered at ends of branches, blade 5–16 cm long, 3–6 cm wide, widest near apex, tip short-pointed, tapered to base, deciduous for a short time in dry season. **Flowers** greenish yellow, 0.3 cm wide, no petals, calyx 5-lobed, stamens 10, longer than calyx; inflorescence of spikes to 15 cm long; blooms Nov.–Mar., mostly Dec. **Fruit** dry, 3-winged, to 2 cm long, 3.8 cm wide (photo), wind dispersed; Jan.–June. **Habitat:** Wet forests, along rivers in

moist and seasonally dry forests. Altitude: Sea level to 900 m. Conservation areas: ARE, CVC, GUA, LAP, OSA, PAC, TEM, TOR. Common at La Selva Bio-logical Station. **Range:** Mex–Bol. **Notes:** Conspicuous for its smooth, whitish bark and thin, flat buttresses.

■ *Diospyros digyna*
Family Ebenaceae

Slender tree 7–28 m tall, to 30 cm diameter, trunk fluted, irregular, buttresses small, flaring, bark black, flaky, finely fissured with tiny white dots (lenticels), young stems green. **Leaves** alternate, stalk to 1.4 cm, blade 9–20 cm long, 4–8 cm wide, narrowly elliptic, dark green, shiny above, yellow green below, tip pointed to blunt, base tapered to rounded. **Flowers** cream white, radially symmetrical, male and female flowers usually on different plants (dioecious), 1.8 cm long, fragrant, 4 petals fused, lobes rounded, 0.6 cm long and wide, calyx to 1 cm long, stamens about 20; flowers solitary or in small clusters in axils; blooms Jan.–June. **Fruit** fleshy, becoming black at maturity (photo), 6–8 cm, flattened globe, base cupped by enlarged calyx, rind thin, brittle, sprinkled with small, pale dots, flesh black, soft, sweet, edible, seeds to 10, to 3 cm long, lens-shaped; fruits June–Feb., eaten by monkeys. **Habitat:** Wet to seasonally dry forests; also cultivated for fruit. Altitude: Sea level to 1200 m. Conservation areas: ARE, GUA, LAP, OSA, PAC, TEM. **Range:** Mex–Col, Ant. **Notes:** There are eight species of *Diospyros* in Costa Rica.

Courtesy of Margaret Gargiullo

■ *Sloanea ampla* (peine de mico, monkey comb)
Family Elaeocarpaceae

Canopy tree to 30 m tall but may reproduce at 5 m tall. **Leaves** alternate, stalk stout, blade to 40 cm long, 25 cm wide, tip and base blunt, blade angled upward from stalk, edges slightly wavy. **Flowers** off-white, small, radially symmetrical, no petals, numerous stamens, fragrant; blooms Feb.–May. **Fruit** woody, densely orange brown spiny (photo), to 8 cm wide, including spines to 3 cm long, husk opening in 5 sections to reveal red lining and seeds covered with fleshy, orange coat (aril); June–Jan., eaten by parrots and black guans. **Habitat:** Moist to wet mountain forests. Altitude: 1200–2300 m. Conservation areas: ARE, CVC, LAC, LAP, PAC **Range:** Mex–W Pan. **Notes:** There are 23 species of *Sloanea* in Costa Rica.

■ *Hieronyma alchorneoides* (pilón, nancitón, plátano)
Family Euphorbiaceae

Tree to 40 m tall, trunk 1.5 m diameter, buttresses thick, to 1.3 m high, bark brown, ridged, with large, irregular flakes, young stems very hairy. **Leaves** alternate, stalk to 9 cm, blade 8–44 cm long, 5–29 cm wide, broadly egg-shaped, tip elongate pointed, base blunt, hairy below, old leaves turn bright red

orange. **Flowers** red, very small, hairy, in branched clusters, males and females on separate plants; blooms most of the year. **Fruit** fleshy, red, becoming purple black, to 0.4 cm oval, above persistent calyx, 1-seeded, eaten by toucans. **Habitat:** Wet to moist forests. Altitude: Sea level to 1000 m, mostly below 600 m. Conservation areas: ARE, CVC, GUA, LAC, OSA, PAC, TOR. **Range:** Mex–Bol and S Brz. **Notes:** Wood reddish, used for heavy construction. There are three species of *Hyeronima* in Costa Rica.

■ *Hura crepitans* (javillo, báchöl, sandbox, white cedar)
Family Euphorbiaceae

Tree 5–40 m tall, trunk to about 1.5 m diameter, straight, cylindrical, base flared, covered with conical, dark spines, bark flaking in circular disks, twigs stout, sap milky, *toxic*. **Leaves** alternate, stalk to 15 cm long, blade 5–25 cm long, 4–17 cm wide, egg- or heart-shaped, tip pointed, base blunt or lobed, veins pale, margin bluntly toothed. **Flowers** red, without petals, sexes separate on same plant, male flowers tiny, numerous, on a fleshy spike 3–5 cm long, female flowers solitary, to 6 cm long, red purple, top 1 cm wide with radiating appendages; blooms Sept.–Apr. **Fruit** woody, to 5 cm high, 11 cm wide (photo), flattened, with rounded sections, these exploding to release seeds; seeds 2 cm wide, poisonous; fruits Jan.–Apr. **Habitat:** Wet to seasonally dry regions in

second growth and gaps. Altitude: Sea level to 1400 m. Conservation areas: ARE, GUA, LAC, OSA, PAC, TEM, TOR. **Range:** Nic–N S Amer, WI. **Notes:** Sap has been used as a fish poison and can cause temporary blindness if gotten in eyes. This is the only species of *Hura* in Costa Rica.

■ *Caesalpinia eriostachys* (sahíno, palo de sahíno)
Fabaceae/Caesalpinioideae

Small to medium tree about 15 m tall with multiple, twisted, grooved or interwoven trunks, habit erect, rather narrow, bark gray, flaky. **Leaves** alternate, blade twice evenly pinnate about 13 cm long, 9 cm wide, pinnae about 5 cm long, leaflets 0.5–1.5 cm long, 0.5 cm wide, sides very unequal, tip rounded, base truncate. **Flowers** yellow, about 2.5 cm wide, bilaterally symmetrical, petals 5, 4 with narrow bases, spreading, the 5th, lower petal, folded over stamens and pistil, calyx rusty-scaly, 5-lobed; inflorescence of large, once-branched clusters, very attractive to ants; blooms Dec.–Feb. **Fruit** dry, pods to 10 cm long, 3 cm wide, flattened. **Habitat:** Moist to seasonally dry forests or second growth; also planted, as a living fence and ornamental. Altitude: Pacific slope, sea level to 700 m. Conservation areas: PAC, TEM. **Range:** Mex–Pan, Cuba. **Notes:** There are seven species of *Caesalpinia* in Costa Rica.

■ *Cassia grandis* (carao, sandal, extranjero, carulo, stinking toe, coral shower tree)
Family Fabaceae/Caesalpinioideae

Tree 8–20 m tall, widely branching, young stems rusty-hairy, bark gray black, grainy, with many thin, raised horizontal ridges. **Leaves** alternate, about 20 cm long, 10 cm wide, evenly pinnate, leaflets 3–6 cm long, about 1.5 cm wide, oblong, blunt at both ends, hairy on both sides, deciduous in dry season. **Flowers** pink to orange pink, bilaterally symmetric, about 0.8 cm, 5 petals, narrowed at base, 2 stamens and stigma longer than petals, curved; inflorescence of unbranched clusters along stems; blooms when leafless, Jan.–Apr. **Fruit** woody, pods to 1 m long, 4 cm diameter (photo), cylindrical, dark brown, margins ribbed, seeds about 2 cm long, 1 cm wide, blackish, flattened, stacked like coins with pulpy partitions between each seed. **Habitat:** Moist to seasonally dry lowland forest; also cultivated. Altitude: Sea level to 500 m, mostly on the Pacific slope; cultivated at higher elevations. Conservation areas: ARE, GUA, HNO, OSA, PAC, TEM. **Range:** S Mex–SE Brz, WI. **Notes:** There are about 34 species of *Cassia* in Costa Rica; *C. grandis* is sometimes used to shade coffee plantations in the Central Valley.

Cassia grandis

■ *Hymenaea courbaril* (guapinol, stinking toe)
Family Fabaceae/Caesalpinioideae

Tall canopy tree, 10–50 m tall, trunk to 1.5 m diameter or more, branched high up, bark smooth, gray, with closely spaced lenticels, buttresses thick, to about 1 m high. **Leaves** alternate, with 2 leaflets to 7 cm long, 3 cm wide, each, asymmetrical, narrowly oblong, tip pointed, base unequal, rounded, surface leathery, sprinkled with tiny dots; leafy during most of dry season. **Flowers** white to purplish white, slightly bilaterally symmetrical, to 4 cm wide, 5 rounded petals, stamens 10, and style both longer than petals; blooms Dec.–Apr.; pollinated by bats. **Fruit** dry, flattened pods, to 17 cm long, 6 wide, 3 cm thick (photo), oblong, reddish brown, rounded at both ends, filled with powdery, sweet, edible but unpleasantly scented pulp, eaten by agoutis and monkeys. **Habitat:** Wet to seasonally dry forests. Altitude: Pacific slope, sea level to 800 m, mostly below 400 m. Conservation areas: ARE, GUA, LAP, OSA, PAC, TEM. **Range:** Mex–Bol and French Guiana, WI. **Notes:** This is the only species of *Hymenaea* in Costa Rica.

■ *Myrospermum frutescens*
(arco, papi, guachipelín ratón)
Family Fabaceae/Caesalpinioideae

Small to medium tree to about 18 m tall, bark gray brown with whitish longitudinal lines. **Leaves** alternate, pinnate, 10–15 cm long, leaflets 2–5 cm long, oblong, tip rounded, base pointed to blunt, thin, pale blue green, deciduous in the dry season. **Flowers** white and pale lavender, lower petal often yellow, bilaterally symmetrical, 1.5 cm long, bean-flower-shaped or like small orchids, fragrant; inflorescence of dense, branched clusters; blooms when tree is leafless, attractive to bees. **Fruit** dry, thin, papery winged, about 10 cm long, 2 cm wide, 1-seeded. **Habitat:** Seasonally dry to moist lowland forests. Altitude: Pacific lowlands 50–300 m. Conservation areas: GUA, PAC, TEM. **Range:** Mex–N S Amer. **Notes:** This is apparently the only species of *Myrospermum* in Costa Rica. Not common but conspicuous in bloom.

■ *Prioria copaifera* (cativo)
Family Fabaceae/Caesalpinioideae

Tree to 35 m tall, trunk to 75 cm diameter, no buttresses, bark gray, rough-grainy but not fissured, sap black, sweet, twigs finely hairy, sprinkled with small dots (lenticels). **Leaves** alternate, stalk to 3 cm, blade pinnate, leaflets 4, stalks stout, to 1 cm long, blades 4–16 cm long, to 8 cm wide, elliptic, leathery, dark green, sides unequal, tip pointed, base unequal. **Flowers** greenish white, 0.4 cm wide, stamens longer than petals; inflorescence of densely branched clusters of flowering spikes, about 10 cm long; blooms and fruits on and off most of the year. **Fruit** dry, broadly egg-shaped to 10 cm long, 7 cm wide (photo), flattened, one side convex, the other indented, one end pointed, dark brown, margin ridged; buoyant, often washed up on beaches; eaten by monkeys. **Habitat:** Wet lowland forests, along rivers, in flood plains and swamp forests. Altitude: Sea level to 300 m. Conservation areas: CVC, LAC, OSA, TOR. **Range:** Nic–N Col, Jam. **Notes:** This is the only species of *Prioria* in Costa Rica. Fallen fruits are the most recognizable feature of this tree.

■ *Schizolobium parahyba*
  (gavilán, gallinzano, cañafístol)
  Family Fabaceae/Caesalpinioideae

Slender tree to 30 m tall, trunk to 1 m diameter, buttresses narrow, low, bark pale gray, hard, flat with minute fissures and lenticels, young plants unbranched, branches on larger trees at right angles to trunk, sap sticky. **Leaves** alternate, spiraled at ends of branches, twice evenly pinnate, to 2 m long in young trees, 30–50 cm long in mature trees, primary pinnae opposite, each with 12–22 pairs of opposite leaflets 2–3 cm long, 1 cm wide, oblong, tip and base rounded, dull green above. **Flowers** yellow, bilaterally symmetrical, fragrant, 4 cm wide, 5 pet-

Courtesy of Margaret Gargiullo

Courtesy of Margaret Gargiullo

als, narrow at base, 10 stamens; inflorescence of large branched clusters 20–30 cm long; blooms while leafless, Nov.–Mar. **Fruit** dry, pods 9–12 cm long, 3–5 cm wide, flattened, drop-shaped, tip rounded, stem end pointed, 1 seed 0.8 cm. **Habitat:** Second growth lowland forests, a pioneer species in disturbed sites. Altitude: Pacific lowlands, sea level to 450 m (photo: distant trees in bloom). Conservation areas: OSA, PAC, TEM. **Range:** SE Mex–Brz. Cultivated in FL and Old World tropics. **Notes:** This is the only species of *Schizolobium* in Costa Rica. Large, feathery leaves of young trees are particularly conspicuous.

■ *Dipteryx oleifera (D. panamensis)* (almendro)
  Family Fabaceae/Faboideae

Tree to 40 m tall, trunk to 1 m diameter, broadly buttressed, bark light orange tan, thick, surface granular, finely flaky. Stipules large, to 15 cm long, 1 cm wide. **Leaves** alternate, stalk narrowly winged, 6–15 cm long, blade evenly pinnate, to 30 cm, midrib (axis) winged, leaflets 7–22 cm long, 3–7 cm wide, elliptical, tip bluntly pointed. Seedling leaves with elongate midrib, leaflets growing out of this (photo). **Flowers** purple, bilaterally symmetrical, about 2 cm wide, bean-flower-shaped, longest petal at base, green; inflorescence of clusters to 40 cm at ends of branches; blooms mostly during wet season, Mar.–July. **Fruit** fleshy, to 6 cm long, 3 cm wide (photo), 1-seeded, gray green, becoming brown, filled with oily, fragrant liquid, eaten by monkeys, coatis, and rodents, gnawed, fuzzy-looking fruits common under parent trees in early dry season. **Habitat:** Wet to moist lowland forests. Altitude: Caribbean slope, sea level to 100 m. Conservation areas: CVC, HNO, LAC, TOR. **Range:** Nic–Col. **Notes:** This is the only species of *Dipteryx* in Costa Rica. Seeds "planted" by agoutis and pacas, which bury the seeds and neglect to retrieve all of them.

■ *Erythrina fusca* (poró, papayo,
poró blanco, pochotillo, popeye)
Family Fabaceae/Faboideae

Tree to 20 m tall, trunk to 1 m diameter, old trees with large buttresses, bark grayish, coarse, with broad, corky prickles, branches also with prickles, leafless during dry season. **Leaves** alternate, stalk to 18 cm long, blade 3-parted, terminal leaflet 8–15 cm long, 7–12 cm wide, lateral leaflets smaller, egg-shaped, rounded at both ends, underside with dense mat of white hairs. **Flowers** pale orange to almost cream color, bilaterally symmetrical, to 5 cm long, 2.5 cm wide, 1.5 cm thick, bluntly rectangular to somewhat cone-shaped, top petal closed over the others; inflorescence of large clusters at ends of branches; blooms Sept.–Apr., pollinated by hummingbirds. **Fruit** dry, pod to 33 cm long, 2 cm wide, brown-hairy, tip pointed, constricted between seeds. **Habitat:** Wet lowland forests or along rivers. In the wild it grows in freshwater swampy areas, but it is frequently planted along the Caribbean Coast. Altitude: Sea level to 600 m, usually below 100 m. Conservation areas: GUA, HNO, ICO, OSA, PAC, TEM. **Range:** Gua–Brz, WI, parts of S Asia, Oceania. Introduced widely as well. **Notes:** Rectangular, pale orange flowers distinctive. There are about 12 species of *Erythrina* in Costa Rica.

■ *Erythrina poeppigiana* (poró, poró gigante)
Family Fabaceae/Faboideae

Large tree to over 25 m tall, bark dark brown with spine-like protuberances. **Leaves** alternate, 3-parted, leaflets to 20 cm long, rather bluntly triangular to egg-shaped, deciduous. **Flowers** bright orange, bilaterally symmetrical, narrowly saber-shaped, the long, narrow top petal enclosing the others; blooms Jan.–Feb., when trees are leafless. **Fruit** dry, pods to 25 cm long, seeds, brown. **Habitat:** Cultivated, commonly planted in and around San José in parks. Altitude: 500–1100 m. Conservation areas: CVC, LAP. **Range:** Ven–Bol. **Notes:** Originally introduced to shade coffee plants.

■ *Lonchocarpus macrophyllus* (chaperno)
Family Fabaceae/Faboideae

Tree 10–30 m tall, bark pale, grainy, patchy, young stems 4-sided, green, finely hairy. **Leaves** alternate, stalk 5 cm, yellowish-hairy, blade odd-pinnate, midrib yellow-hairy, leaflets opposite, stalks short, blade 5–14 cm long, 2–5 cm wide, oblong, tip pointed, base rounded. **Flowers** pale purple, with yellow mark on top petal, bilaterally symmetrical, bean-flower-shaped, about 1.5 cm long, calyx reddish, hairy, flower buds red; inflorescence of dense spikelike clusters, to 27 cm long held erect at ends of branches; defended by ants; blooms Feb.–May. **Fruit** dry, pods green or reddish, becoming brownish, 3–11 cm long, about 2 cm wide, irregularly constricted between the 1–4 seeds; June. **Habitat:** Wet lowland forests, often in marshy sites. Altitude: Sea level to 300 m, mostly below 50 m. Conservation areas: OSA (mostly), PAC, TOR. **Range:** Mex–Col. **Notes:** There are 29 species of *Lonchocarpus* in Costa Rica.

■ *Pterocarpus officinalis* (sangregao, cuajada amarilla, palo de sangre)
Family Fabaceae/Faboideae

Tree to 30 m tall, trunk to 30 cm diameter, upper branches often held horizontally, buttresses wide, high, thin, flat (photo), very often flaring outward then sharply angled downward like a bent knee; bark smooth, pale greenish tan, green just below surface, sap red, trunk irregularly fluted, branched high up, canopy thin during the dry season. **Leaves** alternate, odd-pinnate, leaflets alternate, 8–15 cm long, 4–7 cm wide, oblong to egg-shaped, tip tapered, base blunt. **Flowers** yellow orange with red center, to brownish yellow with purple stripes, about 1 cm, bilaterally symmetrical, bean-flower-shaped; inflorescence of branched clusters to 25 cm long; blooms Mar.–Sept., Dec. **Fruit** dry, flattened, round with asymmetrical wing, about 5 cm diameter, 1-seeded; fruit present June, July, Oct., Jan. **Habitat:** Wet lowlands, mostly along flooded areas of the coastal plains, in shallow water. Altitude: Sea level to 200 m. Conservation areas: LAC, OSA, TOR. **Range:** Bel–Brz. **Notes:** Knee-shaped buttresses are distinctive, but not always present.

■ *Enterolobium cyclocarpum* (gua, choreja, ear tree)
Family Fabaceae/Mimosoideae

Tree to 35 m tall, trunk to 2.5 m diameter, canopy wide, branched near ground, crown widely spreading, bark roughly fissured. **Leaves** alternate, twice pinnate with 4–15 pairs primary pinnae 15–40 cm long, leaflets 15–30 pairs, to 1.5 cm long, 0.4 cm wide, deciduous in dry season. **Flowers** white, tiny, radially symmetrical, stamens longer than petals; in small, ball-shaped clusters to 2 cm diameter; blooms Feb.–Apr. as new leaves unfold. **Fruit** dark brown, fleshy, kidney- or ear-shaped (photos), curved into an overlapping circle, to 14 cm diameter, with central stem, flesh sweet, with 5–20 seeds; pods eaten by horses, which can pass intact seeds; fruits Jan.–Feb. **Habitat:** Wet to seasonally dry forests, in open habitats along roads, and in pastures. Altitude: Sea level to 1200 m, most often below 600 m on the Pacific slope. Conservation areas: ARE, GUA, HNO, OSA, PAC, TEM. **Range:** Mex–N S Amer, introduced in WI and Africa. **Notes:** The other species of *Enterolobium* in Costa Rica, *E. schomburgkii*, has smaller fruit than *E. cyclocarpum* but is otherwise similar.

■ *Inga edulis* (guaba mecate, guaba chillillo, cuajiniquil)
Family Fabaceae/Mimosoideae

Tree 6–15 m tall, wide spreading, bark granular with horizontal lines, twigs brownish hairy, sprinkled with pale dots (lenticels). **Leaves** alternate, stalk about 3 cm long, blade evenly pinnate, axis broadly winged, leaflets stalkless, small nectar-bearing cups between each pair, blades opposite, 5–6 pairs, 8–25 cm long, 3–11 cm wide, elliptic, smaller toward base of leaf, leathery. **Flowers** white, brushlike, petals green, short, stamens numerous to 4 cm long; inflorescence of short, dense clusters; blooms and fruits mostly Nov.–Apr. **Fruit** woody, pulp-filled pod, to 1.2 m, deeply ribbed (photo), more or less cylindrical. **Habitat:** Moist to wet lowland forests; commonly planted. Altitude: Sea level to 550 m. Conservation areas: LAP, OSA, PAC. **Range:** Native from Col–Pr and Brz. Introduced in C Amer. **Notes:** Cultivated for the fleshy, edible covering of the seeds, and as a shade tree. There are about 66 species of *Inga* in Costa Rica.

■ *Inga multijuga* (guabo, guaba de estero)
Family Fabaceae/Mimosoideae

Tree 6–15 m tall, trunk 40 cm wide, young stems densely rusty-hairy. **Leaves** alternate, stalk hairy, blade evenly pinnate, axis not winged, leaflets 5–10 pairs, blades opposite, 7–14 cm long, 2–4 cm wide, smaller toward base, oblong, tip pointed, base blunt, hairy below. Seedling leaves with winged axis (photo). **Flowers** white, brushlike, petals 1–2.5 cm long, silky-hairy, stamens numerous, to 4 cm long, flowers ranked along both sides of an unbranched inflorescence stem; blooms and fruits most of the year. **Fruit** woody, pod, reddish brown, to 19 cm long, 3 cm wide, margins thick, raised. **Habitat:** Wet to seasonally dry lowland forests. Altitude: Sea level to 450 m. Conservation areas: ARE, LAP, OSA, PAC, TEM, TOR. **Range:** Mex–Hon, CR–Ec and Ven.

■ **Inga punctata (guaba, cuajiniquil, puraa, surrí)**
Family Fabaceae/Mimosoideae

Tree 4–15 m tall, trunk to 20 cm diameter, bark smooth, gray, twigs densely, finely hairy. **Leaves** alternate, evenly pinnate, about 15 cm long, axis not winged, nectar cups between leaflets about 0.1 cm wide, leaflets 2–3 opposite pairs, 6–17 cm long, 3–7 cm wide, terminal pair largest, elliptic, tip blunt to pointed, shiny, dark green, new leaves densely, finely hairy. **Flowers** white, brushlike, fragrant, petals much shorter than stamens; inflorescences of 1–7 flowers; blooms on and off most of the year. **Fruit** green, becoming dry, pulp-filled pods 4–20 cm long, 1–3 cm wide, ridged along edges, contracted between seeds; pods eaten by many animals. **Habitat:** Moist and wet second growth forests, roadsides, edges. Altitude: Sea level to 2000 m, mostly above 600 m. Conservation areas: ARE, CVC, GUA, HNO, LAC, LAP, OSA, PAC, TOR. **Range:** Mex–Pr and Brz, Tr, To. **Notes:** Probably the most common species of *Inga* in Costa Rica.

■ **Inga spectabilis (guaba machete, guabo de castilla,**
alówa) Family Fabaceae/Mimosoideae

Tree 5–15 m tall, 1 m diameter, bark patchy gray brown, trunk twisted, grooved, small branches conspicuously 4-sided. **Leaves** alternate, 4-parted, midrib usually winged with nectar cups between upper and lower leaflet pairs, blades 20–30 cm long, 8–18 cm wide, lower leaflets much smaller, broadly elliptic to widest near apex, tip barely pointed, base narrowed, slightly lobed, surface leathery, veins closely spaced, loop-connected near margin. **Flowers** white, brushlike, petal tube about 2 cm long, hairy, stamens to 2.5 cm, numerous; flowers in clusters of 1–6 amid numerous woolly bracts on a hairy stalk to 8 cm long; blooms May–Aug., Nov.–Jan. **Fruit** woody, pulp-filled pods to 70 cm long, 8 cm wide, 3 cm thick, flattened (photo). **Habitat:** Wet to moist forests; also widely cultivated. Altitude: Sea level to 1750 m, mostly below 500 m. Conservation areas: CVC, HNO, LAC, LAP, OSA, PAC, TOR. **Range:** Mex–Ec. **Notes:** White pulp around the seeds is edible, and pods are often sold in markets.

■ *Inga vera* (guaba, atuñá, guaba de rio)
Family Fabaceae/Mimosoideae

Tree 4–15 m tall, usually less than 10 m, trunk to
45 cm diameter, often forked near base, bark pale
gray, twigs rusty-hairy. **Leaves** alternate, evenly pinnate, stalk and midrib winged, leaflets 6–7 opposite pairs, blades 9–17 cm long, 3–4 cm wide, lower
leaflets smaller, narrowly elliptic. **Flowers** white,
powder-puff-like, petals to 2 cm long, dull yellow,
covered with silky hairs, stamens numerous, to 5 cm
long; inflorescence of spikes near ends of branches.
Pollinated by bats and insects; blooms most of the
year. **Fruit** woody, cylindrical pulp-filled pods, furrowed, 8–15 cm long, 1–2 cm wide, brown-hairy; May–Sept.
Eaten by monkeys. **Habitat:** Mostly in seasonally dry forests,
sometimes in wet forests also. Altitude: Sea level to 1900 m.
Conservation areas: ARE, GUA, HNO, LAP, OSA, PAC,
TEM. **Range:** Mex–Ven.

■ *Pentaclethra macroloba* (gavilán, quebracho, sharál)
Family Fabaceae/Mimosoideae

Tree 5–35 m tall, to 1.5 m diameter, base of large trees
slightly buttressed, trunk irregularly fluted, bark pale gray,
smooth. **Leaves** alternate, twice pinnate, feathery, pinnae
15–27 pairs, leaflets very numerous, to 1 cm long, to 0.2 cm
wide, densely arrayed along pinna axis. **Flowers** white,
brushlike; inflorescence of crowded, plumelike, pendant
spikes, to 15 cm long; blooms June–Dec. Trees bloom and
fruit when about 5 m tall. **Fruit** woody pods, brown, 20–
50 cm long, 4–6 cm wide, 1 cm thick, flat, seeds 3–8, large,
flattened, toxic; pods split open explosively, empty seed pods
and seedlings common on forest floor (photo). **Habitat:**
Wet forests, swamps, edges, open and second growth sites,
saplings common along roadsides. Altitude: Caribbean lowlands, sea level to 500 m. Conservation areas: CVC, HNO,
LAC, TOR. Very common at La Selva Biological Station.
Range: S Mex–Amazonia. **Notes:** This is the only species
of *Pentaclethra* in Costa Rica.

■ *Samanea saman (Pithecellobium s.)*
(cenízero, raintree)
Family Fabaceae/Mimosoideae

Large tree 20–30 m tall, crown very widely spreading, dense, trunk 1.4 m diameter, bark black, rough, irregularly flaking, young trees with finely textured, grainy bark, twigs stout, tan gray. **Leaves** alternate, stalk about 6 cm, blade twice evenly pinnate, to about 35 cm long, 23 cm wide, pinnae 2–6, opposite, about 12 cm long, 5 cm wide, leaflets opposite, blade 2–4 cm long, about 1 cm wide, irregularly rectangular, midrib diagonal, dark green above, yellowish-velvety below, leathery; deciduous in seasonally dry areas. **Flowers** pink and white brushlike, petals shorter than stamens; inflorescences of rounded clusters; blooms Feb.–June, usually as leafing-out occurs. **Fruit** woody, pods (photo), brown, 15–20 cm long, about 3 cm wide, 1 cm thick, twisting open to release about 20 seeds, in Mar. Fruit eaten by cattle. **Habitat:** Mostly in seasonally dry forests; also planted in moist regions (where it is evergreen). Altitude: Pacific slope, sea level to 1200 m, mostly below 500 m. Conservation areas: ARE, GUA, HNO, PAC, TEM. **Range:** Mex–Brz and Par but apparently introduced in Nic. Also introduced in much of the tropics worldwide. **Notes:** This is the only species of *Samanea* in Costa Rica.

■ *Quercus bumelioides* (*Q. copeyensis*)
(encino, roble, roble barcino, oak)
Family Fagaceae

Large tree 11–25 m tall, trunk to 1.5 m diameter, bark irregularly flaky, pale gray, shallowly fissured, base buttressed, stipules persistent on juvenile twigs. **Leaves** alternate, often crowded at ends of twigs, stalk to 0.8 cm long, blade 5–17 cm long, 2–7 cm wide, elliptic to slightly wider above middle, tip slightly pointed to rounded, base wedge-shaped to slightly lobed, leathery, surface shiny, veins pale, slightly impressed above, margin often wavy. **Flowers** greenish, inconspicuous, sexes separate on same tree, male catkins 4–9 cm long, females 2–6 cm long; blooms Sept.–Oct., Feb. **Fruit** a nut (acorn), to 2.8 cm long, 2.2 cm wide, egg-shaped, cup to 1.8 cm long, 2–3 cm wide, covering 1/3–1/2 of nut; fruit present Feb.–Oct. **Habitat:** Dominant tree in some wet forests in the mountains. Altitude: 1600–2600 m. Conservation areas: ARE, CVC, LAC, LAP, PAC. **Range:** Mex–Pan. **Notes:** There are 15 species of *Quercus* in Costa Rica, mostly found in mountains where they are often the most abundant trees.

■ *Quercus costaricensis* (encino, roble, oak)
Family Fagaceae

Large tree to 30 m tall, trunk to 1 m diameter, bark of lower trunk dark brown, thick, rough, fissures fairly regular, no buttresses, younger bark smooth. **Leaves** alternate, stalk to 0.4 cm, blade 3–10 cm long, 2–6 cm wide (occasionally larger), oblong, rounded at both ends, base often slightly lobed, surface shiny, leathery, dark green above, paler below, young leaves densely hairy below, veins deeply impressed above, margins wavy to slightly lobed becoming rolled toward underside. **Flowers** greenish, inconspicuous, male catkins to 9 cm long (photo), female flower spike to 5 cm long; blooms Feb.–July. **Fruit** a nut (acorn) to 3 cm long, 3.5 cm wide, cup to 1.5 cm deep, to 3.5 cm wide, shallow, covering only 1/4 of acorn; fruit present most of the year. **Habitat:** Mountain forests. Altitude: 2000–3600 m, rarely down to 1000 m. Conservation areas: LAC, LAP, PAC, mostly between Volcán Irazú and Cerro Chirripó. **Range:** CR, Pan. **Notes:** Sometimes dominant, along with *Q. bumelioides*.

■ *Quercus oleoides* (encino, roble, oak)
Family Fagaceae

Tree to 16 m tall, trunk 80 cm diameter, much-branched, habit wide, spreading, bark thick, rough, fissured, flaking. **Leaves** alternate, 3–11 cm long, 2–5 cm, elliptical, tip pointed or blunt, base blunt, surface shiny dark green above, brown-hairy below, margin sometimes with a few shallow lobes or teeth; retains much foliage during dry season. **Flowers** yellow green, inconspicuous, male catkins 3–4 cm long, female spikes to 3 cm; blooms Oct., Feb.–Mar. **Fruit** a nut (acorn) elliptic, to 2.8 cm long, 1.4 cm wide, cup shallow about 1 cm long, to 1.7 cm wide, scales hairy; Aug.–Sept., Mar., May. **Habitat:** Only in seasonally dry forests. Altitude: Northern Pacific slope, 100–1100 m, mostly below 800 m. Conservation areas: GUA, TEM. Seen in Santa Rosa N.P. **Range:** Mex–CR.

■ *Calatola costaricensis* (azulillo, palo de papa)
Family Icacinaceae

Tree to 25 m tall, sap turns blue on exposure to air. **Leaves** alternate, 6–29 cm long, 4–12 cm wide, elliptic, pointed at both ends, veins loop-connected along margin. **Flowers** greenish, inconspicuous, in thin spikes to 13 cm long; blooms most of the year. **Fruit** fleshy, purple black when ripe, elliptical to 7 cm long, ripe Aug.–Oct., 1 woody seed almost as large as the fruit, highly ornamented with thin longitudinal crests, ridges, and points. Eating seeds reported to cause severe gastric distress. Seeds often found washed up along shores and on beaches. **Habitat:** Wet to moist forests. Altitude: Sea level to 2300 m mostly below 1000 m. Conservation areas: ARE, CVC, GUA, LAC, LAP, OSA, PAC, TOR. **Range:** Mex–Pan. **Notes:** This is the only species of *Calatola* in Costa Rica.

■ *Persea americana* (aguacate, avocado, amó)
  Family Lauraceae

Tree to 40 m tall, blooms and fruits when 6 m, deciduous. **Leaves** alternate, stalk to 6 cm long, blade 6–
30 cm long, 3–19 cm wide, egg-shaped, tip abruptly
pointed to rounded, base blunt, thin, dark green
above, pale green to whitish below, veins prominent. **Flowers** greenish white to yellow, fragrant, to 1 cm long (photo),
finely hairy, radially symmetrical,
in branched clusters 4–12 cm long;
blooms on and off Mar.–Sept. **Fruit**
fleshy, green to blackish, to 12 cm
long, pear-shaped to oval with 1 large
seed 2–5 cm long, skin leathery, flesh
soft, edible, up to 30% fat; fruits ripen
early in rainy season. **Habitat:** Widely
cultivated; wild in wet to seasonally
dry forests. Altitude: 100–2000 m.
Conservation areas: ARE, GUA,
HNO, ICO, LAP, OSA, PAC, TEM.
Range: Apparently native to Mex;
probably cultivated for up to 8000
years in C Amer. **Notes:** There are
13 species of *Persea* in Costa Rica.

Courtesy of Sylvia Peterson

■ *Lecythis ampla* (jicarillo, olla de mono, monkey pot)
  Family Lecythidaceae

Tree to 45 m tall, 1.75 m diameter, trunk straight, cylindrical, buttresses small, bark dark, deeply grooved (photo).
Leaves alternate, to 8 cm long, narrowly oblong, margin
finely toothed, undulating, shiny, deciduous during rainy
season. **Flowers** pale blue and white, petals free, large,
stamens numerous, covered by a hood; inflorescence of
branched clusters at ends of twigs; blooms May–Aug., when
tree is leafless. **Fruit** woody, about 17 cm long, 15 cm wide
(photo), heavy, thick-walled, bluntly elliptical, top detach-
ing like a lid, revealing the edible nuts, to 5 cm long, 2 cm
wide, one end covered by a thick, white, fatty-fleshy attachment eaten by bats, which disperse the seeds; fallen seeds
eaten by agoutis and other rodents; fruits Nov.–Dec. Falling
fruit dangerous to anyone standing below the tree. **Habitat:**
Wet lowland forests. Altitude: 30–500 m. Conservation
areas: CVC, OSA, TOR. **Range:** Nic–Ec. **Notes:** *Lecythis
ampla* is scarce and in danger of extinction, but fallen fruits
are very conspicuous. They are used for crafts. Wood has
been used for heavy construction.

■ *Magnolia poasana* (Magnolia, candelillo)
Family Magnoliaceae

Tree to 20 m tall, twigs with ringlike stipule scar below each leaf stalk. **Leaves** alternate, to 12 cm long, 5 cm wide, elliptic, dark green. **Flowers** cream white, radially symmetrical, 10 cm diameter, fragrant, petals 6, fleshy, spatula-shaped, sepals 3, gray, thin; stamens and stigmas numerous, on a green, nar-

rowly conical structure at center of flower; blooms Mar.–Oct. **Fruit** becoming dry, a cone-shaped aggregate with seeds in individual compartments, valve of each compartment opening to release a seed covered by red fleshy coating; fruit present Mar.–Dec. **Habitat:** Wet mountain forests and remnant trees in pastures, sometimes in swampy areas. Altitude: 1600–2400 m. Conservation areas: ARE, CVC, HNO, LAC, LAP, PAC. **Range:** Mex–Pan. **Notes:** There are two species of *Magnolia* in Costa Rica; M. *sororum* is much less common. *Magnolia grandiflora*, from the southern United States, is sometimes cultivated.

■ *Hampea appendiculata*
(azajardillo, burío, burío ratón)
Family Malvaceae

Tree 6–17 m tall, trunk to 40 cm diameter, bark smooth, twigs reddish brown, densely woolly-hairy. **Leaves** alternate, stalks 3–7 cm long, top with tiny ear-shaped appendages, blade 9–21 cm long, 6–16 cm wide, egg-shaped to elliptic, tip long-pointed, base blunt to slightly lobed, major veins 5, palmate at base, densely woolly-hairy, tan below. **Flowers** white to yellow, radially symmetrical, sexes on separate plants, petals 5, fused at base, 1.5 cm long and wide, tips pointed, male flowers with numerous stamens fused into a central tube, female flowers with style 1 cm long; inflorescence of 1–10 flowers in axils; blooms Mar-Oct., mostly June–July. **Fruit** dry, elliptic, 2–3 cm long, 3-parted, densely hairy-woolly, splitting open explosively to release black seeds, 1 cm long, partly covered by white flesh; Oct.–Nov. **Habitat:** Moist to wet, primary and second growth forests. Altitude: Sea level to 1800 m, usually below 1000 m. Conservation areas: ARE, CVC, GUA, LAC, LAP, OSA, TOR. **Range:** Hon–Pan. **Notes:** The only other species of *Hampea* in Costa Rica is H. *platanifolia*, which is much less common.

■ *Wercklea woodsonii* (Panamá,
burío espinoso)
Family Malvaceae

Tree 10–20 m tall, trunk to 35 cm diameter,
twigs gray-hairy. **Leaves** alternate, stalks elongate, blade almost round, to 28 cm long and
wide, sometimes shallowly angled, base lobed,
pale below, hairy on both sides, veins palmate,
margin coarsely toothed. **Flowers** yellow,
large, showy, trumpet-shaped, petals widest
above, narrow at base, 8–12 cm long, 5–6 cm
wide, stamens fused into a tube about 7 cm
long, stigmas fringed; flowers solitary in axils;
blooms July–Oct., Feb.–Mar. **Fruit** dry, densely
hairy, 5-parted, 5–6.5 cm long, surrounded by old calyx and
small bracts. **Habitat:** Wet mountain forests and second
growth. Altitude: 1300–2900 m. Conservation areas: LAC,
LAP, PAC. **Range:** CR, Pan. **Notes:** There are four species
of *Wercklea* in Costa Rica; all but *W. insignis* have yellow
flowers.

■ *Cedrela odorata* (cedro, cedro maría, Spanish cedar)
Family Meliaceae

Tree to 40 m tall, bark dark reddish brown to grayish, rough,
deeply fissured, sometimes buttressed to 2 m high, wood sap
sweetly aromatic. **Leaves** alternate, once pinnate, to 60 cm
long, leaflets 6–17 cm long, 3–5 cm wide, egg-shaped to
elliptic, tip pointed, base asymmetric, deciduous. **Flowers**
white, about 2 cm wide, radially symmetrical, petals 5, stamens white; blooms Apr.–July. **Fruit** woody, to 4.5 cm long,
2 cm wide (photo), oblong, brown, opening in 5 sections to
release 1-winged seeds about 3 cm long, 0.8 cm wide, fruit
interior 5-grooved; fruit present Apr.–Dec. **Habitat:** Wet
to seasonally dry lowland forests along rivers and streams.
Altitude: Sea level to 1000 m, mostly below 500 m. Conservation areas: ARE, CVC, OSA, PAC, TEM. **Range:**
Mex–S Amer, WI. **Notes:** There are four species of *Cedrela*
in Costa Rica.

■ *Guarea rhopalocarpa* (cocora, ocora, pocora)
Family Meliaceae

Tree to 20 m tall, branches low, trunk to 25 cm diameter, bark aromatic. **Leaves** alternate, evenly pinnate, of different lengths on one tree because leaves grow from tip of the axis, adding leaflet pairs, leaflets 4–5 pairs, blade 13–21 cm long, about 4 cm wide, tip pointed. Leaves can live as long as five years. **Flowers** pink and white, radially symmetrical, tubular, about 1 cm long; in clusters from trunk and older branches, pollinated by moths and hummingbirds; blooms and fruits most of the year. **Fruit** dry, rounded, to 8 cm long, with 6–8 thick sections, opening to reveal seeds with fleshy attachment; bird dispersed. **Habitat:** Wet to moist forests. Altitude: 90–1200 m. Conservation areas: ARE, CVC, GUA, HNO, LAC, TOR. **Range:** Nic–Pan. **Notes:** There are 10 species of *Guarea* in Costa Rica.

■ *Swietenia humilis* (caoba, mahogany)
Family Meliaceae

Tree to 20 m tall, trunk 45 cm diameter, bark black, very rough, deeply fissured longitudinally, flaking in long plates, branches sinuous, elongate. **Leaves** alternate, evenly pinnate, stalk 4 cm long, very slender, blade to 30 cm long, leaflets 4–6 pairs, blade 7–14 cm long, 3–4 cm wide, egg-shaped, sides very unequal, pointed at both ends, tip sometimes threadlike, base tapered, texture leathery but thin, veins pale. **Flowers** white to pale yellow, minute, inconspicuous; inflorescence of branched clusters 8–10 cm long; blooms end of dry season, Mar.–Apr. **Fruit** woody, 8–20 cm long, 10–12 cm wide, splitting open in 5 sections, then appearing star-shaped (photo); seeds woody, 6 cm long, 1.3 cm wide, red brown, 1-winged. **Habitat:** Seasonally dry forests. Altitude: Pacific lowlands, sea level to 250 m. Conservation areas: GUA, TEM. **Range:** Mex–N CR. **Notes:** A species of true mahogany, valued for cabinet making, now becoming rare and endangered. *Swietenia macrophylla* is the only other species of this genus in Costa Rica.

■ *Artocarpus altilis* (fruta de pan, breadfruit)
Family Moraceae

Tree to 20 m tall, bark thin. **Leaves** alternate, stalk stout, to 7 cm long, blade to 1 m long, 65 cm wide, egg-shaped, deeply pinnately lobed, lobes pointed, base tapered; leaf buds enclosed in a sheath to 15 cm long. **Flowers** yellow green, in club-shaped spikes to 40 cm long, 3 cm wide. **Fruit** fleshy, oval to round, to 30 cm, green, spiny when young, yellow brown when ripe, surface with pebbled texture of numerous small, fused segments, edible when cooked. **Habitat:** Widely cultivated in wet lowlands. Altitude: Sea level to 200 m. Conservation areas: OSA, TEM. **Range:** Native to Pacific islands. Cultivated throughout the tropics. **Notes:** There is one other species of *Artocarpus* in Costa Rica, which is less common.

■ *Brosimum alicastrum* (ojoche, lechoso, breadnut)
Family Moraceae

Tree to 45 m tall, buttresses large, thick, sap milky, white to yellow, edible; bark smooth gray, thin with irregular horizontal, raised lines, trunk irregularly fluted, branching low, twigs encircled by prominent leaf scars. **Leaves** alternate, in one plane, stalk about 1 cm long, stout, blade 4–20 cm long, 2–8 cm wide, egg-shaped to elliptic, tip pointed, base wedge-shaped to blunt, glossy, leathery, pale below, veins pale, conspicuous vein around margin. **Flowers** greenish, very small, sexes on separate plants; inflorescences of dense, rounded succulent fruitlike heads, to 1 cm wide, usually in pairs; blooms Feb.–Mar., June, Sept. **Fruit** fleshy, green, round, to 2 cm wide, surface bumpy, tip depressed, 1-seeded, pulp white, pithy, ripens in Apr.; edible. **Habitat:** Wet to seasonally dry forests. Altitude: Sea level to 700 m. Conservation areas: ARE, GUA, OSA, PAC, TEM. **Range:** N Mex–CR, WI. **Notes:** Leaves used as cattle feed. There are six species of *Brosimum* in Costa Rica.

■ *Brosimum utile* (baco, lechoso, milk tree)
Family Moraceae

Tree to 50 m tall, young trees with short, thick buttresses, trunk to 1.5 m diameter, fluted above buttresses, older trees lack buttresses, bark dark gray, grainy with fine horizontal ridges, young stems with ringlike scars, roots orange red, sap milky, drinkable. **Leaves** alternate, stalk about 1 cm long, blade 11–40 cm long, 5–18 cm wide, elliptical, thick, tip pointed, base rounded, secondary veins numerous, parallel, almost at right angles to midrib, loop-connected around margin. **Flowers** greenish, very small, in rounded, solitary, head-like clusters 0.5–1 cm wide; blooms Nov.–Jan. **Fruit** fleshy, to 3 cm wide (photo), becoming brown, with 1 large seed; Dec.–Mar. **Habitat:** Wet to moist forests. Altitude: Pacific slope, sea level to 700 m. Conservation areas: OSA, PAC. **Range:** CR–Pr and Brz. **Notes:** There are often many seedlings under adult trees.

■ *Castilla elastica* (hule, palo de hule, rubber tree)
Family Moraceae

Tree to 30 m tall, low buttresses, sap milky, young growth yellowish-hairy, older bark with vertical rows of small, warty outgrowths. **Leaves** alternate, in one plane along elongate branches, stalk to 2 cm long, densely bristly-hairy, blade 10–55 cm long, 5–25 cm wide, oblong, tip abruptly pointed, base shallowly, slightly unequally lobed, surface rough, golden-hairy, dark green above, yellowish below, margin minutely toothed. **Flowers** yellowish, tiny, densely crowded in fleshy inflorescences, sexes separate on same tree, female inflorescence disk-shaped, of many thick, fused, bractlike parts; male inflorescence fleshy, appearing folded, fan-shaped, flattened, base about 1 cm (photo: three fallen inflorescences), conspicuous in rows along both sides of young stems; blooms mostly Jan.–June. **Fruit** fleshy, yellow orange, a head of fused, individual fruits 4–5 cm long, 1.5 cm wide, edible, seeds numerous, to 1 cm long. **Habitat:** Wet to seasonally dry lowland forests, second growth. Altitude: Sea level to 850 m, mostly below 400 m. Conservation areas: CVC, GUA, LAC, TEM, TOR. **Range:** Mex–W Col and Ec. **Notes:** There is one other species of *Castilla* in Costa Rica: *C. tunu.*

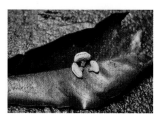

Courtesy of Margaret Gargiullo

■ *Ficus benjamina* (weeping fig)
Family Moraceae
Tree 5–20 m tall, canopy broad, trunk and aerial roots wide, irregular, corded, branching near ground, twigs slender, often drooping, bark smooth, gray, sap milky; stipule enfolds leaf bud, leaving a circular scar around stem. **Leaves** alternate, stalk to 1.5 cm long, blade simple, 4–12 cm long, 2–4.5 cm wide, elliptic, tip long-pointed, base blunt, surface smooth, glossy, secondary veins obscure. **Flowers** minute, inside a fleshy, fruitlike fig, about 1 cm long (see Introduction for description of fig flowers and reproduction). **Fruit** fleshy, bright yellow fig, to about 2 cm long, 1.5 cm wide (photo), rounded with contracted stem-end, usually paired at nodes. **Habitat:** Cultivated as an ornamental, rarely escaping. Altitude: Sea level to 1200 m. Conservation areas: CVC, PAC. **Range:** Native from S Asia to Australia. Cultivated throughout the tropics. **Notes:** There are 42 species of *Ficus* in Costa Rica.

■ *Ficus costaricana* (higo, higuerón, higuerón colorado)
Family Moraceae
Tree 8–20 m tall, usually free standing but sometimes a strangler, trunk usually short, bark smooth, gray brown, young twigs hairy, older twigs ridged, often with small projections from fig attachments above leaf scars, stipules to 3 cm long, 0.5 cm wide, enfolding leaf bud, often persistent on twigs. **Leaves** alternate, clustered at ends of twigs, stalk to 3 cm, blade 5–16 cm long, 3–7 cm wide, very variable on different trees, broadly elliptic to oblong, tip abruptly narrowed, often blunt, narrowed to base. **Flowers** minute, inside fleshy, fruitlike fig; blooms and fruits all year. **Fruit** fleshy fig, about 1 cm diameter when mature (photo), pinkish with red spots, to all red, stalkless, usually paired; fruits most of the year; edible. **Habitat:** Wet to seasonally dry forests, second growth, disturbed sites, also in towns on old walls. Altitude: Sea level to 1600 m. Conservation areas: ARE, CVC, GUA, HNO, LAP, OSA, PAC, TEM, TOR. **Range:** Gua–Pan.

Courtesy of Margaret Gargiullo

Courtesy of Margaret Gargiullo

63

■ *Ficus cotinifolia* (higuerón)
Family Moraceae
Tree 6–20 m tall, broadly spreading strangler, bark gray, trunk of fused aerial roots, fluted, corded, branches with stiltlike aerial roots, twigs densely, softly gray-hairy, stipules enfold leaf bud, 0.5–1.2 cm long, densely gray-hairy, deciduous. **Leaves** alternate, stalk 1–8 cm long, stout, blade 7–15 cm long, 4–8 cm wide, oblong-elliptic to almost round, both ends rounded, glossy above, slightly velvety to touch below, veins weakly joined by loop connections at margin, deciduous in dry season. **Flowers** minute, inside fleshy fruitlike figs; blooms and fruits most of the year. **Fruit** fleshy fig, 0.6–1 cm diameter (photo), 2 per node, round, apex slightly depressed within a raised ring. **Habitat:** Moist to seasonally dry forests, edges. Altitude: Pacific slope, sea level to 900 m. Conservation areas: ARE, CVC, GUA, PAC, TEM. **Range:** Mex–CR.

■ *Ficus insipida* (chilamate higuerón)
Family Moraceae
Tree 8–40 m tall, base buttressed, bark smooth, very pale gray, sap milky, thick, very sticky, copious, twigs stout, to 0.6 cm wide, with prominent leaf or fig scar ridges; stipules enfold leaf bud, very slender, 4–10 cm long. **Leaves** alternate, stalk 2–5 cm long, blade 8–22 cm long, 3–8 cm wide, narrowly elliptic to oblong, tip tapered to pointed, base rounded, secondary veins numerous, weakly connected at margin. **Flowers** minute, inside fleshy fruitlike figs; blooms and fruits on and off Oct.–Apr. **Fruit** fleshy fig, 2.5–5 cm diameter (photo), solitary, green with pale speckles, rounded. **Habitat:** Wet to seasonally dry lowlands, very often along stream or river banks. Altitude: Sea level to 1100 m, usually below 500 m. Conservation areas: ARE, CVC, GUA, HNO, OSA, PAC, TEM. **Range:** S Mex–S Brz.

■ *Ficus maxima* (amate, chilamate)
Family Moraceae

Free-standing tree to 25 m tall, bark smooth, brown with fine horizontal striations and vertical lines of small yellowish dots (lenticels), sometimes peeling in small strips, young stems reddish, flaking, buttresses sinuous, low, long, often merging with surface roots; stipules covering leaf buds 1–3 cm long, very slender. **Leaves** alternate, stalk to 3 cm, blade 7–23 cm long, 3–12 cm wide, elliptic, tip bluntly pointed, base narrowed, truncate at leaf stalk, smooth above, rough below; secondary veins flat above, 2 marginal veins at base of blade, other veins at nearly right angle to midrib, loop-connected near margin. **Flowers** tiny, inside figs; blooms and fruits most of the year. **Fruit** fleshy fig, 2 cm wide (photo), rounded, surface rough, solitary. **Habitat:** Wet to seasonally dry forests, second growth, often growing along streams. Altitude: Sea level to 1600 m, mostly below 500 m. Conservation areas: ARE, GUA, LAC, OSA, PAC, TEM, TOR. **Range:** S Mex–Amazonia.

■ *Naucleopsis naga* (amargo, quina)
Family Moraceae

Tree to 15 m tall, sap brownish to clear yellow, stipules to 1.9 cm long, brown hairy, encircling stem. **Leaves** alternate, stalk to 2 cm long, blade 14–40 cm long, 5–11 cm wide, slightly asymmetric, narrow, elliptic-oblong, pointed at both ends, base often asymmetrical, leathery, smooth, shiny, midrib prominent. **Flowers** dull yellow to whitish, in dense, domed clusters embedded in a mass of woody, narrow spine-like bracts, becoming about 2 cm long in fruit, flower parts similar to bracts; blooms Apr.–Sept. **Fruit** bright orange, embedded within the mass of woody, spinelike

bracts and flower parts, about 6–8 cm diameter; fruit present Apr.–Sept. Old fruit sometimes found on forest floor (photo). **Habitat:** Wet forests of the Caribbean slope. Altitude: Sea level to 1350 m, mostly below 700 m. Conservation areas: CVC, LAC, TOR. **Range:** Hon–CR. **Notes:** Spiny fruit is distinctive. The other species of *Naucleopsis* in Costa Rica, *N. ulei*, is found mostly in the Pacific lowlands.

■ *Virola koschnyi* (bogamaní fruta,
fruta dorada, candelo)
Family Myristicaceae

Tree 30–45 m tall, sap red, trunk straight, cylindrical, base buttressed, bark corky, orange brown, slightly fissured, young trees with branches at right angle to trunk, in spirals up trunk, twigs tan-scaly, straight, stout, seedlings rusty-hairy, attached to persistent seed. **Leaves** alternate, ranked along stem, stalk about 1 cm, blade 7–29 cm long, 2–8 cm wide, oblong, both sides very hairy, tip abruptly pointed, base rounded to slightly lobed, veins numerous, parallel, loop-connected at margin, surface shiny above, paler, yellow-brown-hairy below. **Flowers** yellow, small, radially symmetrical, no petals, calyx 3-lobed; Aug.–Mar. **Fruit** hard-fleshy (photo), splitting open to reveal a large seed covered by a bright red fleshy network (aril) that is attractive to large birds like toucans; fruit present Sept.–June. **Habitat:** Moist to wet forests. Altitude: Sea level to 1000 m. Conservation areas: ARE, CVC, GUA, LAC, OSA, PAC, TOR. **Range:** Gua–Pan. **Notes:** There are five species of *Virola* in Costa Rica.

Seed pod

■ *Eucalyptus deglupta* (eucalipto,
ocalipto, Mindanao gum)
Family Myrtaceae

Tree 7–30 m tall, bark dark gray, peeling, under bark green, with red streaks (photo). **Leaves** alternate on adult trees, 8–23 cm long, 4–9 cm wide, tip with elongate point, base wedge-shaped, blade shiny green above, paler green below, sprinkled with tiny dots containing aromatic oils; leaves of young growth opposite, without leaf stalk. **Flowers** white small, radially symmetrical, 0.3 cm long; in clusters of 6–8. **Fruit** dry, 4-parted, 0.3–0.4 cm long. **Habitat:** Horticultural, used in parks, to shade coffee plantations, not known to escape. Altitude: Sea level to 1100 m. Conservation areas: CVC, LAP, PAC. **Range:** Native to the Philippines, New

Guinea, and Indonesia. Widely cultivated in tropical regions. **Notes:** One of several species of *Eucalyptus* used in tree plantations, agriculture, and horticulture. There are at least four, possibly up to seven species of *Eucalyptus* in Costa Rica; none are native to the new world.

■ *Myrcianthes fragrans*
(albajaquillo, arrayán, murta)
Family Myrtaceae

Slender tree or shrub 3–30 m tall, trunk to about 80 cm diameter, more or less cylindrical, buttresses low, thin, sweeping; bark smooth, orange tan, with brown patches, mottled, flaking in small chips (photo). **Leaves** opposite, ranked along stem, stalk about 0.5 cm long, blade 3–14 cm long, 1.5–5.5 cm wide, elliptic, pointed at both ends, surface smooth, underside pale, densely covered by tiny dots, often with a strong odor, midrib impressed above secondary veins rather obscure. **Flowers** white to cream,

radially symmetrical, sweetly fragrant, about 1 cm wide, petals 4, anthers very numerous, white nearly 1 cm long; inflorescence of 3 or 7 flowers; blooms Mar.–July, Nov. **Fruit** fleshy, becoming red to dark purple, round, about 1 cm wide, flesh juicy, edible, 1- to 3-seeded; Mar.–Nov. **Habitat:** Moist to wet forest, disturbed sites, remnant trees in pastures. Altitude: Sea level to 2600 m, usually above 1000 m. Conservation areas: ARE, CVC, GUA, HNO, LAP, PAC, TEM. **Range:** Mex–Ven and Pr, WI. **Notes:** There is one other species of *Myrcianthes* in Costa Rica, found mostly above 2000 m.

■ *Cespedesia spathulata (C. macrophylla)*
(tabacón, espavel colorado)
Family Ochnaceae

Tree to 35 m tall, trunk to 50 cm diameter, often with stilt roots; stipules to 7 cm long, persistent at ends of stems, becoming almost woody. **Leaves** alternate, spiraled at ends of branches amid persistent stipules, stalk to 1 cm long, blade 0.2–1 m long, 15–25 cm wide, widest near apex, tip blunt, tapered to base, lateral veins numerous, margins unevenly toothed; new leaves red. **Flowers** yellow, about 6 cm wide, showy, 5-parted, nearly radially symmetrical, petals free, stamens numerous, clustered on opposite side of flower

from stigma; inflorescence of large, branched clusters at tips of branches, above upper leaves; blooms Mar.–May, Nov. **Fruit** dry, to 6 cm long, 1 cm wide, splitting into 5 sections to release numerous winged seeds. **Habitat:** Moist to wet forests, second growth. Altitude: 100–950 m. Conservation areas: ARE, CVC, GUA, HNO, PAC, TOR. **Range:** Hon–Col. **Notes:** This is the only species of *Cespedesia* in Costa Rica.

■ *Triplaris melaenodendron*
(hormigo, tabacón, barrabás)
Family Polygonaceae

Tree 5–25 m tall, trunk slender, slightly corded, bark patchy, flaking, brown and pale tan, twigs reddish brown, lenticels in longitudinal ridges, young trunk ringed, hollow stems usually inhabited by aggressive ants, stipules 2–3 cm long, covering leaf bud. **Leaves** alternate, stalk 0.4–2 cm long, blade 15–35 cm long, 6–18 cm wide, egg-shaped, tip pointed, base blunt, slightly unequal, veins closely spaced, loop-connected along margin. **Flowers** pale green to reddish, sexes on different plants, male flowers 0.5 cm long, anthers to 0.7 cm, in dense clusters along a branched inflorescence, female flowers tubular, about 3 cm long, 0.7 cm wide (photo), radially symmetrical, petal lobes 3–4, 2 cm long, 0.6 cm wide, in branched clusters at ends of stems; blooms Jan.–Mar. **Fruit** dry, 3-winged, 4–6 cm long, wings reddish, papery; Feb.–Mar. **Habitat:** Wet to seasonally dry regions, second growth, edges, roadsides. Altitude: Pacific slope, sea level to 1100 m, most often below 500 m. Conservation areas: ARE, GUA, LAP, OSA, PAC, TEM. **Range:** Mex–CR, Col. **Notes:** This is the only species of *Triplaris* in Costa Rica.

■ *Rhizophora mangle* (mangle,
mangle blanco, red mangrove)
Family Rhizophoraceae

Rhizophora mangle photos opposite

Tree to 13 m tall, no central trunk, numerous, large arching, branched stilt roots, growing into mud through water; stipules sheathe the terminal bud. **Leaves** opposite, 7–15 cm long, 2–9 cm wide, elliptical, thick, shiny, smooth, midrib pale, secondary veins obscure. **Flowers** white to yellow, about 1 cm wide, 4-parted, petals deciduous, sepals greenish yellow, thick, flowers 1–2, in axils near ends of branches; blooms Aug.–Mar. **Fruit** about 3 cm long initially, germinating on parent tree to form a fleshy root about 30 cm long, sometimes forming small leaves before dropping into water or mud; fruit present Oct.–July. **Habitat:** Tidal swamps. Altitude: Sea level to 200 m, usually below 10 m. Conservation areas: GUA, LAC, OSA, PAC, TEM. **Range:** NC, SC, FL, Mex–Ec and S Brz, WI, Africa. **Notes:** The most salt tolerant of the mangroves, forming dense tangles of roots that trap sediment and are important shelters for hatchling fish and marine life. Destruction of mangrove forests leads to decreases in fish populations and pollution of coastal waters by suspended sediments. *Rhizophora racemosa* is the only other species of *Rhizophora* in Costa Rica.

■ *Alibertia patinoi* (*Boroja p.*)
Family Rubiaceae

Tree 9–25 m tall, trunk to 32 cm diameter, bark reddish tan, fibrous, thin; stipules between leaf stalk bases, to about 2 cm long, 1 cm wide or more, fused at base, lobes pointed. **Leaves** opposite, clustered at ends of branches, each pair at right angles to the next, stalk to 3 cm long, bade 13–38 cm long, 7–17 cm wide, elliptic, tip long-pointed, base pointed to blunt. **Flowers** white, radially symmetrical, tubular, fragrant, petal tube about 1 cm long, 0.4 cm wide near top, petal lobes 5–6, about 1 cm long, triangular, tips pointed; calyx thick, cup-shaped, lobes tiny; male and female flowers on different plants, male inflorescence of 2–9 flowers, female flowers solitary; blooms Mar.–July. **Fruit** fleshy, thick-walled, yellow green, to 11 cm long, 10 cm wide (photo), crowned by persistent calyx, flesh tough, white, seeds numerous, flattened, embedded in a viscous pulp. **Habitat:** Moist to wet forests; also cultivated. Altitude: Sea level to 600 m. Conservation areas: OSA. **Range:** CR. **Notes:** There are three other species of this genus in Costa Rica.

Rhizophora mangle

Seedling

■ *Calycophyllum candidissimum*
(sálamo, colorado, conejo)
Family Rubiaceae

Tree 5–18 m tall, trunk to 70 cm diameter, branching low, often
with several trunks, deeply corded and often twisted, bark pale
gray mottled with red brown, thin, peeling and flaking, loose,
new growth pale woolly-hairy; stipules to 1 cm long, deciduous,
leaving ridge across stem. **Leaves** opposite, stalk 1–2 cm, blade
4–10 cm long, 2–7 cm wide, broadly elliptical to egg-shaped,
tip abruptly long-pointed, base tapered, hairy below. **Flowers**
white, 0.5–0.9 cm long, radially symmetrical, tubular, fragrant,
in groups of 3, the center flower often with 1 enlarged, heart-
shaped lobe, 2–4 cm long, 2–3 cm wide, white, becoming reddish (photo); inflorescence of branched clusters; blooms most
of the year. **Fruit** dry, about 1 cm long, cylindrical, 8-ribbed;
seeds to 0.5 cm, winged at both ends; fruit present Jan.–Aug.
Habitat: Seasonally dry forests. Altitude: Pacific lowlands, sea
level to 400 m, occasionally to 800 m. Conservation areas:
GUA, LAP, PAC, TEM. **Range:** Mex–Ec, Cuba, PtR. **Notes:**
This is the national tree of Nicaragua. It is the only species of
the genus in Costa Rica.

■ *Genipa americana* (guaitil, guatil blanco, yuguaitil)
Family Rubiaceae

Tree 4–35 m tall, trunk to 50 cm diameter, bark smooth, gray
with raised lenticels, branches and twigs stout, sap turns blue
in air; stipules 1–2.5 cm long, triangular, base fused around
stem, leaving prominent scars. **Leaves** opposite, at ends of
twigs, stalk thick, 0.2–1 cm, blade 12–42 cm long, 6–19 cm
wide, widest at or above middle, pointed at both ends, deciduous in seasonally dry regions. **Flowers** yellow or white, radially symmetrical, tubular, 3–4 cm long, 4 cm wide, petal lobes
5–6, to 0.3 cm long, 1 cm wide, tips rounded; inflorescence
at or near ends of branches; blooms May–July. **Fruit** hard-
fleshy, to 11 cm, elliptic, tip with crater formed by persistent
sepals (photo); seeds numerous, yellow; fruit present all year.
Habitat: Wet to seasonally dry forests, second growth. Altitude: Sea level to 1100 m. Conservation areas: CVC, GUA,
HNO, LAC, OSA, PAC, TEM, TOR. **Range:** Mex–Arg.
Notes: There is one other species of *Genipa* in Costa Rica.

■ *Guettarda crispiflora*
Family Rubiaceae

Tree or shrub 4–25 m tall, bark smooth, branches opposite, young stems 4-sided; stipules between leaf stalk bases (interpetiolar) 1–2 long, 1 cm wide, egg-shaped, keeled on back, tip pointed. **Leaves** opposite, at ends of stems, each pair at right angles to next, stalks 2–7 cm long, blade 8–22 cm long, 5–11 cm wide, egg-shaped, dull green, pointed at both ends, or base blunt, hairy below, veins curved sharply upward. **Flowers** white to pinkish, radially symmetrical, tubular, to 1.8 cm long, petal lobes 4, to 0.6 cm long, curved back, ends of lobes

fringed; inflorescence 2–6 cm long, of 2 diverging, 1-sided, out-curved spikes (bifurcate), to 3 cm long; blooms Jan., Apr.–Nov. **Fruit** fleshy, pinkish purple becoming dark blue, 0.8 long, 0.6 cm wide (photo), oblong, sharply 4-angled, angles sharply ribbed, pulp white; fruit present all year. **Habitat:** Wet forests, second growth, roadsides. Altitude: 100–2300 m, mostly above 1000 m. Conservation areas: ARE, CVC, LAC, LAP, OSA, PAC. **Range:** Bel–Bol, WI. **Notes:** There are 10 species of *Guettarda* in Costa Rica.

■ *Macrocnemum roseum*
(M. glabrescens) **(palo cuadrado)**
Family Rubiaceae

Tree or shrub 4–35 m tall, trunk irregular, deeply fluted, twisted, bark blackish, new growth greenish tan scaly; stipules to 2 cm long, 1 cm wide, oblong, leaving scar above leaf stalks. **Leaves** opposite, stalk 0.5–2 cm, often unequal at same node, blade 7–21 cm long, 4–9 cm wide, egg-shaped, tip blunt to pointed, narrowed to blunt base, surface dark green shiny, veins brown-scaly below. **Flowers** purple pink, showy, radially symmetrical, tubular, to 1 cm long, with 5 ribs, about 1.3 cm across top, petal lobes 5, very angular, buds sharply 5-angled, anthers yellow to green, stigma green; inflorescence of dense, branched clusters at ends of stems; blooms Sept.–Apr.; very attractive to bees and butterflies. **Fruit** dry, to 1.5 cm long, 0.4 cm wide, splitting in two to release numerous small winged seeds. **Habitat:** Moist to seasonally dry forests, second growth, and edges. Altitude: Sea level to 1600 m. Conservation areas: LAC, LAP, OSA, PAC, TEM. **Range:** CR–Bol. **Notes:** This is the only species of *Macrocnemum* in Costa Rica.

71

Simira maxonii (Sickingia m.)
(guaitil, siguaitil, inkwood)
Family Rubiaceae

Tree to 20 m tall, trunk to 30 cm diameter, irregularly corded, usually crooked, branches drooping, bark rough, stipules to 4 cm long, 0.6 cm wide. **Leaves** opposite, stalk about 1 cm long, blade 22–60 cm long, 10–40 cm wide, broadly elliptical, pointed at both ends, minor veins with ladderlike arrangement perpendicular to secondary veins, margin sometimes shallowly lobed near top, young leaves reddish. **Flowers** yellowish to orange, radially symmetrical, funnel-shaped, to 0.5 cm, petal lobes 5, to 0.3 cm long, anthers purplish, longer than petal tube; inflorescence of densely branched clusters to 15 cm long; blooms on and off Jan.– Sept; pollinated by bees. **Fruit** hard, to 9 cm long, 7 cm wide (photo), gray green, rounded; eventually rotting to release flat, winged seeds to 2.5 cm long; fruit present all year. **Habitat:** Wet forests, often along streams. Altitude: Caribbean lowlands and OSA Peninsula sea level to 300 m. Conservation areas: CVC, HNO, LAC, OSA, TOR. **Range:** Nic–Pan. **Notes:** This is the only species of *Simira* in Costa Rica.

Salix humboldtiana photos opposite

Salix humboldtiana (sauce, willow)
Family Salicaceae

Tree to 18 m tall, bark gray brown, furrowed; twigs yellowish, branches often somewhat drooping, evergreen. **Leaves** alternate, stalks to 0.5 cm long, blade 4–10 cm long, 0.4–1 cm wide, lance-shaped to linear, pointed at both ends, margin minutely toothed. **Flowers** green, males and females on separate plants, tiny, inconspicuous, in spikes 3–7 cm long, only females found in Costa Rica. **Fruit** not found on Costa Rican trees due to the lack of male trees. **Habitat:** Planted from cuttings, or growing along rivers from rooted, broken branches. Altitude: Cool, wet regions to 2000 m. **Range:** Native to N C Amer and parts of S Amer. Also escaped from cultivation along rivers. Mex–Arg and Brz, Jam, PtR. **Notes:** *Salix babylonica*, with long, weeping branches, is also planted in Costa Rica.

■ *Billia hippocastanum* (ocora, cocora, resina, ira)
Family Sapindaceae

Tree to 18 m tall, trunk 40 cm diameter, bark smooth, gray. **Leaves** opposite, 3-parted, leaflets to 20 cm long, elliptic to lance-shaped, pointed at both ends. **Flowers** red to white with yellow base, variable, small, petals 5, free, slightly unequal, sepals yellow to red, free; blooms and fruits most of the year. **Fruit** hard-fleshy, brown, 3-parted, to 5.5 cm long (photo), grainy texture, splitting open in 3 parts to release 1 large, 2-parted seed, 4 cm long, 4.5 cm wide, drying dark reddish. **Habitat:** Wet forests. Altitude: 500–2800 m. Conservation areas: ARE, CVC, GUA, LAC, LAP, PAC. **Range:** Mex–Pan. **Notes:** There are three species of *Billia* in Costa Rica. This genus is often included in the family Hippocastanaceae.

Salix humboldtiana

73

■ *Blighia sapida* (akii, seso vegetal, huevo vegetal)
Family Sapindaceae
Tree 8–15 m tall, young stems yellowish woolly-hairy. **Leaves** alternate, evenly pinnate, leaflets opposite, stalk to 0.7 cm, leaflets 3–5 pairs, 4–20 cm long, 3–8 cm wide, elliptic, tip rounded to short-pointed, leathery. **Flowers** greenish white to cream, small, fragrant, petals 5, about 0.4 cm long, stamens 8–10, ovary densely reddish-hairy; inflorescences unbranched, elongate, stiff; blooms May. **Fruit** fleshy, red, 3-sided pod, 6–10 cm wide (photo), splitting open to reveal 3 large black shiny seeds each embedded in a large cream white, fleshy aril 3 cm long and wide (looks like animal fat); fruits Feb., May. **Habitat:** Cultivated in wet lowlands. Altitude: Sea level to about 300 m. Conservation areas: LAC, PAC. **Range:** Native to Africa. Cultivated in Bel-Col, WI. **Notes:** Ripe aril is edible when cooked. However unripe arils, overripe arils and other plant parts are very toxic, causing a sometimes fatal drop in blood sugar levels, called "Jamaica sickness." Genus named for Captain Bligh.

■ *Nephelium lappaceum* (mamón chino rambután)
Family Sapindaceae
Tree to 20 m tall, bark grainy, brown, twigs tan-scaly. **Leaves** alternate, evenly pinnate, 4–6 leaflets, to 28 cm long, 15 cm wide, elliptic, shiny green, leathery. **Flowers** whitish, small, male and female plants separate, no petals; inflorescence of branched clusters; blooms Feb., May, June. **Fruit** leathery, red husk, rounded, soft-spiny, to 6 cm wide (photo, unripe fruit), surrounding a translucent, edible, fleshy layer that covers 1 large central seed; fruit present June. **Habitat:** Cultivated in wet lowlands. Altitude: 100–400 m. Conservation areas: ARE, OSA. **Range:** Native to Malaysia, cultivated in many tropical regions. **Notes:** Oily seed also edible if cooked. Fruit often sold at fruit stands. Very much like *N. mutabile*, also a cultivated Asian tree.

■ *Chrysophyllum cainito* (caimito, sokuikuo, caimito de monte)
Family Sapotaceae

Tree to 20 m tall, trunk about 70 cm diameter, no buttresses, bark longitudinally fissured, gray brown, twigs densely brown-hairy, new growth gold-scaly, sap milky. **Leaves** alternate, stalk to 1.5 cm, gold-scaly, blade 7–12 cm long, 4–6 cm wide elliptic, tip long-pointed, base blunt, glossy dark green above, densely gold-brown-hairy below, lateral veins numerous, closely spaced, nearly at right angles to midrib, loop-connected near margin. **Flowers** cream-white, radially symmetrical, very small, tubular, petal lobes 5, about 0.4 cm long, stigma 7- to 12-lobed; inflorescence of dense axillary clusters, on stalks 1 cm; blooms on and off most of the year. **Fruit** fleshy, purple, 5–10 cm wide (photo); seeds several, asymmetrical about 2.5 cm long. **Habitat:** Moist to seasonally dry forests; also cultivated. Altitude: Sea level to 1200 m. Conservation areas: CVC, HNO, LAC, OSA, TEM. **Range:** Native to WI, naturalized in other regions. Mex–Ec, Brz, WI, Africa. **Notes:** There are eight species of *Chrysophyllum* in Costa Rica.

■ *Manilkara chicle* (níspero, níspero chicle)
Family Sapotaceae

Tree to 45 m tall, trunk to 1.25 m, base slightly fluted, bark brown black with deep, narrow vertical fissures (photo), sap milky, crown dense, dark green, young trees have whorled branches, twigs stout. **Leaves** alternate, clustered in spirals at ends of stems, blade to 18 cm long, 9 cm wide, narrowly elliptic, pointed at both ends, leathery, dark green, evergreen, lateral veins closely spaced, rather obscure. **Flowers** white, small, radially symmetrical, bell-shaped, fragrant, petals fused; blooms Feb.–Oct. **Fruit** fleshy, pale reddish brown, rounded, to 7 cm (photo), skin rough, flesh edible, sweet, seeds black; fruit present Nov.–Jan. **Habitat:** Wet to seasonally dry forests. Altitude: Sea level to 1400 m. Conservation areas: ARE, GUA, HNO, LAC, PAC, TEM. **Range:** Mex–Col. **Notes:** There are three species of *Manilkara* in Costa Rica. Sap is source of chicle used in chewing gum.

■ *Pouteria fossicola* (zapote, sapote, níspero)
Family Sapotaceae
Tree 12–40 m tall, buttresses thick, bark pale, rough, sap milky, sticky, twigs stout, rough with old leaf scars; deciduous in dry season. **Leaves** alternate, spiraled at ends of twigs, stalk to 4 cm, blade 12–30 cm long, 6–13 cm wide, widest near apex, tip rounded or abruptly pointed, tapered to base, texture leathery. **Flowers** whitish, radially symmetrical, 1 cm, tubular, fragrant at night, pollinated by moths; inflorescence of dense clusters on stems below leaves; Apr.–May, Sept.–Oct. **Fruit** fleshy, to 10 cm long, 7 cm wide (photo), with a brittle rind, elliptical, greenish tan, flesh orange at maturity, edible; seed solitary, to 6 cm long, smooth, brown, elliptic,

with pale scar along one side, cut seeds release cyanide (odor of bitter almond); fruit present most of the year; eaten by mammals including agoutis. **Habitat:** Wet to moist forests. Altitude: Sea level to 1600 m. Conservation areas: ARE, LAP, OSA. **Range:** Nic–Pan. **Notes:** There are 35 species of *Pouteria* in Costa Rica.

■ *Pouteria sapota* (P. *mammosa*)
(zapote, zapote colorado, zapote mamey)
Family Sapotaceae
Tree 8–30 m tall, trunk to 60 cm diameter, bark grainy with horizontal lines, sap milky, twigs brown-hairy. **Leaves** alternate, spiraled at ends of branches or on new growth; stalk stout, to 4 cm, blade 10–40 cm long, 4–14 cm wide, narrow, widest near apex, tip abruptly pointed, tapered to base, hairy below, secondary lateral veins at right angles to primary lateral veins. **Flowers** white, radially symmetrical, tubular, to 1 cm long, petal lobes 4–5, sepals 8–12, to 0.6 cm round, densely hairy; clustered at leafless nodes often on older branches and trunk; May–Aug. **Fruit** fleshy, oval, to 20 cm long, 15 cm wide (photo), skin sandpapery, brown, flesh reddish orange, sap milky, edible, very sweet, dense; 1 large seed, to 6 cm, brown, with broad scar along one side; Sept., Feb. **Habitat:** Moist to wet forests; also cultivated. Altitude: Sea level to 600 m. Cultivated to 1500 m. Conservation areas: OSA, TEM. **Range:** FL, Mex–Ec. **Notes:** Fruit used in ice cream and other desserts.

◼ *Sideroxylon capiri* (danto, dri, tempisque)
Family Sapotaceae

Tree 14–28 m tall, trunk 80 cm diameter, straight, bark pale brown tan, flaking in large, flat, rectangular plates, sap milky. **Leaves** alternate, in whorls at ends of twigs, stalk 3–7 cm long with a small leaflike tab at the top forming a pocket at the base of the leaf blade, blade 7–15 cm long, about 5 cm wide, widest near long-pointed tip, tapered to base, evergreen, dark green, margins smooth. **Flowers** cream white, radially symmetrical, tubular, calyx rusty brown, small. **Fruit** fleshy, rounded, green, sap milky, copious; seeds blackish brown. **Habitat:** Wet to seasonally dry forests. Altitude: Sea level to 1000 m, mostly below 500 m. Conservation areas: GUA, LAP, TEM, TOR. **Range:** Mex–Pan, Pr, To. **Notes:** There are seven species of *Sideroxylon* in Costa Rica.

◼ *Guazuma ulmifolia* (guácimo hembra, caulote)
Family Sterculiaceae

Shrub or tree 3–25 m tall, trunk to 60 cm diameter, often multiple, twisted, grooved, most parts densely woolly-hairy. **Leaves** alternate, stalk to 2 cm, blade 6–16 cm long, 2–6 cm wide, widest at base, tip tapered, base rounded, unequal, hairy, rough, dull green, major veins 3–7, palmate at base, margins finely, irregularly toothed; deciduous during dry season. **Flowers** yellow green with red markings, radially symmetrical, very small (photo), petals 5, about 0.2 cm long, tip 2-lobed, with appendages to 0.4 cm, sepals 3, stamens numerous; inflorescence of short, axillary clusters; blooms Feb.–June, Sept.–Oct. **Fruit** dry, to 4 cm, oval, green, warty when developing (photo), appearing conelike when mature; ripening Dec.–Feb., seeds numerous, bat dispersed. **Habitat:** Wet to seasonally dry regions in open areas, second growth. Altitude: Pacific slope, sea level to 1100 m. Conservation areas: ARE, GUA, LAP, OSA, PAC, TEM. **Range:** Mex–Ven and Par, WI. Introduced in Galapagos. **Notes:** *Guazuma invera* is the only other species of *Guazuma* in Costa Rica.

■ *Pterygota excelsa* (probado)
Family Sterculiaceae

Tree 35–60 m tall, trunk straight, cylindrical, to about 1.6 m diameter, with wide buttresses about 1.5 m, bark light gray to brown. **Leaves** alternate, stalk elongate, blade 6–30 cm long, 6–25 cm wide, broadly heart- or egg-shaped, tip pointed, base rounded or broadly lobed, major veins 5, palmate at base, from a broad connection at the top of the leaf stalk, loop-connected around margin; deciduous in dry season. **Flowers** brownish green, small, no petals, calyx green lightly striped with maroon inside; anthers bright yellow; blooms Feb., Mar. **Fruit** woody, thick-walled, asymmetrical, to about 15 cm long, 9 cm wide, 5 cm thick, wider than long; opening to release many, large, winged seeds about 8 cm long, 3 cm wide; May–Oct. **Habitat:** Moist to wet lowland forests. Altitude: Southern Pacific slope, sea level to 550 m. Conservation areas: OSA, PAC. **Range:** CR, Pan. **Notes:** Fallen fruit or leaves may be the most easily recognized part of this tree. This is the only species of *Pterygota* in Costa Rica.

■ *Sterculia apetala* (terciopelo, panamá, árbol de Panamá)
Family Sterculiaceae

Tree 8–40 m tall, canopy umbrella-shaped, trunk cylindrical to irregular, to 1 m diameter, buttresses to 1.5 m, bark pale gray, thin, with many closely spaced, raised dots, sap with strong, pungent odor. **Leaves** alternate, stalk to 25 cm long, blade palmately 3- to 5-lobed, to 35 cm long, 45 cm wide, lobes rounded or pointed at tip, base deeply round-lobed, softly hairy below; deciduous at end of wet season, then leaf-

ing out again. **Flowers** pale green with red markings (photo), radially symmetrical, strong, spicy odor, to 2 cm wide, no petals, calyx bowl-shaped, 5-lobed; blooms and fruits on and off most of the year. **Fruit** woody, of 3–5 elliptical segments each to 10 cm long, 5 cm wide, attached at one end, each splitting open to release seeds, inside covered with sharp orange hairs, seeds 2–4, about 2 cm long, black; seeds taken by birds. **Habitat:** Wet to seasonally dry, lowland forests. Altitude: Pacific slope, sea level to 400 m. Conservation areas: GUA, OSA, PAC, TEM. **Range:** Mex–Bol, DR. **Notes:** There are two other species of *Sterculia* in Costa Rica.

■ *Apeiba membranacea* (botija, peine mico, tapabotija)
Family Tiliaceae
Tree to 30 m tall, trunk to 75 cm diameter, weakly buttressed, ribbed above buttresses, bark thin, flaky, young stems rusty-hairy. **Leaves** alternate, stalk to 3 cm, blade 8–25 cm long, 3–10 cm wide, oblong-elliptic, tip pointed, base rounded or lobed, major veins 3, palmate at base, margin finely toothed; deciduous in early dry season, leafing out again soon after. **Flowers** yellow, radially symmetrical, 5-parted, petals spatula-shaped, to 2 cm long, 1 cm wide, sepals about 2 cm long, narrow, stamens numerous, about 0.5 cm long; inflorescences of small, branched clusters to 8 cm long; blooms and fruits most of the year. **Fruit** dry, to 6 cm wide, 1.5 cm thick, dark, spiny, a flattened globe, resembles a sea urchin with short blunt spines (photo), seeds numerous, 0.4 cm long. Apparently eaten by some parrots and macaws. **Habitat:** Wet forests. Altitude: Sea level to 900 m. Conservation areas: ARE, CVC, GUA, HNO, LAC, OSA, PAC, TOR. **Range:** Hon–Bol. **Notes:** The only other species of this genus in Costa Rica is A. *tibourbou*.

■ *Apeiba tibourbou*
(burío, peine de mico, monkey comb)
Family Tiliaceae
Tree to 20 m tall, trunk to 25 cm diameter, bark thin light brown, weakly fissured, often striped horizontally, twigs stout, most nonwoody parts red-gold-hairy; stipules to 3 cm long, triangular, leaving scars on stems. **Leaves** alternate, in one plane along stems, stalk to 3 cm, bristly-hairy, blade 10–30 cm long, 6–12 cm wide, oblong-elliptic, tip long-pointed, base slightly lobed, densely red-gold-hairy below, veins palmate at base, minor veins ladderlike between major secondary veins, margin finely toothed. **Flowers** yellow to white, radially symmetrical, 4- to 5-parted, petals to 1.5 cm long, thick, sepals densely hairy outside, anthers numerous, flat, yellow; inflorescence of sparse clusters to 11 cm; blooms Feb.–Nov. **Fruit** dry, to 4 cm tall, 8 cm wide, a flattened globe, densely covered with long, flexible bristles to 1.5 cm (photo), seeds numerous, rounded, 0.2 cm; fruits Jan.–Sept. **Habitat:** Wet to seasonally dry forests. Altitude: Pacific slope, sea level to 1100 m. Conservation areas: GUA, LAP, OSA, PAC, TEM. **Range:** Mex–Bol, Tr, To.

Heliocarpus americanus photos opposite

■ **Goethalsia meiantha** (jaunilama, chancho blanco, guácimo)
Family Tiliaceae

Tree 15–30 m tall, trunk about 40 cm diameter, fast-growing pioneer species, trunk straight, cylindrical, often buttressed at base, bark thin, whitish or pale, fibrous, sometimes hanging in strips; leafy only near top. **Leaves** alternate, ranked along twigs, somewhat drooping, blade 10–22 cm long, 3–8 cm wide, elliptic, pointed at both ends, major veins 3, palmate at base, margin toothed. **Flowers** yellow, radially symmetrical, small, fragrant (photo); blooms June–Sept. **Fruit** dry, 3–4 winged, greenish, 3–5 cm long (photo), seed a dark, thicker area in center of flat fruit wing; fruits July–Jan. **Habitat:** Moist to very wet lowlands in open sites, second growth, edges, forest light gaps. Altitude: Sea level to 600 m. Conservation areas: GUA, LAC, OSA, PAC, TOR. **Range:** Nic–Ven. **Notes:** This is the only species of *Goethalsia* worldwide.

■ **Heliocarpus americanus** (burío, burillo)
Family Tiliaceae

Tree 5–25 m tall, trunk to about 1 m wide, ringed, like old *Cecropia* trunks, bark tan with horizontal ridges, corky lenticels and fine longitudinal fissures, twigs stout. **Leaves** alternate, leaf stalk brown-hairy-scaly, blade to 24 cm long, 20 cm wide, dull gray green, hairy, heart-shaped, larger leaves often with 2 shallow lobes near top, tip long-pointed, base broadly lobed, inner edges of basal lobes with small, erect frill, margin toothed; fallen leaves yellow. **Flowers** greenish yellow, becoming pink to dark red, radially symmetrical, 1 cm, petals 5, narrow; inflorescence of masses at tips of branches blooms Aug.–Feb. **Fruit** dry, 1 cm wide, flat, margin densely fringed with dull red, hairs; distant trees appear to be flowering; fruits Dec.–Feb. **Habitat:** Moist to wet secondary forests, old pastures roadsides, landslides, and edges. Altitude: 950–2200 m. Conservation areas: CVC, LAP, PAC. **Range:** Mex–Ven and Par, WI. **Notes:** *Heliocarpus* is fast growing with very soft, balsalike wood. It is a pioneer tree in open areas. There are three species of *Heliocarpus* in Costa Rica. *Heliocarpus appendiculatus* is also common, but mostly found in lowland sites.

■ *Luehea alternifolia (L. speciosa)* (guácimo macho)
Family Tiliaceae

Tree 9–20 m tall, to 70 cm diameter, trunk slightly corded, sometimes crooked, bark rough, dark, fissured, young parts rusty-hairy; stipules narrow, to 2 cm. **Leaves** alternate, stalk stout, rusty-scaly, blade 8–24 cm long, 6–12 cm wide, egg-shaped, tip abruptly pointed or notched, base blunt to slightly lobed, surface leathery, dull, dark green above, pale tan-hairy-scaly below, veins palmate at base, margin toothed; leafless during dry season. **Flowers** white or pale yellow, radially symmetrical, 5-parted, showy, odor unpleasant, petals to 3.5 cm long, 1.5 cm wide, tip irregular, sepals rusty-green-scaly, stamens numerous, 1–2 cm long; inflorescence of branched clusters; blooms Nov.–Jan. **Fruit** thin-woody, to 4 cm long, 1.5 cm wide, narrowly elliptic, rusty-hairy, widest at blunt tip, which opens in 5 sections to release small, winged seeds, 1 cm long, 0.4 cm wide. **Habitat:** Moist to seasonally dry forests, second growth. Altitude: Mostly 100–900 m, sometimes to 1400 m. Conservation areas: ARE, CVC, PAC, TEM. **Range:** Mex–Brz and Arg. **Notes:** There are three species of *Luehea* in Costa Rica; *L. candida* is much like *L. alternifolia* but has 5-ribbed fruit.

Heliocarpus americanus (all three below)

81

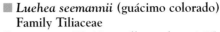

■ *Luehea seemannii* (guácimo colorado)
Family Tiliaceae

Canopy tree 25–40 m tall, trunk to 1.25 m diameter, buttresses sometimes to 3 m high, trunk corded, bark gray, peeling, with prominent, round lenticels, inner bark lighter, young parts rust-hairy. **Leaves** alternate, stalk 1 cm long, blade 5–40 cm long, 2–15 cm wide, oblong-elliptic, tip pointed, base asymmetric, shiny, dark olive green above, densely rusty-brown-hairy below, veins palmate at base, margins irregularly toothed. **Flowers** white or yellow, radially symmetrical, to 2.5 cm wide, petals small, inconspicuous, sepals about 1 cm long, stamens numerous to about 1 cm long; inflorescence of large, branched clusters near ends of branches; blooms Dec.–Mar. **Fruit** woody, 3 cm long, elliptic, deeply 4- to 5-ribbed, densely brown-hairy (photo), seeds winged, numerous, to 1 cm long; fruits Feb.–Nov. **Habitat:** Young secondary forest in wet lowlands and along waterways in seasonally dry regions. Altitude: Sea level to 400 m. Conservation areas: CVC, HNO, LAC, LAP, OSA, PAC, TEM, TOR. **Range:** Bel and Gua–Ven and Bol.

Courtesy of Margaret Gargiullo

■ *Citharexylum donnell-smithii* (dama)
Family Verbenaceae

Tree 3–20 m tall, trunk to about 35 cm diameter, sap milky. **Leaves** opposite, elliptical, to 20 cm long, 6 cm wide, lance-shaped, tip pointed, base blunt, glossy, smooth above with veins paler green. **Flowers** white, small, pleasant odor, petal lobes 5, finely hairy, center green, anthers yellow; inflorescences of narrow, dangling, spikes at ends of twigs; blooms Dec.–May, Sept.–Oct. **Fruit** fleshy, yellow to orange, about 1 cm, densely packed in dangling spikes about 20 cm long, 4 cm wide; eaten by birds, which disperse the seeds; fruit present Jan.–June, Sept.–Oct. **Habitat:** Wet to seasonally dry forests, second growth, remnant trees in pastures; also planted as an ornamental. Altitude: Sea level to 2200 m, mostly above 500 m. Conservation areas: ARE, CVC, GUA, LAP, OSA, TEM. **Range:** Mex–Hon, CR, and Pan. **Notes:** There are eight species of *Citharexylum* in Costa Rica.

■ *Gmelina arborea* (molina, white teak)
Family Verbenaceae

Tree to 30 m tall, trunk 0.5–1.5 m diameter, young tree with smooth, yellow tan bark, becoming grainy and darker with age, branches long, slender. **Leaves** opposite, mostly at ends of stems, each pair at right angles to next blade 10–25 cm long, 5–18 cm wide, egg- to heart-shaped, tip long-pointed, base broad, abruptly contracted at top of leaf stalk with 2 small gland structures, dark green above, pale below, veins palmate at base; young leaves hairy. **Flowers** yellow and brownish orange, bilaterally symmetrical, 2.5–4.5 cm long, about 3.5 cm wide, tubular, 5-lobed, top petal lobes brownish, lower lip yellow with frilly, irregular edges, densely fine-hairy; inflorescence of large branched clusters, sometimes below leaves; blooms June, Sept. Pollinated by large bees. **Fruit** fleshy, yellow orange, aromatic, becoming black, 20–35 cm long, succulent, sweet, containing 2–3 seeds. **Habitat:** Plantations in lowland regions. Sometimes escaping. Altitude: Sea level to 400 m. Conservation areas: GUA, HNO, OSA, PAC. **Range:** Native to SE Asia. Widely grown in tropical regions. **Notes:** This is the only species of *Gmelina* in Costa Rica. Very fast growing, cultivated for wood pulp.

■ *Tectona grandis* (teak)
Family Verbenaceae

Large tree 30–40 m tall, trunk straight, bark gray, deeply fissured, twigs thick, 4-sided, angles ribbed, surface scaly-hairy, pale tan. **Leaves** opposite, simple, blade 25–50 cm long, 15–35 cm wide, elliptic, pointed at both ends, surface rough above, finely tan-hairy below; new leaves often purplish. **Flowers** whitish to greenish tan, small, to 0.8 cm wide, 5-parted; inflorescence of large, open, branched clusters at ends of branches; blooms a few at a time; pollinated by insects. **Fruit** becoming dry, woody, to 2 cm wide, rounded, enclosed in expanded, papery sepals (photo, developing fruit), hard-fleshy, 1–4 seeds. **Habitat:** Grown in plantations, sometimes escaped, widely cultivated. Altitude: Grown

mostly in the Pacific lowlands. **Range:** Native to SE Asia. Now pantropical. Mex–Pr and Brz, WI. **Notes:** Wood is very resistant to fungi and insects, used for timber, boat building. This is the only species of *Tectona* in Costa Rica.

SHRUBS AND SMALL TREES

■ COLOR OF CONSPICUOUS PART BLUE, PURPLE, LAVENDER, OR PINK

Poikilacanthus macranthus
Cordyline fruticosa
Neomirandea angularis
Nopalea cochinellifera
Capparis frondosa
Hirtella racemosa
Cavendishia callista
Cavendishia quereme
Bauhinia monandra
Gliricidia sepium
Zygia longifolia
Symbolanthus calygonus
Wigandia urens
   (*W. caracassana*)
Struthanthus orbicularis
Malpighia glabra
Wercklea insignis
Blakea tuberculata
Conostegia subcrustulata
Monochaetum amabile
Tibouchina urvilleana
   (*T. semidecandra*)

Bougainvillea glabra
Fuchsia microphylla
Fuchsia paniculata
Averrhoa carambola
   (*carambola*)
Piper subsessilifolium
Monnina xalapensis
Faramea suerrensis
Gonzalagunia rosea
Palicourea guianensis
Palicourea purpurea
Psychotria brachiata
Siparuna thecaphora
Brunfelsia grandiflora
   (*B. pauciflora*)
Cestrum megalophyllum
Trichospermum galeottii
Callicarpa acuminata
Cornutia pyramidata
Duranta erecta

■ COLOR OF CONSPICUOUS PART RED, RED ORANGE, BRIGHT ORANGE

Aphelandra lingua-bovis
Aphelandra scabra
Megaskepasma
   erythrochlamys
Odontonema tubaeforme
Razisea spicata
Spondias purpurea
Desmopsis microcarpa
Rauvolfia tetraphylla
Verbesina ovatifolia
Protium ravenii
Podandrogyne decipiens
   (*P. chiriquensis*)

Perrottetia longistylis
Clusia gracilis
Cavendishia bracteata
Satyria warszewiczii
Acalypha costaricensis
Acalypha macrostachya
Euphorbia pulcherrima
   (*Poinsettia pulcherrima*)
Jatropha gossypiifolia
Caesalpinia pulcherrima
Delonix regia
Erythrina berteroana
Erythrina costaricensis

■ COLOR OF CONSPICUOUS PART RED, RED ORANGE, BRIGHT ORANGE, continued

Erythrina gibbosa
Calliandra haematocephala
Tetrathylacium macrophyllum
Drymonia rubra
Solenophora calycosa
Psittacanthus ramiflorus
Hibiscus rosa-sinensis
Malvaviscus concinnus
Souroubea gilgii
Blakea litoralis
Neea sp.
Heisteria acuminata
Rubus glaucus

Coffea arabica
Hamelia patens
Hillia triflora (Ravnia t.)
Ixora coccinea
Psychotria poeppigiana
  (Cephaelis tomentosa)
Warszewiczia coccinea
Allophylus occidentalis
Quassia amara
Herrania purpurea
Trema micrantha
Clerodendrum paniculatum

■ COLOR OF CONSPICUOUS PART YELLOW, ORANGE YELLOW

Justicia aurea
Allamanda cathartica
Stemmadenia donnell-smithii
Tabernaemontana longipes
Thevetia ovata
Lasianthaea fruticosa
Senecio cooperi
Tecoma stans
Buddleja nitida
Carica papaya
Cochlospermum vitifolium
Coriaria ruscifolia
  (C. thymifolia)
Vaccinium poasanum
Croton draco
Hippomane mancinella
Parkinsonia aculeata
Senna pallida (Cassia biflora)
Senna papillosa
Senna reticulata
Cajanus cajan
Diphysa americana
  (D. robinoides)
Ulex europaeus
Acacia collinsii
Acacia farnesiana
Besleria formosa
Hypericum costaricense

Hypericum irazuense
Vismia baccifera
Gaiadendron punctatum
Byrsonima crassifolia
Talipariti tiliaceum var.
  pernambucense (Hibiscus
  tiliaceus)
Psidium friedrichsthalianum
Psidium guajava
Ouratea lucens (O. nitida)
Hamelia magnifolia
Palicourea padifolia
Pentagonia monocaulis
Psychotria marginata
Psychotria parvifolia
Psychotria solitudinum
Citrus spp.
Simarouba glauca
Cestrum warszewiczii
Cuatresia cuneata
Witheringia meiantha
Waltheria indica
Clavija costaricana
Dicraspidia donnell-smithii
Triumfetta bogotensis
Turnera ulmifolia
  (T. angustifolia)
Urera rzedowskii

■ COLOR OF CONSPICUOUS PART WHITE, CREAM, YELLOWISH, GREENISH WHITE

Aphelandra dolichantha
Avicennia germinans
Saurauia montana
Anacardium occidentale
Tabernaemontana alba
Oreopanax nicaraguensis
Ageratina anisochroma
Baccharis trinervis
Clibadium leiocarpum
Montanoa guatemalensis
Verbesina turbacensis
Vernonia patens
Amphitecna latifolia
Bixa orellana
Cordia dentata
Cordia diversifolia
Tournefortia brenesii
Centropogon smithii
Sambucus nigra
    (S. mexicana; S. nigra
    ssp. canadensis)
Viburnum costaricanum
Jacaratia dolichaula
Chrysobalanus icaco
Clusia croatii (C. minor,
    misapplied)
Ipomoea carnea
Weinmannia pinnata
Curatella americana e
Tetracera volubilis e
Comarostaphylis arbutoides
Disterigma humboldtii
Gaultheria erecta
Gaultheria gracilis
Pernettya prostrata
Thibaudia costaricensis
Vaccinium consanguineum
Cnidoscolus aconitifolius
Cnidoscolus urens
Euphorbia cotinifolia
Acacia angustissima
Mimosa pigra e
Pithecellobium lanceolatum
Carpotroche platyptera
Macrocarpaea macrophylla
    (M. auriculata)
Besleria notabilis
Drymonia lanceolata

Escallonia myrtilloides
Phyllonoma ruscifolia
Clinopodium vimineum
    (Satureja viminea)
Ocotea veraguensis
Blakea grandiflora
Clidemia sericea
Conostegia xalapensis
Leandra granatensis
Meriania phlomoides
Miconia argentea
Miconia costaricensis
Miconia nervosa
Miconia tonduzii
Monochaetum floribundum
Tibouchina inopinata
Ardisia pleurobotrya
Ardisia revoluta
Myrsine cubana
Eugenia truncata
Psidium guineense
Ugni myricoides
Piper aequale
Piper auritum
Piper biolleyi
Piper friedrichsthalii
Piper littorale
Piper marginatum
Piper peltatum
Piper tuberculatum
Coccoloba uvifera
Coccoloba venosa
Roupala montana
Rubus roseifolius
Arcytophyllum lavarum
Augusta rivalis (Lindenia r.)
Chomelia spinosa
Hillia loranthoides
Posoqueria latifolia
Psychotria carthagenensis
Psychotria deflexa
Psychotria glomerulata
Randia aculeata
Rudgea skutchii
Sabicea panamensis
Acnistus arborescens
Brugmansia candida
Solanum chrysotrichum

Solanum rugosum
Theobroma cacao
Muntingia calabura
Myriocarpa longipes

Urera baccifera
Lippia myriocephala e
Drimys granadensis

■ COLOR OF CONSPICUOUS PART GREEN TO BROWN, AND SHRUBS GROWN FOR FOLIAGE

Yucca guatemalensis
Annona muricata
Guatteria amplifolia
Montrichardia arborescens
Oreopanax donnell-smithii
Diplostephium costaricense
Crescentia cujete
Acanthocereus tetragonus
Epiphyllum phyllanthus var.
    pittieri
Hylocereus costaricensis
Selenicereus wercklei
Stenocereus aragonii
Semialarium mexicanum
Conocarpus erectus
Laguncularia racemosa
Davilla kunthii
Dracaena fragrans
Diospyros salicifolia
Casearia arguta
Trichilia havanensis
Ficus pertusa
Morella pubescens

Bocconia frutescens
Piper imperiale
Bambusa vulgaris
Chusquea longifolia
Chusquea subtessellata
    (Swallenochloa s.)
Rhipidocladum racemiflorum
Acaena elongata
Alibertia edulis
Elaeagia auriculata
Isertia laevis
Morinda citrifolia
Psychotria graciliflora
Erythrochiton gymnanthus
Zanthoxylum rhoifolium
Cupania guatemalensis
Jacquinia nervosa
    (J. pungens)
Urera laciniata
Rinorea deflexiflora
    (R. squamata)
Dendrophthora costaricensis
Phoradendron tonduzii

Woody plants generally less than 10 m (30 ft) tall, often with multiple stems, including bamboos and some shrubs with vinelike branches, are classed as shrubs or small trees. Here they are listed by the color of the flowers, fruit, bract, or most conspicuous part, then alphabetically by family, genus, and species.

COLOR OF CONSPICUOUS PART BLUE, PURPLE, LAVENDER, OR PINK

■ *Poikilacanthus macranthus*
   Family Acanthaceae

Shrub to 3 m tall, young stems 4-sided. **Leaves** opposite, stalks to 2.6 cm long, blades with pair members unequal, 3–8 cm long, 2–4 cm wide, egg-shaped, tip long-pointed, base rounded. **Flowers** lavender to purple, to 7.8 cm long, tubular, bilaterally symmetrical, narrowly funnel-shaped, petal lobes about as long as tube, upper lip 3.5 cm long, 0.9 cm wide, lower lip to 2.7 cm long, 1.2 cm wide, 3-lobed, stamens 2, as long or slightly longer than upper lip; blooms on and off most of the year. **Fruit** dry, club-shaped, 1.5 cm long, 0.5 cm wide. **Habitat:** Open areas in cloud forests, roadside banks, forest gaps. Altitude: 1000 to 1750 m. Conservation areas: ARE, CVC, LAP, PAC. **Range:** S Mex–CR. **Notes:** This is the only species of *Poikilacanthus* in Costa Rica.

■ *Cordyline fruticosa (C. terminalis)* (caña de indio, ti)
   Family Asteliaceae

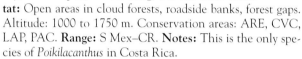

Small shrub 1–3.5 m tall, larger plants may appear palmlike, stem slender, mostly unbranched ringed by old leaf scars, colonial from underground stems (rhizomes). **Leaves** alternate, spiraled, mostly clustered at top of stem, stalk 4–20 cm long, narrow, sharply differentiated from blade, base of stalk clasping stem; blade 14–57 cm long, 3–14 cm wide, strap-shaped, green to red, or with yellow or pink markings, tip bluntly pointed, base blunt, veins parallel, margin smooth. **Flowers** white, yellow, or reddish, to 2 cm long, radially symmetrical, crowded on a branched inflorescence, flowering stems 30–70 cm long, often red; blooms very rarely. **Fruit** fleshy, red, to 1 cm wide, seeds numerous.

Habitat: Moist to wet regions. Cultivated, sometimes seen at sites of abandoned habitations, or used as a boundary marker in second growth forests. Widely grown as an ornamental. Altitude: Sea level to 1350 m or more. Conservation areas: CVC, LAC. **Range:** Native to India, Indonesia, Australia. Cultivated in tropical regions worldwide. **Notes:** It is similar to *Dracaena* but distinguished by its sharply differentiated leaf stalk. In some places it is used both as food and medicine.

Neomirandea angularis

■ *Neomirandea angularis*
Family Asteraceae

Coarse shrub or shrubby herb 2–7 m tall, young stems hairy. **Leaves** opposite, stalks to 15 cm long, blade to 20 cm long and wide, with several pointed lobes, base blunt to lobed, margin toothed, hairy on both sides, especially below, 3-veined from base. **Flowers** lavender purple, 0.4 cm long, radially symmetrical, tubular (no rays), in compact 5-flowered heads, 0.6 cm high, arising from a bract-covered floral base, basal bracts about 15, overlapping in several rows; inflorescence of branched clusters to 27 cm wide; blooms July–Dec., Apr. **Fruit** dry, 1-seeded, with tuft of hairs at one end; dispersed by wind. **Habitat:** Open areas, edges, second growth. Altitude: 450–2300 m, mostly above 1000 m. Conservation areas: ARE, CVC, GUA, LAP, PAC. **Range:** Endemic to CR. **Notes:** There are 16 species of *Neomirandea* in Costa Rica. Most have purplish flowers but some have white.

Nopalea cochinellifera

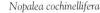

■ *Nopalea cochinellifera (Opuntia c.)*
Family Cactaceae

Large, often treelike cactus 2–4 m tall, much branched, new growth consists of flattened, succulent, green, padlike segments, 12–33 m long, 6–11 cm wide, dotted with small, dark, often spiny projections, new pads and flowers growing from edges of outermost pads; older stems woody, more or less cylindrical. **Leaves** none. **Flowers** white, base 5–6 cm long of red or green bracts, petals numerous. **Fruit** fleshy, red 3–4 cm long, edible. **Habitat:** Cultivated and escaped, specially in open sites of dry forests. Often used for living fences. Altitude: Sea level to 200 m, cultivated to at least 1200 m. Conservation areas: CVC (cultivated), PAC, TEM. **Range:** Native to Mex, Caribbean. Cultivated throughout the tropics and subtropics. Invasive in Hawai'i and the Galapagos islands. **Notes:** There are five species of *Opuntia* in Costa Rica.

■ *Capparis frondosa* (talcacao)
Family Capparaceae

Shrub or small tree 1–7 m tall, occasionally vine-like, bark tan, old leaf and branch scars prominent. **Leaves** alternate, stalk very variable to 20 cm long, swollen at both ends, blade 5–22 cm long, 2–9 cm wide, oblong-elliptical, usually pointed at both ends, glossy green above, pale below. **Flowers** white and purple, radially symmetrical, about 2 cm wide, petals 4, to 1 cm long, stamens numerous, 1.5 cm long, purple with white tip, pistil 2 cm long, stigma green, flower buds dark purple, 0.7 cm on 1 cm stalks; inflorescence of umbrella-shaped clusters; blooms Sept.–Mar. **Fruit** fleshy pods, reddish to dark purple, to 9 cm long, splitting open to reveal round, sticky seeds, 0.8 cm wide. **Habitat:** Moist to seasonally dry forests, second growth and open sites. Altitude: Pacific slope from GUA to the Meseta Central, sea level to 800 m. Conservation areas: GUA, HNO, LAP, PAC, TEM. **Range:** S Mex–Pr and Brz, WI. **Notes:** There are 17 species of *Capparis* in Costa Rica.

■ *Hirtella racemosa* (serrecillo, garrapatillo, seringró)
Family Chrysobalanaceae

Shrub or small tree 1–8 m tall with many slender arching branches, rarely a tree to 25 m tall, trunk irregular, somewhat corded, bark brown, finely fissured, flaky, new growth with linear stipules on each side of leaf. **Leaves** alternate, stalk 0.2 cm, blade 4–10 cm long, 1.5–3 cm wide, elliptic to oblong, tip long-pointed, base rounded to wedge-shaped, dark green, leathery, new leaves reddish. **Flowers** purple, radially symmetrical, about 0.7 cm wide, petals 5, short, calyx green, lobes folded back, stamens 5–7, 1–2 cm long, much longer than petals, pistil longer than stamens, flowers in spikelike clusters, 5–29 cm long, at ends of branches; blooms most of the year. **Fruit** fleshy, purplish brown, turning black, 1.5 cm long, 0.6 cm wide; Jan.–Feb. **Habitat:** Open sites, second growth, roadsides. Altitude: Sea level to 1200 m. Conservation areas: ARE, GUA, HNO, LAP, OSA, PAC, TEM. **Range:** Mex–Bol, NE Brz. **Notes:** There are 11 species of *Hirtella* in Costa Rica.

91

■ *Cavendishia callista*
Family Ericaceae

Epiphytic shrub, to 3 m tall, young stems white-hairy, sap sticky. **Leaves** alternate, stalk to 1.6 cm long, blade 7–26 cm long, 1–10 cm wide, elliptic, tip long-tapered, base rounded to slightly lobed, surface stiff, often rough, puckered, rusty-hairy on veins below, major veins 5, palmate at base, impressed above. **Flowers** white to pinkish, radially symmetrical, tubular, to 3.5 cm long, 0.8 cm wide, narrowly vase-shaped, constricted below petal lobes, petal lobes edged in dark purple, anthers 10, unequal, bracts bright pink (photo), large; inflorescence of crowded flower clustered at ends of branches, sticky, flower buds covered by overlapping bracts in a tight, cone-shaped, mass; blooms all year. **Fruit** fleshy blue black, juicy, rounded, seeds small, numerous. **Habitat:** Moist to wet forests, edges, roadside banks. Altitude: 150–2000 m. Conservation areas: ARE, CVC, GUA, LAC, LAP, OSA, PAC, TOR. **Range:** Gua–N Brz, Ec, Guy. **Notes:** Distinguished by flowers with dark rim on petal lobes, and large pink bracts. There are about 20 species of *Cavendisha* in Costa Rica.

■ *Cavendishia quereme*
Family Ericaceae

Shrub, somewhat vinelike, to 2 m tall, branches and bark reddish brown, twigs angled. **Leaves** alternate, stalk about 0.6 cm, blade to 11 cm long, 4 cm wide, elliptic, tip abruptly tapered, base blunt, veins 5, palmate at base, surface puckered, leathery, shiny. **Flowers** whitish base, orange middle, white tip, radially symmetrical, tubular, bottle-shaped, about 3 cm long, 0.5 cm wide, bluntly 5-angled, bracts pink to red purple (photo), 2 cm long, 0.8 cm wide, often folded along center; inflorescence of branched clusters at ends of branches; blooms and fruits most of the year. **Fruit** fleshy, blue black, juicy, rounded, seeds small, numerous. **Habitat:** Wet forests, also in disturbed sites, second growth, roadside banks. Altitude: 350–1830 m. Conservation areas: ARE, CVC, LAC, LAP. **Range:** CR–Col.

Courtesy of Margaret Gargiullo

■ *Bauhinia monandra*
Family Fabaceae/Caesalpinioideae

Small cultivated tree, to about 6 m tall. **Leaves** alternate, stalk to 6 cm long, blade 7–20 cm long and wide, deeply 2-lobed (cow-hoof-shaped), lobe tips pointed, base rounded, tending to fold like butterfly wings, veins palmate. **Flowers** pink to white with red markings, about 10 cm wide, orchid or lilylike, petals 5, 3–5 cm long, 2–3 cm wide, broadest near the top, tapering to a long slender base, stigmas to 4 cm, style elongate, curving. **Fruit** dry, pods, flat, 15–20 cm long, 2 cm wide, leathery, brown to black. **Habitat:** A garden plant in wet to seasonally dry regions. Altitude: About sea level to 500 m or more. Conservation areas: LAC, OSA. **Range:** Native to Burma. Widely cultivated in tropical regions. Invasive in some regions.

■ *Gliricidia sepium* (madero, madero negro, sangre de drago)
Family Fabaceae/Faboideae

Small tree, 3–10 m tall, deciduous, canopy elongate. **Leaves** alternate, odd pinnate, leaflets opposite along midrib, blades 3–8 cm long, 2–5 cm wide, elliptical, pointed at both ends, pale gray on underside, deciduous during dry season. **Flowers** lavender pink with white and yellow markings, bilaterally symmetrical, bean-flower-shaped, to 2 cm long; inflorescence of clusters to 10 cm; blooms while leafless, mostly Jan.–Mar., also June. **Fruit** dry, pod 8–15 cm long, to 2 cm wide, flattened; seeds 2–9. **Habitat:** Grows wild in open areas of seasonally dry regions on the Pacific slope. Used extensively for living fences in all parts of the country. Altitude: Sea level to 1000 m. Conservation areas: CVC, OSA, PAC, TEM, TOR. **Range:** Mex–Pan, also widely cultivated. **Notes:** This is the only species of *Gliricidia* in Costa Rica. A cut branch easily takes root in moist soil. Dark, rot-resistant heartwood used to build house foundations.

Bauhinia monandra (above)

Gliricidia sepium (below)

Living fence

■ *Zygia longifolia (Pithecellobium l.)*
(sotacaballo, azote de caballo, kitá)
Family Fabaceae/Mimosoideae
Shrub to medium sized tree, 2–15 m tall, to about 60 cm diameter, bark red brown, flaking, new growth green. **Leaves** alternate, twice evenly pinnate, in a Y pattern with 1 pair pinnae, each with 3–5 opposite leaflets, blades narrowly elliptic, to 15 cm long, 5 cm wide, dark green, new leaves red, drooping. **Flowers** pink and white, powder-puff-like, showy, about 1.5 cm long, stamens numerous, long, pink at tips, white below, in dense short clusters along leafless branches and twigs. **Fruit** dry, pod to 30 cm long, 1.5 cm wide, flattened, somewhat twisted, margins ribbed. **Habitat:** Wet to seasonally dry regions, common along rivers and streams. Altitude: Sea level to 1100 m, mostly below 500 m. Conservation areas: CVC, GUA, HNO, LAP, PAC, TEM, TOR. **Range:** SE Mex–Amazonia. **Notes:** There are 13 species of *Zygia* in Costa Rica.

■ *Symbolanthus calygonus*
Family Gentianaceae
Small shrub 1–3 m tall. **Leaves** opposite, blades 6–20 cm long, elliptic, pointed at both ends. **Flowers** bright pink, magenta, or blue, large, tubular, radially symmetrical, trumpet-shaped, 7–11 cm long, 4 cm wide, petal lobes pointed; solitary; blooms most of the year, especially Apr.–Aug. **Fruit** dry, elliptic to egg-shaped, 3–4 cm long. **Habitat:** Wet forest understories and second growth. Altitude: 600–3200 m. Conservation areas: ARE, CVC, GUA, HNO, LAC, LAP, PAC. **Range:** CR, Pr, Bol. **Notes:** This is the only species of *Symbolanthus* in Costa Rica.

■ *Wigandia urens (W. caracassana)*
(ortiga, ortiga blanca)
Family Hydrophyllaceae

Shrub or small tree, to 7 m tall, most often less than 4 m, 18 cm diameter, branches thick, often with many smaller branches around the base, all parts densely hairy and spiny, hairs irritating. **Leaves** alternate, blade 8–42 cm long, 4–19 cm wide, simple, egg-shaped to rounded, tip blunt to pointed, base blunt to lobed, covered with stinging hairs, margin toothed. **Flowers** lavender, radially symmetrical, woolly, petals fused, 5 lobes about 2 cm long, calyx lobes to 1 cm long, persistent, stamens 5; inflorescence of 2 crowded ranks along ends of floral stems, hairy; blooms most of the year; flowers attractive to ants. **Fruit** dry, 0.5–1 cm long, egg-shaped; developing along inflorescence stem below flowers. **Habitat:** Wet to seasonally dry regions often in mountains; in open sites, common on rocky banks, and along roadsides. Altitude: 80–3000 m, usually above 1000 m. Conservation areas: ARE, CVC, GUA, LAP, PAC, TEM. **Range:** Mex–NE S Amer. **Notes:** This is the only species of *Wigandia* in Costa Rica.

■ *Struthanthus orbicularis*
Family Loranthaceae

Parasitic, shrubby vine, stems slender, to 2 m long, fused to those of host at base and points along stems. **Leaves** opposite, early leaves narrow, curved, or twining, helping plant to climb; blade of later leaves 2.5–6 cm long, 1–3 cm wide, elliptic or rounded, tip and base blunt, yellowish green, brittle-fleshy, rather translucent. **Flowers** pale yellow or greenish, 0.4–0.8 cm long, radially symmetrical, in unbranched clusters 3–16 cm long in leaf axils; blooms Feb., Mar., Apr., Oct. **Fruit** fleshy, dull rose becoming dark blue (photo), 1 cm long, 0.7 cm wide, elliptic, on thick, short stems 1 cm long, 0.3 cm wide, wider at top, fruits in Mar., Apr., Sept., Oct., Jan. **Habitat:** On other plants, often in disturbed sites, sometimes in urban areas. Altitude: Sea level to 1600 m. Conservation areas: CVC, HNO, LAC, LAP, OSA, PAC. **Range:** Mex–Brz and Pr. **Notes:** There are 12 species of *Struthanthus* in Costa Rica. All are apparently quite similar.

■ *Malpighia glabra*
  Family Malpighiaceae

Shrub or small tree, to 8 m tall, bark brown to blackish with prominent lenticels, branching opposite, young branches from upper leaf axils, sometimes vinelike, small stems slender, green, nodes with line between leaf stalk bases. **Leaves** opposite, 2–7 cm long, about 2 cm wide, variable, elliptical, pointed at both ends, smooth dark green, veins obscure, midrib slightly raised above. **Flowers** pink lavender (sometimes white) with white markings, about 1.5 cm wide, petals 5, spoon-shaped with narrow bases, stamens yellow, inflorescence of small, stalked clusters; blooms most of the year. **Fruit** fleshy, bright red, about 1 cm wide, slightly lobed, old sepals persistent, 5-lobed, flesh juicy, red, seeds 3, tan, deeply grooved, wedge-shaped. **Habitat:** Wet to seasonally dry regions, second growth or disturbed forest, edges. Often cultivated, used as street plantings in San José. Altitude: 20–1400 m. Conservation areas: ARE, GUA, LAC, OSA, PAC, TEM. **Range:** NE TX–S Amer, Ant. **Notes:** There are seven species of *Malpighia* in Costa Rica.

■ *Wercklea insignis* (Panamá, clavelón, burío)
  Family Malvaceae

Small tree 5–15 m tall, trunk cylindrical, sounds hollow when struck; bark gray, grainy, leafy branches with stipules to 0.4–1 cm long, 0.5–1.5 cm wide, semicircular. **Leaves** alternate, stalk to about 20 cm long, blade about 26 cm long, 38 cm wide, broadly heart- to kidney-shaped, base lobed, veins palmate, margin sometimes with few teeth; fallen leaves with bright yellow blade, stalk becoming pink. **Flowers** pink purple, large, showy, trumpet-shaped, petals 10–15 cm long, widest near apex, narrow at base, stamens fused into a central column around stigma, 3–4.5 cm long; blooms July–Feb., mostly Sept.–Oct. **Fruit** dry, bristly-hairy, 5-parted, 4.5–7 cm long, surrounded by old calyx and small bracts, tip beaked, seeds numerous, 0.3 cm, hairy. **Habitat:** Wet to moist forests. Altitude: 400–1600 m, mostly above 1000 m. Conservation areas: ARE, CVC, GUA, LAC, LAP. **Range:** CR Pan. **Notes:** There are four species of *Wercklea* in Costa Rica. This is the only species with lavender flowers.

■ *Blakea tuberculata*
Family Melastomataceae

Epiphytic shrub or small tree 2–10 m tall, young parts rusty-hairy. **Leaves** opposite, stalk about 5 cm long, stout, blade 10–17 cm long, 6–14 cm wide, large, fleshy, broadly egg- to heart-shaped, tip barely pointed, base shallowly lobed, major veins 3, palmate, parallel, minor veins numerous, ladderlike, between primary veins. **Flowers** dark pink to purplish, radially symmetrical, fragrant, very showy, not pendant, axillary, 6-parted, about 7 cm wide, petals deciduous, about 3.5 cm long, 2 cm wide, fleshy, finely warty, sepals appendaged, attached to the expanded floral base, anthers broad yellow, filaments white; blooms and fruits most of the year. **Fruit** fleshy, surface rusty-hairy. **Habitat:** Moist to wet forests. Altitude: 400–1700 m. Conservation areas: ARE, CVC, GUA, LAC, LAP. Seen at Tapantí N.P. **Range:** CR, Pan.

■ *Conostegia subcrustulata*
Family Melastomataceae

Shrub to about 1–3 m tall, young stems gray green, finely scaly-hairy. **Leaves** opposite, 9–25 cm long, 4–17 cm wide, egg-shaped, thin, hairy on both sides, tip with elongate point, base blunt or slightly lobed, surface of blade puckered, rough-textured, midrib arched, major veins palmate, parallel 3–4 on each side of midrib, sharply impressed above, often dull pink, minor veins numerous, ladderlike between primaries, margin finely toothed, fringed with hairs, new leaves reddish. **Flowers** pale lavender pink, about 1 cm wide, buds bright pink, stamens yellow, petals 5, to 0.5 cm long, 0.3 cm wide, tips rounded, stamens 10; inflorescence 10–20 cm long, of dense, branched, rather cone-shaped clusters, about 12 cm long, 7 cm wide, stems often reddish; blooms and fruits all year. **Fruit** fleshy, becoming red, dark blue, dark purple black at maturity, crowned by old calyx scar. **Habitat:** Seasonally dry to wet regions, in open sites, roadsides, pastures. Altitude: Sea level to 1200 m, mostly below 500 m. Conservation areas: ARE, CVC, GUA, HNO, LAC, LAP, OSA, PAC, TEM. Seen near La Selva Biological Station, Caribbean lowlands. **Range:** Nic–Col and Ec. **Notes:** There are about 25 species of *Conostegia* in Costa Rica.

■ *Monochaetum amabile* (nochebuena)
Family Melastomataceae

Erect shrub, 1–4 m tall, young stems red, hairy, branches arching, older parts woody, bark brown, flaky. **Leaves** opposite,
stalk to 0.4 cm long, blade 1–3 cm long, 0.3–0.9 cm wide,
narrowly elliptic, somewhat hairy on both sides, pointed at
both ends, major veins 3–5, palmate, secondary veins ladderlike in between. **Flowers** dark pink, radially symmetrical, about 4 cm wide, petals 4, widest near tip, to 2 cm long,
nearly as wide, stamens yellow and red, calyx lobes and floral
base red, bracts leaflike; flowers solitary or paired, abundant,
often covering shrub; blooms Dec.–Mar., sporadically until
July. **Fruit** at first red, surrounded by persistent red calyx,

4-parted, becoming
dry, seeds numerous.
Habitat: Mountains
in open sites. Alti-
tude: 2000–3300 m.
Conservation areas:
CVC, LAP, PAC. Very
common at Volcán
Poas N.P., Cerro de la
Muerte area. **Range:**
CR. **Notes:** There are
six species of *Mono-
chaetum* in Costa Rica.

■ *Tibouchina urvilleana (T. semidecandra)*
(magrande, nazareno)
Family Melastomataceae

Shrub 1–4 m tall, all parts hairy; stems ribbed, reddish.
Leaves opposite, no stalk, blade 4–15 cm long, 2–7 cm wide,
elliptic to lance-shaped, tip with elongate point, base blunt,
hairy on both sides, upper side rough, major veins 5–7, secondary veins ladderlike between major veins, new leaves reddish, in groups of 3 at ends of stems. **Flowers** deep purple,
about 7 cm wide, buds encased in bright pink, hairy
bracts, petals 2.5–4 cm long, 2–4 cm wide, anthers
1.5 cm long, style 2–2.5 cm long. **Fruit** dry, 5-parted,
encased in old calyx tube. **Habitat:** Often in mountain regions. Altitude: 1380–2600 m. Conservation
areas: PAC. **Range:** Native to S Brz. Widely cultivated and escaped throughout the tropics. Invasive
on some Pacific islands. **Notes:** There are five species of *Tibouchina* in Costa Rica.

◼ *Bougainvillea glabra*
Family Nyctaginaceae

Shrubs or woody vines, to about 7 m long or high, sometimes spiny. **Leaves** alternate, about 10 cm long, broadly elliptical, tip pointed, base blunt. **Flowers** off-white, small, tubular, surrounded by 3 (very colorful) bracts purple, red, orange, etc. (photo), very showy and persistent; blooms all year. **Fruit** dry, nut-like. **Habitat:** Widely cultivated especially in seasonally dry regions, not escaping. Altitude: Sea level to 1100 m. Conservation areas: CVC, GUA, TEM. **Range:** Native to S Amer. Cultivated throughout the tropics and subtropics. **Notes:** *Bougainvillea spectabilis* is very similar but flower bracts are only purple, young stems are finely hairy and spiny, with a denser growth habit than B. *glabra*.

◼ *Fuchsia microphylla*
Family Onagraceae

Erect to arching or vinelike shrub 1–4 m tall, branches finely brown-hairy. **Leaves** opposite, each pair at right angles to next, stalk very short, blade small, 1–2.5 cm long, about, 0.5 cm wide, oblong to egg-shaped, tip blunt, base pointed, upper surface shiny, pale below, margin with few teeth. **Flowers** dark pink, radially symmetrical, about 1.5 cm long, tubular, 4-lobed, stigma white, longer than petal lobes, calyx lobes longer and darker pink than petals; floral base dark pink, longer than sepals or petals; blooms all year; flowers solitary in leaf axils; pollinated by fiery-throated hummingbirds. **Fruit** fleshy, purple black, shiny, about 0.5 cm wide; fruit present most of the year. **Habitat:** High elevations in second growth forests and open sites, roadsides, edges. Altitude: 1300–3300 m. Conservation areas: CVC, LAC, LAP, PAC. **Range:** Mex–Pan. **Notes:** There are seven species of *Fuchsia* in Costa Rica.

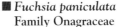

■ *Fuchsia paniculata*
Family Onagraceae

Shrub or small tree 1–8 m tall, young stems often red, some-times vinelike. **Leaves** opposite, each pair at right angles to the next, or sometimes in whorls of 3–4, stalk to 2.5 cm long, often red, blade 5–15 cm long, 3–5 cm wide, ellipti-cal, pointed at both ends, smooth, glossy, margins finely to coarsely toothed. **Flowers** purple pink, tubular, 4-lobed, pet-als and sepals 0.5–1 cm long, stigma knobby, purple, calyx purple; inflorescence of showy branched clusters at ends of branches, flowering and fruits stems red; blooms and fruits all year. **Fruit** fleshy, purple black, glossy, rounded, to 0.9 cm long. **Habitat:** High-elevation forests, second growth, and open sites, roadsides. Alti-tude: 1300–3400 m, most often above 1800 m. Conservation areas: CVC, LAC, LAP, PAC. **Range:** Mex–Pan.

■ *Averrhoa carambola* (carambola)
Family Oxalidaceae

Cultivated tree 3–10 m tall, much branched. **Leaves** alter-nate, pinnate, 10–20 cm long, leaflets 6–11, 5–8 cm long, 2–3 cm wide, smaller at base of leaf, egg-shaped, tips pointed, bases rounded, often drooping along either side of main leaf axis. **Flowers** pale violet, pink, to purple and white, radi-ally symmetrical, petals 0.6–0.9 cm long, about 0.3 cm wide; blooms and fruits on and off most of the year. **Fruit** fleshy, pale, translucent waxy yellow, deeply, sharply 5-ribbed, star-shaped in cross section, 8–13 cm long, 5–6 cm diameter, acid to slightly sweet tasting. **Habitat:** Cultivated for fruit. Appar-ently escaping occasionally. Altitude: Sea level to 400 m. Conservation areas: LAC, OSA, PAC, TOR. **Range:** Native to SE Asia. Cultivated in most of the tropics. **Notes:** The only other species of *Averrhoa* in Costa Rica is *A. bilimbi*, with almost smooth fruit, cultivated much less frequently, also from Southeast Asia.

■ *Piper subsessilifolium*
Family Piperaceae

Vine or vinelike shrub to 2 m tall, sometimes epiphytic, stipules 3–6 cm. **Leaves** alternate, ranked along sides of stems, stalk to 1 cm long, bade 12–24 cm long, 3–9 cm wide, narrowly elliptic, tapered to long-pointed tip, base blunt, unequal, major veins 3–5 per side, from near base of midrib, curved sharply upward, deeply impressed above. **Flowers** purple when young, minute, crowded on unbranched, erect spikes 4–8 cm long, 0.3 cm wide; blooms and fruits Jan.–June. **Fruit** fleshy, less than 0.1 cm wide, in dense, slender spikes, eaten by bats. **Habitat:** Wet forest understories in mountains. Altitude: 1000–2200 m, usually below 1700 m. Conservation areas: ARE, GUA, LAC, LAP. **Range:** Mex–Ec. **Notes:** One of only three *Piper* species with purplish flower spikes.

■ *Monnina xalapensis*
Family Polygalaceae

Shrub, sparsely branched, stems slender, 1–2 m (sometimes to 7 m) long, slightly ridged. **Leaves** alternate, crowded in loose spirals at ends of stems, stalk 0.1–0.5 cm, blade 3–15 cm long, 0.5–6 cm wide, lance-shaped, pointed at both ends, base extending down stalk. **Flowers** blue and yellow, bilaterally symmetrical, more or less bean-flower-shaped, about 0.5 cm long; inflorescence of unbranched, spikelike clusters 2–15 cm long; blooms and fruits all year. **Fruit** dry, to 0.8 cm long. **Habitat:** Wet forests, open sites, second growth, at high elevations. Altitude: 550–3000 m, mostly above 1100 m. Conservation areas: CVC, GUA, LAC, LAP, PAC. **Range:** Mex–Pan. **Notes:** There are four species of *Monnina* in Costa Rica. All are very similar and difficult to distinguish. They are found mostly above 1000 m.

◼ *Faramea suerrensis*
Family Rubiaceae

Shrub 2–6 m, branches 4-sided, slender, opposite, green, elongate; stipules between leaf stalk bases, 0.5–1 cm, often united to form a tube with 1 pointed lobe. **Leaves** opposite, stalk to 1.8 cm, blade narrowly elliptic, 9–20 cm long, 3–8 cm wide cm, tip tapered to a point, base blunt to pointed, surface stiff, leathery, dark green, puckered by impressed veins, secondary veins conspicuous at right angles to midrib, pattern ladderlike, joined by a prominent marginal vein near the edge (very like that in the family Melastomataceae). **Flowers** bright blue, radially symmetrical, tubular, to 1 cm long, narrow, petal lobes 4, to 0.5 cm long; inflorescence with bright blue branches and stalks, at ends of branches; blooms Aug.–Apr. **Fruit** fleshy, deep blue, about 1 cm long, 1.5 cm wide, flattened side to side, wider than long, flesh spongy-foamy, 1-seeded; fruit present all year. **Habitat:** Understories of wet forests. Altitude: Sea level to 1700 m. Conservation areas: ARE, CVC, HNO, LAC, LAP, OSA, TOR. **Range:** Nic–Col. **Notes:** There are 13 species of *Faramea* in Costa Rica.

Gonzalagunia rosea photos opposite

◼ *Gonzalagunia rosea*
Family Rubiaceae

Shrub or small tree 2–4 m tall, branches erect to sometimes vinelike, hairy; stipules between leaf stalk bases, 0.3–0.7cm long, broadly triangular, tips pointed. **Leaves** opposite, stalks to 2 cm, densely hairy, blade 7–18 cm long, 2–6 cm wide, lance-shaped to elliptic, tip long-pointed, base blunt to pointed, hairy above, densely hairy below, veins curving sharply upward. **Flowers** pink, radially symmetrical, tubular, to 1.3 cm long, hairy, petal lobes 4, pointed, anthers slightly longer than petal lobes, flower buds red; inflorescence of hairy spikes 12–35 cm long; blooms Jan.–Sept. **Fruit** fleshy, white, to 1.5 cm, wider than high, 4-lobed, flesh spongy, in long clusters; fruit present all year. **Habitat:** Wet mountain forests, edges, and open habitats. Altitude: 900–2700 m. Conservation areas: ARE, CVC, GUA, HNO, LAC, LAP, PAC. **Range:** CR–Col. **Notes:** Conspicuous for its pink flowers. The other two species are *G. ovatifolia,* with white flowers and fruit (photo), and *G. panamensis,* with white flowers and red to blue fruit.

■ *Palicourea guianensis*
Family Rubiaceae

Shrub or small tree 2–6 m, stems 4-sided; stipules, to 0.8 cm, with 2 rounded lobes. **Leaves** opposite, stalk to 2 cm, blade broadly egg-shaped, 15–28 cm long, 7–18 cm wide, tip pointed, base rounded, thin, secondary veins 10–15 per side. **Flowers** yellow to orange, radially symmetrical, tubular, to 2.5 cm long, hairy, middle of petal tube contracted, top inflated, petal lobes to 0.2 cm, flower stems red orange, turning purple, inflorescence of crowded, pyramid-shaped clusters to 18 cm long, 10 cm wide, at ends of branches; blooms all year. **Fruit** fleshy, dark purple, translucent, to 0.7 cm, oval, seeds 2. **Habitat:** Wet, moist or, occasionally, seasonally dry lowland forests, open areas, and second growth. Altitude: Sea level to 600 m, infrequently to 1200 m. Conservation areas: ARE, CVC, GUA, LAC, OSA, PAC, TEM TOR. **Range:** Mex–Bol and Brz. **Notes:** There are about 30 species of *Palicourea* in Costa Rica. *Palicourea guianensis* is distinguished by its rounded stipules, broad leaves, orange flowers, and lowland habitat.

Gonzalagunia rosea

G. *ovatifolia*

G. *ovatifolia*   G. *panamensis*

103

■ *Palicourea purpurea*
Family Rubiaceae

Shrub, 3–6 m tall; stipules with basal tube to 0.4 cm long, lobes bristle tipped, to 0.5 cm long, persistent. **Leaves** opposite, stalk to 2.5 cm long, blade 7–19 cm long, 2–7 cm wide, elliptic, dark green, pointed at both ends, base slightly extended down stalk. **Flowers** pale blue to purple, pink or white, radially symmetrical, tubular, to 2 cm long, petal lobes to 0.4 cm long, calyx lobes to 0.1 cm, stamens purple; inflorescence stems pink to purple, 4–12 cm long, branched, pyramid-shaped; blooms and fruits most of the year. **Fruit** fleshy, purple black, translucent, round, to 0.6 cm, seeds 2, flat on one side. **Habitat:** Wet forest understories in mountains. Altitude: 1200–2800 m. Conservation areas: CVC, LAP. **Range:** CR, Pan.

■ *Psychotria brachiata*
Family Rubiaceae

Shrub 1.5–3 m tall, sparsely branched, straggling in understory, leaning on other vegetation, new growth green, smooth, 4-sided; stipules between leaf-stalk bases, to 0.7 cm tall, 2-lobed, tips rounded, persistent after leaves fall on older stems. **Leaves** opposite, stalk to 3.5 cm, blade elliptic, 9–17 cm long, 3–7 cm wide, smooth, pointed at both ends. **Flowers** yellow or white, radially symmetrical, tubular, funnel-shaped, small, to 0.5 cm long, petal lobes 5, 0.1 cm long, finely hairy, inflorescence 10–20 cm long, pyramid-shaped, open, branches opposite, widely spaced, at the tips

of stems, flowers in small, dense clusters at tips of inflorescence branches; blooms all year, mostly May–June. **Fruit** fleshy, bright blue to blue black, small, to 0.5 cm long, 0.6 cm wide, shiny, crowned by old calyx lobes, fleshy spongy-foamy, seeds 2; fruits mostly July–Feb. **Habitat:** Wet lowland forests and second growth. Altitude: Sea level to 1000 m, mostly on the Caribbean slope below 500 m. Conservation areas: CVC, GUA, HNO, LAC, OSA, TOR. **Range:** S Mex–Ven and Pr, WI. **Notes:** *Psychotria* is the largest genus in the family Rubiaceae with approximately 117 species in Costa Rica.

■ *Siparuna thecaphora* (limoncillo)
Family Siparunaceae

Shrub or small tree, 1–10 m tall, multistemmed, sap with strong citrus aroma. **Leaves** opposite, stalk 0.5–4.5 cm long, blade 6–15 cm long, 3–12 cm wide, broadly elliptic, tip pointed, base blunt, hairy below, veins pinnate, aromatic, margins toothed to smooth. **Flowers** yellow small, radially symmetrical, the fleshy base spreading into 5–6 petal-like lobes, males and females on separate plants, male flowers 0.3–0.5 cm wide stamens 5–9, to 0.3 cm long; in clusters of 3–25 in leaf axils or nodes; female flowers 0.3–0.4 cm wide, in clusters of 1–8 flowers at nodes; blooms and fruits all year. **Fruit** pinkish (photo), leathery rind of expanded floral base, 0.6–1 cm wide, crowned with remnants of petal lobes, aromatic, splitting open irregularly to reveal bright pink flesh containing gray seeds with red, pointed, caplike fleshy attachments about 0.5 cm long (photo), May. **Habitat:** Wet forests, second growth, edges. Altitude: Sea level to 1300 m. Conservation areas: ARE, CVC, LAC, OSA, PAC, TOR. **Range:** Mex–Pr. **Notes:** There are 15 species of *Siparuna* in Costa Rica.

Early developing fruit

■ *Brunfelsia grandiflora* (B. *pauciflora*)
Family Solanaceae

Shrub to 2 m, spreading, branched from base. **Leaves** alternate, simple, to 10 cm long, 2 cm wide, elliptic, widest at or above middle, glossy above, paler below, pointed at both ends. **Flowers** purple, fading to lavender, then to white, fragrant, tubular at base, showy, nearly radially symmetrical, 5 cm wide, 5 petal lobes, broad, somewhat puckered, edges overlapping; inflorescence of small clusters. **Fruit** leathery, with large seeds. **Habitat:** Cultivated in gardens over much of Costa Rica. Apparently never escaping from cultivation. Altitude: About 200–1200 m. **Range:** Native to Brz, Col–Bol and Brz. Invasive in the Galápagos. **Notes:** *Brunfelsia nitida* is the only other species of this genus in Costa Rica.

Late fruit

■ *Cestrum megalophyllum* (zorillo)
Family Solanaceae

Small tree or shrub 1–8 m tall, twigs stout. **Leaves** alternate, stalk to 2.5 cm long, stout, blade to 30 cm long, elliptic, tip pointed, base pointed to rounded, stiff, surface often wrinkled by impressed, unevenly spaced veins, 5–10 per side. **Flowers** greenish white, inconspicuous, slightly fragrant, petal tube

to 1.5 cm long, bulging, lobes 5, 0.3 cm, stamens free, yellow, stigma green, calyx to 0.4 cm; inflorescence of dense clusters on leafless stems or trunk; blooms and fruits most of the year. **Fruit** fleshy, initially white, turning dark purple black, 0.4–0.8 cm (photo), seeds several to numerous. **Habitat:** Deeply shaded moist to wet forest understories. Altitude: Sea level to 2000 m. Conservation areas: CVC, GUA, LAC, LAP, OSA, TOR. **Range:** Mex–Bol and Brz, WI. **Notes:** There are 24 species of *Cestrum* in Costa Rica. *Cestrum megalophyllum* seems to be the most common by far. It has much larger leaves than most other species.

■ *Trichospermum galeottii* (guácimo, capulín, jucó)
Family Tiliaceae

Tree or shrub 4–20 m tall, usually less than 10 m; bark gray tan, smooth, branches long, slender, new stems purple-hairy, sap gummy. **Leaves** alternate, stalk purple-hairy, swollen at top, blade 8–23 cm long, 2–10 cm wide, egg-shaped, tip pointed, base rounded, major veins 3, palmate at base, smaller veins like ladder rungs between large veins, dull, dark green above, brownish below, finely velvety hairy on both sides, margin finely toothed. **Flowers** white to pinkish, radially symmetrical, petals narrow, inflorescence of branched clusters to 12 cm long; blooms and fruits on and off most of the year. **Fruit** dry, purplish to green, 2-parted, flattened, to about 2 cm long and wide, 0.6 cm thick, velvety-hairy (photo), opening to release small black seeds with tufts of tan bristles. **Habitat:** Open areas, second growth. Altitude: Pacific slope, sea level to 1100 m. Conservation areas: LAP, OSA, PAC. **Range:** Mex–Hon, CR–Ven and Ec. **Notes:** *Trichospermum grewiifolium* is the only other species of his genus in Costa Rica. It is very similar to *T. galeottii*.

■ *Callicarpa acuminata* (cucaracha)
  Family Verbenaceae

Shrub or small tree 2–7 m tall, to 10 cm diameter, often with multiple trunks, stems arching, sometimes climbing, much branched, bark gray, finely scaly, twigs tan-scaly, nodes flattened. **Leaves** opposite, stalk 1–2 cm, bases joined by line across stem, blade 13–28 cm long, 5–12 cm wide, new leaves gray tan, mature blades puckered by impressed veins, green above paler, tan-scaly below, upper margin toothed. **Flowers** white to green, radially symmetrical, tubular, funnel-shaped, about 0.2–0.3 cm long, petal lobes 4, stamens 4, extending from flower tube; inflorescence of dense, branched, umbrella-shaped, pendant clusters, 5–10 cm long and wide; blooms and fruits most of the year. **Fruit** fleshy, dark purple, 0.3–0.5 cm, round, juicy thin flesh with 4 wedge-shaped seeds. **Habitat:** Open areas, edges, second growth, or forest understories in wet regions. Altitude: Sea level to 1000 m, mostly below 300 m. Conservation areas: CVC, GUA, HNO, LAC, OSA, PAC. **Range:** Mex–Bol. **Notes:** This is the only species of *Callicarpa* in Costa Rica.

■ *Cornutia pyramidata*
  Family Verbenaceae

Large shrub or small tree 2–10 m tall, about 20 cm diameter, often multistemmed, younger branches 4-sided, winged, green, hairy. **Leaves** opposite, stalks winged about 1/2 way to base, joined by ridge across stem, blade about 8–28 cm long (including stalk), 5–15 cm wide, broadly egg-shaped to elliptic, tip pointed, base extending down leaf stalk, surface hairy, slightly sticky on both sides; aromatic when crushed, attractive to ants. **Flowers** blue, about 1 cm wide at top, bilaterally symmetrical, tubular, tube 0.7–1 cm long, bulging on one side of base, petal lobes 2-lipped,

upper lip 3-lobed, lower lip 0.3–0.7 cm long, margin toothed, hairy outside, whitish in throat; inflorescence branched, pyramid-shaped, 11–40 cm long, 4–16 cm wide; blooms Mar.–Nov. **Fruit** fleshy, blue, purple, or black, 0.4–0.7 cm wide, 4-seeded; fruits July–Oct. **Habitat:** Wet forests, edges; also planted, sometimes as a windbreak. Altitude: 50–2000 m. Conservation areas: ARE, GUA, OSA, PAC, TEM. **Range:** Mex–Ven and Pr, WI. **Notes:** There are two species of *Cornutia* in Costa Rica. *Cornutia pyramidata* is the most common, *C. grandifolia* is quite similar.

107

■ *Duranta erecta* (cuentas de oro, golden dewdrop)
Family Verbenaceae
Shrub 1–3 m tall, densely, finely branched, often thorny, bark gray, becoming fissured. **Leaves** opposite, 2–8 cm long, elliptic to egg-shaped. **Flowers** blue, lavender, or white, radially symmetrical, tubular, petal lobes 5; inflorescence of showy, spikelike clusters; attractive to butterflies and hummingbirds. **Fruit** fleshy, orange, 5-lobed, with up to 5 seeds, eaten by birds, which disperse the seeds. Fruit and other plant parts toxic to humans. **Habitat:** Native to Central America, especially in dry coastal scrub, but mostly a cultivated ornamental. Altitude: Cultivated. Conservation areas: Not listed. Seen in Sabana Park, San José. **Range:** Mex–Arg and Brz, WI, Madagascar, Tanzania. Invasive on some Pacific islands. **Notes:** The only other species in this genus is *D. costaricense*.

COLOR OF CONSPICUOUS PART RED, RED ORANGE, BRIGHT ORANGE

■ *Aphelandra lingua-bovis*
Family Acanthaceae
Shrub or woody herb 1–3.5 m tall, sparsely branched, if at all, young stems often 4-sided, rough. **Leaves** opposite, each pair at right angles to next, stalk about 1 cm, rough, blade widest at or above middle, to 38 cm long, 12 cm wide, tip tapered to point, base tapered, veins pinnate, curved upward, slightly hairy below. **Flowers** coral red, to 6 cm long, 0.6 cm wide at top, tubular, bilaterally symmetrical, very finely hairy, 5 unequal petal lobes, bracts red to 1.4 cm long and 1 cm wide, tightly overlapping flowers, inflorescence of spikes to 38 cm long, at ends of stems; blooms June–Apr. **Fruit** dry, club-shaped, to 2 cm long, 0.4 cm wide, rough hairy near top, 4-seeded. **Habitat:** Mature lowland rain forest understories. Altitude: Sea level to 900 m, southern Pacific lowlands. Conservation areas: OSA, PAC. **Range:** CR–Col. **Notes:** There are 12 species of *Aphelandra* in Costa Rica.

■ *Aphelandra scabra*
Family Acanthaceae

Shrubs 1–3 m tall, often in large stands. **Leaves** opposite, stalk 0.5 cm or less, blade to 25 cm long, 8 cm wide elliptic, pointed at both ends, margins smooth or wavy. **Flowers** pink, red, or purple red, to 3 cm long, tubular, bilaterally symmetrical, 2-lipped, upper lip 2-lobed, to 1 cm long, lobes very short, lower lip about 1 cm, tip long-pointed; bracts pale green, to 1.5 cm, egg-shaped, upper margin *toothed*, overlapping flowers; inflorescence of spikes, at tips of branches; blooms Aug.–Mar. **Fruit** dry, elliptic, to 1.5 cm long. 0.6 cm wide, seeds flattened, irregular, 0.3 cm wide. **Habitat:** Mostly in seasonally dry forests of the northern Pacific slope, sometimes in moist to wet forests. Altitude: Sea level to 1750 m, mostly on the Pacific slope. Conservation areas: ARE, CVC, GUA, HNO, LAP, PAC, TEM. **Range:** S Mex–N S Amer.

■ *Megaskepasma erythrochlamys*
Family Acanthaceae

Shrub to 4 m tall, stems somewhat 4-sided. **Leaves** opposite, stalks to 4 cm long, finely hairy, blade elliptic, 13–28 cm long, 4–13 cm wide, tip elongated with rounded point, base pointed. **Flowers** white, 5–6 cm long, bilaterally symmetrical, tubular, petal lobes 2-lipped, upper lip 2-lobed, lower lip 3-lobed, stamens 2, extended beyond petal lobes; major bracts deep red purple, to 4.5 cm long, 2 cm wide, smaller bracts to 2 cm long; inflorescence a cluster of drooping spikes to 20 cm long. **Fruit** dry, club-shaped, to 3.5 cm long, 0.7 cm wide, tip pointed, 4-seeded. **Habitat:** Cultivated, sometimes used as a hedge. Altitude: At least 400–1100 m, probably wider. Conservation areas: GUA, CVC, TEM. **Range:** Native to Ven. Cultivated widely in the Neotropics. **Notes:** This is the only species of *Megaskepasma* worldwide.

■ *Odontonema tubaeforme*
Family Acanthaceae

Shrub to 2.5 m tall, stems green, nodes with line across leaf stalk bases. **Leaves** opposite, stalk none or to 3 cm long, blade 11–36 cm long, 4–11 cm wide, elliptic, pointed at both ends, margin sometimes bluntly toothed. **Flowers** red or pink, bilaterally symmetrical, tubular, to 3 cm long, 0.5 cm wide at throat, petal lobes 5, flaring, 2 fused above, 3 below, to 0.8 cm long; inflorescence at ends of branches, spikelike to 35 cm long, flowers in whorls at nodes; blooms all year. **Fruit** dry, club-shaped, to 3 cm long, 0.4 cm wide. **Habitat:** Light gaps in wet forests, edges, stream margins. Altitude: Sea level to 1700 m. Conservation areas: ARE, CVC, LAC, LAP, OSA, PAC, TEM, TOR. **Range:** Mex–Pan. **Notes:** The only other species of *Odontonema* in Costa Rica is O. *cuspidatum*, which is rare.

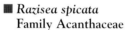

■ *Razisea spicata*
Family Acanthaceae

Shrub to 2.5 m tall, often many stems in same area; young stems 4-sided, slender, nodes swollen, with a line between leaf bases, old stems to 2 cm wide. **Leaves** opposite, stalks to 3.5 cm, blade 10–29 cm long, 4–8 cm wide, elliptic to egg-shaped, shiny, dark green, pointed at both ends, margin sometimes toothed. **Flowers** bright red, bilaterally symmetric, tubular, 4–6 cm long, 0.9 cm wide across top, narrowly funnel-shaped, curved, 2-lipped, both about 1 cm long, much shorter than tube, upper lip narrower than lower, lower lip with 3 small lobes, stamens slightly longer than petal tube, calyx lobes 5, linear, 1 cm long; inflorescence spikelike, at ends of branches; blooms most of the year, especially Sept. **Fruit** dry, club-shaped, 4-seeded. **Habitat:** Moist to wet forest understories, gaps, edges. Altitude: Sea level to 2600 m. Conservation areas: ARE, CVC, GUA, LAC, LAP, OSA, PAC, TOR. **Range:** Gua–Col. **Notes:** There are three other species of *Razisea* in Costa Rica; *R. spicata* is by far the most common and widespread.

■ *Spondias purpurea* (jocote cimarrón)
  Family **Anacardiaceae**

Tree or large shrub 4–15 m, often with multiple trunks, bark tan, mottled, stems stout; often leafless in flower. **Leaves** alternate, stalk about 4 cm long, blade pinnate, about 20 cm long, leaflets 5–12 pairs, 2–8 cm long, 1–3 cm wide, dark green, sides unequal, margin smooth or toothed, tip rounded to pointed, base tapered. **Flowers** red, radially symmetrical, about 0.7 cm, petals 4–6, stamens red, stigma yellowish; inflorescence to 10 cm long, of small branched clusters near ends of stems; blooms Jan.–May. **Fruit** fleshy, turning orange,

then red, when mature, to 5 cm long, 2 cm wide, edible, 1 pale, woody seed; fruit present most of the year. **Habitat:** Wet to seasonally dry forests. Altitude: Pacific slope, sea level to 1200 m. Conservation areas: ARE, CVC, GUA, OSA, PAC, TEM. **Range:** Mex–SE Ec. Introduced in Old World tropics.

■ *Desmopsis microcarpa* (guineo)
  Family **Annonaceae**

Small tree or shrub, 2–6 m tall, bark very fibrous, branches thin. **Leaves** alternate, stalk to 0.4 cm, blade 10–20 cm long, 4–10 cm wide, narrowly elliptic, tip abruptly pointed. **Flowers** yellowish to green, radially symmetrical, 6 petals, 2–3 cm long, 1.5 cm wide, tips pointed, finely hairy outside, stamens small and numerous; flowers usually solitary on a long, very thin stalk, to 8 cm long, with a heart-shaped, leaflike bract at its base; each flower producing up to 7 fruit; blooms Apr.– July, Oct. **Fruit** fleshy, yellow, to red, to dark purple, small, a short cylinder about 0.7 cm long, 0.8 cm wide; in stout umbrella-shaped clusters; July–Feb. **Habitat:** Wet forests, sometimes in temporarily flooded sites. Altitude: Sea level to 1800 m. Conservation areas: ARE, CVC, GUA, HNO, LAC, LAP, OSA, TOR. **Range:** Nic–Pan. **Notes:** There are seven species of *Desmopsis* in Costa Rica.

■ *Rauvolfia tetraphylla*
Family Apocynaceae

Low shrub 0.5–1.5 m, sometimes to 4 m tall, stems woody, tan gray, sap milky. **Leaves** opposite or, more often, in whorls of 4, 2–12 cm long, 1–6 cm wide, elliptic to oblong, tip pointed to blunt, base blunt. **Flowers** white, radially symmetrical, tubular, petal lobes to 0.4 cm long; blooms most of the year; inflorescence in axils of leaves and much shorter than subtending leaf. **Fruit** fleshy, red, rounded, 0.5–0.8 cm wide; in small dense clusters at ends of twigs; fruits most of the year. **Habitat:** Seasonally dry forests. Altitude: Sea level to 800 m, Pacific slope. Conservation areas: GUA, PAC, TEM. **Range:** Mex–Brz, Ant. **Notes:** There are eight species of *Rauvolfia* in Costa Rica. *Rauvolfia tetraphylla*, *R. aphlebia*, found at higher elevations, and *R. littoralis* are the most common.

■ *Verbesina ovatifolia*
Family Asteraceae

Shrub 0.5–1.5 m tall, branches often vinelike, stems sharply 4-angled, young stems green. **Leaves** opposite, stalk 1–2 cm long, extending down stem as winged angles, blade 6–8 cm long, 4–5 cm wide, egg- to heart-shaped, tip pointed, base rounded to sometimes lobed, surface rough, margins toothed. **Flowers** orange to red orange, showy, tiny, in compact heads about 2.5 cm wide, of 150 or more flowers arising from a bract-covered floral base, about 1 cm tall, 1.5 cm wide, basal bracts loose, overlapping, widest at base; flowers tubular, the central, disc flowers, radially symmetrical, the larger peripheral flowers (rays) bilaterally symmetrical, with 1 enlarged petal about 1.2 cm long; inflorescence of a few heads on long stalks at ends of stems; blooms Oct.–Apr. **Fruit** dry, 1-seeded with 2 stiff, winglike bristles. **Habitat:** Seasonally dry to wet regions, scrambling over roadside vegetation, second growth, edges. Altitude: 200–1500 m, mostly on the Pacific slope. Conservation areas: ARE, GUA, PAC. **Range:** Mex–CR. **Notes:** There are 11 species of *Verbesina* in Costa Rica.

■ *Protium ravenii* (alcanfor, canfin)
Family Burseraceae

Small tree 5–13 m tall, sap strongly aromatic,
drying very sticky, insoluble in water. **Leaves**
alternate, variable with 1, 3, or 5 leaflets,
large, elliptic. **Flowers** pale yellow or whitish,
very small; inflorescence of branched clusters
to 21 cm long; blooms Jan.–May, Sept. **Fruit**
fleshy, red, aromatic, 1.5–3 cm long, opening
in sections to reveal large seeds covered by a
white, fleshy coating that is eaten by parrots;
fruit present most of the year. **Habitat:** Wet
forests. Altitude: Sea level to 1200 m, mostly
100–500 m. Conservation areas: CVC, GUA,
HNO, LAC, LAP, OSA (very common), PAC, TOR. **Range:**
Nic–Pan. **Notes:** There are 10 species of *Protium* in Costa
Rica. *Protium ravenii, P. costaricense,* and *P. panamense* are
the most common. All are very similar. Red, aromatic fruit
hull segments are often found along trails below trees. This is
the most likely part of these trees to be observed.

■ *Podandrogyne decipiens (P. chiriquensis)* **Family
Capparaceae**

Shrub or shrubby herb 1–3 m tall, stems greenish, branched
or not. **Leaves** alternate, stalk to 20 cm long, 3-parted, central leaflet larger than laterals, 10–25 cm long, 7–13 cm
wide, elliptical, veins pinnate, deeply depressed above, shiny,
yellow green. **Flowers** pale coral to orange, radially to bilaterally symmetrical, male and female flowers separate, males
near top, females lower, petals 4, free, spatula-shaped, 1.5–
2.7 cm long, 0.5–1 cm wide, sepals fused, stamens 6, anthers
dark blue, pistil long and thin; inflorescence of umbrella-
shaped cluster at tips of stems. **Fruit** becoming dry, a pod,
at first wine red, 5–21 cm long, 0.5 cm wide, dangling below
flowers, splitting open spirally to expose many small dark

brown seeds 0.3 cm long, in whitish, lumpy flesh (aril); blooms and
fruits all year. **Habitat:** Moist, open
or partly shady sites, in low growth,
roadside ditches, stream sides. Altitude: 200–2700 m. Conservation
areas: ARE, CVC, LAC, GUA, LAP,
OSA, PAC. **Range:** Gua–Pan and Pr.
Notes: There is one other species of
Podandrogyne in Costa Rica, which is
very uncommon.

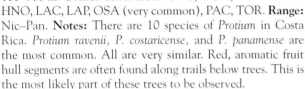

113

◼ *Perrottetia longistylis*
Family Celastraceae

Shrub, or small tree mostly 4–12 m tall, sometimes to 20 m. **Leaves** alternate, arranged in one plane along opposite sides of twigs; blade 7–20 cm long 3–8 cm wide, egg-shaped to oblong, tip long-pointed, base wedge-shaped to blunt, dark green, surface wrinkled, margin toothed. **Flowers** yellowish

to greenish, very small, anthers yellow; inflorescence of branched clusters; blooms July–Feb. **Fruit** fleshy, red, about 0.4 cm long and wide, translucent, flesh watery, gelatinous with several small seeds; at various stages of maturity in dangling, branched clusters on thin stems at nodes along twigs below leaves; Dec.–Aug. **Habitat:** Wet mountains in forests and open sites, roadsides, second growth. Altitude: 900–2400 m. Conservation areas: CVC, LAP, PAC. **Range:** Mex–CR. **Notes:** There are three species of *Perrottetia* in Costa Rica; *P. multiflora* and *P. sessiliflora* have yellow flowers.

◼ *Clusia gracilis* (copey)
Family Clusiaceae

Epiphytic shrub 1–5 m tall, sap milky; a strangler, occasionally terrestrial or on rocks. **Leaves** opposite, stalk 1–4 cm, blade 6–15 cm long, 2.5–7.5 cm wide, elliptic to lance-shaped, pointed at both ends, veins obscure. **Flowers** red to dark red; sexes on separate plants; petals 4, fleshy, sepals 4 often purple, unequal, 0.4–0.7 cm, male flowers with numerous stamens fused onto a central stalk, female flow-

ers with a similar central structure; inflorescence opposite-branched, 5–17 cm long, pendent; blooms Sept.–Mar. **Fruit** fleshy, red to purple, 2–7 cm long, 1–3 cm wide, becoming pendent, 4-angled near the base (stem end), the 4 parts separating at the tip into pointed lobes, each bearing the remnant of 1 style; fruit present most of the year. **Habitat:** Wet forests. Altitude: Caribbean slope, sea level to 1300 m. Conservation areas: ARE, CVC, LAC, TOR. Very common but probably not often observed from ground. **Range:** Nic–Pan. **Notes:** Distinguished by its red, 4-parted fruits.

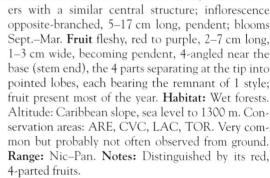

■ *Cavendishia bracteata*
Family Ericaceae

Shrub, terrestrial or epiphytic, much-branched, 1–4 m tall, often sprawling over other vegetation, occasionally treelike to 15 m tall. **Leaves** alternate, stalk to 1.5 cm long, often red, blade 3–20 cm long, 1–10 cm wide, narrowly elliptic to egg-shaped, tip pointed, base blunt to slightly lobed, leathery, shiny green above, veins paler, deeply impressed, lower surface pale yellow green, major veins palmate. **Flowers** red to orange, white at tip, radially symmetrical, narrowly tubular, bottle-shaped to cylindrical, narrowed below flaring petal lobes, base red orange, top white, 1–2.5 cm long, 0.5 cm wide, petal lobes 0.2 cm long; bracts bright pink to dark red, large, 1–4 cm long, 1–2.5 cm

wide, tip rounded; inflorescence of dense clusters surrounded by showy bracts; bud of overlapping pink bracts 3 cm long, 1.5 cm wide; blooms all year; often visited by hummingbirds. **Fruit** fleshy, black, about 1 cm wide. **Habitat:** Mostly in mountain areas. Altitude: 550–3300 m, usually above 1000 m. Conservation areas: ARE, CVC, GUA, LAC, LAP, PAC. **Range:** Mex–Bol. **Notes:** There are over 23 species of *Cavendishia* in Costa Rica. *Cavendishia* species are distinguished by their colorful, often large, bracts.

■ *Satyria warszewiczii* (uva)
Family Ericaceae

Epiphytic or terrestrial vine or vinelike shrub, branches 1–2.5 m long or more, bark brown to gray, new growth often red. **Leaves** alternate, 10–25 cm long, 4–10 cm wide, egg-shaped to elliptic, tip pointed, base wedge-shaped, margin slightly rolled under, palmately 3-veined, leathery, new leaves limp, copper-colored. **Flowers** bright red with white tip, radially symmetrical, to 2.5 cm long, 0.4 cm wide, narrowly tubular, petal lobes 0.2 cm long, floral base, usually red, about 0.2 cm tall, 0.3–0.4 cm wide; inflorescences of tight clusters directly from woody branches, each on a short red stalk; blooms and fruits all year. **Fruit** fleshy, changing from red orange to whitish, finally to purple, to 0.6 cm long, 0.8 cm wide. **Habitat:** Mountain forests. Altitude: 200–2700 m, mostly above 1200 m. Conservation areas: ARE, CVC, GUA, LAC, LAP, OSA, PAC. **Range:** S Mex–Pan. **Notes:** There are four species of *Satyria* in Costa Rica.

115

■ *Acalypha costaricensis*
Family Euphorbiaceae

Woody herb or slender shrub to 2 m or more, stems greenish, sparsely branched, old stems rough, hairy, gray brown. **Leaves** alternate, stalk 2–7 cm long, blade 10–22 cm long, 5–11 cm wide, elliptic, tip long-pointed, base blunt or with small lobes, hairy below, margin bluntly toothed. **Flowers** red, tiny, sexes separate, male flowers in catkinlike spikes to 30 cm long, in axils; female flowers in open, branched clusters to 40 cm long, 12 cm wide, at ends of stems; blooms and fruits on and off most of the year. **Fruit** dry, greenish, warty-spiny, to 0.4 cm wide, 3-lobed. **Habitat:** Understories of wet, lowland forests. Altitude: Caribbean slope, 70–800 m, mostly below 200 m. Conservation areas: CVC, LAC, TOR. **Range:** S Mex–Pan. **Notes:** There are about 25 species of *Acalypha* in Costa Rica.

■ *Acalypha macrostachya*
Family Euphorbiaceae

Small tree or shrub, to 6 m, stems often in clusters, densely hairy, stipules about 1 cm long, deciduous, leaving scars.

Leaves alternate, stalk 3–25 cm long, blade 10–24 cm long, 6–17 cm wide, egg-shaped, tip long, tapered, base blunt, hairy, margins toothed. **Flowers** red, sexes separate, female flowers accompanied by bracts, style red, branched, to 1 cm long, male flowers minute, in drooping spikes to 20 cm; blooms Sept.–June. **Fruit** dry, 3-lobed, explodes to release seeds. **Habitat:** Wet to seasonally dry regions in weedy, open sites, and second growth forests. Altitude: Sea level to 1800 m. Conservation areas: ARE, CVC, GUA, LAC, LAP, OSA, PAC, TEM. **Range:** Mex–Bol and Brz.

■ *Euphorbia pulcherrima*
  (Poinsettia pulcherrima) (poinsettia)
  Family Euphorbiaceae

Shrub to 5 m tall, sparsely branched, sap milky. **Leaves** alternate on leafy stems, whorled below inflorescence, stalk to 8 cm long, blade 8–22 cm long, 4–12 cm wide, elliptic to egg-shaped, pinnately lobed, tips pointed, hairy below. **Flowers** red and yellow, very small, in small branched clusters above a whorl of large, red (sometimes white or pink), petal-like leaves; blooms Nov.–Jan. **Fruit** dry, 3-parted. **Habitat:** Cultivated ornamental, often used for hedges. Occasionally escaping into natural areas. Altitude: Sea level to 1200 m. Conservation areas: CVC, LAC, PAC. **Range:** W Mex. **Notes:** The Christmas poinsettia. There are 18 species of *Euphorbia* in Costa Rica. Most are native.

■ *Jatropha gossypiifolia* (casaba marble,
  frailecillo)
  Family Euphorbiaceae

Short-lived shrub to 2.5 m tall, sparsely branched, multistemmed, bark pale tan, smooth, stipules simple to feathery tufts, soft green bristles with glandular tips. **Leaves** alternate, on new growth at tips of stems, stalk to 7 cm with fringed tufts at top, below blade, blade 5–16 cm long, 3–18 cm wide, thin, sticky-hairy, deeply 3- to 5-lobed, lobe tips pointed, veins palmate, margin finely toothed and bristle-fringed. **Flowers** dark red, with yellow eye, 1 cm wide, petals

falling as a unit; blooms most of the year. **Fruit** dry, ribbed, 2- to 3-lobed, about 1.5 cm wide, splitting open to release seeds. **Habitat:** Wet to seasonally dry regions, in weedy, open sites, often near beaches; also cultivated. Altitude: Sea level to 800 m. Conservation areas: GUA, LAC, OSA, PAC, TEM, TOR. **Range:** Brz. Widely naturalized in other tropical areas; invasive in some Old World regions. **Notes:** Used medicinally to treat high blood pressure and liver problems. Oil from seeds used on skin. There are five species of *Jatropha* in Costa Rica.

117

■ *Caesalpinia pulcherrima*
(clavelina, hoja de sen, malinche)
Family Fabaceae/Caesalpinioideae

Shrub to 5 m tall, stems somewhat thorny. **Leaves** alternate, twice evenly pinnate, feathery, to 30 cm long, 15 cm wide, 3–9 pairs primary leaflets pinnae each with 6–12 pairs of

oblong leaflets 1–3 cm long, about 0.8 cm wide, tips blunt. **Flowers** red or red with yellow petal edge, 5 petals, 2–3 cm wide, slightly asymmetrical, stamens red, very long; in large, terminal clusters, each flower on a long stem from the central axis; blooms Sept.–Jan., May. **Fruit** dry, pods flat, becoming dark brown black, to 12 cm long, 2 cm wide. **Habitat:** Mostly horticultural. Sometimes escaped from cultivation. Altitude: 100–1100 m including planted specimens. Conservation areas: CVC, OSA, PAC. **Range:** Mex–N C Amer, possibly to S Amer, WI. Cultivated in the Old World tropics. Invasive in the Galápagos islands.

■ *Delonix regia* (clavellina, malinche
framboyán, flamboyant, poinciana)
Family Fabaceae/Caesalpinioideae

Small to medium-sized tree to about 15 m tall, with wide crown, bark gray. **Leaves** alternate, twice evenly pinnate, to 60 cm long, 45 cm wide pinnae up to 22 pairs, each with about 40 pairs of small, oblong leaflets, about 1 cm long, 0.6 cm wide, very fine, lacy, deciduous in seasonally dry regions. **Flowers** bright red to red orange, showy, to 10 cm wide, 5 petals, wide, fan-shaped at top, narrowed toward base, in large clusters; blooms May–June. **Fruit** dry, woody,

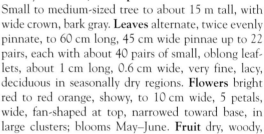

pods, flat, about 30 cm long, 4.5 cm wide, blackish, seeds numerous, wider than long, pods persistent on leafless trees in dry season. **Habitat:** Horticultural, widely planted, sometimes escaped. Altitude: Sea level to 100 m. Conservation areas: ICO, LAC, OSA. **Range:** Native to Madagascar. Cultivated and naturalized throughout the tropics and subtropics. **Notes:** This is the only species of *Delonix* in Costa Rica.

■ *Erythrina berteroana*
(poró, palo de cerca, palo de mona)
Family Fabaceae/Faboideae

Small tree to 7 m tall, armed with stout spines. **Leaves** alternate, 3-parted, leaflets 5–17 cm long, about 5 cm wide, egg-shaped, very pale below. **Flowers** red, saber-shaped, bilaterally symmetrical, upper petal tubular, inflorescence of long, spikelike clusters; blooms mostly Nov.–Apr., July. **Fruit** pods 10–20 cm long, seeds red, sometimes with a black line. **Habitat:** Wet to moist regions in open areas. Also used as living fences especially in the Central Valley. Altitude: Sea level to 2700 m, mostly below 1000. Conservation areas: ARE, CVC, LACLAP, OSA, PAC, TOR. **Range:** Mex–Pr, WI. **Notes:** There are 14 species of *Erythrina* in Costa Rica.

■ *Erythrina costaricensis* (poró cimarrón,
pito, pato trinidad, poró espinoso)
Family Fabaceae/Faboideae

Tree to 10 m tall, 30 cm diameter, sparsely branched, twigs often with silvery mottling, smooth, armed with scattered short spines. **Leaves** alternate, stalks to 34 cm long, often spiny, blade 3-parted, leaflets egg-shaped, middle leaflet 7–23 cm long, 5–25 cm wide, tip narrowed, long-pointed, base broad, blunt, dark green above whitish green below, thin, stiff-papery texture, usually deciduous in flower and especially in fruit. **Flowers** red, to 9 cm long, 1 cm wide, more or less saber-shaped, upper petal tubular, tip tapering with blunt end, calyx red, tubular, 2-lipped, inflated; inflorescence of dense branched clusters; blooms mostly Nov.–Apr. **Fruit** dry, pods 15–23 cm long, about 1 cm wide, reddish, hairy, strongly constricted between seeds, seeds scarlet, about 10, 0.8 cm long. **Habitat:** Wet to seasonally dry forests. Often used for living fences and cultivated as a street trees. Altitude: Sea level to 2150 m, mostly well below 1000 m. Conservation areas: GUA, LAC, OSA, PAC, TEM. **Range:** CR–Col.

119

■ *Erythrina gibbosa* (poró)
Family Fabaceae/Faboideae

Small tree or shrub, about 2–9 m tall, to 10 cm diameter, usually with a straight trunk and wide canopy, bark with longitudinal striations, tan and brown, slightly spiny, branches stout, curved, rough, bumpy with closely spaced leaf scars; leafless Sept.–Oct. **Leaves** alternate, 3-parted, leaflets egg-shaped, 1–30 cm long, 4–15 cm wide, tip pointed, base broad, blunt. **Flowers** rose red, saber-shaped, 5 cm long, 1 cm wide, flattened, calyx red, inflated at far end; inflorescence of spikes, about 13 cm long, at branch tips; blooms July–Jan. **Fruit** dry, pods about 10 cm long, 2 cm wide, cylindrical, constricted between seeds, tip long-pointed, green turning red, then dark purple black, curved, several together twisting into a ball, splitting open to reveal bright red orange seeds attached to white interior. **Habitat:** Wet to moist forests, often along rivers and streams. Altitude: Sea level to 1800 m. Conservation areas: ARE, CVC, GUA, HNO, LAC, LAP, OSA, PAC, TOR. Seen in Tapantí N.P. **Range:** Nic–Pan.

■ *Calliandra haematocephala*
(pon pon rojo, red powder puff)
Family Fabaceae/Mimosoideae

Shrub 1–7 m tall, branches spreading. **Leaves** alternate, stalk 1–2 cm, blade twice evenly pinnate, pinnae each with 6–10 pairs of leaflets 1–4 cm long, 0.5–1.5 cm wide, usually curved, tip with small, abrupt point, base unequal, upper leaflets larger than the lower. **Flowers** pinkish to greenish, radially symmetrical, tubular, to about 0.8 cm long, stamens 3 cm long, bright red; inflorescences showy, rounded, powderpuff-like clusters to 5 cm wide. **Fruit** dry, pod 6–10 cm long, about 1 cm wide, flat with a raised margin, twisting open at maturity to release seeds explosively. **Habitat:** Cultivated, especially in and around San José. Altitude: 1100 m. Conservation areas: CVC. **Range:** Native to Bol, widely cultivated as an ornamental. **Notes:** There are 14 species of *Calliandra* in Costa Rica. All have powder-puff-type flower clusters, border on the fruit pods raised. All are horticultural.

Erythrina gibbosa (above)

Calliandra haematocephala (below)

■ *Tetrathylacium macrophyllum* (cacao de mico, cacao de mono, cacao silvestre, cimarrón, zapote)
Family Flacourtiaceae

Small tree or shrub 3–15 m tall, usually less than 10 m, trunk to 30 cm diameter, bark pinkish to gray brown, smooth, branches long, stout, 0.6 cm thick at ends, slightly drooping, evenly distributed up axis, twigs 2–3 m long, older twigs hollow, occupied by ants. **Leaves** alternate, in 2 ranks along stems, tending to overlap, stalk thick, about 1 cm long, blade 25–40 cm long, 5–14 cm wide, oblong, tip abruptly long-pointed, base slightly unequal, rounded to lobed, surface shiny, dark green, stiff, leathery, new leaves reddish bronze, drooping on either side of twig, veins palmate at base, about 11 per side, curved upward. **Flowers** reddish purple, of rounded sepals, 0.2 cm wide, in 4 knoblike protrusions on several spikes about 9 cm long, from a central axis; blooms and fruits most of the year. **Fruit** red purple, rounded, about 1 cm wide, finely hairy. **Habitat:** Second growth lowlands forests, edges, thickets. Altitude: Southern Pacific lowlands, sea level to 800 m, mostly below 400 m. Conservation areas: OSA (mostly), PAC. **Range:** CR–S Amer. **Notes:** The uncommon *T. johansenii* is the only other species of *Tetrathylacium* in Costa Rica.

■ *Drymonia rubra*
Family Gesneriaceae

Fruit (red); flowers (yellow-green)

Shrub or liana, often epiphytic, to 2 m tall, stems drooping, new growth succulent, older stems woody, bark gray, shiny. **Leaves** opposite, stalks to 4 cm long, blades with pair members often unequal, 7–20 cm long, 3–9 cm wide, elliptic, sides often unequal, tip pointed, base tapered, dark green, shiny above, paler or reddish below, slightly rough-hairy. **Flowers** red orange often with white or yellow stripes, tubular, bilaterally symmetrical, to 6 cm long, about 3 cm wide across top, petal lobes rounded with fringed margin, calyx asymmetrical, to 5 cm long, 3 cm wide, pale green, surrounding base of petal tube; blooms most of the year. **Fruit** fleshy, hollow, white, oval, to 2 cm long, 1 cm wide. **Habitat:** Wet, mountain forests. Altitude: 200–1700 m, mostly above 1000 m. Conservation areas: ARE, CVC, GUA, LAC, LAP, PAC. Seen at Tapantí N.P. and Monteverde. **Range:** CR, Pan. **Notes:** There are about 20 species of *Drymonia* in Costa Rica.

121

■ *Solenophora calycosa*
Family Gesneriaceae

Shrub, small tree, or large herb, 1–8 m tall, stems erect, to 15 cm diameter, stems green to purple or brown. **Leaves** opposite, stalks 2–15 cm, bases joined across stem, blade 14–32 cm long, 7–21 cm wide, egg-shaped to elliptic, tip pointed, base unequal, dark green, rough above, paler green below, sometimes reddish or purple, margin toothed. **Flowers** coral, orange, or deep yellow with dark red spots on inside of petal lobes, large, showy, 6–7 cm long, 2.5 cm across top, petal lobes 5, tips rounded, finely hairy outside, calyx green to reddish, 1–2 cm long, anthers with tips touching; inflorescence of 1–4 flowers in upper axils on a stalk to 15 cm long; blooms all year. **Fruit** dry, hollow, 1 cm wide, tipped by old calyx. **Habitat:** Wet, mountain forest understories. Altitude: 900–3300 m, usually above 1500 m. Conservation areas: ARE, CVC, LAC, LAP, PAC. Seen in Braulio Carrillo, and Tapantí N.P. **Range:** Gua–Hon, CR, Pan. **Notes:** This is the only species of *Solenophora* in Costa Rica.

■ *Psittacanthus ramiflorus*
Family Loranthaceae

Parasitic shrub, about 1 m tall, on branches of host plant, multistemmed, branched. **Leaves** opposite, alternate or in whorls of 3, often on same branch, stalk 0.2–1 cm long, winged, blade 3–8 cm long, 1.5–4 cm wide, elliptic, symmetrical, dull green, tip blunt, base extending down stalk. **Flowers** red orange near base, yellow near tip, 3–4 cm long, very narrow, young flowers appearing tubular, in dense clusters about 4–5 cm long at nodes, top of flower stalk forming cup at base of flowers; blooms and fruits Jan.–Nov. **Fruit** fleshy, blue black. **Habitat:** Moist to wet forests, second growth, roadside, and remnant pasture trees. Altitude: Sea level (rarely) to 2500 m, usually above 1000 m. Conservation areas: ARE, CVC, GUA, LAC, LAP, OSA, PAC. **Range:** Mex–Pan. **Notes:** There are seven species of *Psittacanthus* in Costa Rica.

■ *Hibiscus rosa-sinensis*
(amapola, clavelón, Chinese hibiscus)
Family Malvaceae

Shrub to 3–6 m tall, young leaves and stem hairy. **Leaves** alternate, stalk to 3 cm long, blade egg-shaped, 8–15 cm long, 5–9 cm wide, tip pointed, base often asymmetric, margins toothed. **Flowers** red to yellow, white, lavender, very showy, to 17 cm, solitary, central column of stamens and style longer than petals, tipped by stigma; blooms most of the year. **Fruit** dry, 5 sections. **Habitat:** Mostly horticultural, may occasionally escape, mostly in coastal areas. Altitude: Sea level to 300 m. Conservation areas: GUA, LAC, OSA. **Range:** Native to Asia, cultivated throughout tropics and subtropics. **Notes:** There are about six species of *Hibiscus* in Costa Rica, most are cultivated or very uncommon.

■ *Malvaviscus concinnus* (amapola, quesito)
Family Malvaceae

Shrub 1–8 m tall. **Leaves** alternate, 7–20 cm long, 4–14 cm wide egg-shaped, tip tapered to a long point, base blunt to lobed, veins palmate, margin toothed. **Flowers** red to pink, never fully opening, petals 5, 3–5.5 cm long, asymmetrically wedge-shaped, with a lobe near the base on one side, widest near apex, notched, stamens and pistils joined in a central column longer than petals, calyx about 1.5 cm long, a set of 5 pointed bracts grow just below the calyx lobes; blooms most of the year. **Fruit** white, to 2 cm wide, at first fleshy, becoming dry, 5-parted, wider than tall, **Habitat:** Moist to wet evergreen forests. Altitude: Sea level to 1700 m, mostly below 500 m. Conservation areas: CVC, LAC, LAP, OSA, PAC, TEM, TOR. **Range:** CR–Pr and Brz. **Notes:** There are at least two other species of *Malvaviscus* in Costa Rica. The other common species, *Malvaviscus arboreus*, has velvety-hairy leaves but is otherwise almost identical to M. *concinnus*. It is found in regions of seasonally dry forest in GUA area.

Malvaviscus arboreus

123

▪ *Souroubea gilgii*
Family Marcgraviaceae

Epiphytic shrub, often vinelike, sap milky. **Leaves** alternate, elliptic, leathery. **Flowers** red and yellow, radially symmetrical, 0.5–0.8 cm long, petals fused, lobes 4–5; each flower above a tubular, nectar-producing structure about 1 cm long, with a rounded end; inflorescences to 25 cm long, unbranched; blooms June, Nov., Feb. **Fruit** leathery-fleshy, red; seeds numerous; fruit seen in Oct. **Habitat:** Wet forests and disturbed sites. Altitude: Sea level to 220 m. Caribbean lowlands. Conservation areas: CVC, TOR. Seen at La Selva Biological Station. **Range:** Bel–Pan. **Notes:** There are five species of *Souroubea* in Costa Rica. Often high in the tree canopy and difficult to observe.

▪ *Blakea litoralis*
Family Melastomataceae

Epiphytic shrub, 1.5–5 m tall, often drooping, sometimes vinelike, young parts brown-hairy, becoming smooth with age. **Leaves** opposite, blades 4–12 cm long, 2–5 cm wide, egg-shaped, pointed at both ends, succulent, old leaves often red above, major veins palmate, parallel, minor veins numerous, ladderlike between major veins. **Flowers** red to pink, radially symmetrical, petals 6, 2–3 cm long, 1.5–2.5 cm wide, apex broadly rounded, calyx and basal bracts often purplish, anthers 12, yellow, filaments white to pale pink, all on one side; blooms and fruits on and off most of the year. **Fruit** fleshy, red, rounded, to 2 cm wide, seeds 0.1 cm. **Habitat:** Moist to wet evergreen forests. Altitude: Sea level to 1600 m, mostly below 1000 m. Conservation areas: ARE, CVC, LAC, LAP, OSA, PAC. **Range:** CR. **Notes:** Common but probably not often observed.

■ *Neea* sp.
Family Nyctaginaceae

Shrubs or small trees, appearing, superficially, like plants in the family Rubiaceae, but leaves are without stipules. **Leaves** opposite (or nearly so), in whorls of 3–4, or alternate, often all on the same plant, stalked, blades of a pair often differ in size, margins smooth, veins pinnate. **Flowers** greenish, tubular, small, petal lobes 5, female flowers sometimes urn-shaped, contracted just below the petal lobes, much smaller than male flowers, no calyx; inflorescences at ends of stems, branched, flowers often in groups of 3; stems often red or purple, especially in fruit. **Fruit** fleshy, becoming red, bright yellow, pink, or purple, 1-seeded. **Habitat:** Moist and wet forests, second growth, or open habitats. Altitude: Sea level to 1700 m. Conservation areas: ARE, CVC, GUA, HNO, LAC, LAP, OSA, PAC, TOR. **Range:** The genus occurs in S FL, Mex–Bol, WI. **Notes:** Plants in the genus *Neea* are very difficult to tell apart, they are differentiated on traits that overlap widely. Different taxonomic and herbarium sources list different numbers of species, generally 2–10. The most common species names listed are *N. psychotrioides*, *N. laetevirens*, and *N. amplifolia*.

■ *Heisteria acuminata* (naranjillo)
Family Olacaceae

Shrub or treelet 1–3 m tall, rarely to 8 m, freely branched, young twigs thin, ridged. **Leaves** alternate, stalk about 1 cm long, ridged above, blade 6–23 cm long, 2–7 cm wide, elliptic, tip tapered to a long point, base blunt to pointed, glossy green above, leathery, margin smooth or wavy, veins joined by loop connections at margin, impressed above, raised below. **Flowers** greenish white, radially symmetrical, to 0.3 cm long, flower buds sometimes reddish, calyx 5-toothed, 0.2 cm wide, greatly expanding in fruit, stamens 10; inflorescences of small clusters mostly in leaf axils; blooms mostly Mar.–Oct. **Fruit** thinly fleshy, green, eventually black, to 1 cm, above bright red calyx, expanded to 3 cm wide in fruit; 1-seeded; fruit present most of the year.

Habitat: Moist forests. Altitude: Sea level to 1800 m, usually below 600 m. Conservation areas: GUA, LAC, LAP, OSA, PAC. **Range:** CR–Ven and Pr. **Notes:** There are six species of *Heisteria* in Costa Rica; most have a broad, red calyx in fruit while the fruit itself becomes black. An exception is *H. concinna* (photo) which has white fruit. It is found in lowland forests of the GUA, LAC, OSA, PAC, TOR conservation areas. Another exception is *H. scandens*, a woody vine with red fruit.

■ *Rubus glaucus*
Family Rosaceae

Shrub with vinelike branches, stems with whitish bloom, prickly, prickles to 0.3 cm, base wide, tip curved, stipules linear, to 1 cm long, 0.8 cm wide. **Leaves** alternate, 3-parted, stalk to 5–12 cm long, leaflets 5–13 cm long, 2–6 cm wide, narrowly egg-shaped, smooth above, whitish, feltlike below, margins toothed. **Flowers** white, radially symmetrical, 2 cm wide, petals 5, sepals 5, whitish-feltlike below, stamens numerous; inflorescence of branched clusters to 20 cm long, with 15–22 flowers; blooms and fruits on and off most of the year. **Fruit** fleshy, red to black, 1.5–2.5 cm long and about as wide, of many tiny individual fruits fused together, edible. **Habitat:** Mountain forests, second growth, edges. Altitude: 1600–2300 m. Conservation areas: ARE, CVC, PAC. **Range:** Mex, Hon, CR–Ec, Bol. **Notes:** There are six species of *Rubus* in Costa Rica. All are usually found above 1000 m. Most species of *Rubus* are found in temperate regions of the world.

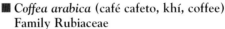

■ *Coffea arabica* (café cafeto, khí, coffee)
Family Rubiaceae

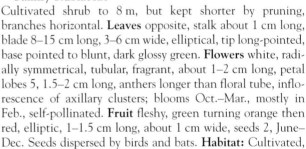

Cultivated shrub to 8 m, but kept shorter by pruning, branches horizontal. **Leaves** opposite, stalk about 1 cm long, blade 8–15 cm long, 3–6 cm wide, elliptical, tip long-pointed, base pointed to blunt, dark glossy green. **Flowers** white, radially symmetrical, tubular, fragrant, about 1–2 cm long, petal lobes 5, 1.5–2 cm long, anthers longer than floral tube, inflorescence of axillary clusters; blooms Oct.–Mar., mostly in Feb., self-pollinated. **Fruit** fleshy, green turning orange then red, elliptic, 1–1.5 cm long, about 1 cm wide, seeds 2, June–Dec. Seeds dispersed by birds and bats. **Habitat:** Cultivated, occasionally escaping. Altitude: 20–2000 m. Cultivated mostly in the Central Valley, 1000–2000 m. Conservation areas: CVC, GUA, ICO, LAC, TOR. **Range:** Native to Ethiopia, Africa. Cultivated Mex–Par, WI. **Notes:** Seeds are separated from pulp, dried, and roasted before being used. The most important export crop from Costa Rica. Traditional cultivars require part shade and are grown under tall trees. Newer cultivars can be grown in the open. Plantations of these lack the habitat diversity of older varieties. The only other species of *Coffea* in Costa Rica is *C. liberica*, grown in lowland sites (photo: flowers), produces a poorer grade of coffee.

▪ *Hamelia patens* (añiñeto, azulillo, clavelillo, scarlet bush)
Family Rubiaceae

Shrub or small tree 2–7 m tall, young twigs 4-angled, rough, often hairy, greenish; stipules between leaf bases, to 0.6 cm, linear, finely hairy. **Leaves** in whorls of 3, stalks 2–5 cm long, often reddish, blade elliptic, 5–17 cm long, 1–7 cm wide, elliptic, tip tapered to a point, base often extending down leaf stem, underside often hairy. **Flowers** orange red, radially symmetrical, narrowly tubular, to 1.8 cm long, petal lobes about 0.2 cm, triangular, floral base to 0.3 cm long, deep red,

flower buds orange; inflorescence of rather 1-sided, branched clusters to 9 cm long, 12 cm wide, at ends of branches, flowering stems often reddish; blooms and fruits all year. **Fruit** fleshy, red becoming purple or black, soft, to 1.3 cm long, 1.0 cm wide, several seeds. **Habitat:** Wet to seasonally dry regions, in open sites, edges, and second growth. Altitude: Sea level to 2200 m. Conservation areas: ARE, CVC, GUA, LAC, LAP, OSA, PAC, TEM, TOR. **Range:** Mex–Guy and Arg. **Notes:** Widely planted as an ornamental.

▪ *Hillia triflora* (*Ravnia t.*)
Family Rubiaceae

Usually epiphytic, shrub 0.5–1.5 m tall with long, drooping branches to 2 m, old stems brown, woody; stipules 2–4 cm long to 1 cm wide, elliptic, deciduous, leaving a linear scar around nodes. **Leaves** opposite, stalk to 0.7 cm, blade 5–13 cm long, 2–4 cm wide, pair members sometimes unequal, narrowly elliptic, thin, smooth, rubbery-textured, shiny green above, tip tapered to a point, base pointed, secondary veins 3–5 per side. **Flowers** bright red, radially symmetrical, narrowly tubular, to 6.5 cm long, 1 cm wide, petal lobes 6 (usually), to 0.4 cm long, calyx lobes 4, linear, small, stamens yellow, grouped at petal lobes; inflorescence of 1 or 3 flowers, above a pair of pale green bracts; blooms most of the year. **Fruit** dry, cylindrical, to 10 cm long, 0.8 cm wide, splitting open to release numerous tiny, plumed seeds. **Habitat:** Moist to wet forests, sometimes low on tree trunks, rarely terrestrial. Altitude: 500–2400 m, above 1000 m on the Pacific slope. Conservation areas: ARE, CVC, GUA, LAC, LAP. **Range:** CR, Pan. **Notes:** The most commonly collected of the 10 species of *Hillia* in Costa Rica.

◾ *Ixora coccinea* (cruz de Malta, flor de fuego, jazmín rojo)
Family Rubiaceae

Ornamental shrub 0.5–3 m, much-branched, stipules 0.1 cm. **Leaves** opposite, stalk small or none, blade 3–10 cm long, 2–4 cm wide oblong-elliptic, tip blunt to pointed, base rounded to slightly lobed. **Flowers** red, radially symmetrical, tubular, to 4 cm long, tube very narrow, petal lobes 4, flaring, 1 cm long, tips pointed, stamens and style slightly longer than petal tube; visited by butterflies; inflorescence to 10 cm long, of dense, rounded clusters at ends of stems. **Fruit** fleshy, about 1 cm wide, a round, red or black berry; eaten by birds. **Habitat:** Widely cultivated, apparently not escaping often. Altitude: Sea level to about 1500 m. Conservation area: HNO, LAC. **Range:** Native to India. Cultivated in Mex–Ec, Bol, and Par, WI, Africa, S Asia, some Pacific islands. **Notes:** *Ixora finlaysoniana* is also cultivated but has white flowers. It is native to Southeast Asia. There are also two native species of Ixora, *I. floribunda* and *I. nicaraguensis;* both are small trees with white flowers.

◾ *Psychotria poeppigiana* (*Cephaelis tomentosa*)
(labios de mujer, labios de novia, ladies lips, hot lips)
Family Rubiaceae

Shrub 0.7–3 m tall, stems hairy; stipules hairy, base a tubular sheath to 0.8 cm high but often obscure, 2 linear lobes to 1.6 cm long. **Leaves** opposite, stalk to 1.8 cm long, hairy, blade 8–18 cm long, 3–8 cm wide, elliptic, hairy on both sides, especially on midrib below, tip long-tapered, base blunt to pointed. **Flowers** yellow or whitish, radially symmetrical, tubular, to 1 cm long, embedded in a tight headlike cluster of bracts above 2 larger, bright red bracts to 3 cm long, 4 cm wide with abruptly pointed tip, united at base; blooms all year. **Fruit** fleshy, bright blue to 2 cm long, 1 cm wide, 2-seeded; fruits all year. **Habitat:** Wet to moist forest understories, second growth, forest edges in evergreen regions. Altitude: Sea level to 1700 m. Conservation areas: CVC, GUA, HNO, LAC, LAP, OSA, PAC, TOR. **Range:** Mex–Brz and Bol. **Notes:** Much like *P. elata*, which is also common but not hairy. *Psychotria* is the largest genus in the family Rubiaceae, with approximately 117 species in Costa Rica.

■ *Warszewiczia coccinea* (pastora, pastora de montaña, zorillo bandera)
Family Rubiaceae

Shrub or tree 2–15 m tall, trunk irregular, twisted, bark smooth; stipules to 4 cm, 1 cm wide, triangular. **Leaves** opposite, stalk to 2.5 cm long, blade 20–36 cm long, 7–15 cm wide, elliptic, widest at or above middle, tip tapered, blunt to pointed, base blunt to pointed. **Flowers** red orange, radially symmetrical, tubular, to 0.5 cm long, petal lobes 5, to 0.4 cm long, pointed, calyx mostly small but 1 in each flower cluster with 1 greatly enlarged, bright red, leaf-shaped lobe to 10 cm long, 4 cm wide; inflorescence 20–80 cm long, spikelike, with flowers in dense clusters, along axis, each cluster with 1 enlarged bractlike calyx lobe; blooms all year, mostly Apr.–Sept. **Fruit** dry, woody, to 0.5 cm, splitting open to release numerous tiny seeds. **Habitat:** Understories of wet to moist, usually lowland, forests, second growth. Altitude: Sea level to 500 m rarely to 1600 m. Conservation areas: CVC, HNO, LAC, LAP, OSA, PAC, TOR. **Range:** Nic–Ven and Bol. **Notes:** This tree is unique for its long, red inflorescences. The only other species of *Warszewiczia* in Costa Rica is *W. uxpanapensis*.

■ *Allophylus occidentalis* (estanquillo)
Family Sapindaceae

Small tree or shrub to 10 m tall, stems slender, woolly-hairy when young. **Leaves** alternate, 3-parted, stalk to 6 cm long, leaflets almost stalkless, blades 5–25 cm long, 3–7 cm wide, elliptic to narrowly diamond-shaped, pointed at both ends, densely fine-hairy below, margin wavy toothed. **Flowers** white to yellow, very small, about 0.1 cm long, hairy, in spikelike clusters to 6 cm long; blooms as leaves expand, Apr. **Fruit** fleshy, yellow orange becoming red, to 0.6 cm wide, slightly hairy, 1 hairy seed; July–Oct. **Habitat:** Understories of wet to seasonally dry forests. Altitude: Pacific slope, sea level to 1400 m. Conservation Areas: ARE, GUA, LAP, PAC, TEM. **Range:** El Salv–Pan, Ven, DR. **Notes:** There are four species of *Allophylus* in Costa Rica.

129

■ *Quassia amara* (cuasia, hombrón, hombre grande)
Family Simaroubaceae

Shrub or small tree 2–5 m tall, rarely to 9 m. **Leaves** alternate, pinnately compound, about 30 cm long, 20 cm wide overall, midrib and leaf stem broadly winged, leaflets 3 or 5, the 3 near tip widely separated from 2 near base by winged midrib, leaflets stalkless, blades 5–16 cm long, 3–6 cm wide, elliptic, tapered at both ends, pale below. **Flowers** red outside, white inside, radially symmetrical, 5-parted, petals to 4.5 cm long, stamens longer than petals, anthers yellow; inflorescence of long clusters at ends of branches, flower stems pinkish; blooms and fruits most of the year. **Fruit** fleshy, black, oval, 1.5 cm, in groups of 4–5 on a broad red base, eaten by monkeys. **Habitat:** Moist to wet lowland forests; also cultivated for flowers and wood. Altitude: Sea level to 700 m. Conservation areas: GUA, HNO, LAC, OSA, PAC. **Range:** Mex–Ven. **Notes:** Used medicinally to reduce fevers and to treat diabetes. *Quassia amara* is the only species of this genus in Costa Rica.

■ *Herrania purpurea* (cacao de mico)
Family Sterculiaceae

Shrub or small tree 3–7 m tall, trunk unbranched, young stems densely hairy. **Leaves** alternate, stalk stout, to 40 cm, densely hairy, blade palmately compound, to 80 cm, leaflets, 5, blades to 53 cm long, 19 cm wide, lateral leaflets smaller, narrow, widest near apex, tip tapered, tapered to base, hairy below; deciduous. **Flowers** violet to purplish red, radially symmetrical, to 1.5 cm wide, rounded, petals 5, fleshy, hood-shaped with a slender appendage to 1 cm long, calyx deeply 3- to 4-parted, lobes broadly egg-shaped, longer than petals, hairy, more or less enclosing other flower parts; flowers borne on trunk; blooms and fruits on and off most of the year. **Fruit** fleshy, orange, 4–10 cm long about 4 cm wide, elliptical, broadly ribbed, like a small *Cacao* pod, covered with irritating hairs, seeds 1.5 cm long, covered with white, edible flesh. **Habitat:** Moist to wet lowland forest understories. Altitude: Sea level to 800 m. Conservation areas: HNO, LAC, OSA, PAC, TOR. **Range:** Nic–Col. **Notes:** This is the only species of *Herrania* in Costa Rica.

Quassia amara (above)

Herrania purpurea (below)

■ *Trema micrantha* (capulín, vara, jucó)
Family Ulmaceae

Tree or shrub usually less than 10 m tall, occasionally to 30 m, to 70 cm diameter in wet regions, older trees with small buttresses, bark slightly fissured, twigs hairy, sap unpleasantly pungent. **Leaves** alternate, in one plane on opposite sides of stem, stalk to 1 cm, blade 5–15 cm long, 2–5 cm wide, narrowly oblong-elliptic, tip tapered, long-pointed, base lobed, unequal, hairy, rough-textured above, veins palmate at base, pinnate above, margin usually finely toothed. **Flowers** white to greenish yellow, tiny, 5-parted, no petals, sepals about 0.1 cm long; inflorescences of small axillary cluster to 1.5 cm long; blooms all year, mostly Apr.–Aug. **Fruit** fleshy, orange to red, to 0.4 cm long, round, 1-seeded; eaten by birds; fruits all year, mostly May–Nov. **Habitat:** Wet to seasonally dry

forests, in open areas, a common pioneer species, secondary forests, roadsides. Altitude: Sea level to 2100 m. Conservation areas: ARE, CVC, GUA, HNO, LAC, LAP, OSA, PAC, TEM, TOR. **Range:** FL, Mex–Ven, Par and Arg, WI. **Notes:** *Trema integerrima* is the only other species of this genus. It is very similar but less common, and more often a canopy tree 10–25 m tall.

Trema micrantha (above)

Clerodendrum paniculatum (below)

■ *Clerodendrum paniculatum* (Java glory bower)
Family Verbenaceae

Shrub or woody herb 1–3 m tall, stems 4-sided. **Leaves** opposite, stalk to 30 cm long, blade 9–25 cm long, 12–30 cm wide, broadly egg- to heart-shaped, lower leaves often shallowly 5-lobed, lower surface velvety-hairy, white-scaly, tip pointed, base lobed, veins palmate at base, margin toothed. **Flowers** red orange to red, radially symmetrical, tubular, 5-parted, petal tube slender, to 2 cm, lobes spreading, 0.6 cm, calyx orange, about 1.3 cm long, lobes spreading; stamens 4, orange, about 3.5 cm long, longer than petals; style purple, longer than petal lobes; inflorescence of large, oppositely branched clusters to 45 cm long and wide, at tops of stems, stems reddish; blooms mostly Sept.–Nov. **Fruit** fleshy, blue green to black, small, enclosed by persistent calyx, 1-seeded. **Habitat:** Common garden plant in moist and wet regions. Altitude: Sea level to 200 m. Conservation areas: LAC, OSA, TOR. **Range:** Native to SE Asia. FL, Hon–Col, Africa. Invasive on some Pacific islands. **Notes:** There are six species of *Clerodendrum* in Costa Rica. Most have white flowers. None is apparently very common.

COLOR OF CONSPICUOUS PART YELLOW, ORANGE YELLOW

■ *Justicia aurea*
Family Acanthaceae

Shrub to 6 m, young stems 4-sided. **Leaves** opposite, stalk to 5.7 cm long, blade 12–40 cm long, 5.5–17 cm wide, egg-shaped to elliptic, pointed at both ends, margins variable. **Flowers** yellow, to 5.5 cm long, bilaterally symmetrical, petal tube 0.3 cm wide, lobes funnel-shaped, 2 lipped, upper lip 2-lobed, lower lip 3-lobed, bracts linear, about 1 cm long; inflorescence of large, branched clusters at ends of stems; blooms all year. **Fruit** dry, club-shaped, 4 seeds. **Habitat:** Cultivated and wild, in most wet regions. Altitude: 100–2000 m. Conservation areas: ARE, CVC, GUA, LAP, PAC. **Range:** Mex–Pan.

■ *Allamanda cathartica*
Family Apocynaceae

Arching, long-branched shrub or short woody vine, sap milky. **Leaves** opposite or in whorls of 4, stalk to 0.5 cm long, blade 8–16 cm long, 3–6 cm wide, narrow, pointed at both ends. **Flowers** bright yellow, radially symmetrical, showy, 8–12 cm wide, tube to 3.5 cm long, petal lobes to 3.5 cm long, rounded, overlapping; blooms most of the year. **Fruit** dry, spiny to 8 cm long, green, becoming brown and splitting open to release flat brown seeds. **Habitat:** Widely cultivated ornamental, also escaped, sometimes along river margins or canals. Altitude: Sea level to 1100 m, mostly below 200 m. Conservation areas: CVC, LAC, OSA, PAC, TOR. **Range:** E S Amer. Naturalized throughout much of the tropics. Has become invasive in Australia and some Pacific islands. **Notes:** This is the only species of *Allamanda* in Costa Rica.

Justicia aurea (above)

Allamanda cathartica (below)

■ *Stemmadenia donnell-smithii* (huevos de caballo,
cojón de chancho, bajarro)
Family Apocynaceae

Tree or shrub 2–14 m tall, mostly less than 10 m, sap milky.
Leaves opposite, 4–18 cm long, 2–5.5 cm wide, elliptic, tip
long-pointed, tapered to base, tufts of hairs in the vein axils
below. **Flowers** yellow to cream, radially symmetrical, tubular, to 6 cm long, petal lobes overlapping; in small clusters of
1–4 at ends of branches, fragrant; blooms and fruits most of
the year. **Fruit** woody, in pairs, 5–9 cm (about same size as
leaves), rounded with pointed tips, thick, green-brown, husk
splits open to reveal seeds embedded in red orange flesh.
Many birds eat the nutritious, oily flesh (aril) and disperse
the seeds, Nov.–Mar. **Habitat:** Wet to seasonally dry forests.
Altitude: Sea level to 1100 m. most often below 500 m. Conservation areas: ARE, GUA, LAC, LAP, OSA, PAC, TEM,
TOR. **Range:** Mex–Pan. **Notes:** There are 7 species of *Stemmadenia* in Costa Rica, all are quite similar.

133

■ *Tabernaemontana longipes* (cojón, cachitos)
Family Apocynaceae

Understory tree to 3–10 m tall, 10 cm diameter, sap milky, sticky, bark smooth, gray, twigs tan, slender. **Leaves** opposite, stalk 2 cm, blade 5–28 cm long, 2–9 cm wide, elliptic, tip abruptly long-pointed, base tapered, veins pinnate, curved upward to margin. **Flowers** yellow-cream or white, radially symmetrical, tubular, about 1.5 cm long, 2 cm across top, petal lobes widely spreading in "pin-wheel" pattern, fragrant; inflorescence of branched clusters to 35 cm long on an elongated stalk; blooms most of the year. **Fruit** woody, bright yellow pods in pairs, each 2.5–4.5 cm long, fused at bases, with pointed, up-curved tips, splitting along base to reveal seeds about 1.5 cm, covered by bright orange fleshy coat. **Habitat:** Moist to wet forests. Altitude: Sea level to 2500 m Conservation areas: ARE, GUA, LAC, LAP, OSA, PAC, TEM, TOR. **Range:** Nic–Col. **Notes:** This is the most common, widespread of the four species of *Tabernaemontana* in Costa Rica.

■ *Thevetia ovata* (chirca)
Family Apocynaceae

Shrub or small tree to 3–5 m, trunk about 15 cm diameter, sap white, sticky, poisonous, bark reddish with conspicuous horizontal bands of small lenticels. **Leaves** alternate, 5–18 cm long, 2–6 cm wide, narrow and long (wider than those of *T. peruviana*), tip rounded with a small point, tapered to base, secondary veins numerous, parallel, at right angles to midrib. **Flowers** bright yellow, radially symmetrical, showy, about 8 cm long, 5 cm wide, tubular, trumpet-shaped, 5 petal lobes broad, overlapping, fragrant, anthers white; blooms and fruits all year. **Fruit** dark reddish, to 3.5 cm long, becoming brown when mature, wider than long. **Habitat:** Open areas and secondary woodlands, often near beaches and in rocky areas. Altitude: Northern Pacific lowlands, sea level to 400 m. Conservation areas: GUA, PAC, TEM. **Range:** Mex–CR. **Notes:** There are four species of *Thevetia* in Costa Rica, *T. ovata* is the most common but *T. peruviana*, a nonnative, is the most commonly cultivated.

■ *Lasianthaea fruticosa* (quitirrí, San Rafael, ira)
Family Asteraceae

Shrub or small tree to 5 m tall, branches slender, bark gray brown, ridged across nodes. **Leaves** opposite, stalk to 0.9 cm long, blade to 14 cm long, egg-shaped, tip long-pointed, base blunt, rough-textured above, softly hairy below, 3 major veins palmate at base, margin toothed. **Flowers** yellow, ray flowers few, to 2 cm long, spatula-shaped, notched at tip, disk about 0.3 cm wide, disk flowers yellow, numerous, anthers dark, flower heads about 2.5 cm wide including rays, to 1 cm long, basal bracts about as long as disk flowers, overlapping; inflorescence of branched, umbrella-shaped clusters; blooms most of the year, especially Aug.–Jan. **Fruit** dry, 1-seeded, shiny, black, 0.5 cm, long, with a tuft of bristles. **Habitat:** Wet to

seasonally dry regions, often along rivers, second growth, edges. Altitude: Sea level to 1800 m. Conservation areas: ARE, CVC, GUA, LAC, LAP, PAC, TEM. **Range:** Mex–Pan, introduced in N Ven. **Notes:** This is the only species of *Lasianthaea* in Costa Rica.

■ *Senecio cooperi*
Family Asteraceae

Coarse shrub or large woody herb, 1–3 m tall, branches and stems of inflorescence rough, with dark-tipped hairs. **Leaves** alternate, stalk about half as long as blade, winged, margin irregularly wavy, base clasping stem, blade 10–40 cm long, 5–20 cm wide, elliptic, larger leaves often contracted in middle, lobed near base, margin toothed, upper leaves stalkless, becoming narrow bracts to 20 cm long. **Flowers** yellow, fragrant, rays 5–8, 1 cm long, disk flowers 10–18, flower heads cylindrical, bract-covered floral base to 1 cm long, bracts in 1 row; Inflorescence large, flat-topped, branched from top of stem; blooms most of the year. **Fruit** dry, 1-seeded, with a tuft of white hairs. **Habitat:** Open sites in mountains. Altitude: 1100–2100 m. Conservation areas: ARE, CVC, LAC, LAP, PAC. **Range:** S Nic–N Pan. **Notes:** There are about 28 species of *Senecio* in Costa Rica. Most have yellow to orange flowers, a few have white.

■ *Tecoma stans*
Family Bignoniaceae
Small tree or shrub, to 10 m tall, 25 cm diameter, bark dark, ridged. **Leaves** alternate, pinnate, stalk 1–9 cm long, leaflets 3–9, 3–1 cm long, 1–6 cm wide, egg-shaped, tip tapered to point, margins toothed. **Flowers** yellow with reddish lines inside, slightly bilaterally symmetrical, tubular, to 5 cm long, trumpet-shaped, fragrant, showy, petal lobes 5, to 1.5 cm long, slightly unequal; inflorescence of unbranched clusters at ends of twigs; blooms Sept.– May. **Fruit** dry, narrow pods to 20 cm long, seeds winged. **Habitat:** Moist or sometimes seasonally dry regions, roadsides, open areas; also widely cultivated. Altitude: Pacific slope, 50–1050 m. Conservation areas: ARE, OSA, PAC, TEM. **Range:** FL, TX–N Arg. **Notes:** This is the only species of *Tecoma* in Costa Rica.

■ *Buddleja nitida* (Salvia)
Family Buddlejaceae
Tree or shrub to 6 m tall, 40 cm diameter, young bark silvery. **Leaves** opposite, 4–12 cm long, 1–3 cm wide, lance-shaped, tip pointed, base blunt, dark bluish-green above, white-woolly below. **Flowers** dark yellow, radially symmetrical, 0.2–0.4 cm wide, 4-parted; inflorescence of dense clusters at ends of branches; blooms on and off most of the year. **Fruit** dry, 0.4–0.5 cm wide. **Habitat:** Open sites and shrubby growth, at high elevations. Altitude: 2200–3700 m. Conservation areas: CVC, LAP, PAC. Seen in Volcán Irazú N.P. **Range:** SE N Amer, Mex–Pan, W S Amer–Bol. **Notes:** There are four species of *Buddleja* in Costa Rica. *Buddleja* is often included with the Family *Loganiaceae*.

■ *Carica papaya* (papaya)
Family Caricaceae

Unbranched tree to 6 m, trunk soft, hollow, covered by persistent leaf scars; sap milky. **Leaves** alternate, blade to 70 cm long, deeply palmately 5–7-lobed, each lobe pinnately divided. **Flowers** dull yellow, small, male and female flowers usually on separate trees, male flowers in dangling clusters to 1 m long; female flowers solitary or few, to 5 cm, next to trunk; blooms July–Jan. **Fruit** fleshy, edible, to 50 cm long, usually oblong, turning yellow, flesh orange, seeds numerous, small round black; fruits Sept.–Jan. **Habitat:** Widely cultivated for fruit, as a garden plant or commercial crop, but also wild in seasonally dry to moist forests, in second growth. Altitude: Wild plants mostly on the Pacific slope, sea level to 800 m. Conservation areas: GUA, OSA, PAC, TEM. **Range:** Tropical Americas. **Notes:** commonly seen in markets. Probably native to Mexico and Central America. Dry sap is the source of meat tenderizer, papain. There are three other species of *Carica* in Costa Rica.

■ *Cochlospermum vitifolium* (poro-poro, broó, silk tree)
Family Cochlospermaceae

Tree 3–12 m tall, trunk to 30 cm or more in diameter, branches few, young twigs densely hairy. **Leaves** alternate, 10–30 cm long and wide, deeply 5–7 palmately lobed, lobe tips tapered, veins conspicuous, margins toothed, deciduous in seasonally dry regions, retains foliage in moist regions. **Flowers** bright yellow, radially symmetrical, showy, 8–12 cm wide, 5 petals, tips notched, stamens numerous; blooms during dry season, Dec.–Feb., pollinated by bees. **Fruit** reddish, becoming dry, egg-shaped to rounded, 5–10 cm long, 3- to 5-parted, splitting open to release numerous seeds buried in cottony fibers, wind dispersed; fruits Jan.–Apr. **Habitat:** Moist to seasonally dry forests, second growth, open sites. Occasionally planted as an ornamental. Altitude: Sea level to 700 m, mostly in the Pacific lowlands below 400 m. Conservation areas: GUA, HNO, LAP, OSA, PAC, TEM. **Range:** Mex–N S Amer. **Notes:** This is the only species of *Cochlospermum* in Costa Rica.

◼ *Coriaria ruscifolia (C. thymifolia)*
Family Coriariaceae

Arching, slender shrub 1–3 m tall, feathery looking, stems opposite, ribbed, leafy branches regularly sized, shorter toward ends of main stems, appearing frondlike, or like pinnate leaves. **Leaves** opposite, all in one plane, little or no stalk, blade about 1–2 cm long, narrowly oblong, tip rounded to pointed, pale green, veins palmate, margins smooth. **Flowers** yellow and dark red, 0.2 cm long, radially symmetrical

with 5 sepals and 5 smaller, fleshy petals; inflorescences of unbranched, dangling clusters below leafy branches; blooms and fruits most of the year. **Fruit** small, seedlike surrounded by fleshy, enlarged petals, red becoming black; in clusters about 10 cm long; eaten by birds. **Habitat:** Mountains, in partial shade or open sites, roadsides, second growth. Altitude: 1700–3300 m. Conservation areas: CVC, LAC, LAP, PAC. **Range:** CR, Pr. **Notes:** This is the only species of *Coriaria* in Costa Rica.

◼ *Vaccinium poasanum*
Family Ericaceae

Shrub or small tree, 2–5 m tall, trunk large, complex, crooked, with flaky, gray bark, new growth reddish, slender. **Leaves** alternate, stalk to 0.4 cm, blade 3–8 cm long, 3–4 cm wide, egg-shaped, tip pointed, base blunt, stiff, leathery, dark green shiny above with pale net veins, primary veins 3–5, palmate at base, new leaves pinkish-bronze. **Flowers** pale greenish white to greenish yellow, tubular, radially symmetrical, cylindrical, about 1 cm long, less than 1 cm wide, petal lobes 5, sometimes with a red rim, stamens 10, gold-yellow, calyx about 0.5 cm long, greenish-red. **Fruit** fleshy, reddish to whitish, translucent, turning dark purple, about 1 cm, top depressed, crowned by old calyx lobes, seeds white; blooms and fruits all year. **Habitat:** Mountain forests and open sites. Altitude: 700–3100 m, mostly above 1500 m. Conservation areas: ARE, CVC, GUA, LAC, LAP, PAC. Seen at V. Poás N.P. **Range:** Gua–W Pan.

■ *Croton draco* (targuá colorado)
Family Euphorbiaceae

Small tree, 2–15 m tall, often rather flat-topped, stems pale, scaly-hairy. **Leaves** mostly alternate, sometimes opposite, near ends of twigs, stalk 4–14 cm long, densely scaly-hairy, with several disk-shaped protuberances near base of blade, blade 11–26 cm long, 6–16 cm wide, egg- to heart-shaped, tip gradually narrowed to long point, base blunt to lobed, hairy on both sides, pale below, woolly-hairy, veins tan-hairy, dying leaves orange yellow, hanging below green leaves. **Flowers** yellowish, small, radially symmetrical, males and female separate, male flowers to 0.6 cm wide, stamens numerous, longer than petals, female flowers smaller, inflorescences of narrow clusters 7–35 cm long; blooms all year. **Fruit** dry, yellowish, scaly-hairy, to 0.6 cm long, 0.8 cm wide, enclosed in old sepals, seeds to 0.5 cm long. **Habitat:** Wet to seasonally dry regions in second growth and open sites, often along roadsides. Common throughout the Central Valley region. Altitude: 125–2500 m, usually above 500 m on the Pacific slope. Conservation areas: ARE, CVC, LAC, LAP, OSA, PAC, TEM. **Range:** S Mex, Gua–Col. **Notes:** There are about 41 species of Croton in Costa Rica. Like C. *draco*, many have leaves that turn orange yellow in age.

■ *Hippomane mancinella*
(manzanillo de playa, manchineel)
Family Euphorbiaceae

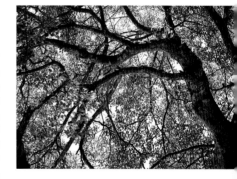

Tree 2–18 m tall, most often under 10 m, 80 cm diameter, often leaning, habit irregular, broad-crowned, sometimes shrubby, bark pale brown, finely fissured, sap milky, very toxic, *all parts toxic-irritating*. **Leaves** alternate, stalk to 4 cm long with a dark pit at top, blade 3–8 cm long, 2–5 cm wide, egg-shaped, tip pointed to blunt, base blunt to slightly lobed, surface medium green, smooth, shiny, midrib pale, margin very finely toothed. **Flowers** cream white, very small, sexes separate on same tree; inflorescences spikelike, to 7 cm long, of small dense clusters of flowers from a central axis; Mar.–May, Sept.–Dec. **Fruit** fleshy, pale yellow, *poisonous*,

rounded, to 2.5 cm long and wide with 1 woody 5-parted nutlike brown seed; fruit present most of the year. **Habitat:** Mostly along the coast, on beaches above high tide line. Altitude: Pacific coast, sea level to 100 m. Conservation areas: GUA, OSA, PAC, TEM. **Range:** FL, Mex–N S Amer, WI. **Notes:** Sap can cause blindness if gotten into eyes, causes burns after contact with skin. This is the only species of *Hippomane* in Costa Rica. Common in Manuel Antonio N.P. Do *not* sit under this tree.

■ *Parkinsonia aculeata* (espino, palo verde, retamola)
Family Fabaceae/Caesalpinioideae

Large shrub or small tree, 2–8 m tall, much-branched, often multistemmed, bark flaky, brown, branches arching almost to ground, with 2–3 small thorns at each node, twigs green. **Leaves** alternate, appearing simple and linear but these are leaflets of once or twice evenly pinnate leaves; pinnae 1–3 pairs on a short midrib (rachis), 20–30 cm long, 0.4 cm wide, flat, leathery, shiny green, leaflets, when present, up to 50 pairs, very small, flat, egg-shaped about 0.3 cm long, 0.1 cm wide along margins of pinnae. **Flowers** yellow, slightly bilaterally symmetrical, fragrant, 2 cm wide, 5 petals with red markings; inflorescence of narrow, unbranched clusters, to 20 cm long, amid leaves; probably flowers on and off most of the year. **Fruit** dry, pods 3–15 cm long, 0.7 cm wide, constricted between seeds. **Habitat:** Seasonally dry regions, in open sites. Also grown as an ornamental. Altitude: Pacific lowlands, sea level to 100 m. Conservation areas: TEM. Common in Palo Verde N.P., near the marsh. **Range:** Native to the S temperate and tropical Americas, site uncertain; widely cultivated and naturalized. Invasive on some Hawaiian islands. **Notes:** This is the only species of *Parkinsonia* in Costa Rica.

■ *Senna pallida (Cassia biflora)* (abejoncillo)
Family Fabaceae/Caesalpinioideae

Small shrub, to 3.5 m tall, stems slender, gray. **Leaves** alternate, stalk bears 2 orange dots, leaf and leaflet stems swollen at their bases, blade evenly pinnate, 5–6 cm long, leaflets 6–7 pairs, 2–3 cm long, about 1.5 cm wide, dull blue green, widest near apex, tip and base rounded, veins rather obscure. **Flowers** bright yellow, about 3 cm wide, slightly bilaterally symmetrical, 5 petals, fragile; flowers in pairs, on a stalk to 2 cm long; blooms Dec.–May, pollinated by bees. **Fruit** dry, flattened pods, 6–8 cm long, 0.3–0.5 cm wide, repeated "x" pattern along surface; ripening during dry season, splitting open to release seeds under parent plant. **Habitat:** Moist to seasonally dry regions, in open sites along roadsides, and in pastures. Altitude: Sea level to 1200 m, mostly on the Pacific slope. Conservation areas: ARE, CVC, GUA, TEM. **Range:** S Mex–Pr, Bh. **Notes:** There are about 20 species of *Senna* in Costa Rica.

Senna papillosa
Family Fabaceae/Caesalpinioideae

Shrub or small tree to 5 m, finely hairy all over, branches zigzag from node to node near ends. **Leaves** alternate, pinnate, leaflets 4, to 24 cm long, 9 cm wide, lower pair smaller than upper, tips tapered, bases blunt, small dots or bumps on stem between leaflet pairs. **Flowers** dull yellow orange, about 5 cm wide, slightly bilaterally symmetrical, 5 petals, rounded with narrow bases, stamens 7; inflorescence of clusters near ends of branches, about 20 cm long and wide; blooms Apr.–Dec. **Fruit** dry pods, to

30 cm long, 1 cm wide, cylindrical, splitting open to release seeds. **Habitat:** Wet to moist regions in second growth forest and open sites, pastures, roadsides. Altitude: Sea level to 1700 m. Conservation areas: ARE, CVC, GUA, HNO, LAC, LAP, OSA, PAC, TOR. **Range:** S Mex–NE S Amer.

Senna reticulata (abejón, saragundí)
Family Fabaceae/Caesalpinioideae

Small tree or shrub 2–8 m tall, young stems green, pithy, sometimes many together. **Leaves** alternate, stalk orange-scaly, 4–13 cm long, blade evenly pinnate, 25–70 cm long, main midrib orange-scaly, leaf folding lengthwise when disturbed, leaflets 7–13 pairs, upper leaflets the largest, blades 7–18 cm long, 3–7cm wide, oblong, tip and base rounded, dull pale green above, finely hairy both sides, margin finely orange-scaly. **Flowers** yellow with dark veins, about 3 cm wide, petals 5, 1.5–2 cm long, tips rounded, curling inward, flower buds with taillike yellow bract 2 cm long; inflorescence of unbranched clusters (racemes) at or near ends of branches; blooms Sept.–Mar. **Fruit** dry, pods flattened, dark, shiny, 10–16 cm long, about 1.5 cm wide, margin ribbed, pod constricted between numerous, narrow seeds, breaking apart across constrictions at maturity. **Habitat:** Moist to wet regions,

sometimes open swampy, disturbed sites. Altitude: Sea Level to 1800 m, mostly below 500 m. Conservation areas: CVC, HNO, LAC, OSA, PAC TOR. **Range:** S Mex–coastal Ec and Amazonia. **Notes:** Planted for use as a medicinal. Very similar to *Senna alata*, an ornamental shrub that has pods winged along the edges.

■ *Cajanus cajan* (gandul, timbolillo, frijol de palo, pigeon pea, gungu bean)
Family Fabaceae/Faboideae

Cultivated shrub, to 4 m tall, bark dark with greenish patches, newer growth hairy. **Leaves** alternate, stalk 1 cm, blade 3-parted, leaflets with stalks to 1 cm long, blades 4–15 cm long, 2–6 cm wide, lance-shaped to elliptic, tips pointed, base wedge-shaped, surface velvety-hairy, dull blue green above, pale gray green below. **Flowers** yellow and orange, bean-flower-shaped, to 1.5 cm long and wide; inflorescences to 9 cm long; seen blooms Feb. **Fruit** becoming dry, pods 6–8 cm long, to 1.4 cm wide, at first green mottled with brown, finely hairy, flattened, 2–9 seeded. **Habitat:** Cultivated. Altitude: Garden plant, apparently not escaping. LAC. **Range:** Native to India or possibly Africa; widely cultivated and escaped. Invasive on some Pacific islands. **Notes:** Plant is said to die if fruit is not picked. Beans are edible, leaves used for tea to treat sore throats.

■ *Diphysa americana* (*D. robinoides*)
(cacique, guachipelín)
Family Fabaceae/Faboideae

Tree, 4–15 m; trunk often crooked, much-branched, bark rough, flaking, with deep, wide furrows and ridges. **Leaves** alternate, pinnate, 8–14 cm long, 9–21 leaflets, blades 2–3.5 cm long, 0.5–1 cm wide, oval, rounded at both ends, thin, dark, dull bluish green above, whitish below. **Flowers** yellow, bean-flower-shaped, small, about 1 cm long, 1.6 cm wide, top petal (banner) curled back, tip notched; inflorescence of branched clusters to 7 cm long; blooms Jan., Mar., Nov. **Fruit** dry, pods tan, inflated, thin-walled, 5–8 cm long, 1–2 cm wide; fruit present in Apr. **Habitat:** Moist to wet regions, open sites, roadsides. Also used as street trees and living fences. Altitude: Sea level to 1900 m. Conservation areas: ARE, CVC, GUA, OSA, PAC. **Range:** Mex–Pan. **Notes:** There are three species of *Diphysa* in Costa Rica.

■ *Ulex europaeus* (gorse) Fabaceae/Faboideae

Shrub to 2 m tall, copiously branched, branches spine-tipped. **Leaves** alternate, linear, spinelike, 0.5–1.5 cm long, numerous, crowded. **Flowers** bright yellow, about 2 cm long, bilaterally symmetrical, bean-flower-shaped, sepals hairy, about 1.5 cm; blooms Mar.–May. **Fruit** dry pod, hairy, 1–2 cm long with 2–4 seeds. **Habitat:** High elevations in open sites. Altitude: 2500–2700 m. Conservation areas: CVC. **Range:** Native to W Europe. Widely introduced worldwide. **Notes:** This is the only species of *Ulex* in Costa Rica.

■ *Acacia collinsii* (cornizuelo, bull-thorn acacia) Family Fabaceae/Mimosoideae

Small tree to 10 m tall, often multistemmed, bark gray, paired thorns, about 1.5 cm long, 0.5 cm wide, bases fused, ants live in hollowed out thorns. **Leaves** alternate, twice evenly pinnate, stalk with 4–5 tiny, cuplike glands along base, pinnae 4–12 pairs, about 15 cm long and wide, feathery, mostly deciduous during dry season, leaflets 12–24 pairs, about 0.8 cm long, 0.2 cm wide. New leaves tipped by small fleshy, oblong yellowish appendages (Beltian bodies) that provide food for one of several protective "Acacia ants" (*Pseudomyrmex ferruginea* and *P. nigocincta,* red ants, and *P. belti,* a black ant). The ants attack anything that touches the plant and often clear an area around small trees of all other vegetation. **Flowers** bright yellow, minute, in dense clusters about 3 cm long, 0.3 cm wide; blooms Aug.–Mar. **Fruit** dry, pods often in whorled clusters, dark, about 2.5 cm long, 1 cm wide, splitting along base to reveal seeds with bright yellow fleshy coats (arils). **Habitat:** Moist to seasonally dry regions, in open sites, second growth. Altitude: Pacific slope, sea level to 1400 m, mostly below 100 m. Conservation areas: GUA, PAC, TEM. **Range:** SE Mex–NE Col. **Notes:** See Costa Rican Natural History (Janzen 1983).

Acacia ants tending Beltian bodies

Ground clearing around small Acacia tree

143

▨ *Acacia farnesiana* (espino blanco, aromo macho)
Family Fabaceae/Mimosoideae

Multistemmed shrub to about 5 m tall, bark densely speck-led with lenticels, spines paired at nodes, very thin, to 3 cm long. **Leaves** alternate, twice evenly pinnate, about 5 cm long, 4 cm wide, very fine, 1 to several at each node, stalk about 0.7 cm, hairy, with tiny cuplike glands, pinnae 4–6 pairs, about 2 cm long, 0.8 cm wide, leaflets 10–20 pairs per pinna, 0.4 cm long, 0.1 cm wide, gray green. **Flowers** yellow, minute, in small, fuzzy, ball-shaped clusters about 0.8 cm wide, fragrant; blooms Sept.–Apr. **Fruit** dry, pods, cylindrical, 6–7 cm long, 1 cm wide, solitary to several in a whorl, slightly constricted between seeds, pod sap very sticky, pulp slightly sweet; about 7 seeds per pod. **Habitat:** Seasonally dry scrub to moist woodlands, old pastures; also cultivated. Altitude: Northern Pacific lowlands sea level to 700 m, mostly below 400 m. Conservation areas: GUA, TEM. **Range:** US–Brz and Pr. Widely introduced in the Old World. **Notes:** Flowers used to make perfume. There are about 11 species of Acacia in Costa Rica.

▨ *Besleria formosa*
Family Gesneriaceae

Shrub, to 3 m, usually less, stems slender, erect to arching. **Leaves** opposite, stalk to 5 cm long, blade 3–13 cm long, 2–5 cm wide, elliptic, tip long-pointed, base blunt, smooth, dark green, shining, margin sometimes sparsely toothed. **Flowers** orange, to 1.5 cm long, 0.6 cm wide, tubular, bilaterally symmetrical, fleshy, petal lobes short, grouped with 2 above, 3 below, calyx cream white to pale green, fleshy, inflorescence of small axillary clusters 1–3; usually blooms 1 at a time; blooms on an off most of the year, especially Feb.–Apr. **Fruit** fleshy, white, to 0.8 cm with black tip, surrounded by persistent calyx; seeds minute. **Habitat:** Wet mountain forest understories. Altitude: 1000–2400 m, mostly above 1700 m. Conservation areas: CVC, LAC, LAP. **Range:** CR, Pan. **Notes:** There are 15 species of *Besleria* in Costa Rica.

144

▩ *Hypericum costaricense* (cimarrón)
Family Hypericaceae

Small shrub, 0.15–1 m tall, much-branched. **Leaves** opposite, needlelike, 0.2–0.4 cm long, to 0.1 cm wide, flattened
against stems, tip pointed. **Flowers** bright yellow,
radially symmetrical, about 1.5 cm diameter, petals about 0.6 cm long, styles shorter than stamens;
blooms most of the year. Pollinated by the bumble
bee *Bombus ephippiatus*. **Fruit** dry, to 0.5 cm long,
broadly egg-shaped, shorter than sepals. **Habitat:**
High elevations, sometimes dominating dry, windy,
open sites. Altitude: 2400–3800 m. Conservation
areas: LAC, LAP, PAC. Common, with *H. irazuense*, at Cerro de la Muerte. **Range:** CR. **Notes:** *H.
pratense* is also fairly common and is found down to
1100 m.

▩ *Hypericum irazuense* (culandro,
St. John's-wort) Family Hypericaceae

Shrub to 4 m, many-branched. **Leaves** opposite,
about 0.3 cm long, 0.2 cm wide, blue green, stiff,
tip pointed; in 4 ranks along stem, each pair at right
angles to the next, crowded at ends of stems, giving stem a sharply 4-angled appearance. **Flowers**
bright yellow, showy, radially symmetrical, about
3 cm wide, 5 petals, stamens numerous, style longer
than stamens, solitary at ends of stems; blooms most
of the year. Pollinated by the bumble bee *Bombus
ephippiatus*. **Fruit** dry. **Habitat:** High mountains in
open areas. Altitude: 2200–3800 m. Conservation
areas: CVC, LAC, LAP, PAC. **Range:** CR. **Notes:** Similar
to *Hypericum strictum* which has smaller leaves lying flat
against stems, and grows in drier, sites. There are six species
of *Hypericum* in Costa Rica.

145

■ *Vismia baccifera* (achotillo, achiote tigre)
Family Hypericaceae
Shrub to 10 m, multistemmed, branches long, slender, drooping, young parts densely rusty-hairy, sap yellow to bright
orange, drying red. **Leaves** opposite, stalk to 2.5 cm long,
blade 7–17 cm long, 3–10 cm wide, egg-shaped, tip pointed,
base blunt, dark green above, tan-hairy below sprinkled with
tiny, red, translucent dots, veins loop-connected along margin. **Flowers** dull orange to orange-striped outside, whitish-
hairy inside, radially symmetrical, to 2.5 cm wide, 5-parted,
petals notched at top, calyx rusty-scaly, stamens feathery,
fan-shaped, stigma yellow; inflorescence of clusters to 8 cm
at ends of branches; blooms most of the year. **Fruit** fleshy,
green, smooth, with numerous small seeds, sepals and petals persistent. **Habitat:** Wet and moist forests in open sites,
edges. Altitude: Sea level to 2000 m. Conservation
areas: ARE, CVC, GUA, HNO, LAC, LAP, OSA,
PAC, TOR. **Range:** S Mex–S Col and Ven. **Notes:**
There are six species of *Vismia* in Costa Rica, *V. baccifera* and *V. billbergiana* are the most common and
are quite similar.

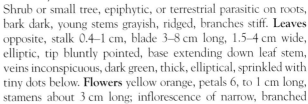

■ *Gaiadendron punctatum*
Family Loranthaceae
Shrub or small tree, epiphytic, or terrestrial parasitic on roots,
bark dark, young stems grayish, ridged, branches stiff. **Leaves**
opposite, stalk 0.4–1 cm, blade 3–8 cm long, 1.5–4 cm wide,
elliptic, tip bluntly pointed, base extending down leaf stem,
veins inconspicuous, dark green, thick, elliptical, sprinkled with
tiny dots below. **Flowers** yellow orange, petals 6, to 1 cm long,
stamens about 3 cm long; inflorescence of narrow, branched
clusters at ends of stems. Visited by hummingbirds and
bumblebees; blooms and fruits most of the year. **Fruit**
fleshy, orange, with dot at top, to 1 cm long, flesh juicy,
yellow, sweet, eaten by birds, seed pale, large. **Habitat:**
Wet mountain forests. Altitude: 900–3700 m, most
often above 2000 m. Conservation areas: ARE, CVC,
GUA, LAC, LAP, PAC **Range:** Nic–Bol. **Notes:** This
is the only species of *Gaiadendron* in Costa Rica. Narrow, bright orange flowers very conspicuous.

■ *Byrsonima crassifolia* (nance, tsiki, shoemaker's tree)
Family Malpighiaceae

Tree to 7 m (rarely to 13 m), trunk to 30 cm diameter, often multistemmed, branching low, gnarled or twisted, bark fissured, horizontally creased, stems with prominent leaf scars, conspicuous lenticels, young stems densely hairy. **Leaves** opposite, stalk to 1 cm long, blade 7–14 cm long, 3–8 cm wide, elliptic, pointed to blunt at both ends, leathery, new leaves densely rusty-hairy below, old leaves turning orange red, deciduous during dry season. **Flowers** bright yellow turning red orange with age, about 2 cm wide, radially symmetrical, petals 5, spoon-shaped, margins ruffled, stamens whitish; inflorescence of spikelike clusters to 20 cm long at ends of twigs; blooms Jan.–Sept. **Fruit** fleshy, yellow to reddish, to 2 cm wide, rounded, 1–3 seeds, dispersed by birds. Edible, also used to make alcoholic beverages. **Habitat:** Wet to seasonally dry regions in open sites, shrub-lands, second growth forests. Altitude: Sea level to 1400 m. Conservation areas: GUA, HNO, LAC, LAP, OSA, PAC, TEM, TOR. **Range:** Mex–Par, WI. **Notes:** There are three species of *Byrsonima* in Costa Rica, *B. crispa* is also common, it is a larger tree, found in wet regions.

■ *Talipariti tiliaceum* var. *pernambucense (Hibiscus tiliaceus)* (majagua, alú, seabiscus, Hibiscus tree)
Family Malvaceae

Tree or shrub 2–13 m tall, nodes ringed by stipule scars. **Leaves** alternate, stalk to 14 cm long, blade to 20 cm long and wide, broadly heart-shaped, tip pointed, base lobed, whitish-hairy below, major veins palmate. **Flowers** yellow orange, 5–8 cm long, never fully expanding, solitary, central column of stamens shorter than petals; blooms most of the year. **Fruit** dry, splitting into 5 sections to disperse seeds. **Habitat:** beaches, mangrove swamps. Altitude: Sea level to 300 m, mostly below 50 m. Conservation areas: GUA, ICO, LAC, OSA, TEM, TOR. **Range:** FL, Mex–Bol, WI, Africa, Asia. **Notes:** This is the only species of *Talipariti* in Costa Rica; its round, heart-shaped leaves, yellow flowers and shoreline habitat are distinctive.

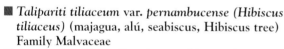

147

■ *Psidium friedrichsthalianum* (cas, cas ácido)
Family Myrtaceae

Small trees to 9 m tall, bark thin mottled tan and reddish brown, peeling in patches, twigs 4-ribbed. **Leaves** opposite, stalks to 0.6 cm long, blade 4–12 cm long, 3–5 cm wide, elliptic to oblong, tip pointed, base rounded, surface smooth, lateral veins about 8 pairs, inconspicuous above. **Flowers** white, petals 5, round, 1–1.5 cm long, stamens numerous, calyx 2–3-lobed, 1 cm long; blooms and fruits Oct.–Feb. **Fruit** fleshy, yellow, round, 3–6 cm wide, crowned by old calyx lobes, flesh white, acidic tasting, seeds numerous. **Habitat:** Wet forests, second growth, cultivated and wild. Altitude: Sea level to 1100 m. Conservation areas: CVC, OSA. **Range:** S Mex–Col. **Notes:** Apparently more common in home gardens than in the wild.

■ *Psidium guajava* (guava)
Family Myrtaceae

Shrub or small tree to 8 m, trunk to 25 cm diameter, bark mottled pale reddish brown, patchy, peeling, young parts hairy. **Leaves** opposite, stalk 0.5 cm, blade elliptic, 7–12 cm long, 4–6 cm wide, sprinkled with tiny, translucent dots, tip pointed to blunt, base blunt, lateral veins conspicuous, 12 or more pairs, raised below, often impressed above. **Flowers** white, to 7 cm wide, radially symmetrical, 5 petals 1.5–2 cm long, egg-shaped, stamens numerous, about as long as petals; blooms Jan.–July. **Fruit** fleshy, becoming yellow outside, 3 to 6 cm diameter, fragrant, edible, sepals persistent as a crown, flesh pinkish, eaten by monkeys, seeds numerous; fruit present most of the year. **Habitat:** Widely cultivated for fruit, escaped into natural areas; also wild in wet to seasonally dry forests, second growth, disturbed sites. Altitude: Sea level to 1700 m. Conservation areas: ARE, CVC, LAC, LAP, OSA, PAC, TEM, TOR. **Range:** FL, LA, Mex–Ven and Arg, WI. Naturalized and invasive in S Africa, Australia and some Pacific islands. **Notes:** There are nine species of *Psidium* in Costa Rica.

Psidium guajava (below)

Psidium friedrichsthalianum (above)

■ *Ouratea lucens (O. nitida)*
Family Ochnaceae

Shrub or small tree to 8 m tall, bark dark brown with yellowish lenticels, twigs crooked, brown. **Leaves** alternate, stalk about 1 cm long, swollen, blade 5–22 cm long, 2–7 cm wide, lance-shaped to elliptic, widest near middle or base, tip tapered, base blunt, secondary veins obscure, margin finely toothed. **Flowers** bright yellow, about 2 cm, radially symmetrical, petals 5, widest near apex, tip notched, stamens about 10, with pointed tips, in a crownlike arrangement surrounding pistil, ovary 5-lobed above petal bases; accompanied by bracts about 1 cm long; inflorescence of clusters to 14 cm long; blooms Nov.–Mar. **Fruit** fleshy, 5-parted, becoming black, each part to 1 cm long, attached at its narrowed

base to rounded, red greatly enlarged flower base, about 1 cm wide; fruit present Nov.–Aug. **Habitat:** Wet to seasonally dry forests. Altitude: Sea level to 1200 m. Conservation areas: ARE, CVC, GUA, HNO, LAP, OSA, PAC, TEM. **Range:** Mex–Col. **Notes:** There are seven species of *Ouratea* in Costa Rica.

■ *Hamelia magnifolia* (zorillo amarillo)
Family Rubiaceae

Large shrub, to 5 m tall, multiple trunks, to 12 cm diameter, twigs 4-sided, nodes often reddish, stipules to 0.9 cm long, linear. **Leaves** opposite, each pair at right angles to next, blade 10–27 cm long, 4–11 cm wide, broadly oblong, tip long-pointed, base rounded, secondary veins numerous, loop-connected near margins. **Flowers** yellow, radially symmetrical tubular, 1.3 cm long, 0.3 cm wide, petal lobes to 0.3 cm long, calyx and base red, calyx lobes minute; inflorescence of dense, branched clusters to 12 cm long, 15 cm wide, stalks opposite, red; blooms Jan.–Oct. **Fruit** fleshy, red, to 1 cm long, 0.4 cm wide, seeds numerous; fruit present June–Jan. **Habitat:** Wet to moist forest understory and edges. Altitude: Mostly on the Pacific slope, sea level to 1900 m, usually below 600 m. Conservation areas: CVC, LAP, OSA (mostly), PAC. **Range:** CR, Pan. **Notes:** There are six species of *Hamelia* in Costa Rica. They are distinguished by funnel-shaped, yellow, orange to red flowers and small fleshy fruit with numerous seeds. Several species have leaves in whorls of 3–4.

■ *Palicourea padifolia* (cafecillo)
Family Rubiaceae

Shrub or small tree, 2–7 m tall, young stems 4-sided, stipules 2-lobed, basal tube to 0.4 cm long, lobes to 1 cm long, bristle tipped. **Leaves** opposite, blade 6–16 cm long, 2–6 cm wide, narrowly elliptic, tip pointed. **Flowers** yellow to orange, radially symmetrical, tubular or funnel-shaped, to 1.5 cm long,

petal lobes to 0.3 cm; inflorescence of branched clusters 7–18 cm long broadly pyramid-shaped, stems red purple to orange; visited by hummingbirds; blooms and fruits all year. **Fruit** fleshy, dark purple black, translucent, to 0.6 cm long, oval to round, seeds 2; fruits Jan.–Aug. **Habitat:** Wet to moist mountain forests, second growth, edges. Altitude: 900–2500 m. Conservation areas: ARE, CVC, GUA, LAC, LAP, PAC. **Range:** Mex–Pan, Ec and Pr. **Notes:** There are about 30 species of *Palicourea* in Costa Rica. Cafecillo is the name applied to most or all species of *Palicourea* in Costa Rica.

■ *Pentagonia monocaulis* (lengua de vaca, tabacón)
Family Rubiaceae

Shrub 2–7 m, often unbranched, stems usually 4-ribbed near top, leaves clustered at top of stem; stipules between leaf-stalk bases, triangular, 3–9 cm long. **Leaves** opposite, stalks 3–12 cm long, blade 26–90 cm long, 13–50 cm wide, elliptic, leathery, tip pointed to blunt, veins raised above, sharp-edged, smaller veins conspicuously parallel, new leaves wine red with pale green veins. **Flowers** yellow to white, radially symmetrical, tubular,

to 3 cm long, 0.5 cm wide near base, about 2 cm across top, petal lobes to 1 cm long, tips pointed, calyx tube to 1 cm long, lobes to 0.8 cm, rounded; inflorescence of dense axillary clusters to 5 cm long, 8 cm wide; blooms Mar.–Nov. **Fruit** fleshy but hard, orange, rounded, to 4 cm wide, flesh white, seeds numerous; fruit present most of the year. **Habitat:** Wet to moist forest understories. Altitude: Sea level to 1500 m, mostly below 700 m. Conservation areas: ARE, CVC, GUA, HNO, LAC, LAP, PAC, TOR. **Range:** CR. **Notes:** There are nine species of *Pentagonia* in Costa Rica, *P. wendlandii* is also common, it has leaf stalks less than 2 cm long.

■ *Psychotria marginata*
Family Rubiaceae

Straggling slender shrub, 1–3 m tall, newer stems dark green, stipules triangular, to 1.5 cm long, 0.5 cm wide, tip pointed, deciduous. **Leaves** opposite, often clustered at ends of stems, blade 6–17 cm long, 2–6 cm wide, usually widest near apex, dark green, smooth, shiny, stiff, but thin, tip pointed, base tapered down stalk, veins closely spaced, impressed above, margin fringed with tiny hairs. **Flowers** clear yellow to white, radially symmetrical, funnel-shaped, to 0.3 cm long, petal lobes 5, 0.1 cm long, curled back, anthers white, often extending beyond petal tube, inflorescences on stalks to 7 cm long, pyramid-shaped, to 17 cm long, 12 cm wide, branches opposite, at right angles to axis; blooms and fruits all year. **Fruit** fleshy, orange becoming red or purple, to 0.6 cm, fleshy, rounded, 2 seeds, flattened on inner side, ridged. **Habitat:** Wet to moist forest understories, edges, second growth. Altitude: Sea level to 800 m. Conservation areas: CVC, GUA, LAC, LAP, OSA, PAC, TOR. **Range:** Mex–Ven and Bol, Jam, Tr. **Notes:** Distinguished by its small fruit and flowers on long stalks.

■ *Psychotria parvifolia* (cafecillo)
Family Rubiaceae

Shrub 70 cm to 3 m tall, flat-topped, branches in layers, leaves in flat planes, young stems dark green, slender, finely reddish-hairy, becoming smooth, stipules to 0.6 cm long, sheathing leaf buds, leaving a scar across node between stalk bases. **Leaves** opposite, clustered at branch tips, blade small, 1–3.5 cm long, 0.5–1.4 cm wide, elliptic, tip blunt to pointed, base tapering, margin wavy, irregularly undulating. **Flowers** white, radially symmetrical, tubular, to 0.4 cm long, petal lobes 4, flaring, to 0.2 cm long tips pointed, inflorescence few-flowered clusters to 2 cm long at or near ends of twigs; blooms most of the year, mostly July–Aug. **Fruit** fleshy, yellow, turning red, with dark spot at flower end, to 0.6 long, rounded, translucent, juicy, 2-seeded; fruits Oct.–May. **Habitat:** Understories of wet forests, second growth. Altitude: 100–2200 m, usually above 1300 m. Conservation areas: ARE, CVC, LAP, OSA, PAC. **Range:** CR, Pan. **Notes:** Similar to *P. graciliflora* which has shorter stipules with 2 narrow lobes.

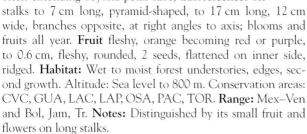

■ *Psychotria solitudinum* (cafecillo)
Family Rubiaceae

Sprawling shrub or small tree 2–6 m tall, sparsely branched; stipules to 0.6 cm, rounded with 2 short lobes, persistent. **Leaves** opposite, blade 10–21 cm long, 5–10 cm wide, egg-shaped to elliptic, tip long-pointed, base blunt to pointed, dark green above, paler below, leathery, secondary veins numerous, slightly raised above, loop-connected along margin. **Flowers** yellow to pale green, (sometimes white), radially symmetrical, funnel-shaped, tube to 0.5 cm, petal lobes 0.1 cm; inflorescence to 26 cm long, pyramid-shaped, branches opposite; blooms and fruits all year. **Fruit** fleshy, blue, purple to black, to 0.4 cm, rounded, finely hairy, 2 seeded, fruits Mar.–Sept. **Habitat:** Wet, forest understories, Altitude: Sea level to 1000 m, mostly on the Pacific slope. Conservation areas: OSA (mostly), PAC, TOR (rarely). **Range:** CR–Pr. **Notes:** Similar species are *P. angustiflora* Caribbean slope; *P. brachiata,* smaller, mostly on the Caribbean slope; *P. microbotrys* much smaller, with larger leaves and much larger stipules.

■ *Citrus* spp. (naranja, lemon, limón, orange)
Family Rutaceae

Trees or shrubs, stems often thorny. **Leaves** alternate, simple, leaf stems winged, blade shiny, margin smooth or finely toothed. **Flowers** white, fragrant, radially symmetrical, 5-parted, small. **Fruit** fleshy, green, yellow to orange, rind finely bumpy, covered with tiny pores containing aromatic oils, flesh divided into wedge-shaped segments full of large, juice-filled cells. **Habitat:** Wet to seasonal dry regions; widely

cultivated in gardens and as agricultural crops. Altitude: Sea level to 2900 m. Conservation areas: GUA, OSA, PAC, TEM. **Range:** Native to Asia. Occasionally escaping from cultivation. **Notes:** Includes numerous species, hybrids and varieties. Hybrids and species sometimes found in natural areas in Costa Rica include: *Citrus aurantifolia* (limón, lime); *C. aurantium* (Seville orange, naranja agria); *C. medica* (citron, cidra); *C. paradisi* (grapefruit); *C. reticulata* (mandarin orange, tangerine, mandarina); *C. sinensis* (sweet orange, naranja dulce; probably a hybrid with pomelo; *C. maxima* x *C. reticulata*); Oils in the fruit skins are insecticidal.

■ *Simarouba glauca* (aceituno, manteco, olivo, negrito)
  Family Simaroubaceae

Small to medium sized tree about 7–13 m tall, young bark smooth, older bark rough, fissured, dark gray, branches sinuous, twigs thick. **Leaves** alternate, pinnate, stalk about 6 cm, base swollen, extending slightly down twig as small ridges, blade to about 27 cm long, 14 cm wide, leaflets 10–20, about 6 cm long, 2 cm wide, oblong, tip blunt to slightly notched, surface dark green, shiny, secondary veins rather obscure. **Flowers** pale yellow to yellow green, radially symmetrical, 0.9 cm wide, petals fused, 5 lobes, ovary 5-lobed; inflorescence of large branched clusters in axils of small leaves near branch tips; blooms in Nov.–Feb. **Fruit** fleshy, red becoming dark purple, about 2 cm, oblong, 1 seed; Feb.–Mar. **Habitat:** Seasonally dry to moist forests. Also used for living fences. Altitude: Pacific lowlands, sea level to 550 m. Conservation areas: GUA, PAC, TEM. **Range:** Mex–Pan. **Notes:** *Simarouba amara* is the only other species of this genus in Costa Rica. It is found in wetter habitats than is S. *glauca*.

■ *Cestrum warszewiczii* (pavoncillo, zorillo)
  Family Solanaceae

Shrub or small tree to 7 m tall twigs finely hairy. **Leaves** alternate, blade to 8 cm long, 5 cm wide, elliptic, tip pointed, base wedge-shaped, shiny, dark green above. **Flowers** orange, petal tube 2 cm long, angled, petal lobes 5, 0.5 cm, egg-shaped, calyx green, to 1.2 cm long; inflorescence of branched, axillary clusters to 25 cm long, on short, stout stalks; Mar., May, Oct. **Fruit** fleshy, white, enveloped by persistent calyx. **Habitat:** High elevations in shrubby, open sites. Altitude: 1400–3000 m. Conservation areas: CVC, LAP. **Range:** Mex, CR, Pan. **Notes:** There are 14 species of Cestrum in Costa Rica.

153

■ *Cuatresia cuneata*
Family Solanaceae

Shrub or herb to 3 m tall, stems slender, arching, often vine-like. **Leaves** appearing opposite, pair members often very unequal, often with small round extra leaves, blade to 25 cm long, elliptic but variable, sides often unequal, shining above, tip long-pointed, base extending down stalk, each pair at right angles to next. **Flowers** dull yellow to greenish, about 0.6 cm long, petal lobes 4–5, often curled back, finely hairy at base inside, calyx lobes small, pointed, stamens clumped around stigma; inflorescence of crowded, branched clusters in axils and at nodes along leafless stem. **Fruit** fleshy, blue-violet, round, to 1.2 cm wide. **Habitat:** Wet forest understories. Altitude: Sea level to 1800 m. Conservation areas: ARE, CVC, LAC, PAC, TOR. **Range:** Nic–Col. **Notes:** There are at least three species of *Cuatresia* in Costa Rica. Formerly included in the genus *Witheringia*.

■ *Witheringia meiantha*
Family Solanaceae

Shrub to 4 m, erect to sprawling. **Leaves** alternate, blade to 20 cm long, elliptic, tip long-pointed, base slightly unequal, wedge-shaped, blunt, sometimes abruptly contracted and extending down leaf stalk as narrow wings, larger leaf often accompanied by smaller, opposite, rounded leaf, about 4 cm long, 2.5 cm wide. **Flowers** pale yellow-cream, 0.5 cm wide, petal tube to 0.3 cm, lobes 4–5, to 0.6 cm long, curled sharply backward, stamens 4, purplish, clustered at center of flower, pistil longer than stamens; inflorescence of solitary or numerous flowers in leaf axils, hanging below leaves; blooms and fruits on and off most of the year. **Fruit** fleshy, turning yellow then orange or red, about 0.8 cm but variable, rounded, translucent, juicy, held at or above leaf level, seeds 0.1 cm, yellow. **Habitat:** Understories or openings of moist to wet forests. Altitude: 300–1600 m. Conservation areas: ARE, CVC, GUA. **Range:** Mex–Pan. **Notes:** There are about 10 species of *Witheringia* in Costa Rica. *Witheringia meiantha* is very similar to *W. solanacea*, which has a smaller calyx and is the most common and widely distributed species of *Witheringia*.

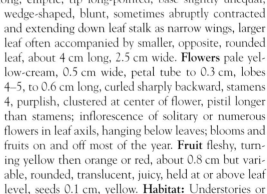

■ *Waltheria indica* (hierba de soldado, sleepy morning)
Family Sterculiaceae

Small shrub, to 2 m tall, stems to 2 cm wide, densely gray-woolly, flowering branches long, straight. **Leaves** alternate, 2–12 cm long, 1–7 cm wide, narrowly heart-shaped to bluntly oblong, woolly-hairy, tip pointed to rounded, base rounded to lobed, surface puckered by impressed veins, veins palmate at base, margin toothed. **Flowers** yellow to orange, radially symmetrical, very small, imbedded in gray green, woolly-hairy bracts, fragrant; in dense, small, stalked clusters in leaf axils; blooms Sept.–Mar., June. **Fruit** dry, 0.2 cm, 1-seeded, seeds black. **Habitat:** Disturbed, open areas, roadsides. Altitude: Sea level to 1100 m. Conservation areas: ARE, CVC, GUA, PAC, TEM. **Range:** Mex–Ven and Arg, WI, introduced in Africa and Oceania, invasive in numerous Pacific islands. **Notes:** The only other species of *Waltheria* in Costa Rica is *W. glomerata,* which is less common and has whitish flowers.

■ *Clavija costaricana*
Family Theophrastaceae

Shrub or small tree to 4 m tall, few or no branches, stem stout, erect with clusters of old leaf scars up stem. **Leaves** alternate, in tight spirals at top of stem, blade 0.3–1.2 m long, 8–23 cm wide, narrowly lance-shaped to widest near apex, tip pointed, gradually tapered to base. **Flowers** pale orange to rose, 1 cm wide, radially symmetrical, petals fused, round, berry-shaped, 4 fleshy petals 0.5 cm long, 0.5–0.7 cm wide, curved inward and overlapping one another, stamens whitish; inflorescence of elongate, dangling, unbranched clusters 3–27 cm long on upper stem, mostly among leaves; blooms Sept.–June. **Fruit** hard-fleshy, bright orange, 2–4.5 cm wide, interior white, seeds 2–20 each to 1 cm long, covered with an gelatinous, orange to white coating (aril); fruits all year. **Habitat:** Moist to wet forest understories. Altitude: Sea level to 1100 m. Conservation areas: ARE, GUA, LAC, OSA, TEM, TOR. **Range:** Nic–Col. **Notes:** The only other species of this genus in Costa Rica is *C. biborrana* which less common and found only on the Pacific slope.

■ *Dicraspidia donnell-smithii*
Family Tiliaceae

Small tree, to 7 m tall, bark dark, rough with small, raised lenticels, twigs brown, hairy; stipules large, oval, about 2 cm long and wide, hairy, appearing almost like smaller leaves; leaves and stipules ranked in one plane along ends of branches. **Leaves** alternate, 10–20 cm long, 3–8 cm wide, elliptic, often widest above middle, tip long-pointed, base unequal, lobed, hairy, dull green above, whitish-tan, finely scaly below, veins palmate at base, impressed above, margin toothed. **Flowers** yellow, showy, radially symmetrical, about 6 cm wide, petals 5, crepelike, stamens numerous in a ring around single stigma, sepals green, margins fringed with long, linear tips; blooms and fruits most of the year. **Fruit** dry, about 1 cm cupped in old calyx, seeds several. **Habitat:** Moist to wet forests, disturbed sites, roadsides, second growth. Altitude: Sea level to 1000 m. Conservation areas: LAC, OSA, PAC. **Range:** CR–Col. **Notes:** This is the only species of *Dicraspidia* in Costa Rica.

■ *Triumfetta bogotensis* (mozote)
Family Tiliaceae

Low shrub, 1–3 m tall, most parts hairy. **Leaves** alternate, stalk 4–6 cm long, blade broadly egg-shaped, 3-lobed to

simple, tip pointed, base rounded to slightly lobed, margin irregularly toothed. **Flowers** yellow, radially symmetrical, about 1.5 cm wide, petals 5, 0.5–1 cm long, broadly egg-shaped, stamens 15–30, elongate, yellow, style 0.9 cm long; blooms Sept.–June. **Fruit** dry, rounded, woolly and spiny, burlike; fruits Sept.–Apr. **Habitat:** Moist to wet forest understories. Altitude: Pacific slope, 300–2200 m. Conservation areas: ARE, CVC, LAP, PAC. **Range:** Mex–Pr, Arg, WI. **Notes:** There are six species of *Triumfetta* in Costa Rica.

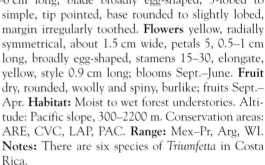

■ *Turnera ulmifolia (T. angustifolia)* (ram goat dash-a-long) Family Turneraceae

Small aromatic shrub 0.4–1.5 m tall, much-branched, slender, bark dark. **Leaves** alternate, stalk 1–2.5 cm with small wartlike outgrowths near top, blade 5–13 cm long, 2–4 cm wide, narrowly elliptic, shiny dark green, pointed at both ends, margin coarsely toothed, flower stalk fused to upper side of leaf stalk. **Flowers** bright yellow, radially symmetrical, showy, about 6 cm wide, 5-parted, petals 2–3.5 cm long, widest near tip, calyx 2 cm long, lobes pointed; 2 linear, toothed bracts below calyx; blooms on and off most of the year, mostly Apr.–Nov. **Fruit** dry, 0.3–0.8 cm long, surface puckered. **Habitat:** In mangrove swamps and low, coastal sites. Also horticultural and escaped. Altitude: Lowlands, at or near sea level. Conservation areas: LAC, TEM. **Range:** Bel, Hon, CR, Pan, Jam. **Notes:** There are six species of *Turnera* in Costa Rica; T. *angustifolia* is often treated as a separate species from T. *ulmifolia*. The others are found mostly on the Pacific slope.

■ *Urera rzedowskii* (ortiga, tabaquillo) Family Urticaceae

Small tree or large shrub, 2–8 m tall, twigs to 1 cm thick, densely hairy when young; stipules to 1.8 cm long, united across base of leaf stalk, densely hairy. **Leaves** sometimes *with stinging spines*, alternate, clustered at ends of branches, blade 10–44 cm long, 7–40 cm wide, broadly egg-shaped, tip long-pointed, base slightly lobed to rounded, softly hairy below, veins palmate at base, margins toothed. **Flowers** white to pinkish, minute, to 0.2 cm, male and female flowers usually on separate plants, males often with pink anthers; inflorescences to 12 cm long (to 30 cm in fruit), of branched clusters in axils on leafless stems; blooms most of the year. **Fruit** fleshy, bright orange, about 0.2 cm long, 1 seed. **Habitat:** Understories and gaps in wet to moist, partly deciduous forests. Altitude: Sea level to 2600 m. Conservation areas: ARE, CVC, GUA, LAC, LAP, OSA, PAC, TEM. **Range:** CR. **Notes:** Very similar to U. *elata* which has smaller inflorescences and leaf blades. Both these species are common and painful to collect.

COLOR OF CONSPICUOUS PART WHITE, CREAM, YELLOWISH, GREENISH WHITE

■ *Aphelandra dolichantha*
Family Acanthaceae

Shrub or woody herb to 1.5 m tall, young stems 4-sided. **Leaves** opposite, blade to 24 cm long, 10 cm wide, elliptic, dark green above with satiny sheen, paler below, pointed at both ends. **Flowers** white, tubular, bilaterally symmetrical, to 7 cm long, longest petal lobes to 2 cm long, 0.9 cm wide, tube mostly hidden by closely overlapping pale, green, finely hairy bracts, to 3.5 cm long, 1 cm wide, sometimes with reddish speckles; flower spikes to 13 cm long, usually solitary at end of stems; blooms most of the year. **Fruit** dry, club-shaped, widest near apex, to 1.7 cm long, 0.4 cm wide. **Habitat:** Understories of wet forests. Altitude: Sea level to 1400 m, mostly on the Caribbean slope. Conservation areas: ARE, CVC, LAC, HNO, OSA, TOR. **Range:** CR–Col. **Notes:** There are 12 species of *Aphelandra* in Costa Rica.

■ *Avicennia germinans* (culamate, mangle negro, palo de sal, black mangrove)
Family Acanthaceae

Shrub or small tree 1–15 m tall, bark black, grainy, roots with numerous aboveground, erect, slender appendages (pneumatophores), 6–7 cm tall, sticking out of mud. **Leaves** opposite, 5–15 cm long, 2–5 cm wide, elliptic, fleshy, green above, finely hairy below, coated with salt, secondary veins obscure. **Flowers** white with yellow center, fragrant, radially symmetrical, small, tubular, 0.9 cm wide across top, petal lobes 4, anthers dark; inflorescence of cone-shaped clusters; blooms most of the year, especially in Mar. **Fruit** dry, to 5 cm long, asymmetrical, flattened, tip pointed. **Habitat:** Upper tidal areas with other mangroves. Altitude: Sea level to 300 m, mostly along Pacific coast. Conservation areas: GUA, LAC, OSA, PAC, TEM. **Range:** Coastal S US, N Mex–Pr and Brz, WI, Bh, Bermuda, Galapagos. **Notes:** There are three species of *Avicennia* in Costa Rica. They are often placed in the family Avicenniaceae or Verbenaceae. New genetic information indicates they belong in Acanthaceae.

◼ *Saurauia montana* (moquillo, moco)
Family Actinidiaceae

Shrub or small tree 2–7 m tall, 25 cm diameter, erect, young parts covered with reddish bristly hairs. **Leaves** alternate, blade 15–25 cm long, 6–11 cm wide, elliptic, tip long-pointed, base wedge-shaped, margins toothed, with longer bristles. **Flowers** white, about 2 cm wide, 5 petals 1 cm long, in 2 series, 3 inner ones shorter than 6 outer, deciduous as a unit, 5 sepals, green to white, stamens numerous, yellow; inflorescence in axils, 5–16 cm long cm, branched; blooms most of the year, especially Jan.–Mar. **Fruit** pale greenish, about 1 cm, splitting open to reveal small, dark seeds in a colorless, gelatinous flesh. **Habitat:** Wet forests, edges, second growth. Altitude: 300–2900 m, mostly above 1000 m. Conservation areas: ARE, CVC, GUA, LAC, LAP, OSA, PAC. **Range:** Hon–Pan. **Notes:** There are four species of *Saurauia* in Costa Rica; all have white flowers similar to *S. montana*, which is the most common.

◼ *Anacardium occidentale* (marañón, cashew)
Family Anacardiaceae

Tree 3–12 m; branches rough with prominent lenticels. **Leaves** alternate, blade 6–15 cm long, 4–9 cm wide, broadest near apex, tip rounded or notched, base tapered, midrib and veins pale, young leaves bright red. **Flowers** white and reddish, radially symmetrical, to 0.8 cm wide, fragrant; inflorescence of broad clusters, 10–25 cm long; blooms Jan.–Mar. **Fruit** fleshy, purple-brown, to 3 cm long, kidney-shaped, borne at the tip of a bright red to yellow, fleshy appendage 5–9 cm long, this "cashew apple" is the swollen fruit stalk; 1-seeded. **Habitat:** Cultivated widely and escaped. Often seen as a garden tree. Altitude: Sea level to 800 m, mostly on the Pacific slope. Conservation areas: GUA, OSA, PAC, TEM, TOR. **Range:** Considered originally native to coastal regions Ven–Brz but now cultivated in tropical regions worldwide. **Notes:** Cashew apples are edible and used for juice and preserves, commonly sold at fruit stands. Also eaten by large birds such as toucans, which disperse the seeds. The sap of the husk is very toxic and can cause blisters. Nuts must be roasted to be edible. However the raw nuts (photo) may be eaten by some parrots and by tapirs. Cashew is also reported to have medicinal uses.

159

■ *Tabernaemontana alba* (huevos de mono)
Family Apocynaceae

Small tree 3–8 m tall, sap milky, copious, bark gray, lines between leaf-stalk bases. **Leaves** opposite, 7–20 cm long, 2–7.5 cm wide, narrowly elliptic, tip rounded or with an abrupt point, base tapered, secondary veins whitish and conspicuous. **Flowers** cream-yellowish, tubular, very fragrant, about 1 cm long, 3 cm across petal lobes, 5 petal lobes twisted slightly, in a pinwheel pattern at center of flower, inflorescence of branched clusters to 14.5 cm long; blooms most of the year. **Fruit** thinly-fleshy, green, of 2 mirror-image parts, end-to-end, each about 5 long, 3 cm wide and deep, tips rounded, splitting open when ripe to release seeds covered by bright colored flesh, eaten by birds, which disperse seeds. **Habitat:** Wet to seasonally dry lowland forests and edges. Altitude: Sea level to 700 m, mostly below 300 m. Conservation areas: GUA, HNO, LAC, OSA, TEM, TOR. **Range:** Mex–Pan. **Notes:** There are seven species of *Tabernaemontana* in Costa Rica. All are quite similar and also similar to species of *Stemmadenia* but with mostly smaller flowers.

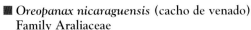

■ *Oreopanax nicaraguensis* (cacho de venado)
Family Araliaceae

Small tree, sometimes epiphytic, to 10 m (sometimes to 40 m) tall, trunk 30 cm diameter, branches about 4 m long. **Leaves** alternate, stalk 4–15 cm long, blade 7–20 cm long, 7–15 cm wide, broadly egg- or heart-shaped, tip blunt to slightly pointed, base rounded to slightly lobed, shiny, smooth, major veins 5–9, palmate at base. **Flowers** cream white, radially symmetrical, sexes separate, petals 5, calyx without lobes, male flowers with 5 stamens, females with 7 styles; in tight, ball-like clusters; inflorescence branched, pyramid-shaped, about 25 cm long, at ends of branches; blooms and fruits on and off through the year. **Fruit** fleshy, greenish white, becoming purple black, to 0.9 cm in clusters of 8–10, about 2 cm wide, on a single stalk, Jan.–July. **Habitat:** Open areas in mountains. Altitude: 1000–3200 m. Conservation areas: ARE, CVC, LAP, PAC. **Range:** Nic–Pan. **Notes:** There are about 13 species of *Oreopanax* in Costa Rica.

■ *Ageratina anisochroma*
Family Asteraceae

Shrub, to 2 m tall, stems slender, nodes ridged between leaf bases. **Leaves** opposite, stalk very short to none, blade to 11 cm long, 4 cm wide, egg-shaped to narrowly lance-shaped, tip pointed, base rounded, surface dark green, smooth, shiny, margin toothed. **Flowers** white to pale lavender or pink tinged, no ray flowers, in heads to 0.5 cm long, and wide, about 17 flowers per head, bracts around base of head 0.3 cm long, often purplish; inflorescence branched, about 8 cm wide, top rounded; blooms most of the year. **Fruit** dry, 1-seeded, 0.1 cm long, crowned by a ring of bristles longer than seed. **Habitat:** Open sites in mountain regions. Altitude: 500–3400 m most often above 1500 m. Conservation areas: ARE, CVC, GUA, LAC, LAP, PAC. **Range:** Nic–W Pan. **Notes:** There are about 19 species of *Ageratina* in Costa Rica; most are found above 1500 m in open sites.

■ *Baccharis trinervis*
Family Asteraceae

Shrub 50 cm to 4 m tall, sometimes vinelike, or a tree to 7 m tall, most parts finely hairy, branches at right angles to main stems. **Leaves** alternate, blade to 8 cm long, elliptic, usually pointed at both ends, finely hairy on both sides, major veins 3, palmate, parallel, impressed above, margin smooth. **Flowers** dull white, 0.5 cm long, no rays, heads, 0.6 cm wide, numerous, small, rounded, basal bracts in 3 rows, straw-color; flower heads in branched clusters near ends of stems; blooms all year. **Fruit** dry, 1-seeded, plumed. **Habitat:** Open sites, mostly at mid- to higher elevations. Altitude: 40–2600 m, mostly 1000–2000 m. Conservation areas: ARE, CVC, GUA, HNO, LAC, LAP, PAC. **Range:** Mex–NW S Amer and Pr. **Notes:** There are three species of *Baccharis* in Costa Rica. *Baccharis pedunculata,* which is not hairy, is almost as common as *B. trinervis* and is found in roughly the same areas.

Clibadium leiocarpum
Family Asteraceae

Shrub 2–5 m tall, bark pale brown, stems woolly-hairy, old leaf scars circling stems. **Leaves** opposite, bases joined across stem, blades 7–19 cm long, 2–10 cm wide, rough-textured, egg-shaped, tip long-pointed, base narrowed, becoming wedge-shaped, dark green above, veins curved sharply upward, margin toothed. **Flowers** white inconspicuous, to 0.3 cm long, with dark anthers, in small rounded heads to 0.7 cm wide, with less than 20 flowers, basal bracts egg-shaped, about 0.4 cm long and wide; inflorescence branched, dome-shaped, at ends of stems; blooms all year. **Fruit** dry, 1-seeded, less than 0.2 cm long, shiny, black, conical, enclosed in the greenish-black enlarged bracts of flower head. **Habitat:** Open, sunny areas in wet to seasonally dry regions. Altitude: Sea level to 2600 m, mostly on the Pacific slope, above 1000 m. Conservation areas: ARE, CVC, GUA, LAP, OSA, PAC, TEM. **Range:** Nic–Pan. **Notes:** There are 13 species of *Clibadium* in Costa Rica, all have inconspicuous flowers almost hidden by bracts of the flower heads.

Montanoa guatemalensis (tubú)
Family Asteraceae

Shrub or small tree to 15 m, often multistemmed and branched to ground, bark pale tan, fissured, new growth tan, woolly-scaly nodes swollen, ridged. **Leaves** opposite, to 17 cm long, 13 cm wide, irregularly egg-shaped with 2–4 shallow, blunt-tipped lobes, dark green above, pale whitish below, tip pointed, base narrowed. **Flowers** white with orange center, daisylike, to 5 cm wide, rays about 8, to 2.5 cm long, disk about 1.2 cm across, inflorescence of branched clusters at ends of stems; blooms Dec.–Mar. **Fruit** dry, flower head becoming ball-shaped, about 1.5 cm wide, of small, soft spinelike bracts, seeds 0.3 cm, round, brown. **Habitat:** Cultivated and wild in open areas. Often used as hedges. Altitude: Pacific slope 1000–1500 m. Conservation areas: ARE, CVC, LAP, PAC. **Range:** Gua–CR. **Notes:** There are five species

of *Montanoa* in Costa Rica. All are fairly similar; *M. tomentosa*, with smaller flowers and hairy leaves, is also used in hedges. It blooms Nov.–Jan, occurs naturally 800–1000 m.

■ *Verbesina turbacensis*
Family Asteraceae

Coarse shrub, small tree to 4 m tall, hairy, sparsely branched at top of stem, stems winged below leaf stalks. **Leaves** alternate, leaf stalk winged, blade to 25 cm long, pinnately lobed, lobes rounded at tips, somewhat rough-hairy above, hairy below. **Flowers** dull white, aromatic, ray flowers 5–8, 0.3 cm long, anthers dark, flower heads about 0.5 high, 0.4 cm wide, basal bracts in several rows, overlapping, finely hairy; inflorescence of large, branched, flat-topped clusters at top of stem; blooms most of the year. **Fruit** dry, 1-seeded, black, 0.2 cm, 4-angled, margins winged, tip with 2 hornlike bristles. **Habitat:** Open sites, roadsides, second growth, mostly in mountain regions. Altitude: 100–2000 m, mostly over 1000 m on the Pacific slope. Conservation areas: ARE, CVC, GUA, LAP, OSA, PAC. **Range:** Mex–Col and Ven. **Notes:** This is the most common species of *Verbesina* in Costa Rica. It is very similar to *Verbesina gigantea* which is less common and found at lower elevations.

■ *Vernonia patens* (tuete, tuetillo, dawaska)
Family Asteraceae

Shrub or small tree 1–8 m tall, often multistemmed, stems erect, bark gray, new growth gray brown, scaly-hairy. **Leaves** alternate, blade narrow, to 15 cm long, 4.5 cm wide, tip pointed, base tapered, hairy below, veins depressed above, surface puckered, margin toothed to entire. **Flowers** white (sometimes purplish), no rays, fragrant, attractive to bees and other insects, flower heads to 0.5 cm high, about 0.6 cm wide, with 20–27 flowers, basal bracts numerous, small, tightly overlapping, midribs brown; flower heads stalkless, mostly along one side of inflorescence stems; blooms Feb.–Apr., July. **Fruit** dry, 1-seeded, less than 0.2 cm long, plumed, wind-dispersed. **Habitat:** Open, disturbed areas, second growth, roadsides. Altitude: Sea level to 1400 m. Conservation areas: ARE, CVC, GUA, HNO, LAC, LAP, PAC, TEM, TOR. **Range:** Mex–N S Amer. **Notes:** There are 14 species of *Vernonia* in Costa Rica. All have blue, purple or white flowers in flower heads without rays, mostly arranged along one side of the inflorescence branches.

■ *Amphitecna latifolia* (cacao silvestre, jícaro, duppy gourd)
Family Bignoniaceae

Small crooked tree or shrub 3–10 m tall, bark pale, smooth or slightly fissured, twigs stout, bumpy, crooked. **Leaves** alternate to almost opposite, stalks very short, blade 6–25 cm long, 3–12 cm wide, oblong, tip rounded with small point, base blunt or tapered, stiff and leathery, secondary veins obscure, midrib pale. **Flowers** greenish or yellowish-white, fleshy, tubular, to 6 cm long, 5 cm wide across top, petal lobes unequal; blooms most of the year. **Fruit** gourdlike 5–10 cm long, and wide, rounded, flesh spongy-white, edible, also eaten by Agoutis; fruit stalk stout, about 4 cm, seeds about 1.5 cm long, dispersed by mammals and water, fruits most of the year. **Habitat:** Marshy

areas along coasts with mangroves. Altitude: Sea level to 300 m. Conservation areas: LAC, OSA (mostly), PAC, TEM, TOR. **Range:** Mex–Ven and Ec, cultivated in S FL. **Notes:** There are six species of *Amphitecna* in Costa Rica. Several are fairly common but *A. latifolia* is the only one found in mangrove swamps.

■ *Bixa orellana* (achiote, kachá) **Family Bixaceae**

Shrub or small tree 2–10 m, sap orange. **Leaves** alternate, stalk 2–10 cm long, blade 5–20 cm long, 3–18 cm wide, heart-shaped to broadly elliptical, tip pointed, veins palmate at base, pinnate above, shiny green. **Flowers** white or pink, radially symmetrical, about 5 cm wide, showy, petals 5, 2–3 cm long, broadest near apex, slightly overlapping, anthers numerous, yellow; inflorescence of branched clusters, pollinated by bees; blooms Aug.–Feb. **Fruit** becoming dry, dark red, 2–4 cm long, elliptical, covered with soft spines, splitting apart to reveal seeds covered with an orange fleshy coat, Dec.–Aug. **Habitat:** Cultivated and wild. Open sites in moist to wet forests, edges, roadsides. Altitude: Sea level to 700 m. Conservation areas: CVC, LAC, OSA, PAC, TEM, TOR. **Range:** Native to tropi-

cal America. **Notes:** Grown commercially for yellow food coloring, Anatto, extracted from seeds. *Bixa urucurana* is the only other species of *Bixa* in Costa Rica. It is uncommon.

■ *Cordia dentata* (tiguilote, jiguilote)
   Family Boraginaceae

Large shrub to small tree, 3–12 m tall, canopy sprawling, dome-shaped, trunk sometimes twisted, irregular, often multistemmed, much branched, branches low, arching to near ground, sometimes vinelike, bark dark, finely fissured. **Leaves** alternate, blade 5–13 cm long, 3–7 cm wide, elliptic to egg-shaped, tip rounded with small, dull point, base rounded to slightly lobed, texture rough, leathery, surface shiny, dark green, veins arching sharply upward to margin, small veins ladderlike between midrib and secondary veins, margin sometimes slightly toothed. **Flowers** pale yellow to cream white, 1–1.5 cm wide, petals fused with 5 shallow lobes, notched at top, texture crepelike, stamens 5; inflorescence branched, 15–20 cm wide; blooms all year. **Fruit** fleshy, translucent-white, dark stigma remnant at tip, 1–1.5 cm long, cupped in old calyx remnant, flesh juicy, sweet and sticky; 1-seeded. **Habitat:** Open sites in seasonally dry regions, pastures, roadsides. Altitude: Northwest Pacific lowlands, sea level to 300 m. Conservation areas: GUA, TEM. **Range:** Mex–S Amer and Ant. **Notes:** Sometimes used as a living fence.

■ *Cordia diversifolia*
   Family Boraginaceae

Shrub or small tree 5–10 m tall, multistemmed, bark tan, finely fissured, new growth densely rusty-hairy. **Leaves** alternate, blade 11–19 cm long, 3–7 cm wide, narrowly elliptical, pointed at both ends, surface rough and hairy on both sides, slightly sticky, clustered at ends of stems. **Flowers** white, fragrant, 5-parted, about 0.8–1 cm long, 5-lobed, lobes bent back, calyx 0.5 cm long, tubular, stamens 5, short, style 0.8 cm long; inflorescence branched, about 12 cm long, 6–11 cm wide, at ends of stems; blooms and fruits May–Nov. also observed in Feb. **Fruit** fleshy, white, about 1.5 cm long, 1 cm wide, cupped by old calyx, tipped by stigma remnant; 1 round, black seed. **Habitat:** Open sites, in wet regions. Altitude: Sea level to 200 m, mostly in Caribbean lowlands. Conservation areas: LAC. **Range:** Mex–Pan. **Notes:** Sometimes used as living fence.

165

■ *Tournefortia brenesii*
Family Boraginaceae

Shrub or small tree, young stems green, woody stems with many horizontal leaf or branch scars, bark smooth. **Leaves** alternate, stalk 2–5 cm long, blade 10–28 cm long, 4–10 cm wide, narrowly elliptic to widest above middle, tip pointed, base extending down leaf stalk, upper surface dark green, shiny, hairless, wrinkled by deeply depressed pinnate and net veins, pale below. **Flowers** greenish white, about 1 cm long and wide, radially symmetrical, tubular, base of tube bulging, petal lobes 5, flaring, with pointed, down-curved tips, sepal lobes very narrow, green; flower clusters mostly one-sided, coiled in bud and curving downward in flower, sparsely branched, 10–28 cm long, including stalk; blooms Feb.–May. **Fruit** fleshy, surrounded by old sepals; fruits Apr.–Nov. **Habitat:** Mountainous areas in open sites or forest edges. Altitude: 900–2300 m. Conservation areas: ARE, GUA, HNO, LAC, PAC. **Range:** CR, Pan. **Notes:** There are 13 species of *Tournefortia* in Costa Rica.

■ *Centropogon smithii*
Family Campanulaceae

Large herb or shrub 1–5 m tall, stout, unbranched, stems hollow, sap milky. **Leaves** alternate, densely clustered at ends of stems, blade 15–36 cm long, 6–10 cm wide, broadly elliptic to widest above middle, tip abruptly point, base tapered, minutely scaly below, margin usually wavy and toothed, teeth dark purplish. **Flowers** cream white, greenish or yellowish, petal lobes often purple or speckled with purple, 6–8 cm long, tubular, bilaterally symmetrical, tube 2 cm long, petal lobes curved, 2 upper lobes 2–4 cm, 3 lower lobes about 2 cm long, *odor skunk-like*, calyx lobes linear, 2–3 cm long; blooms Feb.–Aug. **Fruit** fleshy, rounded 2–3.5 cm wide, shorter than wide, crowned by base of old calyx. **Habitat:** Mountain areas, oak forest, open sites, roadsides. Altitude: 950–3000 m, mostly above 2000 m. Conservation areas: ARE, CVC, LAP, PAC. **Range:** CR–Pan. **Notes:** There are about 12 species of *Centropogon* in Costa Rica.

166

■ *Sambucus nigra (S. mexicana; S. nigra* ssp. *canadensis)* (sauco, European elder)
   Family Caprifoliaceae

Shrub or small tree 2–5 m (sometimes to 10 m) tall, arching, spreading, bark pale gray brown, specked with small, raised dots (lenticels), young stems green, scarcely woody, nodes ridged, old stems with flaky pale bark. **Leaves** opposite, pinnate, leaflets 5–7, the lowest 2 pairs sometimes 3-parted, leaflets 4–15 cm long, 1.5–3.5 cm wide, elliptic to lance-shaped, tip pointed, margin toothed. **Flowers** white, fragrant, radially symmetrical, tubular, 0.3–0.6 cm wide; inflorescences of broad, flat, umbrella-shaped, branched clusters 5–30 cm wide, sometimes to 50 cm, at ends of branches; blooms and fruits all year. **Fruit** fleshy, red, becoming purple black, 0.5 cm, 3–5 seeded. **Habitat:** Mountains in wet, open areas, shrubby second growth. Imported plants often cultivated. Altitude: 800–2000 m, usually over 1200 m. Conservation areas: ARE, CVC, LAC. **Range:** E. Canada and USA, Mex–Pan. **Notes:** *Sambucus mexicana,* is often considered to be a separate species.

■ *Viburnum costaricanum* (colpalchí, cura, paraviento)
   Family Caprifoliaceae

Large shrub or small tree 2–20 m tall, trunk about 20 cm diameter, bark gray, branches elongate. **Leaves** opposite, 5–12 cm long, 2–5 cm wide, smallish, margins smooth. **Flowers** white, small, fragrant, tubular, radially symmetrical, 0.4–0.6 cm wide numerous; inflorescences of umbrella-shaped clusters, flower; blooms Jan-Oct. **Fruit** fleshy, becoming red, then purple black, small, stems often red, 0.5–0.8 cm long, about 0.6 cm wide, stems often red; seed 1, white; fruit present Jan.–Sept. **Habitat:** Open sites, secondary forest, roadsides, and edges in mountains. Altitude: 900–3200 m, mostly above 1500 m. Conservation areas: ARE, CVC, GUA, LAP, OSA, PAC. **Range:** CR, Pan. **Notes:** There are three species of *Viburnum* in Costa Rica.

■ *Jacaratia dolichaula* (palo de barril, ceiba papaya, papaya silvestre)
Family Caricaceae

Tree to 8 m, trunk to 25 cm diameter, often unbranched, sap milky. **Leaves** alternate, palmately compound, 3–5 leaflets, egg-shaped, tip abruptly pointed, base tapered. **Flowers** white, male flowers to 10 cm, very slender, tubular, petal lobes about 2 cm long, 0.5 cm wide, female flowers to 4 cm; blooms Jan.-Apr.; pollinated by moths. **Fruit** fleshy, smaller than Papaya, pale orange; fruit develops Apr.–Nov. Parrots may disperse seeds. **Habitat:** Moist and wet forests, second growth, edges. Altitude: Sea level to 1300 m. Conservation areas: ARE, CVC, GUA, HNO, LAC, LAP, OSA, PAC, TOR. **Range:** CR, Pan. **Notes:** The only other species of *Jacaratia* in Costa Rica, *J. spinosa*, is less common and found more often in OSA than is *J. dolichaula*.

■ *Chrysobalanus icaco* (Icaco, coco-plum)
Family Chrysobalanaceae

Shrub to 5 m, young stems reddish with many small lenticels. **Leaves** alternate, 2-ranked but often held erect, blade 2–8 cm long, 1–6 cm wide, paddle-shaped, widest near apex, tip rounded or notched, base wedge-shaped. **Flowers** white, small, radially symmetrical, to 0.7 cm long, with numerous stamens, in small clusters in axils and ends of branches; blooms June–Feb. **Fruit** fleshy, pink to blackish-purple, 1–4 cm wide, pulp white, edible, 1-seeded; fruit present most of the year. **Habitat:** Mostly coastal back dunes, beaches above high tide line, and forest edges, sometimes inland. Altitude: Sea level to 200 m, mostly near sea level. Conservation areas: CVC, HNO, LAC, OSA, PAC, TEM, TOR. **Range:** FL, Mex–S Brz, PtR, VI, Africa. **Notes:** Leaves and fruit used for black dye, wood hard, fine grained. This is the only species of *Chrysobalanus* in Costa Rica.

■ *Clusia croatii* (*C. minor,* misapplied) (azahar, copey) Family Clusiaceae

Epiphytic shrub, 3–10 m tall, main branches erect; sap milky, becoming orange in air. **Leaves** opposite, stalks joined across stem with line, blade 7–14 cm long, 3–7 cm wide, thick, fleshy, narrowly elliptic, veins numerous, parallel, rather obscure, tip pointed to sometimes rounded, base tapered to stalk. **Flowers** white to pink and red, radially symmetrical, sexes on separate plants (dioecious), fragrant, petals 4–7, base often dark pink, sepals 4, male flowers with numerous stamens fused to a circular, flattened central structure; female flowers with superior ovary, stigmas 10–13 fused to the central ringlike structure, 0.2 cm wide; inflorescences branched, about 3–8 cm long, and wide; blooms and fruits all year. **Fruit** turning dark red, 1.5–3.5 cm, crowned by the floral ring, splitting open to reveal seeds with orange fleshy coating. **Habitat:** Wet to moist forests, sometimes in remnant pasture trees. Altitude: Sea level to 1700 m. Conservation areas: ARE, CVC, GUA, HNO, LAC, LAP, OSA, PAC, TOR. **Range:** Nic–Pan, NE S Amer. **Notes:** There are 24 species of Clusia in Costa Rica.

■ *Ipomoea carnea* (sapo)
Family Convolvulaceae

Shrub, herb or woody vine, 1–5 m tall, often forming large tangled mounds, woody base about 40 cm diameter, splitting into numerous, vining, woody branches just above base, stems smooth, sinuous, elongate, prostrate and climbing over one another, ends of stems with new growth velvety-hairy, gray green, sap milky. **Leaves** alternate, blade 10–25 cm long, broadly heart-shaped, tip long-pointed, base shallowly lobed. **Flowers** pink to white and purple, radially symmetrical, 5–9 cm long, to 11 cm across top, trumpet-shaped, petals fused into a 5-sided tube flaring out at top; blooms all year. **Fruit** dry, rounded, 2 cm long, seeds brown-woolly. **Habitat:** Most often in wet, open areas of seasonally dry lowlands. Tolerates flooding. Altitude: Sea level to 2000 m.; mostly below 100 m. Conservation areas: ARE, CVC, GUA, LAC, LAP, PAC, TEM, TOR. Seen in Palo Verde N.P. **Range:** Mex–Pr; now pantropical, invasive in some regions. **Notes:** There are up to 50 species of *Ipomoea* in Costa Rica, many are very similar. This is the only woody species.

■ *Weinmannia pinnata* (loro, lorito, arrayán blanco)
Family Cunoniaceae

Shrub or small tree 1–10 m, sometimes a tree to 35 m in sheltered sites, trunks stout, sometimes with prop roots, sinuous, bark blackish, grainy, new growth yellowish-scaly-hairy, nodes swollen marked by linear stipule scar, stipules between leaf bases, leaflike, curled back, 1 cm long and wide. **Leaves** opposite, ranked along stem, stalkless, blade pinnate 5–10 cm long, 2.5 cm wide, midrib winged, rusty-hairy below, leaflets 9–20, egg-shaped, to 2 cm long, margins toothed. **Flowers** white, to 0.2 cm long, stigmas pinkish, buds, and ovary red; inflorescences of bottle-brush-like spikes, to 10 cm long, 2 cm wide; blooms mostly Aug.–Jan. **Fruit** dry, at first red, to 0.5 cm long, tipped by elongate, remnant style, 2-parted. **Habitat:** Moist to wet regions in open areas. Most common in mountains. Altitude: 700–3100 m, mostly above 2000 m. Conservation areas: ARE, CVC (mostly), GUA, LAC, LAP, PAC. Very common at Volcán Poás N.P. **Range:** Mex–S Amer, WI. **Notes:** There are nine species of *Weinmannia* in Costa Rica.

■ *Curatella americana* (chumico, lija, hoja de chigüe)
Family Dilleniaceae

Small, crooked tree or shrub about 3–7 m tall, trunk 30 cm diameter, bark gray, flaking, trunk stout, very crooked, branches few. **Leaves** alternate, blade 8–18 cm long, 5–9 cm wide, elliptic to egg-shaped, tip blunt to notched, base abruptly contracted, extending part-way down leaf stalk, blade stiff, leathery, very rough on both sides, dull yellow green above, tan-green below, veins pinnate, numerous, parallel, 10–20 per side, midrib raised above and below, margin wavy. **Flowers** white, yellowish, or orange, radially symmetrical, fragrant, about 1 cm wide, petals 4–5, soon falling, sepals 4, pale green, about as long as petals, persistent, stamens numerous; inflorescence of small, dense, branched clusters along older parts of stems; blooms Sept.–May. **Fruit** dry, becoming yellow, hairy, splitting open to release 4 black seeds with white fleshy attachment (aril); fruit present Dec.–May. **Habitat:** Open, shrubby areas, in moist to seasonally dry lowlands. Altitude: Pacific slope, sea level to 400 m. Conservation areas: GUA, LAP, PAC, TEM. **Range:** C Mex–Brz, Ant. **Notes:** This is the only species of *Curatella* in Costa Rica.

■ *Tetracera volubilis*
Family Dilleniaceae

Shrub or woody vine. **Leaves** alternate, stalk winged, blade 10–18 cm long, 4–8 cm wide, broadly elliptic to widest above middle, tip pointed to rounded, base extended down stalk, leathery, rough, dark green, veins 15–25, deeply impressed above, margins toothed. **Flowers** cream white and orange, radially symmetrical, 0.5 cm wide, petals 2–4, stamens numerous, sepals 0.3 m densely hairy; inflorescence of branched clusters at or near ends of stems; blooms July–Oct. **Fruit** dry, to 0.7 cm long, tipped by persistent style, seeds with fleshy coating; fruit present Sept.–Mar. **Habitat:** Forests to open, shrubby lowlands, in seasonally dry regions, rarely in moist to wet forests. Altitude: Sea level to 600 m. Conservation areas: CVC, GUA, HNO, PAC, TEM (mostly). **Range:** Mex–Brz and Pr, Cuba, Jam. **Notes:** There are four species of *Tetracera* in Costa Rica.

■ *Comarostaphylis arbutoides*
Family Ericaceae

Shrub 1–4 m tall, young stems rusty or grayish finely hairy; leaves mostly at ends of stems. **Leaves** alternate, blade 5–7 cm long, 1–2.5 cm wide narrowly elliptic, young leaves rusty-hairy, mature leaves leathery, shiny above, waxy rusty or grayish woolly below, pointed at both ends. **Flowers** cream white, radially symmetrical, urn-shaped, about 0.6 cm long, 0.4 cm wide; in dense, branching clusters at ends of stems; very attractive to bees; blooms and fruits all year. **Fruit** fleshy, becoming red, then dull black, rounded, about 0.5 cm wide, surface finely warty. **Habitat:** High elevations in open sites, second growth, roadsides. Common in the mountains along the Interamerican Highway (Ruta 2). Altitude: 1200–3500 m. Conservation areas: CVC, LAC, LAP, PAC. **Range:** S CA–Pan. **Notes:** This is the only species of *Comarostaphylis* in Costa Rica.

Tetracera volubilis (above)

Comarostaphylis arbutoides (below)

171

■ *Disterigma humboldtii*
Family Ericaceae

Shrub, 50 cm to 1 m tall, sometimes epiphytic, twigs grooved, 3–4 angled, bark flaky, reddish brown, young stems red brown, hair-scaly, branches stiff, straight. **Leaves** alternate, spiraled along stems, almost no stalk, blade small, 0.6–1.5 cm long, 0.4–0.9 cm wide, egg-shaped to elliptic, blunt at both ends, stiff, smooth, dark green above, pale below, veins obscure, margins smooth. **Flowers** pink to white, radially symmetrical, small, to 0.8 cm long, 0.4 cm wide, vase-shaped, constricted below 4 short petal lobes, stamens purple, inflorescence of 1–3 flowers in leaf axils, bracts small; blooms all year. **Fruit** fleshy, white, often translucent, to 0.5 cm wide, with about 10 brown seeds. **Habitat:** Open sites, second growth forest, in mountain regions. Altitude: 950–3200 m, mostly above 1500 m. Conservation areas: ARE, CVC, LAC, LAP, PAC. **Range:** Mex, Gua, CR–Ven and Ec. **Notes:** There are four species of *Disterigma* in Costa Rica; *D. humboldtii* is by far the most common.

■ *Gaultheria erecta*
Family Ericaceae

Erect to arching shrub 0.5–3.0 m tall, usually epiphytic, bark cracking longitudinally, reddish brown to gray, twigs slightly ridged, rusty-hairy. **Leaves** alternate, stalk to 0.8 cm long, young leaf stalks whitish, often becoming red, blade 5–11 cm long, 3–6 cm wide, elliptic to almost round, leathery, tip abruptly pointed, base rounded to lobed, blade dark, dull green, hairy, surface sprinkled with tiny dark dots, rusty-hairy below, midrib impressed above, margin finely toothed, teeth tipped with glandular hairs. **Flowers** white to red, radially symmetrical, to 0.7 cm long, 0.6 cm wide, tubular, urn-shaped, surrounded by numerous white to red bracts, spoon-shaped to 1.6 cm long, 0.6 cm wide, usually hairy; inflorescence of narrow, unbranched clusters about 7 cm

long; blooms all year. **Fruit** fleshy, black, with persistent stigma at top, fruiting calyx to 1.2 cm, crowning fruit. **Habitat:** Open, shrubby sites in mountains. Altitude: 1200–3300 m, mostly above 1500 m. Conservation areas: ARE, CVC, GUA, LAC, LAP, PAC. **Range:** N Mex–N Arg. **Notes:** *Gaultheria gracilis* is the only other species of *Gaultheria* in Costa Rica.

▪ *Gaultheria gracilis*
Family Ericaceae

Shrub 40 cm to 1 m tall, terrestrial or epiphytic, young stems yellow-rusty-hairy, older bark blackish, often fissured, twigs hairy. **Leaves** alternate, stalk about 0.5 cm long, finely warty, often hairy, blade to 4–6 cm long, about 2 cm wide, elliptical, tip pointed, base rounded to wedge-shaped, stiff, surface rough-textured, may appear sprinkled with tiny pores, dull dark green above, paler, hairy below, young leaves hairy above, veins pinnate, arching sharply upward parallel to midrib, often reddish, margins minutely toothed. **Flowers** white to red, radially symmetrical, urn-shaped, to 0.8 cm long, 0.4 cm wide, contracted just below petal lobes, finely hairy, inflorescence bracts dull red to white, to 1 cm long, 0.6 cm wide; inflorescence of unbranched clusters 3–7 cm long, axis hairy; blooms all year. **Fruit** fleshy, becoming red, then black when mature, to 0.7 cm wide. **Habitat:** Open sites, in mountains, roadsides, pastures. Altitude: 1100–3300 m, mostly above 2000 m. Conservation areas: ARE, CVC, LAC, LAP, PAC. **Range:** Endemic to CR and W Pan. **Notes:** Both species of *Gaultheria* are common in open high-elevation areas.

▪ *Pernettya prostrata*
Family Ericaceae

Erect to prostrate, 20 cm to sometimes 3 m tall, often forming dense tufts or mats, stems often densely hairy, base swollen, rusty-hairy. **Leaves** alternate, stalk to 0.4 cm, blade 0.6–1.4 cm long, 0.4–0.7 cm wide, elliptic, tip blunt to pointed, base blunt, margin thickened, often reddish, very finely toothed, teeth bristle-tipped, new leaves often pinkish, shiny. **Flowers** white to rose tinted, radially symmetrical, petal tube cylindrical to urn-shaped, 0.6 cm long, petal lobes 5, bent back; inflorescence in upper leaf axils, nodding on stalk 0.4–1.0 cm long; blooms all year.

Fruit fleshy, becoming red then dark blue black, rounded 0.6–1.6 cm, cupped by persistent calyx, tipped by persistent stigma. **Habitat:** Open sites, usually in the mountains. Altitude: 650–3800 m, mostly above 2000 m. Conservation areas: ARE, CVC, GUA, LAC, LAP, PAC. **Range:** Mex–NW Arg. **Notes:** Very common around Cerro de la Muerte.

■ *Thibaudia costaricensis*
Family Ericaceae

Epiphytic shrub, stems elongate, slender, to 2 m long, gray. **Leaves** alternate, stalk to 0.3 cm long, blade 12–24 cm long, 3.5–5 cm wide, lance-shaped to elliptic, base wedge-shaped, tip long-pointed, stiff, shiny, margin slightly rolled under, palmately 5-veined, major veins depressed above. **Flowers** white to pinkish, radially symmetrical, tubular, cylindrical, about 1 cm long, 0.3 cm wide, slightly contracted at both ends, petal lobes 0.1 cm, sometimes pink, calyx red, to 0.2 cm long,

floral base pink to rose about 0.2 cm long and wide, stigma purple; inflorescences of dense, branched, pink-stemmed clusters along branches; blooms and fruits most of the year, most often Mar.–Apr. **Fruit** fleshy, becoming whitish then red finally dark purple, crowned by old calyx lobes. **Habitat:** Wet forests in trees or on steep banks along roads and in open sites. Altitude: 800–2200 m, mostly above 1200 m on the Caribbean slope. Conservation areas: ARE, CVC, LAC, LAP, PAC. **Range:** Endemic to CR and W Pan. **Notes:** This is the only species of *Thibaudia* in Costa Rica.

■ *Vaccinium consanguineum* (arrayán, madroño)
Family Ericaceae

Shrub, 50 cm to 4 m tall, many stiff, rigid branches, twigs short. **Leaves** alternate, stalk to 0.3 cm long, blade 1.5–3 cm long, 0.5–1 cm wide, elliptic, pointed at both ends, margins thickened, barely toothed, mature leaves stiff, dark green, new leaves often dull, matte pink. **Flowers** white, often pink-tinged, radially symmetrical, vase-shaped or cylindrical, 0.5–0.7 cm long, 0.4 cm wide, petal lobes about 0.1 cm long; inflorescence of unbranched clusters 1–4 cm long in leaf axils; blooms and fruits all year. **Fruit** fleshy, blue to reddish, turning black, about 0.5 cm wide, crowned by old calyx lobes. **Habitat:** Open sites in mountains. Altitude: 1500–3400 m. Conservation areas: CVC, LAC, LAP, PAC **Range:** CR, W. Pan. **Notes:** There are nine species of *Vaccinium* in Costa Rica, *V. consanguineum* and *V. poasanum* are the two most common.

■ *Cnidoscolus aconitifolius* (chicasquil)
Family Euphorbiaceae

Shrub or small tree 1–4 m tall, stems leafy, to about 1 cm diameter, often with *stinging hairs or thorns*. **Leaves** alternate, stalk 6–30 cm long, stinging hairs few to many, disk-shaped glands about 0.1 cm at top, blade 11–28 cm long, 14–36 cm wide, 3–5 deep lobes above, 2 smaller lobes at base, margins deeply, sharply lobed and toothed, veins palmate. **Flowers** white, sexes separate, male flowers tubular, to 0.6 cm, female flowers 0.6–1 cm, in branched clusters 11–40 cm long; blooms Mar.–Nov. **Fruit** dry, to 1.8 cm long, 1 cm wide, 3-parted, with stinging hairs. **Habitat:** Common patio shrub with edible leaves, hedgerows and gardens, naturalized in some Pacific lowlands. Altitude: Sea level to 120 m. Conservation areas: GUA, OSA, PAC, TEM. **Range:** Native to Mex, cultivated in C Amer. **Notes:** Trees used as fence posts. There are four species of *Cnidoscolus* in Costa Rica.

■ *Cnidoscolus urens* (hierba santa, mala mujer)
Family Euphorbiaceae

A weedy herb or shrub 0.5–2.5 m tall, stems to 1 cm diameter, succulent, *densely covered with fiercely stinging hairs* to 0.9 cm long. **Leaves** alternate, stalk 7–18 cm long, stinging-hairy, glands at top of stalk fingerlike to 0.1 cm long, blade 6–19 cm long and wide, 3 large sharp-tipped lobes near top, 2 broad lobes at base, margins smooth or with very short, broad teeth to 0.3 cm, finely hairy on both sides. **Flowers** white, sexes separate, male flowers about 1 cm long tubular, female flowers to 0.6 cm long; in umbrella-shaped clusters to 16 cm long, 8 cm wide on a stalk-12 cm long; blooms June–Jan. **Fruit** dry, about 1 cm, green with white-stripes and stinging hairs. **Habitat:** Moist to seasonally dry lowlands. Altitude: Pacific slope, sea level to 300 m. Conservation areas: GUA, LAP, PAC, TEM **Range:** Mex–Arg. **Notes:** An infamously painful plant.

175

◼ *Euphorbia cotinifolia* (sapo barbasco, barrabás,
Caribbean copper plant)
Family Euphorbiaceae

Shrub or small tree 2–9 m tall, stems wine red, *sap* milky,
sticky, *caustic, toxic;* stem ridged between leaf stalk bases.
Leaves in whorls of 3 per node sometimes opposite, stalk
to 6 cm long, blade 4–11 cm long, 2–9 cm wide, broadly
egg-shaped, tip and base rounded, gray green to deep wine
red, veins pinnate, texture dull, soft, deciduous in dry season. **Flowers** pale yellowish, about 0.6 cm, 5-parted, stamens red; inflorescence of small clusters in axils and ends
of stems; blooms Nov.–June. **Fruit** dry, to 0.5 cm, 3-lobed.
Habitat: Planted in evergreen and partly deciduous regions,
as hedges and living fences along pastures and fields, apparently not often escaping from cultivation. Altitude: Sea level
to 1800 m. Conservation areas: CVC, LAP, PAC. **Range:** S
Mex–N S Amer.

◼ *Acacia angustissima* (carboncillo)
Family Fabaceae/Mimosoideae

Shrub or small tree, to about 5 m tall, bark smooth, gray,
multistemmed, freely branched, habit rounded. **Leaves** alternate, twice pinnate, pinnae 6–15 pairs, leaflets about 60 pairs
per pinna, 0.6 cm long, 0.1 cm wide, sides very unequal.
Flowers white, very small, in round heads, inflorescence
large, branched, at ends of stems; blooms Aug.–Jan. **Fruit**
dry, pods flat, 4–8 cm long, 0.5–1 cm wide. **Habitat:** Moist
to wet regions, in open sites and second growth. Altitude:

800–2000 m. Conservation areas: ARE, CVC,
LAP, PAC. Common around the Central Valley. **Range:** S US–Col. **Notes:** There are 18
species of *Acacia* in Costa Rica. All have very
small white to yellow flowers in dense clusters.
Most have spines.

■ *Mimosa pigra* (dormilona, zarza)
Family Fabaceae/Mimosoideae

Weedy shrub 0.5–3 m tall, usually wider than tall, rather flat-topped, branches hairy and spiny. **Leaves** alternate, stalks hairy, bristly, blade twice pinnate, 10–20 cm long, 8 cm wide, pinnae opposite, 8–15 pairs, 3–6 cm long, hairy, leaflets 20–30 pairs, about 1 cm long, 0.2 cm wide, oblong, hairy. **Flowers** whitish to pinkish, tiny, stamens longer than petals, in dense, rounded heads, about 2 cm diameter; blooms Aug–Feb. **Fruit** pods 4–8 cm long, to 1.5 cm wide, flat, bristly, with 7–20 segments, often in dense, tight, flat, spiraled clusters of 10–15. **Habitat:** Wet to seasonally dry regions in open sites, often along roadsides. Altitude: Sea level to 1700 m. Conservation areas: ARE, CVC, GUA, LAC, OSA, PAC, TEM, TOR. **Range:** US, Mex–Par, WI, Africa. Introduced in E Asia, and invasive in some Pacific islands and Australia. **Notes:** There are 24 species of *Mimosa* in Costa Rica.

■ *Pithecellobium lanceolatum* (michiguiste)
Family Fabaceae/Mimosoideae

Small tree or large shrub 4–10 m tall, often multistemmed sprawling, low-branched, trunks stout, arching or leaning, bark yellow-tan with prominent horizontal ridges, younger stems thorny at old nodes, thorns in pairs on twigs, to 1 cm long, broad-based. **Leaves** alternate, evenly twice pinnate, 2 opposite pinnae, each with 2 broad leaflets, in a cow-hoof pattern, blades 2–10 cm long, 1–4 cm wide, inner sides shorter than outer, tough, leathery, stiff. **Flowers** white, about 2 cm long, brushlike with numerous stamens, no petals, fragrant, in spikes to 7 cm long, inflorescence of many spikes about 20 cm long, 15 cm wide; blooms most of the year. **Fruit** pods dark, about 10 cm long, 1 cm wide, twisted, red inside when mature. **Habitat:** Wet to seasonally dry lowlands, in open sites or second growth. Often near streams or marshes. Altitude: Sea level to 600 m, mostly below 200 m. Conservation areas: GUA, PAC, TEM, TOR. **Range:** SE Mex–Col. and Ven. **Notes:** There are 20 species of *Pithecellobium* in Costa Rica.

■ *Carpotroche platyptera* (caraña)
Family Flacourtiaceae

Small tree 2–5 m tall, branches stout, few, leafy at tips. **Leaves** alternate, blade large, 15–55 cm long, 3–19 cm wide, elliptic, tip blunt to long-pointed, base tapered, midrib very prominent below, veins impressed above, arching upward, loop-connected along margin, margin coarsely wavy-toothed.

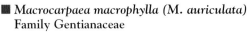

Flowers pinkish-white, radially symmetrical, about 0.6 cm wide, petals about 8, sexes separate, male flowers with 24 stamens, in axillary clusters, female flowers solitary on branches; blooms and fruits most of the year. **Fruit** dry, reddish to orange, to 6 cm long, 4.5 cm wide, with 6–10 hairy, winglike longitudinal ridges. **Habitat:** Wet to moist lowland forests understories. Altitude: Sea level to 1150 m, mostly below 400 m. Conservation areas: ARE, CVC, HNO, LAC, LAP, OSA, PAC TOR. **Range:** Gua–Pan. **Notes:** This is the only species of *Carpotroche* in Costa Rica.

■ *Macrocarpaea macrophylla (M. auriculata)*
Family Gentianaceae

Shrub to about 5 m tall. **Leaves** opposite, blade 20–30 cm long, 13–20 cm wide, hairy, pointed at both ends. **Flowers**

cream white, tubular, bilaterally symmetrical, showy, 3.5–4 cm long, 2.5–3.5 cm wide, more or less funnel-shaped; inflorescence of branched clusters at ends of stems; blooms most of the year. **Fruit** dry, 1.5–3 cm long, elliptic, tip pointed. **Habitat:** Moist to wet forests, and open sites, at midelevations. Altitude: 1000–2000 m. Conservation areas: ARE, CVC, LAP. Seen in Tapantí and Braulio Carrillo N.P. **Range:** CR, Col. **Notes:** There are four species of *Macrocarpaea* in Costa Rica.

■ *Besleria notabilis*
Family Gesneriaceae

Coarse shrub, or large herb to 2 m tall, stems to 1 cm diameter, herbaceous above, woody toward base, unbranched, new growth 4-sided, leaves all at ends of stems. **Leaves** opposite, stalk to 4.5 cm long, blade 14–30 cm long, 4–13 cm wide, elliptic, tip abruptly pointed, base wedge-shaped, shiny, slightly fleshy, surface puckered from deeply impressed veins, margin often sparsely toothed. **Flowers** cream to red, tubular, bilaterally symmetrical, to 1.2 cm long, 0.3 cm wide, translucent, petal lobes small, calyx reddish, hairy, stalks to 1.6 cm long; inflorescence of many-flowered, axillary clusters often below leaves; blooms all year. **Fruit** fleshy, hollow, white or green, to 0.6 cm, surrounded by pale lavender persistent calyx, flesh Styrofoam-textured; on leafless stems below leaves (photo). **Habitat:** Wet forest understories. Altitude: 20–1800 m, mostly above 500 m. Conservation areas: ARE, CVC, GUA, LAC, LAP, OSA (rarely). Found at Tapantí, Rincón de la Vieja, and Braulio Carrillo N.P. **Range:** CR, Pan.

■ *Drymonia lanceolata*
Family Gesneriaceae

Shrub, or woody-based herb, to 2 m tall, stems about 1 cm wide, new growth rather succulent and translucent, stems square, slightly winged at corners, conspicuous ridge across stem between leaf stalk bases. **Leaves** opposite, stalk to 14 cm, blade 10–34 cm long, 5–14 cm wide, broadly elliptic, thin, tip long-pointed, base wedge-shaped, margin with small rounded teeth, hairy on both sides, especially below, veins depressed above. **Flowers** white outside, yellow inside, showy, fragrant, hairy, bilaterally symmetrical, tubular, to 4.5 long, 1 cm wide, constricted below, petal lobes fringed, calyx pale green, about 5 cm long, 1.5 cm wide, buds winged by corners of closed sepals, flowers on individual stems, in rings around nodes; blooms most of the year. **Fruit** fleshy, greenish white, oval. **Habitat:** Wet forest understories. Altitude: 700–1700 m, usually above 1300 m. Conservation areas: ARE, CVC, GUA, LAC, LAP. Seen at Tapantí and Braulio Carrillo N.P. **Range:** CR. Pan. **Notes:** Winged, pale green buds conspicuous. There are about 20 species of *Drymonia* in Costa Rica.

■ *Escallonia myrtilloides*
Family Grossulariaceae

Shrub or small tree 2–6 m tall, trunk to 25 cm diameter, bark brown, fibrous, flaky, fissured, branches numerous, held at right angles to trunk, ends of branches slightly upturned. **Leaves** alternate, in tight spirals (rosettes) on short twigs along top sides of branches, blade 0.8–2 cm long, 0.4–1 cm wide, widest near apex, rounded, leathery, dark green above, pale below. **Flowers** greenish white to pale yellow, radially symmetrical, petals about 1 cm long, free, ovary inferior, yellow; blooms Apr.–Oct. Flowers very attractive to bees. **Fruit** dry, about 0.6 cm wide, tipped by persistent style and calyx lobes; seeds numerous. **Habitat:** High mountains in open areas (páramo), and along roadsides. Often the dominant plant on rocky slopes. Altitude: 2500–3400 m. Conservation areas: CVC, LAP, PAC. Very common along the Interamerican Highway (Ruta 2) near Cerro de la Muerte. **Range:** CR–Bol. **Notes:** There is one other species of *Escallonia* in Costa Rica, *E. paniculata* is much less common and found at slightly lower elevations.

■ *Phyllonoma ruscifolia*
Family Grossulariaceae

Shrub or small tree 1.5–6 m tall, occasionally epiphytic, secondary branches arise in leaf axils with inflorescence, branches sometimes vinelike. **Leaves** alternate, 4–10 cm long, 1–3 cm wide, tip narrow and elongate. **Flowers** pale yellow green, 0.2–0.3 cm wide, radially symmetrical; borne in small groups at the end of the leaf blade; blooms and fruits most of the year. **Fruit** fleshy, white. **Habitat:** Wet mountain forests. Altitude: 700–2000 m, mostly above 1300 m. Conservation areas: ARE, CVC, LAC, LAP, PAC. **Range:** CR–Bol. **Notes:** The inflorescences borne near the tip of the leaf surface is extremely unusual. There are two other less common species of *Phyllonoma* in Costa Rica.

■ *Clinopodium vimineum (Satureja viminea)* (menta)
Family Lamiaceae

Small shrub about 1–2 m tall, strong mint odor. **Leaves** opposite, about 0.7–2 cm long, narrow, tip rounded, base tapered, veins slightly impressed. **Flowers** white to pale lavender, about 1 cm long, slightly bilaterally symmetrical, tubular, 5-parted, lowest petal lobe longer than others; blooms Sept.– Jan. **Fruit** dry, small. **Habitat:** Nonnative, cultivated in home gardens, apparently not escaping. Altitude: 1100–1300 m. Conservation areas: CVC (probably also in other areas). **Range:** DR, Jam. **Notes:** There is one other species of *Clinopodium* in Costa Rica, uncommon, found at high elevations in the Cordillera Talamanca.

■ *Ocotea veraguensis* (canelo, sigua, quina)
Family Lauraceae

Tree 4–10 m tall, 80 cm diameter (often blooms and fruits at 5 m), trunk erect, bark gray, grainy, twigs slender, green. **Leaves** alternate, stalk to 1 cm long, blade 6–14 cm long, 2–5 cm wide, narrowly elliptic, tip bluntly pointed, base tapered to stalk, stiff, smooth, shiny, midrib pale, secondary veins rather obscure. **Flowers** white, radially symmetrical, sweetly fragrant (jasmine-scented), 0.5–1 cm wide, 6 petals about

0.4 cm long, 0.3 cm wide, flat, stamens yellow, clustered in center in a cushionlike arrangement; inflorescence of branched clusters, on a stalk 5–16 cm long; blooms and fruits most of the year. **Fruit** fleshy, becoming black when ripe, to 2.5 cm long, 1.8 cm wide, elliptic, in a cuplike red base formed by top of stalk, to 1.6 cm wide, 0.5 cm deep, 1 large seed. **Habitat:** Wet to seasonally dry forests. Altitude: Sea level to 1600 m, mostly on the Pacific slope, below 1000 m. Conservation areas: ARE, GUA, LAP, OSA, PAC, TEM. **Range:** Mex–Pan. **Notes:** There are about 59 species of *Ocotea* in Costa Rica. All are quite similar.

■ *Blakea grandiflora*
Family Melastomataceae

Epiphytic shrub or sometimes a small tree to 15 m tall, branches very stiff, hard, young stems brown-hairy, often rooting at nodes. **Leaves** opposite, stalk finely brown-hairy, blade 10–18 cm long, 6–12 cm wide, broadly egg-shaped, blunt at both ends, new leaves brown-hairy, major veins palmate at base, becoming parallel above, minor veins numerous, ladderlike-like between primaries. **Flowers** white to pinkish, radially symmetrical, large, petals 6, about 2.5 cm long, 2 cm wide, broadly egg-shaped, thick, tips often pink, anthers yellow, filaments white, all on one side, flower buds often red or pink; blooms Apr.–Dec. **Fruit** red, about 2 cm long with persisting calyx lobes. **Habitat:** Moist to wet forests, mostly in mountain regions. Altitude: 700–2700 m, usually above 1500 m. Conservation areas: ARE, CVC, GUA, HNO, LAP **Range:** CR. **Notes:** There are about 18 species of *Blakea* in Costa Rica.

◼ *Clidemia sericea*
Family Melastomataceae

Shrub or woody herb 50 cm to 3.5 m tall, woody stems gray brown, scaly-hairy, all young parts hairy, hairs to 0.2 cm long. **Leaves** opposite, 3–10 cm long, 2–6 cm wide, elliptic, tip pointed to blunt, base pointed to rounded, surface dull green above, paler below, hairy on both sides, major veins 5–7, palmate, secondary veins numerous, ladderlike between major veins, all veins depressed above, margin sometimes finely toothed. **Flowers** white to pinkish, petals 4, 2.5 cm long, 1 cm wide, anthers pink, longer than petals, calyx and floral base red-hairy; inflorescence of tight axillary clusters; blooms and fruits most of the year. **Fruit** fleshy, turning red then blue purple to black, hairy, to 1 cm wide, flesh juicy, seeds 0.1 cm. **Habitat:** Wet to seasonally dry regions in open sites, old pastures, roadsides. Altitude: Sea level to 1800 m. Most often below 1000 m. Conservation areas: ARE, CVC, GUA, HNO, LAP, OSA, PAC, TEM. **Range:** SMex–Bol and Brz, Tr. **Notes:** There are about 30 species of *Clidemia* in Costa Rica.

◼ *Conostegia xalapensis* (canallito)
Family Melastomataceae

Shrub or small tree to 10 m tall, most parts densely brown-hairy, twigs slender, gray. **Leaves** opposite, stalk 1–2.5 cm, blade 5–25 cm long, 2–8 cm wide, lance-shaped, tip long-pointed, base blunt to wedge-shaped, dull, dark green above, tan or whitish, hairy-scaly below, major veins palmate at base, becoming parallel above, minor veins numerous, ladderlike between primaries. **Flowers** white, sometimes pinkish, about 1 cm wide, fragrant, petals 5, widest above middle, stamens 10, yellow, all on one side of the flower along with the stigma, inflorescence of dense, branched, pyramidal clusters at ends of branches; blooms and fruits most of the year. **Fruit** fleshy, becoming reddish, then purple black when mature, densely hairy, to 0.8 cm, seeds numerous. **Habitat:** Moist to wet forests, also as horticultural planting. Altitude: Sea level to 1600 m. Conservation areas: ARE, CVC, GUA, HNO, LAC, LAP, PAC, TOR. **Range:** Mex–Col, Cuba.

■ *Leandra granatensis*
Family Melastomataceae

Shrub 1–5 m tall, most parts densely bristly hairy, hairs to 0.2 cm long. **Leaves** opposite, stalk about 3.5 cm long, blade 10–30 cm long, 6–12 cm wide, tip with elongate point, densely, stiffly hairy, major veins 7, palmate, parallel, secondary veins numerous, ladderlike between major veins. **Flow-**

ers white, to pale pink, radially symmetrical, petals 5, 2 cm long, linear, hairy, anthers yellow 0.5 cm; inflorescence 7–19 cm long, stems red with opposite branches, flowers stalkless, covering one side of inflorescence branch; blooms mostly July–Nov. **Fruit** fleshy, to 0.5 cm wide, red-hairy, becoming red then purple; fruits mostly July–Nov. **Habitat:** Moist to wet forests, also in disturbed sites, second growth. Altitude: Sea level to 1100 m, usually below 600 m. Conservation areas: CVC, GUA, HNO, LAC, OSA, PAC, TOR. **Range:** Nic–Ven and Ec. **Notes:** There are nine species of *Leandra* in Costa Rica.

■ *Meriania phlomoides*
Family Melastomataceae

Large shrub or treelet, 4–7 m tall, twigs brown, hairy. **Leaves** opposite, stalk about 3 cm long, sometimes purplish, blade 11–23 cm long, 6–14 cm wide, elliptic, pointed at both ends, upper surface dark green, shiny, lower surface paler, shiny, major veins 5, palmate at base, becoming parallel above,

minor veins numerous, ladderlike between primaries, margin very faintly toothed. **Flowers** white, radially symmetrical, about 2.5 cm wide, petals 5, 1–2 cm long, 1.5 cm wide, tips blunt, anthers yellow, numerous, style 2 cm long, petals and anthers deciduous as one unit; blooms Apr.–Oct. **Fruit** fleshy, rusty green-brown when young; fruits Feb., Mar., Aug.–Nov. **Habitat:** Wet mountain forest understories. Altitude: 1000–2300 m. Conservation areas: ARE, CVC, GUA, HNO, LAP, PAC. **Range:** CR–Col. **Notes:** There are five species of *Meriania* in Costa Rica.

■ *Miconia argentea* (María, santamaría, lengua de vaca)
Family Melastomataceae

Tree 3–15 m, trunk to 50 cm diameter, blooms when 3–4 m, bark coarse, pale gray, flaking, peeling, shaggy in age, young parts pale tan-scaly, stems flattened, edges twisted at nodes. **Leaves** opposite, stalk to 6 cm, stout, blade 8–30 cm long, 6–18 cm wide, broadly egg-shaped, tip rounded with small, abrupt, pointed tip, base rounded, dull, dark green above, tan-scaly below, leathery, major veins 5, palmate, secondary veins ladderlike between major veins. **Flowers** white, small, numer-

ous, about 0.5 cm wide, petals 5, folded back, stamens yellow, 10; inflorescence branched, pyramid-shaped clusters to 25 cm long at ends of stems; blooms Jan.–Mar. **Fruit** fleshy, blue purple, hairy, to 0.8 cm wide, seeds numerous. **Habitat:** Wet to seasonally dry regions, second growth and scrub, roadsides, edges. Altitude: Sea level to 1200 m. Conservation areas: ARE, CVC, GUA, LAP, OSA, PAC, TEM. **Range:** S Mex–Pan. **Notes:** There are about 100 species of *Miconia* in Costa Rica.

■ *Miconia costaricensis* (lengua de vaca, uña de gato)
Family Melastomataceae

Shrub 1–3 m tall, stems slender, rusty scaly-hairy. **Leaves** opposite, stalk pinkish, blade about 15 cm long, 6 cm wide, elliptic, hairy on both sides, hairs often reddish, dull green above, tip tapered, base rounded, major veins, parallel to midrib, secondary veins ladderlike between major veins. **Flowers** white to pink, hairy, enclosed in pinkish calyx, about 0.3–0.4 cm wide, rounded, stamens yellow with red anthers, longer than petals; flowering stems pinkish, reddish-hairy, in branched clusters at ends of branches; blooms Mar.–July. **Fruit** fleshy, pale blue to dark purple, 0.5–1 cm wide, seeds numerous, tiny; fruit present Feb.–Oct. **Habitat:** Wet mountain forests, open sites, and second growth. Altitude: 220–2100 m, usually above 1500 m. Conservation areas: ARE, CVC, LAC, LAP. **Range:** Mex, CR–Col.

Miconia argentea (above)

Miconia costaricensis (below)

185

■ *Miconia nervosa* (canilla de mula, burro, zorrillo)
Family Melastomataceae

Shrub to 5 m tall, multistemmed, bark gray, shredding, new growth green, densely white-hairy. **Leaves** opposite, pairs often unequal, stalk 0.5–2 cm long, blade 7–28 cm long, 4–12 cm wide, elliptic, tip pointed, base tapered to stalk, hairy on both sides, young leaves often purplish below, major veins 5–7, parallel to midrib, secondary veins ladderlike between major veins. **Flowers** white, hairy, appearing tubular, petals 5, tips rounded, bent outward, anthers longer than petals, inflorescence often spikelike, to 15 cm long with tuftlike clumps of flowers on red stalks; blooms and fruits all year. **Fruit** fleshy, at first white, becoming red orange, then blue, densely hairy, 1 cm diameter, seeds brown, sticky. **Habitat:** Wet to moist lowland forests, edges, second growth. Altitude: Sea level to 600 m. Conservation areas: CVC, GUA, HNO, LAC, OSA, PAC, TOR. Seen near Carate, OSA Peninsula. **Range:** Bel–Bol and Brz, Tr.

■ *Miconia tonduzii* (canilla de mula, burro, zorrillo)
Family Melastomataceae

Shrub about 4 m tall, bark smooth, gray brown, twigs rusty green, finely hairy, 4-sided, slender. **Leaves** opposite, stalk 1.5 cm, blade 6–16 cm long, 3–5 cm wide, elliptical, pointed at both ends, tip arched downward, blade shiny, hairless, dark, dull green above, rusty-scaly below, wrinkled, major veins deeply depressed above, 3–5, palmate at base, becoming

parallel above, secondary veins ladderlike between major veins, margin slightly toothed. **Flowers** white with purple pink, radially symmetrical, 5- to 6-parted, about 1 cm wide, petals 0.2 cm long, stamens yellow, longer than petals; inflorescence 4–8 cm long, of branched clusters; attractive to bees; blooms Jan.–Apr., Aug., Nov. **Fruit** fleshy, pink, becoming blue, 0.4–0.7 cm wide; fruit present most of the year. **Habitat:** Mountain forests, second growth, open sites. Altitude: 900–3400 m, mostly above 1900 m. Conservation areas: ARE, CVC, GUA, LAP, PAC. **Range:** Nic–Pan.

186

■ *Monochaetum floribundum*
Family Melastomataceae

Low, erect shrub, 0.5–2.5 m tall, stems slender, about 0.3 cm wide, arching, usually drooping in flat sprays, hairy, brown, young stems often red, older parts woody, bark flaking; aggressively colonial. **Leaves** opposite, stalk 0.1–0.5 cm long, blades in unequal pairs, the larger 2–5 cm (rarely to 8 cm) long, 0.6–2 cm wide, egg-shaped, tip pointed, base rounded, major veins 3–5, parallel, palmate at base, sharply impressed above as parallel grooves, secondary veins ladderlike, between major veins, surface hairy on both sides. **Flowers** white to pale pink, about 2 cm wide, petals 4, rounded, tips notched to barely pointed, 0.6–1.4 cm long, 0.6–1 cm wide, calyx red, hairy, stamens with red "tails," anthers red to yellow, floral base urn-shaped; flowers solitary or in small clusters with candelabralike branching; blooms most of the year, especially Oct.–Mar. **Fruit**

at first red, surrounded by persistent red calyx, becoming dry; seeds numerous. **Habitat:** Open mountain sites, roadsides, edges, burned areas, pastures. Altitude: 1100–2700 m. Conservation areas: ARE, CVC, GUA, LAC, LAP. **Range:** S Mex–Pan. **Notes:** There are six species of *Monochaetum* in Costa Rica.

■ *Tibouchina inopinata*
Family Melastomataceae

Small tree or shrub 2–6 m tall. **Leaves** opposite, 5–12 cm long, 1.5–3 cm wide, old leaves turning red. **Flowers** white to pink, petals 5, free, about 1 cm long, stigma red, anthers yellow; inflorescence branched; blooms May–Aug. **Fruit** red, becoming dry, hollow, 5-parted, 0.6 cm wide, brown, enveloped in old calyx; fruit present July, Feb. **Habitat:** Wet mountain forests and second growth. Altitude: 900–2000 m. Conservation areas: CVC, LAP **Range:** CR, Pan. **Notes:** The most common species of *Tibouchina* is *T. longifolia,* an herb, with very similar flowers.

Courtesy of Margaret Gargiullo

■ *Ardisia pleurobotrya* (tucuico)
Family Myrsinaceae

Shrub or tree 3–15 m tall, stems rusty scaly-hairy, new growth fleshy, brown, stout, finely scaly with purple black sap. **Leaves** alternate, stalk 1 cm, blade 5–11 cm long, 1.5–3.5 cm wide, elliptic, pointed at both ends, dark green above, pale below, sprinkled with tiny yellow dots, firm, shiny, midrib impressed above. **Flowers** dull white with patches of tiny lavender spots in center of each petal, about 1 cm wide, radially symmetrical, petals 5, tips pointed, bases fused, anthers dull yellow; inflorescence of dense, sparsely branched, drooping clusters 7–13 cm long, with a stalk 3–6 cm long; blooms Apr.–Oct. **Fruit** fleshy, becoming red then black, about 1 cm wide, shiny, rounded, persistent style at top, flesh foamy-pulpy, white with 1 large, pale seed; fruit present June–Oct., Feb., Mar. **Habitat:** Mountain forests and second growth. Altitude: 1100–3300 m. Conservation areas: CVC, GUA, LAC, LAP. **Range:** CR, Pan. **Notes:** There are about 25 species of *Ardisia* in Costa Rica.

■ *Ardisia revoluta* (papaturro de pava, guastomate, tucuico) Family Myrsinaceae

Shrub or small tree usually 2–10 m tall, rarely to 17 m, larger trees with erect trunk, older trunks corded, stump sprouts readily, bark gray with prominent lenticels, horizontal ridges, twigs rather stout. **Leaves** alternate, spiraled at ends of twigs, stalk 1–2 cm, blade 9–22 cm long, 3–10 cm wide, narrowly elliptic, tip blunt to pointed, base wedge-shaped, glossy green, surface smooth, leathery-textured, paler below, marked with numerous tiny black dots, midrib raised below, other veins obscure, leaf buds pointed with hooked tip. **Flowers** white, radially symmetrical, fragrant, 5-parted, petals about 1 cm long, fused at base, tips pointed, stamens about 0.7 cm long, style 0.5–0.7 cm long, ovary superior; inflorescence of large, dense, once-branched, pyramid-shaped clusters, about 30 cm long; blooms and fruits on and off most of the year. **Fruit** fleshy, turning red then black, round, 0.4–0.8 cm wide, flesh juicy, dark purple, edible; fruits Jan.–Mar. **Habitat:** Moist to seasonally dry forests, second growth, and open sites. Altitude: Sea level to 1200 m, mostly on the Pacific slope. Conservation areas: ARE, CVC, GUA, LAP, PAC, TEM. **Range:** Mex–Pan. **Notes:** Many species of *Ardisia* are very similar.

■ *Myrsine cubana* (ratón, ratoncillo)
Family Myrsinaceae

Shrub or small tree 1–15 m tall, trunks thick, bark gray. **Leaves** alternate, closely spiraled at ends of stems, stalks 0.4–0.7 cm long, blade 4–13 cm long, 1–5.5 cm wide, narrowly elliptic, tips usually rounded or notched, base pointed, surface dark green above, paler green below, smooth leathery, midrib pale above, secondary veins obscure. **Flowers** off-white, about 0.5 cm long, 5-parted, radially symmetrical, sexes on separate plants; petals fused below, lobes about 0.2 cm long; inflorescences of 3–9 flowers in clusters along leafless parts of stems; fruits and blooms Mar.–Dec. **Fruit** fleshy, black, 0.4–0.7 cm wide, with 1 large seed, stalkless; fruit present most of the year. **Habitat:** Open sites, pastures, and second growth in mountain areas. Altitude: Sea level to 2800 m. Conservation areas: CVC, GUA, LAC, LAP, TOR. **Range:** Mex–CR, WI. **Notes:** There are seven species of *Myrsine* in Costa Rica. They are much like *Ardisia* species.

■ *Eugenia truncata* (escobo, cacique, carro caliente) Family Myrtaceae

Shrub or tree 2–8 m tall, bark fairly smooth, small branches thin, gray, twigs brown, hairy-scaly. **Leaves** opposite, to not quite opposite, ranked along ends of twigs, stalk short, swollen, blade 6–14 cm long, 3–6 cm wide, oblong, narrowly egg-shaped or elliptic, dark green above, tip gradually tapered to a blunt point, base blunt to slightly lobed, veins raised below, rather obscure above, joined near margin by loop connections, new leaves reddish, velvety below. **Flowers** white and pink, radially symmetrical, about 2 cm wide,

4 free petals, about 0.9 cm long, 0.4 cm wide, blunt at both, ends curled inward, soon falling, white inside, pink outside, 4 sepals, 2 smaller than the others, persistent, stamens numerous, pistil elongate, about 1.3 cm, flowers arising in small clusters from twigs below leaves; blooms Sept.–Mar. **Fruit** fleshy, turning pink then purple when mature, about 1.5 cm wide; 1-seeded; fruit present Nov.–July. **Habitat:** Moist to seasonally dry forests and second growth. Altitude: 300–1200 m. Conservation areas: ARE, CVC, GUA (mostly), PAC. **Range:** CR, Pan. **Notes:** There are about 25 species of *Eugenia* in Costa Rica.

SHRUBS AND
SMALL TREES

■ *Psidium guineense* (güizaro, cas, guayaba, wild guava)
Family Myrtaceae

Shrub or tree 1–3 m tall, sometimes to 7 m, bark smooth, thin, peeling, young stems rusty-hairy becoming greenish hairy. **Leaves** opposite to subopposite; blade 4–14 cm long, 3–8 cm wide, elliptic to oblong, dull gray green with lighter,

pinnate veins, reddish-hairy below, new leaves reddish, hairy. **Flowers** white, radially symmetrical, to 1.8 cm wide, showy, fragrant, 5-parted, sepals 5 curved back, stamens numerous, flowers in groups of 3, in axils; blooms Mar.–Nov. **Fruit** fleshy, yellow, 1–2.5 cm wide, pulp white, edible but acidic, fragrant, seeds numerous; fruit present May–Nov. **Habitat:** Wet to seasonally dry forests, second growth, open sites, roadsides. Altitude: Sea level to 1900 m. Conservation areas: ARE, GUA, HNO, LAP, TEM. **Range:** Mex–S Amer, WI. **Notes:** There are seven species of *Psidium* in Costa Rica.

■ *Ugni myricoides* (arrayán)
Family Myrtaceae

Shrub or small tree 1–4 m tall, bark tan brown, stems numerous, rough, scaly, branches opposite, often in 2–4 ranks along a main stem, intervals between leaf stalks short, stipules on stem between bases of leaf stalks, twigs whitish-hairy. **Leaves** opposite, stalk 0.2 cm, blade 0.7–2 cm long, 0.2–1.5 cm wide, egg-shaped, tip pointed, base blunt, stiff, dark green, with fine translucent dots above and below, new leaves bronze-tinged. **Flowers** white, with dark pink markings, bell-shaped, about 1.5 cm diameter, nodding, petals 5, free, overlapping, stamens and stigma pink, calyx lobes (sepals) dark pink to green, folded back; solitary on stalks 1–2 cm long; blooms in Mar.–June. **Fruit** fleshy, purple black, 0.5–1 cm long,

finely hairy, crowned by old calyx lobes, edible, seeds numerous; Mar. **Habitat:** Mountain forests and open sites, old pastures, scrub. Altitude: 1800–3700 m, mostly above 2500 m. Conservation areas: CVC, LAC, LAP, PAC. **Range:** S Mex–Ven and Pr. **Notes:** This is the only species of *Ugni* in Costa Rica.

◼ *Piper aequale*
Family Piperaceae

Shrub usually not more than 2 m tall, stems slender, green, bamboolike with swollen nodes, stipules about 1 cm long, 0.2 cm wide, deciduous as new leaf expands, leaving a scar around each node. **Leaves** alternate, usually ranked along stem and drooping below plane of stem, stalk 0.6–1 cm long, blade narrow, 6–15 cm long, 3–7 cm wide, elliptic to lance-shaped, tip tapered, long-pointed, base blunt, sides unequal, dark green, glossy above, veins rather fine and inconspicuous. **Flowers** white, minute, crowded on unbranched spikes 5–10 cm long, 0.3 cm wide (0.4 cm in fruit), held above leaves, a spike opposite almost every leaf; blooms most of the year. **Fruit** fleshy, about 0.1 cm long, 1-seeded, eaten by bats. **Habitat:** Wet to seasonally dry forests, second growth, disturbed sites, roadsides. Altitude: Sea level to 2200 m, mostly below 1100 m. Conservation areas: ARE, CVC, GUA, HNO, LAC, LAP, OSA, PAC, TEM, TOR. **Range:** NE Hon–SE Brz. **Notes:** There are about 124 species of *Piper* in Costa Rica.

◼ *Piper auritum* (alcotán, estrella, anisillo, anise piper)
Family Piperaceae

Shrub or small tree 1.5–8 m tall, to 10 cm diameter, trunk usually single, base sometimes with stilt roots, stipules not evident. **Leaves** alternate, stalk 4–10 cm long, winged, blade large, 20–55 cm long, 12–30 cm wide, narrowly heart-shaped, tip abruptly tapered, base lobed, lobes very unequal, hairy below, margin densely hairy, foliage with a sarsaparilla or aniselike odor when crushed. **Flowers** white, minute, crowded on thin unbranched spikes about 30 cm long, 0.2–0.5 cm thick (to 0.8 cm wide in fruit), arching or drooping; blooms and fruits all year; pollinated by small bees and beetles. **Fruit** fleshy, less than 0.1 cm wide, eaten by bats. **Habitat:** Moist to wet forests, edges, second growth, open sites. Altitude: Sea level to 1700 m. Conservation areas: ARE, CVC, GUA, LAC, LAP, OSA, PAC, TEM, TOR. **Range:** Mex–Ec, Haiti, Jam. **Notes:** One of the most common species of *Piper*. Conspicuous for its treelike habit and large leaves, with unequally lobed bases.

■ *Piper biolleyi*
Family Piperaceae

Shrub 2–4 m tall, new leaves and inflorescence emerging from within sheathing leaf-base, stipule 5 cm long, covering emerging leaves, deciduous, leaving scar around stem, old nodes thickened. **Leaves** alternate, blade 15–30 cm long, 10–18 cm wide, broadly elliptic, tip abruptly pointed, base blunt, sides mostly equal, sometimes slightly lobed, surface

dark green, shiny, slightly fleshy and stiff, corrugated from 10–20 pairs of closely spaced, impressed veins at acute angle to midrib. **Flowers** pale greenish white, minute, in rather short and stout spikes, 5–13 cm long, becoming 0.6–0.8 cm in fruit, erect; blooms and fruits Feb., Aug.–Oct. **Fruit** fleshy, large, to 0.3 cm wide, tightly packed on fruits spike, eaten by bats. **Habitat:** Shady, wet forest understories and stream sides, forest edges. Altitude: Sea level to 1400 m. Conservation areas: CVC, LAC, LAP. **Range:** Nic–Pan. **Note:** Rather uncommon but conspicuous for its large, stiff, puckered leaves.

■ *Piper friedrichsthalii*
Family Piperaceae

Shrub 1–4 m tall, with bamboolike appearance, often many stems together, nodes thickened, stems green, clumped, upright, young stems finely hairy, older stems often marked with purple, branches at right angle to main stem, stipule to 1 cm long enclosing leaf bud. **Leaves** alternate, 2-ranked and drooping along stems, blade 7–16 cm long, 2–3 cm wide, lance-shaped, tip gradually tapered, long-pointed, base blunt, surface smooth, sides unequal, veins impressed above, curved sharply upward, almost parallel to midrib. **Flowers** white, minute, crowded on unbranched spikes 4–9 cm long, 0.2–0.3 cm wide, becoming 0.4 cm wide in fruit, arching, solitary, each opposite a leaf; blooms and fruits all year. **Fruit** fleshy, less than 0.1 cm wide, eaten by bats. **Habitat:** Open, sunny areas, along roadsides, in wet, evergreen, regions. Altitude: Sea level

to 1500 m, mostly on the Pacific slope. Conservation areas: ARE, CVC, LAC, LAP, OSA, PAC. **Range:** Nic–Ec. **Notes:** Conspicuous in large stands along roadsides. Very similar to the common species *P. aduncum*, which has rough-textured leaves.

▓ *Piper littorale*
Family Piperaceae

Low shrub 1–2 m tall, stems slender, smooth, green, stipules small, deciduous. **Leaves** alternate, 2-ranked along sides of stem, blade 7–15 cm long, 2–6 cm wide, elliptic, sides unequal, tip pointed, base unequal, often slightly lobed, surface shiny, rubbery, dark green above, paler below, quite smooth. **Flower** spike bright white, becoming grayish white, erect, 4–8 cm long, 0.3 cm wide (0.5 cm thick in fruit). **Fruit** fleshy, to nearly 0.1 cm wide, eaten by bats. **Habitat:** Coastal swamps, forests behind beaches, disturbed, wet forests. Altitude: Caribbean coast, at or near sea level. Conservation areas: LAC, TOR. **Range:** Mex, Nic–Col. **Notes:** The only species of *Piper* growing along the seashore.

▓ *Piper marginatum* (anisillo)
Family Piperaceae

Shrub to 3 m tall, sap with strong licorice odor, young stems green, nodes thickened, leaves emerging from sheathing leaf stalk base, no stipule apparent. **Leaves** alternate, stalk 3–5 cm long at flowering nodes, to 10 cm at nonflowering nodes, deeply grooved, margins winged, blade 8–18 cm long, 5–13 cm wide, broadly heart-shaped, often almost round in outline, tip gradually tapered to a point, base round to deeply lobed, sides about equal, veins palmate 7–13 major veins, slightly raised above. **Flowers** white, becoming gray, minute, crowded on unbranched, elongate, spikes 10–25 cm long, 0.3 cm thick (to 0.4 cm in fruit), held above leaves, base erect, tip drooping; blooms all year. **Fruit** fleshy, less than 0.1 cm wide. **Habitat:** Moist to seasonally dry forests, second growth, partial shade, roadside banks. Altitude: Sea level to 1300 m, mostly on the Pacific slope. Conservation areas: ARE, CVC, GUA, LAP, PAC, TEM. **Range:** Mex–Ven and Ec, WI. **Notes:** Conspicuous for its heart-shaped leaves with parallel veins and slender, drooping flower spikes.

■ *Piper peltatum (Pothomorphe peltata)*
Family Piperaceae
Shrub 0.5–2 m tall, stems green, often rough-textured with dark speckles, zigzagged, hollow, to 1 cm diameter, few branches. **Leaves** alternate, leaf stalk 10–26 cm long, attached to underside of blade about 5 cm in from edge, deeply grooved, base sheathing stem, blade almost round, 20–30 cm long, 15–26 cm wide, tip abruptly pointed, base round to slightly lobed, dark green, paler below, slightly puckered, veins palmate, radiating from leaf stalk insertion, pinnate above. **Flowers** white, minute, crowded on unbranched spikes 4–10 cm long, about 0.3 cm wide, erect, in umbrella-shaped clusters of 3–20 spikes from 1 stalk about 5 cm long in leaf axils; blooms most of the year. **Fruit** fleshy, less than 0.1 cm wide, probably eaten by bats. **Habitat:** Wet to seasonally dry but evergreen regions, open areas or part shade, along roadsides. Altitude: Sea level to 1900 m, usually below 500 m. Conservation areas: CVC, GUA, HNO, LAC, OSA, PAC, TEM, TOR. **Range:** Mex–Pr and Brz, WI. **Notes:** There are only a few *Piper* species with leaf stalks attached to the blade underside. The common *P. umbellatum* also has multiple flower spikes, but the leaf stalk is attached to the deeply lobed base of the leaf margin.

■ *Piper tuberculatum* (cigarillo)
Family Piperaceae
Shrub 2–3 m, sometimes trees to 6 m tall, 18 cm diameter, older nodes swollen. **Leaves** alternate, ranked along sides of stem, stalk very short, often with small pinkish warts, blade oblong, 4–12 cm long, 2–6 cm wide, tip tapered to a blunt point, base lobed, very unequal, veins pinnate. **Flowers** whitish to greenish, minute, crowded on unbranched, erect

spikes 4–14 cm long, to 0.5 cm thick; blooms all year. **Fruit** fleshy, less than 0.1 cm wide, spike becoming pale tan in fruit; eaten by bats. **Habitat:** Understories of moist, evergreen forests to seasonally very dry, deciduous forests and second growth. Altitude: North Pacific slope, sea level to 1000 m. Conservation areas: GUA, HNO, PAC, TEM. **Range:** Mex–Ven and Pr, WI. **Notes:** One of the few *Piper* species adapted to seasonally dry, deciduous forests.

■ *Coccoloba uvifera* (papaturro, uvita, sea grape)
Family Polygonaceae

Shrub or small tree 2–8 m tall, trunk usually crooked, stems stout, old bark gray, mottled. **Leaves** alternate, stalk to 1.5 cm long, base clasping branch, blade 6–18 cm long, 8–27 cm wide, usually wider than long, round to kidney-shaped, tip broadly rounded, sometimes slightly notched, base round-lobed, sides often unequal, thick, stiff, veins 3–5 pairs, often red. **Flowers** white, radially symmetrical, very small, to 0.4 cm long, fragrant, in spikes 15–30 cm long, at ends of stems; blooms most of the year. **Fruit** fleshy, green, turning purple, rounded, to 2 cm long, in narrow, unbranched clusters, edible. **Habitat:** Shores, along beaches above high-tide line. Altitude: Near sea level. Conservation areas: GUA, LAC, PAC, TEM, TOR. **Range:** Native to WI. Now found in FL, Mex–N S Amer. **Notes:** There are 15 species of *Coccoloba* in Costa Rica. A similar species, *C. caracasana*, is found only in the seasonally dry northwest below 500 m. The leaves are longer than wide with 6–12 pairs of secondary veins.

■ *Coccoloba venosa* (papaturro, papaturro negro macho, gateador)
Family Polygonaceae

Shrub 4–7 m tall, widely arching branches, bark, dark gray, smooth, twigs gray, nodes thick, stems stout, trunk often twisted. **Leaves** alternate, stalk to 1 cm long, thick, often reddish or brown, blade 5–20 cm long, 3–10 cm wide, broadest near apex, tip rounded to pointed, base rounded with very small lobes, leathery, veins pinnate, raised below, margins and surface wavy and irregular. **Flowers** cream to pale yellow, about 0.5 cm wide, radially symmetrical, stamens white; inflorescence of erect, slender, crowded spikes 6–12 cm long, in leaf axils near ends of stems; blooms on and off all year. **Fruit** fleshy, becoming red, then white when mature, to 0.6 cm long. **Habitat:** Moist to seasonally very dry, deciduous forests, edges. Altitude: Sea level to 300 m, seasonally dry northwest Pacific lowlands. Conservation areas: GUA, PAC, TEM. **Range:** Mex–CR.

Coccoloba uvifera

Coccoloba venosa

195

■ *Roupala montana* (ratón, danto, danto carne, zorrillo)
   Family Proteaceae
Shrub or tree 2–8 m, often multistemmed, trunks stout, old bark gray, with large fissures and plates, young bark gray. **Leaves** alternate, stalk 2–6 cm, blade egg-shaped, 4–14 cm long, 2–8 cm wide, tip long-pointed, entire or with few shallow teeth, base rounded, leathery, stiff, dark green above, slightly paler below, sides partially folded inward, fishy smelling when crushed; young plants have compound leaves, leaflets toothed. **Flowers** cream white, fragrant, 0.7–0.9 cm, fragile, petals lacking, sepals petal-like, linear, curled back, soon deciduous, stamens attached near tips of petals, pistil 0.6 cm; inflorescence of numerous, crowded spikes, 7–15 cm long, among leaves near ends of branches; blooms Nov.–Mar. **Fruit** dry, 3–4 cm long, about 1 cm wide, asymmetrical, flattened, elliptic, splitting open along one side to release 2-winged seeds, about 2 cm long, 1 cm wide; June–Oct. **Habitat:** Wet to seasonally dry forests, open sites, flood plains. Altitude: Sea level to 1200 m. Conservation areas: ARE, GUA, LAP, OSA, PAC, TEM. **Range:** Mex–Bol and Ven. **Notes:** There are two other species of *Roupala* in Costa Rica.

■ *Rubus roseifolius* (frambuesa)
   Family Rosaceae
Shrub with vinelike branches, stems prickly, 1–2 m long, young stems green, prickles to 0.4 cm long, base elongate, tip curved backward, stipules threadlike, to 0.8 cm long. **Leaves** alternate, blade pinnate, about 12 cm long, leaf axis prickly, leaflets 7, 2–8 cm long, 1–3 cm wide, broadly egg-shaped, somewhat hairy, tip pointed, base blunt, margin toothed, upper leaves often with 5 lobes. **Flowers** white, radially symmetrical, petals 5, 1–2 cm long, base very narrow, sepals finely woolly-hairy, to 1.5 cm long, tips threadlike, stamens numerous, flowers 1–3 in axils; blooms and fruits Sept.–Apr. **Fruit** fleshy, translucent red, 1.5–3.5 cm long, of many tiny individual, 1-seeded fruits fused together, ripe fruit easily removed from floral base. **Habitat:** Second growth forest, open areas, pastures, roadsides, forest edges. Altitude: 550–2300 m, usually above 1100 m. Conservation areas: ARE, CVC, GUA, LAP, PAC. **Range:** Native to Asia, Australia. Introduced and naturalized in CR. Invasive on some Pacific islands.

■ *Arcytophyllum lavarum*
Family Rubiaceae

Small shrub 10–40 cm tall, sometimes forming mats but root-ing only at base, stems thin, many-branched, nodes thick-ened, new stems often red. **Leaves** opposite, stalkless, blade 0.4–0.8 cm long, 0.2–0.4 cm wide, egg-shaped, tip and base blunt, stiff, dark green, in small clusters at ends of stems. **Flowers** white, about 0.7 cm long, radially symmetrical, trumpet-shaped, petal lobes 4, tips pointed, bluish outside, white, hairy inside, inflorescence of small clusters at ends of stems; blooms most of the year. **Fruit** dry, to 0.2 cm, rounded, crowned by old sepals, splitting open to release 4–8 seeds. **Habitat:** Open sites or second growth in mountains. Altitude: 2500–3500 m, and on newer volcanic sites 800–900 m. Conservation areas: CVC, GUA, LAC, LAP, PAC. **Range:** CR, Pan. **Notes:** The other species of *Arcytophyllum* (*A. muticum*) in Costa Rica is a prostrate, mosslike plant that roots at nodes.

■ *Augusta rivalis (Lindenia r.)*
(jazmincillo, lirio de agua)
Family Rubiaceae

Low shrub 0.4–1 m tall, branches dark, thick; stipules to 0.5 cm long, bristle-tipped, brown. **Leaves** opposite, clustered toward ends of stems, blade 3–12 cm long, 0.8–3 cm wide, narrowly elliptic to widest above middle, tip tapered to a point or spinelike, base tapered, extending down stalk, stiff. **Flowers** white, showy, radially symmetrical, tube often pink, 1.7 cm, finely hairy, petal lobes elongate to 2.7 cm long, tips pointed; inflorescence of 1–7 flowers, opening at night and on cloudy days; blooms Feb.–Oct. **Fruit** woody, to 4 cm long, including persistent calyx, about 1 cm wide, pear-shaped, twisting open to release numerous small seeds; fruit present Feb.–Nov. **Habitat:** Moist to seasonally dry forests along streams, often on rocks. Altitude: Sea level to 700 m. Conservation areas: GUA, PAC, TEM. **Range:** Mex–Col. **Notes:** Possibly pollinated by sphingid moths. This is the only species of *Augusta* in the American tropics.

■ *Chomelia spinosa* (malacacahüite, chocolatico)
Family Rubiaceae

Shrub or small tree 1–6 m tall, spines straight (photo), 1–4 cm long, mostly paired at nodes on older stems, leafy branches finely whitish-hairy, stipules 0.4–0.8 cm long, linear, persistent. **Leaves** opposite, often crowded at ends of twigs, blade 4–9 cm long, 2–5 cm wide, elliptic to egg-shaped, tip pointed, base pointed to blunt, veins white-hairy below, prominent, curved sharply upward. **Flowers** cream white, fragrant, radially symmetrical, tubular, finely hairy outside, about 1.5 cm long, petal lobes 4, about 0.5 cm long, tips pointed, inflorescence of small axillary clusters; blooms June–Sept. **Fruit** fleshy, becoming black, 0.6–0.9 cm long, 0.3–0.6 cm wide, 2-seeded, May–Dec. **Habitat:** Understories of seasonally dry forests, occasionally in moist forests. Altitude: Pacific lowlands, sea level to 400 m, rarely to 700 m. Conservation areas: GUA, LAP, PAC, TEM.

Range: Mex–Ven and Pr. **Notes:** There are nine species of *Chomelia* in Costa Rica; *C. spinosa* is the only one found in seasonally dry regions.

■ *Hillia loranthoides*
Family Rubiaceae

Epiphytic shrub 0.4–1.5 m tall, stems woody, brown, branches vinelike, stipule scars between leaf bases, stipules 2 cm long, 1 cm wide, oblong. **Leaves** opposite, purplish, blade 4–10 cm long, 2–4 cm wide, rather thick, elliptic to egg-shaped, tip pointed, base blunt to pointed, rubbery, smooth, dull green, veins obscure. **Flowers** white, showy, radially symmetrical, tubular, 4–6 cm long, petal lobes 4, to 2.5 cm long, 1 cm wide, curled back, tips rounded, calyx lobes 4, linear, to 1 cm; flowers solitary at ends of stems, each above a pair of reddish bracts to 2.5 cm long; blooms Feb.–Nov. **Fruit** woody, to 8 cm long, 1 cm wide, splitting open to release seeds each encircled by a thin wing. **Habitat:** On trees in wet forests. Altitude: 250–1400 m. Conservation areas: ARE, GUA, LAC, OSA, PAC. **Range:** Mex, CR. **Notes:** There are 10 species of *Hillia* in Costa Rica. Most are epiphytes.

■ *Posoqueria latifolia* (boca de vieja, fruta de mono, guayabo de mico)
Family Rubiaceae

Shrub or small tree to 10 m, trunk to 25 cm diameter, cylindrical, bark smooth; stipules about 1 cm long, triangular. **Leaves** opposite, blade 10–20 cm long, 4–10 cm wide, elliptic, tip pointed to blunt, base abruptly narrowed, surface leathery, shiny dark green above, veins conspicuous. **Flowers** white, radially symmetrical, long-tubular, 8–16 cm long, fragrant, petal lobes usually 5, about 2 cm long, tips rounded, folded back against tube; pollinated by moths; inflorescence 7- to 18-flowered; blooms all year. **Fruit** fleshy, yellow or orange, to 6 cm, rounded, with small navel-like disk at tip, seeds numerous, triangular, about 1 cm long embedded in white to orange edible pulp. **Habitat:** Understories of moist to wet forests, along waterways in seasonally dry forests; also cultivated. Altitude: Sea level to 1700 m. Conservation areas: ARE, CVC, GUA, HNO, LAC, LAP, OSA, PAC, TEM, TOR. **Range:** Mex–Brz and Bol. **Notes:** There are four, less common species of *Posoqueria* in Costa Rica.

Courtesy of Margaret Gargiullo

■ *Psychotria carthagenensis* (cafecillo)
Family Rubiaceae

Shrub 0.3–3 m tall, multistemmed, slender, bark dark grainy, twigs green, smooth, internodes very short; stipules to 0.8 cm long, deciduous leaving scar across node. **Leaves** opposite, stalk to 1 cm long, blade 6–13 cm long, 2–5 cm wide, usually widest above middle, tip pointed, base tapered, veins pinnate, meeting in loop connections at margin. **Flowers** white, radially symmetrical, tubular funnel-shaped, to 0.3 long, petal lobes 0.2 cm, flaring; inflorescence 3–8 cm long, dense, branched; blooms mostly Feb.–July, sometimes Nov.–Aug. **Fruit** fleshy, red to orange, 0.5 cm, translucent, shiny, flesh red, juicy, 2 seeds with flat inner sides; fruit present all year. **Habitat:** Moist to seasonally dry forests, second growth. Altitude: Sea level to 1400 m. Conservation areas: CVC, GUA, LAP, PAC, TEM. **Range:** Mex–Arg and Brz, WI. **Notes:** Much like *P. graciliflora*, which has smaller leaves and 2-lobed stipules.

■ *Psychotria deflexa* (cafecillo)
  Family Rubiaceae

Low shrub 0.5–3 m tall, stems green, slender, nodes swollen, stipules with base fused, 2 lobes, needle-shaped, to 0.8 cm long between leaf stalk bases, stipule base persistent. **Leaves** opposite, blade 7–18 cm long, 2–7 cm wide, narrowly elliptic, tip tapered, narrow, long-pointed, base pointed to blunt, stiff, leathery, shiny, smooth, dark green above, paler below. **Flowers** white, tubular, radially symmetrical, funnel-shaped, to 0.3 cm long, petal lobes 4 or 5, 0.1 cm long, inflorescences at ends of stem, to 11 cm long, branched; blooms June–Aug. **Fruit** fleshy, bright white, or blue to purple, to 1 cm, with dark indentation at top, flesh foamy-textured, white, juicy, ripening few at a time, seeds 2, fruits stems wine red; blooms July–Mar. **Habitat:** Along trail edges, open, second growth, or understories of wet to moist forests. Altitude: Sea level to 1400 m. Conservation areas: ARE, GUA, HNO, LAC, LAP, OSA, PAC, TOR. **Range:** Mex–Sur and Par.

■ *Psychotria glomerulata*
  Family Rubiaceae

Shrub 0.6–2 m tall, new growth dark green, smooth, leafy stems 4-sided; stipules with short sheath, 0.2 cm, persistent (young stipules often fringed with brown hairs). **Leaves** opposite, blade 5–17 cm long, 2–6 cm wide, narrowly elliptic, tip long-pointed, base wedge-shaped, surface dark green, shiny, veins raised slightly above, secondary veins loop-connected at margin. **Flowers** white, radially symmetrical, funnel-shaped, tube to 1.5 cm long, petal lobes 5, to 0.3 cm long, tips pointed, embedded in a dense head of whitish bracts to 2.5 cm long, 3.5 cm wide, above 4 larger rounded, white to greenish bracts, about 1.5 cm long, margins sometimes purplish; inflorescences at ends of branches; blooms most of the year. **Fruit** fleshy, bright blue, about 1 cm long, widest above middle, bracts becoming dark reddish, fruit flesh blue, spongy, seeds 2. **Habitat:** Understories of wet forests. Altitude: Sea level to 1100 m. Conservation areas: CVC, GUA, HNO, LAC, OSA, TOR. **Range:** Mex–Ec. **Notes:** Distinguished by its solitary flower heads with whitish bracts.

■ *Randia aculeata* (espino, espino blanco cafecillo)
Family Rubiaceae

Spiny shrub or small tree 1.5–3 m tall, trunk usually single, bark smooth, gray, branches mostly opposite, generally horizontal, secondary branches in one plane, forming "fish-bone" pattern, spines paired, to 2 cm long, cylindrical; stipules to 0.3 cm long, triangular, brownish. **Leaves** in tight whorls on small twigs along upper sides of branches, or opposite on new growth, blade mostly 1–6 cm long, 0.8–3 cm wide, egg-shaped to elliptic, tip rounded, to barely pointed, base tapering abruptly. **Flowers** white, radially symmetrical, tubular to 0.8 cm long, petal lobes 4–5, flaring, to 0.6 cm long, tips pointed; usually solitary at ends of short twigs; blooms Apr.–July. **Fruit** fleshy, white with black, juicy pulp, rounded, to 1.4 cm long, crowned by old calyx, seeds disk-shaped; fruits Apr.–Jan. **Habitat:** Understories of wet to seasonally dry forests, second growth. Altitude: Sea level to 1700 m. Conservation areas: CVC, GUA, LAC, LAP, OSA, PAC. **Range:** FL, Mex–Ven and Pr, WI. **Notes:** There are 18 species of *Randia* in Costa Rica. Many have paired spines, all have fruit with black to brown pulp and disk-shaped seeds.

■ *Rudgea skutchii*
Family Rubiaceae

Shrub or small tree 1–6 m tall, nodes thickened; stipules to 0.8 cm long, egg-shaped, upper margin toothed, at first forming a leathery, 4-angled cap over the shoot tip, stipules soon deciduous. **Leaves** opposite, blade 6–14 cm long, 2–6 cm wide, elliptic, or wider above middle, tip long-pointed, base variable, from pointed to slightly lobed. **Flowers** white,

Randia aculeata (above) fruit detail

radially symmetrical, tubular, to 0.7 cm long, petal lobes 5, to 0.7 cm long, tips thickened or bent inward, fragrant; inflorescence branched, to 14 cm long, few-flowered; blooms Feb.–Nov. **Fruit** fleshy, to 0.8 cm, rounded, crowned by persistent calyx tube, 2-seeded; fruits July–Jan. **Habitat:** Understories of wet forests, second growth, edges. Altitude: Sea level to 1300 m. Conservation areas: CVC, LAC, LAP, OSA, PAC, TOR. **Range:** CR–Bol. **Notes:** There are nine species of *Rudgea* in Costa Rica; they are distinguished by their often-toothed stipules, petal lobes mostly with tips bent inward, and smooth seeds with concave inner surfaces.

201

■ *Sabicea panamensis*
Family Rubiaceae

Vine or shrub with climbing branches to 5 m high, older stems red brown; stipules to 1 cm long, persistent. **Leaves** opposite, blade 5–16 cm long, 2–7 cm wide, elliptic, tip long-pointed, base blunt to pointed, sparsely hairy above, densely hairy on veins below. **Flowers** white, radially symmetrical, tubular, to 0.8 cm long, finely hairy, petal lobes 5,

to 0.4 cm long, narrowly triangular; inflorescences to 3 cm long, branched, in axils; blooms and fruits all year. **Fruit** fleshy, pink or red becoming purple black, to 0.9 cm, round, finely hairy, crowned by old calyx. **Habitat:** Wet to moist forests, edges, second growth, sometimes climbing into canopy. Altitude: Sea level to 1700 m, mostly 300–1000 m. Conservation areas: ARE, CVC, GUA, HNO, LAC, LAP, OSA, PAC, TOR. **Range:** Bel and Gua–Pr. **Notes:** There are only two species of *Sabicea* in Costa Rica. *Sabicea villosa* is hairier, has smaller flowers in smaller clusters, and leaf bases extend down stalk.

■ *Acnistus arborescens* (guitite)
Family Solanaceae

Shrub or small tree 2–10 m tall, usually multistemmed, bark pale tan, very corky, spongy, deeply grooved, with narrow, ridges in a longitudinal network, easily colonized by epiphytes. **Leaves** alternate, blade 5–20 cm long, 3–14 cm wide, narrowly elliptic, tip and base pointed, shiny, dark green above, finely hairy below. **Flowers** white, radially symmetrical, about 1 cm long, tubular, bell-shaped, fragrant; in dense clusters of 30 or so, on stems below leaves; pollinated by bees, flies, wasps, beetles, butterflies, sometimes hummingbirds; blooms May–Sept. **Fruit** fleshy, orange, 0.5–1 cm,

wide, above persistent calyx; seeds flat, numerous, fruit eaten by many birds, which disperse the seeds; fruits July–Oct. **Habitat:** Midelevations in second growth, open areas, roadsides, pastures. Altitude: 800–1500 m. Conservation areas: ARE, CVC, PAC. **Range:** Mex–Bol and Brz, WI. **Notes:** This is the only species of *Acnistus* in Costa Rica. Used medicinally. May have anticancer properties.

■ *Brugmansia candida (Datura arborea)*
Family Solanaceae
Shrub or small tree 5 m tall, twigs stout, green, finely hairy.
Leaves alternate, blade to 25 cm long, elliptic, tip pointed,
base blunt, finely hairy above. **Flowers** white, to 30 cm
long, about 15 cm across top, radially symmetrical, trumpet-shaped, facing downward, petal lobes about 3 cm long,
flaring outward, tips pointed, turned upward, calyx to 12 cm
long, narrowly tubular fitting snugly around lower petal tube,
stamens free, about 5 cm long; blooms all year. **Fruit** dry,
smooth, with numerous seeds. **Habitat:** Widely cultivated
in moist regions, apparently sometimes escaping from waste
piles in open areas. Altitude: 1100–2100 m. Conservation
areas: CVC, LAP, PAC. **Range:** Possibly native to Pr. Found
in Mex–Ven and Pr, Madagascar. **Notes:** There are two other
species of *Brugmansia* in Costa Rica; *B. suaveolens*, is very
similar and sometimes has pinkish flowers.

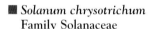

■ *Solanum chrysotrichum*
Family Solanaceae
Shrub or small tree 2–6 m tall, twigs green, stout, covered
with yellowish rusty hair, moderately *spiny*, spines 0.6 cm
long, curved, young stems often purplish. **Leaves** alternate,
about 17 cm long, 14 cm wide, egg-shaped, densely hairy
on both sides, margin lobed, new leaves and stems densely
rusty-yellow-woolly. **Flowers** white, 3 cm wide, star-shaped,
base tubular, petal lobes 5, pointed, anthers yellow, grouped
around stigma; pollinated by large bees; inflorescence of
tight, branched clusters along internodes near ends of stems;
blooms and fruits all year. **Fruit** fleshy, dull yellow orange, to
2 cm wide, round, cupped in old calyx, stalk swollen; apparently eaten by bats, which disperse the seeds, possibly also
by birds. **Habitat:** Second growth, disturbed, open areas in
mountains. Altitude: 700–2400 m, mostly above 1500 m.
Conservation areas: ARE, CVC, LAC, LAP, PAC. **Range:**
Mex–Pan, Pr. **Notes:** There are about 50 species of *Solanum*
in Costa Rica.

Brugmansia candida (above)

*Solanum chrysotrichum
(all two below)*

203

■ *Solanum rugosum* (zorro)
Family Solanaceae

Shrub or small tree to 5 m, stems rough, densely finely rusty-hairy, bark tan, new growth greenish. **Leaves** alternate or with a small leaf almost opposite, blade 8–25 cm long, 3–7 cm wide, narrowly elliptic, pointed at both ends, hairy, rough on both sides, dark green, shiny above. **Flowers** white, about 1.5 cm wide, 5-parted, anthers yellow, united in center of flower, 0.3 cm long; inflorescence of branched, dense, clusters to 20 cm long, stems hairy, becoming flat-topped in fruit; blooms and fruits all year. **Fruit** fleshy, yellow, about 1 cm wide with numerous seeds. **Habitat:** Open areas and roadsides in wet regions. Altitude: Sea level to 1500 m, mostly below 900 m. Conservation areas: ARE, CVC, GUA, HNO, LAC, LAP, TOR. **Range:** Bel–Brz and Bol, WI. Introduced in the Old World.

■ *Theobroma cacao* (cocoa, tsirú, chocolate)
Family Sterculiaceae

Tree to 8 m tall, branched near base, often widely spreading. **Leaves** alternate, stalk swollen at top and base, blade oblong, 15–50 cm long, 4–15 cm wide, tip tapered, base rounded, young leaves reddish hairy on both sides, pendant, major veins 3–5, palmate at base. **Flowers** white, radially symmetrical, 5 free petals, petals to 0.4 cm long, sepals to 0.8 cm long, stamens often purple; flowers borne on trunk and larger branches, pollinated by small flies. **Fruit** fleshy, red, yellow to purple, oblong, thick-walled pod with 10 broad ribs, to 25 cm long, finely hairy, seeds 20–40, to 4 cm wide, in sweet, edible pulp, dispersed by monkeys. **Habitat:** Forest understories; cultivated in wet lowland regions, many abandoned plantations in secondary forests. Altitude: Sea level to 600 m. Conservation areas: HNO, CVC, LAC, OSA, PAC,

TOR. **Range:** Native to Amazon River basin. Mex–Bol and Brz, WI, Africa. **Notes:** Dried, fermented seeds are processed into cocoa. Cultivated in Mexico and Central America for at least 3000 years by Aztec, Mayan, and other native people. There are four other species of *Theobroma* in Costa Rica.

◼ *Muntingia calabura* (capulín, Jamaican cherry)
Family Tiliaceae

Tree or tall shrub to 10 m tall, trunk 15 cm diameter, often multistemmed, wide-spreading, bark dark gray, small branches striped brown and pale gray, new growth green, hairy. **Leaves** alternate, in one plane along stem, blade 4–18 cm long, 2–6 cm, elliptical, tip tapered, base unequal, rounded to slightly lobed, both sides softly hairy, dull green above, whitish below, veins palmate at base, margin toothed. **Flowers** white, radially symmetrical, about 2.5 cm wide, petals 5, fragile, odor unpleasant, stamens numerous, yellow, pistil green, bulbous; pollinated by bees; blooms most of the year. **Fruit** fleshy, red, 1.5 cm diameter, sweet, with numerous seeds, about 0.5 cm long; fruit matures mostly Aug.–Jan. **Habitat:** Wet to seasonally dry regions, open sites, second growth, roadsides. Altitude: Mostly on the Pacific slope, sea level to 1100 m. Conservation areas: ARE, GUA, LAC, OSA, PAC, TEM.
Range: Mex–Ven and Arg.
Notes: This is the only species of *Muntingia* worldwide.

◼ *Myriocarpa longipes* (estrella, ortiga)
Family Urticaceae

Large shrub, 2–6 m tall, often leaning, stems stout, twigs hairy; stipules to 2.5 cm long, strap-shaped, fused at base. Leaves alternate, stalk 2–35 cm long, blade 12–45 cm long, 8–25 cm wide, broadly elliptic to egg-shaped, tip pointed to blunt, base blunt, thin, often rough above, hairy on both sides, margin toothed. **Flowers** white, cream, or greenish, tiny, about 0.1 cm long; inflorescences of drooping, elongate, multiple, threadlike strings, female inflorescences to 60 cm long, branched only near base, males to 12 cm long; blooms July–Mar., but mostly Nov.–Jan. **Fruit** dry, tiny, about 0.1 cm long, green. **Habitat:** Understories of wet forests. Altitude: Sea level to 2000 m, but most often below 500 m. Conservation areas: ARE, CVC, GUA, LAC, LAP, OSA, PAC, TEM, TOR. **Range:** Mex–Col. **Notes:** There are four species of *Myriocarpa* in Costa Rica.

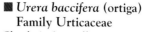

■ *Urera baccifera* (ortiga)
Family Urticaceae

Shrub 1–6 m tall, most parts covered with *stinging bristles or spines*, stems 4-sided, angles ridged, grooved, hollow, arching, 1–2 cm wide; stipules to 1.5 cm, fused except for tips. **Leaves** alternate, stalk 3–30 cm long, stinging-spiny, blade 10–40 cm long, 6–40 cm wide cm, egg-shaped, tip pointed, base lobed to rounded, upper surface puckered, hairy with stinging spines on veins below, veins palmate at base, margin coarsely few-toothed. **Flowers** white, minute, to 0.3 cm, male and female flowers usually on separate plants; inflorescence to 12 cm long, branched, wider than long, slightly 1-sided, stems often pink or red; blooms and fruits on and off most of the year. **Fruit** fleshy, white, to 0.3 cm, ripening few at a time, 1 seed; fruits stems often wine red. **Habitat:** Open areas, in wet forests and second growth. Also planted as hedgerows. Altitude: Sea level to 1300 m, usually below 500 m. Conservation areas: ARE, GUA, LAC, LAP, OSA, PAC, TOR. **Range:** Mex–Ven and Arg, WI. **Notes:** There are seven species of *Urera* in Costa Rica; *U. baccifera* and *U. laciniata* are the most consistently and painfully stinging species.

■ *Lippia myriocephala* (caraigre)
Family Verbenaceae

Shrub or small tree 3–7 m tall, sometimes to 15 m, often with several trunks, to about 20 cm diameter, bark tan, young stems 4-sided, sap very sticky. **Leaves** opposite, blade 8–21 cm long, 2–8 cm wide, tip with elongate point, base pointed, lance-shaped to elliptic, surface puckered, dark green above, paler green below. **Flowers** white to yellow, 0.2–0.3 cm long, crowded in bract-covered heads, 0.4–0.7 cm long and wide, bracts yellowish white; inflorescence of numerous heads each on a stalk, in umbrella-shaped clusters on a long common stalk (umbel); blooms Aug.–May. **Fruit** dry, very small, wrapped in persistent calyx; eventually separating into 2 hard segments, one of which contains a seed; rarely seen; Nov. **Habitat:** Second growth, open areas. Altitude: 700–2700 m. Conservation areas: ARE, CVC, LAP, PAC. **Range:** Mex–Pan. **Notes:** There are seven species of *Lippia* in Costa Rica.

■ *Drimys granadensis* (chile, chilemuela, quiebramuelas, winter's bark)
Family Winteraceae

Small tree, multistemmed, about 5–6 m tall, very leafy, bark aromatic. **Leaves** alternate, spiraled at ends of stems, blade about 11 cm long, 3 cm wide, narrowly elliptic, tip blunt, base tapered, dark green above, pale bluish white below, thick. **Flowers** white, radially symmetrical, 1–2 cm diameter with numerous petals, many short yellow anthers, pistils about 6, rounded, green with black dot at tip, calyx 2-parted; inflorescence of short, umbrella-shaped clusters near ends of stems; blooms and fruits most of the year. **Fruit** fleshy, black, about 1 cm long, 0.6 cm wide, 1-seeded, in small, tight, branched clusters at ends of elongate, branched, stalks. **Habitat:** Open areas in wet mountains, pastures, roadsides. Often used as living fences. Altitude: 1100–3700 m, most often above 2000 m. Conservation areas: ARE, CVC, GUA, LAC, LAP, PAC. **Range:** Mex–Hon, CR–Ven and Pr. **Notes:** This is the only species of *Drimys* in Costa Rica. The bark was once used as a cure for scurvy (winter's bark) and has also been used to relieve toothache and stomach problems.

COLOR OF CONSPICUOUS PART GREEN TO BROWN, AND SHRUBS GROWN FOR FOLIAGE

■ *Yucca guatemalensis* (itabo, izote)
Family Agavaceae

Shrub or small tree to 10 m tall, sparsely branched near top, stems ringed by old leaf scars, trunk swollen at base, surface rough. **Leaves** alternate, stalkless, closely spiraled at ends of stems, 23–80 cm long, 2–6 cm wide, sword-shaped, stiff, fibrous, spine-tipped, base clasping stem, margin minutely toothed. **Flowers** white, radially symmetrical, 6-parted, to 4 cm long, fragrant; inflorescence of large, branched, erect clusters to 70 cm long, on a stout stalk from the center of the plant; blooms Feb.–June. **Fruit** fleshy, to 8 cm long, 4 cm wide, oval. **Habitat:** Cultivated, some escaped. Commonly used as a living fence posts in moist to wet regions. Altitude: Sea level to about 1100 m. Conservation areas: CVC, GUA. **Range:** Native to S Mex and Gua. Widely cultivated elsewhere. **Notes:** This is the only species of *Yucca* in Costa Rica. It is sometimes grown in plantations for its flowers, which are edible.

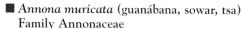

■ *Annona muricata* (guanábana, sowar, tsa)
Family Annonaceae

Small tree or shrub to 8 m, bark gray, smooth. **Leaves** alternate, in one plane on opposite sides of the stem, stalks very short, blade 8–15 cm long, 3–6 cm wide, oblong, pointed at both ends. **Flowers** yellowish outside, cream inside, radially symmetrical, to 3.5 cm, rounded, 3 outer petals thick, leathery; flowers solitary from branches and trunk; blooms most of the year. **Fruit** fleshy, green, large, asymmetric, oblong to 20 cm long, covered with hooked, fleshy, spinelike appendages, edible; seen fruiting Feb. **Habitat:** Cultivated and naturalized in moist and wet areas. Altitude: Sea level to 1000 m. Conservation areas: CVC, LAC, OSA, TEM. **Range:** Probably native to tropical America. Widely introduced in tropical regions worldwide. Has become an invasive in the Galapagos (Ec) and some other Pacific islands. **Notes:** There are 13 species of *Annona* in Costa Rica.

Annona muricata (above)

Guatteria amplifolia (below)

■ *Guatteria amplifolia* (malagueto, anonillo)
Family Annonaceae

Small tree or shrub 3–12 m tall, occasionally to 20 m, bark smooth, twigs green, smooth, branches long, arching. **Leaves** alternate, stalk thick, blade 15–35 cm long, 7–15 cm wide, oblong-elliptic, blade shiny, dark green above, shiny, slightly lighter below, leathery, veins pinnate, curved upward, joining around margin in loop-connections, impressed above, raised below, tip tapered, base abruptly narrowed. **Flowers** greenish to cream yellow, rusty-woolly, radially symmetric, stiff, flat, 3 sepals, 6 petals to 2 cm long, 1.5 cm wide, middle of flower cushionlike, broad with green pistil at center; blooms mostly Aug.–Apr. **Fruit** hard-fleshy, red, then purple black, about 1 cm long, 0.8 cm wide, in a rounded cluster from the end of a stalk; fruit stalks red, sap aromatic, red, 1 seed; fruits Apr.–Jan. **Habitat:** Wet lowlands, second growth woodlands; swamps in the Caribbean lowlands. Altitude: Sea level to 800 m. Conservation areas: LAP, LAC, OSA (mostly). **Range:** S Mex–Col. **Notes:** There are 15 species of *Guatteria* in Costa Rica. All are quite similar.

■ *Montrichardia arborescens*
Family Araceae

Semiaquatic or terrestrial shrub or woody herb, generally growing in dense stands, stems prickly, 2–6 m tall, 4 cm diameter near base, *sap toxic, very irritating;* branched sparsely, if at all. **Leaves** alternate, spiraled near top of stem; stalk 20–45 cm long, base clasping stem, blade 22–41 cm long 15–30 cm wide, arrow-shaped, 2 large basal lobes often larger than upper portion of blade, lobes and tip pointed; margin smooth. **Flowers** white, minute, very fragrant, spikes 10–13 cm long, inflorescence bract to 18 cm long, white near top, base green, wrapped around spike, widest near base; blooms and fruits most of the year. **Fruits** fleshy, yellow to green, to 3 cm diameter, 1-seeded, in large round clusters to 11 cm long, 8 cm wide, edible when ripe, eaten by birds, seeds also dropping into water and floating to shore. **Habitat:** Wet soil or shallow water of the coastal plain and freshwater flood plains. Altitude: Caribbean slope, sea level to 100 m. Conservation areas: CVC, LAC, TOR. **Range:** Bel–Brz and Pr, Ant. **Notes:** This is the only species of *Montrichardia* in Costa Rica.

■ *Oreopanax donnell-smithii* (cacho de venado)
Family Araliaceae

Shrub or small tree to 8 m tall, 45 cm diameter, bark whitish, stems thick. **Leaves** alternate, stalks 5–40 cm long, blade broadly egg-shaped, 10–36 cm long, 9 30 cm wide, very variable, tip pointed, base rounded, veins palmate at base, spiraled at ends of branches. **Flowers** whitish to pale green, radially symmetrical, petals free, calyx without lobes; inflorescence of dense clusters at ends of stems; blooms in Mar. **Fruit** fleshy, whitish to green, 0.3–0.5 cm wide (dry), in tight, round, headlike clusters, heads in large branched pyramidal clusters 7–30 cm long and wide, at ends of stems, very variable; fruit present Apr., May. **Habitat:** Moist to wet regions, open areas, roadsides. Altitude: 900–1750 m. Conservation areas: ARE, CVC, LAC, LAP. **Range:** Not known except for CR. **Notes:** There are 17 species of *Oreopanax* in Costa Rica.

■ *Diplostephium costaricense*
Family Asteraceae

Shrub or woody herb 1–4 m tall, larger stems stout, to 13 cm diameter, crown dense, pale gray green. **Leaves** alternate, crowded at ends of stems, no stalk, blades small, to 4 cm long, 0.6 cm wide, narrowly lance-shaped, tip abruptly pointed, base tapered, bluish gray, pale below, margin in-rolled. **Flowers** white; ray flowers 21, white, disk flowers 36, purple, heads densely woolly, to 0.9 cm high, 1.2 cm wide, basal bracts reddish; inflorescence 3–5 cm wide; blooms Aug.–May. **Fruit** dry, 1-seeded, plume purple-tipped. **Habitat:** Open sites in high mountains (paramo). Altitude: 2400–3800 m. Conservation areas: LAC, LAP, PAC. **Range:** Possibly confined to CR. **Notes:** Common on Cerro de la Muerte. There is one other species of *Diplostephium* in Costa Rica, which is quite uncommon.

■ *Crescentia cujete* (jícaro, calabazo,
raspaguacal, gourd tree)
Family Bignoniaceae

Small, open tree to 10 m tall, trunk to 30 cm diameter, branching near ground, bark gray black, branches crooked, stout, elongate. **Leaves** alternate, in tuftlike clusters at nodes along branches, stalkless, blade variable, 4–26 cm long, 1–

7 cm wide, broadest near apex, tip blunt to pointed, base tapered, margins smooth. **Flowers** yellow to pale green with purple veins, tubular, 4–7 cm long, 3–4 cm wide across top of tube, petal lobes triangular to 4 cm long, solitary or paired, growing from trunk and branches, unpleasant odor, open at night, bat pollinated; blooms most of the year. **Fruit** gourd-like, round, large, to 30 cm long, 20 cm wide, turning from green to yellow to brown, with numerous small seeds embedded in pulp. **Habitat:** Cultivated and wild, pastures, roadsides, gardens. Altitude: Sea level to 1200 m, mostly above 50 m on the Pacific slope. Conservation areas: ARE, GUA, HNO, PAC, TEM. **Range:** Native to C Amer; also extensively cultivated. **Notes:** Fruit used for rattles, carvings, and utensils. The only other species of *Crescentia* in Costa Rica, *C. alata,* is very similar but has smaller fruit and some leaves that are 3-parted.

■ *Acanthocereus tetragonus* (cactus)
  Family Cactaceae

Large, terrestrial, often treelike, cactus 1–3 m tall, often many stems together, young stems 3-ribbed, older stems with 4–6 thick ribs, to 15 cm wide, often woody at base, spines 0.5–7 cm long, in clusters along tops of ribs. **Leaves** none. **Flowers** cream white more or less ball-shaped on a long, thick, stalklike, pale green tube 10–18 cm long, petals short, numerous in many rows, bracts at base few, green, Apr.–July. Open only at night, pollinated by bats. **Fruit** fleshy, bright pink to red, spiny, 4–8 cm wide, edible, Apr.–Oct. **Habitat:** Dry shores, and upland of mangrove swamps, open sites, second growth in wet to seasonally dry lowlands; also cultivated in the Central Valley. Altitude: Sea level to 200 m. Conservation areas: GUA, LAC, LAP, TEM. **Range:** S US–Ven, WI. **Notes:** The only other species of *Acanthocereus* in Costa Rica is *A. pentagonus*, which is quite uncommon.

■ *Epiphyllum phyllanthus* var. *pittieri* (cactus)
  Family Cactaceae

Epiphytic, shrublike cactus to 2 m long, stems 20–60 cm long, 2–6 cm wide long, stiff, green, usually pendant, varying from thin, cylindrical near base to broadly 3-ribbed, flattened, near ends of stems, margins shallowly blunt-lobed. **Leaves** none. **Flowers** cream white to yellow, very fragrant, 10–25 cm long, 5–6 cm wide across top, base covered by bracts, petals 2–5 cm long, 0.4–0.8 cm wide, numerous, sepals pale green, floral base 8–18 cm long; blooms at night, Mar.–Dec. **Fruit** fleshy, green elliptic, berries 3–8 cm long, 1.5–3.5 cm wide, pulp with numerous seeds; fruit present Mar.–Oct. **Habitat:** Moist, wet, or rarely, seasonally dry lowland forests, often high in trees, but also near ground on fallen logs, in open sites. Altitude: Mostly sea level to 500 m, rarely to 2000 m. Conservation areas: ARE, CVC, GUA, HNO, LAC, LAP, OSA, PAC, TOR. **Range:** CR–Ec. **Notes:** There are about seven species of *Epiphyllum* in Costa Rica; *E. phyllanthus* var. *pittieri* is the most common.

Acanthocereus tetragonus (above)

Epiphyllum phyllanthus **var**.
pittieri (below)

■ *Hylocereus costaricensis* (cactus)
Family Cactaceae

Epiphytic or terrestrial cactus, stems to 70 cm long, 3–7 cm diameter, 3-ribbed, each angle forming a thick-based ridge, much-branched, often in masses, hanging from tree branches, rooting along stem on flattened side, gray green, spines very short, in small, raised cushions along tops of ridges. **Leaves**

none. **Flowers** white, large, 20–30 cm long, fragrant, with numerous petals, tube trumpet-shaped, sepals green, sometimes with red margins, stamens numerous, whitish, floral base covered with overlapping scales; open only at night; blooms May–Sept. **Fruit** fleshy, fuchsia to red, 5–10 long, 6–8 cm wide with persistent scales, edible; June–Oct. **Habitat:** Moist to seasonally dry forests. Altitude: Sea level to 1400 m. Conservation areas: ARE, CVC, GUA, PAC, TEM. **Range:** Nic–Pan. **Notes:** There are four species of *Hylocereus* in Costa Rica; *H. costaricensis* is by far the most common.

■ *Selenicereus wercklei* (cactus)
Family Cactaceae

Epiphytic cactus, hanging from trees, often in large masses of branched stems; stems gray green, about 1 cm wide, with 6–12 fine ribs, not spiny, old stems gray, woody. **Leaves** none. **Flowers** cream white or yellow, often reddish outside with many petals, tube elongate, 16–23 cm; blooms Apr.–Aug. **Fruit** fleshy, yellow or greenish yellow, spiny, 0.5–1 cm, June–Sept. Fallen fruit often seen along trails. **Habitat:** Moist to seasonally dry forests; sometimes cultivated. Altitude: Mostly on the Pacific slope, 500–1100 m. Conservation areas: ARE, GUA. **Range:** Endemic to CR. **Notes:** There are three species of *Selenicereus* in Costa Rica; *S. werklei* is the most common.

■ *Stenocereus aragonii* (cactus)
Family Cactaceae

Large, treelike, columnar terrestrial cactus to 8 m tall, stems
erect, thick, mostly green, 25–35 cm diameter, 7- to 11-ribbed
with white, V-shaped ridges across ribs, creating a pattern of
narrow arches around stems, spines in cushions along top of
ribs, gray with black, tips white, about 1 cm long, old stems
with brown, woody base, cut stem turns orange. **Leaves** none.
Flowers white to pinkish, to 3 cm long, many petals, sepals
green and red, anthers pale yellow; blooms Apr.–June. **Fruit**
fleshy, 2.5 cm long, reddish to reddish green, spiny. **Habitat:**
Open woods of seasonally dry Pacific lowlands. Altitude: Sea
level to 600 m. Conservation areas: CVC (rarely), GUA,
LAP (rarely), TEM. Most likely to be seen in Santa Rosa,
GUA, and Palo Verde N.P. **Range:** Endemic to CR. **Notes:**
This is the only species of *Stenocereus* in Costa Rica.

■ *Semialarium mexicanum* (crucillo, guacharo) Family
Celastraceae

Shrub or small tree 2–7 m tall, trunk to about 12 cm diameter, much-branched, branches often vinelike, often at right
angle to trunk. **Leaves** opposite, 7–10 cm long, elliptic, tips
rounded, velvety hairy, margins toothed, new leaves finely
scaly. **Flowers** yellow green, radially symmetrical, 5-parted,
petals free, overlapping; blooms Feb.–Mar. **Fruit** dry, 3-
parted, 5–7 cm long, flattened, seeds 3 cm long, winged;
fruit present most of the year, mature in middle of wet season. **Habitat:** Moist or, more often, seasonally dry forests
and second growth. Altitude: Pacific lowlands, near sea level
to 400 m. Conservation areas: GUA, PAC, TEM. **Range:**
Mex–Pan. **Notes:** This is the only species of *Semialarium* in
Costa Rica. *Semialarium* was formerly included in the family
Hippocrateaceae.

■ *Conocarpus erectus* (mangle torcido, mangle botoncillo, buttonwood mangrove)
Family Combretaceae

Shrub or tree 4–10 m tall, to 20 cm diameter, often with multiple stems, bark fissured, pitted. **Leaves** alternate, 2–11 cm long, 1–4 cm wide, elliptic, leathery, shiny, pointed at both ends, sharp-tipped, somewhat succulent, light green, veins widely spaced. **Flowers** greenish white, tiny, radially symmetrical, stamens longer than petals; in branching clusters of small, dense heads, about 0.5 cm wide, at ends of branches; blooms and fruits most of the year. **Fruit** dry, very small, round, reddish with 2 wings, in small conelike, warty structures, 1–1.5 cm wide. **Habitat:** Landward part of mangrove forests, open areas above high-tide line. Altitude: Sea level to 750 m, mostly below 100 m, Pacific coast. Conservation areas: GUA, LAC, OSA, PAC, TEM. **Range:** Mex–N Pr and Brz. **Notes:** This is the only species of *Conocarpus* in Costa Rica.

Conocarpus erectus (fruit)

■ *Laguncularia racemosa* (mangle blanco, mangle salado, white mangrove)
Family Combretaceae

Tree or shrub 4–12 m tall, bark light gray, older bark fissured, often with stilt roots and/or many small vertical roots above soil (pneumatophores) to take in air. **Leaves** opposite, stalk with a pair of conspicuous glands, blade 3–11 cm long, 2–5 cm wide, oblong, rounded at tip and base, glossy, stiff, light green, lateral veins inconspicuous. **Flowers** white, small, radially symmetrical, stamens longer than petals, in branched clusters to 20 cm long; blooms most of the year. **Fruit** red,

Laguncularia racemosa (below)

to 2 cm long, oval, 3-ribbed, in branched clusters; fruit present July–Dec. **Habitat:** Higher ground of mangrove forests. Altitude: Pacific coast, sea level to 200 m, mostly below 50 m. Conservation areas: GUA, OSA, PAC, TEM. **Range:** Mex–N Pr, Ant, E Africa. **Notes:** This is the only species of *Laguncularia* in Costa Rica.

■ *Davilla kunthii*
Family Dilleniaceae

Woody vine or sprawling shrub, semierect to vinelike, bark gray, branches elongate, sinuous, new growth densely brown-hairy. **Leaves** alternate, blade 6–22 cm long, 4–11 cm wide, broadly elliptic, tip pointed to rounded with very small point, base rounded, texture very rough, sandpapery above, yellow green, hard, rather brittle, tan-hairy below, veins pinnate, numerous, 14–29, sharply impressed above. **Flowers** green, becoming reddish, radially symmetrical, round, 0.8–1.5 cm wide, at first enclosed in the 2 hairy, capsulelike inner sepals 0.8 cm long and wide, petals yellow, 4–6, to 0.9 cm long, 0.5 cm wide, stamens numerous, stigma wide at top; blooms on and off most of the year. **Fruit** yellowish to orange, round, very small, enclosed in hairy inner sepals and persistent stamens, seed 1, black, covered by a fleshy white aril. **Habitat:** Open areas in wet to seasonally dry lowlands. Altitude: Sea level to 800 m, mostly 100–400 m. Conservation areas: CVC, GUA, HNO, LAP, OSA, PAC, TEM. **Range:** S Mex–Brz, Tr. **Notes:** There are three species of *Davilla* in Costa Rica; *D. nitida* is also common.

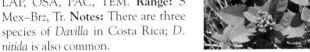

■ *Dracaena fragrans* (itabo, dracena)
Family Dracaenaceae

Large shrub or small tree 1–6 m tall, unbranched or sparsely branched (if cut), stems ringed by old leaf scars, palmlike in appearance. **Leaves** alternate, clustered at top of stem, no stalk, blade 40–90 cm long, 5–10 cm wide, straplike, thin, tip pointed, base expanded and clasping stem, center often with a yellow green or whitish stripe, margin smooth. **Flowers** white, 6-parted, radially symmetrical, small, about 1.5 cm wide, very fragrant; inflorescence 0.2–1 m long, elongated clusters from top of stem. Only very large, mature plants known to bloom; Feb. **Fruit** fleshy, red orange, about 2 cm diameter, sweet, rarely seen. **Habitat:** Cultivated for export as houseplants, often grown in plantations, sometimes escaping. Also often used for living fences. Altitude: Sea level to about 1200; widely cultivated as a foliage plant from lowlands to midelevations in wet to seasonally dry regions. Conservation areas: GUA, PAC, also horticultural in many parts of the country. **Range:** Native to W Africa. Cultivated throughout the world. **Notes:** Very similar to *Cordyline* species. The other species of *Dracaena* in Costa Rica, *D. americana*, is native and has longer, narrower leaves.

■ *Diospyros salicifolia*
Family Ebenaceae

Small tree to 15 m tall, bark gray, twigs hairy. **Leaves** alternate, to 9 cm long, 4 cm wide, lance-shaped, widest above middle, pointed at both ends, hairy below. **Flowers** off-white, about 1.2 cm long, petal lobes 3, 0.3 cm long, 0.1 cm wide, densely hairy outside, calyx 0.6–0.9 cm, 3-lobed, hairy outside, stamens about 9 in male flowers, female flowers with 3 fleshy 2-lobed stigmas; blooms Sept.–Oct. **Fruit** fleshy, becoming orange yellow, 3 cm wide, rounded, cupped by calyx enlarged to about 1.5 cm, hairy on both sides, seeds 6, 1.7 cm long, 0.7 cm wide, brown; fruit present all year. **Habitat:** Swamp forests to seasonally dry forests. Altitude: Sea level to 800 m. Conservation areas: ARE, GUA, PAC, TEM. Seen at Palo Verde N.P. **Range:** Mex–Pan. **Notes:** *Diospyros hartmanniana* is another common species and is found mostly above 800 m.

■ *Casearia arguta* (cerito, cerillo, raspaguacal)
Family Flacourtiaceae

Shrub or small tree 2–12 m tall, to 20 cm diameter, branches slender, elongate, bark tan, young twigs often densely rusty-hairy, smooth with age, lenticels conspicuous. **Leaves** alternate, drooping in ranks along each side of branch, blade 9–17 cm long, 3–6 cm wide, narrowly elliptical, tip pointed, base blunt, shiny green above, usually sprinkled with translucent dots, margins coarsely toothed. **Flowers** greenish white, radially symmetrical, somewhat fragrant, small, to 0.5 cm long, calyx lobes 5, no petals, stamens 10, shorter than calyx, in crowded clusters to 2 cm wide, along leafy and leafless parts of branches; blooms Aug.–Feb. **Fruit** fleshy, becoming yellow, to 2.5 cm wide, seeds numerous, embedded in sweet orange flesh, bird dispersed; fruit present Dec.–June. **Habitat:** Wet to seasonally dry regions in open sites and second growth. Also used for living fences. Altitude: Sea level to 950 m, mostly along Pacific slope. Conservation areas: ARE, CVC, GUA, HNO, LAC, LAP, OSA, PAC, TEM. **Range:** Mex–N S Amer. **Notes:** There are 13 species of *Casearia* in Costa Rica.

■ *Trichilia havanensis* (caracolillo, cedro cóbano, uruca)
Family Meliaceae

Small tree about 3–15 m tall, twigs slender, bark aromatic. **Leaves** alternate, pinnate, leaf axis slightly winged, leaflets 5–11, opposite, 5–10 cm long, 2–5.5 cm wide, lower leaflet pairs smaller, shape widest above middle, tip bluntly pointed, base tapering down leaflet stalk, dark green, veins somewhat obscure. **Flowers** white to greenish, fragrant in clusters to 7 cm long, often along stems below leaves; blooms Dec.–Apr., Aug. **Fruit** dry, 3-parted, to 1.5 cm long, opening to reveal seeds with an orange fleshy attachment; fruit present Feb.–June, Sept.–Oct. **Habitat:** Moist to wet mountain forests and second growth sites. Altitude: 600–2500 m, mostly above 1000 m. Conservation areas: ARE, CVC, GUA, HNO, LAC, LAP, PAC, TEM. **Range:** Mex–Ven, WI. **Notes:** There are 14 species of *Trichilia* in Costa Rica.

■ *Ficus pertusa* (higuito, higuerón)
Family Moraceae

Small tree 5–12 m tall, often an epiphyte or strangler; stipules covering leaf buds 0.5–1 cm long. **Leaves** alternate, blade 5–11 cm long, 2–4 cm wide, elliptic, tip pointed, base blunt to pointed, upper surface often sprinkled with tiny dots, secondary veins closely parallel, loop-connected near margin. **Flowers** tiny, inside figs; blooms and fruits all year. **Fruit** is fig, small, 0.8–1.4 cm diameter, rounded to somewhat conical, dull yellow green with wine red speckles, stalks about 0.5 cm long. **Habitat:** Wet evergreen forests, especially in wet areas of Central Valley. Altitude: Sea level to 2100 m, mostly above 500 m. Conservation areas: ARE, CVC, GUA, HNO, LAC, LAP, OSA, PAC, TOR. **Range:** Mex–Par, Jam. **Notes:** Very common but difficult to observe when epiphytic.

■ *Morella pubescens (Myrica p.)* (encinillo)
Family Myricaceae

Shrub or small tree 1.5–7 m tall, leafy stems densely fine-hairy, sap aromatic, bark pale pinkish gray, becoming dark brown with age, lenticels prominent, in horizontal lines, branches almost at right angles to trunk, ends often curving upward. **Leaves** alternate, blade 4–14 cm long, 1–3 cm wide, narrowly elliptic, tip and base pointed, surface shiny, wrinkled, rough-textured, both sides sprinkled with minute dots, secondary veins numerous yellowish, rusty-hairy, impressed above, raised below, underside pale, densely hairy on veins below, margins toothed. **Flowers** minute, inconspicuous, no petals or sepals, accompanied by hairy bracts to 0.5 cm long, surface sprinkled with translucent dots; inflorescence a spike to 4 cm long in leaf axil, often persisting after leaf falls; blooms Jan.–Aug. **Fruit** hard, waxy-coated, round, about 0.3 cm wide, minutely warty, 1-seeded; fruit persistent, present most of the year. **Habitat:** Open sites and second growth in mountains. Altitude: 1300–3000 m, mostly above 2000 m. Conservation areas: CVC, LAC, LAP, PAC. **Range:** CR–Bol. **Notes:** There are two other species of *Morella* in Costa Rica. The other common species, M. *cerifera*, is found below 2000 m and has smaller leaves.

■ *Bocconia frutescens* (tabaquillo,
   guacamaya, tree celandine)
   Family Papaveraceae

Shrub or small tree 2–7 m tall, branches thick, sap orange. **Leaves** alternate, spiraled at ends of branches, stalk to 3 cm long, blade 14–50 cm long, 4–20 cm wide, pinnately lobed, blue green above, whitish below, lobe margins finely toothed. **Flowers** cream white to yellow green, radially symmetrical, no petals, sepals to 1 cm long, in large, branched clusters 20–60 cm long at ends of stems; blooms Sept.–Mar. **Fruit** dry, orange becoming grayish at maturity, splitting open to reveal 1 black seed partially covered by red flesh, attractive to birds, which disperse seeds; fruit present most of the year. **Habitat:** Moist to wet regions, second growth and open sites, roadsides. Altitude: 100–3200 m, usually above 700 m. Conservation areas: ARE, CVC, GUA, LAC, LAP, OSA, PAC, TEM. **Range:** Mex–Ven and Bol. **Notes:** This is the only species of *Bocconia* in Costa Rica.

■ *Piper imperiale*
Family Piperaceae

Coarse, often treelike shrub 2–6 m tall, stems thick, to 2 cm wide, sparsely branched, younger stems green, with pointed warts or soft spines, stipule attached to leaf stalk, pale, curling back. **Leaves** alternate, usually 2-ranked along stem, stalk 3–12 cm long, usually warty, clasping stem at base, blade 20–60 cm long, 15–35 cm wide, narrowly heart-shaped, tip pointed, base unequally lobed, variable, large, stiff, surface puckered, veins depressed above, raised below, midrib warty, texture rubbery. **Flowers** greenish, occasionally purplish, minute, crowded on unbranched, pendant spikes 15–55 cm long, 0.4–0.8 cm wide in flower; blooms and fruits all year. **Fruit** fleshy, green to reddish brown, to 0.2 cm wide, eaten by bats; spike becoming 1.5–2 cm thick in fruit. **Habitat:** Moist to wet forests, forest edges, part shade. Altitude: Sea level to 2500 m. Conservation areas: ARE, CVC, GUA, LAC, LAP, OSA, PAC, TOR. **Range:** Nic–Ec. **Notes:** conspicuous for its large leaves and warty texture.

■ *Bambusa vulgaris* (bamboo)
Family Poaceae

Very large woody grass to 20 m tall, arching toward top, spreading by underground runners growing in loose clumps that form large thickets excluding other vegetation, stems to 10 cm diameter, jointed, hollow between jointlike, nodes, yellow, often with irregular green stripes, nodes ridged, branches thin, emerging from a papery sheath. **Leaves** alternate, clustered toward ends of thin straight twigs, blades narrow, 15–25 cm long, 2–4 cm wide, veins parallel, tip pointed, base rounded, almost stalkless. **Flowers** rarely seen, grasslike. Colony blooms all at once, then dies. **Habitat:** Horticultural, planted mainly in vicinity of banana plantations, also as an ornamental. Altitude: Sea level to 1100 m. Conservation areas: CVC, LAC, PAC, TEM. **Range:** Native to tropical Asia. Naturalized worldwide in the tropics. **Notes:** Used mainly to prop up banana plants, sometimes for other construction. There are four species of *Bambusa* in Costa Rica. *Bambusa* species have hollow stems. The genus *Guadua* is very much like *Bambusa* or *Chusquea*, but it has thorns.

219

■ *Chusquea longifolia* (bamboo, caña brava, cañuela)
Family Poaceae

Woody grass to 15 m tall, colonial in dense stands, stems to 4 cm diameter, nodes ridged, stem interior pithy between nodes, not hollow, many stems clumped together, arching or drooping, main stems with leaf sheaths about 12 cm long, blade of sheath erect, about 13 cm long, 3 cm wide, tip long-pointed, whisker-tipped; leafy branches arising at nodes in dense clusters, to 60 cm long, not branched again,

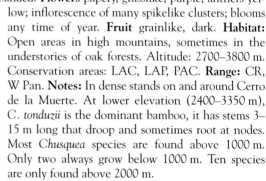

leaf sheaths of branches lobed at top. **Leaves** alternate, blades very fine, grasslike, 14–27 cm long, about 1 cm wide, tip long-pointed. **Flowers** rarely seen, grasslike. Bamboos flower rarely, most die after producing seed. **Habitat:** Open areas in mountains, forest gaps, roadsides. Altitude: 1700–3100 m. Conservation areas: ARE, CVC, LAP, PAC. **Range:** CR, W Pan. **Notes:** There are 21 species of *Chusquea* in Costa Rica. All are found at high altitudes. They differ from *Bambusa* in mostly having solid, pith-filled stems, each main branch bears many small leafy branches.

■ *Chusquea subtessellata* (*Swallenochloa s.*)
(batamba, matamba)
Family Poaceae

Shrublike woody grass 1–3 m tall, in large, very dense clumps, stems yellow, stiff, erect or leaning outward from clumps, branches numerous, erect, nodes ridged, branched again, foliage dense, leaf sheaths overlapping, persistent. **Leaves** alternate, blade 2–11 cm long, 0.5–1 cm wide, yellow green, tip abruptly pointed, stiff, base rounded, margins very rough, white-banded. **Flowers** papery, grasslike, purple, anthers yellow; inflorescence of many spikelike clusters; blooms

any time of year. **Fruit** grainlike, dark. **Habitat:** Open areas in high mountains, sometimes in the understories of oak forests. Altitude: 2700–3800 m. Conservation areas: LAC, LAP, PAC. **Range:** CR, W Pan. **Notes:** In dense stands on and around Cerro de la Muerte. At lower elevation (2400–3350 m), *C. tonduzii* is the dominant bamboo, it has stems 3–15 m long that droop and sometimes root at nodes. Most *Chusquea* species are found above 1000 m. Only two always grow below 1000 m. Ten species are only found above 2000 m.

▦ *Rhipidocladum racemiflorum*
Family Poaceae

Woody grass 10–15 m long, often vinelike, stems in dense clumps, very slender, 0.5–1 cm wide, hollow, green; new stems unbranched, whiplike, eventually drooping over, lying on other vegetation, nodes not ridged, sheaths of main stems with small triangular blades 3–4 cm long, older stems sprouting dense, fan-shaped bundles of 60–80 leafy branches per node, branches about 30 cm long. **Leaves** alternate, 2-ranked along ends of branches, essentially stalkless, blades grasslike, 6–12 cm long, 0.5–1 cm wide, midrib visible only at base.

Flowers papery, whitish, to nearly 2 cm long, about 10, in 2 rows along one side of a narrow spike to 8 cm long; spikes solitary at ends of leafy branches; blooms most of the year, especially Dec. **Habitat:** Forest edges and gaps in wet to seasonally dry regions. Altitude: Pacific slope, sea level to 1700 m. Conservation areas: CVC, GUA, LAP, OSA, PAC, TEM. **Range:** Mex–Ec and Ven. **Notes:** There are five species of *Rhipidocladum* in Costa Rica. The other fairly common one, *R. pittieri,* is similarly slender and graceful, but stems are not as long, it has much wider leaves, and is found mostly above 1000 m.

▦ *Acaena elongata*
Family Rosaceae

Low, cushionlike shrub about 30–40 cm tall, often many plants together. **Leaves** alternate, stalk flattened, base clasping stem, blade pinnate, about 5 cm long, leaflets about 7–11, about 2 cm long, 1 cm wide, elliptic, dark green, shiny (typical rose leaf), folded upward along midrib. **Flowers** green, inconspicuous amid spines, not different in appearance from fruit; inflorescence of elongate, narrow clusters above leaves; blooms and fruits all year. **Fruit** dry, reddish green, becoming brown, about 0.5 cm long, covered with small, hooked spines, for dispersal by clinging to fur or clothing. **Habitat:** Open sites, high in mountains. Altitude: 2200–3450 m. Conservation areas: CVC, LAP, PAC. **Range:** Mex, Gua, CR–Ven and Pr. **Notes:** *Acaena cylindristachya* is the only other species of this genus in Costa Rica.

221

■ *Alibertia edulis* (lagartillo, trompillo, wild guava)
Family Rubiaceae

Shrub or small tree 1–4 m tall, sometimes forming thickets; bark red brown, shredding, stipules 0.7–1.5 cm long narrowly triangular, brownish, persistent with older leaves. **Leaves** opposite, clustered at ends of stems, blade 5–14 cm long, 2–5 cm wide, elliptic to egg-shaped, tip tapered to a long point, base tapered to blunt point, yellow green. **Flowers** white, usually 4-parted, radially symmetrical, tubular 2–3 cm long, petal lobes to 2 cm long, 1 cm wide, in sparse clusters at ends of branches; blooms Apr.–Nov. **Fruit** fleshy, green turning yellow then black, 2–3 cm, slightly flattened globe, crowned with old calyx, flesh brown, sticky, seeds numerous, flat, brown, about 0.5 cm; fruit present June–Jan. **Habitat:** Understories of wet to seasonally dry forests, second growth and forest edges. Altitude: Sea level to 1400 m, usually below 500 m. Conservation areas: ARE, GUA, HNO, LAC, LAP, OSA, PAC, TEM, TOR. **Range:** Mex–Bol and Brz, Cuba. **Notes:** There are two other species of *Alibertia* in Costa Rica, neither is common.

■ *Elaeagia auriculata* (huesillo, madroño)
Family Rubiaceae

Small tree 3–10 m tall, twigs stout, 4-sided when young; stipules 2–5 cm long, to 2 cm wide, oblong to widest above middle, tip rounded; deciduous leaving prominent scars encircling stem. **Leaves** opposite, crowded at ends of twigs, each pair at right angles to next, stalk small to none, blade large, 15–40 cm long, 9–25 cm wide, elliptic or widest above middle, tip abruptly pointed, narrowing below middle, base with small ear-shaped lobes, hairy below, veins impressed above, closely parallel, 11–16 pairs, at right angles to midrib, curving upward. **Flowers** white, radially symmetrical, tubular, to 0.7 cm long with flaring petal lobes; blooms Nov.–Mar. **Fruit** dry, rounded, to 0.5 cm, crowned by old calyx, splitting open at top to release dark brown, small, winged seeds; fruit present Jan.–June. **Habitat:** Understory tree in wet forests. Altitude: 350–1750 m, Conservation areas: ARE, CVC, GUA, LAP. **Range:** CR, Pan. **Notes:** There are five species of *Elaeagia* in Costa Rica; *E. auriculata* is conspicuous for its very large, almost stalkless leaves.

■ *Isertia laevis*
Family Rubiaceae

Tree or shrub 3–13 m tall, erect, often with several trunks, bark finely fissured, twigs 4-sided, densely yellowish-hairy; stipules 4, 1.2 cm long, 0.6 cm wide, triangular, in pairs, hugging each corner of the twig above the leaf stalk, tip pointed, base broad, eventually leaving a scar around the stem. **Leaves** opposite, stalks stout, to 7.5 cm long, blade large 15–60 long, 7–22 cm wide, oblong, leathery, dark green above, whitish-hairy below, tip pointed, base blunt, surface slightly puckered, veins loop-connected along leaf margin. **Flowers** white with yellowish hairs inside, fragrant, radially symmetrical, tubular, 3–5 cm long, petal lobes 6–7, to 1.4 cm long,

widely spreading; inflorescence large, branched clusters to 35 cm long, 15 cm wide; blooms Apr.–Oct., mostly June. **Fruit** fleshy, becoming black, to 1 cm long and wide, smooth, top flattened, seeds numerous, small; fruit present most of the year. **Habitat:** Moist to wet forests, second growth, open sites. Altitude: Sea level to 800 m. Conservation areas: ARE, CVC, LAC, OSA (mostly), PAC. **Range:** Nic–Ven and Bol. **Notes:** There are two other species of *Isertia* in Costa Rica.

■ *Morinda citrifolia* (yema de huevo, Indian mulberry) Family Rubiaceae

Shrub or small tree 2–8 m tall, branches to 1 cm thick, stipules to 2 cm long, 1 cm wide, tip rounded. **Leaves** opposite, stalk to 2 cm, slightly winged, blade 12–28 cm long, 7–16 cm wide, oblong, tip and base blunt to pointed, shiny, veins prominent. **Flowers** white, radially symmetrical, tubular, small, to 1 cm long, petal lobes 5, to 0.8 cm long, fleshy, bases fused in fleshy heads to 2 cm long and wide, solitary; blooms and fruits Feb.–Oct. **Fruit** fleshy, rounded, 4–12 cm wide, becoming white, lumpy, irregularly oval,

made up of fused individual fruits each with a central "eye" from the old calyx (like *Annona* fruits), not edible. **Habitat:** Ocean shores and wet areas. Altitude: Caribbean shore, sea level to 30 m. Conservation areas: HNO (infrequently), LAC, TOR. **Range:** Native to India, widely naturalized. Bel–Ven, WI, Madagascar, some Pacific islands. **Notes:** *Morinda panamensis* is native to Costa Rica, it has fruit only to 3 cm wide, inflorescence heads 1–3 together. Often found further inland, to 600 m (mostly below 50 m) on the Caribbean slope.

■ *Psychotria graciliflora*
Family Rubiaceae

Shrub 60 cm to 2 m tall, much-branched, often flat-topped, branches horizontal, conspicuously layered, twigs slender, rough with closely spaced leaf scars, at about right angles to branches in more or less one plane; stipules with 2 linear lobes to 0.2 cm long, reddish brown, deciduous. **Leaves** opposite, clustered near ends of twigs, blade 2–6 cm long, 0.7–3 cm wide, elliptical to egg-shaped, thin, margins wavy-fluted, tip and base blunt to pointed, dark green, shiny above, paler below, midrib raised above, secondary veins obscure. **Flowers** white, radially symmetrical, tubular, to 0.3 cm long, petal lobes 5, to 0.2 cm long; inflorescences at ends of branches 6 cm long and wide; blooms Jan.–Aug. **Fruit** fleshy, red when mature, to 0.6 cm, in loose clusters above leaves, seeds 2, flat sides together; fruits all year. **Habitat:** Understories of wet forests. Altitude: Sea level to 1700 m. Conservation areas: ARE, CVC, GUA, LAC, LAP, TOR. **Range:** Mex–Pr. **Notes:** Similar to *P. parvifolia*, which has smaller leaves and is found at higher elevations, and *P. carthagenensis*, which has larger leaves and is found mostly in seasonally dry regions.

■ *Erythrochiton gymnanthus* (cafecillo)
Family Rutaceae

Shrub or small tree 1.5–6 m tall, many stems in the same site. **Leaves** alternate, spiraled at ends of branches, stalk 0.5–3 cm long, base swollen, blades 18–36 cm long, 5–11 cm wide, lance-shaped, widest near apex, surface leathery, dark green, shiny, somewhat puckered, paler below, pointed at both ends. **Flowers** white, slightly bilaterally symmetrical, showy, tubular, petal tube 2.5–4 cm long, lobes 5, 1.8 cm long, 1.5 cm wide, tip rounded, calyx tube 1.5 cm, lobes 5, to 1.7 cm long, 1 cm wide, tips pointed, stamens 5, fused to petal tube, style to 4.4 cm long; inflorescence stems elongate, above leaves; blooms May–June. **Fruit** dry, of 5 hard, 2-lipped structures 1.5–3.5 cm long, 2–2.5 cm wide, surrounded by persistent sepals, each fruit segment opening to release 2 dark, warty seeds 0.6 cm long, 0.5 cm wide; fruit present Sept.–Oct., Mar.–June. **Habitat:** Understories of moist to seasonally dry lowland forests. Altitude: Sea level to 600 m. Conservation areas: PAC, TEM. **Range:** CR. **Notes:** This is the only species of *Erythrochiton* in Costa Rica. It is abundant in Carara Biological Reserve.

■ *Zanthoxylum rhoifolium* (lagarto amarillo, lagartillo)
Family Rutaceae

Small, spiny tree 4–15 m tall, bark tan gray, *spines* flattened top to bottom, 1.5 cm long with very sharp tip, fewer spines on branches. **Leaves** alternate, evenly pinnate, to 45 cm long, 8 cm wide, leaflets, 7–23 pairs, about 5 cm long, 1–2 cm wide, elliptic, almost stalkless, hairy, sprinkled with tiny, translucent dots, leaf axis and leaflet midribs often reddish, margin coarsely toothed. **Flowers** whitish, small, radially symmetrical, in branched clusters 10–20 cm long; blooms Apr.–Aug. **Fruit** dry, surface finely glandular-warty; present Sept.–Nov. **Habitat:** Wet to seasonally dry regions, in open sites and second growth. Altitude: 30–1200 m. Conservation areas: ARE, CVC, GUA, HNO, PAC. **Range:** Mex, El Salv, Hon, CR, Col–Arg. **Notes:** There are 15 species of *Zanthoxylum* in Costa Rica.

■ *Cupania guatemalensis* (huesillo, pozolillo, tarzano)
Family Sapindaceae

Small tree or shrub 3–10 m tall, young stems yellow-woolly-hairy. **Leaves** alternate, pinnate, leaflets 3–11, alternate, blades 5–20 cm long, 2–6 cm wide, egg-shaped to narrowly oblong, tip pointed, base pointed, sides unequal, reddish-brown-hairy below, margin often remotely toothed. **Flowers** white, petals 5, about 0.2 cm long, sepals 5, hairy, 0.3 cm long, inflorescence to 10 cm long, branched; blooms Dec.–Apr. **Fruit** dry, about 1.5 cm long, top-shaped, 3-lobed, sharply angled with concave sides, densely reddish-brown-hairy; seeds 1 cm, with a fleshy aril; fruits Mar.–Nov. **Habitat:** Wet to seasonally dry forest understories and edges. Altitude: Sea level to 1400 m. Conservation areas: ARE, GUA, HNO, LAP, PAC, TEM. **Range:** Mex–Pan. **Notes:** There are 11 species of *Cupania* in Costa Rica.

◼ *Jacquinia nervosa* (*J. pungens*)
(burriquita, false evergreen needle bush)
Family Theophrastaceae

Shrub to 5 m tall, often appearing stunted, leafless in wet season. **Leaves** alternate, in tufts at ends of branches, blade 4–10 cm long, about 3 cm wide, narrowly elliptical, tip sharp, needlelike, yellow green, smooth; leafy during dry season. **Flowers** red orange, radially symmetrical, fleshy aromatic, tubular, petals fused, 5 lobes; blooms and fruits Oct.–June. **Fruit** hard-fleshy, becoming yellow, to 3 cm, thick rind, sharp-tipped, flesh sweet, seeds 2–10. **Habitat:** Seasonally dry forest understories, second growth, ridge tops. Altitude: Pacific lowlands, near sea level to 300 m. Conservation areas: GUA, PAC, TEM. **Range:** Mex–CR. **Notes:** The only species of *Jacquinia* in Costa Rica.

◼ *Urera laciniata* (ortiga comestible, tririkueko)
Family Urticaceae

Tall woody herbs or sparsely branched shrubs 1–5 m tall, often many stems in one area, stems stout, to 2 cm diameter, hollow, tan, *densely covered with stinging spines* to 0.9 cm long; stipules to 1.5 cm long. **Leaves** alternate, stalk 6–30 cm long, with stinging spines, blade 15–40 cm long, 10–45 cm wide, broadly egg-shaped to triangular in outline, deeply lobed, especially near base, lobes often toothed, tips pointed, lobes

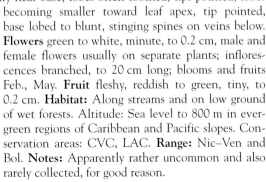

becoming smaller toward leaf apex, tip pointed, base lobed to blunt, stinging spines on veins below. **Flowers** green to white, minute, to 0.2 cm, male and female flowers usually on separate plants; inflorescences branched, to 20 cm long; blooms and fruits Feb., May. **Fruit** fleshy, reddish to green, tiny, to 0.2 cm. **Habitat:** Along streams and on low ground of wet forests. Altitude: Sea level to 800 m in evergreen regions of Caribbean and Pacific slopes. Conservation areas: CVC, LAC. **Range:** Nic–Ven and Bol. **Notes:** Apparently rather uncommon and also rarely collected, for good reason.

■ *Rinorea deflexiflora (R. squamata)*
Family Violaceae

Shrub or small tree to 12 m tall, stems to 10 cm diameter, new growth green, or minutely rusty-hairy; stipules small, pointed. **Leaves** opposite or in whorls of 3, blade elliptic to widest above middle, 6–3 cm long, 3–5 cm wide, tip long-pointed, base blunt, often unequal, dark green above, paler below, margin toothed. **Flowers** white, about 0.5 cm long, radially symmetrical, 5-parted, inflorescence unbranched to 6 cm long at ends of stems; blooms Jan.–May, also Aug., Oct. **Fruit** dry, 3-sided, egg-shaped, about 2 cm long, 1.5 cm wide, obscurely ribbed, on short stout stalks, seeds round, few; fruits Mar.–July. **Habitat:** Wet to moist forest understories. Altitude: Sea level to 1300 m. Conservation areas: ARE, CVC, GUA, LAP, OSA, PAC, TEM. **Range:** Bel and Gua–Pan. **Notes:** There are nine species of *Rinorea* in Costa Rica.

■ *Dendrophthora costaricensis* (Mistletoe)
Family Viscaceae

Shrubby epiphyte to 1 m tall and wide, stems green, compact, much branched. **Leaves** opposite, small, dull yellow green, stalk to 0.6 cm, bases joined across stem, not well differentiated from blade, blade 2–6 cm long, 1–4 cm wide, broadly egg-shaped to nearly round, rather featureless, tip rounded, base narrowed, extending down stalk, veins obscure. **Flowers** minute, greenish, inconspicuous, in small depressions along inflorescence axis; inflorescence 1–3 cm long, spikelike, solitary in leaf axils. **Fruit** fleshy, to 0.6 cm round, whitish, translucent, 1-seeded; flesh sticky, dispersed by birds, which eat the fruit and wipe the sticky seeds off their beaks onto tree branches where a new plant can grow; fruits all year. **Habitat:** Parasitic on branches of other shrubs or trees in mountains. Altitude: 1100–3500 m. Conservation areas: CVC, LAC, LAP, PAC. **Range:** Mex–Hon, CR–Ec. **Notes:** There are eight species of *Dendrophthora* in Costa Rica. Another common species is *D. squamigera*, which only grows above 3000 m and has leaves reduced to scales.

■ *Phoradendron tonduzii*
Family Viscaceae

Small epiphytic shrub to 1 m wide, often pendant, often yellowish brown. **Leaves** opposite, blade 6–20 cm long, 0.5–3 cm wide, narrowly lance-shaped, scythe-shaped, dark yellowish, tip and base tapered to long points, veins palmate but obscure. **Flowers** greenish, tiny and inconspicuous, inflorescences spikes 1–3, 3–7 cm long, in leaf axils; blooms all year. **Fruit** rounded, fleshy, to 0.4 cm long, white, becoming orange in sunlight, translucent, 1-seed, eaten by birds which disperse the seeds; fruits all year **Habitat:** Branch parasite on trees in wet mountains. Altitude: 90–2200 m. Conservation areas: ARE, LAP, PAC **Range:** Mex–Pan. **Notes:** There are 21 species of *Phoradendron* in Costa Rica. *Phoradendron tonduzii* is distinguished by its narrow, curved leaves.

WOODY VINES (LIANAS)

■ COLOR OF CONSPICUOUS PART BLUE, PURPLE, OR LAVENDER

Thunbergia grandiflora
Aristolochia gigantea
Podranea ricolasiana

Xylophragma seemannianum
Ipomoea phillomega
Solanum wendlandii

■ COLOR OF CONSPICUOUS PART RED, RED ORANGE

Combretum fruticosum
Smilax subpubescens
Cissus erosa

■ COLOR OF CONSPICUOUS PART YELLOW OR ORANGE YELLOW

Pyrostegia venusta
Caesalpinia bonduc
Solandra brachycalyx

■ COLOR OF CONSPICUOUS PART WHITE, CREAM, YELLOWISH, OR GREENISH WHITE

*Allomarkgrafia
    brenesiana*
Tournefortia hirsutissima
Mucuna mutisiana

Muehlenbeckia tamnifolia
Solanum aturense
Byttneria aculeata
Cissus verticillata

■ COLOR OF CONSPICUOUS PART GREEN TO BROWN

Macfadyena unguis-cati
*Mansoa hymenaea
    (Pachyptera h.)*
*Pithecoctenium crucigerum
    (P. echinatum)*
Bauhinia glabra
Bauhinia guianensis

Dioclea wilsonii
*Entada gigas
    (E. monostachya)*
*Stigmaphyllon
    lindenianum*
Uncaria tomentosa
Smilax vanilliodora

Woody vines, also called lianas, are high-climbing plants with woody stems. Here, they are listed by the color of the flowers or the most conspicuous part, then alphabetically by family, genus, and species.

COLOR OF CONSPICUOUS PART BLUE, PURPLE, OR LAVENDER

■ *Thunbergia grandiflora*
Family Acanthaceae

Slender woody twining vine, or somewhat shrubby. **Leaves** opposite, stalk to 6 cm long, blade 8–16 cm long, 3–13 cm wide, egg- to heart-shaped, somewhat angular, margin sparsely toothed, veins palmate at base, curved strongly upward. **Flowers** blue to pale purple, 5–8 cm long, about 6–8 cm wide, bilaterally symmetrical, tubular, petal lobes 5, large, round-tipped, wavy margins, throat white; blooms Oct.– May. **Fruit** dry, cone-shaped, 3–5 cm long, splitting open to forcibly eject flat, scaly seeds, about 1 cm long. **Habitat:** Moist to seasonally dry forests climbing in trees; widely cultivated and escaped. Altitude: Sea level to 850 m. Conservation areas: ARE, CVC, GUA, OSA, TEM (mostly). **Range:** Native to Bangladesh. Cultivated throughout the tropics; an invasive pest species in many countries. **Notes:** Fallen flowers are often the only part seen. There are six species of *Thunbergia* in Costa Rica. All are cultivated vines or shrubs native to Africa or Asia.

■ *Aristolochia gigantea*
Family Aristolochiaceae

Slender liana, twining, scarcely woody, young stems herbaceous. **Leaves** alternate, to 15 cm long, 11 cm wide, heart- to egg-shaped, tip long pointed, base blunt to shallowly lobed, whitish hairy below. **Flowers** dark reddish with a dense, whitish mottled pattern, more or less bilaterally symmetrical, tubular, large and very irregular, inflated, base to 8 cm long, then contracted and bent in middle then expanded to 20 cm long; blooms Sept.–Dec. **Fruit** dry, cylindrical, to 13 cm long, 3 cm wide, splitting into 7 sections from near the base but held together at top and base in a "Chinese lantern" pattern. Seeds numerous, about 0.8 cm, flat, wind dispersed. **Habitat:** Mostly cultivated, occasionally escaped. Altitude: 700–1100 m. Conservation areas: GUA, HNO. **Range:** Native only to Pan. **Notes:** There are 17 species of *Aristolochia* in Costa Rica. All have similar flowers and fruit. Flowers often carrion-scented.

231

■ *Podranea ricasoliana*
Family Bignoniaceae

Woody vine or vining shrub. **Leaves** opposite, pinnate, short-stalked, leaflets 7–9, blades about 3 cm long, 2 cm wide, egg-shaped, tips pointed, margins toothed. **Flowers** pale lavender with dark patch at base of 2 petal lobes, bilaterally symmetrical, tubular 6–8 cm long, tube whitish with deep magenta lines inside, 5-lobed, showy, petal lobes broad, flaring; inflorescence of branched clusters at ends of stems; blooms most of the year. **Fruit** leathery-dry, hollow, linear, splitting open to release seeds. **Habitat:** Widely cultivated, rarely escapes into natural areas. Altitude: 1100–1600 m. Conservation areas: CVC. **Range:** Native S Africa. **Notes:** This is the only species of *Podranea* in Costa Rica.

■ *Xylophragma seemannianum* (pie de gallo)
Family Bignoniaceae

Woody vine, bark with prominent lenticels, young parts densely hairy, tendrils simple, few, becoming large and woody. **Leaves** opposite, 3-parted, stalk to 12 cm long, leaflet stalks 1–7 cm long, center leaflet often may be replaced by a tendril, blades 4–28 cm long, 2–14 cm wide, egg-shaped but variable, tip abruptly pointed, base blunt, young leaves woolly-hairy. **Flowers** lavender pink and white, bilaterally symmetrical, tubular, fragrant, showy, to 6 cm long, about 3 cm across top, petal lobes 5, slightly unequal; inflorescence of oppositely branched clusters, on leafless stems; blooms Feb.–May. **Fruit** dry pods, oblong, somewhat flattened, smooth, to 18 cm long, 5 cm wide, splitting open to release winged seeds, to 2.5 cm long, 4.5 cm wide, body lobed at base, wings transparent. **Habitat:** Seasonally dry or occasionally moist forests, climbing in trees and along fences. Altitude: Sea level to 400 m, Pacific lowlands. Conservation areas: GUA, PAC, TEM. **Range:** Mex–N Brz. **Notes:** There is one other species of *Xylophragma* in Costa Rica, which is very uncommon.

▪ *Ipomoea phillomega*
Family Convolvulaceae

Shrubby, twining woody vine, sap milky, bark brown, leafy stems about 1 cm thick. **Leaves** alternate, stalk stout, 2–16 cm long; blade 7–20 cm long, 5–20 cm wide, broadly heart-shaped, tip abruptly pointed, base round-lobed, dark, dull green, young leaves often purple below. **Flowers** pale purple to pink purple, radially symmetrical, funnel-shaped, narrow below, flaring above, showy, fragrant, to 6 cm long, 5 cm across top, petal lobes shallow, notched at top, sepals pink, about 1.5 cm long, rounded, stamens on purple red filaments, borne on a ring of knobby structures; inflorescence of small branched clusters in leaf axils; blooms July–Feb. **Fruit** dry, hollow, rounded to 1.5 cm, cupped in persistent sepals, seeds 4. **Habitat:** Wet to moist forests, often in low vegetation, open areas, roadsides, forest understories, climbing on shrubs and trees. Altitude: Sea level to 1500 m. Conservation areas: ARE, CVC, GUA, HNO, ICO, LAC, OSA PAC, TOR. **Range:** Gua–Guy and Pr, WI.

▪ *Solanum wendlandii* (volcán)
Family Solanaceae

Spiny woody or herbaceous vine, high climbing to prostrate, stems green, usually with curved spines. **Leaves** alternate, stalk to 5 cm long, spiny; blade to 20 cm long, 15 cm wide, variable, entire to deeply 3- to 7-lobed on same plant, lobe tips long-pointed, midrib spiny. **Flowers** blue purple, showy, 5 cm wide, shallowly trumpet-shaped, petal lobes short; inflorescence of branched clusters; blooms all year. **Fruit** fleshy, yellow green, about 4 cm wide, possibly to 6 or 8 cm. **Habitat:** Open areas; also widely cultivated. Altitude: 700–1700 m. Conservation areas:

ARE, CVC, LAP, PAC. **Range:** Native Gua–CR, now found Mex–Par, DR, PtR. **Notes:** Seen in a garden in San José.

233

COLOR OF CONSPICUOUS PART RED, RED ORANGE

■ *Combretum fruticosum*
Family Combretaceae

Woody vine about 2 m long, bark tan, becoming fibrous, peeling. **Leaves** opposite, blade 6–12 cm long, 2–6 cm wide, elliptic, yellow green, tip pointed, base blunt to wedge-shaped, veins pinnate, few, loop-connected near margin. **Flowers** red orange to yellow, radially symmetrical, brush-like, petals minute, calyx 1 cm, stamens 8, to 2 cm long; inflorescence of dense, 1-sided spikes to 12 cm long, at ends of stems; visited by hummingbirds; blooms Oct.–Feb. **Fruit** dry, red brown to purplish, to 1.8 cm long, 2.5 cm wide, 4-winged, circular, dispersed by wind; fruit present Nov.–Mar. **Habitat:** Wet to seasonally dry, lowland forests, in trees along roadsides, pasture edges, second growth. Altitude: Sea level to 500 m. Conservation areas: HNO, LAP, OSA, PAC, TEM. **Range:** Mex–N S Amer. **Notes:** There are seven species of *Combretum* in Costa Rica, all are woody vines with winged fruit. *Combretum fruticosum* is one of the more common species.

■ *Smilax subpubescens* (cuculmeca, raíz de chino, zarza)
Family Smilacaceae

Woody vine without thorns, stems bluntly 4-sided, green to wine red, young stems hairy, becoming smooth; base of leaf stalk expanded into a sheath, with a pair of tendrils arising from juncture of leaf stalk and sheath. **Leaves** alternate, stalk about 2–5 cm long, thickened at base; blade 4–17 cm long, 4–10 cm wide, egg-shaped, tip pointed, base rounded to lobed, often finely hairy on underside, major veins palmate, 5–7. **Flowers** whitish to green, radially symmetrical, small, petals 0.3–0.5 cm long, males and females on different plants; inflorescence stems about 2–5 cm long, finely hairy, often reddish. Clusters lie below leaf axils, knoblike in bud; blooms and fruits Jan.–Aug. **Fruit** fleshy, bright orange, about 1 cm wide, top slightly pointed, in tight, dense, rounded clusters about 4 cm wide. **Habitat:** Open, second growth, climbing in low trees, wet forests, second growth. Altitude: 500–3400 m, mostly above 1100 m. Conservation areas: ARE, CVC, GUA, LAC, LAP, OSA, PAC. **Range: Notes:** Seen near Volcán Poas N.P. Common in disturbed sites in mountains.

■ *Cissus erosa*
Family Vitaceae

Slender woody, tendriled vine, to 3.6 cm diameter, most parts reddish-hairy, stem angled to winged; coiling tendrils opposite leaves. **Leaves** alternate, stalk variable, blade 3-parted, leaflets without stalks, blades 5–13 cm long, to about 6 cm wide, middle leaflet bluntly diamond-shaped, lateral leaflets with sides unequal, tips pointed, margin toothed. **Flowers** whitish yellow, 4-parted, tiny, buds and stems bright red, in dense inflorescence of flat-topped clusters; blooms, fruits Mar.–May, Aug.–Oct. **Fruit** fleshy, black at maturity, to 1 cm long with 1–2 seeds. **Habitat:** Open second growth, roadsides, climbing over low shrubs and trees Altitude: Sea level to 3000 m. Conservation areas: CVC, HNO, LAP, OSA, PAC. **Range:** Mex–Brz and Bol, DR, PtR. **Notes:** There are 16 species of *Cissus* in Costa Rica.

COLOR OF CONSPICUOUS PART YELLOW OR ORANGE YELLOW

■ *Pyrostegia venusta* (flame vine)
Family Bignoniaceae

Woody vine. **Leaves** opposite, 2-parted with a terminal, 3-parted tendril, leaflets egg-shaped, 4–6 cm long, 3–4 cm wide, tip pointed, base rounded. **Flowers** bright orange, bilaterally symmetrical, narrowly tubular, 5-lobed, about 6 cm long, 1 cm wide across top, petal lobes about 1 cm long; inflorescence of dense clusters at ends of stems; blooms most of the year. **Fruit** dry, linear, 25–30 cm long, 1.5 cm wide, pointed at both ends. **Habitat:** Widely cultivated in the central valley and elsewhere, rarely escaping into natural areas. Altitude: Cultivated 500–2240 m at least. Conservation areas: CVC, GUA, LAP. **Range:** Native to Brz–Arg, cultivated in many tropical and subtropical areas worldwide. **Notes:** This is the only species of *Pyrostegia* in Costa Rica.

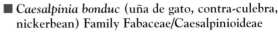

■ *Caesalpinia bonduc* (uña de gato, contra-culebra, nickerbean) Family Fabaceae/Caesalpinioideae
Woody vine or vining shrub, stems 6 m long or more, densely covered with curved spines, young plants shrubby, developing long vining branches, stems to 5 cm diameter; new growth bright green. **Leaves** alternate, stalk and midrib spiny, blade twice evenly pinnate, 25–80 cm long, to about 30 cm wide, 4–9 pairs of pinnae, each about 15 cm long, with 4–8 pairs leaflets, about 5 cm long, 2 cm wide, elliptic to oblong, tip pointed, base rounded to slightly lobed. **Flowers** yellow, slightly bilaterally symmetrical, 1–2 cm wide, 5 petals; inflorescence of dense spikes; blooms Aug.–Dec.; very attractive to bees.

Fruit dry, inflated, pods, densely prickly, 5–10 cm long, red becoming dark brown, splitting open to release 1–2 round, gray seeds 2 cm long. **Habitat:** Scrubby, second growth woodlands, especially along beaches above high-tide line. Altitude: Sea level to 300 m, rarely to 1700 m. Conservation areas: CVC, GUA, ICO, OSA, PAC, TEM. **Range:** Native to the Caribbean islands, or possibly pantropical along beaches. **Notes:** There are seven species of *Caesalpinia* in Costa Rica; *C. bonduc* is the most common.

■ *Solandra brachycalyx*
Family Solanaceae
Woody vine or vinelike shrub from 7–30 m, high in large trees. Stems to 5 cm diameter, near round, spongy, old bark flaking in rectangles, young bark silvery brown, twigs stout about 0.8 cm, with netted, corky markings. **Leaves** alternate, stalk to 6 cm, blade about 11 cm long, broadly elliptical to egg-shaped, tip pointed, base blunt to pointed, thick, leathery, midribs, white-hairy below, veins 5 per side. **Flowers** orange to greenish white and yellow, dark yellow with age, tubular, goblet-shaped, 15–25 cm long, fleshy, 5 strong green ribs on tube, 5 purple lines inside of tube, petal lobes 3 cm long, rounded, margins irregular, calyx warty, 8 cm long, 5-angled, loose; blooms Dec., Mar.–Sept. **Fruit** leathery, to 25 cm slender, whitish, enclosed by old calyx, apparently edible; fruits Apr.–Sept. **Habitat:** Mountain forests; often cultivated, sometimes wild. Altitude: 1100–2700 m. Conservation areas: CVC, GUA, LAP. **Range:** Hon–Pan. **Notes:** *Solandra grandiflora* is the only other species of this genus in Costa Rica. It has much smaller flowers and is less common than *S. brachycalyx*.

COLOR OF CONSPICUOUS PART WHITE, CREAM, YELLOWISH, OR GREENISH WHITE

■ *Allomarkgrafia brenesiana*
Family Apocynaceae

Woody vine, sap milky, sticky, stems 0.1–1 cm wide. Leaves opposite, 7–14 cm long, 2–5 cm wide, narrowly elliptic, dark green, thin, shiny. Flowers white to pink, fragrant, radially symmetrical, tubular, pendant; tube 2–3 cm long cm long, petal lobes 1–2 cm long, asymmetrical, with overlapping edges, pinwheel-like; blooms Mar.–Oct. Fruit green, becoming dry, about 30–60 cm long, 0.3 cm wide, splitting open to release seeds. Habitat: Wet forests, high in trees. Altitude: 500–1600 m. Conservation areas: ARE, CVC, LAC, LAP. Range: CR was the only listing found. Notes: There are three species of *Allomarkgrafia* in Costa Rica.

■ *Tournefortia hirsutissima*
Family Boraginaceae

Woody vine to vinelike shrub or small tree to about 5 m, stems hairy. Leaves alternate, blades 7–20 cm long, 3–8 cm wide, narrowly egg-shaped, tip pointed, thin but rough-textured. Flowers white, bilaterally symmetrical, tubular, 5-parted, tube 0.4–0.5 cm long, petal lobes 0.1 cm long, fragrant, stamens dark; inflorescence of pairs of curling spike-like clusters; blooms most of the year. Fruit fleshy, white, 0.3–0.4 cm, round, translucent, with foamlike flesh, slightly hairy; 4 seeds. Habitat: Wet, moist, and seasonally dry forests, edges, disturbed sites. Altitude: Sea level to 1800 m. Conservation areas: ARE, CVC, LAC, LAP, OSA, PAC, TEM. Range: Mex–S Amer, Ant. Notes: There are about 11 species of *Tournefortia* in Costa Rica; *T. glabra* and *T. hirsutissima* are the most common in Costa Rica.

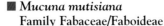

■ *Mucuna mutisiana*
Family Fabaceae/Faboideae

Woody or herbaceous vine to 15 m long. **Leaves** alternate, stalk to 9 cm long, blade 3-parted, leaflets 7–16 cm long, 4–7 cm wide, elliptic to egg-shaped, tip pointed, base unequal. **Flowers** dull white to purplish, bilaterally symmetrical, bean-flower-shaped, 5 modified petals, 1 larger petal at the top to 5 cm long, 1.5 cm wide, blunt tipped, petals folded over one another, calyx covered with *irritating hairs*; inflorescence of umbrella-shaped clusters hanging at the ends of very long, hairy stalk, 2–5 m; blooms Aug.–Jan. **Fruit** dry, pods, very reddish-hairy, to 13 cm long, 6 cm wide, ringed by numerous, winglike ridges to 1.5 cm high; seeds 1–2, to 4 cm wide; fruit present on and off most of the year. **Habitat:** Wet, lowland forests, hanging in trees. Altitude: Sea level to 300 m. Conservation areas: CVC, ICO, OSA, PAC, TOR. **Range:** CR–Ven. **Notes:** There are seven species of *Mucuna* in Costa Rica. The other common species, M. *urens*, is found at much higher elevations.

■ *Muehlenbeckia tamnifolia*
Family Polygonaceae

Scarcely woody vine to 15 m, sometimes in dense masses, young stems shiny, smooth, often red, nodes reddish brown, thick, stipules translucent, sheathlike, deciduous, leaving scar around stem. **Leaves** alternate, in one plane along sides of stem, stalk 0.5–1.5 cm, often red; blade 3–9 cm long, 1–4 cm wide, elliptical to narrowly heart-shaped, tip pointed, base rounded to slightly lobed, slightly succulent, midrib often red, margins smooth. **Flowers** greenish white to yellow, 0.2 cm wide, 5-parted, regular, in dense, branched axillary clusters; blooms all year. **Fruit** dry, enclosed in old flower parts, 0.5 cm, 5-lobed, rounded. **Habitat:** Mountains, in weedy, open sites, second growth, roadsides. Altitude: 1400–3500 m. Most often above 2000 m. Conservation areas: ARE, CVC, LAC, LAP, PAC. **Range:** Mex–Ven and Arg. **Notes:** There are three species of *Muehlenbeckia* in Costa Rica; M. *tamnifolia* is the most common.

■ *Solanum aturense*
Family Solanaceae

Sprawling woody vine or shrub with vinelike branches, stems very spiny, rough, most parts rusty-hairy. **Leaves** alternate to nearly opposite, stalk to 5 cm long, spiny, blade 5–15 cm long, about 3 cm wide, lance-shaped, tip with elongate point, base blunt, hairy on both sides, margin irregularly, broadly toothed or lobed, midrib spiny below. **Flowers** white inside, purple outside, 3–5 cm wide, petal lobes 5, narrowly triangular, tips pointed, about 1.2 cm long, 0.3 cm wide, pink-purple-hairy outside, anthers 1 cm long, yellow with white ends, gathered around stigma, calyx spiny, small; inflorescences along internodes, unbranched; blooms and fruits all year. **Fruit** fleshy, orange to red, 2–3 cm wide, cupped by persistent calyx; seeds circular, flat. **Habitat:** Shady roadsides and forest edges to primary forest, climbing or terrestrial. Altitude: Sea level to 1800 m. Conservation areas: ARE, GUA, LAC, LAP, OSA, PAC, TOR. **Range:** Mex–Brz, Ec, Ven. **Notes:** Seen in Jaco along roadside.

■ *Byttneria aculeata*
Family Sterculiaceae

Prickly woody vine or shrub with climbing stems, prickles curved, older stems 5-angled, hollow, often breaking into 5 separate stems. **Leaves** alternate, stalks to 2 cm with curved prickles; blade 4–11 cm long (to 19 cm on young stems), 2–4 cm wide, elliptic to lance-shaped, tip long-pointed, base blunt, often blotched with silver above, major veins 3–5, palmate at base, margin entire to slightly toothed. **Flowers** white, yellow, or greenish, occasionally dark wine red, 5-parted, star-shaped, radially symmetrical, about 1 cm wide, petals to 0.4 cm long, linear;

inflorescence of few-flowered, umbrella-shaped clusters in axils on stalk to 1 cm, finely hairy; blooms Sept.–Feb., May. **Fruit** dry, to 2.5 cm, 5-lobed, spine-covered, burlike; seeds 5, kidney-shaped. **Habitat:** Moist to seasonally dry lowland forests; open areas, edges, roadsides climbing on trees and shrubs. Altitude: Sea level to 1000 m. Conservation areas: CVC, GUA, HNO, LAP, OSA, PAC, TEM, TOR. **Range:** Mex–Ven and Bol. **Notes:** Of the three species of *Byttneria* in Costa Rica, *B. aculeata* is by far the most common.

■ *Cissus verticillata* (iazú)
Family Vitaceae

Woody, tendriled vine, coiling tendril opposite leaves, new stems hairy. **Leaves** alternate, stalk 1–8 cm long, blade 3–15 cm long, 2–12 cm wide, narrowly heart-shaped, egg-shaped, sometimes nearly arrow-shaped, tip pointed, base rounded to slightly lobed, leaves on new growth blue green with white veins, red below. **Flowers** pale yellow green, tiny, 0.1–0.2 cm long; inflorescence 3–10 cm long, of branched, more or less flat-topped clusters; blooms and fruits all year. **Fruit** fleshy, purple black, 0.7–1 cm long, seed solitary about 0.5 cm long. **Habitat:** Climbing on shrubs or trees. Altitude: Sea level to 1500 m. Conservation areas: ARE, CVC, GUA, HNO, LAC, LAP, OSA, PAC, TEM, TOR. **Range:** FL, TX–Arg and Brz, DR, PtR. **Notes:** There are 16 species of *Cissus* in Costa Rica; this is most common.

COLOR OF CONSPICUOUS PART GREEN TO BROWN

■ *Macfadyena unguis-cati* (uña de gato, cat-claw, bignone) **Family Bignoniaceae**

Woody vine, stem to 6 cm diameter, attached to tree by small roots growing from stem, juvenile plants climbing straight up tree trunks, with 3-parted tendrils with hooked tips like cat's claws, about 1 cm long, from between leaflets, clinging to tree bark, adult plants lack tendrils. **Leaves** opposite, stalk 1–4 cm long, blade, 2-parted, leaflets of juvenile leaves small, to 2 cm long, adult leaflets 5–16 cm long, 1–6 cm wide, lance- to egg-shaped, thin, tip pointed, base wedge-shaped to truncate, veins often reddish below. **Flowers** orange yellow, tubular, 5–10 cm long, about 2 cm wide across throat, petal lobes 1–3 cm long, tips rounded; pollinated by bees; blooms Jan.–July. **Fruit** dry, linear pods 26–95 cm long, 1–2 cm wide, splitting open to release winged seeds, about 4.5 cm wide, wind dispersed; May–Oct. **Habitat:** Cultivated and wild, in wet to seasonally dry regions. Altitude: Sea level to 1400 m. Conservation areas: GUA, HNO, LAC, LAP, OSA, PAC, TEM. **Range:** Mex–Arg, WI. **Notes:** *Macfadyena uncata* is the only other species of this genus in Costa Rica.

■ *Mansoa hymenaea (Pachyptera h.)* (josmeca, ajillo)
Family Bignoniaceae

Woody vine to 5 cm diameter, sometimes shrublike in stands with many short stems forming a ground cover, about 1 m tall, bark smooth, gray, plant smelling strongly of garlic when crushed. **Leaves** opposite, 2-parted, often with a 3-pronged tendril between leaflets, blades 5–9 cm long, 4–7 cm wide, broadly egg-shaped, tip pointed to blunt, base blunt to slightly lobed, thin, shiny green, major veins pale. **Flowers** purple pink, to nearly white, garlic-scented, tubular, 4–5 cm long, about 1 cm wide across top of tube, petal lobes about 1 cm long; blooms Jan.–Apr., June. **Fruit** dry, linear, flattened, 15–25 cm long, 2 cm wide, splitting open to release numerous winged seeds 1 cm long. **Habitat:** Seasonally dry forests, sometimes in wet to moist forests; sometimes cultivated. Altitude: Sea level to 1100 m, mostly on the Pacific slope. Conservation areas: ARE, GUA (mostly), LAP, OSA, PAC, TEM. **Range:** Mex–Brz. **Notes:** Used medicinally by indigenous people. There are five species of *Mansoa* in Costa Rica; all are woody vines.

■ *Pithecoctenium crucigerum (P. echinatum)*
Family Bignoniaceae

Liana, stems 6–8 angled, most parts whitish-scaly, old stems ribbed. **Leaves** opposite, 2- or 3-parted, 2- to 3-branched tendril often replacing terminal leaflet, stalk to 6 cm long, leaf and leaflet stalks slender, white-scaly; leaflet blade 7–14 cm long, 6–10 cm wide, heart-shaped, tip abruptly pointed, base lobed, whitish-scaly on both sides, veins palmate at base. **Flowers** cream white, becoming pale yellow in age, hairy, tubular, to 6 cm long, 5-lobed, tube curved, odor unpleasant; in hairy, unbranched clusters to 20 cm long; blooms Jan.–June. **Fruit** woody, to 32 cm long, 8 cm wide, flattened side to side, densely covered with short, warty spines, abruptly pointed at both ends, splitting in 2 parts lengthwise; seeds flat, 4 cm long, 10 cm wide, including broad, transparent wing; green or ripe fruit present most of the year. **Habitat:** Wet to seasonally dry forests. Altitude: Sea level to 1050 m. Conservation areas: ARE, CVC, GUA, LAC, OSA, PAC, TEM, TOR. **Range:** Mex–Arg, WI. **Notes:** This is the only species of *Pithecoctenium* in Costa Rica. Woody fruit hulls are distinctive.

241

■ *Bauhinia glabra* (escalera de mono, sibö, kaparuwo)
Family Fabaceae/Caesalpinioideae

Woody liana, older stems with undulating, S-shaped pattern, flattened, wide marginal ribs, central part with occasional spines or small twig on raised part of undulation, with a cleft running along center, younger stems with tendrils. **Leaves** alternate, stalk slender, elongate, blade 4–10 cm long and wide, broadly egg-shaped to rounded, tip deeply 2-lobed giving the leaf a "cow-hoof" appearance, base round-lobed.

Flowers greenish white to pink, with purple dots, fragrant, open, slightly bilaterally symmetrical, petals 5, to 2 cm long, egg-shaped, somewhat unequal; blooms mostly Nov.–Mar. **Fruit** dry, woody pods, becoming red then brown, 6–7 cm long, about 2 cm wide; splitting open to release seeds. **Habitat:** Moist to seasonally dry forests. Altitude: Pacific lowlands, sea level to 300 m. Conservation areas: GUA, PAC, TEM. **Range:** Mex–Bol, Cuba. **Notes:** There are 14 species of *Bauhinia* in Costa Rica. They include trees, shrubs, and woody vines. Most of the vines have the same flat, undulating form as B. *glabra*.

■ *Bauhinia guianensis* (escalera de mono, sibö, kaparuwo)
Family Fabaceae/Caesalpinioideae

Woody vine (liana) with flat, undulating stem, to 20 cm wide, thickly ridged or winged on each side, thornlike appendages at out-pouching of stem, undulations fuse with other stems they contact (possibly a climbing/holding aid), young stems cylindrical, tendrils unbranched, coiling. **Leaves** alternate, stalk to 3 cm long, blade 6–10 cm long, 4–10 cm wide, "cow-hoof"-shaped, cleft to at least 1/3 of length from tip, finely rusty-hairy below, base lobed. **Flowers** white,

slightly bilaterally symmetrical, about 4 cm wide, fragrant, 5 petals, 4 alike, 1 shorter and narrower; inflorescence of unbranched hairy clusters to 15 cm long; blooms in July. **Fruit** woody, hollow pods flat, oblong, to 8 cm long, 2.5 cm wide, tip pointed with 2–4 disk-shaped seeds. **Habitat:** Moist to wet lowland forests. Altitude: Sea level to 550 m. Conservation areas: CVC, LAC, OSA, PAC, TOR. **Range:** Mex–Bol, Tr.

■ *Dioclea wilsonii* (sea purse, ojo de buoy)
  Family Fabaceae/Faboideae

Woody vine. **Leaves** alternate, 3-parted, leaflets 7–15 cm long, 4–13 cm wide, elliptic to rounded, base blunt, hairy below. **Flowers** purple, to 3 cm long, bean-flower-shaped, in dense, narrow, unbranched clusters to 45 cm long, stems dark, rusty-hairy, flowers arising from warty knobs along inflorescence stalk; blooms Sept.–Jan. **Fruit** pods, more or less rectangular, 10–14 cm long, 5 cm wide, 1.7 cm thick, purplish-hairy, not splitting open, developing by Nov., ripe by May; seeds 3–4, woody, blackish brown with a tan margin, 3 cm diameter, often found along shores, dispersed by water, but also by animals that eat the pods. **Habitat:** Wet lowlands, shores. Altitude: Sea level to 100 m. Conservation areas: LAC, OSA. **Range:** SE Mex–Guy and Brz. **Notes:** There are eight species of *Dioclea* in Costa Rica. It is one genus of several that produce "drift seeds" dispersed by rivers or along shores.

■ *Entada gigas* (*E. monostachya*) (sea heart)
  Family Fabaceae/Mimosoideae

Woody vine, tendriled, trunk to 40 cm wide near base, often twisted, bark finely fissured, reddish brown. **Leaves** twice pinnate, 2 pairs of opposite pinnae, to 10 cm long, axis ending in a tendril, each pinna with about 5 pairs of leaflets to 5 cm long, 3 cm wide, asymmetrically oblong, tips blunt or notched, bases unequal. **Flowers** green white, powder-puff type, sweet, unpleasant odor, 0.6 cm long, stamens much longer than petals, in dense, unbranched clusters; blooms Sept.–May. **Fruit** dry, very large pod to 1.2 m long, 13 cm wide, broadly spiraled, eventually separating between seeds; seeds woody, to 6 cm diameter and 2 cm thick, bluntly heart-shaped, dark purplish black, requires about a year to mature; seeds dispersed by water. **Habitat:** Wet to moist lowlands. Very often washed up on beaches of both coasts. Altitude: Sea level to 900 m, mostly below 400 m. Conservation areas: CVC, HNO, ICO, LAP, OSA, PAC, TOR. **Range:** SE Mex–Ec and Guy, WI. Apparently also native to Africa. **Notes:** There are three species of *Entada* in Costa Rica; all are woody vines.

■ *Stigmaphyllon lindenianum*
Family Malpighiaceae

Woody vine, most parts finely hairy. **Leaves** opposite, stalk to 5 cm long, two prominent nector glands at the top; blade 5–16 cm long, 4–11 cm wide, egg- to heart-shaped, tip blunt to long-pointed, base lobed, to pointed, surface dark green above, paler and finely hairy below, veins palmate at base, margin sometimes toothed. **Flowers** yellow, somewhat bilaterally symmetrical, about 2 cm wide, petals 5, about 0.8 cm long, widest near apex, very narrow at base; blooms and fruits most of the year. **Fruit** dry, 3-parted, winged, sometimes reddish, wings 3–4 cm long. **Habitat:** Moist to wet lowland forests, disturbed sites. Altitude: Sea level to 900 m, mostly below 300 m. Conservation areas: ARE, CVC, GUA, HNO, LAC, LAP, OSA, PAC, TOR. **Range:** S Mex–Col. **Notes:** There are eight species of *Stigmaphyllon* in Costa Rica.

Nector glands

■ *Uncaria tomentosa* (rangayo)
Family Rubiaceae

Woody vine climbing to 30 m, sharp, hooked *spines* to 1.5 cm long, paired at nodes, aid climbing; stems to 2.5 cm diameter near base, leafy stems bristly-hairy; stipules to 1.4 cm, tip pointed. **Leaves** opposite, usually ranked in one plane, stalk to 1.8 cm long; blade 7–15 cm long, 4–9 cm wide, broadly oblong to egg-shaped, tip blunt to pointed, base blunt to slightly lobed, often whitish below, veins impressed above.

Flowers yellow to whitish, radially symmetrical, tubular, to 0.6 cm, petal lobes 5, about 0.1 cm long, flaring outward, anthers and stigma slightly longer than petal tube; inflorescences axillary, to 15 cm long, of 3–5 dense, ball-shaped flower clusters about 2 cm wide, on opposite branches of inflorescence, main stalk much like spines; blooms Jan.–May. **Fruit** dry, 2-parted, splitting open to release numerous winged seeds 0.4 cm long, old fruit clusters persistent. **Habitat:** Wet regions, in weedy edges and second growth. Altitude: Caribbean lowlands, sea level to 400 m. Conservation areas: CVC, HNO, LAC, TOR. **Range:** Bel and Gua–Guy and Bol. **Notes:** This is the only species of *Uncaria* in Costa Rica.

■ *Smilax vanilliodora*
Family Smilacaceae

Woody vine with flat, wide-based, triangular thorns, stems smooth, green, 4-sided, winged or ridged, stipules expanded into a sheath, with a pair of tendrils arising from juncture of leaf stalk and sheath. **Leaves** alternate, blade 6–24 cm long, 3–12 cm wide, egg- to lance-shaped, tip pointed to blunt, base rounded to slightly lobed, major veins 5–9, palmate. **Flowers** yellow to green, radially symmetrical, fragrant, small, petals 0.4–0.6 cm long; males and females on different plants; inflorescences of umbrella-shaped clusters on stalks much longer than the adjacent leaf stalk; blooms and fruits most of the year. **Fruit** fleshy, red orange, becoming dark red to black, flesh yellow, to 1.8 cm wide. **Habitat:** Climbing to about 3 m in low trees and shrubs of wet forests. Altitude: Sea level to 1600 m. Conservation areas: ARE, CVC, GUA, HNO, LAC, OSA, PAC, TOR. **Range:** S Mex–Pan. **Notes:** Winged stems and long inflorescence stalks are distinctive.

■ *Vitis tiliifolia* (bejuco negro)
Family Vitaceae

Liana, stems often very thick, bark peeling in strips, young stems densely white-woolly, coiling tendrils opposite leaves. **Leaves** alternate, blade 8–18 cm long, about as wide, typical grape leaf shape, shallowly to deeply 3- to 5-lobed, young leaves densely woolly above, becoming dark green above, brown- to gray-hairy below, margin toothed. **Flowers** greenish yellow, radially symmetrical, fragrant, very small, petals 5, deciduous; inflorescence branched, narrow, branches woolly. **Fruit** fleshy, purple, 0.6–0.8 cm wide, edible.

Habitat: Often a canopy vine. Altitude: 60–1300 m. Conservation areas: ARE, CVC, GUA, LAC, PAC, TEM. **Range:** Mex–Ven. **Notes:** This is the only wild grape in Costa Rica. The cultivated grape, *V. vinifera*, which is the European wine grape, is grown in Costa Rica but does not escape into natural areas.

HERBACEOUS VINES

■ COLOR OF CONSPICUOUS PART
  BLUE, PURPLE, LAVENDER, OR PINK

Anthurium clavigerum
Weberocereus trichophorus
Ipomoea pes-caprae
Evodianthus funifer

Canavalia rosea
  (C. maritima)
Centrosema plumieri
Passiflora edulis

■ COLOR OF CONSPICUOUS PART
  RED OR RED ORANGE

Bomarea acutifolia
Bomarea costaricensis
Pseudogynoxys
  chenopodioides
  (P. cumingii)
Ipomoea quamoclit

Dioscorea bulbifera
Cissampelos pareira
Passiflora costaricensis
Passiflora vitifolia
Trichostigma polyandrum

■ COLOR OF CONSPICUOUS PART
  YELLOW OR YELLOW ORANGE

Mandevilla hirsuta
Merremia umbellata
Gurania makoyana
Luffa aegyptiaca
Momordica charantia

Sechium edule
Rhynchosia minima
Vigna luteola
Pavonia cancellata

■ COLOR OF CONSPICUOUS PART WHITE, CREAM,
  YELLOWISH, OR GREENISH WHITE

Anthurium scandens
Monstera deliciosa
  (M. dilacerata)
Monstera dissecta
Gonolobus edulis

Begonia glabra
Rytidostylis gracilis
Sechium pittieri
Vanilla planifolia
Cobaea aschersoniana

■ COLOR OF CONSPICUOUS PART
GREEN TO BROWN

Anthurium caperatum
Monstera tenuis
Philodendron aurantiifolium
Philodendron crassispathum
Philodendron hederaceum
Philodendron radiatum
Philodendron verrucosum
Syngonium hoffmanii
Syngonium podophyllum
Mikania guaco

Asplundia microphylla
Scleria secans
Dioscorea convolvulacea
Dioscorea spiculiflora
Dalechampia scandens
Calopogonium caeruleum
Pueraria phaseoloides
Peperomia hernandiifolia
Peperomia rotundifolia

Herbaceous vines are climbing or twining herbs. Some have tendrils, and the stems are usually green and not woody.

COLOR OF CONSPICUOUS PART BLUE, PURPLE, LAVENDER, OR PINK

▩ *Anthurium clavigerum*
Family Araceae

Stout epiphytic vine, stem to 2 m long, 3–4 cm thick, large leaf scars, thick aerial roots. **Leaves** alternate, crowded near top of stem; stalk 0.6–1.5 m long, base clasping stem; blade 0.5–2 m long, palmately compound, leaflets 0.25–1 m long, 4–25 cm wide, with 2–5 deep pinnate lobes, central leaflet longer than lateral leaflets, juvenile leaves simple, unlobed, narrow; leaves becoming palmately compound and progressively more divided as plant matures. **Flowers** dark purple, or grayish, minute, densely crowded

on a fleshy spike 20–70 cm long, to 2 cm wide, tapered at both ends, above a maroon bract 18–65 cm long, 1–3.5 cm wide; inflorescence drooping below leaves; blooms all year. **Fruit** fleshy, red purple, 0.7 cm long, crowded, fruiting spike to 6 cm wide; seeds 1 or 2; Mar.–Oct. **Habitat:** Wet lowland forests, usually 2–7 m from ground. Altitude: Sea level to 600 m, mostly below 200 m. Conservation areas: ARE, GUA, HNO, LAC, LAP, OSA, TOR. **Range:** Nic–Brz. **Notes:** There are 87 species of *Anthurium* in Costa Rica.

▩ *Weberocereus trichophorus*
Family Cactaceae

Epiphytic, succulent, hairy cactus, stems climbing, to 12 m long, about 1 cm diameter, cylindrical, pale gray green, spines, bristles, and wooly hairs in short tufts along stem. **Leaves** none. **Flowers** bright, deep pink outside, white inside, 4–6 cm long, petals numerous, 1.5–2.5 cm long, flower base reddish-hairy, covered with short bracts, flowers solitary at ends of stems; seen blooming in Feb. **Fruit** fleshy, reddish, 2–3 cm long, egg-shaped; seeds black, embedded red purple fruit pulp. **Habitat:** High climbing and pendant in trees. Altitude: Southern Caribbean lowlands, sea level to 100 m. Conservation areas: LAC. **Range:** CR. **Notes:** There are six species of *Weberocereus* in Costa Rica; *W. trichophorus* is the only one found in and near Cauhita N.P. and Gandoca-Manzanillo Wildlife Refuge.

■ *Ipomoea pes-caprae* (pudre oreja,
beach morning glory)
Family Convolvulaceae
Vine, stems purplish, to 30 m long, rooting at nodes, extending underground. **Leaves** alternate, broadly elliptical, to
10 cm long, thick, tip often notched, veins conspicuous.
Flowers pinkish purple, with 5 darker stripes, to 9 cm wide,
funnel-shaped, open for only 1 day; blooms July–Feb. **Fruit**
dry, splitting into 4 parts each containing 1 seed. **Habitat:**
Beaches, above high-tide line. Altitude: Mostly at or near sea
level, occasionally to 200 m. Conservation areas: GUA, ICO,
LAC, OSA, PAC, TEM, TOR. **Range:** Pantropical. **Notes:**
Long roots and underground portions of stems help hold sand
in place. Often found with *Canavalia rosea*, a bean vine.

■ *Evodianthus funifer* (chidra, chirravaca, tucuso)
Family Cyclanthaceae
Epiphytic vine, sparsely branched, often with drooping aerial
roots, climbing tree trunks. **Leaves** alternate, stalk longer
than or equal to blade, partially winged, blade 35–80 cm
long, narrow, tips forking into 2 lobes for 1/2–2/3 of its
length, lobes 2–8 cm wide, tips long-pointed, surface corrugated by impressed veins, shiny, dark green. **Flowers** pinkish
with long white stamens; inflorescence of spikes, bulblike in
bud (photo of inflorescence bud), bracts dark pink red, overlapping, 6 cm long, 4 cm wide, 3 cm thick, on a stalk about
6 cm long; pollinated by small bumblebees; blooms and fruits
most of the year, especially Apr.–Aug. **Fruit** fleshy, yellow,
unripe fruits spike patterned with geometric grooves and
bumps. **Habitat:** Wet forests. Altitude: Sea level to 1600 m,
most often below 500 m. Conservation areas: ARE, CVC,
GUA, HNO, LAC, OSA, TOR. **Range:** S Nic–Ven, Pr,
Tr, To, Brz. **Notes:** This is the only species of *Evodianthus*
worldwide.

■ *Canavalia rosea (C. maritima)*
Family Fabaceae/Faboideae
Vine to 10 m long, creeping along sand. **Leaves** alternate, with three thick, shiny leaflets, about 12 cm long, oval to oblong, blunt at tip and base. **Flowers** pink purple with white center, bilaterally symmetrical, bean-flower-shaped, about 2 cm wide; inflorescence of sparse clusters; blooms most of the year. **Fruit** dry, bean pods, about 15 cm long, 2 cm wide, flattened. **Habitat:** Beaches above high-tide line. Altitude: Sea level to 200 m, mostly below 10 m. Conservation areas: GUA, LAC, OSA, PAC, TEM,

TOR. **Range:** Beaches throughout the tropics. **Notes:** Often mixed with *Ipomoea pes-caprae* (beach morning glory). There are eight species of *Canavalia* in Costa Rica.

■ *Centrosema plumieri*
Family Fabaceae/Faboideae
Herbaceous twining vine to 1 m long, slender, green. **Leaves** alternate, 3-parted, leaflets 5–15 cm long, broadly egg-shaped, tips sharply pointed, base blunt, white-hairy below. **Flowers** white margin with dark purple center, bilaterally symmetric, flattened, bean-flower-shaped, 5–6 cm wide, 5 modified petals, 1 larger petal at the top rounded; flowers solitary or few in leaf axils; blooms Nov.–Apr. **Fruit** dry, pod, black when dry, 10–14 cm long, 1 cm wide, flattened with squared edges, seeds brown, to 0.9 cm long. **Habitat:** Wet to seasonally dry lowlands, in open, weedy sites. Altitude: Pacific lowlands, sea level to 500 m. Conservation areas: GUA, LAP, OSA, PAC, TEM. **Range:** Mex–Brz, WI, introduced in Africa. **Notes:** There are six species of *Centrosema* in Costa Rica. The other common species, *C. pubescens*, has lavender flowers.

■ *Passiflora edulis* (tococa, granadilla)
Family Passifloraceae

Tendriled vine 5–15 m long, young parts green, older parts woody, bark pale brown, flaky, base of stem to 7 cm wide. **Leaves** alternate, stalk 3–6 cm long, with 2 warty outgrowths at top, blades 5–15 cm long, 4–10 cm wide, deeply 3-lobed, base shallowly lobed, margins toothed. **Flowers** white and purple, large, showy, solitary in leaf axils, 5–10 cm wide, petals and sepals 5 each (photo: flower bud), below a central crown of long fleshy, purple and white threads about 4 cm long, the stamens and stigma large, fused onto a stalk, elevated above the center of the flower; blooms Feb., Apr., July. **Fruit** fleshy, smooth, round 4–7 cm wide, thick skin, surrounding seed cavity with numerous black seeds each in a juice-filled sac, edible when black and fully ripe, *immature fruit very toxic;* fruit present Apr., Nov. **Habitat:** Widely cultivated, escaping occasionally. Altitude: Sea level to 2900 m. Conservation areas: ARE, CVC, LAC, PAC. **Range:** Native to Brz. Widely cultivated throughout the tropics. Invasive in Africa and on some Pacific islands. **Notes:** Fruit used for juice.

COLOR OF CONSPICUOUS PART RED OR RED ORANGE

■ *Bomarea acutifolia*
Family Alstroemeriaceae

Herbaceous vine about 2 m long. **Leaves** alternate, stalk 1 cm, blade about 7–10 cm long, 3–5 cm wide, elliptic, smooth, veins inconspicuous. **Flowers** red orange, sometimes with yellow margins, yellow inside often with purple spots, radially symmetrical, of 3 free petals and 3 free sepals, all similar, closely overlapping, flower appearing tubular, flower about 3–7 cm long, 1 cm wide across top, nodding on thin stalks; inflorescences of umbrella-shaped clusters of about 10 flowers at ends of stems; blooms most of the year. **Fruit** becoming dry, hollow, greenish, hairy, angular, about 2 cm long; seeds red. **Habitat:** High elevations in open habitats. Altitude: 1300–3200 m. Conservation areas: CVC, LAC, LAP, PAC. **Range:** Mex–Pan. **Notes:** There are 11 species of *Bomarea* in Costa Rica; most are herbaceous vines with red flowers, two have white or pinkish flowers.

■ *Bomarea costaricensis*
Family Alstroemeriaceae

Herbaceous vine about 2 m long. **Leaves** alternate, stalk 1 cm, blade 7–10 cm long, 3–5 cm wide, elliptic, smooth, veins inconspicuous. **Flowers** red orange, often with purple spots inside, radially symmetrical, of 3 free petals and 3 free sepals, all similar closely overlapping, flower appearing tubular, 4–6 cm long, about 1 cm wide; inflorescence of pendant, umbrella-shaped clusters of about 10 flowers at ends of stems; blooms Aug., Sept., Dec.–Apr. **Fruit** greenish, becoming dry, hollow. **Habitat:** High elevations in open habitats. Altitude: 1300–3200 m. Conservation areas: CVC, LAC, LAP, PAC. **Range:** Endemic to CR.

■ *Pseudogynoxys chenopodioides (P. cumingii)*
Family Asteraceae

Vine, stem eventually becoming woody, deeply grooved, reaching 4–5 m high, most parts hairy, young stems slender, green. **Leaves** alternate, stalk 1–3 cm long, blade 3–12 cm long, 1–7 cm wide, triangular to egg-shaped, about 10 cm long, 4.5 cm across base, tip pointed, base truncate to slightly lobed, margin coarsely toothed. **Flowers** bright red orange, showy, in compact heads, individual flowers tubular; the central, disc flowers radially symmetrical, the peripheral flowers bilaterally symmetrical with 1 enlarged petal (ray), rays 1–2 cm long, about 0.6 cm wide, tips pointed, disk flowers yellow, turning red in age, heads about 5 cm wide including rays, bract-covered base large, vase-shaped, about 1.5 tall, 1.7 cm wide, bracts loosely bowed outward; heads solitary at ends of stems; blooms Dec.–May. **Fruit** dry, 1-seeded, with a tuft of soft, white bristles. **Habitat:** Wet to seasonally dry regions, open woodland, second growth, draping over other vegetation. Altitude: 150–2100 m, Pacific slope. Conservation areas: GUA, OSA, PAC. **Range:** N Mex–Arg. **Notes:** This is the only species of *Pseudogynoxys* in Costa Rica, showy but not very common.

■ *Ipomoea quamoclit* (Cypress vine)
Family Convolvulaceae

Annual vine, stems slender, twining, to 5 m long. **Leaves** alternate, stalk to 3 cm long, blade about 9 cm long, 6 cm wide, pinnately divided to the midrib, feathery, delicate, lobes linear, about 3 cm long, 0.2 cm wide. **Flowers** red, tubular, 2 cm wide at top, lobes 5, flat, tube 2 cm long, 0.2 cm wide, pistil white, anthers pinkish, both extending slightly beyond petal lobes; inflorescence of few-flowered clusters; blooms most of the year. **Fruit** dry, 4-parted, conical cupped by persistent sepal lobes, seeds 4, black. **Habitat:** Wet to seasonally dry regions in weedy open areas, roadsides. Altitude: Sea level to 1800 m, most often below 500 m. Conservation areas: CVC, GUA, LAC, LAP, OSA, PAC, TEM. **Range:** Mex–S Amer. Now pantropical, invasive in some places. **Notes:** Sometimes sold as a garden plant.

■ *Dioscorea bulbifera* (papa Caribe, papa de aire, yam)
Family Dioscoreaceae

Twining, climbing vine to 20 m long, branching; tubers grow from stems in leaf axils, to 12 cm wide, rounded to pear-shaped (photo). **Leaves** alternate, 20–30 cm long and wide, heart-shaped, tip abruptly pointed, base deeply lobed, major veins palmate, converging at leaf tip, small veins numerous, more or less perpendicular to major veins. **Flowers** dark reddish to off-white, radially symmetrical, about 0.4 cm wide, fragrant, petals 6, male and female flowers on separate plants; inflorescences of multiple, dangling spikes 12 cm long or more; blooms Oct.–Jan. **Fruit** dry, winged, wings 1.5 cm long, 0.9 cm wide, gray to brown, both ends rounded. **Habitat:** Cultivated, sometimes escaped in wet to moist weedy areas, roadsides. Altitude: Sea level to 1100 m. Conservation

areas: CVC, HNO, PAC. **Range:** Native to Asia and E Africa. Cultivated throughout the tropics. **Notes:** Tubers of cultivated varieties edible, those of wild types are toxic, can be fatal. *Dioscorea alata* is another cultivated Asian species. It has winged stems. There are 24 species of *Dioscorea* in Costa Rica. *Dioscorea* is grown for its starchy tubers in many tropical areas of the world.

Cissampelos pareira
Family Menispermaceae

Twining vine, stems hairy, older stems slightly woody.
Leaves alternate, stalk to 7 cm, hairy, blade 2–12 cm
long and wide, broadly heart- or egg-shaped, pale
gray green, finely hairy on both sides, tip rounded
or with small point, base broadly lobed to truncate.
Flowers greenish to white, 0.3 cm, radially symmetrical; in many-branched clusters amid small, rounded,
hairy, leaflike bracts, decreasing in size toward end of
inflorescence; blooms Nov.–Aug, mostly Feb.–June.
Fruit fleshy, red, 0.5 cm, round, finely hairy, juicy, 1-
seeded; fruit present most of the year. **Habitat:** Moist to wet
regions in forests, second growth, edges, open areas. Altitude:
Near sea level to 2200 m. Conservation areas: ARE, CVC,
GUA, HNO, LAC, LAP, PAC, TOR. **Range:** Pantropical
and subtropical. **Notes:** There are five species of *Cissampelos*
in Costa Rica.

Passiflora costaricensis
Family Passifloraceae

Herbaceous vine, stem green rather succulent about 0.5 cm
diameter, 3-sided, angles slightly, winged, coiling tendrils in
axils opposite each leaf. **Leaves** alternate, stalk 2–5 cm long,
blade 8–17 cm long, 5–13 cm wide, apex with 2 hornlike
lobes, 1 at either side, about 3 cm long, blade thus terminating
in a bitelike cut-out, base rounded, dark green, slightly hairy,
shiny above, veins palmate at base. **Flowers** yellow green, to
greenish white, radially symmetrical, 5-parted, 2.5–4 cm
wide, petals 1–5 cm long, center crownlike, sepals 1.5–2 cm
long, brownish, often with purple spots inside; blooms Apr.–
Dec. **Fruit** fleshy, dark red, 1–2 in axils, a narrowly elliptical pod, 6–8 cm long, 1.5–3 cm wide, pointed at both ends,
deeply, unevenly 6-ribbed, ribs of one side narrower than the
other, seeds dark, numerous in a thin, white pulp; fruit present May–Nov. **Habitat:** Wet forests, edges, second growth.
Altitude: Sea level to 1300 m, mostly below 500 m. Conservation areas: ARE, GUA, LAC, OSA (mostly), PAC.
Range: Mex–Col and Ec. **Notes:** There are about 48 species
of *Passiflora* in Costa Rica.

■ *Passiflora vitifolia* (granadilla del monte, passion flower) Family Passifloraceae

Vine or liana, stems to 3 cm diameter, all parts densely rusty-hairy, tendrils from leaf axils. **Leaves** alternate, deeply 3-lobed, 7–14 cm long, 9–14 cm wide, lobes tapered at tips, base round-lobed, margin toothed. **Flowers** bright red, very showy, 10–15 cm wide, petals 5, 4–6 cm long, narrow, crown-like floral center of 3 rows of filaments to 2 cm long, anthers

5, green; on leafless, lower branches in forest understory, sepals 5, 6–8 cm long, 1–2 cm wide, tips with a long, slender appendage; blooms on and off much of the year, mostly Jan.–Mar., often pollinated by hummingbirds. **Fruit** fleshy, yellow green with purple markings, egg-shaped, to 10 cm, with numerous black seeds about 1 cm long, probably eaten by mammals; fruit present Jan.–Sept. **Habitat:** Wet to moist forests. Altitude: Sea level to 1500 m, mostly below 800 m. Conservation areas: ARE, CVC, GUA, LAC, LAP, OSA, PAC, TOR. **Range:** Nic–Pr.

■ *Trichostigma polyandrum* Family Phytolaccaceae

Shrub or vine 1–3 m long, long stems may appear as herbaceous vine, sometimes in trees. **Leaves** alternate, stalks 1–3 cm long, blade 7–16 cm long, 2–7 cm wide, narrowly elliptic to egg-shaped, dark green, pointed at both ends, margin smooth, veins often loop-connected near margin. **Flowers** white to greenish, 0.2–0.4 cm long, nearly radially symmetri-

cal, 4 petal-like sepals, stamens about 20, very short, falling early, 1 pistil; inflorescence unbranched, 7–15 cm long (to 25 cm in fruit), stem usually red to purple; blooms and fruits all year. **Fruit** fleshy, red at first, becoming black, 0.5–0.8 cm wide, above bright red, persistent sepals 0.6–1 cm long. **Habitat:** Wet forests, second growth, disturbed sites. Altitude: Sea level to 1300 m, usually below 500 m; mostly on the Caribbean slope. Conservation areas: ARE, CVC, HNO, LAC, LAP, TOR. **Range:** Nic–Pan. **Notes:** The only other species, *T. octandrum*, is very similar but has only 10 stamens. Flowers much like those of *Phytolacca*.

COLOR OF CONSPICUOUS PART YELLOW OR YELLOW ORANGE

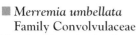 *Mandevilla hirsuta*
Family Apocynaceae

Herbaceous vine, hairy, sap milky, copious, internodes about 13 cm long, stem 0.2–0.3 cm wide. **Leaves** opposite, stalk about 3.5 cm long, blade 3–13 cm long, 1–5 cm wide, oblong to elliptic, hairy on both sides, tip abruptly long-pointed, base with narrow lobes, veins pinnate. **Flowers** pale yellow with bright red center, fragrant; radially symmetrical, tubular, 5–6 cm long, 5.5 cm wide, trumpet-shaped, 5 petal lobes, 1 cm long, each lobe very asymmetric but all 5 alike, one side rounded, the other narrowed to a point, slightly fleshy, tube abruptly narrowed, calyx with 5 narrow lobes 1 cm long; blooms most of the year. **Fruit** dry, 0.5 cm wide; 2 cylindrical pods, connected end to end, green to reddish brown, hairy. **Habitat:** Moist to wet regions, climbing in trees and shrubs. Altitude: Sea level to 1800 m. Conservation areas: ARE CVC, GUA, HNO, LAC, LAP, OSA, PAC, TOR. **Range:** Gua–Brz and Bol. **Notes:** There are seven species of *Mandevilla* in Costa Rica.

 *Merremia umbellata*
Family Convolvulaceae

Twining vine, slender. **Leaves** alternate, stalk 1–8 cm long, blade 5–14 cm long, 3–8 cm wide, narrow to egg-shaped, smaller on flowering stems, tip pointed, base deeply lobed, with wide gap between lobes, veins palmate at base. **Flowers** bright yellow, radially symmetrical, about 2 cm long, 3 cm wide across top, trumpet-shaped, petals fused to top, rim slightly notched, inflorescence of unbranched clusters; blooms Nov.–Mar. **Fruit** dry, round, about 0.8 cm, splitting into 4–6 sections to release several brown, hairy seeds. **Habitat:** Wet to seasonally dry regions in open to partly shady disturbed sites. Altitude: Sea level to 800 m. Conservation areas: ARE, GUA HNO, LAP, OSA, PAC, TEM. **Range:** Pantropical, invasive in a few places. **Notes:** There are seven species of *Merremia* in Costa Rica, all have white to yellow flowers.

Gurania makoyana
Family Cucurbitaceae

Stout, herbaceous, tendriled vine, usually hairy, stems finely grooved, tendrils coiling around other plant stems to climb. **Leaves** alternate, each opposite a thick tendril, stalk to 10 cm long, blade 15–40 cm long and about as wide, 3- to 7-lobed, upper lobes pointed at tips, base with rounded lobes, hairy on both sides, veins palmate, margin finely toothed. **Flowers** orange and yellow, radially symmetrical, 5-parted, sexes on different plants (dioecious), petals fused, tube bright yellow; calyx lobes bright orange, linear, to 4 cm, longer than petal tube; inflorescence of dense, rounded clusters; blooms all year. **Fruit** fleshy, green, cylindrical, to 6 cm long, 2.5 cm wide, old flowers persistent at tip, seeds white, numerous, to 0.9 cm long, 0.5 cm wide. **Habitat:** Wet to moist forests, on edges, in gaps, open to partly shaded sites, climbing in other vegetation. Altitude: Sea level to 1400 m. Conservation areas: ARE, CVC, GUA, HNO, LAC, LAP, OSA, PAC, TOR. **Range:** S Mex–Col. **Notes:** There are eight species of *Gurania* in Costa Rica.

Luffa aegyptiaca (estropajo, paste)
Family Cucurbitaceae

Herbaceous vine, stems green, slender, with watch-spring tendrils 3- to 5-branched opposite each leaf. **Leaves** alternate, stalks slender, 4–12 cm, blade 10–25 cm long and about as wide, broadly heart-shaped with 5 lobes, lobe tips pointed, basal lobes rounded, veins palmate, margin toothed. **Flowers** yellow, radially symmetrical, 2–3 cm long, about 7 cm wide, showy, petals 5, free, male flowers on an axis 10–35 cm long with 10–30 flowers along the upper half, female flowers solitary in axils; blooms most of the year. **Fruit** fleshy and edible when young, cylindrical, 10–30 cm long, striped with darker markings, becoming dry, fibrous, opening at the conical top to release gray seeds, about 1 cm long, with winged margins. **Habitat:** Cultivated for its long, fibrous fruit, used for scrubbing. Occasionally escaped in wet to seasonally dry regions in open, lowland sites. Altitude: Sea level to 400 m. Conservation areas: CVC, HNO, OSA, PAC, TEM, TOR. **Range:** Native to Old World tropics, now pantropical. Invasive in some Pacific islands. **Notes:** Naturalized plants often fiercely defended by ants. There are three other species of *Luffa* in Costa Rica, all but *L. operculata* are native to the Old World tropics.

■ *Momordica charantia* (sorosí, pepino de
monte, balsampear)
Family Cucurbitaceae

Slender vine, tendrils simple, climbing on fences and
other vegetation. **Leaves** alternate, stalk 1–6 cm,
blade 3–6 cm long and wide, deeply divided into 5–7
palmately arranged lobes, narrower at base than middle, tips blunt, margin toothed. **Flowers** yellow, radially symmetrical, 5-lobed about 1 cm wide, on stalks
4–15 cm long, male flowers with 3 short stamens,
female flower with a warty ovary below base of petal
tube; blooms and fruits May–Jan. **Fruit** bright yellow
orange, oval to spindle-shaped, 4–8 cm long, 2–4 cm
wide, surface warty or blunt-spiny, tip
pointed, gourdlike, splitting open into
3 segments to reveal bright red fleshy-
coated seeds about 1 cm long. **Habitat:**
Wet regions in part shade or open weedy
sites, roadsides, vacant lots. Altitude:
Sea level to 800 m. Conservation areas:
ARE, CVC, HNO, LAC, LAP, OSA,
PAC, TEM, TOR. **Range:** Native to the
Old World tropics. Naturalized in the
Neotropics and invasive in some Pacific
islands. **Notes:** This is the only species of *Momordica* in Costa Rica. Fleshy
seed coat is edible, as are green fruits and
leaves when cooked.

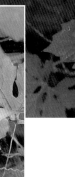

Ripe fruit detail

■ *Sechium edule* (chayote)
Family Cucurbitaceae

Herbaceous vine, high-climbing perennial, tendrils
1- to 5-branched. **Leaves** alternate, stalk 4–15 cm
long, blade broadly egg-shaped to rounded, 6–22 cm
long, and almost as wide, 3–5 shallow lobes, tips
pointed, base deeply round-lobed, margin finely
toothed, rough-hairy above. **Flowers** yellow green,
about 1–2 cm long, radially symmetrical, male flowers in small clusters of 2–6 on a long stalk, female
flowers 1–2 in axils. **Fruit** fleshy, pale green, 7–20 cm
long, pear-shaped, grooved surface spiny or smooth,
fleshy, 1-seeded, seed lens-shaped, 3–6 cm long. **Habitat:** Cultivated and naturalized, in open weedy areas.
Altitude: To at least 1100 m. Conservation areas:
CVC. **Range:** Neotropical native. **Notes:** Fruit, tubers
(called *raiz*), and shoots edible when cooked. Fruit is
common in markets. There are five other species of
Sechium in Costa Rica, all of which are wild.

259

■ *Rhynchosia minima*
Family Fabaceae/Faboideae

Herbaceous or shrubby vine, straggling, ground cover, stems green, finely hairy, more or less prostrate. **Leaves** alternate, 3-parted, leaflet stalks 1 cm long, blades 2–4 cm long, 1–3 cm wide, egg-shaped, sides often slightly curved inward, tip pointed to blunt, base blunt to wedge-shaped. **Flowers** yellow with purplish stripes, small, bilaterally symmetrical, bean-flower-shaped, to 0.7 cm long, 0.5 cm wide, 5 modi-

fied petals, 1 larger petal at the top; inflorescence of spikelike clusters 7–13 cm long, as long or longer than leaves; blooms Oct.–Jan., Apr. **Fruit** dry, pod hairy, flat, small to1.5 cm long, 0.4 cm wide, constricted between seeds; seeds 0.3 cm, brown, mottled with black. **Habitat:** Wet to seasonally dry lowlands in open, weedy sites, roadsides. Altitude: Sea level to 240 m, mostly on the Pacific slope. Conservation areas: GUA, LAC, LAP, OSA, PAC, TEM. **Range:** Mex–Arg. Also widely introduced, and/or possibly native, throughout much of the tropics. **Notes:** There are five species of *Rhynchosia* in Costa Rica.

■ *Vigna luteola* (cowpea)
Family Fabaceae/Faboideae

Prostrate vine, rooting at nodes and along internodes, or climbing on other vegetation. **Leaves** alternate, 3-parted, leaflets 2–8 cm long, lance-shaped to egg-shaped, tip blunt, shiny green. **Flowers** yellow, bilaterally symmetrical, bean-flower-shaped, upper (banner) petal wider than long, about 2 cm long and wide, much larger than side and lower petals; inflorescence of small unbranched clusters at ends of erect, stout stalks about 6 cm long; blooms Oct.–Feb. **Fruit** dry, pods, 4–6 cm long, about 0.4 cm wide. **Habitat:** Open sites, sometimes along beaches. Altitude: Sea level to 1200 m. Conservation areas: LAC, LAP. **Range:** Native to much of the Old World tropics and S US, introduced in tropical Amer. **Notes:** Seen on beach at Puerto Viejo, Limón. There are 17 species of *Vigna* in Costa Rica. The most common species is probably *V. vexillata*, which has white flowers with purple markings.

■ *Pavonia cancellata*
Family Malvaceae

Stems to 2 m long, trailing along ground, green, most parts densely bristly-hairy. **Leaves** alternate, stalk 0.5–3.5 cm, blade 2–3.5 cm long, asymmetrical, more or less triangular, 3-lobed, tip blunt to pointed, base with rounded to pointed lobes, veins palmate, margin toothed. **Flowers** pale yellow with dark red center, 3 cm across top, trumpet-shaped, 5 petals, 1.5–2.5 cm long, overlapping, calyx lobes to 0.8 cm long, hairy, stamens fused into a central column 0.9 cm long surrounding base of pistil, basal bracts about 15, 1–1.5 cm long, linear lobes with feathery margins; flowers solitary or in pairs; blooms most of the year. **Fruit** dry, to 0.8 cm wide, broadest near apex. **Habitat:** Seasonally dry regions in open sites, roadsides, pasture edges. Altitude: Pacific lowlands, sea level to 800 m, mostly below 400 m. Conservation areas: GUA, PAC, TEM. Seen near Rincón de la Vieja N.P. **Range:** CR–Pr and Brz. **Notes:** There are 11 species of *Pavonia* in Costa Rica.

COLOR OF CONSPICUOUS PART WHITE, CREAM, YELLOWISH, OR GREENISH WHITE

■ *Anthurium scandens*
Family Araceae

Epiphytic, vining herb, stem creeping, to about 1 m long, usually less, slender, lower nodes with long aerial roots; leaf bud sheaths brown, often wearing into fibers. **Leaves** alternate, stalk 1–9 cm long, swollen at top and bottom, usually bent at top; blade 2–14 cm long, 1–5 cm wide, elliptic, tapered to a point at both ends, surface smooth, dull green, somewhat leathery, lower surface (and sometimes upper) often sprinkled with tiny, dark dots; lateral veins obscure. **Flowers** greenish white to lavender, densely crowded on a fleshy spike, 0.5–3 cm long, inflorescence bract pale green, small, 0.3–2 cm long, 0.1–0.8 cm wide, lance-shaped, tip long-pointed, bent back; blooms and fruits all year, especially Jan.–July. **Fruit** fleshy white to purple, flesh clear, gelatinous; seeds 5–9. **Habitat:** Moist to wet forests often on mossy trees, or rocks. Altitude: 20–2500 m. Conservation areas: ARE, CVC, GUA, HNO, ICO, LAC, LAP, OSA, PAC, TOR. **Range:** S Mex–S Brz, Tr, Ant.

■ *Monstera deliciosa (M. dilacerata)* (chirrivaca, costilla de Adán, hoja de piedra, mano de trigre)
Family Araceae

Epiphytic vine to 10 m long, rooting at nodes to hold tree trunk. **Leaves** alternate, stalk winged, attachment of blade and stem at a sharp angle, blades of young leaves unlobed, resembling water-lily pads, closely adhering to tree bark and increasing in size as they ascend, older juvenile leaves simple, heart-shaped, free from tree trunk, mature blades to 1 m long, 75 cm wide, deeply, pinnately lobed and perforated, base lobed. **Flowers** off-white, minute, densely crowded on a fleshy spike to 25 cm long, inflorescence bract cream white, to 30 cm long, thick, waxy, decaying as fruits develop; blooms Jan.–Aug. **Fruit** fleshy, yellow, edible when ripe; fruits Feb.–Nov. **Habitat:** Wet forests mostly in mountains; also frequently cultivated. Altitude: 500–2200 m. Conservation areas: ARE, CVC, LAC, LAP, PAC. **Range:** Mex–Pan. **Notes:** There are 24 species of *Monstera* in Costa Rica. Many resemble *Philodendron* species. *Monstera* is distinguished by the winged leaf stalk, the bend at the attachment of leaf stalk and blade, and the often perforated leaves.

Early fruit

Juvenile leaves

Monstera dissecta photos opposite

■ *Monstera dissecta*
Family Araceae

Large epiphyte, stems vining, clinging to tree trunks. **Leaves** alternate, stalk 4–46 cm long, base sheathing stem, blade 8–50 cm long, 4–30 cm wide, deeply pinnately lobed, 2–7 lobes per side, occasionally also with perforations, tip pointed, base blunt or with shallow lobes. **Flowers** minute, white, densely crowded on a fleshy spike 5–16 cm long, 1–2.5 cm wide, inflorescence bract white, about 50 cm long, 30 cm wide, cowl-shaped, tip pointed, base rounded; inflorescence stalk 9–25 cm long; blooms most of the year. **Fruit** fleshy, white, fruiting spike to 30 cm long, seeds about 1 cm long; fruits Jan., July. **Habitat:** Wet forests, on tree trunks. Altitude: Sea level to 2000 m, mostly above 1000 m. Conservation areas: ARE, CVC, GUA, LAP, OSA, TOR. **Range:** Bel–W Pan.

■ *Gonolobus edulis*
Family Asclepiadaceae

Vine climbing on other low vegetation, sap milky, copious, stems slender, green. **Leaves** opposite, 3–8 cm long, 1–6 cm wide, oblong, tip pointed, base lobed, slightly hairy, basal lobes narrow, curved inward, margin smooth. **Flowers** pale green to cream white with purple speckles, center dark yellow, solitary, 1.5–3 cm long, 5-parted, petals 0.8–1.5 cm long, 1 cm wide, egg-shaped, overlapping, veins darker green, sepals egg-shaped, 0.6 cm, greenish white, tip pointed, bases overlapping, flat about 0.3 cm wide; blooms Mar., June–July, Sept. **Fruit** dry, pods splitting open to release plumed seeds. **Habitat:** Moist to wet forests. Altitude: 600–2800 m. Conservation areas: ARE, CVC, GUA, LAP, PAC. **Range:** Mex–Col. **Notes:** There are six species of *Gonolobus* in Costa Rica.

Monstera dissecta

■ *Begonia glabra*
Family Begoniaceae

Succulent epiphytic vine to 4 m or more, old stems sometimes woody; stipules 0.5–3 cm long, persistent, old stems ringed by stipule scars at nodes. **Leaves** alternate, in one plane along opposite sides of the stem, blade 1–14 cm long, 0.8–10 cm wide, broadly elliptic to egg-shaped, tip pointed, base blunt to slightly lobed, margin sparsely toothed. **Flowers** white to pink, bilaterally symmetrical, male and female flowers separate, male flowers with 4 petals about 0.5 cm long, 0.3 cm wide, stamens yellow, numerous; female flowers with 5 petals 0.5 cm long, 0.1–0.3 cm wide, ovary inferior; inflorescence with forked branching, flowers numerous; blooms Sept.–June, mostly Dec.–Mar. **Fruit** dry, about 1 cm long, 3-winged, one wing much larger than the other two; seeds tiny, numerous. **Habitat:** Wet and very wet forests. Altitude: Sea level to 2600 m, mostly 400–1100 m. Conservation areas: ARE, GUA, LAC, LAP, PAC TOR. **Range:** Mex–Pr, Ant. **Notes:** There are about 34 species of *Begonia* in Costa Rica; this is the only vinelike species.

■ *Rytidostylis gracilis*
Family Cucurbitaceae

Herbaceous vine climbing in low vegetation, stems green, tendrils coiled, with 2–3 branches. **Leaves** alternate, stalk

1–6 cm, blade 6–8 cm long, 5–7 cm wide, broadly heart-shaped to rounded, often with 3–5 shallow lobes with pointed tips, basal lobes deep, rounded, veins palmate, margin toothed. **Flowers** white to pale yellow, narrowly tubular, 2–3 cm long, petal lobes linear, tips pointed, elongate, bent back, male flowers in small clusters on a stalk to 20 cm long, female flowers solitary, in axils, ovary below petal tube, spiny; blooms most of the year. **Fruit** green, becoming dry, 2–4 cm long, 1–2 cm wide, covered with short, spiny bristles 0.5 cm long, asymmetrically oval, splitting open to release winged seeds about 1 cm long; fruit present July–Jan. **Habitat:** Wet to seasonally dry regions, in open weedy sites, roadsides. Altitude: Sea level to 2000 m. Conservation areas: ARE, CVC, GUA, LAC, LAP, OSA, PAC, TEM, TOR. **Range:** Mex–Pr and Brz. **Notes:** There is one other species of *Rytidostylis* in Costa Rica. It is uncommon.

■ *Sechium pittieri* (tacaco de monte)
Family Cucurbitaceae

Herbaceous vine, covering ground and climbing over other vegetation, tendrils 3- to 5-branched. **Leaves** alternate, stalk 5–15 cm long, blade 10–28 cm long, and about as wide, broadly egg-shaped, top usually 3- to 5-angled or -lobed, the central lobe the largest, tips pointed, base lobed, margin slightly wavy, with a few teeth. **Flowers** white to pale yellow green, sexes separate, male flowers small, about 1 cm wide, petals 0.3–0.5 cm long, numerous, in groups of unbranched clusters 4–25 cm long (photo: inflorescence), female flowers solitary, petals similar to males; blooms and fruits all year. **Fruit** fleshy, 4–6 cm long, 3–4 cm wide, elliptic-oblong, pale green to red, slightly grooved, covered with low spines, becoming netted with deep olive brown and conspicuous veins when mature, eventually splitting open in 10 sections to release 1 seed 2–3 cm long. **Habitat:** Wet forest understories. Altitude: 380–2000 m. Conservation areas: ARE, CVC, LAC, LAP, OSA, PAC. **Range:** Nic–Pan. **Notes:** This is by far the most common wild species of *Sechium* in Costa Rica.

■ *Vanilla planifolia*
Family Orchidaceae

Terrestrial or epiphytic vine, stem elongate to about 3 m long, fleshy, no bulblike swellings at base. **Leaves** alternate, 9–23 cm long, 4–7 cm wide, elliptic to oblong, fleshy, tip pointed, folded along midrib, secondary veins obscure. **Flowers** white to yellowish green, bilaterally symmetric, 3 sepals and 2 side petals similar, 5–6 cm long, about 1 cm wide, lower or central petal 5 cm long, 1.5–3 cm wide, appearing tubular, narrower at base, lip 3-lobed white with orange veins, margin frilly; flowers opening one at a time, lasting only 1 day; blooms Apr.–June, Dec.–Jan. **Fruit** yellow green, 10–25 cm long, about 1 cm wide, becoming dry, elongate, beanlike, in clusters; splitting open to release seeds. **Habitat:** Very wet forests; also widely cultivated. Altitude: Sea level to 200 m. Conservation areas: HNO, LAC, OSA, TEM, TOR. **Range:** Mex–Pan. **Notes:** There are 10 species of *Vanilla* in Costa Rica, all are vines, some to 30 m long; *V. planifolia* is the most common species cultivated for vanilla flavoring, which is extracted from the fruit. It is unusual to see it in flower.

Courtesy of Frederick Williams

■ *Cobaea aschersoniana*
Family Polemoniaceae

Tendriled liana or vine, stems green, hairy. **Leaves** alternate, pinnate, terminal leaflet replaced by a branched tendril, leaflets 6, opposite, 6–10 cm long, 2–3 cm wide, lance-shaped, tip pointed, base blunt, often unequal, dark green above. **Flowers** pale green to cream, with purplish highlights, radially symmetrical but appearing bilaterally symmetrical, large, showy, tubular, about 6–9 cm long, 4 cm wide, across top, base of floral tube very narrow, petal lobes 5, 6 cm long, 2 cm wide, tips abruptly contracted into tendril-like ends 6–9 cm long, calyx green, 5 free lobes 2–4 cm long, 0.8 cm wide, anthers 5, yellow, filaments purple, 6–9 cm long, style 6–9 cm long, stigma green, with 6–8 small branches; inflorescence of 1–2 flowers with 2 or more bracts at ends of stalk about 25 cm long; blooms Oct, Feb. **Fruit** dry, 5–6 cm long, splitting open to release 9–18 seeds 0.3 cm long, 0.1 cm wide; fruit present Dec., Mar., Apr. **Habitat:** Open sites and weedy areas in mountains, roadsides. Altitude: 2000–3000 m. Conservation areas: CVC, LAP, PAC. **Range:** Endemic to CR. **Notes:** There are four species of *Cobaea* in Costa Rica.

COLOR OF CONSPICUOUS PART GREEN TO BROWN

■ *Anthurium caperatum*
Family Araceae

Epiphytic vine on tree trunks, or terrestrial, stem to 1.2 m long, 3–5 cm wide. **Leaves** alternate, stalk 0.2–1 m long, blade 0.34–1.2 m long, 22–69 cm wide, egg- to heart-shaped, with deep gap between basal lobes, about 10 cm, tip pointed, surface wrinkled, thick, rubbery, dull green, a prominent marginal vein extending from base of lobes to tip of blade.

Flowers pale green, minute, crowded on an erect spike 7–25 cm long, 1–2 cm thick, inflorescence bract pale green, 10–20 cm long, 2–4 cm wide, lance-shaped to oblong, rolled back and soon falling; inflorescence stalk 10–54 cm long, about 1 cm wide; blooms Mar.–May, Sept., Dec. **Fruit** fleshy, pale yellow green, to 0.9 cm long, 0.5 cm wide, egg-shaped; fruits Apr., July, Dec. **Habitat:** Wet forests. Altitude: 500–2000 m. Conservation areas: ARE, CVC, LAC, LAP, PAC. **Range:** CR–Pan. **Notes:** There are 87 species of *Anthurium* in Costa Rica, most have a marginal vein along edge of leaf.

Monstera tenuis
Family Araceae

Epiphytic vine, clinging to tree trunks, stems about 2 cm thick, nodes with many short aerial roots, juvenile stems flattened. **Leaves** alternate, stalk 20–60 cm long, mature blade 0.5–1.1 m long, 30–65 cm wide, becoming progressively larger and more pinnately cleft, lobes narrow, appearance rather fernlike; juvenile leaves heart-shaped and flat against bark of host tree, overlapping one another along stem. **Flowers** minute, white, densely crowded on a fleshy spike 15–30 cm long, 3–5 cm wide, inflorescence bract hooding flower spike, at first white to pinkish, blunt tipped, deciduous

as fruit develops; blooms and fruits most of the year. **Fruit** fleshy, yellowish, fruit spike enlarging, base of inflorescence bract splitting open to reveal fruit; seeds numerous, each surrounded by a sweet fleshy layer. **Habitat:** Moist to wet forests. Altitude: Sea level to 1800 m. Conservation areas: ARE, GUA, LAP, PAC, TOR. **Range:** SE Nic–W Pan. **Notes:** When a seed germinates the seedling grows toward the darkness of a tree and, upon reaching the trunk, begins to produce flat, undivided leaves that press tightly against the bark. As the vine grows upward, leaves become free and the edges become progressively more divided (see Janzen 1983 for more).

Philodendron aurantiifolium
Family Araceae

Herbaceous vine, freely branching, reaching at least 10 m long; stem about 1 cm wide, much-branched, slightly woody; rooting at every node. **Leaves** alternate, stalk 5–17 cm long, about 1 cm wide, broadly winged the entire length; blade 8–23 cm long, 3–14 cm wide, narrowly egg-shaped, tip pointed, base blunt to slightly lobed, secondary veins widely diverging from midrib. **Flowers** inconspicuous, densely crowded on a fleshy spike 7–13 cm long, inflorescence bract tubular at base, wrapped around spike, dark green outside; blooms Mar.–Nov. **Fruit** fleshy, white-translucent, seeds deep red purple at maturity; fruits Mar., Apr., June. **Habitat:** Wet forests, mostly lowlands; often covering tree trunks and forest understory vegetation. Altitude: Sea level to 1750 m, usually below 500 m. Conservation areas: ARE, CVC, LAC, LAP, OSA, PAC, TOR. **Range:** S Mex–Pan. **Notes:** There are about 62 species of *Philodendron* in Costa Rica.

■ *Philodendron crassispathum*
Family Araceae

Herbaceous, low epiphytic vine, occasionally terrestrial, stems 2–3.5 cm wide, sap with spicy odor. **Leaves** alternate, stalk 12–24 cm long, margins rounded, blade 13–30 cm long, 10–23 cm wide, heart-shaped to broadly arrow-shaped, tip pointed, base deeply lobed, surface dark green, smooth,

leathery, midrib pale. **Flowers** white densely crowded on a fleshy spike 8–11 cm long, male flowers above, females below, about 2 cm wide, inflorescence bract 7–4 cm long, 5–10 cm wide, wall to 1 cm thick, elliptic, tip blunt, green outside, red inside, fleshy; inflorescences solitary in leaf axils, stalk 4–7 cm long; blooms Mar., Apr., Sept. **Fruit** fleshy, becoming orange to whitish, seeds yellow orange; fruiting spike 5 cm long (female part), 4 cm wide. **Habitat:** Wet mountain forests. Altitude: Caribbean slope, 1300–2600 m. Conservation areas: LAC. Seen in Tapantí N.P. **Range:** CR, W Pan.

■ *Philodendron hederaceum* (hoja de hombre, heart-leaved Philodendron) **Family Araceae**

High-climbing herbaceous vine, usually epiphytic, stems hanging downward, leafy stems about 1.5 cm wide, short-hairy. **Leaves** alternate, stalk 12–40 cm, blade 14–46 cm long, 11–35 cm wide, heart-shaped, tip pointed, base deeply lobed, leaves of young plants tightly clinging and flattened against tree trunks or rocks, blades overlapping, shinglelike. **Flowers** inconspicuous, densely crowded on a fleshy spike 11–18 cm long, 1–2 cm wide; inflorescence bract tubular, bulbous at base, to 19 cm long, to 3.5 cm wide, greenish white; inflorescences solitary in leaf axils; blooms Jan.–Mar., June–July. **Fruit** fleshy, pale orange to off-white, 1 cm; cluster to 9 cm long, 5 cm wide, inflorescence bract deciduous; seeds 4–5 per fruit; fruits Feb.–Mar. **Habitat:** Moist to wet forests, along rivers, on remnant trees in pastures. Altitude: Sea level to 900 m. Conservation areas: CVC, HNO, ICO, LAC, LAP, OSA, PAC, TEM, TOR. **Range:** Mex–Bol, E Brz, Ant. **Notes:** Familiar house plant in North America.

■ *Philodendron radiatum* (mano de tigre)
Family Araceae

Large, epiphytic vine, stems thick, to 12 cm diameter, clinging to tree trunks with aerial roots, other aerial roots grow downward like slender cables, ends becoming densely branched; leaf bud sheaths sometimes pale pink, lance-shaped, to 30 cm long. **Leaves** alternate, mostly near end of stem, stalk to 1 m long, base sheathing stem, blade 0.3–1 m long, 30–90 cm wide, deeply split into many narrow lobes, 2–4 cm wide, lobes sometimes split again, juvenile leaves much smaller, heart-shaped, mostly unlobed. **Flowers** incon-spicuous, densely crowded on a fleshy spike 11–23 long, 1.5–2.4 cm wide, tightly covered by bottle-shaped inflorescence bract, about 35 cm long, 10 cm wide, off-white above, some-times red-tinged, base greenish; stalk stout, 3–13 cm long; inflorescences 1–5 together; blooms Mar., May–Dec. **Fruit** fleshy, white, seed numerous, oblong, sticky; fruits Mar., July, Nov. **Habitat:** Wet lowland forests; also cultivated. Altitude: Caribbean lowlands, sea level to 250 m, sometimes to 700 m. Conservation areas: CVC, GUA, LAC, TOR. **Range:** Mex–Pan. **Notes:** Most conspicuous for its foliage, much like that of some *Monstera* species.

■ *Philodendron verrucosum*
Family Araceae

Epiphytic or terrestrial vine, stem to 2 cm diameter, densely covered with coarse hairlike projections; leaf bud sheath to 8 cm long, pink, scaly-hairy, blunt-tipped. **Leaves** alternate, stalk 35–70 cm long, dark red, becoming green in age, densely covered with pale green, coarse hairs about 1 cm long; blade 36–67 cm long, 28–52 cm wide, heart-shaped, tip pointed, base deeply round-lobed, upper side dark green with a metal-lic sheen, veins light green, underside red with light green veins, becoming all green as leaf ages. **Flowers** inconspicuous, densely crowded on a fleshy spike to about 10–16 cm long, 0.9–1.8 wide, covered by inflorescence bract, pale green, densely coarse-hairy, tip pointed, stalk about 10–20 cm long, 1 cm wide, densely green-hairy-scaly; blooms on and off most of the year. **Fruit** fleshy, pale yellow, about 1 cm long, in a cluster to 7 cm long, 3 cm wide; fruits Feb., Aug. **Habitat:** Wet forest understories or on trees or rocks. Altitude: 200–1500 m. Conservation areas: ARE, CVC, LAC, LAP, PAC. **Range:** CR–Pr. **Notes:** Easily recognized by its colorful, coarsely green-hairy appearance.

269

■ *Syngonium hoffmanii*
Family Araceae

Epiphytic vine, sap milky, stems green; blooms when about 12 m above the forest floor. **Leaves** alternate, stalk 11–38 cm long, winged for at least 3/4 of its length; blade 3-parted, middle leaflet elliptic, 10–27 cm long, 3–9 cm wide, tip long-pointed, base wedge-shaped, lateral lobes smaller, variably 2- to 4-lobed, in a more or less palmate arrangement, thin, dark green to white-splotched, lustrous, prominent marginal vein. **Flowers** inconspicuous, densely crowded on a fleshy spike, inflorescence bract off-white, becoming orange, envel-

oping flower spike, base tubular, to 8 cm long, upper blade to 8 cm long, 6 cm wide, tip pointed; male flowers above, female below; blooms and fruits most of the year. **Fruit** fleshy, white; fruiting part of spike to 5 cm long, 2 cm wide. **Habitat:** Moist to wet forests. Altitude: 300–2100 m, mostly above 1000 m on the Pacific slope. Conservation areas: ARE, GUA, LAC, LAP, PAC. **Range:** CR, Pan. **Notes:** Also a common houseplant. There are 16 species of *Syngonium* in Costa Rica. Milky sap distinguishes plants in the genus *Syngonium* from species of *Philodendron* with 3-parted leaves.

■ *Syngonium podophyllum* (garrobo, goosefoot plant)
Family Araceae

Epiphytic vine, sap milky, stems to 2 cm wide, green. **Leaves** alternate, stalk 15–50 cm long, sheathing stem; blade of adult leaves to 30 cm long with 3–5 or more, deep lobes, lobes may be outgrowths of other lobes, middle lobe 10–30 cm long, 4–15 cm wide, with prominent marginal veins; juvenile leaves smaller, simple, heart-shaped, blades becoming arrow-shaped as the vine climbs a tree trunk, progressing to lobed leaves. **Flowers** inconspicuous, densely crowded on a fleshy spike, inflorescence bract enveloping flower spike, dark green, fleshy, bulbous basal tube to 5 cm long, 2 cm wide, upper blade about 6 cm long, to 5 cm wide, off-white or pink inside; inflorescence stalk stout, in axillary clusters of 4–9 inflorescences; blooms and fruits Jan.–Sept. **Fruit** fleshy, white, spike about 4 cm long, 2.5 cm wide,

Plant with flower buds

bract becoming bright red outside, yellow inside, fruit pulp

sweet. **Habitat:** Moist to wet forests. Altitude: Near sea level to 1100 m. Conservation areas: CVC, GUA, LAC, LAP, OSA, PAC, TEM, TOR. **Range:** Mex–Guy, Brz, Bol, Ant, Bh. **Notes:** Juvenile form is the common houseplant *Syngonium*, often mottled with white.

Mikania guaco
Family Asteraceae

Slender, herbaceous twining vine, finely hairy, new stems purple, becoming brownish. **Leaves** opposite, stalk to 4 cm long, blade to 25 cm long, 15 cm wide, egg-shaped, tip long-tapered, base wedge-shaped, slightly extended down stalk, hairy on both sides, young leaves dark green with paler veins above, purple between veins below, surface shiny. **Flowers** white to greenish yellow, no rays, heads to 1 cm long, 4-flowered, basal bracts to 0.6 cm long; in clusters of 3; inflorescence large, branched; blooms June–Jan. **Fruit** dry, 1-seeded with tan to reddish tuft of long hairs for wind dispersal. **Habitat:** Wet to moist forests. Altitude: Sea level to 1100 m or more. Conservation areas: CVC, LAC, LAP, OSA, TOR. **Range:** Mex–Brz. **Notes:** There are 21 species of *Mikania* in Costa Rica. Most are vines. *Mikania micrantha* is the most common but does not have the distinctive variegated young leaves of M. *guaco*.

Asplundia microphylla
Family Cyclanthaceae

Epiphytic herbaceous vine, to about 10 m long, much-branched, stems green, to 1.3 cm wide, rooting at nodes, clinging to tree trunks and branches, often in large masses, young stems slender; leaf sheath brown, fibrous above. **Leaves** alternate, stalk about 8 cm, blade 12–30 cm long, forking into 2, narrow lobes for more than half its length, lobes 2–4 cm wide, tips pointed, pleated by sharply impressed, parallel veins running to leaf tip. **Flowers** off-white, inconspicuous, crowded on a thickened spike, very fragrant; inflorescence bud red, elliptic, 5 cm long, 2 cm wide, pointed at both ends; blooms and fruits Sept.–June, mostly Jan.–June. **Fruit** fleshy green, often with black markings, becoming yellow, unripe fruiting spike 3–5 cm long, about 2 cm wide, rounded to cylindrical, patterned with geometric grooves and bumps; opening at top when ripe to reveal juicy, pale orange to pink pulp, with many seeds. **Habitat:** Wet forests. Altitude: 550–2000 m, mostly above 1000 m. Conservation areas: ARE, CVC, GUA, LAC, LAP, PAC. **Range:** Nic–Pan. **Notes:** There are 19 species of *Asplundia* in Costa Rica.

271

■ *Scleria secans* (navajuela)
Family Cyperaceae

Herbaceous vinelike sedge, stems 1–6 m long, 3-sided, with *sharp, cutting edges* lined with minute, sharp, backward facing teeth, top of leaf sheath with brown appendages to 0.6 cm long. **Leaves** alternate, grasslike, to 35 cm long, 0.2–0.5 cm wide, midrib deeply impressed above, *margins lacerating*. **Flowers** purplish, 0.3–0.5 cm, dry, shiny; inflorescence 4–12 cm long, branched, bracts leaflike, male flowers in many flowered clusters, female flowers solitary, bracts thread-like; blooms and fruits all year. **Fruit** dry, 0.2–0.4 cm long, hard, white, shiny, beadlike. **Habitat:** Wet forests and open weedy areas, overgrown pastures, in low trees and shrubs. Altitude: Sea level to 1300 m. Conservation areas: ARE, LAC, OSA, PAC. **Range:** S Mex–E S Amer, Par, Tr, Ant, Bh. **Notes:** Very memorable for its ability to cling to clothing and cut skin. A plant to avoid.

■ *Dioscorea convolvulacea*
Family Dioscoreaceae

Herbaceous twining vine, stems to about 4 m long. **Leaves** alternate, blade 7–20 cm long, 4–18 cm wide, heart-shaped, tip pointed, base lobed, fleshy, usually finely hairy, major veins 7 or 9, palmate, converging at leaf tip. **Flowers** greenish white to reddish, tiny, radially symmetrical, petals 6, about 0.2 cm long; male inflorescence of long unbranched clusters, 8–35 cm long, stalks sometimes purplish, female flowers solitary in axils; blooms June–Dec., Jan.–Mar. **Fruit** dry, 1 cm wide, oblong to elliptical, 3-angled. **Habitat:** Seasonally dry to very wet forests, in open sites or forest edges, climbing on trees, roadside vegetation, fences. Altitude: 50–1950 m, most often 500–1300 m. Conservation areas: ARE, CVC, GUA, HNO, LAP, LAC, PAC, TEM **Range:** Mex–Pan. **Notes:** There are 24 species of *Dioscorea* in Costa Rica. It appears similar to *Smilax*, but *Dioscorea* has no tendrils.

■ *Dioscorea spiculiflora*
Family Dioscoreaceae

Twining vine, old stems often somewhat woody. **Leaves** alternate, blade 8–26 cm long, 5–26 cm wide, heart-shaped to triangular, tip long-pointed, base truncate to deeply lobed, major veins 7–11, palmate, converging at leaf tip, margin entire; leaves on new shoots with silvery white stripes between deeply impressed palmate veins, leaf color completely green on mature vine. **Flowers** greenish to purple, very small, radially symmetrical, petals 6; inflorescence a cluster of slender spikes 8–40 cm long; blooms all year. **Fruit** dry, 3-winged, 2–3 cm wide, green, becoming tan. **Habitat:** dry to very wet forests, climbing in trees or understory vegetation. Altitude: Sea level to 1100 m. Conservation areas: ARE, GUA, LAC, LAP, OSA, PAC, TEM. **Range:** Mex–Pan.

Winged fruit

Juvenile

■ *Dalechampia scandens* (mala)
Family Euphorbiaceae

Climbing, herbaceous vine, base woody, often with *stinging hairs*; stems hairy, stipules 0.4–0.9 cm, lance-shaped, tip bent back. **Leaves** alternate, stalks 2–9 cm long, densely hairy, blade 4–13 cm long, 5–16 cm wide, deeply 3-lobed, middle lobe 3–10 cm long, lobe tips pointed to rounded, base round-lobed, surface leathery, puckered, hairy on both sides, major veins 5, palmate. **Flowers** dark, cupped by 2 sets of cream white or greenish, hairy, 3-lobed bracts, to about 3 cm long and wide; blooms Aug.–Oct. **Fruit** dry, to 0.7 cm long, 0.9 cm wide, cupped by 8–12 sepals, splitting explosively into 3 parts to disperse seeds; fruits Oct.–Feb. **Habitat:** Moist to seasonally dry forests and second growth. Altitude: Pacific slope, sea level to 1200 m, mostly below 500 m. Conservation areas: GUA, PAC, TEM (mostly). **Range:** Mex–Arg, WI. **Notes:** There are nine species of *Dalechampia* in Costa Rica, almost all are vines.

■ *Calopogonium caeruleum*
Family Fabaceae/Faboideae

Herbaceous vine to 5 m long, all parts softly orange-hairy, stems green. **Leaves** alternate, stalk 3–10 cm long, blade 3-parted, leaflet stalks about 0.5 cm long, blade egg- to diamond-shaped, 5–11 cm long, 4–8 cm wide, tip pointed to rounded, base slightly lobed, major veins 3. **Flowers** blue, bilaterally symmetrical, bean-flower-shaped, to 1 cm long, 5 petals, 1 larger petal at the top, tip notched, flat, erect, green at center, calyx bilaterally symmetrical, hairy; inflores-

cence of unbranched, axillary clusters 2–40 cm long; blooms Dec.–May. **Fruit** dry, pods linear, 4–6 cm long, 0.6–0.8 cm wide, tip long-pointed; seeds 4–8, 0.5 cm long. **Habitat:** Wet to seasonally dry regions, in open sites, covering the ground and climbing in trees. Altitude: Sea level to 1400 m, mostly below 600 m. Conservation areas: ARE, GUA, LAC, OSA, PAC, TEM. **Range:** Mex–N S Amer. **Notes:** There are three species of *Calopogonium* in Costa Rica. This is one of many similar "kudzulike" leguminous vines encountered along roadsides.

■ *Pueraria phaseoloides* (tropical kudzu)
Family Fabaceae/Faboideae

Twining, hairy, herbaceous vine covering ground, 5–6 m long, rooting at nodes, branching, young stems densely brown-hairy. **Leaves** alternate, stalk 5–10 cm long, blade 3-parted, leaflets 3–15 cm long, egg- to diamond-shaped, tip pointed, base rounded to wedge-shaped, lateral leaflets asymmetrical, surface finely hairy. **Flowers** purple and white, small, bilaterally symmetrical, bean-flower-shaped, top (banner) petal to 1.8 cm long, base lobed; inflorescences 15–30 cm long, unbranched; blooms Dec.–Mar. **Fruit** dry, linear pods 5–10 cm long, becoming black, hairy with 10–20 brown seeds. **Habitat:** Open, disturbed, lowland sites, covering ground and small trees, second growth, roadsides. Altitude: Sea level to 300 m, rarely to 1000 m, usually on the Pacific slope. Conservation areas: CVC, LAP, OSA, PAC. **Range:** Native to tropical Asia and some Pacific islands. Widely introduced. **Notes:** This is the only species of *Pueraria* in Costa Rica. Another Asian species, *P. lobata* (kudzu), is an infamous invasive pest in the southern United States, originally planted for erosion control.

Peperomia hernandiifolia
Family Piperaceae

Epiphytic or terrestrial very succulent vine, rooting at nodes, stems and leaf stalks mottled red. **Leaves** alternate, stalk 4–18 cm long, attached to leaf underside (peltate), blade 5–20 cm long, 4–14 cm wide, broadly egg-shaped to almost round, thick, rubbery, succulent, smooth, tip long-pointed, base round, veins obscure. **Flowers** pale green, minute, without stems or petals, densely packed on a solitary, erect, fleshy spike. **Fruit** fleshy, pale green, tiny; spike to 25 cm long, 0.3 cm, thick in fruit, especially the lower part; blooms all year. **Habitat:** Wet forest understories on tree trunks and logs. Altitude: Sea level to 2300 m, usually above 1000 m. Conservation areas: ARE, CVC, GUA, LAC, LAP, TOR. **Range:** Gua–Brz. **Notes:** There are about 120 species of *Peperomia* in Costa Rica.

Peperomia rotundifolia
Family Piperaceae

Tiny epiphytic vine often low on mossy tree trunks, stems creeping, rooting at nodes. **Leaves** alternate to almost opposite below inflorescences, stalk 0.1–0.4 cm, blade rounded to egg-shaped, 0.5–1.5 cm long 0.3–1.2 cm wide, tip rounded, often reddish below, veins obscure. **Flowers** pale green, minute, densely packed on fleshy spikes 1–4 cm long, at ends of stems, usually solitary; blooms and fruits most of the year. **Fruit** fleshy, less than 0.1 cm wide. **Habitat:** Moist to wet forests, second growth, remnant trees in pastures. Altitude: Sea level to 2500 m, usually below 1200 m. Conservation areas: ARE, CVC, GUA, HNO, LAC, LAP, OSA, PAC, TOR. **Range:** Mex–Pr and Brz, WI, Tanzania.

HERBACEOUS PLANTS

■ COLOR OF CONSPICUOUS PART BLUE, PURPLE, LAVENDER, OR PINK

Hypoestes phyllostachya
Ruellia biolleyi
Ruellia inundata
Eryngium carlinae
Anthurium formosum
Anthurium upalaense
Ageratum conyzoides
Dahlia imperialis
Emilia fosbergii
Erechtites valerianifolia
Fleischmannia pycnocephala
Gnaphalium roseum
Impatiens walleriana
Heliotropium indicum
Aechmea mariae-reginae
Tillandsia leiboldiana
Centropogon gutierrezii
Commelina erecta
Floscopa robusta
Tradescantia poelliae
Desmodium axillare
Lupinus costaricensis
Mimosa pudica
Geranium guatemalense
Drymonia turrialvae
Episcia lilacina
Monopyle maxonii

Sisyrinchium micranthum
Hyptis suaveolens
Prunella vulgaris
Salvia carnea
Utricularia unifolia
Spigelia anthelmia
Cuphea carthagenensis
Ctenanthe dasycarpa
Thalia geniculata
Arthrostemma ciliatum
Clidemia globuliflora
Triolena hirsuta
Musa acuminata
Arundina graminifolia
Elleanthus glaucophyllus
Epidendrum pfavii
Phytolacca rivinoides
Phytolacca rugosa
Polygala paniculata
Eichhornia crassipes
Psychotria guapilensis
Digitalis purpurea
Browallia americana
Pilea pteropodon
Lantana trifolia
Stachytarpheta frantzii
Verbena litoralis

■ COLOR OF CONSPICUOUS PART RED, RED ORANGE, OR BRIGHT ORANGE

Aphelandra aurantiaca
Anthurium bakeri
Anthurium ranchoanum
Anthurium scherzerianum
Asclepias curassavica
Begonia multinervia
Tillandsia insignis
Werauhia ororiensis
  (*Vriesea o.*)
Centropogon ferrugineus
Centropogon granulosus

Lobelia laxiflora
Canna indica
Costus malortieanus
Costus woodsonii
Euphorbia tithymaloides
  (*Pedilanthus t.*)
Indigofera hirsuta
Alloplectus tetragonus
Columnea consanguinea
Columnea magnifica
Columnea nicaraguensis

■ COLOR OF CONSPICUOUS PART RED, RED ORANGE, OR BRIGHT ORANGE, continued

Kohleria spicata
Gunnera insignis
Heliconia danielsiana
Heliconia imbricata
Heliconia irrasa
Heliconia latispatha
Heliconia mathiasiae
Heliconia pogonantha
Heliconia psittacorum
Heliconia rostrata
Heliconia wagneriana
Crocosmia × crocosmiiflora
Cuphea appendiculata
Epidendrum radicans
Maxillaria fulgens
Galium hypocarpium

Hoffmannia
   subauriculata
Nertera granadensis
Notopleura uliginosa
   (Psychotria u.)
Castilleja irasuensis
Russelia sarmentosa
Capsicum annuum var.
   aviculare
Lantana camara
Alpinia purpurata
Etlingera elatior
   (Nicolaia e., Phaeomeria
   magnifica, P. speciosa)
Renealmia alpinia
Renealmia cernua

■ COLOR OF CONSPICUOUS PART YELLOW OR YELLOW ORANGE

Barleria oenothereides
Pachystachys lutea
Anthurium ochranthum
Anthurium subsignatum
Acmella oppositifolia
Baltimora recta
Cirsium subcoriaceum
Erato volcanica
Hypochoeris radicata
Jaegeria hirta
Melampodium perfoliatum
Munnozia wilburii
Neurolaena lobata
Senecio oerstedianus
Sphagneticola trilobata
   (Wedelia t.)
Tithonia diversifolia
Tridax procumbens
Youngia japonica
Bromelia pinguin
Guzmania nicaraguensis
Guzmania plicatifolia
Nopalea guatemalensis
Canna glauca
Cleome viscosa
Costus curvibracteatus
Euphorbia heterophylla
   (Poinsettia h.)

Phyllanthus urinaria
Ricinus communis
Chamaecrista nictitans
Aeschynomene scabra
Arachis pintoi (A. glabrata)
Crotalaria retusa
Crotalaria vitellina
Sesbania herbacea
   (S. emerus)
Halenia aquilegiella
Lisianthius seemannii
Alloplectus ichthyoderma
Chrysothemis
   friedrichsthaliana
Columnea purpurata
Kohleria allenii
Heliconia longiflora
Hypoxis decumbens
Sida rhombifolia
Calathea crotalifera
   (C. insignis)
Calathea lutea
Ludwigia octovalvis
Ludwigia peruviana
Oncidium stenotis
Psygmorchis pusilla
Telipogon storkii
Argemone mexicana

■ COLOR OF CONSPICUOUS PART YELLOW OR YELLOW ORANGE, continued

Peperomia pernambucensis
Notopleura polyphlebia
   (Psychotria p.)

Calceolaria irazúensis
Hemichaena fruticosa
Solanum quitoense

■ COLOR OF CONSPICUOUS PART WHITE, CREAM, OR GREENISH WHITE

Blechum pyramidatum
Justicia comata
Justicia orosiensis
Justicia valerioi
Nothoscordum gracile
Gomphrena serrata
Iresine diffusa
Hymenocallis littoralis
Hydrocotyle leucocephala
Myrrhidendron
   donnell-smithii
Sanicula liberta
Anthurium consobrinum
Anthurium obtusilobum
Spathiphyllum
   friedrichsthalii
Spathiphyllum montanum
Xanthosoma undipes
Zantedeschia aethiopica
Bidens pilosa
Chaptalia nutans
Galinsoga quadriradiata
Melanthera nivea
Begonia convallariodora
Begonia involucrata
Begonia semiovata
Aechmea mexicana
Rhipsalis baccifera
   (R. cassytha)
Hippobroma longiflora
Arenaria lanuginosa
Drymaria cordata
Stellaria prostrata
Dichorisandra amabilis
Tradescantia zanonia
Maianthemum gigas
Costus laevis
Costus speciosus
Croton argenteus
Diastema affine
Koellikeria erinoides

Xiphidium caeruleum
Hyptis verticillata
Gossypium hirsutum
Malachra fasciata
Calathea gymnocarpa
Calathea marantifolia
Calathea micans
Maranta arundinacea
Pleiostachya pruinosa
   (Ischnosiphon p.)
Centradenia inaequilateralis
Tococa platyphylla
Brassavola nodosa
Epidendrum trialatum
Maxillaria inaudita
Nidema boothii
Prosthechea fragrans
   (Encyclia f.)
Prosthechea ionophlebia
   (Encyclia i.)
Prosthechea vespa
   (Encyclia v.)
Sobralia luteola
Xylobium elongatum
Petiveria alliacea
Rivina humilis
Peperomia palmana
Peperomia pellucida
Peperomia poasana
Peperomia tetraphylla
Heteranthera reniformis
Coccocypselum hirsutum
Geophila repens (lechuga)
Hoffmannia congesta
Notopleura capitata
   (Psychotria aggregata)
Psychotria aubletiana
Spermacoce assurgens
Spermacoce latifolia
Leucocarpus perfoliatus
Solanum acerifolium

■ COLOR OF CONSPICUOUS PART WHITE, CREAM, OR GREENISH WHITE, continued

Solanum americanum (S. nigrum var. americanum)
Valeriana prionophylla
Priva lappulacea
Viola stipularis
Alpinia zerumbet
Hedychium coronarium
Kallstroemia maxima

■ COLOR OF CONSPICUOUS PART GREEN TO BROWN

Agave angustifolia
Furcraea cabuya
Amaranthus spinosus
Cyathula achyranthoides
Eryngium foetidum
Alocasia macrorrhizos
Anthurium salvinii
Colocasia esculenta
Dieffenbachia nitidipetiolata (D. longispatha)
Dieffenbachia oerstedii
Dracontium gigas
Philodendron wendlandii
Pistia stratiotes
Xanthosoma wendlandii
Delilia biflora
Aechmea magdalenae
Ananas comosus
Puya dasylirioides
Werauhia gladioliflora (Vriesea g.)
Werauhia kupperiana (Vriesea k.)
Burmeistera almedae
Burmeistera vulgaris
Cochliostema odoratissimum
Kalanchoe pinnata
Chamaesyce hirta
Chamaesyce lasiocarpa
Manihot esculenta
Plectranthus scutellarioides (Coleus blumei, Solenostemon s.)
Dorstenia contrajerva
Eulophia alta
Stelis guatemalensis
Peperomia galioides
Rumex nepalensis
Typha domingensis
Laportea aestuans

Herbaceous plants are those with predominantly nonwoody stems. For climbing or twining nonwoody plants, see Chapter 5.

COLOR OF CONSPICUOUS PART BLUE, PURPLE, LAVENDER, OR PINK

■ *Hypoestes phyllostachya* (polka-dot plant)
Family Acanthaceae

Herb to 70 cm long, stems weak, often trailing, young stems hairy. **Leaves** opposite, stalk to 2.5 cm, blade pink-spotted on both sides, 2–4.5 cm long, about 2 cm wide, tip pointed, base blunt. **Flowers** pink purple, to 2.5 cm long bilaterally symmetrical, tubular, 2-lipped, upper lip 3-lobed, lower lip not lobed; inflorescence of narrow spikes with small, green bracts; blooms Sept.–Feb. **Fruit** dry, club-shaped. **Habitat:** Disturbed sites, open or partly shady, roadsides and pastures. Altitude: Sea level to 2000 m. Conservation areas: ARE, CVC, LAP, OSA, PAC. **Range:** Native to Africa; escaped from cultivation in many tropical regions worldwide. **Notes:** This is the only species of *Hypoestes* in Costa Rica.

■ *Ruellia biolleyi*
Family Acanthaceae

Shrubby herb to 1 m tall, stem 4-sided, dark. **Leaves** opposite, stalks 1–2 cm long, yellowish; blade 4–14 cm long, 2–5 cm wide, elliptic, silvery pale when young, back of blade often dark red, pointed at both ends, margins wavy, often yellow along midrib above. **Flowers** purple to pale lavender, to 2.4 long, 0.7 cm wide across top, bilaterally symmetric, tube bent, petal lobes 5; inflorescence of branched clusters at the top of long, 4-sided, slightly winged stalk to 23 cm; blooms, Jan.–Mar., July–Sept. **Fruit** dry, club-shaped, to 1.7 cm long, 0.4 cm wide. **Habitat:** Very wet lowland forests, cut-over sites. Altitude: Sea level to 900 m, Caribbean slope. Conservation areas: ARE, CVC, LAC, TOR. **Range:** CR, Pan. **Notes:** There are 18 species of *Ruellia* in Costa Rica.

■ *Ruellia inundata*
Family Acanthaceae

Herb, aromatic, sometimes shrubby, to 1.5 m tall, stems somewhat 4-sided, hairy, old stems tan, leaf axils often with tufts of small leaves. **Leaves** opposite, stalk to 8 cm long, blade 4–15 cm long, 1–8 cm wide, pointed at both ends, pale, dull green, hairy-sticky on both sides, margins toothed. **Flowers** pink or pink purple, to about 3 cm long, 5-parted,

narrowly funnel-shaped, tube slightly curved, petal lobes equal, flaring, tips rounded, sepal lobes linear about 1 cm long with 1 lobe longer than others, finely glandular-hairy, blooms few at a time amid a mass of hairy bracts; inflorescence branched, of dense, headlike clusters; Nov.–June. **Fruit** dry, club-shaped to 1 cm long, 0.3 m wide. **Habitat:** Open sites or part shade in disturbed areas, pastures, road-sides. Altitude: Sea level to 900 m, Pacific slope. Conservation areas: CVC, GUA, LAP, PAC, TEM (mostly). Seen in Palo Verde N.P. **Range:** Mex–S Amer. **Notes:** Much like *R. paniculata*, which grows in similar habitats but has blue flowers.

■ *Eryngium carlinae*
Family Apiaceae

Small, stiff, spiny herb 6–30 cm tall, stems erect to pros-trate, mostly leafless. **Leaves** alternate, in a basal rosette, lying flat in older plants, stalk almost none, blade 3–10 cm long, about 0.7 cm wide, tip blunt, base tapered nearly to stem, surface stiff, margin toothed to irregularly lobed, these spine-tipped. **Flowers** dark blue, minute, radially symmet-ric, each with a small, stiff bract, in a dense, conical head, about 0.8 cm long, 0.6 cm wide, above a collar of 8–10 spine-tipped bracts 1–1.5 cm long, forming a star-shaped ruff, bract margins green, center white or bluish white, margins with a few spine-tipped teeth; inflorescence and stem about 3 cm tall; blooms Dec., May, July, Oct. **Fruit** dry, 2-seeded, small. **Habitat:** Open, rocky sites, pastures in mountains. Altitude: 1600–3400 m. Conservation areas: CVC, PAC. Seen at Vol-cán Irazú N.P. **Range:** Mex–Pan. **Notes:** There are four spe-cies of *Eryngium* in Costa Rica.

■ *Anthurium formosum*
Family Araceae

Large epiphytic or terrestrial herb, stems to 1 m long. **Leaves** alternate, stalk 40–150 cm long, pinkish near top, blade 30–80 cm long, 20–50 cm long, heart-shaped, shiny on both sides, basal lobes 13–20 cm long, widely separated, midrib raised on both sides, secondary veins connected by a marginal vein along edge of blade. **Flowers** purple to white, minute, densely crowded on a fleshy inflorescence spike (spadix) 5–14 cm long, to 1.5 cm wide, inflorescence bract (spathe) greenish white to pale purple, 13–24 cm long, 3–8 cm wide, narrowly elliptic to egg-shaped, tip with small, abrupt point, base rounded, held close to spike, inflorescence stalk stout, 21–47 cm long; blooms mostly Apr. and Sept. **Fruit** fleshy, purple red, 1 cm long, 0.5 cm wide, 2-seeded; fruiting spike 18–32 cm long; fruits Sept.–Oct. **Habitat:** Moist to wet forest understories, secondary forest, shaded roadside banks. Altitude: Sea level to 2500 m, most often 500–1500 m. Conservation areas: CVC, LAC, LAP, TOR. **Range:** CR–Col. **Notes:** Often forming large stands. There are 87 species of *Anthurium* in Costa Rica.

■ *Anthurium upalaense* (tabacón)
Family Araceae

Epiphytic herb, stems short, less than 10 cm long or none, 2–3 cm wide. **Leaves** alternate, in a rosette or vaselike arrangement, stalk 8–43 cm long, to 1 cm wide, 3-ribbed, somewhat 4-sided, blade 0.3–1 m long, 5–32 cm wide, narrowly oblong to elliptic, midrib raised below, secondary veins conspicuous, rather closely spaced, connected by a marginal vein. **Flowers** purple to brown, minute, densely crowded on a fleshy spike 9–30 cm long, 0.6–1.5 cm wide, tip narrowed, inflorescence bract yellow green, sometimes purplish on underside, 3–26 cm long, 1–4 cm wide, narrowly lance-shaped, widest at base, narrowed to the pointed tip, bent downward; inflorescence stalk 10–52 cm long, longer than leaf stalks; blooms most of the year. **Fruit** fleshy, red, 1–1.5 cm long, oblong, pointed at both ends, 2-seeded; fruiting spike pendent, to 55 cm long, to 6 cm wide; fruits Jan., June, Oct., Nov. **Habitat:** Wet forest understories. Altitude: Sea level to 900 m, most common below 400 m, on the Caribbean lowlands. Conservation areas: HNO, LAC, TOR. **Range:** Nic–CR. **Notes:** Often used as a garden plant in the Caribbean lowlands.

■ *Ageratum conyzoides* (Santa Lucía)
 Family Asteraceae

Woody-based herb to 1.5 m tall, usually 20–40 cm and herbaceous, sparsely branched, old stems brown or reddish, usually hollow, hairy. **Leaves** usually opposite, stalk, almost none, blade to 10 cm long, 7 cm wide, heart- to egg-shaped, with 3 palmate veins at base, tip pointed to blunt, base rounded, somewhat hairy, underside paler, sprinkled with tiny dots, margin toothed. **Flowers** blue, purple, occasionally white, less than 0.2 cm long, no ray flowers, disk flowers about 50, in heads about 0.5 cm wide on a base of small bracts, basal bracts numerous, about 0.4 cm long, hairy, in 2 cycles; inflorescence of flat topped clusters; blooms all year. **Fruit** dry, 1-seeded, ribbed, crowned by 5 pointed scales. **Habitat:** Wet to seasonally dry regions in open sites. Altitude: Sea level to 2700 m, most often above 1000 m. Conservation areas: ARE, CVC, GUA, LAP, OSA, PAC, TEM. **Range:** C and S Amer. Naturalized in much of the tropics and subtropics worldwide. **Notes:** There are 10 species of *Ageratum* in Costa Rica. All are quite similar; *A. conyzoides* is by far the most common and widespread.

■ *Dahlia imperialis*
 Family Asteraceae

Straggling woody-based herb to 4 m tall, sparsely branched, stems hollow. **Leaves** opposite, lower leaves pinnate, to 35 cm long, with 1–5 egg-shaped leaflets, hairy, tip pointed, base blunt, margins toothed. **Flowers** pale purple, to white, of two types, in heads of small flowers on a base of bracts, central disk flowers tubular, peripheral ray flowers petal-like with extended petal lobe; heads large, showy, rays about 9, about 5 cm long, 2 cm wide, disk yellow, 3 cm wide, basal bracts in 2 rows, to 2 cm long, leafy; blooms in Sept.–Mar. **Fruit** dry, 1-seeded to 1.7 cm long. **Habitat:** Mountains; also cultivated and escaped in open areas, roadsides. Altitude: 1500–2700 m. Conservation areas: CVC, LAP, PAC. **Range:** Mex–Col. **Notes:** There is one other species of *Dahlia* in Costa Rica: *D. rosea* is smaller and has white flowers.

■ *Emilia fosbergii* (dandelion)
Family Asteraceae

Erect, slender herb 10–50 cm tall, often hairy. **Leaves** alternate, lower leaves stalked, stalks winged, blade 5–10 cm long, 2–5 cm wide, broadly egg-shaped, often waxy pale blue green, margin toothed to lobed near base of blade, upper leaves small, triangular, stalkless, base clasping stem. **Flowers** pink purple, very small, radially symmetrical (no rays), densely crowded in a compact head of 15–30 flowers that arises from a bract-covered floral base, heads appearing pufflike, longer than wide, basal bracts 8–13, to 1 cm long; inflorescence branched; blooms May– Jan. **Fruit**s dry, 1-seeded, 0.4 cm long, with a white plume; wind-dispersed. **Habitat:** Weeds of open sites, roadsides, pastures, vacant lots in wet to seasonally dry regions. Altitude: Near sea level to 1800 m. Conservation areas: ARE, CVC, GUA, LAC, LAP, OSA, PAC, TEM, TOR. **Range:** Native to the Old World, probably Africa. Now widely naturalized in tropical regions. **Notes:** Used medicinally to treat high blood pressure. Very similar to E. *sonchifolia,* also an Old World weed, usually found below 500 m elevation and has flower heads with 10–20 flowers.

■ *Erechtites valerianifolia* (diente de león)
Family Asteraceae

Slender herb 1–2 m tall, smooth to very hairy, stem simple to much-branched. **Leaves** alternate, blade narrowly egg-shaped, 8–12 cm long, 2–4 cm wide, lower leaves undivided, margins toothed, middle and upper leaves pinnately divided with toothed margins, the uppermost leaves becoming small, stalkless bracts. **Flowers** pale purple, radially symmetrical, small, surrounded by long pink, soft bristles, densely crowded in narrow heads about 1 cm tall, 0.3 cm wide, above a ring of small, narrow bracts; inflorescence of branched clusters at top of plant; blooms most of the year. **Fruit** dry, 1-seeded with numerous ribs, bristles becoming white. **Habitat:** Wet to very wet regions; a weed of open, disturbed habitats, fields, and roadsides. Altitude: 800–2200 m. Conservation areas: ARE, CVC, HNO, LAP, PAC. **Range:** Mex–Arg. Now invasive in tropical Asia, Pacific islands, and Australia. **Notes:** The only other species of *Erechtites* in Costa Rica, E. *hieracifolia,* has pale yellow flowers.

■ *Fleischmannia pycnocephala*
Family Asteraceae

Herb or small shrub to 1 m tall, stems hairy. **Leaves** opposite (except some upper alternate leaves), egg-shaped to 5.5 cm long, 3.5 cm wide, tip pointed, base blunt to lobed, hairy on both sides, 3 major veins from base (palmate), margin toothed. **Flowers** lavender to white, tiny, radially symmetrical, crowded in small heads, 0.5 cm tall, about 25 flowers per head, basal bracts hairy, numerous, inflorescence branched, flat-topped, about 7 cm wide; blooms Dec.–June, mostly in Feb.–Mar. **Fruit** dry, 1-seeded, plumed. **Habitat:** Wet regions in open sites, mostly in mountains. Altitude: 100–2500 m, mostly above 1000 m. Conservation areas: ARE, CVC, GUA, GUA, LAC, LAP, OSA, PAC. **Range:** SW US–N S Amer. **Notes:** There are 13 species of *Fleischmannia* in Costa Rica.

■ *Gnaphalium roseum*
Family Asteraceae

Silvery herb about 25 cm tall, sometimes to 1 m, branched from base, stems densely white woolly with matted hairs. **Leaves** alternate, linear, to 3 cm long, 0.3 cm wide, tip pointed, base slightly extending down stem, white-woolly below, young leaves silvery-hairy above becoming smooth when mature. **Flowers** yellow, inconspicuous, densely crowded in heads 0.4–0.6 cm long, covered with wine red, to sometimes yellowish dry, papery bracts, in numerous rows, more prominent than flowers; inflorescence at top of stem, branched, with numerous crowded flower heads aggregated into rounded clusters; blooms July–Dec. **Fruit** dry, plumed, reddish 1-seeded, 0.8 cm long. **Habitat:** Open sites at high elevations. Common on Cerro de la Muerte. Altitude: 1600–3400 m. Conservation areas: ARE, LAP, PAC. **Range:** C Mex–Pan, possibly N S Amer. **Notes:** There are at least four species of *Gnaphalium* in Costa Rica. The most common species is *G. attenuatum*, but it is rather inconspicuous. *Gnaphalium rhodarum* also has reddish flower heads but is quite uncommon.

■ *Impatiens walleriana*
Family Balsaminaceae

Herb 30–90 cm tall, stems succulent, translucent. **Leaves** alternate, stalk elongate, blade 4–12 cm long, elliptic to egg-shaped, dull dark green, margin toothed. **Flowers** pink, purple, red, or white, showy, to 4 cm wide, 5 broad petals, fused at base, slightly bilaterally symmetrical, 1 sepal with an elongate nectar-filled tube (spur) 3–5 cm long; inflorescence of small clusters in leaf axils; blooms all year. **Fruit** green, about 2 cm long, 0.7 cm wide, splitting open explosively to scatter seeds. **Habitat:** Cultivated, escaped in many disturbed forest understories, espe-

cially along trails, shady edges, and roadsides in wet and moist regions. Altitude: Sea level to 2000 m. Conservation areas: ARE, CVC, LAP, PAC. **Range:** Native to Africa. Invasive in many other tropical regions. **Notes:** There are two other species of *Impatiens* in Costa Rica. *Impatiens balsamina*, a native of India, is another familiar cultivated herb but rarely escapes. *Impatiens turrialbana* is native to Costa Rica, an herb to 2 m tall, stems succulent, reddish, sometimes vinelike, with red orange flowers, found mostly above 1200 m but occasionally down to sea level.

■ *Heliotropium indicum* (alacrán, alacrancillo)
Family Boraginaceae

Roadside herb 0.3–1.5 m tall, usually less than 0.5 m, hairy. **Leaves** alternate, stalks 1–8 cm long, often winged, blade egg-shaped, 4–14 cm long, 2–7 cm wide, tip pointed, base blunt, extending down stalk, surface slightly hairy on both sides, dull green, wrinkled, margin coarsely toothed. **Flowers** lavender to blue, radially symmetrical, small, about 0.5 cm long, petal lobes flaring, inflorescence of 1-sided, curved, spikes to 28 cm long; blooms all year. **Fruit** dry, with 4 small nutlike parts, 0.3 cm long. **Habitat:** Wet to seasonally dry regions in weedy, open areas, pastures, roadsides. Altitude: Sea level to 900 m. Conservation areas: GUA, HNO, OSA, PAC, TEM. **Range:** Native to the Old World tropics, now a pantropical weed. Invasive in parts of SE Asia and the Pacific islands. **Notes:** There are six species of *Heliotropium* in Costa Rica, *H. indicum* is the most common.

■ *Aechmea mariae-reginae*
Family Bromeliaceae

Epiphytic herb to 2.5 m tall, no stem. **Leaves** alternate, in a dense spiral, forming a spreading rosette, inner leaves progressively shorter, no stalk, blades 65–95 cm long, 7–14 cm wide, straplike; tip pointed, base broad, forming a sheath, surface finely scaly especially below, margins spiny-toothed. **Flowers** white with blue tip, about 1 cm long, small, asymmetrical, densely crowded among small whitish bracts on a cylindrical spike, 10–20 cm long, 5 cm wide, atop the inflorescence stalk 45–76 cm long, covered with bright pink strap-shaped bracts; blooms Sept.–May. **Fruit** dry, red, inside white. **Habitat:** Wet forests. Altitude: Sea level to 1800 m, Caribbean slope. Conservation areas: ARE, CVC, LAC, TOR. **Range:** SE Nic, CR. **Notes:** There are 17 species of *Aechmea* in Costa Rica.

■ *Tillandsia leiboldiana*
Family Bromeliaceae

Epiphytic herb to 40 cm tall, no stem. **Leaves** alternate, but mostly basal, 11–32 cm long, 1.5–2.5 cm wide, green, red or mottled with purple, tip elongate, pointed, base broad, sheathing, pinkish-cream. **Flowers** dark purple to lavender, inflorescence bracts red, to green or mottled with purple; inflorescence 12–27 cm long, branched once, branches 4–9 cm long; inflorescence stalk 9–24 cm long covered by bracts; blooms mostly May–Sept. **Fruit** dry, 2.5–4 cm long, splitting open to release plumed seeds. **Habitat:** Wet forests, often low in understory, also on trees in pastures. Altitude: 100–1900 m. Conservation areas: ARE, GUA, CVC, LAC, LAP, OSA, PAC, TOR. **Range:** Mex–Pan. **Notes:** There are 39 species of *Tillandsia* in Costa Rica. They are very similar to the species of *Werauhia* and *Guzmania*.

■ *Centropogon gutierrezii*
Family Campanulaceae

Sprawling herb to 1.2 m long, stems vinelike, hollow, hairy, often red. **Leaves** alternate, stalk about 1 cm long, blade 5–14 cm long, 2–7 cm wide cm, egg- to heart-shaped, tip pointed, base wedge-shaped to lobed, surface dull pale green, veins impressed above, margin finely toothed. **Flowers** deep pink to red purple, tubular, bilaterally symmetrical, to 4.3 cm long, 1 cm across top, very finely hairy, petal lobes 5, fringed, 2 upper lobes to 2.5 cm long, 3 lower lobes to 3 cm long, anthers gray with pink stalks, calyx lobes narrow, to 1.5 cm long; flowers solitary in leaf

axils, on a stalk to 12 cm long; blooms most of the year. **Fruit** leathery, white, 2–3.7 cm long, 1–2 cm wide with numerous flattened seeds. **Habitat:** Mountains, in disturbed sites and second growth. Altitude: 1900–3300 m, rarely down to 600 m. Conservation areas: CVC, LAP, PAC. **Range:** CR–Pan.

■ *Commelina erecta*
Family Commelinaceae

Sprawling herb to 1 m long, stem trailing, branched, succulent, sometimes with purple red lines; leaf sheath 1–2 cm long. **Leaves** alternate, nearly stalkless, blade 3–14 cm long, 0.3–3 cm wide, narrowly lance-shaped, tip tapered to a long point, base wedge-shaped to rounded. **Flowers** blue and white, bilaterally symmetrical, 3-parted, about 1.5 cm wide, petals 3, the larger 2 blue to white, 0.6 cm long, 1 cm wide, base very narrow, the smaller one usually white, sepals translucent, 1 very small; flowers emerging from a folded bract, 2–3 cm long, about 1 cm wide, bract edges partially fused; inflorescence at or near end of stem; blooms most of the year. **Fruit** fleshy, 0.5 cm long, 2-lobed, splitting open to release seeds. **Habitat:** very wet to seasonally dry regions in clearings, disturbed, open habitats, roadsides. Altitude: Sea level to 850 m. Conservation areas: CVC, GUA, LAC, OSA, PAC, TEM. **Range:** Tropics and subtropics of both New and Old Worlds. **Notes:** There are seven species of *Commelina* in Costa Rica. All are very similar.

■ *Floscopa robusta*
Family Commelinaceae

Small forest floor herb 10–20 cm tall, usually in groups, stems dark red, rooting at nodes; leaf sheaths to 1.5 cm long, hairy. **Leaves** alternate, spirally arranged, almost stalkless, blade 10–30 cm long, 3–8 cm wide, narrowly elliptic, pointed at both ends, surface glossy, very dark green, sometimes with a

silvery sheen below, texture rough. **Flowers** purple and white, 3-parted, bilaterally symmetrical, about 0.3 cm wide, petals white, calyx rounded, densely purple-hairy; inflorescence 4–10 cm long, very densely hairy, purple, branched, with numerous flowers; blooms most of the year. **Fruit** dry, about 0.3 cm long and wide, brown. **Habitat:** Shady understory of very wet undisturbed forests. Altitude: Sea level to 1000 m. Conservation areas: CVC, HNO, LAC, OSA, PAC, TOR. **Range:** Hon–Pr and Brz. **Notes:** There is one other species of *Floscopa* in Costa Rica, but it is very uncommon.

■ *Tradescantia poelliae*
Family Commelinaceae

Creeping herb, ground cover, stems succulent, to 70 cm long, lower stems rooting at nodes, sometimes purplish, branching; flowering stems erect, leafy, finely hairy, often purplish, leaf sheaths hairy. **Leaves** alternate, stalk less than 0.5 cm, blade 3–9 cm long, 1–2 cm wide, lance- to egg-shaped, tip pointed, base pointed to rounded, often unequal, often purple below. **Flowers** bright pink, occasionally white, 3-parted, petals about 0.6 cm long, flowers flat-faced, all 3 petals the same,

stamens and stigma white, anthers yellow; flowers usually solitary, at ends of stems; blooms all year. **Fruit** dry, about 0.3 cm long. **Habitat:** Very wet forest understories, in mountains. Altitude: 1000–2900 m. Conservation areas: ARE, CVC, LAC, LAP, PAC. **Range:** S Mex–Pan. **Notes:** There are eight species of *Tradescantia* in Costa Rica. *Tradescantia poelliae* is one of the two most common, along with *T. zanonia*. The cultivated plant, *T. zebrina*, also has pink purple flowers, but the petals are fused at the base and it usually has purple-striped leaves. It sometimes escapes from cultivation.

■ *Desmodium axillare* (pega pega, tick-trefoil)
  Family Fabaceae/Faboideae

Small herb, trailing ground cover, rooting at nodes. **Leaves** alternate, 3-parted, stalk 4–7 cm long, base swollen, leaflets egg-shaped, 4–8 cm long, 3–6 cm wide, sides often unequal, smooth above, white-hairy below. **Flowers** bright pink to reddish violet, bilaterally symmetrical, about 0.5 cm long, often paired, bean-flower-shaped, top petal notched, base narrow; inflorescence erect, a slender spikelike cluster on a stalk to 20 cm long. **Fruit** dry, usually with 2 flat, kidney-shaped segments, each about 1 cm long, covered with hooked bristles adhering to clothes or fur. **Habitat:** Open sites or forest understories, roadsides, edges, in wet to seasonally dry regions. Altitude: Sea level to 800 m. Conservation areas: ARE, GUA, HNO, LAC, OSA, PAC, TEM, TOR. **Range:** S Mex–Bol and Brz, WI. **Notes:** There are about 20 species of *Desmodium* in Costa Rica. They are distinguished, in part, by their flat, segmented fruit pods. All have blue, purple, or white flowers.

■ *Lupinus costaricensis*
  Family Fabaceae/Faboideae

Erect to sprawling small herb, stems 15–30 cm long, branching from base, stems hairy. **Leaves** alternate, palmately compound, stalk 4–6 cm long, very slender, leaflets 8–11, 2–3 cm long, to 0.6 cm wide, usually folded along midrib. **Flowers** purple, bilaterally symmetrical, bean-flower-shaped, to 1 cm long; inflorescence of spikes 5–12 cm long, amid leaves and at top of stem; blooms Aug–Jan. **Fruit** dry, pods 2–3 cm long, to 0.7 cm wide, hairy, somewhat constricted between the 7–8 small seeds. **Habitat:** Open sites in high mountains. Altitude: 3200–3800 m. Conservation areas: CVC, LAP. **Range:** CR, Pan. **Notes:** There are six species of *Lupinus* in Costa Rica, this is the most common.

291

■ *Mimosa pudica* (dormilona, sensitive plant)
Family Fabaceae/Mimosoideae

Herb or prostrate shrub 1–2 m tall, usually much less, stems reddish, weakly ribbed, spiny. **Leaves** alternate, twice pinnate, 2 pairs of pinnae to 6 cm long, leaflets 10–20 pairs, 0.3–1 cm long, folding over when disturbed. **Flowers** pink,

minute, petals to 0.2 cm, stamens to 0.7 cm, inflorescences of small, rounded, puff-ball clusters; blooms most of the year. **Fruit** dry, pods to 1.5 cm long, 0.3 cm wide, linear, brown, in clusters, each with 3–4 seeds. **Habitat:** Disturbed, open sites, old pastures, common roadside weed. Altitude: Sea level to 1700 m. Conservation areas: ARE, CVC, GUA, LAP, OSA, PAC, TEM, TOR. **Range:** Mex–Brz. Introduced throughout the tropics and invasive in some Pacific islands and Australia. **Notes:** Used to treat insomnia. There are 15 species of *Mimosa* in Costa Rica.

■ *Geranium guatemalense*
Family Geraniaceae

Small herb, stems 10–80 cm long, finely hairy, older stems often rooting at nodes. **Leaves** alternate, stalk 2–8 cm long, blade 2–5 cm long, 2–6 cm wide, deeply 3- to 5-lobed, lobes narrowed toward the base, lobe margins lobed again or deeply toothed, hairy on both sides. **Flowers** lavender to pink, radially symmetrical, about 1 cm long, 0.8–2 cm wide, petals 0.8–1.4 cm long, 0.4–0.7 cm wide, widest above middle, tip sometimes notched; blooms and fruits most of the year. **Fruit** dry, linear, 2 cm long, tip long-pointed, splitting into 5 seg-

ments from the base, each curling upward and outward, carrying a seed at its tip. **Habitat:** Open sites in mountains, edges, roadsides. Altitude: 1700–3500 m. Conservation areas: CVC, LAC, LAP, PAC. Common near Cerro de la Muerte. **Range:** Mex–Pan. **Notes:** The only other species of *Geranium*, *G. costaricense*, is smaller, stems are short and shaggy from old overlapping stipules. It is found only in Cordillera de Talamanca, mostly above 3000 m. Cultivated geraniums are *Pelargonium* spp., a genus from South Africa, bred for large, showy flower clusters.

■ *Drymonia turrialvae*
Family Gesneriaceae

Terrestrial or epiphytic herb or small shrub to 50 cm tall, stems reddish to purple, 4-sided, succulent, stout, hollow center sometimes occupied by ants, unbranched. **Leaves** opposite, stalk stout, to 21 cm, purplish, blade 9–29 cm long, 4–25 cm wide, broadly egg- to heart-shaped, tip pointed, base rounded to lobed, fleshy, veins palmate at base of blade, deeply impressed above, dark green above, sometimes reddish below. **Flowers** bright pink and white to lilac, to 6 cm long, tubular, showy, petal tube and lobes lilac to pink or yellowish white, broad, deciduous, calyx lobes bright pink purple (photo of calyx lobes), to 3 cm long, persistent; blooms all year. **Fruit** fleshy, hollow, lavender to purple, rounded, 1 cm. **Habitat:** Wet forest understories, often along streams. Altitude: 200–1700 m. Conservation areas: ARE, CVC, GUA, HNO, LAC, LAP, OSA, PAC. **Range:** CR–Ec. **Notes:** Persistent pink calyx lobes distinctive. Found often at Volcán Tenorio N.P. There are 17 species of *Drymonia* in Costa Rica.

■ *Episcia lilacina*
Family Gesneriaceae

Low, prostrate herb, rooting at nodes, stems hairy, green to dark red, slender, lax. **Leaves** opposite, at ends of stems, blade 3–14 cm long, 2–9 cm wide, elliptic, tip pointed, base rounded, slightly unequal, hairy, succulent, dark green to reddish above, often paler around deeply impressed veins, pale below, margin bluntly toothed. **Flowers** pale blue violet and white with yellow center, bilaterally symmetric, tubular, about 5 cm long, 3 cm across top, showy, petal lobes wide, flat, finely toothed, 3 above, 2 below, blooms once at a time; blooms all year. **Fruit** fleshy, to 0.8 cm long, hairy. **Habitat:** Wet to moist forests, shady roadside banks. Altitude: Sea level to 1000 m, mostly below 500 m. Conservation areas: CVC, GUA, HNO, LAC, OSA, PAC. **Range:** Nic–Col. Also widely cultivated. **Notes:** This is the only species of *Episcia* in Costa Rica.

■ *Monopyle maxonii*
Family Gesneriaceae

Large herb or shrub to 1.5 m tall, slender, purplish, mostly unbranched. **Leaves** opposite, pair members strongly unequal, stalk to 3.5 cm, blades 7–18 cm long, 4–9 cm wide, smaller of the pair to 3.5 cm long, elliptic, hairy, thin, tip pointed, bases unequal, dark green above, paler or purplish below, margin toothed. **Flowers** pale blue violet to white with purple petal lobes, tubular, somewhat bilaterally symmetrical, to 1.8 cm long, to 1.8 cm wide near top, finely hairy outside, petal lobes flaring, calyx lobes purplish, curved outward, 0.2–0.6 cm long; blooms Jan.–July. **Fruit** dry, red brown, cylindrical, curved at base, to 1.5 long, 0.3 cm wide. **Habitat:** Wet forests, second growth and open sites. Altitude: 200–1400 m. Conservation areas: ARE, CVC, LAC, LAP. **Range:** CR, Pan. **Notes:** The only other species of *Monopyle* in Costa Rica, M. *macrocarpa* is apparently more common and is very similar to M. *maxonii* but calyx lobes 0.5–1.5 cm long.

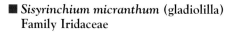

■ *Sisyrinchium micranthum* (gladiolilla)
Family Iridaceae

Small, fan-shaped herb 5–15 cm tall, occasionally to 30 cm; flowering stems flat, branched. **Leaves** alternate, mostly from base of plant, blades flat, linear, 5–12 cm long, 0.2-0.4 cm wide, tip pointed, bases sheathing inner leaves, leaves of flowering stems much shorter. **Flowers** blue to lavender pink, with darker stripe down center of each petal, radially symmetrical, about 1 cm wide, petals 6, stamens 3, yellow; inflorescences of a few flowers emerging from leaflike, pointed bracts, 2–4 cm long; blooms Sept.–May. **Fruit** dry, about 0.3 cm wide, brownish, 3-lobed, rounded, small; seeds numerous. **Habitat:** Wet to very wet forest understories or (more often) in open, disturbed areas, low vegetation, forest edges, roadsides, vacant lots; often a garden weed in San José. Altitude: 700–2800 m or more. Conservation areas: ARE, CVC, GUA, LAC, LAP, PAC. **Range:** Mex–Arg. **Notes:** There are eight species of *Sisyrinchium* in Costa Rica; S. *micranthum* is the most common. Most of the others have yellow flowers.

■ *Hyptis suaveolens* (chan)
Family Lamiaceae

Herb 40 cm to 1.6 m tall, stems 4-sided, hairy. **Leaves** opposite, stalk to 3 cm long, blade 3–7 cm long, 1–5 cm wide,
egg-shaped to widest above middle, lower surface densely
hairy, strongly mint-scented, margin with large, irregular
teeth. **Flowers** blue lavender, about 0.8 cm long, bilaterally
symmetrical, tubular, 5-parted, 2-lipped, lower lip 3-lobed,
calyx lobes bristle-tipped; inflorescence of clusters in axils
of small leaves; blooms Sept.–June, mostly Oct.–Dec. **Fruit**
dry, small, surrounded by dry calyx to 1 cm long, with spine-
tipped lobes, becoming attached to fur or clothing to disperse
seeds. **Habitat:** Wet, moist, and seasonally dry regions, in
open, disturbed sites, roadsides, old pastures. Altitude: Sea
level to 1900 m, usually below 1000 m. Conservation areas:
ARE, CVC, GUA, LAP, OSA, PAC, TEM, TOR. **Range:**
Mex–S Amer, WI. **Notes:** There are about 14 species of
Hyptis in Costa Rica.

■ *Prunella vulgaris*
Family Lamiaceae

Small herb 10–50 cm tall. **Leaves** opposite, few, 2–9 cm
long, 1–4 cm wide, lance-shaped to broadly egg-shaped, lowest broader with rounded base. **Flowers** blue purple,
bilaterally symmetrical, tubular, 5-parted, to 2 cm
long, calyx to 1 cm, among small, hairy, green to
purple bracts to 1 cm long, in spikes to 5 cm long,
2 cm wide; blooms most of the year. **Fruit** small, dry
nutlets. **Habitat:** Open sites and forest understories
in mountains. Altitude: 1200–3100 m, rarely as low
as 50 m. Conservation areas: ARE, CVC, LAP, OSA
(rarely), PAC. **Range:** Native to both Europe and N
Amer. Widely naturalized in temperate and tropical
regions. **Notes:** This is the only species of *Prunella* in
Costa Rica.

■ *Salvia carnea*
Family Lamiaceae

Herb to 1.5 m tall, lower stem sometimes reclining on ground. **Leaves** opposite, blade 3–10 cm long, 3–8 cm wide, heart-shaped, tip pointed, base lobed, margins toothed. **Flowers** purple lilac, showy, bilaterally symmetrical, 5-parted, petal tube 1–1.5 cm long, 0.3–0.5 cm wide, pouched on one side, 2-lipped, lips 0.5–1 cm long, 1 lip 3-lobed; inflorescence of whorls spaced 0.5–2.5 cm apart along flowering stem, calyx often purple green, 2-lipped, to 0.8 cm long, upper lip pointed, lower lip 2-lobed; blooms Oct.–May. **Fruit** dry, small enclosed by persistent, enlarged, calyx to 1 cm long. **Habitat:** Mountain forests, second growth and open sites. Altitude: 2100–3300. Conservation areas: LAC, LAP, PAC. **Range:** Mex–Gua, CR–Ec. **Notes:** There are about 10 species of *Salvia* in Costa Rica.

■ *Utricularia unifolia*
Family Lentibulariaceae

Small epiphytic herb, sometimes terrestrial; very small, rounded traps, 0.1 cm, grow from fleshy, roots. **Leaves** 1–4, stalk 2–3 times as long as blade, blade 5–15 cm long, to 2.5 cm wide, lance-shaped, stiff, leathery. **Flowers** violet or pale purple with yellow markings, bilaterally symmetrical, very orchidlike in appearance, 3–5 cm long, upper lip rounded, lower lip larger, wider than long, back side of flower with a prominent conical, white spur curved to one side, calyx pale green with red-pink veins, 2 lobes, top and bottom, 2–4 cm long, 1–2 cm wide, heart-shaped;

inflorescence of 1–3 flowers, stalk to 30 cm long, with narrow, bracts 1–3 cm long, curved to one side; blooms Sept.–Oct. **Fruit** dry, about 1 cm, round, seeds numerous. **Habitat:** Cloud forests. Altitude: About 1600–2500 m. Conservation areas: CVC, LAC. **Range:** CR–Pr. **Notes:** There are 10 species of *Utricularia* in Costa Rica. All but four are aquatic or rare. The traps on *Utricularias* capture and digest small insects. Like other carnivorous plants, they obtain nutrients from these animals and so can live in very low nutrient habitats.

■ *Spigelia anthelmia* (worm grass)
Family Loganiaceae

Slender annual herb to 1 m tall, usually less, sparsely branched, stems mostly leafless except near top, stipules between leaf stalk bases about 0.5 cm long. **Leaves** opposite, 3–18 cm long, 1–6 cm wide, 2 closely spaced pairs appearing to be whorled, blade narrow, pointed at both ends, dull green. **Flowers** white with pink stripes, appearing pink, tubular, radially symmetrical, to 1.5 cm long, tube narrow, petal lobes 5, pleated; flowers crowded along 1-sided spikes, fruits and blooms at same time; blooms and fruits all year. **Fruit** dry, small, 0.4 cm long, 0.6 cm wide, green warty, in pairs down flower stalk, seeds dispersed by explosive opening of fruit. **Habitat:** Wet to seasonally dry regions, in open sites or forest understories. Altitude: Sea level to 1700 m, mostly below 200 m. Conservation areas: ARE, GUA, HNO, LAC, OSA, PAC, TEM. **Range:** S FL, Mex–Brz and Bol, WI. Introduced into Old World tropics. **Notes:** Used as a treatment for worms in small children. Contains the toxic alkaloid spigeline. There are four species of *Spigelia* in Costa Rica, this is the most common.

■ *Cuphea carthagenensis* (cuna de niño)
Family Lythraceae

Low shrubby herb 20–80 cm tall, branches alternate. **Leaves** opposite, stalk 0.1–1 cm long, blade 1.5–4 cm long, 0.5–2 cm wide, narrowly elliptic to egg-shaped, leaves on outer branches often much smaller than those of main stems, leaves gradually smaller upward on stems. **Flowers** purple, bilaterally symmetrical, tubular, petal lobes 6, 0.1–0.2 cm long; inflorescence, leafy, spikelike, with 1–4 flowers each at node; blooms Mar.–Dec. **Fruit** dry; seeds 3–6, rounded, 0.1–0.2 cm wide. **Habitat:** Wet to seasonally dry regions in disturbed, weedy sites, pastures, roadsides. Altitude: Sea level to 1800 m. Conservation areas: ARE, CVC, HNO, GUA, LAC, LAP, OSA, PAC, TEM. **Range:** S US–Arg. Introduced and invasive on some Pacific islands. **Notes:** Very similar to *C. calophylla*. There are eight species of *Cuphea* in Costa Rica.

■ *Ctenanthe dasycarpa*
Family Marantaceae

Stems about 1.5–3 m tall; leaves mostly from base, 1–2 along stem. **Leaves** alternate, stalk hairy, conspicuously swollen, jointlike at top, base winged and grooved, sheathing stem, blade 20–90 cm long, 10–27 cm wide, oblong, leathery, dark green above, hairy along midrib, olive green below. **Flowers** white, asymmetrical, about 0.6 cm long, several pairs in each bract; bracts dark red purple, purple green, greenish white, or pale yellowish, flaring outward at top; 12–22, in 2 ranks along each flower spike; Inflorescences branched with 3–15 narrow, conelike spikes in leaf axils and top of stem, each 7–17 cm long, 2 cm wide, bracts persistent; blooms all year; pollinated by bees. **Fruit** dry, egg-shaped, red purple; seed solitary, black with a white fleshy attachment. **Habitat:** Very wet forests, second growth. Altitude: Sea level to 1300 m, occasionally to 1500 m. Conservation areas: CVC, LAP, OSA, PAC, TOR. **Range:** CR–Col. **Notes:** This is the only species of *Ctenanthe* in Costa Rica.

■ *Thalia geniculata* (platanilla)
Family Marantaceae

Large herb 0.7–3 m tall, colonial from underground stems (rhizomes), stem formed by overlapping leaf sheaths. **Leaves** alternate, mostly basal, stalk often longer than blade, blade 20–60 cm long, 4–26 cm wide, narrowly egg-shaped, widest near base, tapered to pointed tip, base rounded, dull green above, often waxy white below. **Flowers** purple, small, irregular, to 2 cm long, about 1 cm wide; inflorescence of drooping, few-flowered, zigzag spikes to 7 cm long, widely branched, diffuse, often longer than leaves, main stalk to 1 m long, slender; blooms most of the year. **Fruit** dry, nutlike, small, elliptic, cupped by a bract, 1-seeded. **Habitat:** Seasonally dry to very wet regions in open wet soil or shallow water. Altitude: Sea level to 100 m. Conservation areas: HNO, OSA, TEM (mostly), TOR. **Range:** SE US, Mex–Arg, Ant, W Africa. **Notes:** Very common in the marsh at Palo Verde N.P., often with *Canna glauca*. This is the only species of *Thalia* in Costa Rica.

■ *Arthrostemma ciliatum*
Family Melastomataceae

Sprawling, vinelike herb, stems 4-sided, 1–4 m long, pale green, rather succulent, about 0.3 cm wide, angles sharp, reddish hairy. **Leaves** opposite, stalk 1–3 cm long, often red, blade 3–9 cm long 1.5–4.5 cm wide, narrowly egg-shaped, tip long-pointed, base blunt to lobed, both sides hairy, major veins 5–7, palmate with numerous, ladderlike minor veins, surface puckered by impressed veins, margins red-hairy, finely toothed. **Flowers** lavender pink, radially symmetrical, about 4 cm wide, petals 4, 2–3 cm long, about 1 cm wide, easily deciduous, anthers yellow, with lavender filaments, flower buds red, solitary in axils; blooms all year. **Fruit** dry, elongate, to 2 cm long, to 0.9 cm wide, with persistent calyx lobes at tip, green to red. **Habitat:** Wet to moist forests and open sites, roadsides, ditches. Altitude: Sea level to 1700 m. Conservation areas: ARE, CVC, GUA, HNO, LAC, LAP, OSA, PAC, TOR. **Range:** Mex–Bol, WI. **Notes:** There is one other species of *Arthrostemma* in Costa Rica, *A. alatum*, which is similar but less common.

■ *Clidemia globuliflora*
Family Melastomataceae

Herb, 0.5–1 m tall, usually many stems together, stems, about 0.5 cm wide, reddish, densely covered with thick, coarse, appressed, whitish hairs. **Leaves** opposite, stalks 1–3 cm, blade 8–26 cm long, 5–18 cm wide, broadly heart-shaped, densely hairy, tip pointed, base lobed, major veins palmate (1 pair marginal) 5 or 7, all deeply, sharply impressed above, with numerous, ladderlike cross veins, surface deeply, densely puckered in small squares and rectangles, older leaves very dark, dull green, new leaves brownish green, dark reddish, hairy. **Flowers** white with red calyx, radially symmetrical, 4–5 free petals 0.6 cm long, stamens white, usually with an elbowlike bend, anthers all at one side of the flower; inflorescence a tight flower cluster on a stalk in upper leaf axils, old flower bases bright pink; blooms Mar., Apr., July. **Fruit** fleshy, at first red, becoming bright blue, about 0.5 cm wide, Nov.–Mar. **Habitat:** Moist to wet forests in shady understories. Altitude: 700–1900 m. Conservation areas: ARE, CVC, GUA, LAC, LAP. **Range:** CR. **Notes:** There are 36 species of *Clidemia* in Costa Rica.

■ *Triolena hirsuta*
Family Melastomataceae

Low herb 10–40 cm tall, sometimes woody, stems slender, often trailing, hairy, pinkish in dark sites, green in brighter sites. **Leaves** opposite, 7–16 cm long, 4–10 cm wide, elliptic, tip pointed, base rounded to slightly lobed, hairy on both sides, major veins 5–7, secondary veins ladderlike; in dark sites blade is dark bronze green above, pinkish purple below, in bright sites leaves are green. **Flowers** deep pink in dark sites, to white in bright sites, flowers 5-parted, about 0.7 cm long, 0.4 cm wide, radially symmetrical, petals 0.5–0.7 cm long, 0.4 cm wide, broadest near apex, stamens 10; inflorescence of elongate, 1-sided, unbranched clusters 4–14 cm long, coiled at tip; blooms Nov.–Aug. **Fruit** dry, reddish, to 0.4 cm long, 0.8 cm wide, sharply 3-angled, depressed in center of top. **Habitat:** Wet to moist forest understories, often along streams especially in drier regions. Altitude: Sea level to 1600 m, rarely above 900 m. Conservation areas: ARE, CVC, GUA, HNO, LAC, TOR. Seen at La Selva Biological Station. **Range:** Nic–Ec. **Notes:** There are two other species of *Triolena* in Costa Rica, both are rather uncommon.

■ *Musa acuminata* (banano, claret, guineo, banana)
Family Musaceae

Large, treelike herb 3–5 m tall, colonial from short underground stems; stem about 25 cm wide, formed from overlapping leaf sheaths. **Leaves** alternate, spirally arranged, stalk 60–90 cm long, often waxy pale green, base sheathing stem, blade 2–2.5 m long, 40–60 cm wide, broadly elliptic, simple but often tattered in age, lower surface waxy white, secondary veins closely parallel, at right angles to midrib. **Flowers** white or yellow, asymmetrical, at the tip of a long, pendant inflorescence, surrounded by a large dark red to violet bract; blooms in Nov. **Fruit** fleshy, yellow at maturity, elongate, edible, develops without pollination and no seeds are formed. **Habitat:** Widely cultivated in garden plots and large plantations in the wet lowlands. Altitude: Sea level to 1200 m throughout Costa Rica. **Range:** Sweet bananas are native to India, SE Asia, and the Pacific islands. Now cultivated in all tropical areas of the world. **Notes:** Starchy plantains, used for cooking, are hybrids of *M. acuminata* and *M. balbisiana*, collectively named *Musa* × *paradisiaca* (*M. sapientum*; chato, curare, guineo, plátano). *Musa coccinea*, with bright pink bracts, sometimes escapes. There are five species of *Musa* found in Costa Rica, all are native to the Old World tropics.

■ *Arundina graminifolia* (bamboo orchid, bird orchid)
  Family Orchidaceae

Tall terrestrial orchid 1–2.5 m tall, stems in crowded clusters, canelike. **Leaves** alternate, ranked along stem, blade 8–30 cm long, 0.5–2 cm wide, narrowly lance-shaped, leathery, folded along midrib, tip pointed, base tapered to sheath 2–4 cm long. **Flowers** pink purple, bilaterally symmetrical, 3 sepals and 2 petals similar, lower petal (lip) highly modified, elabo-

rate, sepals lance-shaped, 3–4.5 cm long, about 1 cm wide, pale purple, lateral petals egg-shaped, about 3 cm long, 2.5 cm wide, lower petal (lip) 4–5 cm long, appearing tubular, lower part larger, yellow in throat, margin purple; inflorescence 10–70 cm long, at top of stem, branched, blooms a few at a time; blooms Sept.–Oct. **Fruit** dry, cylindrical, 3.5–5.5 cm long, 6-ribbed; splitting open to release numerous tiny seeds. **Habitat:** Cultivated, occasionally escaped along roadsides. **Range:** Native to SE Asia, India. Widely naturalized. **Notes:** This is the only species of *Arundina* in Costa Rica.

■ *Elleanthus glaucophyllus*
  Family Orchidaceae

Terrestrial on steep banks or epiphytic, often in dense clusters; stems 0.3–1.4 m long, unbranched; canelike, slender, dark, stiff, leaf base sheathing stem, often purplish. **Leaves** alternate, 2-ranked near ends of stems, stiff, stalkless, blade 13–24 cm long, 2–6 cm wide, lance-shaped, tip tapered to a elongate point, base blunt, surface pleated by impressed veins, often whitish to gray. **Flowers** red purple or white, bilaterally symmetrical, about 1.5 cm long, 3 sepals and 2 petals similar, lower petal (lip) highly modified, sepals and side petals about 1 cm long, 0.2–0.5 cm wide, red purple, lower petal about 1 cm long and wide, throat often white with orange dot, base pouch-shaped, margin fringed; inflorescence at top of stem, unbranched, densely flowered, 4–15 cm long, 2–3 cm wide, bracts red purple; blooms Feb.–Nov. **Fruit** dry, seeds numerous, dustlike. **Habitat:** Wet mountain forests, cloud forests. Altitude: Mostly 1000–2100 m, occasionally down to 450 m. Conservation areas: ARE, CVC, LAC, LAP. **Range:** CR, Pan. **Notes:** There are 21 species of *Elleanthus* in Costa Rica; most are slender with 2-ranked leaves, blade pleated or folded; inflorescence unbranched, flowers fairly small with base of lower petal pouch-shaped.

■ *Epidendrum pfavii*
Family Orchidaceae

Epiphytic or sometimes terrestrial herb 0.6–1.8 m tall, stems solitary, 0.6–1.7 cm thick, flattened near top, leaf base sheathing stem. **Leaves** alternate, 6–10, in 2 ranks along stem, no stalk, blade 17–26 cm long, 3–5 cm wide, lance-shaped, tip pointed, secondary veins obscure but parallel to midrib. **Flowers** pink purple, bilaterally symmetric, lateral petals to 1.9 cm long, 0.6 cm wide, with widened, toothed tips, central petal appearing tubular, to 1.3 cm long, 1.5 cm

wide, lip 3-lobed, white patch inside, sepals 2 cm long, 0.6–0.8 cm wide; inflorescence at top of stem, 16–52 cm long, unbranched, fairly dense, flower cluster emerging from bracts; blooms July, Sept. **Fruit** dry, seeds numerous, dustlike. **Habitat:** Very wet mountain forests; also frequently cultivated. Altitude: 800–2000 m. Conservation areas: CVC. **Range:** Endemic to CR. **Notes:** There are about 158 species of *Epidendrum* in Costa Rica. They are distinguished by slender, canelike stems, 2-ranked leaves, blades folded along midrib; *E. pfavii* may be more common as a cultivated plant than in the wild.

■ *Phytolacca rivinoides*
Family Phytolaccaceae

Large, sprawling herb 1–2 m tall, stems red, smooth, to 1 cm thick. **Leaves** alternate, stalks 2–7 cm long, often red, sides with ridges extending from base of leaf blade down stem, blade 5–17 cm long, 2–7 cm wide, elliptic to egg-shaped, tip tapered to point, base blunt, surface shiny, margin smooth. **Flowers** white, to pink or red, about 0.5 cm wide, radially symmetrical, 5 petals, stamens and styles numerous; flowers on very short, pink to red stalks along narrow, spikelike inflo-

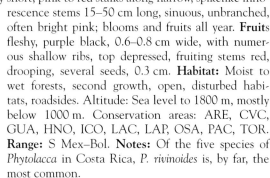

rescence stems 15–50 cm long, sinuous, unbranched, often bright pink; blooms and fruits all year. **Fruits** fleshy, purple black, 0.6–0.8 cm wide, with numerous shallow ribs, top depressed, fruiting stems red, drooping, several seeds, 0.3 cm. **Habitat:** Moist to wet forests, second growth, open, disturbed habitats, roadsides. Altitude: Sea level to 1800 m, mostly below 1000 m. Conservation areas: ARE, CVC, GUA, HNO, ICO, LAC, LAP, OSA, PAC, TOR. **Range:** S Mex–Bol. **Notes:** Of the five species of *Phytolacca* in Costa Rica, *P. rivinoides* is, by far, the most common.

■ *Phytolacca rugosa*
Family Phytolaccaceae

Large herb 0.3–2 m tall, base often woody, stems to 0.8 cm diameter, usually smooth. **Leaves** alternate, stalk 0.2–3 cm long, lateral ridges extending from base of leaf blade down stem, blade 6–12 cm long 2–4 cm wide, narrowly elliptic, pointed at both ends, surface corrugated with impressed veins, margins smooth. **Flowers** pink to red, 0.5 cm wide, radially symmetrical, 5 petals, stamens 6–12, styles 8; inflorescence of short dense, spikelike clusters 5–10 cm long, inflorescence stems scaly, often red or pink, flower stalks about 0.5 cm long, reddish; blooms and fruits all year. **Fruit** fleshy, black, shiny, about 0.3 cm, top depressed, several seeds. **Habitat:** High-elevation forests, second growth, open, disturbed sites, roadsides. Altitude: 1500–3700 m, mostly above 2000 m. Conservation areas: ARE, CVC, LAC, LAP, PAC. **Range:** Mex–Ven and Pr.

■ *Polygala paniculata*
Family Polygalaceae

Small, erect, weedy herb 5–50 cm tall, much-branched. **Leaves** opposite, or in whorls of 4, at the base of the stem, upper leaves alternate, stalk short, blade 0.5–3 cm long, 0.1–0.3 cm wide, linear, tip with a small point, base wedge-shaped. **Flowers** lavender, pink, or white, bilaterally symmetrical, about 0.2–0.3 cm long; inflorescence of spikes 2–10 cm long; blooms all year. **Fruit** dry, podlike, 0.2–0.3 cm long, splitting open to release 2, black, hairy seeds. **Habitat:** Wet to, less often, seasonally dry forests, open, disturbed sites, pastures, roadsides. Altitude: Sea level to 2100 m, usually above 500 m. Conservation areas: ARE, CVC, GUA, HNO, LAC, LAP, OSA, PAC, TEM, TOR. **Range:** Mex–Ven, Pr, and Brz, WI. Naturalized in Tanzania and Vietnam, invasive in Australia and some Pacific islands. **Notes:** There are 13 species of *Polygala* in Costa Rica, *P. paniculata* is, by far, the most common.

■ *Eichhornia crassipes* (choreja, lirio de agua,
  water hyacinth)
Family Pontederiaceae

Floating aquatic herb, almost stemless, about 40 cm tall, with
long, trailing plumelike roots that form new plants, sometimes
rooting in mud, aggressively colonial, covering water surface.
Leaves alternate, erect, in a rosette from base of plant, stalks
very inflated, 2–30 cm long, acting as floatation devices,
blade 3–16 cm long and wide, round to kidney-shaped, shiny
green, veins parallel curving upward and converging at the
leaf tip. **Flowers** blue lavender, occasionally white, with yellow center, tubular, slightly bilaterally symmetric, 6-parted,
petal lobes 2–4 cm long; inflorescence a broad spike, 4–15 cm

long, unbranched above leaves; blooms most of the
year. **Fruit** dry, about 1.5 cm long, 3-parted; seeds
numerous. **Habitat:** Shallow water, ditches, open
marshes in lowlands. Altitude: Sea level to 100 m.
Conservation areas: GUA, HNO, LAC, OSA, PAC,
TEM, TOR. **Range:** Native to Brz. Naturalized in SE
US, S Mex–Arg, and the Old World tropics; invasive in Hawai'i and other Pacific islands, Australia,
SE Asia, and S Africa. **Notes:** An aggressive weed,
often clogging waterways. There are four native species of *Eichhornia* in Costa Rica; all are aquatic herbs,
much less common than *E. crassipes*.

■ *Psychotria guapilensis*
  Family Rubiaceae

Herb 25–90 cm tall, often slightly woody, stems 1 or 2,
unbranched; stipules between leaf stalk bases to about 1 cm,
2-lobed, often deciduous. **Leaves** opposite, stalk to 9 cm
long, blade 9–24 cm long, 4–10 cm wide, elliptic, abruptly
narrowed above, tip pointed, base pointed to blunt, new
leaves often red. **Flowers** pink to purple, radially symmetrical, funnel-shaped, tube about 0.2 cm long, petal lobes 5,
to 0.2 cm, surrounded by numerous bracts to 1 cm long and
wide, becoming purple; inflorescence solitary, headlike, at
top of stem, 2–3 long, 3–5 cm wide; blooms May–Nov. **Fruit**
fleshy, bright blue, about 1 cm long, pear-shaped, bracts purple, in a ball at top of stem; fruit present July–Nov. **Habitat:**
Wet forest understories. Altitude: Caribbean slope, sea level
to 1000 m. Conservation areas: ARE, CVC, GUA, LAC,
TOR. **Range:** Nic–Ec. **Notes:** Similar in form to *P. glomerulata*, which has white flowers and inflorescence bracts.

Digitalis purpurea
Family Scrophulariaceae

Erect herb 50 cm to 1.8 m tall, stems stout, finely hairy. **Leaves** alternate, 13–25 cm long, lance-shaped, pointed at both ends, hairy below, margin blunt-toothed. **Flowers** purple to white, darker purple spots inside, bilaterally symmetrical, broadly tubular (much like flowers of some Gesneriaceae), 4–5.5 cm long, petal lobes 5, very short, rounded, sepals 5, 1–1.5 cm overlapping; inflorescence unbranched, at top of stem; blooms all year. **Fruit** dry, splitting open to release seeds. **Habitat:** Open sites at high elevation. Altitude: 2600–3300 m. Conservation areas: CVC, LAC, LAP. **Range:** Native to Europe. Escaped from cultivation in NW US, Mex–Pr, France, New Zealand. **Notes:** All parts toxic; the chemicals (cardiac glycosides) from *D. purpurea* are the original source of the heart medicine digitalis.

Browallia americana
Family Solanaceae

Herb to 70 cm tall, straggling, stems branched, green, finely hairy. **Leaves** alternate, stalk to 2.5 cm, slightly winged, blade to 5 cm, egg-shaped, tip pointed, base blunt to pointed, finely hairy below. **Flowers** blue, purple, or white, radially symmetrical, 5-parted, tubular, petal tube to 1.5 cm long, slender, to 1.4 cm wide across top, petal lobes broadly flaring, calyx to 1 cm, lobes short, stamens 4, yellow; blooms most of the year. **Fruit** dry, embedded in the old calyx; seeds numerous. **Habitat:** Open areas, roadsides, pastures, vacant lots, in moist and seasonally dry regions. Altitude: 150–1200 m. Conservation areas: ARE, CVC, LAP, PAC. **Range:** Mex–Ven and Bol, WI. **Notes:** The only other species of *Browallia* in Costa Rica is *B. speciosa*. It is much less common and has much larger flowers than *B. americana*.

305

■ *Pilea pteropodon*
Family Urticaceae

Slender herb 15–40 cm tall, succulent, lower stem often kneeling, rooting at nodes, hairless, stipules to 0.8 cm, tip blunt. **Leaves** opposite, pair members at a node usually equal, stalk to 1.8 cm long, blade 6–20 cm long, 3–8 cm wide, ellip-

tic, tip long-pointed, base often extending down leaf stalk as wings, surface puckered, major veins 3, palmate, with lateral veins ladderlike between major veins, margins toothed. **Flowers** dull pink to white, tiny; in branching, flat-topped clusters to 6 cm long, in axils or ends of stems; blooms Feb.–July, mostly Mar. and Apr. **Fruit** dry, tiny, less than 0.2 cm, flat, yellowish. **Habitat:** Very wet to wet regions in forest understories. Altitude: Sea level to 1800 m, usually above 800 m. Conservation areas: ARE, CVC, HNO, LAC, LAP, TOR. **Range:** CR–Ec. **Notes:** See also *P. microphilla*.

■ *Lantana trifolia*
Family Verbenaceae

Shrubby herb to treelet 50 cm to 2 m tall, young stems 4-sided, bristly-hairy. **Leaves** in whorls of 3, or sometimes opposite, stalk hairy blade 5–16 cm long, 3–8 cm wide, lance-shaped, pointed at both ends, softly hairy on both sides, fragrant when crushed, scent wintergreenlike, margins toothed. **Flowers** blue purple to dark pink, center yellow, radially symmetrical, tubular, 0.4–0.7 cm long; inflorescence dense axillary headlike clusters; blooms and fruits most of the year. **Fruit** fleshy, purple, 0.2–0.3 cm wide, in clusters 1–4 cm long, 0.5–1 cm wide. **Habitat:** Moist to wet forest, second growth, disturbed sites, roadsides. Altitude: Sea level to 2100 m, usually below 500 m. Conservation areas: ARE, CVC, GUA, HNO, LAC, LAP, OSA, PAC, TOR. **Range:** Mex–Arg and Brz, WI, Africa.

■ *Stachytarpheta frantzii*
Family Verbenaceae

Shrubby herb to 1.5 m tall, densely branched, young stems green, roughly hairy. **Leaves** opposite, blade 3–13 cm long (including stalk), 2–6 cm wide, egg- to heart-shaped, tip pointed, base blunt to slightly lobed, dull, dark green above, hairy on both sides, deeply puckered, veins palmate at base, pinnate above. **Flowers** deep purple to dark pink, center pale yellow, tubular, bilaterally symmetrical, about 0.7 cm wide across top, tube narrow, about 1.5 cm long, 0.2 cm wide, white at base, petal lobes 5, 2 larger above, fused nearly to tips, calyx tubular 0.7–1 cm long, green, purplish near top, lobes needlelike; inflorescence a spike 15–60 cm long, 0.2–0.6 cm wide. **Fruit** dry, linear, 0.5 cm long, surrounded by persistent calyx. **Habitat:** Wet to seasonally dry regions in open areas, roadsides, pastures. Altitude: Sea level to 1300 m. Conservation areas: ARE, GUA, OSA, PAC, TEM. **Range:** Mex–Pan, DR, PtR. **Notes:** Five species of *Stachytarpheta* are listed as occurring in Costa Rica, only two are native. The other native species is *S. jamaicensis*, which is almost identical, except the leaves are not hairy. It is more common than *S. frantzii*.

■ *Verbena litoralis*
Family Verbenaceae

Slender herb 40 cm to 2 m tall, stems angled, branching opposite, often woody at base. **Leaves** opposite, 3–10 cm long, 1–1.5 cm wide, lance-shaped to widest above middle, pointed at both ends, surface slightly rough, margin toothed on upper half. **Flowers** blue to purple, tubular, somewhat bilaterally symmetrical, small, to 0.3 cm long, petal lobes 5; inflorescence of spikes, 3–12 cm long, about 0.3 cm wide; blooms Jan.–Sept. **Fruit** dry, small. **Habitat:** Wet to very wet regions in weedy, open areas, roadsides, pastures, mostly at higher elevations. Altitude: 600–3500 m. Conservation areas: ARE, CVC, GUA, LAP, PAC. **Range:** Mex–Chile, Arg, Ur. Invasive on the Galapagos, Hawai'i, and some other Pacific islands. **Notes:** This is the only species of *Verbena* in Costa Rica. It has been used medicinally in parts of South America.

COLOR OF CONSPICUOUS PART RED, RED ORANGE, OR BRIGHT ORANGE

■ *Aphelandra aurantiaca*
Family Acanthaceae

Shrubby herb to 1 m tall, young stems 4-sided. **Leaves** opposite, stalk to 1 cm long, blade 8–28 cm long, 3–12 cm wide, elliptic, shiny green, tip long-pointed, base tapered, secondary veins conspicuous, margins often wavy. **Flowers** red

orange, about 6 cm long, showy, tubular, bilaterally symmetrical, tube narrow, petal lobes 4, about 2 cm long, 1 cm wide, unequal, finely hairy, upper lip forming a partial hood over anthers, bracts at base of each flower overlapping, elliptic, to 3 cm long, 1 cm wide, margin fringed with small spines; inflorescence a terminal, 4-sided spike to 17 cm long; blooms July–Feb. **Fruit** dry, 1.6 cm long, club-shaped. **Habitat:** Understories of wet to moist forests. Altitude: Sea level to 1400 m. Conservation areas: ARE, CVC, GUA, HNO, LAC, OSA, TOR. **Range:** Mex–Bol. **Notes:** There are 12 species of *Aphelandra* in Costa Rica. Most have showy flowers.

Courtesy of Margaret Gargiullo

■ *Anthurium bakeri*
Family Araceae

Epiphytic herb, often low on trees, stem short, thick, to 10 cm long, 1.5 cm wide, rooting at nodes; sheath covering leaf bud 3–5 cm long, persistent as coarse brown fibers. **Leaves** alternate, stalk 3–17 cm long; blade 19–44 cm long, 3–9 cm wide, lance-shaped, tip and base pointed, dark green above, pale below, sprinkled with tiny dots, midrib deeply

impressed, prominent lateral veins run very close to margin, smaller veins rather obscure. **Flowers** white, minute, densely crowded on a fleshy, erect, spike (spadix) 2–11 cm long, to 0.7 cm wide in flower; inflorescence bract (spathe) green, to 5 cm long, 2 cm wide, usually folded back, tip pointed; blooms and fruits all year. **Fruit** fleshy, red, berrylike, 0.6 cm long, suspended from spike on 2 fibers, seeds 2, white; spike 15 cm long, 2.5 cm wide in fruit. **Habitat:** Wet to moist forests. Altitude: Sea level to 1300 m. Conservation areas: ARE, CVC, GUA, HNO, LAC, LAP, OSA, PAC, TOR. **Range:** S Mex–Ven and Ec.

■ *Anthurium ranchoanum*
Family Araceae
Large epiphytic or terrestrial herb, stem to 1 m long, 4.5 cm
wide; aerial roots green, thick, appearing fuzzy. **Leaves** alternate, stalk 0.09–1 m long, blade 17–67 cm long, 9–37 cm
wide, arrow-shaped to triangular, tip pointed, base wedge-
shaped, truncate to shallowly lobed, midrib raised on both
sides, secondary veins conspicuous, connected to one another
along leaf margin. **Flowers** dark red purple, minute, densely
crowded on a fleshy spike (spadix) 4–19 cm long, 1–1.5 cm
wide; inflorescence bract (spathe) green to purple-tinged, 4–
21 cm long, 2–8 cm wide, lance- to egg-shaped, base slightly
lobed; inflorescence stalk 13–56 cm long; blooms and fruits
on and off most of the year. **Fruit** fleshy, bright red orange, to
1.4 cm long; fruiting spike to 50 cm long, 3 cm wide, arching
downward. **Habitat:** Wet mountain forests, high to low on
tree trunks or on rocks. Altitude: 1200–2700 m. Conservation areas: ARE, CVC, LAC, LAP, PAC. **Range:** CR–Pan.

■ *Anthurium scherzerianum*
Family Araceae
Usually an epiphyte on tree trunks or branches, stems none
or very short, to about 20 cm, aerial roots thin, numerous.
Leaves alternate, stalk 3–30 cm long, blade 8–33 cm long,
2–7 cm wide, narrowly lance-shaped, straplike, tip pointed,
base blunt to wedge-shaped, surface leathery, both sides
sprinkled with tiny dark dots, midrib sharply raised above.
Flowers bright orange, minute, densely crowded on a fleshy
spike (spadix) 2–8 cm long, about 0.4 cm wide, usually
coiled upward, tip tapered, bract bright red orange, 4–12 cm
long, 3–6 cm wide, heart-shaped, tip abruptly pointed, base
lobed; inflorescence stalk 12–58 cm long, erect; blooms
most of the year, especially July. **Fruit** fleshy, red to orange;
fruits Apr., July. **Habitat:** Wet mountain forests; also widely
cultivated. Altitude: 700–2100 m, mostly above 1300 m.
Conservation areas: ARE, CVC, HNO, LAC, LAP. **Range:**
Endemic to CR.

■ *Asclepias curassavica* (bailarina, mata caballo,
mal casada, milkweed) Family Asclepiadaceae

Herb to 1.5 m tall, young parts of stem hairy. **Leaves** opposite, stalk 1–2 cm long, blade 5–18 cm long, 1–4 cm wide,
narrow, tapered to points at both ends. **Flowers** orange red
and yellow, 0.8 cm long, radially symmetrical, 5-parted, floral parts fused in a central, crownlike arrangement; inflores-

cence of umbrella-shaped clusters at ends of
branches, insect pollinated; blooms all year.
Fruit dry, pods, held upright, to 10 cm long,
1.5 cm wide; splitting open to release plumed
seeds. **Habitat:** Wet to seasonally dry regions
in open sites, clearings, roadsides, and pastures. Altitude: Sea level to 2700 m. Conservation areas: ARE, CVC, GUA, HNO, LAC,
LAP, OSA, PAC, TEM, TOR. **Range:** Entire
Neotropics and subtropics. Naturalized in Old
World tropics. Invasive in the Galapagos and
other Pacific islands. **Notes:** There are five
species of *Asclepias* in Costa Rica; *A. curassavica* is the only common one.

■ *Begonia multinervia*
Family Begoniaceae

Epiphytic or terrestrial herb, to 1.5 m tall, stems erect, succulent, stipules paired, 1–4 cm long, leaving a ringlike scar at
node. **Leaves** alternate, stalk 3–16 cm long, blade 5–15 cm
long, 6–25 cm wide, mostly wider than long, asymmetrically
egg-shaped, underside and stalk often red, tip pointed, base
lobed, margin toothed. **Flowers** white to pink, bilaterally
symmetrical, male and female flowers separate, petals 2, about
0.5–1 cm long, and wide; male flowers with numerous yellow
anthers; female flowers with 3-winged ovary below petals;
inflorescence stems often red, branched main stalk 10–34 cm
long, flowers numerous; blooms Jan.–June. **Fruit** dry, about
1 cm long, very unequally 3-winged, the largest wing about

1.5 cm wide; seeds minute, numerous. **Habitat:** Wet and very wet regions, in open sites
or forest understory, often along streams. Altitude: Sea level to 1700 m. Conservation areas:
ARE, CVC, GUA, LAC, LAP, OSA, PAC.
Range: Nic–Pan. **Notes:** Distinguished by its
bright red leaf undersides. There are about 34
species of *Begonia* in Costa Rica.

■ *Tillandsia insignis* (chira)
Family Bromeliaceae

Small epiphytic or terrestrial herb, stem to 25 cm long. **Leaves** alternate, spirally arranged along length of stem, blade linear, 7–18 cm long, 0.3–.9 cm wide, soft, tip pointed, base dark brown to bluish purple, broadly sheathing, margin minutely toothed. **Flowers** dark blue purple to sometimes yellow green with dark spots, sepals yellow to red, often not opening except at tip, bracts red with greenish tips, narrow, pointed at tips; inflorescence spikelike at top of stem; blooms Sept.–May. **Fruit** dry, about 1.5 cm long, red, becoming brown, splitting open to release plumed seeds. **Habitat:** Wet forests and cloud forests. Altitude: 900–2000 m. Conservation Areas: ARE, CVC, GUA, LAC, LAP. Seen in Tapantí N.P. **Range:** CR, Pan. **Notes:** There are 39 species of *Tillandsia* in Costa Rica. They are distinguished from species of *Guzmania* and *Werauhia* by small differences in the flower structures.

■ *Werauhia ororiensis* (*Vriesea o.*)
Family Bromeliaceae

Epiphytic or terrestrial herb, with leafy rosette about 50 cm wide. **Leaves** alternate, straplike 18–47 cm long, 3–7 cm wide, tip pointed, base sheathing, marked with red purple. **Flowers** green about 3 cm long, 1.5 cm wide, irregular; inflorescence 14–38 cm long, with numerous small branches held close to the main stem, appearing unbranched; inflorescence stalk 33–75 cm tall, covered by bracts heavily marked or striped with red, purple, or green mottled with purple; blooms most of the year. **Fruit** dry, about 3 cm long, hollow, splitting open to release plumed seeds. **Habitat:** Wet mountain forests. Altitude: 1500–3300 m. Conservation areas: CVC, LAC. Especially above 2500 m, in the Cordillera de Talamanca, where it is the dominant species of Bromeliaceae. Very common on Volcán Poas. **Range:** CR, W Pan. **Notes:** There are 58 species of *Werauhia* in Costa Rica.

311

■ *Centropogon ferrugineus*
Family Campanulaceae

Slender shrubby or vinelike herb, stems arching, finely rusty-hairy, sap milky. **Leaves** alternate, stalk 1–3 cm, blade 5–15 cm long, 2–5 cm wide, elliptic to egg-shaped, hairy below, tip pointed, base rounded to tapered, surface dull green, wrinkled, margin sharply toothed. **Flowers** red and orange, tubular, bilaterally symmetrical, about 3 cm long, 1 cm wide,

hairy, tube red, throat yellow, slightly curved, base bulging, top expanded, petal lobes 5, orange-tipped, flaring, 2 upper lobes about 1 cm long, 3 lower lobes slightly shorter, anthers fused above into a single white-hairy tube longer than petal lobes; flowers solitary in upper axils on stalks 4–9 cm long; blooms most of the year. **Fruit** leathery, white, crowned by old calyx rim to 0.3 cm high; seeds numerous, flattened. **Habitat:** Mountain regions in open sites. Altitude: 2000–3000 m. Conservation areas: CVC, LAP. **Range:** Gua–Pr. **Notes:** There are 16 species of *Centropogon* in Costa Rica.

■ *Centropogon granulosus*
Family Campanulaceae

Terrestrial or epiphytic, shrubby herb, stems vinelike to 2.5 m long, hollow, to 1.5 cm diameter, green, sap milky. **Leaves** alternate, stalk about 1 cm long, blade 10–20 cm long, 5–10 cm wide, broadly elliptic to egg-shaped, tip pointed, base pointed to slightly lobed, surface wrinkled, margin finely toothed. **Flowers** bright red orange and yellow, tubular, bilaterally symmetrical, tube 3–4 cm long, base slightly swollen, petal lobes 5, bright yellow, about 1 cm long, 2 upper lobes orange yellow, bent back, 3 lower lobes red to orange, anthers fused into a tube longer than petal lobes by about 0.6 cm, pale yellow, hairy, calyx lobes linear, about 1–2 cm long; inflorescence of unbranched, pendant clusters at ends of stems; blooms all year. **Fruit** leathery, white, 1–1.5 cm wide, barrel-shaped, tipped with persistent red calyx lobes, flesh foamlike; seeds, numerous, minute. **Habitat:** Moist to wet forests. Altitude: 60–2700 m. Conservation areas: ARE, CVC, LAC, LAP, OSA, PAC. **Range:** CR–Pr. **Notes:** This is the by far most common species of *Centropogon*.

■ *Lobelia laxiflora*
Family Campanulaceae

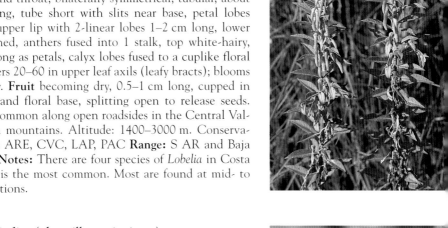

Shrubby herb about 1 m tall, sap milky. **Leaves** alternate, spiraled around stem, 4–12 cm long, 1–4 cm wide, lance-shaped to broadly elliptical, pointed at both ends, margins usually finely toothed. **Flowers** red or orange often with yellow base and throat, bilaterally symmetrical, tubular, about 3–5 cm long, tube short with slits near base, petal lobes 2-lipped, upper lip with 2-linear lobes 1–2 cm long, lower lip 3-toothed, anthers fused into 1 stalk, top white-hairy, about as long as petals, calyx lobes fused to a cuplike floral base, flowers 20–60 in upper leaf axils (leafy bracts); blooms Sept.–May. **Fruit** becoming dry, 0.5–1 cm long, cupped in old calyx and floral base, splitting open to release seeds. **Habitat:** common along open roadsides in the Central Valley and in mountains. Altitude: 1400–3000 m. Conservation areas: ARE, CVC, LAP, PAC **Range:** S AR and Baja CA–Col. **Notes:** There are four species of *Lobelia* in Costa Rica; this is the most common. Most are found at mid- to high elevations.

■ *Canna indica* (platanilla, periquitoya)
Family Cannaceae

Tall herb 1–3 m tall, stems formed by overlapping leaf sheaths, often many stems together sprouting from underground stems (rhizomes). **Leaves** alternate, stalk sheathing stem, blade 15–45 cm long, 7–20 cm wide, tip long-pointed, egg-shaped to elliptic, surface shiny green, fleshy texture. **Flowers** bright red, with yellow markings, irregular, 4–5 cm long, about 2 cm wide, petals 3, narrow, sepals 3, petal-like, stamens 2–6, petal-like, narrow, ovary inferior; inflorescence of short unbranched stalks at top of stem; blooms all year. **Fruit** dry, bluntly triangular, about 4.5 cm long, 2 cm wide, surface warty; seeds shiny, black. **Habitat:** Wet to very wet regions in open areas, along roadsides and pasture edges; also cultivated widely and escaped. Altitude: Sea level to 1300 m. Conservation areas: GUA, LAC, LAP, OSA, PAC. Seen in the Caribbean lowlands near Limón. **Range:** Mex–Arg, Ant. **Notes:** There are three species of *Canna* in Costa Rica; *C. tuerckheimii* is similar to *C. indica*, it has red orange flowers 6–7 cm long and larger leaves and is found from 300–1800 m.

313

■ *Costus malortieanus* (caña agria)
Family Costaceae

Herb 1–1.5 m tall, often many plants together, stem unbranched, hairy, spiraled, lower leaves reduced to sheaths, purplish green. **Leaves** alternate, spiraled around stem, blade 20–35 cm long, 9–18 cm wide, elliptic, tip pointed, base blunt; surface hairy on both sides, young leaves mottled or striped lighter and darker green above, pale silvery green below. **Flowers** striped red and pale yellow, asymmetrical, blooming a few at a time from among a dense, rounded cluster of tightly overlapping bracts at top of stem, bracts bright red in bud, becoming brownish with age; blooms all year. Visited by hummingbirds and euglossine bees. **Fruit** white, seeds black with a white, fleshy coat. Dispersed by birds. **Habitat:** Very wet forest understories, second growth forest, edges. Altitude: Sea level to 850 m, Caribbean slope. Conservation areas: ARE, CVC, GUA, HNO, TOR. **Range:** Nic. CR. **Notes:** Flowers much like those of *C. laevis,* which is a larger, hairless plant. There are about 22 species of *Costus* in Costa Rica.

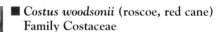

■ *Costus woodsonii* (roscoe, red cane)
Family Costaceae

Herb 1–2 m tall, colonial from underground stems, above ground stems spiraled. **Leaves** alternate, spiraled, blade 8–26 cm long, 4–10 cm wide, texture leathery, shiny on both sides, paler below. **Flowers** yellow, tubular, 3 cm long, 2 cm wide, blooming a few at a time; from between red bracts; inflorescence conelike, 3–11 cm long, 2–3 cm wide, oval to cylindrical; blooms June, July, Nov., Dec., Feb. **Fruit** white, containing black seeds with a fleshy, white aril. **Habitat:** Behind beach in open woodland, among coconut palms. Altitude: At and near sea level, Caribbean shore. Conservation areas: LAC, TOR. **Range:** Nic–Col. **Notes:** Very similar to *C. pulverulentus,* the most common and widespread species of *Costus* in Costa Rica; it is somewhat taller with larger leaves than *C. woodsonii,* and often has red flowers. *Costus pulverulentus* is found from sea level to 1400 m elevation.

■ *Euphorbia tithymaloides (Pedilanthus t.)*
(pie de niño, bítamo, pie de santo, zapatillo)
Family Euphorbiaceae
Herb or shrub, stems green, arching, branches 1–3 m long,
often vinelike. **Leaves** alternate, stalk short to none, blade
4–16 cm long, 2–10 cm wide, fleshy, egg-shaped to elliptic, tip tapered, long-pointed, base blunt, veins obscure;
deciduous. **Flowers** red, 0.7–1.5 cm long, shoe- or insect-
head-shaped, bilaterally symmetrical, not appearing flower-

like. **Fruit** dry, deeply 3-lobed,
0.6 cm wide. **Habitat:** Mostly
cultivated, sometimes used for
hedges, occasionally escaping
into moist to wet forests and
open sites. Altitude: Sea level
to 900 m. Conservation areas:
CVC, LAP, OSA, PAC. **Range:**
Mex–NE S Amer. **Notes:** Used
medicinally for coughs. The
only other species of *Pedilanthus* in Costa Rica is *P. nodi-
florus*. Neither is common but
flowers are very unusual.

■ *Indigofera hirsuta*
Family Fabaceae/Faboideae
Shrubby herb about 50 cm tall, sometimes to 1.5 m, stems
hairy. **Leaves** alternate, odd pinnate, about 11 cm long, 7 cm
wide, 5–7 leaflets, to 4 cm long, 2 cm wide, elliptic,
rounded at both ends, oblong, pale green, hairy on
both sides. **Flowers** red, about 0.7 cm wide, bilaterally symmetrical, inflorescence dense, spikelike
to 30 cm long, blooming a few at a time from base
upward; blooms and fruits mostly July–Mar. **Fruit**
dry, pods, brown, hairy, 1–2 cm long, 0.3 cm wide,
closely overlapping down the stem, giving fruiting
stem a "thatched" appearance; seed 6–9, angular,
pitted. **Habitat:** Wet to seasonally dry lowlands, in
open sites roadsides, pastures. Altitude: Sea level to
700 m, most often below 300 m. Conservation areas:
ARE, GUA, HNO, LAC, LAP,
OSA, PAC, TEM, TOR. **Range:**
Native to Africa and Asia. Widely
naturalized throughout the tropics.
Notes: There are nine species of
Indigofera in Costa Rica, *I. hirsuta* is
probably the most common and conspicuous.

Flower detail   *Fruit detail*

315

■ *Alloplectus tetragonus*
Family Gesneriaceae

Shrublike herb to 3 m tall, rather hairy, stem 4-sided, to 1 cm diameter, younger growth green, succulent, yellowish-hairy, old stems brown, woody, scaly. **Leaves** opposite, stalk 5–8 cm long, blade 14–25 cm long, 4–11 cm wide, narrowly elliptic, tip long-pointed, base tapered, shiny, somewhat succulent and puckered, hairy on both sides especially below, margin toothed. **Flowers** red to orange, tubular, bilaterally symmetrical, showy, to 5 cm long, densely yellow-hairy, calyx winged, hairy, with fringed margins, to 2.7 cm long, green, red, or edges red, in axillary clusters of 1–4 flowers; blooms all year. **Fruit** fleshy, green, seeds numerous. **Habitat:** Wet forests. Altitude: 200–2900 m, mostly 1000–2000 m. Conservation areas: ARE, CVC, GUA, LAC, LAP. Seen at Tapantí N.P. and at Monteverde Cloud Forest Reserve. **Range:** Mex–N S Amer. **Notes:** This is the most common species of *Alloplectus* in Costa Rica.

■ *Columnea consanguinea*
Family Gesneriaceae

Shrublike herb, terrestrial or epiphytic, stems stout, to 1 m long, pale brown, hairy. **Leaves** opposite but extremely unequal and appearing alternate, stalk to 1 cm, larger blades 12–16 cm long, 3–6 cm wide, lance-shaped, sides unequal, hairy, underside blotched with bright red, these appear yellow green on upper surface, tip long-pointed, base unequal, the smaller leaf of a pair 1–2 cm long, to 0.6 cm, base fused to stem. **Flowers** yellow, bilaterally symmetrical, tubular, hairy, about 3 cm long, 0.8 cm wide, petal lobes 2 cm long, calyx green to red, lobes 2 cm long, pointed, hairy, bracts yellow to orange; flowers in leaf axils; blooms all year. **Fruit** fleshy, yellow, seeds, small, numerous. **Habitat:** Wet forests. Altitude: 300–1900 m. Conservation areas: ARE, CVC, GUA, LAC, LAP. **Range:** CR, Pan. **Notes:** There are 36 species of *Columnea* in Costa Rica. *Columnea consanguinea* is conspicuous due to the red markings on leaf undersides.

■ *Columnea magnifica*
Family Gesneriaceae

Shrublike, epiphytic herb, stems slender, brownish-hairy. **Leaves** opposite, pair members somewhat unequal, stalk to 1.5 cm long, blade 3–7 cm long, 1–3 cm wide, egg- to lance-shaped, tip pointed, base blunt to wedge-shaped, rough-textured, finely hairy, dark green above, sometimes reddish below, clustered at ends of stems. **Flowers** bright red orange with yellow markings, bilaterally symmetric, tubular, very showy, to about 7.5 cm long, 3 cm wide across top, red-hairy, center petal lobe broad, side lobes narrow, anthers united and extend beyond petal tube; flowers single in axils; blooms all year. **Fruit** fleshy, pale purple, flesh sticky, seeds small, numerous. **Habitat:** Wet forests, mostly in mountains. Altitude: 700–3000 m, mostly above 1500 m. Conservation areas: ARE, CVC, GUA, HNO, LAC, LAP, PAC. **Range:** CR, Pan.

■ *Columnea nicaraguensis*
Family Gesneriaceae

Shrubby, pendent, epiphytic herb, stems to 5 m long, whitish-hairy. **Leaves** opposite in unequal pairs, the larger narrow, 6–11 cm long, 1–3 cm wide, lance-shaped, tip long-pointed, base unequal, underside often pink to red. **Flowers** red to red orange with yellow markings, to 7.7 cm long, tubular, hairy, funnel-shaped, bilaterally symmetric, calyx lobes to 3 cm, green to red; blooms all year. **Fruit** fleshy, white, to 1 cm, fleshy sticky, seeds small, numerous. **Habitat:** Wet forests and second growth. Altitude: Sea level to 1900 m. Conservation areas: ARE, CVC, HNO, LAC, LAP, OSA, TOR. **Range:** Nic–Pan.

317

■ *Kohleria spicata*
Family Gesneriaceae

Coarse, red-hairy herb to 1.5 m tall, unbranched, or branched from base; colonial from rhizomes. **Leaves** opposite, or in whorls of 3–4, stalk about 2 cm long, blade 7–28 cm long, 3–6 cm wide, smaller above, narrowly elliptic, tip pointed, base blunt, hairy on both sides, often red below, major veins often red above, margin finely toothed. **Flowers** red orange, paler, red-spotted inside, broadly tubular, bilaterally symmetrical, hairy outside, to 2 cm long, 0.7 cm wide, petal lobes 5, flaring outward, nearly equal, rounded; inflorescence of small axillary clusters, green calyx enclosing red ovary remains after petal tube falls; blooms all year. **Fruit** dry, red to brown, round to 0.7 cm wide, hairy, surrounded by old calyx. **Habitat:** Seasonally dry to wet forests, second growth and open sites, roadside banks. Altitude: Sea level to 2700 m, mostly below 1500 m. Conservation areas: ARE, CVC, HNO, LAC, LAP, OSA, PAC, TEM. **Range:** S Mex–N S Amer. **Notes:** There are three species of *Kohleria* in Costa Rica, this is the most common.

■ *Gunnera insignis*
Family Gunneraceae

Herbaceous plant to about 1 m tall, colonial from a creeping underground or prostrate stem. **Leaves** alternate, in a huge rosette, stalk 1.5–2.5 m long, erect, often red, blade nearly round, to 2 m wide, umbrellalike, margin shallowly 5-lobed, lobe tips pointed, leaf base deeply lobed, surface very rough, veins sometimes red. **Flowers** dark red, individually inconspicuous, very small, with small red or whitish bracts, anthers red; inflorescence to 2 m tall, hairy, shaped like a very large bottle-brush or fox tail, central axis reddish purple, to 1 m long, with numerous thin branches 10–30 cm long, densely covered with flowers; blooms on and off Jan.–Nov. **Fruit** fleshy, 0.2 cm long, and about as wide, red to orange. **Habitat:** Open sites in mountains, roadsides, banks. Altitude: 800–2500 m, mostly above 1500 m. Conservation areas: ARE, CVC, LAC, LAP, PAC. **Range:** Endemic to CR. **Notes:** There are two species of *Gunnera* in Costa Rica; *G. talamancana* has smaller, deeply divided leaves and is much less common. *Gunnera* is able to grow in poor quality soil due to its symbiotic relationship with a nitrogen-fixing cyanobacterium (*Nostoc punctiforme*), which takes nitrogen from the air and converts it to a form usable by the plant.

■ *Heliconia danielsiana* (platanilla)
   Family Heliconiaceae

Large herb 5–8 m tall, growth form like a banana plant.
Leaves alternate, 2–4 per stem, long-stalked, blade 2–2.8 m
long, 45–57 cm wide, midrib sometime red purple, underside sometimes waxy white, margin smooth. **Flowers** yellow
with white base, asymmetrical (irregular), 6-parted, about
5 cm long, 1 cm wide, 15–20 tucked into each bract; bracts
red orange, densely reddish brown woolly-hairy, 10–11 cm
long, 8–10 cm deep, Inflorescence pendant, about 1 m long,
with 20–30, overlapping bracts, slightly, spirally arranged or
ranked in one plane; blooms and fruits mostly Sept.–May.
Fruit fleshy, blue, 1-seeded; eaten by birds and mammals.
Habitat: Very wet regions in open or partly shaded roadsides,
edges, second growth. Altitude: Sea level to 900 m, southern Pacific slope. Conservation areas: OSA, PAC. **Range:**
Endemic to CR. **Notes:** Distinguished by its pendant, rusty-
hairy inflorescence. There are 38 species of *Heliconia* in
Costa Rica.

■ *Heliconia imbricata* (platanilla)
   Family Heliconiaceae

Herb 3.5–6 m tall, growth form like a banana plant. **Leaves**
alternate, 3–4 per stem, stalks long to 1 m, blade 1.3–2.3 m
long, 30–50 cm wide held upright, undersides often violet,
especially in young plants. **Flowers** green above, base yellow
or white, asymmetrical, 6-parted, about 3 cm long, 0.6 cm
wide, 10–15 per bract; bracts mostly red above, fading to
yellow below; the middle ones 4–5 cm long, 8–11 cm deep,
rounded-oval, nearly cup-shaped, base bulbous, upper margin
often black, decayed; inflorescence erect about 60 cm long,
bracts 20–30, tightly overlapped in a flattened, 2-ranked
arrangement; blooms mostly Jan.–Oct. **Fruit** fleshy, greenish yellow to blue, 1-seeded; eaten by birds and mammals.
Habitat: Very wet regions, in open sites or part shade, often
near streams. Altitude:
Sea level to 600 m,
mostly south and central
Pacific lowlands. Con-
servation areas: CVC
(infrequent), OSA,
PAC. **Range:** CR–Col.
Notes: Rounded, closely
overlapping bracts are
distinctive.

Inflorescence with fruit

319

■ *Heliconia psittacorum*
Family Heliconiaceae

Herb to 1.5 m tall. **Leaves** like those of banana. **Flowers** orange, green, yellow, bracts red to pale orange, 4–6, many cultivars, lowest bract slender, elongate often with green tip; inflorescence erect, short, as wide or wider than tall. **Fruits** fleshy, blue; eaten by birds and mammals. **Habitat:** Cultivated, garden plant with many cultivars. Altitude: Sea level to roughly 1500 m. Conservation areas: Not escaping from cultivation. **Range:** Mex–Bol and Brz; WI.

■ *Heliconia rostrata* (platanilla)
Family Heliconiaceae

Herb to 1–6 m tall, growth form like a banana plant. **Leaves** alternate, midrib often dark near base. **Flowers** bright yellow, base white, asymmetrical, 6-parted, narrow; bracts mostly red, tip yellow, margin greenish, 12–20 cm long, about 5 cm wide, in one plane or spiraled, at first overlapping becoming separated and horizontal; inflorescence pendant, axis red, bracts 4–35; blooms all year. **Fruit** fleshy, blue. **Habitat:** Garden plant, widely cultivated, apparently not escaping from cultivation. **Range:** Native Ec–Bol.

■ *Heliconia wagneriana* (platanilla)
Family Heliconiaceae
Herb 2–4 m tall, stem flattened, growth form like a banana plant. **Leaves** alternate, 3–4 per stem, stalk to over 1 m long, grooved above, blade 0.95–1.5 m long, 24–30 cm wide, oblong, tip pointed, base blunt often unequal, new leaves often pale waxy, with red midrib. **Flowers** dark green, base white, 6 cm long, 0.8 cm wide, bracts red, bordered by yellow, margins green, the middle ones 12–15 cm long, 11–12 cm high at base, tip pointed, bases overlapping; inflorescence erect, stalk to 50 cm long, bracts 6–20, ranked along inflorescence; blooms Dec.–Sept. **Fruit**s fleshy, 1.5 cm, blue, 1- to 3-seeded; eaten by birds and mammals. **Habitat:** Very

wet lowland regions, edges, open sites or part shade, second growth. Altitude: Sea level to 700 m. Conservation areas: CVC, LAC, OSA (mostly), PAC, TOR. **Range:** Bel and Gua–Ec. **Notes:** Distinguished by its erect inflorescence with overlapping, tricolor red, yellow, and green bracts.

■ *Crocosmia* × *crocosmiiflora*
(chispa, montbretia, crocosmia)
Family Iridaceae
Herb 25–50 cm tall, sometimes to 1 m, from a from a flattened bulblike rootstock (corm) about 2 cm wide, forming colonies as bulbs multiply, stems clustered, 2- to 4-branched. **Leaves** alternate mostly from base, 5–8 in a fanlike arrangement, 30–50 cm long, 0.8–2.0 cm wide, stem leaves smaller than those at base, blade lance- to sword-shaped. **Flowers** bright red orange, asymmetrical, tubular, to 5 cm wide, 6 petal-lobes, lance-shaped, 1.6–2.5 cm long, to 0.9 cm wide, stamens 3, inflorescence bracts below flowers, purple, about 1 cm long; inflorescence of zigzagged, branched, curved spikes; blooms Mar.–Nov. **Fruit** dry, to 0.8 cm long, seeds black. **Habitat:** Cultivated and escaped in wet mountains, part shade, edges, roadsides. Altitude: 1100–2800 m. Conservation areas: CVC, LAP, PAC. **Range:** Cultivated hybrid of *Crocosmia aurea* and *C. pottsii*, both from Africa, now naturalized in many tropical regions. Invasive in Hawai'i and New Zealand.

■ *Cuphea appendiculata*
Family Lythraceae

Herb or small shrub 0.5–1.5 m tall, sparsely branched, often may stems together, upper stem dark-hairy. **Leaves** opposite, each pair at right angle to those adjacent, stalk about 0.2–1 cm long, blade 2.5–15 cm long, 2–6 cm wide, narrowly elliptic to lance-shaped, tip long-pointed, base extending down stalk, dark green, sandpapery above, paler below, hairy, veins numerous, parallel, depressed above, raised below, leaf size abruptly reduced upward on stems. **Flowers** red orange, bilaterally symmetrical, narrowly tubular, showy, 2.5–3.5 cm long, 0.5 cm wide, sticky-hairy, petal lobes 2-lipped, 4 bottom lobes with a dark reddish bristle between each lobe, stamens 11, filaments red orange, 5–9 of them longer than petal tube and clustered toward lower lip; inflorescence at apex of stem, about 15 cm long, 10 cm wide; blooms Mar.–Dec. **Fruit** dry, with 7–11 seeds, about 0.2 cm wide. **Habitat:** Wet to very wet regions in disturbed sites, open areas, roadsides. Altitude: 600–2700 m. Conservation areas: ARE, CVC, GUA, LAC, LAP, OSA, PAC. **Range:** Mex–Pan. **Notes:** There are eight species of *Cuphea* in Costa Rica.

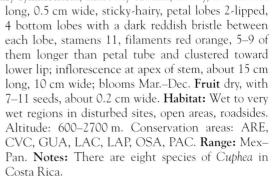

■ *Epidendrum radicans* (bandera, española, gallito, crucifix orchid)
Family Orchidaceae

Terrestrial orchid, stem 0.3–1.5 m tall, unbranched; often in large stands, rooting along partially prostrate stems; leaf base sheathing stem. **Leaves** alternate, 10 or more, ranked along upper stem, no stalk, blade 2–9 cm long, about 2 cm wide, lance-shaped, straplike, somewhat fleshy, veins inconspicuous. **Flowers** red orange with red markings, bilaterally symmetrical, about 2 cm wide, sepals and lateral petals very similar, about 1.5 cm long, 0.5 cm wide, elliptic, lower petal appearing narrowly tubular, often yellow, lip with 3 large, fringed lobes, 1.3 cm long and wide; inflorescence at top of stem, 27–42 cm long, unbranched, flowers usually blooming several at a time; blooms all year, mostly Dec.–June, Aug. **Fruit** dry, about 3 cm long, elliptic, seeds dustlike. **Habitat:** Moist to very wet regions in disturbed habitats, along roads. Altitude: 200–2300 m, mostly above 900 m. Conservation areas: ARE, CVC, GUA, LAP, OSA, PAC. Common in Central Valley, outside San José and Ruta 32 through Braulio Carrillo N.P. **Range:** Mex–Col. **Notes:** The most frequently observed orchid in Costa Rica due to its bright red orange flowers and weedy, terrestrial habit.

■ *Maxillaria fulgens*
Family Orchidaceae

Epiphyte to about 70 cm tall, branchlike stems 10–20 cm
long, upper end swollen, bulblike, each with a single leaf.
Leaves appearing alternate or clustered, blade 9–20 cm long,
2–4 cm wide, stiff, lance-shaped, folded inward along midrib,
rather yellow green, veins parallel, obscure, except for midrib.
Flowers bright red orange, rounded, small, sepals 3, broadly
egg-shaped, tips pointed, to 0.7 cm long, about 0.4 cm wide,
petals 2, narrow, smaller than sepals, lip yellow, shorter than
sepals, bulging at base, flower stalk orange, drooping; inflorescences 2–8 at the base of each stem, numerous flowers in
a dense cluster; blooms most of the year. **Fruit** not known.
Habitat: Very wet regions in forest or pasture trees. Altitude:
100–2000 m. Conservation areas: ARE, CVC, GUA, LAC,
LAP, TOR. **Range:** Nic–Ec and Ven. **Notes:** A similar species
with pinkish or white flowers is M. *pittieri*. There are about
107 species of *Maxillaria* in Costa Rica. Most are branched,
blades 2-ranked, folded along midrib; inflorescences arising
from side of stem or from the bulblike base.

■ *Galium hypocarpium*
Family Rubiaceae

Small vining or prostrate herb to 60 cm, stems slender,
4-sided, angles ridged, sometimes purplish, all parts usually
rough, hairy, stipules leaflike, included with leaves. **Leaves**
whorls of 4 per node, stalkless, blades 0.3–1.3 cm long,
0.2–0.4 cm wide, oblong, hairy on both sides, tip blunt with
tiny point, base blunt. **Flowers** white, radially symmetrical,
tubular, to 0.2 cm long, petal lobes 4, flowers solitary in leaf
axils, above 4 leaflike bracts; blooms and fruits all year. **Fruit**
fleshy, orange, to 0.3 cm, 2- or 3-lobed, often slightly hairy, 2
white seeds. **Habitat:** Moist to wet mountain forests, second
growth, roadsides, pastures, edges. Altitude: 1000–3600 m.
Conservation areas: CVC, LAC, LAP, PAC. **Range:** Mex–
Arg, Jam, DR. **Notes:** There are five species of *Galium* in
Costa Rica. All are found in mountain regions, G. *hypocar-*
pium is by far the most common. All species are weak, trailing herbs with small whorled leaves and slender, 4-angled
stems.

■ *Hoffmannia subauriculata*
Family Rubiaceae

Large understory herb 1–2 m tall, colonial by stout, creeping stems, rooting at nodes, nodes ringed, leafy stems erect, flowers and fruits produced along prostrate stems, or on erect stems, below leaves; stipules small, budlike, to 0.2–0.3 cm, between bases of leaf stalks. **Leaves** opposite, crowded near tops of erect stems, stalk short broadly winged, blades 8–25 cm long, 3–10 cm wide, broadly elliptic to widest above middle, tip pointed, base tapered to stalk, surface dark green, shiny, puckered by deeply impressed, closely spaced veins, curving upward, loop-connected near margin. **Flowers** red, small, about 0.1 cm long, radially symmetrical, anthers white; inflorescence of small branched clusters, often 1-sided below leafy part of stem; blooms June–July, Nov. **Fruit** fleshy, bright red, 0.8 cm long, 0.6 cm wide, elliptic, crowned by fleshy, 4-lobed calyx, fruit flesh spongy, white; seeds tiny, numerous, brown; fruits Dec.–Jan. **Habitat:** Wet forest understories. Altitude: 100–1900 m. Conservation areas: ARE, CVC, LAC, LAP. **Range:** CR–Ec. **Notes:** Conspicuous for its bright red fruit on leafless stems. There are about 26 species of *Hoffmannia* in Costa Rica.

■ *Nertera granadensis*
Family Rubiaceae

Tiny creeping herb to 5 cm tall, to about 1 m long, rooting at nodes, terrestrial or low epiphyte, much-branched, often forming mats, stems 4-sided, stipule minute. **Leaves** opposite, stalk to 0.6 cm long, blade 0.3–1 cm long, 0.2–1 cm wide, egg-shaped to triangular, tip and base blunt, in tight clusters at nodes, semisucculent. **Flowers** greenish, yellow, or white, solitary in axils, inconspicuous, to 0.3 cm, covered by surrounding leaves. **Fruit** fleshy, orange to red orange, translucent, to 0.7 cm, rounded; fruits all year. **Habitat:** Wet mountain forests, edges, or open sites, also on stone walls. Altitude: 1000–3500 m, mostly above 1800 m. Conservation areas: ARE, CVC, GUA, LAC, LAP, PAC. **Range:** Gua–Ven and Pr. **Notes:** *Nertera granadensis* is the only species of this genus in the American tropics and is unique in its creeping habit, high-altitude distribution, and bright orange to orange red translucent fruit.

■ *Notopleura uliginosa (Psychotria u.)*
Family Rubiaceae
Somewhat woody herb 0.5–1.5 m tall, upper stem
erect, green, stout, succulent, usually unbranched, to
1 cm diameter, nodes often thickened; stipules fleshy,
"snout-shaped" to 0.6 cm long, or more, pointing
downward between leaf stalks. **Leaves** opposite, stalk
to 6 cm long, blade 15–35 cm long, 5–13 cm wide,
elliptic, tip narrowed, long-pointed, base pointed,
slightly extending down stalk, blade shiny, dark
green above, veins slightly impressed above, curving upward, often joined in loop connections near
margin. **Flowers** white to pale purple, radially symmetrical, tubular, tube about 0.2 cm long, 0.6 cm wide at top,
petal lobes widely spreading, inflorescence axillary, of dense
branched clusters, to 5 cm long, near tops of stems (10 cm in
fruit); blooms and fruits all year. **Fruit** fleshy, bright red, to
1 cm long, 0.8 cm wide, flesh white, seeds 2. **Habitat:** Wet to
moist forest in shady understories and second growth. Altitude: Sea level to 1400 m. Conservation areas: ARE, CVC,
GUA, LAC, LAP, OSA, PAC, TOR. **Range:** Mex–Guy and
Pr. **Notes:** Similar to *Psychotria macrophylla*, and *P. aggregata*,
but those both have white fruit and 2-lobed stipules.

■ *Castilleja irasuensis*
Family Scrophulariaceae
Herb, often shrublike, 30–50 cm tall, partially parasitic on
the roots of other plants. **Leaves** alternate, 0.6–3 cm long,
narrow, deeply divided with 2–6 pinnate lobes near top, dark
red purple in full sun. **Flowers** yellow to green, narrowly tubular, bilaterally symmetrical, each flower above a larger, red
bract, petal-like, dark red at base, often yellow along margins
at top; inflorescence of spikelike clusters; blooms Mar.–Nov.
Pollinated by hummingbirds. **Fruit** dry, splitting
open to release numerous seeds. **Habitat:** Open areas
in high mountains. Altitude: 1800–3400 m. Conservation areas: CVC, LAC, LAP. **Range:** CR. **Notes:**
There are six species of *Castilleja* in Costa Rica; the
other common species are *C. arvensis*, which occurs
at lower altitudes and blooms Oct.–Apr., and *C. tala-
mancensis*, which is very similar in appearance.

◧ *Russelia sarmentosa*
Family Scrophulariaceae

Woody-based herb or weak shrub 1–2 m tall, or sometimes reclining, branches 4- to 6-ribbed, slender, green, long, arching. **Leaves** opposite, or in whorls of 3, stalk about 0.3 cm long, blade broadly egg-shaped, 2–8 cm long, 1–5 cm wide (at base), rough above, dull green, paler below, tip bluntly pointed, base broadly truncate, abruptly contracted at leaf

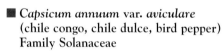

stalk to a small wedge, margins coarsely blunt-toothed. **Flowers** bright red, interior white, tubular, bilaterally symmetric, about 1–1.5 cm long, 0.3 cm wide, petal lobes 3 above, 1 below, stamens yellow; inflorescence of small clusters along ends of stems, in axils of very small leaves. **Fruit** dry, small, round, splitting open to release numerous seeds. **Habitat:** Moist to seasonally dry forest understories. Altitude: Sea level to 1600 m. Conservation areas: ARE, CVC, GUA, LAC, LAP, OSA, PAC, TEM. **Range:** Mex–Col, Cuba. **Notes:** The only species of this genus in Costa Rica.

◧ *Capsicum annuum* var. *aviculare*
(chile congo, chile dulce, bird pepper)
Family Solanaceae

Straggling herb or small shrub to 2 m tall, occasionally to 4.5 m, sometimes climbing, stems branched, green, nodes often purplish. **Leaves** alternate, stalk to 3 cm, slightly winged, blade to 10 cm long, egg-shaped, sometimes lobed. **Flowers** white, about 0.8 cm wide, petal lobes 5, pointed, anthers blue gray to violet, calyx tube blunt rimmed; flowers solitary or few at nodes; blooms and fruits most of the year. **Fruit** bright red or orange, to 3 cm long, 0.9 cm wide (usually much smaller), becoming dry, thin-walled, conical to

egg-shaped, taste is extremely *pungent-hot*. **Habitat:** Weedy forest or second growth, edges, often tangled in roadside vegetation. Altitude: Sea level to 1400 m. Conservation areas: ARE, CVC, GUA, LAP, PAC, TEM, TOR. **Range:** Most likely native to S Amer, now found in S US, Mex–Bol and Brz, WI, Madagascar, India. **Notes:** *Capsicum annuum* is the ancestor of many cultivated hot and mild peppers. The only other wild species of *Capsicum* in Costa Rica is *C. frutescens*, with flowers dull or greenish white, fruit soft, deciduous. It is much less common than *C. annuum*.

■ *Lantana camara* (cinco negritos, lantana)
  Family Verbenaceae

Herb or small shrub, old stems often woody, to about 1 m tall, most parts hairy, occasionally spiny. **Leaves** opposite, stalk to 2 cm long, blade egg-shaped, 4–11 cm long, 2–5 cm wide, tip pointed, base blunt, upper surface rough, hairy, net veins depressed, margin toothed. **Flowers** red orange, to 1 cm long, tubular, 4 petal lobes flaring, inflorescence of dense axillary, headlike clusters to 2 cm wide, flower buds yellow; blooms all year. Pollinated by butterflies, also visited by hummingbirds for nectar. **Fruit** fleshy, purple, to 0.6 cm, sweet, 2-seeded; in small, dense

clusters. Eaten by birds which disperse the seeds. **Habitat:** Wet to seasonally dry regions, a weedy plant of open, disturbed sites, roadsides. Altitude: Sea level to 1800 m. Conservation areas: ARE, CVC, LAP, GUA, HNO, OSA, PAC, TEM. **Range:** TX and Mex–Bol and Brz, WI. Introduced in Africa. Pantropical. Invasive in S Asia and Oceania. **Notes:** The leaves are poisonous. There are six species of *Lantana* in Costa Rica.

■ *Alpinia purpurata* (red ginger)
  Family Zingiberaceae

Cultivated herb 1–5 m tall, sometimes to 7 m, stems formed by overlapping leaf sheaths, usually in clumps. **Leaves** alternate, ranked along stem, stalk short to none, blade 30–75 cm long, 10–20 cm wide, oblong to narrowly elliptical, tip pointed. **Flowers** white, tubular, irregular, 2–2.5 cm long, ephemeral, often hidden by bright red bracts, showy, persistent, 3 cm long, becoming 4–6 cm long in fruit; inflorescence at top of plant, a loose conelike spike 15–30 cm long, eventually much longer, bracts spirally arranged. **Fruit** dry, 2–3 cm wide, rounded, small plants sometimes grow from old inflorescence. **Habitat:** Widely cultivated ornamental, occasionally escaping in wet forests. Altitude: Sea level to 400 m. Conservation areas: CVC, TOR. **Range:** Native to parts of Melanesia in the Pacific islands, but widely naturalized throughout the tropics. **Notes:** Both species of *Alpinia* in Costa Rica are nonnative ornamentals. *Zingiber officinale* is the ginger root used in cooking.

■ *Etlingera elatior (Nicolaia e., Phaeomeria magnifica, P. speciosa)* (bastón de emperador, torch ginger) Family Zingiberaceae

Ornamental herb 4–6 m tall, stems in clumps. **Leaves** alternate, stalk 1–4 cm long, blade to 90 cm long, 20 cm wide. **Flowers** pink, irregular, 4–5 cm long, hidden by showy red bracts with a pale margin, 7–35 cm long; inflorescence of dense, rounded or conical, headlike clusters 10–15 cm long, 7–20 cm wide, on a thick, leafless stalk, 50 cm to 2 m tall, arising from base of plant; blooms in June. **Fruit** red to yellow, 2–3 cm wide, round, becoming dry, hollow, splitting open to release seeds. **Habitat:** Widely cultivated, also escaped in very wet regions. Altitude: Sea level to 1300 m. Conservation areas: At least OSA. **Range:** Native to Java but cultivated throughout the tropics. **Notes:** This is the only species of *Etlingera* in Costa Rica. It is also used to delineate property lines.

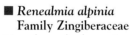

■ *Renealmia alpinia*
Family Zingiberaceae

Very large herb to 4 m tall, colonial from underground stems; leaf sheath covering stem below blade. **Leaves** alternate, 2-ranked along sides of stem, stalk short or none, blade 0.3–1.5 m long, 6–23 cm wide, elliptic, pointed at both ends, margin and midrib sometimes red, secondary veins numerous. **Flowers** red, and yellow, to 2.7 cm long, irregular, petal tube 3-lobed, lip yellow, calyx 3-lobed, red; inflorescence arising from base of plant, leafless, 12–55 cm long, 4–8 cm wide, flowers in small clusters along the floral axis, stalk 15–70 cm long; blooms and fruits July–Mar. **Fruit** with thick rind, red orange turning reddish-black, to 3.5 cm long

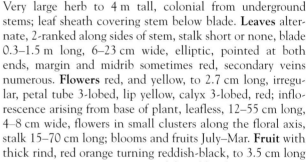

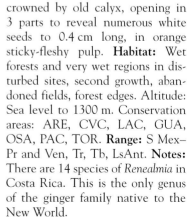

crowned by old calyx, opening in 3 parts to reveal numerous white seeds to 0.4 cm long, in orange sticky-fleshy pulp. **Habitat:** Wet forests and very wet regions in disturbed sites, second growth, abandoned fields, forest edges. Altitude: Sea level to 1300 m. Conservation areas: ARE, CVC, LAC, GUA, OSA, PAC, TOR. **Range:** S Mex– Pr and Ven, Tr, Tb, LsAnt. **Notes:** There are 14 species of *Renealmia* in Costa Rica. This is the only genus of the ginger family native to the New World.

■ *Renealmia cernua*
  Family Zingiberaceae

Herb 0.5–5 m tall, aromatic, colonial from underground stems; leaf sheath covering stem below blade, hairy, overlapping. **Leaves** alternate, 2-ranked along sides of stem, blade 10–40 cm long, 4–12 cm wide, oblong, tip pointed, secondary veins closely spaced, conspicuous on underside. **Flowers** red orange and yellow, to 1 cm long, fragrant, irregular, petal tube 3-lobed, lip orange, 3-lobed slightly longer than petal lobes, calyx 3-lobed, red to yellow, crown-shaped; inflorescence at top of stem, 4–15 cm long, 2–6 cm wide, conelike, egg-shaped, bracts yellow to red, 2–3 cm long, about 1 cm wide, thick, narrow, boat-shaped; blooms all year. **Fruit** fleshy, becoming orange then black, with whitish lines, round about 1 cm wide, crowned by orange calyx, seeds 8–15 in stringy orange pulp. **Habitat:** Wet forests, gaps, stream margins. Altitude: Sea level to 1600 m. Conservation areas: ARE, CVC, GUA, HNO, LAC, LAP, OSA, PAC, TOR. **Range:** S Mex–Pr and Ven. **Notes:** The only species of *Renealmia* in Costa Rica with inflorescence at top of the leafy stem.

COLOR OF CONSPICUOUS PART YELLOW OR YELLOW ORANGE

■ *Barleria oenothereides*
  Family Acanthaceae

Erect herb to 75 cm tall, stems green, finely hairy, nodes swollen. **Leaves** opposite, stalk, to 1.5 cm long, blade 6–23 cm long, 2–5 cm wide, lance-shaped, pointed at both ends, both sides appressed-hairy, dull green. **Flowers** bright yellow, tubular, bilaterally symmetrical, to 4 cm long, 3 cm across top, 2-lipped, lower lip with 4 narrow lobes, lobes flaring, upper lip 2 cm, not lobed, calyx hairy, lobes to 2.5 cm long, 1 cm wide, unequal, margins finely spiny; inflorescence a dense spike to 7 cm long, 3 cm wide, of overlapping, hairy, green, egg-shaped, bracts, about 3 cm long, 1 cm wide, in 4 ranks, tip long-pointed, margins finely spiny, bract folded sharply along midrib, making floral spike star-shaped in cross section; blooms Nov.–Apr., June. **Fruit** dry, 2 cm long, 1.6 cm wide, flattened, with 4 seeds. **Habitat:** Open sites or edges, weedy growth along roadsides, seasonally dry to moist regions. Altitude: Pacific slope, sea level to 1300 m. Conservation areas: ARE, CVC, GUA, LAP, PAC, TEM. **Range:** Mex–Col. **Notes:** The only other species of *Barleria*, *B. micans*, is very much like *B. oenothereides*. They are often considered one species.

331

■ *Pachystachys lutea* (shrimp plant)
  Family Acanthaceae

Horticultural herb or small shrub 0.5–1.5 m tall; stems often several, angular, becoming woody. **Leaves** opposite, stalk none, blade 7–15 cm long, 3–4 cm wide, elliptic, tip and base pointed, shiny above, veins conspicuous. **Flowers** white, bilaterally symmetric, about 5 cm long, tubular, 2-lipped, upper lip 2-lobed, lower lip 3-lobed; bracts bright yellow, 1–2 cm long, egg-shaped, in 4 rows, in dense spikelike clusters to 8 cm long at tips of stems. **Fruit** dry. **Habitat:** Garden plant, widely cultivated but not escaping. **Range:** Native to Pr. **Notes:** This is the only species of *Pachystachys* in Costa Rica.

■ *Anthurium ochranthum*
  Family Araceae

Terrestrial herb to 1.5 m tall or more, stem short, creeping, leafy tip erect, to 45 cm high, 2–4 cm thick. **Leaves** alternate, tufted, stalk, slender, 30–70 cm long, 0.5–0.8 cm wide, widened only at base, dark greenish brown; blade 40–75 cm long, 18–48 cm wide, arrow-shaped, tip long-pointed, lobes 11–22 cm long, broadly rounded, ends curved back, midrib raised on both sides, surface firm, slightly puckered, secondary veins loop-connected at margin. **Flowers** bright yellow, minute, densely crowded on a fleshy spike 7–22 cm long, to 0.8 cm wide, inflorescence bract green to purplish, 8–18 cm long, 1–2 cm wide, lance-shaped, tapered to a point; inflorescence stalk 15–50 cm long, stiff, slender, erect, greenish brown; blooms and fruits all year. **Fruit** fleshy, deep purple violet, to 0.9 cm long, fruiting spike 11–24 cm long. **Habitat:** Wet forest understories. Altitude: Sea level to 2300 m, mostly above 1000 m. Conservation areas: ARE, GUA, HNO, LAC, OSA, PAC, TOR. **Range:** SE Nic–NW Col.

■ *Anthurium subsignatum* (mano de tigre)
  Family Araceae

Epiphytic herb, creeping on tree trunks, stem to about 15 cm long, 2 cm diameter; aerial roots pale green, thin, to 0.4 cm thick. **Leaves** alternate, stalk 21–60 cm long; blade 20–65 cm long, 25–60 cm wide, arrow-shaped to heart-shaped, more or less deeply 3-lobed, tip pointed, basal lobes 4–20 cm long, widely spreading, tips blunt, undersurface pale, midrib raised on both sides, secondary veins joined by a marginal vein. **Flowers** bright yellow, to yellow green, minute, densely crowded on a fleshy spike 8–28 cm long, to 0.9 cm wide, tapered to a point; inflorescence bract pale green, long, thin, 7–29 cm long, 1–3 cm wide, lance-shaped, tip tapered to a long point, base blunt, angled away from spike; inflorescence stalk 13–37 cm long; blooms and fruits on and off most of the year, mostly Mar.–Oct. **Fruit** fleshy, red to dark purple, about 0.5 cm long, tip pointed; 1–2 seeds; fruit spike to 30 cm long. **Habitat:** Wet, lowland forests, often low on tree trunks. Altitude: Sea level to 350 m, Caribbean slope. Conservation areas: CVC, LAC, TOR (most common). **Range:** SE Nic–Col.

■ *Acmella oppositifolia* (oppositeleaf spotflower)
  Family Asteraceae

Low herbaceous ground cover 20–60 cm tall, sprawling, rooting at lower nodes, stems green, hairy, flowering stem erect. **Leaves** opposite, stalk 0.5–2 cm long, blade 3–8 cm long, 0.5–3 cm wide, egg-shaped to lance-shaped, tip pointed, base blunt or tapered, veins palmate at base, margin coarsely toothed. **Flowers** yellow, in compact heads arising from a bract-covered base, flowers tubular, of two forms, tiny, radially symmetrical flowers in a slightly cone-shaped central disk, about 0.5–0.7 cm wide, surrounded by a ring of about 8 bilaterally symmetrical flowers with 1 enlarged petal (rays), ray flowers 0.3–1 cm long, 0.5 cm wide, tip 3-toothed; heads solitary, on stalk about 5.5 cm, long; blooms June–Sept. **Fruit** dry, inconspicuous, 1-seeded; floral disk elongated in fruit. **Habitat:** Wet, disturbed forest understories, along old roads, edges, pastures in mountains. Altitude: 1100–2200 m. Conservation areas: ARE, CVC, LAP. **Range:** Mex–Par, Cuba. **Notes:** There are six species of *Acmella* in Costa Rica. The most common is *A. radicans*, which is taller and has whitish flowers and a disagreeable odor.

■ *Baltimora recta* (florecilla)
Family Asteraceae

Annual herb 0.7–3 m tall, branching opposite, stems very rough near top. **Leaves** opposite, stalk 1–7 cm long, blade 3–15 cm long, 2–12 cm wide, egg-shaped, 3-veined from base, tip long-pointed, base blunt to pointed, both sides rough-textured. **Flowers** yellow, in compact heads 1–2 cm wide, to 0.8 cm tall, arising from a bract-covered base, flowers tubular, of two forms, a central disk of 16 or more, tiny, yellow, radially symmetrical flowers with black anthers, surrounded by a ring of 3–8 bilaterally symmetrical flowers with 1 enlarged petal (rays), ray flowers about 0.5 cm long, 0.2 cm wide, tips usually notched, basal bracts 3–8, about 0.5 cm long, overlapping; blooms Apr.–Nov. **Fruit** dry, 1-seeded, 0.3 cm long, 3-sided, sometimes warty. **Habitat:** Wet to seasonally dry regions, in open sites, wet roadsides, pastures. Sometimes found in dense stands. Altitude: Sea level to 800 m, mostly in the Pacific lowlands. Conservation areas: GUA, OSA, PAC, TEM. **Range:** Mex–Pan. **Notes:** This is the only species of *Baltimora* in Costa Rica.

■ *Cirsium subcoriaceum*
Family Asteraceae

Coarse, spiny annual herb to 4 m tall, young parts densely woolly. **Leaves** alternate, lower leaves 40 cm long, 25 cm wide, smaller upward on stem, deeply lobed and toothed, lobes spine- tipped, spines to 1 cm long, leaf bases clasping stem, blades woolly below, margins spiny. **Flowers** pale yellow to rose pink, very small, densely crowded in a compact head to 6 cm tall, 4 cm wide, that arises from a bract-covered floral base, flowers tubular, radially symmetrical, bracts of base overlapping, spine-tipped; blooms most of the year. **Fruit** 1-seeded, with a tuft of hairs, wind dispersed. **Habitat:** Open sites of high-elevation areas, roadsides, pastures. Altitude: 1700–3500 m. Conservation areas: CVC, LAC, LAP, PAC. **Range:** Mex–Pan. **Notes:** Much like *C. mexicanum*, which has purple flowers.

■ *Erato volcanica*
Family Asteraceae

Shrub or woody herb 1.5–3.5 m tall, sap milky. **Leaves** opposite, 8–26 cm long, 4–23 cm wide egg-shaped with a few large teeth, stalks clasping stem, densely white-woolly below, upper leaves lance-shaped. **Flowers** yellow, in heads of small, bilaterally symmetrical, petal-like flowers on a bract covered base, collectively showy, heads 2–3 cm wide; blooms most of the year. **Fruit** dry, 1-seeded, plumed. **Habitat:** Open, shrubby, second growth sites in mountains. Altitude: 900–2000 m. Conservation areas: ARE, CVC, LAP. **Range:** CR–Col at least. **Notes:** There is one other species of *Erato* in Costa Rica.

■ *Hypochoeris radicata* (cat's ear)
Family Asteraceae

Small herb, flowering stems to 60 cm tall, hairy, sap milky, flowering stem slender, sometimes branched. **Leaves** whorled in a rosette at base of plant, numerous, to 8 cm long, lance-shaped, broadest near apex, surface coarsely hairy, margin toothed to pinnately lobed. **Flowers** yellow, small, bilaterally symmetrical, tubular, with 1 enlarged petal (rays), about 1.5 cm long, tips toothed, flowers densely crowded in showy, dome-shaped heads, about 2 cm wide, on a bract covered base; basal bracts green, about 1 cm long, in several rows; inflorescence branched, heads at ends of stalks to 25 cm long; blooms most of the year. **Fruit** dry, 1-seeded, to 0.7 cm long, with a white plume on a long, thin neck; dispersed by wind. **Habitat:** Very common in open areas, along roadsides in mountains. Altitude: 1100–3400 m. Conservation areas: ARE, CVC, HNO, LAP, PAC. **Range:** A weed native to Eurasia found in temperate and cool tropical regions, north into Canada. **Notes:** This is the only species of *Hypochoeris* in Costa Rica.

335

■ *Jaegeria hirta*
Family Asteraceae

Annual herb to 55 cm tall, often rooting at lower nodes, stems reddish green, hairy, especially at nodes. **Leaves** opposite, mostly stalkless, blade 1–6 cm long, 0.3–2 cm wide, narrowly elliptic to egg-shaped, tip pointed, base rounded, hairy on both sides, major veins 3, conspicuous below, margin often toothed. **Flowers** yellow to white, of two types in very small heads 0.3–1 cm wide, 0.3–0.6 cm tall, on a bract-covered base, central disk flowers tubular, numerous, yellow,

peripheral ray flowers bilaterally symmetrical, 0.2–0.5 cm long, about 0.1 cm wide, tip 2- to 3-lobed, basal bracts 5–12, hairy, in 1 row, about 0.2–0.5 cm long, about 0.1 cm wide; flower heads solitary on long slender stalks; blooms most of the year. **Fruit** dry, 1-seeded, shiny, black, about 0.1 cm long. **Habitat:** Weedy herb of disturbed habitats, pastures, roadsides, at mid- to high elevations. Altitude: 800–3200 m. Conservation areas: ARE, CVC, LAC, LAP, PAC. **Range:** N Mex–Ur. **Notes:** This is the only species of *Jaegeria* in Costa Rica.

■ *Melampodium perfoliatum*
Family Asteraceae

Annual herb to 2 m tall, stems darkish. **Leaves** opposite, 5–17 cm long, 2–12 cm wide, triangular, bases joined across stem with a cup, margin toothed. **Flowers** yellow, of two

types, in heads on a bract-covered base, central disk flowers tubular, radially symmetrical, peripheral ray flowers bilaterally symmetrical, 8–13, with 1 large petal lobe, tips toothed, basal bracts 5, sepal-like, longer and wider than ray flowers; heads solitary on long, thin stalks from upper axils; blooms July–Nov. **Fruit** dry, 1-seeded, enclosed in old flower parts. **Habitat:** Open areas. Altitude: Sea level to 1100 m. Conservation areas: CVC, PAC. **Range:** Mex, Gua, CR. **Notes:** There are six species of *Melampodium* in Costa Rica.

■ *Munnozia wilburii*
Family Asteraceae

Herb or shrub to 3 m tall, sap milky, most parts densely white-woolly, stems about 0.8 cm wide; stipules paired, round tipped, lobed at base, 1.5 cm wide, sometimes purplish. **Leaves** opposite, stalk 8 cm long, blade about 60 cm long, 13 cm wide across base, pale green, densely fine-woolly on both sides, hairs matted, arrow-shaped or triangular, tip pointed, base flat, with flaring to horizontal lobes at corners, central part of base extending down leaf stalk, veins palmate above base, margin coarsely toothed. **Flowers** yellow, of two types in heads about 2 cm wide, on a bract-covered base about 0.7 cm long, 0.6 cm wide, central disk flowers tubular, peripheral ray flowers with 1 extended petal lobe, about 30 per head, disk 1 cm wide, basal bracts green, overlapping in 3 series, appressed; inflorescence of widely branched clusters, about 25 cm tall, at top of plant; blooms Jan.–Mar. **Fruit** dry, 1-seeded. **Habitat:** Open areas in mountains. Altitude: 1300–2200 m. Conservation areas: ARE, CVC, LAP, TEM. **Range:** Endemic to CR. **Notes:** The only other species of *Munnozia* in Costa Rica is M. *senecionidis*, which is less common.

■ *Neurolaena lobata* (gavilana)
Family Asteraceae

Herb to 3 m tall, sometimes shrubby, lower stem unbranched, green, stout, ribbed, hairy. **Leaves** alternate, stalk about 3 cm long, blade 8–26 cm long, 2–7 cm wide, narrowly oblong, mostly 3-lobed near base of blade, tapered at both ends, hairy on both sides, sticky on underside, margins coarsely toothed. **Flowers** yellow, small, radially symmetrical, tubular; densely crowded in heads of about 30 flowers, 0.4–0.8 cm tall, about 0.3 cm wide, above small basal bracts in 3–4 rows, bracts overlapping, straw color; inflorescence of large clusters of flower heads at ends of branches; blooms all year, mostly Jan.–Mar. **Fruit** dry, 1-seeded, whitish-plumed. **Habitat:** Moist to wet regions, open sites, edges, roadsides. Altitude: Sea level to 1800 m. Conservation areas: ARE, CVC, GUA, HNO, LAC, LAP, OSA, PAC, TEM, TOR. **Range:** Mex–S Amer, Ant. **Notes:** Leaves used to make tea for stomach ailments. This is the only species of *Neurolaena* in Costa Rica.

■ *Senecio oerstedianus*
Family Asteraceae
Stout herb 0.3–1.5 m tall, arising from underground stems, often forming large stands; most parts white-woolly. **Leaves** alternate, stalk to about 12 cm long, sheathing stem and making blade appear stalkless, blade 6–25 cm long, 2–10 cm wide (upper leaves smaller), lance-shaped, tip pointed or rounded, base slightly lobed; thick, leathery, dark green, shiny, midrib white, densely white woolly below, margin toothed. **Flowers** yellow, tiny, densely crowded in heads, outer flowers (rays) about 8, yellow, bilaterally symmetrical with 1 large petal, to 1 cm long, 0.4 cm wide, disk flowers radially symmetrical, tubular, smaller, darker; flower heads about 3 cm long, basal bracts narrow, woolly; inflorescence of a large, branched cluster at top of plant; blooms most of the year, especially Nov.–Feb. **Fruit** dry, 1-seeded, crowned by long, white, hairlike bristles. **Habitat:** Rocky, open sites, roadsides, in mountains. Altitude: 3000–3500 m. Conservation areas: CVC, LAP, PAC. **Range:** CR, Pan. **Notes:** There are at least 16 species of *Senecio* in Costa Rica.

■ *Sphagneticola trilobata (Wedelia t.)*
(clavellin de playa, wedelia)
Family Asteraceae
Low, trailing or vining, herb, rooting at nodes, often in large patches, stems 10–40 cm long, flowering stems erect. **Leaves** opposite, stalk to 0.5 cm long, blade 4–9 cm long, 2–5 cm wide, egg-shaped, often 3-lobed, tip pointed, base wedge-shaped, margins with large, irregular teeth, sometimes lobed. **Flowers** yellow, of two types, in heads about 2 cm wide, about 1 cm tall, on a base of small stiff, papery bracts, central disk flowers tiny, numerous, peripheral ray flowers petal-like 4–8,

with 1 extended petal lobe, 0.5–1.5 cm long, tips toothed; heads solitary at ends of stalks 3–10 cm long; blooms most of the year, especially June–Sept. **Fruit** dry, 1-seeded, finely warty, to 0.5 cm long. **Habitat:** Wet regions in open sites, especially near beaches; also cultivated. Altitude: Sea level to 200 m, usually below 100 m. Conservation areas: ICO, LAC, OSA, PAC, TEM, TOR. **Range:** Mex–Pr. Has become an invasive weed in Australia, Hawai'i, many parts of Oceania. **Notes:** This is the only species of *Sphagneticola* in Costa Rica. It is often included in the genus *Wedelia*.

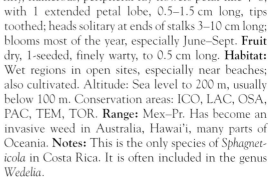

■ *Tithonia diversifolia*
Family Asteraceae

Large herb, often shrublike, to 2 m tall. **Leaves** alternate, stalk slender, base clasping stem, margin sometimes lobed, blade egg-shaped, 2- to 3-lobed, pointed at both ends, lobe tips pointed, dark green, rough above. **Flowers** dark yellow, densely crowded in heads, outer ring bilaterally symmetrical (rays) showy, 4–5 cm long, tips 2–3 toothed, central disc of numerous, tiny, radially symmetrical flowers 3–4 cm wide, anthers black with yellow tips; base of flower heads to 4 cm wide, basal bracts in several rows, outer bracts egg-shaped, to 1 cm long, inner bracts twice as long; flower stalks 8–15 cm long, expanded at tops; blooms Sept.–Nov., Mar., Apr. **Fruit** flat, 1-seeded 0.5 cm long with 2 awns 0.5 cm long. **Habitat:** Cultivated and wild in open sites. Altitude: 70–1800 m. Conservation areas: CVC, LAC. **Range:** Mex–Pan. Introduced in S Africa; invasive on Hawai'i and other Pacific islands. **Notes:** Very similar to *T. rotundifolia*, which has ray flowers 2–3 cm long and is more common, found from sea level to 1000 m, mostly on the Pacific slope. There are two other species of *Tithonia* in Costa Rica, both are uncommon.

■ *Tridax procumbens*
Family Asteraceae

Small trailing herb 14–40 cm tall, stems branching, often reddish, hairy. **Leaves** opposite, stalk 0.2–2 cm, blade 1–6 cm long, 0.5–4 cm wide, egg- to lance-shaped, often lobed near base, pointed at both ends, hairy on both sides, margins often coarsely toothed, bases clasping stem. **Flowers** pale yellow to white, of two types in very small heads on a base of small bracts, central disk flowers tubular, radially symmetrical, numerous, yellow, often purple-tinged; peripheral ray flowers 3–6, petal-like with 1 extended lobe, to 0.4 cm long, tip 2- to 3-lobed; inflorescence of solitary heads about 1–2 cm wide including rays, about 1 cm tall, broader than tall, basal bracts hairy, in 2–3 rows, margins often purple, stalks to 18 cm long, hairy. **Fruit** dry, 1-seeded plumed, about 0.2 cm long. **Habitat:** Very wet to seasonally dry regions, a very common weed, in open sites, roadsides. Altitude: Sea level to 1300 m, Pacific slope. Conservation areas: ARE, CVC, GUA, OSA, PAC, TEM. **Range:** Mex–Ven, Col–Bol. Has become invasive in the Galápagos Islands, some other Pacific islands, parts of SE Asia. **Notes:** This is the only species of *Tridax* in Costa Rica.

339

■ *Youngia japonica*
Family Asteraceae

Herb 10–50 cm tall, flowering stalk leafless, sap milky. **Leaves** all in a basal rosette, stalk to 6 cm long, blade 3–15 cm long, to 5 cm, wide, lance-shaped, broadest near apex, lower part pinnately divided, apical lobe enlarged, rounded at tip, base narrowed to stalk, margin often bluntly toothed. **Flowers** yellow, very small, bilaterally symmetrical with 1 large petal, to 0.7 cm long, tip 5-toothed, sometimes reddish, flowers, about 15, densely crowded in a compact head that arises from a bract-covered floral base about 0.5 cm long, anthers dark green and black, flowers heads 0.5 cm tall, 0.4 cm wide, basal bracts in 2 rows, outer bracts 0.1 cm, pinkish, inner bracts 0.6 cm, green with purplish midrib, tips dark, inflorescence branched, leafless, hairy, often reddish; blooms all year. **Fruit** dry, 1-seeded, white-plumed, about 0.2 cm long. **Habitat:** Open, disturbed sites, curbs, vacant lots roadsides, pastures, occasionally epiphytic. Altitude: 550–3000 m. Conservation areas: ARE, CVC, GUA, LAP, PAC. **Range:** Native to E Asia. Invasive in some Pacific islands. **Notes:** This is the only species of *Youngia* in Costa Rica.

■ *Bromelia pinguin* (piñuela, piro)
Family Bromeliaceae

Large colonial, terrestrial herb 1–1.5 m tall, forming dense stands. **Leaves** alternate, spirally arranged, forming a large, dense rosette, blade 1–2.2 m long, 2.5–4.5 cm wide, narrow, elongate; tip pointed, base very broad, sheathing, surface densely woolly-scaly, dark green above, margins armed with stout spines to 1 cm long; leaves near center often becoming red when plant blooms. **Flowers** rose to lilac with white base and margins, 1.5–2 cm long; inflorescence bracts cream; inflorescence whitish-scaly, 20–40 cm, long, elongate, branches 5–13 cm long; stalk 22–58 cm tall covered with bracts; blooms on and off most of the year, especially May–

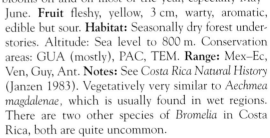

June. **Fruit** fleshy, yellow, 3 cm, warty, aromatic, edible but sour. **Habitat:** Seasonally dry forest understories. Altitude: Sea level to 800 m. Conservation areas: GUA (mostly), PAC, TEM. **Range:** Mex–Ec, Ven, Guy, Ant. **Notes:** See *Costa Rica Natural History* (Janzen 1983). Vegetatively very similar to *Aechmea magdalenae*, which is usually found in wet regions. There are two other species of *Bromelia* in Costa Rica, both are quite uncommon.

■ *Guzmania nicaraguensis*
Family Bromeliaceae

Epiphyte, low on tree trunks and logs, to 40 cm tall, no stem. **Leaves** alternate, 10–15, spirally arranged, forming a rosette, no stalk, blade 23–41 cm long, 1–2.5 cm wide, thin, flexible; tip pointed, base broad, sheathing, striped with red longitudinal lines, dotted with purple, margins smooth. **Flowers** bright yellow about 2 cm long, 3 petals, anthers black, inflorescence bracts bright orange to greenish, 5–6.6 cm long; inflorescence unbranched; blooms Jan.–Apr. **Fruit** dry, 3 cm long, opening along sutures to release plumed seeds. **Habitat:** Wet mountain forests. Altitude: 600–1700 m. Conservation areas: ARE, CVC, GUA, LAC. **Range:** Mex–Pan. **Notes:** There are 28 species of *Guzmania* in Costa Rica. They are very similar to *Tillandsia* and *Werauhia*.

■ *Guzmania plicatifolia*
Family Bromeliaceae

Epiphytic or terrestrial herb to 1 m tall, no stem. **Leaves** alternate, spirally arranged, no stalk, blade 1–1.5 m long, cm 1–2 cm wide, conspicuously pleated lengthwise, flexible; tip pointed, base broad, sheathing, sheath purple, often striped with green above, margins smooth. **Flowers** yellow, 3 petals, 1.5–2 cm long; flower bracts pale orange and yellow, to red brown, 2–2.5 cm long, overlapping; inflorescence 15–41 cm long, branched once, erect, branches 4–9 cm long densely 12–15 flowered; blooms Jan.–Aug. **Fruit** dry, 2 cm long, splitting open to release plumed seeds. **Habitat:** Very wet forests. Altitude: 700–1700 m. Conservation areas: ARE, CVC, LAC, LAP. **Range:** CR, Pan.

■ *Nopalea guatemalensis* (cactus)
Family Cactaceae

Low terrestrial cactus about 1.5 m tall, often hanging or trailing, stems consisting of flat, dull green, elliptic pad-like segments, each 6–18 cm long, 5–8 cm wide, generally widest above middle, dotted with small cushions of bristles

and spines 1–6 cm long. **Leaves** none. **Flowers** clear yellow, showy, 4–5 cm long, about 2 cm wide, petals numerous, about 2 cm long, shield-shaped, with a small abrupt point at top; blooms Jan.–Mar. **Fruit** fleshy, red, with truncate top from flower scar, 3–4 cm long, dotted with small cushions of bristles, seeds numerous; Mar.–July. **Habitat:** Seasonally dry scrub, rocky cliffs. Altitude: Pacific lowlands, sea level to 500 m. Conservation areas: CVC, GUA, TEM. **Range:** Gua–CR. **Notes:** There are about five species of *Opuntia* in Costa Rica; this is the most common.

■ *Canna glauca* (platanilla)
Family Cannaceae

Herb 1–2 m tall, waxy gray green, stems formed by overlapping leaf sheaths, sap gummy. **Leaves** alternate, spirally arranged, stalk winged merging with leaf sheath, blade 25–70 cm long, 6–12 cm wide, narrowly elliptic, tip pointed, base tapered to a stalk, surface gray green, margin entire. **Flowers** pale yellow, showy, irregular, 6–7 cm long, about 6 cm wide, petals 3, sepals 3, petal-like, stamens 2–6, petal-like, narrow, ovary inferior; inflorescence densely branched, contracted, spikelike, flowers emerging amid bracts, not much taller than leaves; blooms June–Mar. **Fruit** pale green, drying brown, 2–3 cm wide, almost ball-shaped, surface finely warty, crowned by old calyx lobes; seeds numerous, black. **Habitat:** Seasonally dry regions in open, sunny marshes, wet soil, or shallow water. Altitude: Sea level to 50 m, Pacific lowlands. Conservation areas: TEM. Common in Palo Verde marsh with *Thalia geniculata*. **Range:** S Mex–Arg. **Notes:** There are five species of *Canna* in Costa Rica.

■ *Cleome viscosa*
Family Capparaceae

Herb 0.1–1.6 m tall, erect, all parts sticky-hairy, stems green, slender, branched, aromatic. **Leaves** alternate, 3- to 5-parted, stalk 1–6 cm, leaflets 1–6 cm long, 0.5–3 cm long, narrowly egg-shaped, tip pointed to rounded, base wedge-shaped. **Flowers** yellow, base sometimes purple, bilaterally symmetrical, petals 4, about 1 cm long, anthers 14–25, purplish, some shorter than others, pistil green; flowers mostly solitary; blooms May–Dec. **Fruit** linear, cylindrical pod, 3–8 cm long, to 0.4 cm wide, sticky-hairy, tipped by old stigma, splitting open to release numerous, small, round seeds. **Habitat:** Wet to seasonally dry lowlands, in open areas, roadsides, Altitude: Sea level to 400 m, Pacific slope. Conservation areas: GUA, LAP, OSA, PAC, TEM. **Range:** Weedy plant native to Asia, now pantropical. Invasive on some Pacific islands. **Notes:** There are eight species of *Cleome* in Costa Rica. The other common species is *C. pilosa*, which has white to violet flowers.

■ *Costus curvibracteatus* (caña agria)
Family Costaceae

Stout unbranched herb 1–3.5 m tall, colonial from underground stems; aboveground stem canelike, about 2.5 cm wide; leaf sheaths hairy, with 2 small lobes at top, 0.5–1 cm, long, with red margin. **Leaves** alternate, spirally arranged, stalk short, hairy, blade 15–35 cm long, 5–10 cm wide, tip pointed, base wedge-shaped to blunt, dark green above, veins at an acute angle to midrib. **Flowers** yellow, red, or orange, about 3 cm wide, irregular, petals 3, fused at base, stamens petal-like, forming a lip about 3 cm long, 2 cm wide, calyx red, 1–1.5 cm long; inflorescence bracts orange with yellow tips to red or yellow, tips pointed, leathery; inflorescence broadly egg-shaped, conelike, 6–18 cm long, 3–9 cm wide, at top of stem; blooms most of the year, especially Mar.–June. **Fruit** dry, about 1.5 cm long; splitting open to reveal numerous, seeds with a white fleshy coating. **Habitat:** Wet and very wet forest understories, second growth, roadsides. Altitude: 50–1600 m. Conservation areas: ARE, CVC, LAC, LAP. **Range:** Nic–Col. **Notes:** There are 24 species of *Costus* in Costa Rica. Most are quite similar to one another.

343

■ *Euphorbia heterophylla (Poinsettia h.)*
Family Euphorbiaceae

Upright herb to 70 cm tall, sap milky, stems green. **Leaves** alternate below, opposite above, stalk to 3 cm long, blade 2–11 cm long, 2–7 cm wide, irregularly elliptic, broadly, irregularly lobed, tip pointed, base wedge-shaped. **Flowers** yellow, very small, without petals, surrounded by leaflike bracts with white base, just below flowers; inflorescences to 15 cm long, branched, with small clusters of flowers at ends of stems;

blooms most of the year, but during the rainy season in seasonally dry regions. **Fruit** dry, about 0.5 cm, 3-lobed, splitting open to release seeds; fruit present most of the year. **Habitat:** Open, sunny sites, roadsides, second growth. Altitude: Sea level to 1800 m. Conservation areas: ARE, CVC, GUA, LAC, LAP, OSA, PAC, TEM. **Range:** S US–Arg, WI. Naturalized in Old World tropics; invasive in SE Asia and some Pacific islands. **Notes:** A weedy species appearing much like the familiar Christmas poinsettia, *E. pulcherrima*, a shrub with red bracts. There are about 18 species of *Euphorbia* in Costa Rica.

■ *Phyllanthus urinaria* (chancapiedras, riñoncillo)
Family Euphorbiaceae

Shrubby herb 10–90 cm tall, mostly with 1 main stem and pinnately arranged branches, appearing like pinnate leaves. **Leaves** alternate, ranked along lateral branches, almost stalkless, blade 0.4–1.4 cm long, 0.2–0.5 cm wide, narrowly oblong, tip blunt, base often asymmetric, dull green, margins minutely hairy-fringed. **Flowers** yellow small, inconspicuous mostly less than 0.1 cm long, in leaf axils, males and females

separate; blooms and fruits most of the year. **Fruit** dry, about 0.2 cm, grooved, in rows along underside of leafy stems. **Habitat:** Moist to wet regions, in open, often weedy sites, roadsides, pastures, vacant lots. Altitude: Sea level to 1400 m. Conservation areas: ARE, CVC, GUA, ICO, LAC, LAP, OSA, PAC, TEM, TOR. **Range:** Native to Asia but naturalized throughout the tropics. **Notes:** Formerly used as a medicinal. Similar species are *P. niruri*, found above 1000 m elevation, and *P. stipularis*, found in wet habitats or shallow water. There are about 14 species of *Phyllanthus* in Costa Rica.

■ *Ricinus communis* (higuerillo,
si-krá, castor bean plant)
Family Euphorbiaceae

Shrubby herb 1–4 m tall. **Leaves** alternate, stalk 20–
60 cm long, attached inside edge of blade, often reddish, blade 12–48 cm long and wide, palmately 6- to
11-lobed, lobe tips pointed, margins toothed. **Flowers** pale yellow to white, very small, without petals,
in long spikes, males and females separate, anthers
white, stigmas red; blooms and fruits July–Feb.
Fruit becoming dry, purplish brown, round, spiny,
to 1.5 cm wide, opening in 3 sections to release red
or green seeds or with a mottled brown and white
pattern. **Habitat:** Cultivated, escaping into open areas, along
roadsides. Altitude: Sea level to 1550 m. Conservation areas:
CVC, GUA, LAP, PAC, TEM, TOR. **Range:** Native to
Africa, naturalized throughout the tropics and subtropics.
Notes: Used for 5000 years in southern Europe. Castor oil is
pressed from seeds. *Seeds are very toxic*. This is the only species of *Ricinus* worldwide.

■ *Chamaecrista nictitans*
Family Fabaceae/Caesalpinioideae

Herb or shrubby herb 10–80 cm tall, branched, stems
hairy, green, often with reddish upper surface; stipules narrow, paired, on either side stalk base, 1.3 cm long, 0.3 cm
wide. **Leaves** alternate, evenly pinnate, about 10 cm long,
3 cm wide, midrib hairy, stalk 0.7 cm, with 2 dark, stalked
structures, leaflets 7–26 pairs, oblong, 0.6–2 cm long, about
0.2 cm wide, hairy below, leaf folding slowly when touched.
Flowers yellow, 1 cm wide, bilaterally symmetrical, petals 5,
unequal, the largest to 0.8 cm long, others much smaller, all
very narrow at base, stamens 5, very short, unequal,
sepals 5, narrow; flowers bloom a few at a time in leaf
axils along underside of stem; Aug. Jan., May. **Fruit**

dry, pods, 2–4 cm long, 0.3–0.6 cm wide, flat, oblong,
splitting open to release seeds. **Habitat:** Wet to sea-
sonally dry regions in open sites, roadsides, pastures.
Altitude: Sea level to 2150 m, mostly below 1200 m.
Conservation areas: ARE, CVC, GUA, HNO, LAP,
OSA, PAC, TEM, TOR. **Range:** Widely distributed
through temperate and tropical Americas. **Notes:**
There are seven species of *Chamaecrista* in Costa
Rica, this is the most common.

■ *Aeschynomene scabra*
   Family Fabaceae/Faboideae

Sprawling or vinelike herb or shrub 2–3 m tall, stems green, bristly-hairy. **Leaves** alternate, finely pinnately compound, leaflets 30–55, 0.5–1.5 cm long, 0.2–0.3 cm wide, linear to oblong, both ends blunt. **Flowers** yellow, sometimes with reddish veins, bilaterally symmetrical, about 1 cm long, bean-flower-shaped, petals 5, upper petal rounded, very narrow at base, the 2 side petals about as long as upper one, lower petal (keel) curved inward, widest at top, calyx 2-lipped, 0.7 cm long; inflorescence of unbranched, spikelike clusters; blooms Oct.–Nov. **Fruit** dry, flattened, becoming blackish when ripe, composed of 9–14 jointed segments 0.3 cm long, and about as wide, usually hairy, the upper margins smooth, the lower margins bluntly toothed, each with a single dark seed about 0.3 cm long. **Habitat:** Moist to seasonally dry regions in open sites. Altitude: Pacific lowlands, sea level to 90 m. Conservation areas: PAC, TEM. Seen in La Palma, OSA. **Range:** Mex–Brz. **Notes:** There are nine species of *Aeschynomene* in Costa Rica.

■ *Arachis pintoi (A. glabrata)* (perennial peanut)
   Family Fabaceae/Faboideae

Creeping colonial herb, spreading by underground stems (rhizomes), forming dense mats; widely used as a ground cover; stems weak, prostrate, rooting at nodes, covered with weak prickles. **Leaves** alternate, stalk to 7 cm long, evenly pinnate with 4 leaflets to 4 cm long, 2 cm wide, lance-shaped to widest above middle, tip with a bristle. **Flowers** yellow, bilat-

erally symmetric, bean-flower-shaped, 1.5–2.5 cm wide, upper petal (banner) the largest; flowers solitary in upper nodes, stalk 10 cm long. **Fruit** dry, pod underground but rarely produced, about 1 cm long. **Habitat:** Cultivated horticultural ground cover, seen mostly in lowland areas. Altitude: Seen in lowland to midelevation regions. Conservation areas: Probably not escaping from cultivation. **Range:** Native to Brz, Arg, Par. **Notes:** There are 22 species of *Arachis*; *A. hypogea* is the common peanut. *Arachis pintoi* is also used as forage for cattle and other animals in some countries.

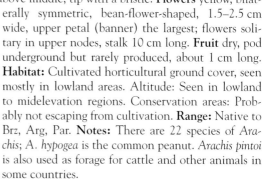

■ *Crotalaria retusa* (pitillo, gallinita)
Family Fabaceae/Faboideae

Stout, branched herb 0.4–1 m tall, stems ribbed, foliage and stems waxy bluish green. **Leaves** alternate, stalk little to none, blade simple, 3–10 cm long, 1.5–2.5 cm wide, widest above middle, tip rounded to notched, base tapered. **Flowers** yellow with reddish markings on back, bean-flower-shaped, top petal 2.5 cm long, 3 cm wide, side petals smaller; along unbranched stalks at tips of branches; blooms all year. **Fruit** dry, pods inflated, about 4 cm long, 1 cm wide, often purplish, becoming black; seeds 0.2 cm, black, kidney-shaped. **Habitat:** Open sites, along roadsides, rivers, beaches, in sandy soil. Altitude: Sea level to 1100 m. Conservation areas: ARE, GUA, LAC, LAP, PAC, TEM. Seen along beach in Puerto Viejo, Limón. **Range:** FL, Mex–Ec and Ven, Pr, Par, WI. **Notes:** There are 11 species of *Crotalaria* in Costa Rica, most have yellow flowers and inflated pods; *C. retusa* and *C. sagittalis* are the most common.

■ *Crotalaria vitellina*
Family Fabaceae/Faboideae

Shrubby herb to about 1.5 m tall, branched from base, bark tan, new growth green finely appressed rusty-hairy. **Leaves** alternate, 3-parted, stalk to 5 cm, leaflets 5–7.5 cm long, about 2 cm wide, elliptic, dark green above, waxy pale below, tip abruptly pointed, base wedge-shaped. **Flowers** yellow with red or purple markings, bean-flower-shaped, to 1.5 cm, top petal erect, bottom petal (keel) sharply hooked forward; inflorescence of axillary, unbranched, spikelike clusters; blooms Sept.–Dec. **Fruit** dry, pods inflated, 2 cm long, 0.6 diameter, gray green, becoming purple black. **Habitat:** Open sites, second growth. Altitude: Pacific slope, sea level to 1800 m. Conservation areas: CVC, LAP, PAC, TEM. Seen near El Rodeo. **Range:** Mex–Brz.

■ *Sesbania herbacea (S. emerus)*
(guanacastillo, pata de garza)
Family Fabaceae/Faboideae

Very large annual herb 2–3 (rarely to 6) m tall, main stem 2–3 cm diameter, branches numerous, short, slender, plant appearing rather diaphanous and open. **Leaves** alternate, once pinnate, 15–25 cm long, fine, leaflets 70–100, opposite, 2–3 cm long, 1 cm wide, oblong, tip and base rounded. **Flowers** yellow, to 1.8 cm long, bilaterally symmetrical, bean-flower-shaped; inflorescences of 3–5 flowers in leaf axils; blooms Aug.–Nov. **Fruit** dry, pods, linear, elongate, about 7–24 cm long, less than 0.5 cm wide, containing up to 50 cylindrical seeds about 0.3 cm long, mottled dark green and black. **Habitat:** Open lowland sites, pastures, roadsides. Altitude: Pacific lowlands, sea level to 150 m, rarely to 1100 m. Conservation areas: GUA, OSA, PAC, TEM. Common around Palo Verde N.P. **Range:** S US–N S Amer, WI. **Notes:** This is the only species of *Sesbania* in Costa Rica.

■ *Halenia aquilegiella*
Family Gentianaceae

Small pale green herb, stem unbranched. **Leaves** opposite, stalkless, blade straplike 2–8 cm long, 0.2–0.6 cm wide, pale green. **Flowers** pale yellow green, tubular, bilaterally symmetrical, 1.2–1.5 cm long, pendant, with 4 spurs facing upward; inflorescence at top of stem; blooms on and off Aug.–Apr. **Fruit** dry, splitting open to release seeds. **Habitat:** Open sites in high mountains. Altitude: 2500–3400 m. Conservation areas: LAC, LAP, PAC. Seen near television towers on Cerro de la Muerte. **Range:** CR, Pan. **Notes:** *Halenia rhyacophila* is the only other species of *Halenia* in Costa Rica. It is very similar to *H. aquilegiella* and is often found in the same areas.

348

■ *Lisianthius seemannii*
Family Gentianaceae

Shrubby herb or small shrub to 2 m tall. **Leaves** opposite, joined across stem in a ridge, those on vegetative stems stalked, those in flowering stems stalkless, blade 5–15 cm long, 1.5–4 cm wide. **Flowers** pale yellow with white tips, 3–5 cm long, tubular, 5-parted, radially symmetrical, petal lobes about 1.2 cm long, narrow; blooms Aug.–Mar. **Fruit** dry, splitting open to release seeds. **Habitat:** Moist forests or open sites, roadside banks. Altitude: 300–1600 m. Conservation areas: ARE, GUA, HNO, PAC. **Range:** CR, Pan. **Notes:** There are two other species of *Lisianthius* in Costa Rica.

■ *Alloplectus ichthyoderma*
Family Gesneriaceae

Stout, shrublike herb, epiphytic or terrestrial, often colonial, stems hairy, to 1.5 m tall, to 1 cm diameter, mostly unbranched, leaves mostly near top of stem. **Leaves** opposite, stalk 1–5 cm long, blade 7–20 cm long, 3–8 cm wide, egg-shaped to widest above middle, pointed at both ends, rather fleshy, finely hairy above, margin toothed. **Flowers** pale yellow to reddish yellow outside, very hairy, yellow inside, bilaterally symmetrical, tubular, showy, tube 1.5–2 cm long, base bulging, mouth small, petal lobes 5, almost radially symmetrical, calyx bright red to green, hairy; inflorescence a dense cluster surrounding stem, in upper axils and along stem; blooms all year. **Fruit** fleshy, white, surrounded by old calyx, seeds numerous; fruit present most of the year. **Habitat:** Wet mountain regions in open sites and forest understories. Altitude: 1300–3700 m Conservation areas: CVC, LAC, LAP, PAC. **Range:** CR–N S Amer. **Notes:** There are seven species of *Alloplectus* in Costa Rica.

■ *Chrysothemis friedrichsthaliana*
Family Gesneriaceae

Herb, terrestrial or epiphytic, erect, to 60 cm tall, pale green somewhat translucent, most parts hairy, stem 4-sided. **Leaves** opposite, each pair at right angles to next, stalk to 1 cm long, winged, blade 8–37 cm long, 3–13 cm wide, elliptic to lance-shaped, tip pointed, base narrowed to wings, surface puckered, hairy on both sides, lower surface sometimes purple, margin toothed. **Flowers** orange with red stripes in throat, to about 3 cm long, tubular, slightly asymmetrical,

petal tube flaring above winged calyx, blooms a few at a time in axils at branch tips in a mass of pale green calyx wings of flower buds; blooms May–Jan. **Fruit** fleshy, to 1 cm, surrounded by persistent calyx, yellowish before maturity. **Habitat:** Moist to wet forests, partly shaded roadsides, oil palm plantations, weedy sites. Altitude: Sea level to 750 m. Conservation areas: CVC, GUA, HNO, LAC, OSA, PAC, TOR. **Range:** Nic–Ec. **Notes:** Used medicinally by the by Chocó Indians for diarrhea and snake bite. There is only one other species of *Chrysothemis* in Costa Rica.

■ *Columnea purpurata*
Family Gesneriaceae

Shrubby herb, terrestrial or epiphytic, most parts densely hairy, stems to 2 m tall, stout, yellow-hairy. **Leaves** opposite but pair members very unequal and appearing alternate, densely hairy on both sides, larger leaves 16–32 cm long, 6–11 cm wide, lance-shaped, broadest near apex, tip long-pointed, base unequal, tapered to leaf stalk, small leaves egg-shaped, 2–5 cm long, 0.5–2 cm wide, flattened along top side of stem, overlapping stalks of large leaves, young leaves purple-hairy. **Flowers** bright orange and yellow, bilaterally symmetrical, tubular, hairy, about 4 cm long 1 cm wide, petal tube yellow or red striped, embedded in a mass of feathery, hairy, orange bracts and calyx lobes; flowers in tight, stalkless clusters along underside of stem; blooms all year. **Fruit** fleshy, orange, about 1.8 cm long, 1 cm wide, flesh sticky, seeds numerous. **Habitat:** Wet to very wet forests. Altitude: Sea level to 1600 m, most often on the Caribbean slope, above 500 m. Conservation areas: ARE, CVC, GUA, HNO, LAC, TOR. **Range:** Nic–Col.

■ *Kohleria allenii*
Family Gesneriaceae

Woody terrestrial herb to 1.5 m tall, stems red-hairy. **Leaves** opposite or in whorls of 3–4, stalk about 2 cm long, blade 5–17 cm long, 3–7 cm wide, lance- to egg-shaped, tip pointed, base blunt, sides slightly unequal, hairy, margin finely toothed. **Flowers** yellow with dense red hairs, interior yellow with dark red dots in lines showy, tubular, bilaterally symmetrical, short, wide, about 3 cm long, 2.5 cm across top, petal lobes 5, triangular, curled back, calyx 5-lobed, green with red margins, hairy, flowers in axils of small, upper leaves on stalks to 4 cm long; blooms Aug.–Feb. **Fruit** dry, 2-parted, enclosed in persistent calyx, seeds numerous. **Habitat:** Wet regions in open sites, second growth, roadside banks. Altitude: Southern Pacific slope, 50–1100 m, mostly below 300 m. Conservation areas: LAP, OSA. **Range:** CR, Pan. **Notes:** There are three species of *Kohleria* in Costa Rica.

■ *Heliconia longiflora*
Family Heliconiaceae

Herb to 1.5–2 m tall, occasionally to 5 m. **Leaves** alternate, 10–16 per stem, ranked in one plane, held horizontally, like those of gingers, stalk short, about 0.4 cm long, base sheathing stem, blade 26–36 cm long, 6.5–8 cm wide, bright, shiny green above, pale, waxy below. **Flowers** pale yellow to white, base orange, asymmetrical, 6-parted, about 7 cm long, 0.5 cm wide, 7–8 per bract; bracts orange, tip sometimes red, in one plane, the middle ones about 7 cm long, 2 cm wide; Inflorescence erect, about 16 cm long, axis orange, bracts 4–8; blooms Jan.–Nov. **Fruit** fleshy, orange becoming blue; eaten by birds and mammals. **Habitat:** Wet to very wet regions, open areas or forest understories, edges, flood plains of streams, roadside ditches. Altitude: Sea level to 1000 m, mostly below 700 m. Conservation areas: ARE, GUA, HNO, LAP, OSA, PAC. **Range:** Nic–Ec. **Notes:** Recognized by its long, conspicuous flowers, and leaves ranked along stem.

■ *Hypoxis decumbens*
  Family Hypoxidaceae

Small tufted herb to about 50 cm tall, arising from a bulb about 2.5 cm long. **Leaves** alternate, tufted, grasslike, 5–55 cm long (much smaller if cut as when growing in lawns or patios), 0.1–0.8 cm wide, linear, folded along midrib, surface, long-hairy. **Flowers** yellow, radially symmetrical, 3-parted, petals and sepals free, 0.6–1.0 cm long, stamens 6, ovary inferior; inflorescence stalk 5–40 cm long, hairy, from amid leaves with 1–4 flowers per stalk; blooms June–Nov. **Fruit** dry, 2 cm wide, pale green at first, mature fruit splitting open at top to release black, warty seeds. **Habitat:** Wet to very wet regions, in open sites, mountains, rocky areas, roadsides, often a lawn weed. Altitude: 700–1400, occasionally to nearly 3000 m. Conservation areas: ARE, CVC, LAP. **Range:** Mex–Arg. **Notes:** The only other species of *Hypoxis* in Costa Rica is H. *humilis*, which is very uncommon.

■ *Sida rhombifolia* (escobilla)
  Family Malvaceae

Woody based herb to 1.5 m tall, finely hairy, stems much-branched, stipules linear, to 0.5 cm, about as long as leaf stalk. **Leaves** alternate, stalk to 0.5 cm long, hairy, blade 1.5–7.5 cm long, 0.8–2.5 cm wide, variable, often rhombic, tip and base pointed or blunt, dull green, margins toothed, 3 palmate veins. **Flowers** yellow orange, radially symmetrical, 1 cm wide, petals strongly asymmetrical, egg-shaped, notched at tip, base very narrow, stamens fused in a central tube around style, about 0.4 cm long; flowers solitary in axils or clustered at ends of stems; blooms most of the year. **Fruits** dry, 8- to 12-parted, each segment 3-sided, 0.5 cm long with 1 beak. **Habitat:** Common weed in pastures, edges, along roadsides. Altitude: Sea level to 1700 m, mostly below 700 m. Conservation areas: ARE, CVC, LAC, LAP, OSA, PAC, TEM. **Range:** Pantropical and subtropical, worldwide. Invasive in Australia, Galapagos, Hawai'i, and some other Pacific islands. **Notes:** There are 16 species of *Sida* in Costa Rica but only four are common. All very similar, S. *acuta* and S. *rhombifolia* are the most common; S. *acuta* has much larger stipules, and flowers are pale orange to white.

■ *Calathea crotalifera* (*C. insignis*)
(cascabel, bijagua, platanilla)
Family Marantaceae

Large herb 1.6–3 m tall, sometimes to 5 m, often in large clumps. **Leaves** alternate, all at base, except 1 along stem, leaf stalk to over 1 m long, top part olive green, slightly swollen, jointlike, base winged and grooved, sheathing stem; blade 0.33–1.1 m long, 16–55 cm wide, elliptic to narrowly oblong, tip rounded to short-pointed, base blunt, often gray green below, midrib usually pale. **Flowers** white, irregular, narrowly tubular, emerging from bracts in pairs; bracts bright yellow to brownish orange, flattened, broadly kidney-shaped, upper margin rounded; 16–43 bracts 2-ranked along sides of floral stem, bases tightly overlapping; inflorescence 2–5 per stem, 12–25 cm long, 5–7 cm wide, flattened, with appearance of a rectangular rattlesnake tail; blooms all year; pollinated by bees. **Fruit** dry, yellow, splitting open to release 3 dark blue seeds with a white fleshy attachment. **Habitat:** Moist to very wet regions, open sites, forest gaps, edges, flood plains. Altitude: Sea level to 1800 m. Conservation areas: ARE, CVC, GUA, HNO, LAC, LAP, OSA, PAC, TOR. **Range:** S Mex–Ven and Bol. **Notes:** There are 41 species of *Calathea* in Costa Rica.

■ *Calathea lutea* (bijagua, hoja
blanca, platanilla, chaguite)
Family Marantaceae

Large herb 1.6–4 m tall, in clumps, stem composed of overlapping leaf sheaths. **Leaves** alternate, mostly basal, stalk to 2 m long, cylindrical, top part slightly bent, jointlike, swollen, olive green, longer than blade; blade 0.3–1.5 m long, 20–60 cm wide, broadly elliptic to nearly round, tip round or short-pointed, base blunt, abruptly extended down stalk, surface green above, underside waxy white. **Flowers** yellow, tubular, irregular, about 3–4.5 cm long, petal lobes purple brown; blooms 1–2 at a time; bracts yellow, becoming brown or reddish in age, 7–18, to 5 cm long, overlapping, upper margin rounded to lobed with an abrupt point, appearing cone-shaped, spirally arranged; inflorescences, branched, spikes several 9–30 cm long, 3–6 cm wide, slightly flattened, cylindrical; blooms about Sept.–May; pollinated by bees. **Fruit** dry, orange, egg-shaped, crowned by old sepal lobes; opening to reveal 3 greenish seeds with bright orange, fleshy attachment (aril). **Habitat:** Wet to very wet lowlands, open areas roadsides, floodplains, river banks. Altitude: Sea level to 300 m, rarely to 700 m. Conservation areas: CVC, HNO, LAP, OSA, PAC, TOR. **Range:** Mex–Brz, Ant. **Notes:** Distinguished by the white underside of leaf blades.

353

■ *Ludwigia octovalvis* (cangá,
yerba de clavo, swamp root)
Family Onagraceae

Shrubby herb to 2 m tall, stems to 1 cm diameter, branched, usually reddish, ribbed. **Leaves** alternate, stalk short to none, reddish, blade 2–16 cm long, 0.5–3 cm wide, narrow, pointed at both ends; midrib reddish to pale, pinnate veins conspicuous. **Flowers** yellow, showy, to 3 cm wide, 4-parted, petals heart-shaped, notched to rounded at top, base very narrow, soon falling, calyx lobes pointed, arising from a reddish floral base, stamens 8; blooms all year. **Fruit** dry, cylindrical, ribbed, to 5 cm long, crowned by persistent calyx lobes; seeds wedge-shaped, dispersed by water. **Habitat:** Seasonally dry to wet regions in wet soil, river banks, wet pastures, marshes. Altitude: Sea level to 1800 m. Conservation areas: ARE, CVC,

GUA, HNO, LAC, LAP, OSA, PAC, TEM, TOR. **Range:** Native to some Pacific islands (Micronesia); now pantropical. **Notes:** There are 18 species of *Ludwigia* in Costa Rica. Several species are very similar in appearance and habitat to *L. octovalvis*. All are erect herbs with showy yellow flowers, 4 petals, in wet, lowland habitats; the most common, by far, is *L. octovalvis*. Sometimes used medicinally.

■ *Ludwigia peruviana*
Family Onagraceae

Herb 1–3 m tall, sprawling, stems hairy, much-branched, base often woody. **Leaves** alternate, 5–10 cm long, 1–3 cm wide, egg-shaped, rough-textured, secondary veins closely parallel, curved upward. **Flowers** yellow, 2–4 cm wide, petals 4, 1–3 cm long, soon falling, tip rounded, base narrow, stamens 8, sepals 4, green, about 1 cm long, pointed; blooms all year. **Fruit** dry, narrowly cylindrical, crowned by persistent sepals, seeds tiny, numerous. **Habitat:** Mountains, in wet, open sites, ditches, pond edges. Altitude: 600–2000 m, usually above 1200 m. Conservation areas: ARE, CVC, LAP, TEM. Common. **Range:** US–S Chile and Arg. Introduced and invasive in Australia and some Pacific islands.

■ *Oncidium stenotis* (lluvia de oro)
   Family Orchidaceae

Epiphyte, uppermost leaf stalk swollen, bulblike, 7–12 cm long, 3 cm wide, grooved. **Leaves** alternate, all stalks, except topmost, sheathing stem blade 20–30 cm long, 4 cm wide, straplike to narrowly egg-shaped, narrowed at base, thin. **Flowers** yellow with dark brown markings, bilaterally symmetrical, 3 sepals and 2 side petals similar, about 1.5 cm long, 0.7 cm wide, elliptical, tips pointed, surface deeply wavy, lower petal (lip) about 1.5 cm long, 1 cm wide, 3-lobed, lateral lobes winglike, small, lower lobe wider, fan-shaped, yellow, margin wavy, tip notched,

central part of flower with a fleshy, snout-shaped protuberance, above a red saddle-shaped area, often with red marking; inflorescence 0.5–1.5 m long, branched, often vinelike, with numerous flowers; blooms Oct.–June. **Fruit** dry, seeds dustlike. **Habitat:** Wet to very wet forests. Altitude: Sea level to 1400 m, Caribbean slope. Conservation areas: ARE, HNO, TOR. **Range:** CR, W Pan. **Notes:** There are 30 species of *Oncidium* in Costa Rica.

■ *Psygmorchis pusilla*
   Family Orchidaceae

Small epiphyte 3–14 cm wide, stem not bulblike. **Leaves** alternate, in a fan-shaped pattern, blade 2.5–5 cm long, 0.4–0.6 cm wide, shorter than flower stalks, tip blunt, surface smooth, midrib impressed, secondary veins obscure. **Flowers** yellow, with brown spots, bilaterally symmetrical, sepals about 0.4 cm long, 0.1 cm wide, side petals slightly larger, lower petal about 1.5 cm long, 1.5–2 cm wide, deeply 3-lobed, center lobe in turn 4-lobed, petal edges fluted and ruffled, center with mottled brownish pattern; inflorescence 3–5 cm long, of several stems, from leaf axils, stalks very slender with 1–2 small bracts, flowers solitary on stem; blooms most of the year. **Fruit** dry, 1.5–2.5 cm long, about 1 cm wide; seeds numerous, dustlike. **Habitat:** Wet to very wet forests. Altitude: Sea level to 300 m, sometimes to 1100 m. Conservation areas: CVC GUA, LAC, LAP, PAC, TOR. **Range:** Mex–Col and Ven, Brz. **Notes:** Seen at Las Cruces Botanical Garden. There is one other species of *Psygmorchis* in Costa Rica; *P. pumila* is smaller and has yellow flowers without any spots.

■ *Telipogon storkii*
Family Orchidaceae

Epiphytic or terrestrial herb to 20 cm tall, branched from upper nodes, stem slender, not bulblike. **Leaves** about 6, much smaller than flowers, ranked on a short stem at base of flowering stem, blade 3–6 cm long, about 2 cm wide, small, broadly elliptic, folded along midrib, tips rounded. **Flowers** yellow to dark yellow, center darker, veins red brown, flower appearing 3-parted, triangular, sepals about 1.5 cm long, 0.5 cm wide, all 3 petals roughly equal, about 2–2.5 cm long, 2–3 cm wide, broadly egg-shaped, bases overlapping, tips pointed, flowers blooms one at a time; inflorescence slender, long-stemmed, sometimes branched, 20–40 cm tall, 6–9 flowered; blooms Mar., May, Aug.–Nov. **Fruit** dry, seeds dustlike. **Habitat:** Mountains, in cloud forests, oak forests, open shrubby areas (páramo). Altitude: 1700–3200 m. Conservation areas: CVC, LAC, LAP. **Range:** Endemic to CR. **Notes:** There are about 22 species of *Telipogon* in Costa Rica. All are found above 1300 m. Flowers appear to have 3 fairly equal petals, not appearing very "orchidlike." They are difficult to tell apart; many are found only in Costa Rica (endemic).

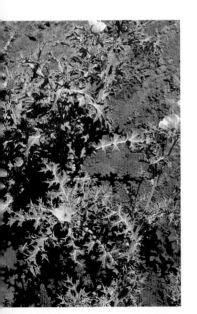

■ *Argemone mexicana* (chicalote, Mexican prickly poppy)
Family Papaveraceae

Herb about 30 cm tall, stems prickly, sap milky yellow. **Leaves** alternate, base clasping stem, blade to 22 cm long, oblong, irregularly pinnately lobed and toothed, lobe tips spiny, surface pale, waxy green, veins slightly prickly. **Flowers** yellow radially symmetrical, to 6 cm wide, showy, petals 2–3 cm long, stamens 30–50, flower buds prickly. **Fruit** dry, broadly elliptical, 3–4 cm long, sparsely covered with prickles to 1 cm long; opening in sections to release numerous small seeds; blooms Mar.–May. **Habitat:** Open sites, fields; also a garden plant. Altitude: 700–1100 m. Conservation areas: ARE, CVC. **Range:** Native to Mex, WI. Now found from S US–Ur, occasional weed north to New York, Old World, invasive in Hawai'i and some other Pacific islands. **Notes:** This is the only species of *Argemone* in Costa Rica.

Courtesy of Margaret Gargiullo

■ *Peperomia pernambucensis*
Family Piperaceae

Usually an epiphytic herb, stem to 10 cm tall, erect. **Leaves** alternate, crowded at end of short stem, stalk 2–7 cm, margin continuous with blade margin and clasping stem at base, blade large, 15–30 cm long, 5–11 cm wide, succulent, elliptic to widest above middle, tip pointed, base tapered, veins obscure. **Flowers** pale yellow, minute, crowded on spikes 0.8–2.5 cm long, slender, in clusters of up to 25 spikes, alternate or whorled on a central axis; inflorescence stalk to 10 cm, branches often pinkish or reddish; blooms all year. **Fruit** fleshy, less than 0.1 cm wide. **Habitat:** Wet forests. Altitude: Sea level to 1600 m. Almost always on the Caribbean slope. Conservation areas: ARE, CVC, GUA, LAC, TOR. **Range:** Nic–SE Brz. **Notes:** Distinctive for its large leaves and inflorescence of many short spikes radiating from a central axis.

■ *Notopleura polyphlebia (Psychotria p.)*
Family Rubiaceae

Herb 15–50 cm tall, slender, stem usually unbranched, colonial from below ground stems (rhizomes); stipules to 0.3 cm long, to 0.6 cm wide, broadly triangular, deciduous. **Leaves** opposite, stalk to 4 cm long, often hairy, blade 7–16 cm long, 3–7 cm wide, oblong to widest above middle, tip blunt, base extending down stalk, stiff, held horizontally, very dark green above, hairy below, surface corrugated by numerous, closely spaced, parallel, secondary veins, curving upward, raised above, usually loop-connected near margin. **Flowers** white, radially symmetrical, funnel-shaped, to 0.5 cm long, petal lobes 5, about 0.1 cm long, embedded in green bracts; inflorescence of dense, rounded, headlike clusters of bracts and flowers, about 3 cm wide in leaf axils, on a stalk to 6 cm long; blooms Feb.–Sept. **Fruit** fleshy, to 0.9 cm, oblong, becoming orange then black, seeds 2; fruit present all year. **Habitat:** Very wet, dark forest understories. Altitude: Sea level to 1500 m. Conservation areas: ARE, CVC, GUA, HNO, LAC, LAP, OSA, TOR. **Range:** Nic–Pr. **Notes:** The short stature and dark green, stiff, corrugated leaves make this a very distinctive and easily recognized understory herb.

357

■ *Calceolaria irazúensis*
Family Scrophulariaceae
Shrubby herb 20 cm to 2 m tall, sometimes vinelike, stems long, slender, bark brown, smooth, new growth finely brownish to purplish-hairy, ridges between leaf stalk bases. **Leaves** opposite, each pair at right angles to next, stalk to 1.5 cm, hairy, blade 5–12 cm long, 2–4 cm wide, elliptic to lance-shaped, tip pointed, base blunt, surface dark green, margin toothed. **Flowers** yellow, bilaterally symmetrical, rounded, pouchlike, slipper or shoe-shaped, 2.5 cm long, 1.5 cm wide, calyx radially symmetrical, 4-parted, sepals to 0.9 cm long, egg-shaped; inflorescence of sparse, single-stemmed clusters to 12 cm long, at ends of branches; blooms all year. **Fruit** dry, rounded, to 0.8 cm long, brown to purplish, splitting open to release seeds. **Habitat:** Wet, high mountain regions in open areas, roadside ditches. Altitude: 2200–3500 m. Conservation areas: CVC, LAC, LAP, PAC. **Range:** CR, Pan. **Notes:** There are six species of *Calceolaria* in Costa Rica, all are distinguished by flowers with a pouched lower lip.

■ *Hemichaena fruticosa*
Family Scrophulariaceae
Large, coarse herb or small shrub 1–2 m tall, most parts hairy and slightly sticky, stems simple or branched, thick, nodes slightly swollen. **Leaves** opposite, at ends of stems, bases fused across stem, blade to about 16 cm long, about 3 cm wide, elliptic or lance-shaped, tip pointed, narrowed toward base, base

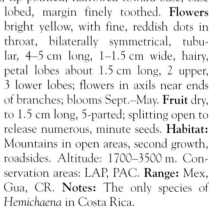

lobed, margin finely toothed. **Flowers** bright yellow, with fine, reddish dots in throat, bilaterally symmetrical, tubular, 4–5 cm long, 1–1.5 cm wide, hairy, petal lobes about 1.5 cm long, 2 upper, 3 lower lobes; flowers in axils near ends of branches; blooms Sept.–May. **Fruit** dry, to 1.5 cm long, 5-parted; splitting open to release numerous, minute seeds. **Habitat:** Mountains in open areas, second growth, roadsides. Altitude: 1700–3500 m. Conservation areas: LAP, PAC. **Range:** Mex, Gua, CR. **Notes:** The only species of *Hemichaena* in Costa Rica.

■ *Solanum quitoense* (naranilla)
Family Solanaceae

Large, coarse herb or small shrub to 3 m tall, all parts woolly-hairy, often with long stinging hairs and stout yellowish spines. **Leaves** alternate, stalks to 15 cm long, hairy, often spiny, blade to 45 cm long, 30 cm wide, shallowly pinnate-lobed, lobe tips pointed, hairy above, densely purple-hairy below, major veins often spiny. **Flowers** white, 5 cm wide, petal lobes often unequal, divided almost to base, densely hairy outside, anthers stout, yellow, gathered together into a central, beaklike cluster; calyx densely purple woolly-hairy, to 1 cm, lobed 1/2 way down; inflorescence branched, crowded, stems densely purple-hairy; blooms and fruits most

of the year. **Fruit** fleshy, orange, to 6 cm wide, round, hairy, often spiny, cupped in persistent calyx, ripe fruit edible, juicy, interior with containing numerous seeds. **Habitat:** Open sites in mountain areas, roadsides, pastures; also widely cultivated for fruit. Altitude: 900–2000 m, mostly above 1300 m. Conservation areas: ARE, CVC, LAP, PAC. **Range:** Native to mountains of S Amer. Now found Nic–Pr; introduced and invasive in the Galapagos.

COLOR OF CONSPICUOUS PART WHITE, CREAM, OR GREENISH WHITE

■ *Blechum pyramidatum*
Family Acanthaceae

Herb to 50 cm tall, erect or leaning, young stems 4-sided. **Leaves** opposite, stalks to 1.4 cm, blade 2–6 cm long, 1–3 cm wide, egg-shaped, tip pointed, base blunt to wedge-shaped, margins sometimes wavy. **Flowers** white to pale lavender and pink, to 1.5 cm long, bilaterally symmetrical, tubular, funnel-shaped, slightly longer than surrounding bracts; bracts green, egg-shaped, to 1.4 cm long, 1 cm wide, densely hairy; inflorescence a 4-sided spike to 7 cm long, at top of stem. **Fruit** dry, to 0.6 cm long, 0.3 cm wide. **Habitat:** Seasonally dry, to very wet regions in disturbed sites, roadsides, edges. Altitude: Sea level to 1450 m. Conservation areas: ARE, CVC, GUA, HNO, LAC, LAP, OSA, PAC, TEM, TOR. **Range:** Mex–S Amer, WI, Galapagos. Introduced in Taiwan, Oceania, invasive on Hawai'i and some other Pacific islands. **Notes:** Similar to *B. costaricense*, the only other species of *Blechum* in Costa Rica, which has larger flowers and is less common.

■ *Justicia comata*
   Family Acanthaceae
Herb or shrubby herb to 1 m tall. **Leaves** opposite, stalkless, blade elliptic to egg-shaped 4–10 cm long, 2–3 cm wide, tip long-pointed, base pointed to blunt. **Flowers** white to pale purple or white with purplish markings, to 0.6 cm long, bilaterally symmetrical, tubular, 2-lipped, upper lip linear, barely 2-toothed, purple, bottom lip 3-lobed, dotted with purple, inflorescence of many thin spikes whorled around a central axis, from upper parts of stems; blooms most of the year. **Fruit** dry, club-shaped, to 0.5 cm long. **Habitat:** Seasonally dry to wet regions in weedy, disturbed, open, or partly shady sites. Altitude: Sea level to 500 m. Conservation areas: CVC, GUA, HNO, LAC, LAP, OSA, PAC, TEM, TOR. **Range:** Throughout the Neotropics. **Notes:** There are about 34 species of *Justicia* in Costa Rica.

■ *Justicia orosiensis*
   Family Acanthaceae
Herb or shrubby herb to 1.2 m tall, sparsely branched, young stems 4-sided, often dark maroon. **Leaves** opposite, stalk to 2 cm long, blade 8–23 cm long, 2–7 cm wide, elliptic, pointed at both ends. **Flowers** greenish white to pale purple, to 1.7 cm long, bilaterally symmetrical, tubular, upper lip 1 cm long, 0.6 cm wide, tip notched, curved over stamens, lower lip 3-lobed, sharply bent downward, lobes to 0.7 cm; flowers amid small, green shiny bracts, to 0.8 cm long; inflorescence a spikelike arrangement of appressed branches at top of stems; blooms Jan.–Sept. **Fruit** dry, club-shaped 0.5 cm long. **Habitat:** Wet forests. Altitude: 450–1800 m, Caribbean slope, mostly near Orosi, Tapantí N.P. Conservation areas: CVC, LAC, LAP, OSA. **Range:** CR.

■ *Justicia valerioi*
   Family Acanthaceae

Small herb to 30 cm tall, often many stems together, young stems green, slightly 4-angled, swollen just above node. **Leaves** opposite, to 4–13 cm long, 2–5 cm wide, elliptic, dark green above, puckered by impressed veins, pointed at both ends, margins entire to slightly blunt-toothed. **Flowers** white or bluish white, to 1 cm long, tubular, bilaterally symmetric, 2-lipped, lower lip 3-lobed, upper lip tiny; blooms few at a time in dense, sharply 4-angled spikes of overlapping, pale green, hairy bracts at tops of stems; blooms Oct.–Apr. **Fruit** dry, to 0.8 cm long, 0.2 cm wide, club-shaped, finely hairy. **Habitat:** Pastures, along trails of mountain rain forests. Altitude: 550–2000 m. Conservation areas: ARE (mostly), GUA, LAP, PAC. **Range:** CR.

■ *Nothoscordum gracile* (false onion weed)
   Family Alliaceae

Garliclike herb 0.4–1 m tall, without garlic odor, from a white bulb, about 2 cm wide, producing many small offshoot-bulbs at base; flowering stems 1–2, cylindrical, 30–60 cm tall. **Leaves** alternate, 2–9, all from base, linear, 20–40 cm long, 0.4–1 cm wide, flat but slightly folded along the prominent, purple midrib. **Flowers** white, radially symmetrical, fragrant, 6-parted, petals 1–1.5 cm long, 0.4 cm wide, elliptic, base narrowed, green, tips pointed, midvein often pink; anthers yellow to dark brown; inflorescence umbrella-shaped, above

2 papery bracts, each flower on a short stalk about 4 cm long from the top of a main stem, to about 48 cm long; blooms Jan.–Nov. **Fruit** dry, 3-parted, 0.7 cm long and wide, seeds numerous, black. **Habitat:** A weed of urban vacant lots, roadsides and other disturbed sites. Altitude: 1100–2200 m. Conservation areas: CVC. Seen in San José. **Range:** Mex–Bol, WI. Native to S Amer, introduced in parts of the US. **Notes:** This is the only species of *Nothoscordum* in Costa Rica. It is much like *Allium* species but easily distinguished from them, as its leaves lack garlic odor.

■ *Gomphrena serrata*
Family Amaranthaceae

Herb 10–50 cm tall, prostrate to erect, most parts usually whitish hairy. **Leaves** opposite, stalk short to 0.6 cm, continuous with the blade base, blade 2–7 cm long, 0.5–2 cm wide, elliptic, tip pointed to blunt, often spine-tipped, base extending down stalk, finely hairy on both sides. **Flowers** greenish white, dry, very small, radially symmetrical, in small heads or short spikes, bearing numerous small spine-tipped bracts 0.4–0.6 cm long; blooms most of the year. **Fruit** dry, 1-seeded, contained in hairy flower heads. **Habitat:** Wet to seasonally dry regions in weedy open, disturbed sites, roadsides. Altitude: Sea level to 1200 m, mostly below 100 m on the Pacific slope. Conservation areas: GUA, OSA, PAC, TEM. **Range:** FL–Par, WI. **Notes:** The only other species of *Gomphrena* in Costa Rica is G. *globosa*, which is much less common than G. *serrata*.

■ *Iresine diffusa*
Family Amaranthaceae

Herbs or weak shrubs to 3 m tall, stems erect or partially climbing in other vegetation, nodes swollen below leaf bases, with a ridge between leaf stalk bases, often hairy, dark pinkish. **Leaves** opposite (or nearly opposite), stalk 0.5–8 cm long, blade 2–16 cm long, 1–10 cm wide, egg-shaped to narrowly elliptic, becoming very small and linear in the flowering branches, tip pointed, base pointed to rounded, extending down leaf stalk as ridges. **Flowers** pinkish white, about 0.1 cm long, each above a bract, 0.1 cm long; in small, crowded clusters, arranged alternately along branches at tops of plant; inflorescence 5–50 cm long, variable, much-branched, appearing rather open; blooms all year, most often Dec.–Mar. **Fruit** dry, enclosed in old flower parts. **Habitat:** Wet to seasonally dry regions in open to partly shaded second growth and disturbed sites, roadsides. Altitude: Sea level to 2600 m. Conservation areas: ARE, CVC, GUA, HNO, LAC, LAP, OSA, PAC, TEM. **Range:** FL, TX, Mex–Ven, Par, and Arg, WI. **Notes:** There are five species of *Iresine* in Costa Rica.

■ *Hymenocallis littoralis* (spider lily)
Family Amaryllidaceae

Herb growing from a bulb 5–10 cm wide; no stem. **Leaves**
alternate, arising directly from bulb, stalkless, blade straplike, 0.5–1.5 m long, 2–4 cm wide, somewhat succulent,
veins parallel, obscure. **Flowers** white, showy, radially symmetrical, 6-parted, fragrant, tubular base, 10–19 cm long,
petal lobes elongate, narrow, to 15 cm long, from the base
of a central, cup-shaped structure (corona) supporting purple stamens to 6 cm long; inflorescence an umbrella-shaped
cluster at top of a leafless stalk; possibly pollinated by large
hawk moths; blooms on and off most of the year, especially
May–July. **Fruit** dry, small pods in a tight cluster. **Habitat:**
Along beaches mostly along the Caribbean shore, just above
high-tide line, Manzanillo to Tortuguero; also cultivated.
Altitude: Usually near sea level, occasionally to 400 m in
Tempisque. Conservation areas: LAC, TEM, TOR. **Range:**
S Mex–Ec. **Notes:** This is the only species of *Hymenocallis*
in Costa Rica. A very similar species is *Crinum erubescens*,
which lacks the corona of *Hymenocallis* and is found along
the fresh and brackish water canals of TOR. Other species
of *Crinum* from Africa and Asia are cultivated, but most are
purple or purple-tinged.

■ *Hydrocotyle leucocephala*
Family Apiaceae

Small creeping ground cover, rooting at nodes. **Leaves** alternate, stalk elongate, blade rounded, 1–5 cm wide, about as
wide, veins 9–11, margin round-toothed or shallowly
lobed. **Flowers** white radially symmetrical, small,
petals egg-shaped; inflorescence of small, round,
dense headlike clusters of 20–30 flowers each on a
stalk 0.2 cm long, each cluster arising from a leaf axil,
inflorescence stems becoming longer than leaf stalks.
Fruit dry, 2-seeded. **Habitat:** Edges, part shade, roadsides. Altitude: Sea level to 1250 m. Conservation
areas: ARE, CVC, GUA, LAP, PAC, TOR. **Range:**
S Mex–Brz and Bol. **Notes:** There are nine species
of *Hydrocotyle* in Costa Rica. *Hydrocotyle mexicana*
is apparently the most common and is very similar.
Apparently used in aquariums.

■ *Myrrhidendron donnell-smithii* (arracachillo)
Family Apiaceae

Very large, coarse herb 0.5–4 m tall, sometimes to 10 m, base woody, stems hollow, finely ribbed, sap aromatic. **Leaves** alternate, very large, lower leaves long-stalked, upper leaves with base of stalk sheathing stem, blade 3 times pinnately compound, coarsely fernlike, ultimate leaflets 2.5–5 cm long, egg-shaped, tip pointed, irregularly toothed. **Flowers** dull white to pale yellow, radially symmetrical, very small, in very large, umbrella-shaped clusters at tops of stems, plant dies back after going to seed, brown stalks and inflorescence remain standing for some time; blooms most of the year. **Fruit** dry, about 1 cm long, 2-seeded. **Habitat:** Open areas in mountains. Altitude: 1300–3800 m. Conservation areas: CVC, LAC, LAP, PAC. **Range:** Gua–CR. **Notes:** The only other species of *Myrrhidendron* in Costa Rica is M. *chirripoense*, which is uncommon.

■ *Sanicula liberta*
Family Apiaceae

Low herb 10–50 cm tall. **Leaves** alternate, mostly basal, stalk elongate, blade 4–10 cm wide, irregularly, palmately compound, leaflets 3–5, irregularly elliptic, deeply lobed and toothed, margin finely bristle-fringed. **Flowers** greenish white, very small, radially symmetrical, petals triangular; inflorescences of small headlike clusters; blooms and fruits most of the year. **Fruit** dry, small, 2-seeded, burlike, covered with hooked bristles that cling to clothing or fur. **Habitat:** Common herb of cloud forests. Altitude: Sea level to 2600 m, mostly above 1000 m. Conservation areas: ARE, CVC, GUA, LAC, LAP, OSA, PAC. **Range:** Mex–NW S Amer. **Notes:** This is the only species of *Sanicula* in Costa Rica.

■ *Anthurium consobrinum*
Family Araceae

Low epiphytic herb, stems short with masses of pale green aerial roots at each node, these covering leaf bases, the aerial roots are usually short and point upward like thick, pale green bristles. **Leaves** alternate, simple, in a rosette or vaselike arrangement, stalk 2–11 cm long, blade 20–80 cm long, 4–20 cm wide, widest near upper end, tip abruptly pointed, base contracted, then tapered to stalk, stiffly erect, surface leathery, shiny dark green, veins raised above. **Flowers** whitish, minute, densely crowded on a curved, fleshy spike 3–10 cm long, inflorescence bract pale green, 2–9 cm long, 0.3–1.4 cm wide; inflorescence shorter than leaves, stalk 10–55 cm long; blooms all year. **Fruit** fleshy, reddish at tip, translucent greenish white below, 1 cm long, 0.5 cm wide, 2-seeded; fruiting spike pendent, to 13 cm long. **Habitat:** Wet lowland and midelevation forests. Altitude: Sea level to 1000 m. Conservation areas: ARE, CVC, GUA, HNO, TOR. **Range:** Nic–Pan.

■ *Anthurium obtusilobum*
Family Araceae

Epiphytic or terrestrial herb to about 70 cm tall, stem to 30 cm long, about 1.5 cm wide, leaves crowded at top of stem. **Leaves** alternate, stalk 16–75 cm long, blade 15–50 cm long, 10–30 cm wide, heart-shaped, tip long-pointed, base deeply lobed, lobes 9–16 cm long, rounded, new leaves tinged with red; veins palmate at base, midrib raised, lateral veins impressed above, joined by a marginal vein. **Flowers** white, becoming purple, minute, densely crowded on a fleshy spike (spadix) 4–10 cm long, 1 cm wide, often with an odor of mint, inflorescence bract (spathe) white to greenish, 5–14 cm long, 2–3 cm wide, broadly lance-shaped, tip pointed, base blunt, inflorescence stalk 15–40 cm long, shorter than leaf stalks; blooms and fruits all year. **Fruit** fleshy, dark red purple, fruiting spike to 15 cm long, thickened, bract becoming green. **Habitat:** Wet forest understories. Altitude: 300–1600 m. Conservation areas: ARE, CVC, GUA, LAC, LAP. **Range:** Bel–Guy and Pr.

365

■ *Spathiphyllum friedrichsthalii* (calita, peace lily)
Family Araceae

Large, stemless herb, usually many plants together (colonial) in shallow water. **Leaves** alternate, all from base of plant, stalk 0.33–1 m long, base sheathing stem, blade 30–63 cm long, 9–23 cm wide, narrowly elliptic, pointed at both ends, secondary veins numerous, parallel. **Flowers** white, minute, densely crowded on a fleshy spike 4–8 cm long, 1–2 cm wide, fragrant, inflorescence bract white, 13–32 cm long, 5–11 cm wide, narrowly elliptical, erect, hoodlike above and around spike; inflorescence stalk 0.5–1.4 m long; blooms and fruits most of the year. **Fruit** spike green, to 3 cm wide, appearing densely spiny from tips of old flowers, bract becoming green; seeds 12–24. **Habitat:** Common in wet pastures, shallow water of open marshes. Altitude: Sea level to 200 m, Caribbean lowlands. Conservation areas: CVC, HNO, LAC, TOR. **Range:** Hon–Col. **Notes:** Cultivated commercially for cut flowers. There are eight species of *Spathiphyllum* in Costa Rica; all are stemless, terrestrial herbs with lance-shaped leaves; S. *friedrichsthalii* is the only one growing in swampy habitats.

■ *Spathiphyllum montanum*
Family Araceae

Stemless understory herb. **Leaves** alternate, stalk 23–50 cm long, occasionally to 80 cm, base sheathing stem, blade 22–35 cm long, 9–16 cm wide, elliptical, tip abruptly pointed, base abruptly tapered to stalk, surface smooth. **Flowers** green, minute, densely crowded on a fleshy spike 3–4 cm long, occasionally to 10 cm, about 1 cm wide, green with regularly spaced white points, inflorescence bract bright white, 12–22 cm long, 4–7 cm wide, elliptical, erect, longer than the spike and shielding but not covering it, midrib often green on back, bract becoming green in fruit; inflorescence stalk 16–60 cm; blooms most of the year. **Fruit** fleshy, white. **Habitat:** Wet forest understories in mountains, cloud forests. Altitude: 1100–2000 m. Conservation areas: ARE, CVC, LAC, LAP, PAC. **Range:** CR, W Pan. **Notes:** The only species of *Spathiphyllum* found above 1300 m. The most common and widespread species of *Spathiphyllum* is probably S. *laeve*, which has a yellow green inflorescence bract and greenish white floral spike. It is found up to about 1100 m in wet forests in most of Costa Rica.

■ *Xanthosoma undipes* (hoja de pata)
   Family Araceae
Large terrestrial herb, trunklike stem 1–3 m tall,
10–15 cm diameter, densely ringed with leaf scars,
several stems often present, sap milky. **Leaves** alternate, stalk 0.3–1.4 m long, blade 35–80 cm long,
37–90 cm wide, arrow- to heart-shaped, tip blunt,
base deeply lobed, lobes widely separated, veins raised
above and below, forming a fish-bone pattern, margin encircled by a vein. **Flowers** white (upper, male
flowers) and red orange (lower, female flowers),
minute, densely crowded on a fleshy spike (spadix)
10–18 cm long, about 1 cm wide, inflorescence bract
(spathe) wrapped around flower spike, base usually
red, bulging, upper portion white, open, hoodlike
around spike, constricted near center; inflorescences
5–7 in leaf axils, stalk 9–34 cm long; blooms most of
the year. **Fruit** fleshy, pale greenish. **Habitat:** Moist
to wet forest understories. Altitude: 200–1800 m.
Conservation areas: CVC, GUA, HNO, LAC,
LAP, OSA, PAC. **Range:** CR–Ec and Ven. **Notes:**
Enclosed portion of inflorescence sometimes full of
small beetles. There are seven species of *Xanthosoma*
in Costa Rica; all are native, except X. *sagittifolium*, a
common ornamental that occasionally escapes from
cultivation.

■ *Zantedeschia aethiopica* (cala, calla,
   cartucho, calla lily)
   Family Araceae
Herb to 1.5 m tall in flower, colonial from poisonous underground stems (rhizomes). **Leaves** alternate, stalk 33–80 cm
long, spongy, blade 15–40 cm long, 7–24 cm wide, arrow-
to heart-shaped, leathery. **Flowers** yellow, minute, densely
crowded on a fleshy spike (spadix) 4–9 cm long, inflorescence bract (spathe) bright white 11–23 cm long, 5–13 cm
wide, funnel-shaped, top broadly flaring, tip pointed, base
tubular, wrapped around base of spike; blooms Apr., June–
Nov. **Fruit** fleshy berries, green, becoming orange. **Habitat:**
Escaped from cultivation in wet forests, roadside ditches,
wet ground in the mountains. Altitude: 1200–3000 m.
Conservation areas: CVC, LAP, PAC. **Range:** Native to
Africa. Naturalized throughout the Neotropics. Invasive in
Hawai'i and some other Pacific islands. **Notes:** This is the
only species of *Zantedeschia* in Costa Rica. Used as pig food
in some places.

367

■ *Bidens pilosa*
Family Asteraceae

Annual herb to 1.5 m tall, erect to sprawling, stems green, angled. **Leaves** opposite, stalk widened near base, slightly clasping stem, blade 3-parted, leaflets to 7 cm long, egg-shaped, tip and base blunt to pointed, margins toothed, finely hairy on both sides, veins pinnate. **Flowers** white and yellow or all yellow; of two types in heads of tiny flowers on a base of small bracts, central disk flowers yellow to greenish, tubular, radially symmetrical, numerous, very small, anthers black,

peripheral ray flowers usually white, occasionally yellow, petal-like with 1 extended lobe, about 1 cm long, tip 3-toothed (or rays absent); blooms all year. **Fruit** dry, black, linear, 1-seeded about 0.2 cm long with 2–3 spines each 0.3 cm long. **Habitat:** Open weedy areas. Altitude: Sea level to 2900 m. Conservation areas: ARE, CVC, HNO, LAC, LAP, OSA, PAC. **Range:** S US, Mex–Ven and Arg. Naturalized in the Old World tropics. Invasive in SE Asia, the Galapagos, and other Pacific islands. **Notes:** There are 11 species of *Bidens* in Costa Rica, *B. pilosa* is apparently the most common.

■ *Chaptalia nutans*
Family Asteraceae

Herb about 50–85 cm tall, flowering stems leafless. **Leaves** all basal, 9–34 cm long, 3–10 cm wide, lobed near base, base tapered, densely woolly below. **Flowers** white, very small, in a compact head that, arises from a bract-covered floral base, flowers tubular, of two forms: radially symmetrical (disk flowers), and bilaterally symmetrical with 1 enlarged petal (rays); outer rays, about 1 cm long; flower heads solitary, to 4 cm long, 6 cm wide at ends of stems, usually nodding when young and in seed, basal bracts of the head linear with bright red tips, densely woolly; blooms most of the year. **Fruit** dry, 1-seeded, 0.1 cm long, brown or green with fine white stripes, plumed with pink bristles. **Habitat:** Open sites, wet to seasonally dry regions. Altitude: 100–2100 m. Conservation areas: ARE, CVC, GUA, LAC, LAP, PAC, TEM. **Range:** SE US–Arg. **Notes:** This is the only species of *Chaptalia* in Costa Rica.

■ *Galinsoga quadriradiata*
  Family Asteraceae

Annual herb to 55 cm tall, often rooting at lower
nodes, stems usually hairy. **Leaves** opposite, stalks
present, blade 2–6 cm long, 1–4 cm wide, egg-
shaped both ends pointed to blunt, margins coarsely
toothed, hairy on both sides, major veins 3, from
base. **Flowers** white and yellow, tiny, of two types
in heads 0.3–0.7 cm wide, on a base of small bracts,
central disk flowers tubular, peripheral ray flowers
petal-like with 1 extended petal lobe, rays 5, 3-lobed
at tip, 0.1–0.2 cm long, sometimes pink or reddish,
disk flowers yellow, numerous, basal bracts about

0.3 cm long, green, 1 or 2 outer bracts, about 7 inner bracts,
some purplish; blooms all year. **Fruit** dry, black, about 0.1 cm
long, 1-seeded. **Habitat:** Wet and very wet regions, a weed of
open sites, often in cities along roadsides, curbs, vacant lots,
at mid- to high elevations. Altitude: 800–2600 m. Conservation areas: ARE, CVC, HNO, LAC, LAP, PAC. **Range:**
US, Mex–Ven and Pr, WI. Naturalized in the Old World
tropics. Invasive in the Galapagos and Hawai'i. **Notes:** The
only other species of *Galinsoga* in Costa Rica is the much less
common G. *parviflora*.

■ *Melanthera nivea* (paira)
  Family Asteraceae

Herb about 60 cm tall, or often a vinelike shrub 2–4 m tall,
stems slender, ridged across nodes. **Leaves** opposite, stalk
1–3 cm long, blade 5–11 cm long, egg-shaped, tip long-
pointed, base blunt, often lobed, dull green, 3 major veins
palmate at base, margin toothed. **Flowers** white, tubular,
radially symmetrical, 0.7 cm long, anthers black, flowers numerous in heads about 1 cm wide, round, but-
tonlike, basal bracts hard, in 2–3 rows, tips green,
hairy, flower heads on long stalks at ends of stems
in groups of 1–3; blooms most of the year. **Fruit**
dry, 0.2 cm long, 1-seeded. **Habitat:** Open areas,
roadsides, edges, near beaches, wet to seasonally
dry regions. Altitude: Sea level to 1700 m. Conservation areas: ARE, CVC, LAC, LAP, OSA, PAC,
TEM **Range:** Illinois–FL, LA, VI, Bel–Pan. **Notes:**
There are three species of *Melanthera* in Costa Rica.
Melanthera aspera is also common and very similar to
M. *nivea*.

■ *Begonia convallariodora*
Family Begoniaceae

Climbing epiphytic herb or shrublike, stems to 4 m long, green or sometimes pink, succulent, ringed by stipule scars at nodes. **Leaves** alternate, in one plane along opposite sides of the stem, fleshy, stalk 0.5–3.5 cm long, blade about 4.5–16 cm long, 1.6–8.0 cm wide, very asymmetrical, irregularly elliptic, one side wider than the other, upper surface with satinlike sheen, often reddish below, tip pointed, base unequal, veins 14–19 per side, margin irregularly toothed. **Flowers** white to

pale pink, bilaterally symmetrical, male and female flowers separate, petals 2 (rarely 3–4), 0.4–0.8 cm wide, male flowers with numerous yellow anthers, female flowers with 3-winged ovary below petals (inferior); inflorescence with forked branching, flowers numerous; blooms Sept.–May. **Fruit** pale green to reddish, becoming dry, about 0.8 cm long, 3-winged, one wing much larger than the other two; seeds minute, numerous. **Habitat:** Wet and very wet forests, cloud forests, open sites at high elevations. Altitude: 400–2350 m. Conservation areas: ARE, CVC, LAC, LAP, OSA, PAC. **Range:** S Mex–Pan. **Notes:** There are about 34 species of *Begonia* in Costa Rica.

■ *Begonia involucrata*
Family Begoniaceae

Terrestrial herb to 1.5 m tall, stems succulent; stipules paired, triangular, 1.5–4.5 cm long, surrounding stem at nodes, persistent, eventually leaving a ringlike scar. **Leaves** alternate, stalk about 2–24 cm long, often rusty-hairy; blade 2–15 cm long, 2–26 cm wide, sides very unequal, one side forked into 2 wide-based, pointed lobes, the other side rounded, margin toothed, slightly bristly-hairy. **Flowers** white to pale pink, bilaterally symmetrical, male and female flowers separate, about 1 cm wide, petals 2, rounded, about 1 cm long and

wide, male flowers with numerous yellow anthers; female flowers with ovary below petals; inflorescence of long-stalked, branched clusters with numerous flowers; blooms on and off July–Apr. **Fruit** becoming dry, about 0.9 cm long, with 3 very unequal wings, the largest about 1.5 cm wide; seeds numerous, minute. **Habitat:** Very wet forests, in gaps, partly shady roadsides, banks, trail edges in mountains. Altitude: 750–2700 m, mostly above 1500 m, on the Pacific slope. Conservation areas: ARE, CVC, GUA, LAP, PAC. Common in GUA N.P. and Monteverde Biological Reserve. **Range:** Gua–Pan.

■ *Begonia semiovata*
Family Begoniaceae

Small herb to about 40 cm tall, terrestrial or epiphytic, stems reddish, succulent, forming colonies from underground stems (rhizomes). **Leaves** alternate, stalk 0.1–4 cm long, blade 1–9 cm long, 0.5–4 cm wide, asymmetrically egg- to lance-shaped, tip pointed, base unequal, veins pale, margin deeply, irregularly toothed. **Flowers** white, small, male flowers with 2 petals, to about 0.2 cm long and wide, stamens no more than 15; female flowers with 4–5 petals, about 0.1 cm long and wide, ovary below petals; blooms most of the year, especially Mar.–June. **Fruit** dry, about 0.8 cm long, round in outline, 3-winged, each wing about 0.4 cm wide. **Habitat:** Wet forest understories, edges, gaps. Altitude: Sea level to 1400 m, Caribbean slope. Conservation areas: ARE, CVC, HNO, LAC, TOR. Common at La Selva Biological Station and Barbilla N.P. **Range:** Nic–Pr.

■ *Aechmea mexicana*
Family Bromeliaceae

Epiphytic herb to 1.5 m tall. **Leaves** alternate, in a dense rosette, no stalk, blade 0.57–1.4 m long, 6–10 cm wide, dark blue green, shiny above, pale-scaly below, stiff; tip pointed, base broadly sheathing, margins spiny. **Flowers** red lilac, about 1 cm long, petals straplike; each on a slender stalk, on few flowered stems; inflorescence 55–85 m tall, once- or twice-branched, cylindrical or pyramidal, on a stalk 30–50 cm long, covered with cream white to pale pink bracts, to 18 cm long, scaly; blooms Dec.–Mar. **Fruit** fleshy, white, spine tipped, about 1 cm long; fruits in Mar. **Habitat:** Wet forests, often in trees close to ground. Altitude: 300–2700 m. Conservation areas: ARE, CVC, LAC, LAP, PAC. **Range:** Mex–Ec.

■ *Rhipsalis baccifera (R. cassytha)* (cactus)
Family Cactaceae
Epiphytic cactus, stems numerous, thin, green, cylindrical, unarmed, branches forking, pendulous, to 2 m or more long, about 0.3 cm diameter, hanging from trees. **Leaves** none. **Flowers** white to pale greenish, translucent, petals about 0.2 cm long, stamens numerous; flowers growing from sides of stems; blooms most of the year. **Fruit** fleshy, greenish white, 0.9 cm long, 0.6 cm wide, with several seeds. **Habitat:** Moist to wet lowland forests. Altitude: Sea level to 800 m, primarily on the Caribbean slope. Conservation areas: ARE, CVC, GUA, HNO, LAC, OSA, PAC, TOR. **Range:** FL, Mex–Bol and Par, WI. **Notes:** There are five species of *Rhipsalis* in Costa Rica, *R. baccifera* is by far the most common.

■ *Hippobroma longiflora* (horse poison)
Family Campanulaceae
Herb 30–50 cm tall, sap milky, unpleasant odor, *strong eye irritant*. **Leaves** alternate, crowded on stem, stalkless, blade 10–20 cm long, 2–5 cm wide, elliptic, finely hairy, tip pointed, base extending to plant stem, margin irregularly pinnately lobed, lobes shallow, pointed, margins toothed. **Flowers** white, showy, long-tubular, radially symmetrical, sweet scented, tube 5–13 cm long, 0.4 cm wide, petal lobes 5, about 2 cm long, 0.5 cm wide, calyx lobes toothed, about 1 cm long, stigmas green; flowers solitary to few, in axils,; blooms all year. **Fruit** dry, 1–2 cm long, splitting open to release cylindrical seeds. **Habitat:** Wet to seasonally dry regions, in moist, open or partly shaded, weedy sites, roadside banks, stream margins. Altitude: Sea level to 1300 m. Conservation areas: ARE, CVC, GUA, HNO, LAC, LAP, OSA, PAC, TEM, TOR. **Range:** Native Mex–Brz and Pr, WI. Now pantropical; invasive in the Galapagos and other Pacific islands. **Notes:** This is the only species of *Hippobroma* worldwide. *Plant is very toxic.*

■ *Arenaria lanuginosa* (spreading sandwort)
   Family Caryophyllaceae

Herb 30–100 m long, stems slender, prostrate or draping over
other vegetation, much-branched from base. **Leaves** opposite,
stalk to 0.3 cm or none, blade 1–3 cm long, 0.1–1.6 cm wide,
linear to lance-shaped, tip pointed to blunt, base tapered,
clasping stem, midrib prominent. **Flowers** white, radially
symmetrical, petals 5, to 0.8 cm long, free, soon deciduous,
sepals 5, to 0.5 cm long, center green, margins translucent;
flowers solitary in leaf axils near tips of branches on thin
stalks 0.5–5 cm long; blooms all year. **Fruit** dry, 0.3–0.6 cm
long, oval, yellowish. **Habitat:** Open sites, roadsides, pastures, mostly in mountains. Altitude: 700–3400 m. Conservation areas: ARE, CVC, LAC, LAP, PAC. **Range:** S US–Pr
and Brz. **Notes:** There is one other species of *Arenaria* in
Costa Rica, which is quite uncommon.

■ *Drymaria cordata* (nervillo)
   Family Caryophyllaceae

Weedy herb, prostrate to erect, stems to 70 cm long, often
rooting at nodes, stipules at bases of new leaves, 0.2 cm long,
fringed or shredding. **Leaves** opposite, rather distant along
stem, stalks 0.2–1.5 cm long, blades broadly egg-shaped
to rounded or kidney-shaped, 0.5–2 cm long and wide, tip
rounded, base rounded to lobed. **Flowers** white, radially
symmetrical, petals 5, free, about 0.3 cm long, split down
center into 2 linear lobes, sepals 5, about 0.3 cm
long, margins translucent; inflorescence of small,
branched clusters on a longish stalk above small
bracts; blooms all year. **Fruit** dry, 3-parted, about
0.2 cm long, splitting open to release seeds. **Habitat:**

Very wet to seasonally dry regions in open or shaded
secondary forest, weedy sites, roadsides, pastures.
Altitude: Sea level to 2100 m. Conservation areas:
ARE, CVC, HNO, ICO, LAC, OSA, PAC, TEM,
TOR. **Range:** FL, Mex–Arg, WI. **Notes:** There are
three species of *Drymaria* in Costa Rica, *D. cordata*
is the most common.

■ *Stellaria prostrata* (prostrate sandwort)
Family Caryophyllaceae

Slender weedy herb, trailing or draped over other low vegetation, pale, bight green, stems to 60 cm long, finely hairy. **Leaves** opposite, stalks 1–2.5 cm long, winged, blade 0.5–3 cm long, 0.5–2 cm wide, egg-shaped, tip pointed, base blunt or slightly lobed, extending down stalk. **Flowers** white, radially symmetrical, petals 5, free, 0.2–0.3 cm long, tip deeply 2-lobed, often almost to base, sepals about as long as petals; inflorescence hairy, bracts 0.6–2 cm long, leaflike, stalked; blooms all year. **Fruit** dry, about 0.5 cm long, elliptic, with 6 valves that curl back to release seeds. **Habitat:** Moist, shaded sites. Altitude: 600–2000 m. Conservation areas: CVC, PAC. **Range:** FL–TX, Mex–Col. **Notes:** There are five species of *Stellaria* in Costa Rica, all very similar. *Stellaria ovata* is the most common, but the species are difficult to tell apart.

■ *Dichorisandra amabilis*
Family Commelinaceae

Erect, shrubby terrestrial herb to about 2 m tall, main stem green, stiff, about 1 cm wide, slightly rough with pale speckles, branches forking almost into 2 equal parts, nodes very swollen; leaf bases sheathing stem. **Leaves** alternate, in one plane, blade 11–20 cm long, 2–5 cm wide, elliptic, tip tapered to a point, base pointed to rounded, smooth on both sides. **Flowers** white to pale blue, about 1 cm long, 1.5 cm wide, petals 3 all equal, sepals 3, green to white, shorter than

petals, anthers blue; inflorescence 2–7 cm, on a stalk to 1–3 cm long; blooms all year except Dec. **Fruit** fleshy, dark purplish green, deeply 3-lobed, above persistent sepals. **Habitat:** Seasonally dry to very wet forests, along edges and understories, roadsides. Altitude: Sea level to 1800 m. Conservation areas: CVC, GUA, LAC, PAC, TEM, TOR. **Range:** S Mex–Pan. **Notes:** There is one other species of *Dichorisandra* in Costa Rica. *Dichorisandra hexandra* is by far the most common. It is a trailing herb, often climbing on tree trunks. The leaves and flowers are much like those of *D. amabilis*.

374

■ *Tradescantia zanonia* (cañutillo, matalomoyo)
Family Commelinaceae

Herb 1–2 m tall, stems usually erect, stout, often unbranched, green with brown rings at tops of leaf sheaths, sheaths 1–2 cm long, tight, top rim and edges with dense, brown fibers. **Leaves** alternate, clustered at ends of stems, stalk very short or none, blade 12–25 cm long, 3–8 cm wide, lance-shaped, tip long-pointed, base narrowed to top of sheath, veins numerous, parallel, obscure. **Flowers** white and dark purple, 3-parted, radially symmetrical, petals 0.6–1.0 cm long, bluntly triangular, calyx purple, flowers blooms few at a time in a dense cluster of

buds and fruit above a pair of wide, leaflike bracts, 1–3 cm long, about 1.5 cm wide; inflorescence stalk elongate, 4–27 cm long; blooms all year. **Fruit** fleshy, dark purple, to 0.5 cm long, enclosed in fleshy calyx. **Habitat:** Wet to very wet forest understories. Altitude: Sea level to 2000 m. Conservation areas: ARE, CVC, GUA, LAC, LAP, OSA, PAC, TOR. **Range:** S Mex–Brz, WI. **Notes:** There are eight species of *Tradescantia* in Costa Rica. This is, by far, the most common.

■ *Maianthemum gigas*
Family Convallariaceae

Terrestrial, or occasionally, epiphytic herb 0.5–2.5 m tall, colonial from long underground stems, aboveground stem unbranched, usually arching, often reddish. **Leaves** alternate, in 2 ranks along stem, almost stalkless, blade 10–30 cm long, 2–10 cm wide, egg-to lance-shaped, pleated longitudinally along parallel veins, tip pointed, base blunt. **Flowers** white, radially symmetrical, about 1 cm wide, petals and sepals alike, 6, tips pointed, stigma purple red, anthers violet; inflorescence at end of stem, cone-shaped, with many short branches, often reddish; blooms and fruits most of the year especially Mar.–July. **Fruit** fleshy, 3-lobed, rounded, to

about 1 cm diameter, dull whitish with red speckles when immature, becoming translucent and bright red at maturity. **Habitat:** Wet mountain forest understories, or in open or partly shady sites, along roadsides, trails. Altitude: 1300–3400 m. Conservation areas: CVC, GUA (infrequent), LAC, LAP, PAC. **Range:** S Mex–Pan. **Notes:** There are four species of *Maianthemum* in Costa Rica; all are very similar, M. *gigas* is the most common.

375

■ *Costus laevis* (caña agria, wild ginger)
Family Costaceae

Stout, unbranched herb 1–6 m tall, stem spiraled; leaf sheath 0.5–1.5 cm long, 2 lobes at top. **Leaves** alternate, spirally arranged, stalk 0–3 cm, blade 15–60 cm long, 5–15 cm wide, lance-shaped, tip tapered to a long point, base wedge-shaped, leaves near top and base of stem smaller, lowest leaves bladeless; young leaves often red below. **Flowers** white with yellow center, asymmetrical, 5–9 cm long, large projecting lip dark red with pale yellow stripes, 5–7 cm long, about 5 cm wide, top 3-lobed, middle lobe ragged, calyx about 1 cm; blooms few at a time; inflorescence bracts green to red with green tips, about 3 cm long, interior bright red in fruit; inflorescence conelike, 5–10 cm long, 3–7 cm wide; blooms all year. **Fruit** white, to 2.5 cm long, crowned by red calyx, seeds small, black with white fleshy coat. Dispersed by birds. **Habitat:** Wet regions, forests, second growth, open roadsides, or part shade; also cultivated. Altitude: Sea level to 900 m. Conservation areas: ARE, CVC, GUA, LAC, LAP, OSA, PAC, TOR. **Range:** Gua–Bol. **Notes:** There are 22 species of *Costus* in Costa Rica.

■ *Costus speciosus* (caña agria, wild ginger)
Family Costaceae

Large unbranched herb 0.5–3 m tall, colonial from underground stems, roots very aromatic, aboveground stem reddish, spiraled, leaf base sheathing stem. **Leaves** alternate, spiraled on stem, stalk short, blade 12–25 cm long, 3–6 cm wide, lance-shaped, shiny above, finely velvety-hairy below, tip pointed. **Flowers** white with yellow or orange throat, showy, 6–7 cm long, 8–10 cm wide, irregular, widely spreading, silky-hairy, calyx about 2.5 cm long, blooms a few at a time; bracts dark red, to 3 cm long, 2 cm wide, overlapping; inflorescence 4–7 cm long, 3–5 cm wide, broadly egg-shaped, conelike, at top of stem; July–Oct. **Fruit** red, crowned by old calyx; seeds black with a white aril. **Habitat:** Cultivated and escaped along roadsides, second growth, oil palm plantations. Altitude: Sea level to 200 m. Conservation areas: CVC, LAC, OSA, PAC. **Range:** Native to India, SE Asia, parts of Oceania. Escaped from cultivation throughout the tropics. Invasive in Hawai'i and some other Pacific islands.

■ *Croton argenteus*
Family Euphorbiaceae

Gray green herb 0.2–1 m tall, most parts appressed-hairy, crushed leaves aromatic, stipules to 1 cm long, linear. **Leaves** alternate, often densely clustered below inflorescences, stalks 0.3–1 cm, blade 2–10 cm long, 1–6 cm wide, egg-shaped, tip blunt, base blunt to wedge-shaped, dull green above, whitish-hairy below, major veins 5, palmate at base, margin vaguely toothed. **Flowers** greenish white, small, to 0.8 cm long, in headlike clusters at ends of stems, often enclosed by the leaflike bracts below inflorescence. **Fruit** dry, 0.5 cm. **Habitat:** Open sites in moist to seasonally dry regions, roadsides, pastures. Altitude: Pacific lowlands, sea level to 300 m. Conservation areas: LAP, PAC, TEM. **Range:** TX–Arg. **Notes:** There are about 41 species of *Croton* in Costa Rica. They are distinguished from one another by technical details of flower structure. They vary from herbs to shrubs or small trees.

■ *Diastema affine*
Family Gesneriaceae

Small hairy herb to 15 cm tall, colonial from underground stems (rhizomes) aerial stems unbranched slender, pale green, sometimes reddish, somewhat translucent, succulent, often reclining and rooting at nodes. **Leaves** opposite, stalk 0.5–2 cm long, green to reddish, hairy, blade 2.5–6.5 cm long, 1.5–4 cm wide, tip pointed, base pointed to blunt, surface hairy-bristly above, covered with small dots, wrinkled from depressed veins, lower surface very pale green, finely hairy, veins pinnate, curved upward, margin coarsely toothed. **Flowers** white marked with purple, 5-parted, tubular, slightly bilaterally symmetrical, tube 0.4 cm wide, hairy, petal tube sometimes flushed with pink, funnel-shaped to cylindrical, 1–2 cm long, lobes short, 0.1 cm long, rounded, calyx green, short; blooms all year; inflorescences of 1–4 flowers. **Fruit** dry, round, 2-parted, membranous, splitting in two to release dark brown, numerous, minute seeds. **Habitat:** Moist to wet forests. Altitude: 150–1700 m. Conservation areas: ARE, CVC, LAC, LAP. **Range:** CR–Pr. **Notes:** The only other species of *Diastema* in Costa Rica is *D. racemiferum*.

■ *Koellikeria erinoides*
Family Gesneriaceae

Small terrestrial herb, colonial from underground stems, aerial stems often very short, unbranched. **Leaves** opposite, usually all in a basal rosette, stalks very short, blade 2–11 cm long, 1–5 cm wide, egg-shaped, pointed at both ends, hairy, dark green, surface often with reddish veins and white dots, margin toothed. **Flowers** white, tubular, 1–2 cm long, upper lip red inside, base of tube wine red outside, upper lip 2-

lobed, lower lip 3-lobed, longer than upper lip, calyx lobes as long as petal tube; inflorescence, slender, unbranched, about 7 cm long, stalk red, hairy; blooms most of the year, especially July–Oct. **Fruit** dry, 0.5 cm long. **Habitat:** Wet to seasonally dry regions, roadside banks; also cultivated as a house plant. Altitude: Sea level to 1300 m, mostly on the Pacific slope, above 400 m. Conservation areas: ARE, CVC, GUA, LAP, PAC, TEM. **Range:** CR–Ven and Bol. **Notes:** This is the only species of *Koellikeria* in Costa Rica. White or silvery spots on leaves are distinctive.

■ *Xiphidium caeruleum* (cola de gallo, espadaña, palma bruja)
Family Haemodoraceae

Terrestrial herb 0.3–1 m tall, flattened side-to-side, colonial from thick, creeping underground stems with red sap. **Leaves** alternate, in a 2-ranked, fanlike arrangement, along end of stem, blade 20–50 cm long, 1–6 cm wide, stiff, narrowly sword-shaped, tip pointed, bases sheathing stem and overlapping, veins all parallel, margin finely toothed. **Flowers** white, radially symmetrical, petals 6, 0.4–1.6 cm long, 0.1–0.6 cm wide, ovary superior; inflorescence 2–45 cm long, 2–15 cm wide, branched once from central axis, held horizontally, with 5–25 flowers along upper sides; blooms Mar., July–Nov. **Fruit** at first fleshy, dull red, becoming black, dry, 0.5–1.0 cm wide, splitting open to release numerous red seeds; fruits July–Mar.

Habitat: Wet to very wet forests, edges and second growth in part shade; also cultivated. Altitude: Sea level to 1400 m, most often about 100–500 m. Conservation areas: ARE, CVC, GUA, LAC, LAP, OSA, PAC, TEM, TOR. **Range:** S Mex–Bol and Ven, Brz, Guy, WI. **Notes:** *Xiphidium caeruleum* is the only representative of the family Haemodoraceae in Costa Rica.

Fruit
Courtesy of Margaret Gargiullo

■ *Hyptis verticillata*
Family Lamiaceae

Erect, shrub or woody herb 0.5–2.5 m tall, often many stems together, slender, freely branched, branches leafy, elongate. **Leaves** opposite, lance-shaped, small, 2–8 cm long, pointed at both ends, tip elongate, aromatically scented, margins irregularly toothed. **Flowers** white, bilaterally symmetrical, tubular, 5-parted, 0.3 cm long, stamens purple; inflorescence of small dense axillary clusters along branches; blooms May–Jan. **Fruit** dry, of 4 small nutlike parts, encased in old calyx. **Habitat:** Wet to seasonally dry open, lowlands sites, a weed of pastures, roadsides, and second growth. Altitude: Sea level to 600 m. Conservation areas: CVC, GUA, HNO, LAC, LAP, OSA, TEM. **Range:** Mex–Ec, WI. **Notes:** Used as a medicinal in Mexico and other parts of Central America. There are about 14 species of *Hyptis* in Costa Rica.

■ *Gossypium hirsutum* (algodón, upland cotton, wild cotton)
Family Malvaceae

Shrublike herb to 2 m tall, new stems hairy, green, sometimes woody at base. **Leaves** alternate, stalk 3–8 cm long, blade 5–10 cm long, and wide, broadly 3- to 5-lobed, tips pointed, base rounded or lobed, margins smooth, dotted with black oil glands. **Flowers** yellow to white, fading to reddish purple, radially symmetrical, showy, to 8 cm long, 5 petals, overlapping, 5 sepals, stamens united into a central column; flowers solitary; blooms Aug.–Nov. **Fruits** dry, oval with sharp tip, to 5 cm, 3- to 5-parted, held within persistent bracts, opening to expose seeds embedded in white cotton fibers; fruit present Nov.–Mar. **Habitat:** Open sites or part shade, disturbed areas, roadsides, ditches of the Pacific lowlands. Altitude: Sea level to 50 m. Conservation areas: GUA, OSA, PAC, TEM. **Range:** Mex–Ven and Ec, Par, WI. Introduced in parts of Africa. **Notes:** The world's major species of cultivated cotton. Cultivated as a fiber crop in all cotton producing countries. Wild plants often defended by ants. There are three other species of *Gossypium* in Costa Rica, all of them are very uncommon.

■ *Malachra fasciata* (malva, malva salvaje)
Family Malvaceae
Herb 0.6–2 m tall, stems with very irritating bristly hairs. **Leaves** alternate, stalk 2–10 cm, blade 3–15 cm long, 3–12 cm wide, rounded to egg-shaped, angled to palmately 3- to 5-lobed, lobe tips pointed, base blunt to lobed, surface hairy, dull green, many marked or dotted with red, major veins 3–7, palmate at base, margin toothed. **Flowers** white (rarely yellow), radially symmetrical, petals 5, to 1.5 cm long, overlapping at edges, stamens fused in a central tube to 1 cm long, surrounding stigmas; inflorescence of axillary clusters; blooms July–Feb. **Fruit** dry, 5-parted, top blunt, base pointed, splitting apart to release seeds. **Habitat:** Wet to seasonally dry, disturbed, open sites, pastures, roadsides. Altitude: Sea level to 1200 m, mostly below 300 m. Conservation areas: ARE, GUA, LAC, PAC, TEM, TOR. **Range:** Mex–Pan, Bol, Ec, and Ven, WI. Invasive in the Galapagos and Hawai'i. **Notes:** Sometimes used with milk as a cough medicine. There are four species of Malachra in Costa Rica. *Malachra alceifolia* is also fairly common, it has yellow flowers.

■ *Calathea gymnocarpa*
Family Marantaceae
Herb 0.6–2 m tall, terrestrial, leaves all basal. **Leaves** alternate, top of stalk slightly swollen, jointlike, olive green, base winged and grooved, sheathing stem, blade 18–80 cm long, 12–43 cm wide, broadly elliptic, tip with small point, base blunt but slightly unequal, new leaves purple below, veins often pink or white above, all fading to green in older leaves. **Flowers** cream white to pale yellow, very irregular, about 2.5 cm long; bracts pale yellow, 30 or more, narrow, erect, spiraled, decomposing as fruit develops; inflorescence 1 per stem, 7–15 cm long, 6–10 cm wide, egg-shaped; blooms all year except May and June. **Fruit** fleshy, pale orange becoming red orange, 3-parted, about 2 cm long, 1.5 cm wide, in a ball-shaped cluster on a stalk about 60 cm long; seeds 3, dark blue; fruits Sept.–Apr. **Habitat:** Wet to very wet forest understories. Altitude: Sea level to 800 m. Conservation areas: ARE, CVC, GUA, LAC, OSA, PAC, TOR. **Range:** Nic–Col. **Notes:** The only species of Marantaceae in Costa Rica in which flower bracts decay entirely and fruit is bright red, forming a dense cluster. There are 41 species of *Calathea* in Costa Rica.

■ *Calathea marantifolia*
Family Marantaceae

Herb 1–2 m tall; leaves both basal and along stem. **Leaves** alternate, stalk to about 15 cm long, sometimes absent, olive to yellow green, jointlike, slightly swollen near top, base winged and grooved, sheathing stem; blade 10–70 cm long, 6–37 cm wide, oblong, tip abruptly short-pointed, base blunt, abruptly extended down stalk; young leaves hairy above, mature leaves with midrib finely hairy above, lower surface gray green. **Flowers** cream white and yellow, 2–3 cm long, irregular, tubular, sepals yellow, persistent; bracts yellow, 6–33, spirally arranged, about 1 cm high, wider than high; inflorescence spike solitary, at top of stem, elliptical to cylindrical, greenish yellow, 4–9 cm long, 3–6 cm wide, bracts slightly overlapped, rounded; blooms all year, mostly Sept.–Oct. **Fruit** dry, yellow, crowned by old sepals; seeds 3, gray with white fleshy attachment. **Habitat:** Wet to very wet forest understories, stream banks, shady, wet roadsides. Altitude: Sea level to 1600 m. Conservation areas: ARE, CVC, GUA, LAP, OSA, PAC. **Range:** Gua–Ec.

■ *Calathea micans*
Family Marantaceae

Low, stemless, colonial herb 10–30 cm tall; leaf sheath finely hairy, narrow. **Leaves** all from base, stalk often hairy, and as long as blade, top slightly swollen, jointlike, olive green to purple-tinged, base winged, grooved; blade 3–15 cm long, 1–5 cm wide, narrowly egg-shaped to elliptic, tip pointed, base blunt to wedge-shaped, midrib sometimes pale, surface silvery gray green above, green to purple below, midrib finely hairy below. **Flowers** white, lip often tinged with purple, irregular, tubular, 0.7–0.9 cm long; bracts green, few, narrow, spirally arranged; inflorescence spikes at tops of stems, 2, 1–2.3 cm long, 0.4–1 cm wide, smaller inflorescences at base; blooms all year, mostly May, Aug.–Sept. **Fruit** purplish green, becoming brown, dry, small; seeds brown, dispersed by ants. **Habitat:** Wet to very wet forest understories, trail margins. Altitude: Sea level to 1100 m, occasionally to 1400 m. Conservation areas: ARE, CVC, GUA, LAC, LAP, OSA, PAC, TOR. Seen at La Selva Biological Station. **Range:** Mex–Brz. **Notes:** This is the smallest species of Marantaceae in Costa Rica. Often locally abundant.

381

■ *Maranta arundinacea* (periquitoya, arrowroot)
Family Marantaceae

Slender herb 0.3–1.3 m tall, often branched above; from a cylindrical, fleshy rootstock, upper stem often dying back to the ground during the dry season. **Leaves** alternate, 4–8 from base, 1–8 along stem, basal leaves with stalk 4–20 cm long, stem leaves with stalk 0–7 cm long, swollen, jointlike at top, olive green, hairy along upper surface, base of stalk sheathing stem; blade 4–25 cm long, 3–11 cm wide, egg-shaped, finely hairy above, pale green below. **Flowers** white, small, asymmetrical, about 1.5 cm long, in pairs on elongate stalks; inflorescence with stiff, slender branches, bracts leaflike; blooms June–Dec. **Fruit**, dry, orange tan, becoming green at maturity; seed solitary with white, fleshy attachment. **Habitat:** Very wet to seasonally dry regions, lowland forests, edges, roadsides, part shade. Altitude: Pacific lowlands, sea level to 800 m, mostly below 400 m. Conservation areas: GUA, OSA, PAC, TEM. **Range:** Mex–Brz, Ant. **Notes:** There are three species of *Maranta* in Costa Rica; *M. arundinacea* is the only common one. The dried roots are sometimes ground up and used as a thickener in foods. Plants with green and white variegated leaves are sometimes cultivated.

■ *Pleiostachya pruinosa* (*Ischnosiphon p.*)
Family Marantaceae

Herb 1–2.5 m tall. **Leaves** alternate, mostly from base, 1 or 2 stem leaves, stalk to 80 cm long, usually hairy-bristly, often purple, upper part olive green to dark purple, cylindrical; blade 25–90 cm long, 10–35 cm wide, tip pointed, bent sideways, dark green above, often wine red below, midrib hairy, pale. **Flowers** white and purple, asymmetrical, about 3 cm long, 1 cm wide, in pairs; bracts pale waxy yellow, smooth to densely white-hairy-bristly, flattened, about 4.5 cm long, narrow, tip pointed, folded along back, closely overlapping; flower spikes 6–18 cm long, about 2 cm wide; inflorescence of 5–16 palmately arranged flower spikes on a stalk to 43 cm long in upper leaf axils; blooms all year except Apr. and May, mostly Aug.–Oct. **Fruit** dry, to 1.3 cm, papery when mature; 1 seed, dark with a white, fleshy attachment. **Habitat:** Wet to very wet regions in partial shade and open areas, roadsides. Altitude: Sea level to 900 m, usually below 300 m, mostly in the Pacific lowlands. Conservation areas: ARE, HNO, OSA, PAC, TEM. **Range:** Mex–Ec. **Notes:** There is one other species of *Pleiostachya* in Costa Rica, *P. leiostachya*, found mostly above 400 m.

■ *Centradenia inaequilateralis*
Family Melastomataceae

Herb about 0.3 to sometimes 1.5 m tall, stems reddish, slender, young stems herbaceous, dark reddish, 4-angled, branches alternate. **Leaves** opposite but those on secondary branches appear alternate due to much smaller opposite leaf, larger leaves with short stalk, blades 2–4 cm long, 0.3–0.7 cm wide, small pair members about 0.2 cm long, 0.1 cm wide, lance-shaped, sides unequal, tip blunt to pointed, base tapered, surface dull green, finely hairy, very pale below, major veins 3, palmate at base, side veins almost at margin, old leaves reddish. **Flowers** white to pale pink, radially

symmetrical, about 0.6 cm wide, petals 4, sides unequal, tips notched, sepals 4, fused to expanded floral base, stamens yellow with pink stalks; flowers solitary or few at ends of branches; blooms all year. **Fruit** initially red, becoming dry, 4-parted; seeds numerous, minute. **Habitat:** Moist to wet forests but also common along roadside banks in part shade and second growth, mostly in mountains. Altitude: 150–1700 m, usually above 1000 m. Conservation areas: ARE, CVC, GUA, LAC, LAP, PAC. **Range:** Mex–Pan. **Notes:** There are two other species of *Centradenia* in Costa Rica both are similar but less common.

■ *Tococa platyphylla*
Family Melastomataceae

Herb or shrub 0.5–1.5 m tall, rarely to 3 m, densely bristly, stems 4-sided, stout. **Leaves** opposite, stalk thick, 3–7 cm long, bristly, blade 30–50 cm long, 20–30 cm wide, broadly egg-shaped or elliptic, hairy, dark green above, pale or sometimes purple below, major veins 5, palmate, deeply impressed, secondary veins numerous, ladderlike, at right angles to major veins. **Flowers** white to pink, small, petals 0.4 cm long, floral base bright red, hairy, no sepals, stamens white, style to 1 cm long; inflorescence 5–15 cm long, of dense, branched, axillary clusters, stems densely bristly, pink or reddish; blooms Dec.–June. **Fruit** fleshy, becoming red, then purple; fruits Jan.–Aug. **Habitat:** Wet to moist forest, understories, also in open sites, pastures, roadsides. Altitude: 70–1500 m, most often above 900 m. Conservation areas: ARE, CVC, HNO, LAC, LAP, OSA, PAC, TOR. **Range:** CR–Ven and Ec. **Notes:** The other species of *Tococa* in Costa Rica, *T. guianensis*, is similar and also moderately common. It is found at lower elevations.

Courtesy of Margaret Gargiullo

383

■ *Brassavola nodosa* (huele de noche,
lady of the night orchid)
Family Orchidaceae

Epiphyte 30–40 cm tall, stems clustered, succulent. **Leaves** 1 per stem, 5–15 cm long, 0.5–1.5 cm wide, fleshy, often nearly cylindrical. **Flowers** white or often with small purple spots, bilaterally symmetrical, 3 sepals and 2 side petals similar, 6–8 cm long, 0.2–0.4 cm wide, linear, sometimes yellow or greenish, lower petal (lip) highly modified, broad, large, appearing heart-shaped, 5–6 cm long, 2.5–3.5 cm wide, tip pointed, margin smooth; blooms Jan.–Oct., especially July–Sept. **Fruit** dry, seeds numerous, dustlike. **Habitat:** Seasonally dry, to very wet forests, usually near the shore on coconut palms or mangroves. Altitude: Sea level to 300 m. Conservation areas: CVC, GUA, LAC, OSA, PAC, TEM. **Range:** Mex–Col, Ven, Pr, Brz, WI. **Notes:** There is one other species of *Brassavola* in Costa Rica, it has drooping leaves and is found in mountain forests.

Courtesy of Margaret Gargiullo

■ *Epidendrum trialatum*
Family Orchidaceae

Epiphyte 15–30 cm tall, stems slender, flattened, leaf base sheathing stem. **Leaves** alternate, 4–7, ranked along stem, no stalk, blade 7–8 cm long, about 1–2 cm wide, narrowly elliptic, fleshy, tip notched. **Flowers** greenish white, very fragrant, sepals and lateral petals very similar, about 1.4 cm long, 0.1–0.6 cm wide, lower petal arched, lip about 1 cm long, 1.5 cm wide, tip shallowly 4-lobed, fringed along top and sides; inflorescence at top of stem, with 3–6 flowers; blooms Oct.–Feb. **Fruit** dry, seeds numerous, dustlike. **Habitat:** Very wet forests. Altitude: 350–1300 m. Conservation areas: CVC, LAP, PAC. Observed in Tapantí N.P. **Range:** Endemic to CR.

■ *Maxillaria inaudita*
Family Orchidaceae

Epiphytic herb 1 m tall, erect, fairly robust, leaf bases sheathing stem. **Leaves** alternate, numerous, ranked along stem, stalk short, broad, blade 5–20 cm long, 2–5 cm wide, straplike, veins parallel to midrib, rather obscure, midrib slightly depressed above, surface shiny, edges folded together at base, tip blunt to slightly notched. **Flowers** cream white to pale yellow, fragrant, showy, bilaterally symmetric, about 9 cm wide, sepals and lateral petals similar, about 0.3–6 cm long, 0.5–1.0 cm wide, slightly twisted, lower petal appearing tubular at base, lip 3-lobed, 1.5–2 cm long, 1–1.5 cm wide, often darker yellow; flowers solitary in leaf axils; blooms on and off July–Mar. **Fruit** dry, 5–6 cm long; seeds numerous, dustlike. **Habitat:** Very wet mountain forests.

Altitude: 800–1800 m. Conservation areas: ARE (mostly), CVC, GUA, LAC, LAP. Observed on a stump in Monteverde. **Range:** CR, Pan. **Notes:** There are 107 species of *Maxillaria* in Costa Rica. Most are branched, leaves folded along midrib; inflorescences arising from side of stem or bulblike base.

■ *Nidema boothii*
Family Orchidaceae

Creeping colonial epiphyte, stems to 20 cm long, with elliptic, bulblike leaf stalks 2–4 cm long. **Leaves** solitary, blade 7–20 cm long, 0.4–0.9 cm wide, straplike, tip pointed, longer than inflorescence. **Flowers** white to pale yellow, fragrant, bilaterally symmetric, 3 sepals and 2 side petals similar, sepals about 1.5 cm long, 0.4 cm wide, longer than petals, lower petal (lip) about 0.9 cm long, 0.3 cm wide, blunt-tipped, curved downward; inflorescence erect, unbranched, 4–8 cm long; blooms on and off most of the year. **Fruit** dry, seeds numerous, dustlike. **Habitat:** Very wet forests. Altitude: Sea level to 1500 m, Caribbean slope. Conservation areas: ARE, CVC, LAC. **Range:** Mex–Pan, Ant. **Notes:** There is one other species of *Nidema* in Costa Rica; it is less common and has smaller flowers.

■ *Prosthechea fragrans (Encyclia f.)*
   Family Orchidaceae

Epiphytic or terrestrial orchid to 20 cm tall from an elliptic bulblike stem 5–12 cm long, 1–1.5 cm wide, with a thick sheath, stems usually clustered. **Leaves** solitary, 1 per stem, 9–31 cm long, 2–4 cm wide, strap-shaped, tip somewhat blunt, secondary veins rather obscure. **Flowers** cream to greenish white with purple stripes, bilaterally symmetric, spicy-fragrant; 3 sepals 2–3 cm long, about 0.5 cm wide, lance-shaped, tips elongate, pointed; 2 side petals elliptic or almost 4-sided; upper petal (lip) 1.5–2 cm long, about 1 cm wide, broadly egg-shaped, concave, striped with purple, tip elongate-pointed; inflorescence arising directly from swollen stem (pseudobulb), 2- to 6-flowered, 5–9 cm long; blooms Feb., Mar., May–July, Nov., Dec. **Fruit** dry, seeds numerous, dustlike. **Habitat:** Very wet, forests; also cultivated. Altitude: Sea level to 1000 m. Conservation areas: ARE, CVC, GUA, LAC, OSA, PAC, TOR. **Range:** Mex–Ec, WI. **Notes:** There are 24 species of *Prosthechea* in Costa Rica. Many are often included in the genus *Encyclia*.

■ *Prosthechea ionophlebia (Encyclia i.)*
   Family Orchidaceae

Epiphytic orchid to 45 cm tall, from an egg-shaped bulblike stem, 4–6 cm long, 2–3 cm wide, often broadly ribbed. **Leaves** 2 or 3 per stem, alternate, 13–30 cm long, 2–3.5 cm wide, strap-shaped, secondary veins obscure. **Flowers** greenish yellow or cream, with purple markings; bilaterally symmetric, 3 sepals and 2 lateral petals similar, about 2.5 cm long, 0.9 cm wide, third petal (lip) 3-lobed, about 2.5 cm long, 2 cm wide, broadly egg-shaped, concave, cream white with violet stripes, margin wavy; inflorescence with 2–5 flowers arising directly from bulbous stem; blooms Mar.–May. **Fruit** dry, seeds numerous, dustlike. **Habitat:** Very wet forests. Altitude: 800–1600 m. Conservation areas: CVC, LAP. **Range:** CR, W Pan. **Notes:** Not as common as *P. fragrans*.

■ *Prosthechea vespa (Encyclia v.)*
Family Orchidaceae

Epiphytic or terrestrial herb to 70 cm, stem base bulblike, 15–40 cm long, 1–2 cm wide. **Leaves** alternate, 2–4, blade 10–25 cm long, 2–4 cm wide, narrowly elliptic, leathery, flat, veins dark green, not impressed. **Flowers** greenish white or pale yellow with maroon spots and markings, bilaterally symmetric, 3 sepals and 2 lateral petals similar, sepals about 1 cm long, 0.4–0.6 cm wide, lower petal (lip) broad, lip about 0.8 cm long, 0.5 cm wide, inconspicuous, undivided, anther cap yellow orange; inflorescence 12–20 cm long, unbranched, at end of stem; blooms all year. **Fruit** dry, 3-sided 2 cm long, 4 cm wide; seeds numerous, dustlike. **Habitat:** Very wet forests. Altitude: 550–1650 m. Conservation areas: ARE, CVC, GUA, LAC, LAP. **Range:** Nic–Brz, WI.

■ *Sobralia luteola*
Family Orchidaceae

Epiphyte 30–90 cm tall, stems clustered, slender, reedlike, covered with bladeless sheaths. **Leaves** alternate, ranked along sides of stem, blade 8–17 cm long, 2–4 cm wide, elliptic, tip tapered to a long point, surface pleated by impressed veins. **Flowers** yellowish white to greenish white, bilaterally symmetrical, delicate, sepals and 2 lateral petals similar, about 3 cm long, less than 1 cm wide, lower petal (lip) tubelike, 3 cm long, 2 cm wide, tip notched, with purple margin, throat orange-hairy; inflorescence at end of stem, flowers bloom 2–3 at a time, lasting less than 1 day; blooms Jan., Feb., Apr. **Fruit** dry, linear, to 9 cm long, 0.6 cm wide, seeds numerous, dustlike. **Habitat:** Very wet forests. Altitude: 450–900 m, sometimes to 2500 m. Conservation areas: CVC, LAP, OSA. **Range:** Nic, CR. **Notes:** There are 27 species of *Sobralia* in Costa Rica.

■ *Xylobium elongatum*
Family Orchidaceae

Epiphytic herb, stems swollen, elongate, bulblike, 18–35 cm long. **Leaves** 2 (rarely 3) per stem, stalk 5–6 cm long, blades 20–47 cm long, 3–9 cm wide, narrowly elliptic, fairly thin, surface slightly pleated by impressed veins. **Flowers** white to cream, often with red speckles or streaks, somewhat fragrant, 3 sepals, and 2 side petals similar, about 1.5–2.5 cm long, 0.5 cm wide, lance-shaped, tip long-pointed, third petal (lip) often purple pink, about 1.5–2 cm long, 0.6 cm wide, 3-lobed, surface finely warty; inflorescence 8–24 cm long, unbranched, flowers numerous; blooms mostly Nov.–Dec. **Fruit** dry, seeds numerous, dustlike. **Habitat:** Very wet forests. Altitude: 700–1800 m. Conservation areas: ARE (mostly), CVC, GUA, LAC, LAP, OSA. **Range:** Mex–Pr. **Notes:** There are five species of *Xylobium* in Costa Rica, *X. elongatum* is the only one that is fairly common.

■ *Petiveria alliacea* (garlic weed)
Family Phytolaccaceae

Herb 0.5–1.5 tall, often many stems together, woody at base in age, cut parts with garlic scent, stipules 0.2 cm long, brownish, persistent. **Leaves** alternate, stalk 0.4–1.8 cm long, blade 5–16 cm long, 2–6 cm wide, narrowly egg-shaped or elliptic, tip pointed, base wedge-shaped, surface dark green shiny above, margins smooth. **Flowers** white, very small, about 0.4 cm long, radially symmetrical, 4-parted, anthers 8, often pinkish, petals linear, each flower above a tiny triangular bract; flowering few at a time along thin, pink-stemmed spikes 10–40 cm long, at top of plant; blooms all year. **Fruit** dry, small, 0.6–0.8 cm long, 0.2 cm wide, rectangular with 4 small hooks 0.3 cm long, dispersed by attaching to fur of passing animals. **Habitat:** Wet to seasonally dry forest understories, second growth, disturbed, shady sites. Altitude: Sea level to 1300 m, usually below 400 m. Conservation areas: ARE, GUA, HNO, LAC, OSA, PAC TEM. **Range:** FL, Tx–Arg, WI. **Notes:** This is the only species of *Petiveria* in Costa Rica.

■ *Rivina humilis*
Family Phytolaccaceae
Herb, sometimes shrubby, 0.3–1 m tall, stems green, base often woody. **Leaves** alternate, spirally arranged, stalk 0.4–4 cm long, blade 4–12 cm long, 2–6 cm wide, egg-shaped to lance-shaped, tip long-pointed, base rounded, margin smooth. **Flowers** white or pale pink, about 0.5 cm wide, radially symmetrical, 5 petals, 0.2 cm, 4 stamens, flower stalk about 0.3 cm; inflorescence unbranched clusters 4–12 cm long (longer in fruit); blooms and fruits all year. **Fruit** fleshy, bright red, somewhat translucent, 0.4–0.6 cm long, 1 black seed. **Habitat:** Wet to seasonally dry

areas, moist sites in dry, deciduous regions, roadsides, ditches, open sun, part shade. Altitude: Sea level to 1200 m. Conservation areas: ARE, CVC, GUA, LAC, LAP, PAC, TEM, TOR. **Range:** S US–S Amer, WI. **Notes:** This is the only species of *Rivina* worldwide.

■ *Peperomia palmana*
Family Piperaceae
Epiphytic or terrestrial herb to 40 cm tall, sometimes branched, stems fleshy, often pinkish, sometimes reaching out horizontally from tree trunks. **Leaves** opposite or in whorls of 4 per node, stalk 0.1–0.6 cm, blade 1–4 cm long, 0.6–2 cm wide, fleshy, egg-shaped to narrowly elliptic, tip bluntly pointed, base rounded to pointed, veins palmate, 3 major veins, midrib impressed above, raised below. **Flowers** white, minute, crowded on spikes 2–10 cm long, 0.2 cm thick, 1–4 (occasionally up to 8), in leaf axils; blooms and fruits all year. **Fruit** fleshy, less than 0.1 cm wide, reddish. **Habitat:** Moist to wet mountain forests and disturbed open sites. Altitude: 1000–3000 m, usually above 1600 m. Conservation areas: ARE, CVC, LAC, LAP, PAC. **Range:** CR, Pan. **Notes:** Common low epiphyte on tree trunks. There are about 120 species of *Peperomia* in Costa Rica.

389

■ *Peperomia pellucida*
Family Piperaceae

Small, translucent, weedy herb to 35 cm tall, usually terrestrial, often with 1 main stem and treelike branching. **Leaves** alternate, becoming crowded and almost opposite near stem tips, stalks 0.3–1.5 cm, base extending down stem, blade 1–3 cm long, 1–2 cm wide, broadly egg-shaped, tip bluntly pointed, base rounded to slightly lobed. **Flowers** greenish white, minute, crowded on spikes, mostly opposite leaves, 1–2 spikes per node or several at stem tip, to 8 cm long, on a stalk to 0.8 cm long; blooms all year. **Fruit** fleshy, less than 0.1 cm wide. **Habitat:** Wet to seasonally dry regions, a weed in shady, disturbed habitats; often in gardens and other cultivated sites. Altitude: Sea level to 1500 m. Conservation areas: CVC, LAC, OSA, PAC, TEM. **Range:** Mex–Ur, WI. Introduced in Old World tropics, invasive in some Pacific islands and Australia.

■ *Peperomia poasana*
Family Piperaceae

Epiphytic or terrestrial herb to 70 cm long, stems pale green, fleshy, translucent, to 1 cm wide, rooting at nodes. **Leaves** alternate, stalk flattened, grooved above, margins slightly winged, clasping stem at base, blade 5–15 cm long, 3–5 cm wide, elliptic, tapered to point at both ends, base extending down sides of leaf stalk, fleshy, veins pinnate, often impressed above, curving sharply upward. **Flowers** white, minute, densely packed on small fleshy spikes, 0.4–1.8 cm long; inflorescence, 6–15 cm long, twice-branched, with 15–40 flower spikes in small clusters, at ends of stems, sometimes pinkish; blooms and fruits Dec.–May. **Fruit** fleshy, less than 0.1 cm wide. **Habitat:** Wet forests. Altitude: 1000–2500 m. Conservation areas: ARE, CVC, LAC. **Range:** CR, Pan. **Notes:** Distinctive for its very short spikes and twice-branched inflorescence.

■ *Peperomia tetraphylla* (garrapatillo,
hilotillo, corredera)
Family Piperaceae

Small epiphyte, stems creeping, flowering stems erect, to
about 15 cm long, nodes often hairy. **Leaves** usually in
whorls of 4, sometimes opposite, stalk 0.1–0.2 cm, blade 1–
2 cm long, 0.5–1.4 cm wide, elliptic, tapered at both ends,
tip blunt, sometimes notched, succulent, veins obscure.
Flower white to pale green, minute, crowded on spikes 2–
5 cm long, solitary at ends of stems; blooms and fruits all
year. **Fruit** fleshy, greenish, less than 0.1 cm wide. **Habitat:**
Moist to wet forests, often on tree trunks and large branches.
Altitude: 600–3000 m, mostly above 1500 m. Conservation
areas: ARE, CVC, GUA, LAC, LAP, PAC. **Range:** Mex–Ur,
WI, Africa.

■ *Heteranthera reniformis* (guacalillo,
lengua de sapo, oreja de agua, kidneyleaf)
Family Pontederiaceae

Small floating or rooted aquatic herb, colonial from root
sprouts, rooting at nodes, stems long, creeping. **Leaves** alternate, stalk sheathing stem, blade floating or above water,
1–4 cm, heart- to kidney-shaped, tip rounded base deeply
lobed, lobes rounded. **Flowers** white, tubular, slightly bilaterally symmetric, 6-parted, about 1 cm wide, tube
0.5–1 cm long, petal lobes 0.3–0.6 cm long, stamens
yellow; inflorescence unbranched, to 5 cm long, with
2–8 flowers, at ends of stems above water; blooms
all year. **Fruit** dry, about 1 cm long; seeds numerous.
Habitat: Open, shallow, quiet water, including roadside ditches, disturbed habitats in seasonally dry to
very wet regions. Altitude: Sea level to 1300 m or
more. Conservation areas: ARE, CVC, GUA, HNO,
LAC, OSA, PAC, TEM, TOR. **Range:** US–N Arg.
Notes: There are two other species of *Heteranthera*
in Costa Rica.

391

■ *Coccocypselum hirsutum*
Family Rubiaceae

Creeping, prostrate, hairy herb, stipules with awns to 0.5 cm long. **Leaves** opposite, stalks 0.4–1 cm long, hairy, blade 2–4 cm long, 1.5–2.5 cm wide, egg-shaped, tip bluntly pointed, base blunt, hairy above and below. **Flowers** blue, white, or white marked with purple, radially symmetrical, floral tube to 0.7 cm long, petal lobes 4, 0.2–0.4 cm long, tip pointed, calyx lobes about as long as petal lobes; Inflorescence stalks 0.3–2.4 cm long, with clusters of 3 flowers; blooms most of the year. **Fruit** fleshy, blue to blue purple, 0.9–2 cm long, about 1 cm wide, crowned by old calyx, flesh foamy-spongy, seeds small, numerous. **Habitat:** Wet to very wet forests, partly shady banks and edges, pastures. Altitude: Sea level to 2500 m, mostly above 1000 m. Conservation areas: ARE, CVC, GUA, HNO, LAP, OSA. **Range:** Mex–Par and Brz. **Notes:** There are four species of *Coccocypselum* in Costa Rica. The other common species, *C. herbaceum*, has shorter petal lobes, no inflorescence stalk, and shorter leaf stalks. It is very similar to, and possibly not distinct from, *C. hirsutum*.

■ *Geophila repens* (lechuga)
Family Rubiaceae

Creeping herb to about 10 cm tall, stems slender, stipules to 0.2 cm long, egg-shaped. **Leaves** opposite, stalks to 6 cm long, blade 1–5 cm long and wide, broadly heart-shaped, tip blunt, base lobed, lobes overlapping. **Flowers** white, sometimes becoming pink, radially symmetrical, funnel-shaped, to 1.4 cm long, petal lobes 5, to 0.5 cm tips blunt to pointed;

blooms May–Oct., Feb. **Fruit** fleshy, bright red orange, rounded, to 1 cm wide, seeds 2, to 0.5 cm long; fruit present all year. **Habitat:** Wet to seasonally dry, forest floors, shady sites of second growth, river banks. Altitude: Sea level to 1200 m, mostly below 400 m. Conservation areas: GUA, LAC, OSA, PAC, TEM, TOR. **Range:** Mex–Ven and Arg, DR, PtR, VI, Africa. **Notes:** There are two other species of *Geophila* in Costa Rica. *Geophila repens* is the most common. It is distinguished by its small size, lack of hairiness, overlapping lobes of the leaf base and bright red fruit.

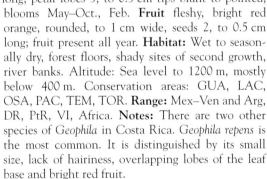

■ *Hoffmannia congesta*
Family Rubiaceae

Herb 0.5–2 m tall, stems to 1.5 cm diameter, stem thick, upright, cylindrical, usually not branched, leaf scars conspicuous, stipules to 1.5 cm long, triangular to rounded, deciduous. **Leaves** opposite, often clustered at ends of branches, stalk to about 1 cm, often reddish, blade 15–30 cm long, 8–15 cm wide, broadly elliptic, tip abruptly pointed, base often slightly extending down stalk, dark green, veins impressed above. **Flowers** white, radially symmetrical, tubular, about 0.3 cm long, petal lobes flaring, about 0.3 cm long, calyx red, lobes to 0.6 cm long, emerging from a tight mass of small red bracts; inflorescence almost surrounding stem at leaf axils to 2 cm long, 6 cm wide; blooms Jan.–Oct. **Fruit** fleshy, white, about 0.5 cm long, flesh spongy-foamy; June–Mar. **Habitat:** Wet forest understories.

Altitude: 500–1900 m, most often above 1000 m. Conservation areas: ARE, CVC, LAC, LAP. **Range:** CR, Pan. **Notes:** There are about 31 species of *Hoffmannia* in Costa Rica. *Hoffmannia congesta* is the most common and is distinguished by its dense, red, stalkless inflorescences, white fruit, and large leaves.

■ *Notopleura capitata (Psychotria aggregata)*
Family Rubiaceae

Shrubby herb 0.5–2 m tall, stems stout, unbranched, succulent, 4-sided, angles often slightly winged; stipules about 1 cm long, triangular with 2 deciduous appendages above. **Leaves** opposite, stalk to 1 cm long, blade 12–38 cm long, 5–17 cm wide, elliptic to widest above middle, tapered gradually above, tip pointed, base blunt to pointed. **Flowers** white, radially symmetrical, tubular, funnel-shaped, to 0.4 cm long, petal lobes 5, 0.1 cm long, tips blunt; inflorescence dense, axillary, 4–15 cm long, flowers crowded in headlike clusters at the ends of 1–2 pairs of branches; blooms and fruits all year. **Fruit** fleshy, white, to 1 cm long, rounded, flesh foamy-spongy. **Habitat:** Understories of wet forests. Altitude: Near sea level to 2100 m, usually above 800 m. Conservation areas: ARE, CVC, GUA, LAC, LAP, OSA, TOR. **Range:** Nic–Col. **Notes:** Most often in cloud forests but common at La Selva Biological Station (100 m elevation).

■ *Psychotria aubletiana*
Family Rubiaceae

Herb or small shrub 0.5–4 m tall, sparsely branched, internodes often elongate; stipules to 1 cm long, base fused for 0.5 cm, top with 2 irregular, blunt lobes. **Leaves** opposite, stalk to 4 cm long, blade 4–18 cm long, 1–6 cm wide, narrowly elliptic, tip long-pointed, base pointed. **Flowers** white, radially symmetrical, tube to 1 cm, petal lobes 5, about 0.3 cm long, triangular; inflorescences axillary, to 2 cm wide,

stalkless, of tight, rounded flower clusters with green to purple bracts to 0.7 cm long; blooms and fruits all year. **Fruit** fleshy, bright blue, to 0.7 cm. **Habitat:** Wet to moist mountain forests understories. Altitude: 600–3200 m, mostly 1200–2300 m. Conservation areas: ARE, CVC, GUA, LAC, LAP, OSA, PAC. **Range:** S Mex–Guy and Pr, WI. **Notes:** *Psychotria aubletiana* is distinguished by its small, dense axillary clusters of white flowers and bright blue fruit.

■ *Spermacoce assurgens*
Family Rubiaceae

Herb 20–80 cm tall, often spreading, stems 4-sided; stipules fused to base of leaf stalk forming a sheath, 0.2–0.8, cm high, beginning below leaf base, upper margin fringed with 3–9 bristles to 0.6 cm long. **Leaves** opposite, blade 1–7 cm long, 0.5–3 cm wide, lance-shaped, tip and base pointed to blunt, upper surface rough, veins 4–6 pairs, deeply impressed above.

Flowers white, radially symmetrical, tube 0.2 cm long, petal lobes 4, 0.1 cm long, calyx lobes 4, triangular, stems often purple; inflorescences crowded, to about 1.5 cm wide, headlike, often surrounding axils; blooms all year. **Fruit** dry, 2-lobed, about 0.2 cm long and wide, above persistent calyx lobes. **Habitat:** Moist to wet regions in weedy, open sites, roadsides, pastures. Altitude: Sea level to 1700 m. Conservation areas: ARE, CVC, LAC, LAP, OSA, TOR. **Range:** FL, El Salv, CR–Pr, Par. **Notes:** There are 12 species of *Spermacoce* in Costa Rica, *S. assurgens* is the most common.

■ *Spermacoce latifolia* (mielcillo, chiritillo)
Family Rubiaceae

Sprawling herb, covering large areas, or climbing to 1 m high, stems reddish, 4-sided, angles ridged or winged, branched near base, stipules forming a small sheath to 0.3 cm high, upper margin fringed by 5–7 bristles to 0.6 cm long. **Leaves** opposite, blade 1–4.5 cm long, 0.5–2.5 cm wide, elliptic, tip pointed, base blunt or extending down stalk. **Flowers** white to blue or lavender, radially symmetrical, tubular, to 0.5 cm, petal lobes 4, flaring outward; inflorescence of small, dense, axillary or terminal clusters, to 1 cm wide with only 3–7 flowers; blooms and fruits all year. **Fruit** dry, to 0.4 cm, 2-lobed, each lobe splitting open to release a single seed, about 0.2 cm long. **Habitat:** Moist to wet regions, in open sites, roadsides, pastures. Altitude: Sea level to 1200 m. Conservation areas: ARE, CVC, HNO, GUA, LAC, LAP, PAC. **Range:** Mex–Guy and Pr, Par, Tr. **Notes:** *Spermacoce latifolia* is distinguished by its ridged, angular stems.

■ *Leucocarpus perfoliatus*
Family Scrophulariaceae

Large, coarse herb 0.5–2 m tall, stems stout, green, 4-sided, angles conspicuously winged, branches few to none. **Leaves** opposite, blade 10–25 cm long, about 6 cm wide, lance-shaped, tip pointed, base lobed, clasping stem, margin toothed. **Flowers** white to yellow, with yellow throat, bilaterally symmetrical, tubular, about 1.5 cm long, rim 2-lipped, 1 lip 3-lobed, sepals fused, lobes needle-shaped; inflorescence of small axillary clusters; blooms most of the year. **Fruit** fleshy, white, succulent, 1 cm wide or more. **Habitat:** Wet areas, stream banks, sand bars or forests in mountains. Altitude: 600–2500 m Conservation areas. ARE, CVC, LAC, LAP, PAC. **Range:** Mex–Ven and Bol. **Notes:** This is the only species of *Leucocarpus* in Costa Rica.

■ *Solanum acerifolium*
Family Solanaceae

Wickedly armed herb or low shrub to 1.5 m tall, stems green, sticky-hairy, *densely covered with spines* to 1.5 cm. **Leaves** alternate, stalk to 12 cm long, blade broadly egg-shaped, about 17 cm long, 14 cm wide, deeply 3- to 9-lobed, lobe tips pointed, base of blade round or blunt lobed, slightly unequal, surface dull green, both sides sticky-hairy, midrib and major veins with long, erect spines to 2 cm long on both sides. **Flowers** greenish white to yellowish white, radially symmetrical, to 2 cm wide, star-shaped, with 5 pointed petal lobes, stamens yellow, in a central beaklike cluster; inflorescence of small, unbranched clusters in axils; blooms and fruits most of the year. **Fruit** fleshy, greenish white with dark green marbled pattern, round, about 1.4 cm wide, surface sticky, seeds numerous, flat, brown, fruit stem swollen near top. **Habitat:** Open sites, forest edges, pastures, in mountains. Altitude: 900–2100 m. Conservation areas: ARE, CVC, LAC, LAP, PAC. **Range:** Mex–Brz and Pr, Tr. **Notes:** *Solanum* is one of the larger genera of Costa Rican plants with about 92 species. It includes potatoes *(S. tuberosum)* and a number of ornamentals.

■ *Solanum americanum*
   (S. nigrum var. americanum)
   Family Solanaceae

Weedy herb 0.15–1.0 m tall, stems branched, often purplish, most parts usually finely hairy. **Leaves** alternate, stalked, blade 2–8 cm long, rarely to 20 cm, 1–5 cm wide, egg-shaped but variable, base blunt or slightly extending down stalk, tip pointed, margin usually irregularly toothed. **Flowers** white to pale blue, about 1 cm wide, petals 5, bent back, tips pointed, bases fused, anthers yellow, in a central, beaklike cluster; blooms and fruits all year. **Fruit** fleshy, black to 0.8 cm wide, rounded, seeds flat, numerous, about 0.1 cm wide; fruit eaten by birds, which disperse the seeds. **Habitat:** Open areas, vacant lots, roadsides, pastures. Altitude: Near sea level to 1800 m. Conservation areas: ARE, CVC, GUA, HNO, LAP, OSA, PAC, TEM. **Range:** Native to S Amer, now pantropical. S and W US, Mex–Arg and Brz, WI, Africa, SE Asia, Oceania. Invasive on some Pacific islands. **Notes:** Plant toxic, fruit toxic, at least when young.

■ *Valeriana prionophylla*
Family Valerianaceae

Small herb to about 0.4–1.5 m tall in flower, tap-rooted, stem tinged with dark purple. **Leaves** opposite, mostly in a dense, basal rosette, stalk wide, blade narrow, 3–20 cm long, 0.5–2.5 cm wide, dark green above, very pale below, hairy on both sides, tip blunt, base tapered to stalk, margins bluntly toothed, 1–2 pairs of stem leaves on flowering plants. **Flowers** white marked with purple, radially symmetrical, 0.5 cm wide, 5 petal lobes, buds and tips of calyx lobes purplish, inflorescence of dense, branched, flat topped clusters at top of stem; blooms most of the year. **Fruit** dry, small, 1-seeded. **Habitat:** High mountains in rocky, open areas. Altitude: 2800–3700 m. Conservation areas: CVC, LAP, PAC. Seen on Cerro de la Muerte. **Range:** Mex, Gua, CR, Pan. **Notes:** There are nine species of *Valeriana* in Costa Rica. The most common is *V. candolleana*, a climbing herb found at somewhat lower altitudes.

■ *Priva lappulacea*
Family Verbenaceae

Small herb less than 1 m tall. **Leaves** opposite, 3–12 cm long, 2–6 cm wide, narrowly egg-shaped, tip pointed base blunt to slightly lobed. **Flowers** white to purple, tubular, 0.3–0.5 cm long, calyx to 0.3 cm long, densely hairy; inflorescence of axillary or terminal spikes 5–15 cm long; blooms and fruits most of the year. **Fruit** dry, 0.3–0.5 cm long, 0.3 cm wide, enveloped by persistent, inflated calyx, covered with tiny hooks that stick to clothes or fur. **Habitat:** Wet to seasonally dry regions in open areas, part shade, a roadside weed. Altitude: Sea level to 400 m. Conservation areas: GUA, LAC, LAP, OSA, PAC, TEM seen from OSA to Palo Verde. **Range:** Mex–Ven and Bol, WI. **Notes:** There is one other species of *Priva* in Costa Rica, which is uncommon.

■ *Viola stipularis*
Family Violaceae

Small trailing or creeping herb rooting at nodes, stems jointed, sometimes reddish; stipules paired, about 1.5 cm long, 0.5 cm wide, tip pointed, upper margin with bristlelike teeth. **Leaves** alternate, young stems with leaves crowded, 2-ranked, stalk 1 cm, blade 3–10 cm long, 1–4 cm wide, elliptic, finely toothed, midrib raised above and below, tip bluntly pointed, base tapered. **Flowers** pale lavender to white with purple markings, bilaterally symmetric, about 1.5 cm long

and 1 cm wide, 3 petals 1 lower, 2 at sides meeting at top; blooms all year. **Fruit** dry, 0.8 cm long, 0.3 cm wide, splitting open to release numerous seeds. Seeds of violets often have a fleshy attachment attractive to ants, which disperse them. **Habitat:** Open areas, pastures, roadsides, in low vegetation, usually in mountains. Altitude: 100–2000 m, mostly above 1300 m. Conservation areas: ARE, CVC, LAC, LAP, OSA, PAC. **Range:** CR–Ven and Pr. **Notes:** There are four species of *Viola* native to Costa Rica; *V. stipularis* is probably the most common. The three other species are found at elevations well above 2000 m.

■ *Alpinia zerumbet* (collar de la reina, grano de oro, lágrimas de Nazareno, shell ginger)
Family Zingiberaceae

Cultivated herb to 3 m tall, stems usually in clumps. **Leaves** alternate, little or no stalk, blade to 60 cm long, 12 cm wide, lance-shaped, tip pointed, base tapered. **Flowers** white and pink, showy, asymmetrical when open, to 4 cm long, petal tube yellow, ephemeral, barely longer than the persistent, showy white calyx lobes with pink purple tips, fused into an elliptic bell or shell shape; inflorescence of numerous flowers on loose, drooping spikes to 30 cm long. **Fruit** red, becoming dry, splitting open to reveal seeds with fleshy appendage. **Habitat:** Ornamental, seldom if ever escaping, but a common horticultural plant. Altitude: Sea level to 1200 m or more. Conservation areas: ARE. **Range:** Native to tropical E Asia, Indonesia. Widely cultivated throughout the tropics.

■ *Hedychium coronarium* (flor de San Juan,
   heliotropo, lirio blanco, white ginger)
   Family Zingiberaceae

Herb 1–2 m tall, stems in clumps, colonial from root
sprouts. **Leaves** alternate, ranked along sides of stem, blade
28–40 cm long, 4–7 cm wide, narrowly elliptical, tip pointed,
hairy below. **Flowers** white, showy, very fragrant, irregular,
11–12 cm long, cm wide, petal lobes 2, about 5 cm long, lip,
2-lobed, larger than petals, base narrowly tubular 7–9 cm;
inflorescence to 20 cm long at top of stems with green bracts;
blooms Jan., Apr.–Nov., especially in June. **Fruit** orange,
seeds numerous, red with fleshy, orange attachments. **Habitat:** Widely cultivated; escaped and naturalized in very wet to
seasonally dry regions, roadsides, ditches, weedy sites. Altitude: Sea level to 1600 m. Conservation areas: ARE, CVC,
GUA, LAC, LAP, OSA, PAC, TOR. **Range:** Native to
China. Widely naturalized in tropical America. Introduced
in Oceania, invasive in Australia, Hawai'i, the Galapagos,
and other Pacific islands **Notes:** This is the only species of
Hedychium in Costa Rica.

■ *Kallstroemia maxima* (muelle de paquera)
   Family Zygophyllaceae

Herb, freely branched, creeping, stems often reddish, about
0.2–1 m long, often forming dense mats. **Leaves** opposite,
evenly pinnate, of 3–4 pairs of leaflets 0.5–2 cm long, asymmetrically oval, tip usually blunt, the largest leaflets at the
top of the leaf. **Flowers** yellow to white, radially symmetrical,
about 2 cm wide, petals 5, about 0.8 cm long, widest at top,
stigmas and stamens 10–12, rounded, yellow; flowers solitary
in axils. **Fruit** dry, 10 small, bony, nutlike segments around a
central axis. **Habitat:** A weedy plant of wet to seasonally dry
regions in open areas, roadsides, fields, lawns. Altitude: Sea
level to 850 m. Conservation areas: CVC, GUA, LAP, PAC,
TEM. **Range:** Mex–Pan, Ven, and Brz, Cuba, PtR. **Notes:**
There are two species of *Kallstroemia* in Costa Rica. *Kallstroemia pubescens* is much less common than *K. maxima*.

Courtesy of Margaret Gargiullo

COLOR OF CONSPICUOUS PART GREEN TO BROWN

■ *Agave angustifolia* (agave, maguey)
Family Agavaceae

Large herb, usually stemless or with a short, trunklike stem to 60 cm long. **Leaves** alternate, densely spiraled in a large rosette, stalkless, blade 0.5–1.2 m long, 4–10 cm wide, thick, fleshy, straplike, tip sharply pointed, pale gray green, margin with small, spine-tipped teeth. **Flowers** yellowish green, radially symmetrical, 6-parted, on a stalk 2–5 m tall from amid leafy rosette; blooms all year, blooms and fruits once then dies, may resprout from roots. **Fruit** dry, about 5 cm long, splitting open to release flat, black seeds about 1 cm wide. **Habitat:** Moist and seasonally dry regions in rocky, open areas, cliff sides. Altitude: Sea level to 500 m. Conservation areas: GUA, LAC, TEM. **Range:** Mex–Pan. **Notes:** There are three species of native *Agave* in Costa Rica. *Agave angustifolia* is the most common wild species; *A. wercklei*, with much wider, shorter leaves, is endemic to Costa Rica. *Agave americana* is a widely cultivated nonnative.

■ *Furcraea cabuya* (cabuya, penca, olancho, itabo)
Family Agavaceae

Large herb, usually stemless or sometimes with a short, thick trunk, to about 1 m tall. **Leaves** alternate, densely spiraled in a large rosette, stalkless, blade 0.6–2 m long, 5–20 cm wide, straplike, thick, fleshy, tip sharply pointed, pale gray green, margin sometimes spiny, base broadened, clasping. **Flowers** greenish white to yellowish green, radially symmetrical, about 4 cm, in large branched clusters along a stalk to 5 m tall, from amid leaves; blooms July–Aug, Feb.; blooms and fruits once, then dies, may resprout from roots. **Fruit** dry, about 5 cm long, 3 cm wide, splitting open to release flat seeds about 1 cm wide. Sometimes producing small plants from tiny bulbs at flower bases, instead of fruit. **Habitat:** Crop plant for fiber. Also wild, in moist to wet forests and on open, rocky slopes. Altitude: 50–2000 m. Conservation areas: ARE, GUA, OSA, TEM. **Range:** S Mex–Pan. **Notes:** *Furcraea cabuya* is the only species of this genus in Costa Rica and is the most common species of Agavaceae in the country. The fiber is used to make rope and hammocks.

Amaranthus spinosus
Family Amaranthaceae

Herb 0.5–1.5 m tall, branched, stem often reddish or purple, with pairs of thin, sharp spines 1–1.5 cm long at many nodes. **Leaves** alternate, stalk to 6 cm long, blade 1–12 cm long, about 1–5 cm wide, narrowly elliptic, tip narrowed to a sharp or blunt point, often with small spine, base extending down stalk, margin entire. **Flowers** tan or green, very small, dry, densely crowded in spikes, among small bracts, bracts often spinelike; inflorescence spikes, very variable in size 1–8 cm long to 1 cm wide; blooms most of the year. **Fruit** dry, about 0.1 cm, seeds shiny, brown. **Habitat:** Open, second growth, weedy sites, roadsides. Altitude: Sea level to 2100 m. Conservation areas: LAP, OSA, PAC, TEM. **Range:** US–Arg. Introduced in the Old World tropics. Invasive in SE Asia, Hawai'i, the Galapagos, and other Pacific islands. **Notes:** There are six species of Amaranthus in Costa Rica; A. spinosus is the most common.

Cyathula achyranthoides
Family Amaranthaceae

Herb or shrubby herb to 1 m tall, sometimes reclining near base and rooting at lower nodes, nodes hairy. **Leaves** opposite, each pair at right angles to those above and below, stalks to 0.6 cm, blade 3–20 cm long, 2–7 cm wide, elliptic, pointed at both ends, base extending down leaf stalk, finely hairy on both sides. **Flowers** pale green, tiny, radially symmetrical, dry, in spikes 5–20 cm long, to 1 cm wide, of dense, small rounded clusters to 0.3 cm long that bend away from the main axis, each flower cluster bears numerous fine, hooked spines 0.4 cm long, making it appear bristly; blooms all year. **Fruit** dry, 1-seeded, 0.2 cm, tightly enclosed in old flower parts. **Habitat:** Wet to seasonally dry lowlands in disturbed, open or partly shaded sites. Altitude: Sea level to about 700 m, mostly below 400 m. Conservation areas: CVC, HNO, LAC, OSA, PAC, TEM, TOR. **Range:** Native to Africa, now common Mex–Pr and Brz, WI. **Notes:** The only other species of Cyathula in Costa Rica is C. prostrata, also an Old World weed; it has smaller leaves but is otherwise much like C. achyranthoides.

401

■ *Eryngium foetidum* (culantro coyote)
Family Apiaceae
Spiny herb 15–60 cm tall, flowering stem much-branched, tough, from a stout taproot, smelling strongly of coriander (*Coriandrum sativum*, cilantro). **Leaves** mostly in a basal rosette, blade 10–16 cm long, 3–4 cm wide, narrow, tip rounded, base tapered, margin toothed, spiny; stem leaves

opposite, stalkless, blade 2–3 cm long, 0.5–1.5 cm wide, often 3-parted, margins with spine-tipped teeth. **Flowers** pale green, minute, in dense, conical heads to 1 cm long, above a ring of spiny bracts, longer than inflorescence, Feb.–Mar. **Fruit** dry, 0.2 cm, spiny, 2-seeded. **Habitat:** common weed of open habitats in wet regions, lawns, edges. Altitude: Sea level to 1200 m. Conservation areas: CVC, GUA, LAC, OSA, PAC. **Range:** Mex–Pr and Brz. Widely cultivated. Introduced to Africa and Asia. Invasive on some Pacific islands. **Notes:** Leaves used as a seasoning and also medicinally.

■ *Alocasia macrorrhizos* (pato, hoja de pato)
Family Araceae
Large herb to over 4 m tall, forming large colonies from shoots at base of stem, stem short, thick, fleshy, mostly buried, with closely spaced, horizontal leaf scars. **Leaves** alternate, all at top of stem, near ground level, stalk to 1.5 m long, base clasping, top attached to leaf blade edge (see description of *Colocasia esculenta*), blade to about 90 cm long, 75 cm wide, broadly arrow-shaped, fleshy, surface shiny, tip pointed, base deeply lobed, lobe tips pointed. **Flowers** pale yellow, minute, crowded on a fleshy spike (spadix), surrounded by a hood-like bract (spathe); rarely blooms. **Fruit** fleshy, red orange; rarely fruits. **Habitat:** Cultivated, sometimes escaping, moist to wet lowlands, abandoned gardens. Altitude: Sea level to about 700 m or more. Conservation areas: CVC, OSA, PAC. **Range:** Native to SE Asia and Oceania. Cultivated throughout the tropics. **Notes:** Horticultural varieties are grown for leaves, which may be patterned in various ways. The root is grown for starchy food called *taro*. Raw plant is toxic, the cut leaves smell of bitter almonds (cyanide). There are three species of *Alocasia* in Costa Rica; *A. macrorrhizos* is the most common and largest.

■ *Anthurium salvinii* (tabacón)
Family Araceae

Large rosette herb, terrestrial or epiphytic, no stem; often with masses of white aerial roots around leaf bases. **Leaves** alternate, erect and crowded in a "bird's nest" formation, stalk 3–15 cm long, 1–2 cm wide, nearly cylindrical, blade 0.5–1.7 m long, 14–52 cm wide, narrow, lance-shaped, broadest near apex, tip pointed, base often with small lobes, midrib and secondary veins raised on both sides. **Flowers** greenish becoming lavender pink, minute, densely crowded on a fleshy spike (spadix) 14–45 cm long, to 0.5–3 cm wide, pendant, inflorescence bract

(spathe) purple to purple green, 4–50 cm long, 1–5 cm wide, narrowly lance-shaped, tip pointed, base blunt; inflorescence stalk 0.3–1.0 m long, usually drooping; blooms Jan.–May, Sept., Nov., Dec. **Fruit** fleshy, red, pink, or purple, 1–1.5 cm long, tip rounded, 2-seeded, fruiting spike to 60 cm long. **Habitat:** Moist to wet forest understories; also cultivated, a common patio plant. Altitude: 200–1650 m. Conservation areas: ARE, CVC, GUA, LAP, TEM. **Range:** S Mex–Col. **Notes:** Recognized by its large size and small lobes at bases of leaf blades.

■ *Colocasia esculenta* (malanga, ñampí, cocoyam, dachín, macal, taro, elephant's ear)
Family Araceae

Stemless herb to 5 m tall, from a large, trunklike tuberous rootstock (corm) to 6 cm wide, colonial from corm buds. **Leaves** alternate, spiraled, stalk 0.3–1 m long attached to underside of leaf blade (peltate); blade 20–85 cm long, 12–70 cm wide, heart- to arrow-shaped, underside pale, waxy whitish, usually with a purple marking near stalk attachment. **Flowers** pale yellow, minute, densely crowded on a fleshy spike (spadix) 10–30 cm long, inflorescence bract (spathe) greenish white or purple-tinged, hoodlike, enveloping spike; blooms Aug., Oct. **Fruit** fleshy, greenish white, 0.5 cm, seeds numerous; rarely fruits. **Habitat:** Wet, open lowlands, swamps; widely cultivated, sometimes escaped or in abandoned gardens. Altitude: Near sea level to 1600 m. Conservation areas: ARE, CVC, HNO, LAP, PAC. **Range:** Native to SE Asia and Oceania. **Notes:** This is the only species of *Colocasia* in Costa Rica. Roots are a source of starch; young leaves can be cooked as greens. Tuber contains sharp calcium oxalate crystals and must be cooked and processed to be edible. *Alocasia*, a very similar cultivated plant, has the stalk attached at the edge of the blade (see above).

■ *Dieffenbachia nitidipetiolata (D. longispatha)*
(lotería, sahinillo, little peccary plant)
Family Araceae

Terrestrial herb to 1.5 m tall, stem to 6 cm diameter, dark green, ringed by tan leaf scars, sap milky, crushed foliage very irritating, with an unpleasant skunklike, sweaty odor; plant usually grows in dense stands. **Leaves** alternate, stalk thick, 30–63 cm long, sheath extending up to middle of stalk, blade 32–68 cm long, 11–25 cm wide, broadly elliptic to egg-shaped, tip pointed, base blunt, surface shiny, usually dark green, midrib somewhat pale, veins impressed above, raised below. **Flowers** white, minute, densely crowded on a fleshy spike (spadix) to 14–25 cm long; inflorescence bract (spathe) pale green to white, tubular, wrapped around flower

spike; blooms July–Sept. **Fruit** fleshy, yellow to orange, to 2 cm diameter, sweet, edible when ripe; seeds 1–3; inflorescence bract persistent in fruit, becoming orange. **Habitat:** Understories of wet and moist forests, often along streams. Altitude: Sea level to 800 m. Caribbean slope. Conservation areas: CVC, LAC, TOR. Common at La Selva Biological Station. **Range:** SE Nic–Pan. **Notes:** The largest *Dieffenbachia* in Central America. Odor is similar to that of wild peccaries, which can usually be smelled before they are seen. There are 13 species of *Dieffenbachia* in Costa Rica.

■ *Dieffenbachia oerstedii* (lotería, sahinillo)
Family Araceae

Terrestrial herb to about 75 cm tall, usually less than 50 cm, stem to 2 cm diameter, lower stem creeping over ground, internodes short, sap milky. **Leaves** alternate, stalk 4–20 cm, base often white, sheathing, sheath lobed at top, blade 7–26 cm long, 2–13 cm wide, thin, egg- to lance-shaped, tip abruptly pointed, base blunt to wedge-shaped, sides often unequal, green to white-speckled, midrib flat above, to 0.8 cm wide, often with a pale green streak along upper half but not speckled, veins 4–11 pairs, impressed above. **Flowers** white, minute, densely crowded on a fleshy spike

(spadix) 7–12 cm long, inflorescence bract (spathe) green, tubular, wrapped around flower spike; often turning orange in age; inflorescences 3–5 in leaf axils, stalks 4–12 cm long; blooms and fruits mostly Mar.–Oct., Feb. **Fruit** fleshy, orange red, to 0.8 cm, edible when ripe. **Habitat:** Wet forest understories. Altitude: Sea level to 1500 m. Conservation areas: ARE, CVC, GUA, HNO, LAP, OSA, PAC, TEM. **Range:** S Mex–Pan. **Notes:** By far the most common, widespread *Dieffenbachia* in Costa Rica. Very variable.

■ *Dracontium gigas*
Family Araceae

Large, 1-leaved herb 3–4 m tall, from a large tuber to 20 cm wide. **Leaf** solitary, stalk to 3.5 m tall, to 9 cm wide, splotched with lighter green or purplish brown, blade 1.5–2.5 m wide, 3-parted, each part deeply and irregularly pinnately lobed 2 or more times; leaflets and lobes more or less triangular, tips pointed. **Flowers** deep brownish purple, minute, densely crowded on a fleshy spike to about 16 cm long, with unpleasant odor, surrounded by a large, hoodlike blotchy, maroon bract, 58–78 cm long, 13–21 cm wide, tip blunt; inflorescence arising separately on its own stalk, much shorter than leaf; blooms Dec.– Jan. **Fruit** fleshy, orange, about 1.5 cm wide, 1–2 seeded. **Habitat:** Wet forest understories, sometimes in disturbed, open sites. Altitude: Sea level to 700 m, Caribbean slope. Conservation areas: CVC, HNO, LAC, TOR. Seen most often in La Selva Biological Station. **Range:** Nic, CR. **Notes:** There are four species of *Dracontium* in Costa Rica, of which *D. gigas* is the largest. The most common is *D. pittieri,* found in lowlands of OSA and PAC. The leaves of the two species are indistinguishable.

■ *Philodendron wendlandii* (filodendron nido de ave, tabacón, bird's nest philodendron)
Family Araceae

Large, rosette-forming epiphytic herb, often fairly low on tree trunks, sometimes on logs, stem short to none. **Leaves** alternate, in a dense rosette, stalk 10–25 cm long, swollen, spongy, flattened above, convex below, continuous with broad midrib of the blade, margins sharply defined, blade 32–68 cm long, 9–20 cm wide, narrowly oblong, to elliptic, base blunt to slightly lobed. **Flowers** white, minute, densely crowded on a fleshy spike 13–17 cm long, about 1 cm wide, inflorescence bract green outside, red inside, 12–18 cm long, constricted near middle, lower part pale reddish, upper part cream white outside, red inside; inflorescences 1–3 in leaf axils, on stalks 3–11 cm long; blooms Feb.–July, Sept., Nov. **Fruit** fleshy, bright orange. **Habitat:** Wet forests; also widely cultivated as an ornamental. Altitude: Near sea level to 1200 m, Caribbean slope. Conservation areas: CVC, HNO, LAC, TOR. **Range:** SE Nic–Pan. **Notes:** There are 62 species of Philodendron in Costa Rica; but the only species similar to *P. wendlandii* is *P. auriculatum,* which is found on the Pacific slope.

■ *Pistia stratiotes* (lechuga de agua, water lettuce)
Family Araceae

Floating aquatic herb, forming large colonies; almost stemless except for small stems (stolons) producing new leaf rosettes at tips, feathery roots dangling in water. **Leaves** alternate, spiraled, in a dense rosette, no stalk, blade 1–17 cm long, 1–8 cm wide, more or less wedge-shaped, widest near the top, tip truncate to notched, tapered to base, surface thick, spongy, finely hairy, pale green, veins parallel, numerous, deeply impressed above. **Flowers** greenish white, very small, inconspicuous, among leaf bases. **Fruit** inconspicuous, seeds minute. **Habitat:** Quiet, open fresh water of marshes, canals, and ponds. Altitude: Sea level to 200 m, rarely to 750 m. Conservation areas: ARE, HNO, OSA, PAC, TEM, TOR. **Range:** Pantropical and subtropical. Probably originally from Lake Victoria, Africa. **Notes:** This is the only species of *Pistia* worldwide. An aquatic pest plant, clogging waterways. Leaves with air-filled tissues and fine hairs help plant stay afloat, feathery root mass keeps plant from being lifted by wind (see Brown 1988 for more).

■ *Xanthosoma wendlandii* (comida de culebra, comida de perro)
Family Araceae

Herb from a bulbous root stock (corm) to 3 cm wide, sap milky. **Leaf** solitary, stalk 0.5–1.3 m long, mottled with purple, blade palmately compound, 3- to 9-parted, lateral leaflets 2-lobed, central leaflet 17–50 cm long, 6–17 cm wide. **Flowers** white, minute, densely crowded on a fleshy spike (spadix) 11–16 cm long, about 1 cm wide, inflorescence bract (spathe) white above, green below, often with a dark red ring at base inside, inflorescence stalk 23–37 cm long; blooms June–Aug.; pollinated by beetles. **Fruit** fleshy, white. **Habitat:** Wet to seasonally dry forest understories; occasionally grown as an ornamental. Altitude: Sea level to 1300 m, Pacific slope. Conservation areas: ARE, PAC, TEM. Most frequently in the PAC area. **Range:** Mex–Ven. **Notes:** There are six other species of *Xanthosoma* in Costa Rica, this is the only one with a compound leaf. Plant dies back to the root stock (corm) during dry season.

■ *Delilia biflora*
Family Asteraceae

Annual herb 10–90 cm tall, erect. **Leaves** opposite, stalks to 1 cm, blade narrowly egg-shaped, 3–8 cm long, 2–3 cm wide, pointed at both ends, covered with short, stiff hairs, margin toothed. **Flowers** pale green, appearing more like winged seeds than like flowers, each flower head about 0.5 cm in diameter, of 2 tiny flowers enclosed by small flattened bracts, these heads in rounded clusters near ends of stems. **Fruit** dry, gray 1-seeded, 0.2 cm, enclosed within inflorescence bracts; blooms Sept.–Mar. **Habitat:** Wet to seasonally dry regions in weedy, open sites, vacant lots, roadsides. Altitude: Sea level to 1600 m. Conservation areas: ARE, CVC, PAC, TEM. Seen in a vacant lot in San José. **Range:** Mex–S Amer. **Notes:** This is the only species of *Delilia* in Costa Rica.

■ *Aechmea magdalenae* (piñuela)
Family Bromeliaceae

Very large terrestrial herb 1.5–2 m tall, colonial from root sprouts. **Leaves** alternate, in a large rosette blade, narrow, elongate 2–3 m long, 5–8 cm wide, dark green, thick; tip pointed, base broadly sheathing, margins conspicuously spiny-toothed. **Flowers** yellow, fleshy, asymmetrical, to 4 cm long; inflorescence 10–20 cm long, to 12 cm wide, branched but appearing as a rounded mass of red bracts, each 4–9 cm long, at the top of a central stalk, to 65 cm long, from among leaves; blooms most of the year. **Fruit** fleshy, yellow, becoming orange when ripe, to 6 cm long, 2 cm wide, angular, sweet, edible; seeds 6–12. **Habitat:** Very wet to seasonally dry, partly deciduous forests. Altitude: Sea level to 1100 m. Conservation areas: GUA, LAC, OSA, PAC, TEM, TOR. **Range:** Mex–Ec and Ven. **Notes:** Vegetatively very similar to *Bromelia pinguin*, which is found in Guanacaste, Puntarenas, and Limón. There are 17 species of *Aechmea* in Costa Rica.

■ *Ananas comosus* (piña, pineapple)
Family Bromeliaceae
Crop plant 50–90 cm tall, often in large plantations; reproduces vegetatively by small offshoot rosettes in leaf axils.
Leaves alternate, in a dense rosette, blade 0.6–1 m long, to
4 cm wide, gray green, often with a reddish caste, stiff, narrow, sharp, spine-tipped, base broadly sheathing, margins
sharp, serrated. **Flowers** pink, bracts bright pink, sharp-tipped
in a headlike arrangement 10–15 cm long, at top of a large
stalk; blooms in Mar. **Fruit** fleshy, yellow brown, of many
fused berries without seeds, 17–33 cm tall, oval with distinctive tilelike pattern, topped by a crown of short, spine-tipped
leaves; on a stalk at the center of the leafy rosette. **Habitat:**
Plantations, often covering large areas, occasionally escaping
very locally. Altitude: Near sea level to 450 m, mostly on the
southern Pacific slope. Conservation areas: CVC,
OSA. **Range:** Native to Brz. Cultivated throughout
the tropics. **Notes:** Cultivated variety does not produce seeds. *Ananas ananassoides* is the only other species of *Ananas* in Costa Rica. It is terrestrial, found
along rivers in moist, Pacific lowland forests and is
apparently very uncommon.

■ *Puya dasylirioides*
Family Bromeliaceae
Terrestrial herb, colonial, appearing pale blue green,
1.5–2.5 m tall (in bloom), young plant rounded, extending
upward as inflorescence develops. **Leaves** alternate, in dense
basal rosette, blade narrowly triangular, 30–55 cm long,
2–5 cm wide, becoming smaller toward center of rosette, and
extending up flowering stalk, surface dark green above, white
below; tip elongate, pointed, base broad, sheathing, margin
serrate-spiny. **Flowers** blue, bracts rusty green, in a dense
cylindrical spike to 2 m tall; blooms Mar.–Oct, mostly in
June and July. **Fruit** dry, hollow, persistent. **Habitat:** Open bogs in high
mountains. Altitude: 2600–3300 m.
Conservation areas: CVC, LAC, LAP,
PAC. Seen in the Reserva Forestal
de Río Macho, along Ruta 2. **Range:**
Endemic to CR. **Notes:** There is one
other species of *Puya* in Costa Rica,
P. floccosa, found at lower altitudes in
LAP, mostly around Ujarras.

■ *Werauhia gladioliflora (Vriesea g.)*
  Family Bromeliaceae

Terrestrial or epiphytic stemless herb, a "tank"-type bromeliad about 70 cm diameter. **Leaves** alternate, in a rosette,
purplish when young, becoming yellow green, 38–67 cm
long, 4–8 cm wide, broadly strap-shaped, tip rounded with
an abrupt point, base broadly sheathing, red brown, surface
smooth, margins smooth. **Flowers** cream white to greenish white, petals 3, rounded, 4–7 cm long, emerging from
between bracts, bracts 4–6 cm long, green with purplish tip in
flower, becoming pale red brown, tightly overlapping, ranked
along floral axis; inflorescence a spike 22–65 cm long, to
about 5 cm wide on a stalk 33–59 cm long, covered by overlapping bracts; blooms Mar.–June, Sept.–Dec.

Fruit dry, 3–4 cm long, brown and black,
splitting open to release plumed seeds. **Habitat:** Wet and very wet forests. Altitude: Sea
level to 1300 m. Conservation areas: ARE,
CVC, GUA, HNO, LAP, OSA, PAC, TOR.
Range: Mex–Ec and N Brz. **Notes:** "Tank"
bromeliads are those with wide, overlapping
leaf bases that collect water. There are 58 species of *Werauhia* in Costa Rica. They are very
similar to one another. Most were formerly
combined with *Vriesea* species, to which they
are very similar. They are also very similar to
Tillandsia and *Guzmania* species.

■ *Werauhia kupperiana (Vriesea k.)*
  Family Bromeliaceae

Large epiphytic or terrestrial stemless herb, a "tank"-type
bromeliad, about 60 cm across. **Leaves** alternate, in a large
rosette, blade 0.75–1.1 m long, 9–12 cm wide, surface mottled dark and light green; tip rounded with a small point, base
dark brown, broadly sheathing, margins smooth. **Flowers**
greenish white, minute, inconspicuous; inflorescence to 1 m
tall, branched once, flowers and brownish green bracts in
spikelike arrangements along branches, stalk 65–95 cm long;
blooms Apr., Sept.–Dec. **Fruit** dry, about 3 cm long, splitting
open to release plumed seeds. **Habitat:** Wet and very wet
forests. Altitude: Sea level to 1100 m. Conservation areas:
ARE, CVC, HNO, LAC, TOR. **Range:** Nic–Pan. **Notes:**
Most likely to be observed when fallen from a tree, the wide,
mottled leaves are distinctive.

■ *Burmeistera almedae*
Family Campanulaceae

Epiphytic or terrestrial herb or vinelike shrub 70 cm tall or more, branches elongate, sap milky. **Leaves** alternate, 1.5–5 cm long, 0.7–2 cm wide, ranked along branches, hard, leathery, curved downward. **Flowers** pale green and purple, tubular, bilaterally symmetrical, 2.5–6 cm long, petal lobes 5, 2-lipped; blooms Feb.–Oct. **Fruit** fleshy, white, inflated; fruit present in Oct. **Habitat:** Wet mountain forests. Altitude: 1300–2900 m. Conservation areas: CVC, LAC, LAP, PAC. Seen in Tapantí N.P. **Range:** CR. **Notes:** There are about eight species of *Burmeistera* in Costa Rica.

■ *Burmeistera vulgaris*
Family Campanulaceae

Terrestrial herb or shrubby herb, stems hollow, 1–3 m tall. **Leaves** alternate, 2-ranked, stalk to 2 cm, blade 5–15 cm long, 3–5 cm wide, elliptic, tip long pointed, base tapered to stalk rounded, leathery, margin toothed. **Flowers** pale green, bilaterally symmetrical, petal tube about 1.5 cm long, inflated at base, lobes 5, sharply curved, hoodlike, 2 longest, upper lobes about 1–2 cm, anthers and stigma on 1 stalk erect, above petal lobes, about 3 cm long, calyx lobes all equal lance-shaped, about 0.5–1 cm long, margins usually toothed, flower base (hypanthium) below calyx lobes about 1 cm long, 0.5 cm wide, developing into the fruit, flowers solitary in upper leaf axils, on a stalk 7–10 cm long; blooms and fruits most of the year. **Fruit** fleshy, green, inflated, 2.5–5 cm long, 2.5–4 cm wide, seeds numerous, very small. **Habitat:** Wet mountain forests. Altitude: 1100–2500 m. Conservation areas: CVC, LAC, LAP, PAC. **Range:** CR–Ec.

■ *Cochliostema odoratissimum* (príncipe azul)
Family Commelinaceae

Large epiphyte, no stem, leaves in a very large rosette, sometimes low on small trees. Appearance is much like a bromeliad. **Leaves** alternate, densely spiraled, 0.4–1 m long, 10–15 cm wide, straplike, leathery, tip pointed, base narrowing, then widening into a sheath, midrib conspicuous below. **Flowers** purple, 3-parted, irregular, about 3 cm long, petals densely fringed, sometimes white, shorter than sepals, sepals 1.5–3 cm long, 0.5–1 cm wide; inflorescence in leaf axils, 30–80 cm long, with bracts 2–6 cm long. **Fruit** dry, 3-parted, 3 cm long, 0.5 cm wide, splitting open to release seeds. **Habitat:** Wet to very wet lowland forests. Altitude: Sea level to 250 m. Conservation areas: CVC, LAC, OSA, TEM, TOR. **Range:** Nic–Ec. **Notes:** This is the only species of *Cochliostema* in Costa Rica. There is one other species from South America.

■ *Kalanchoe pinnata* (leaf-of-life, air plant, coirama)
Family Crassulaceae

Straggling, succulent, colonial herb, stems stout, hollow, to 2 m long, becoming woody, new growth pale gray green. **Leaves** opposite, crowded at ends of stems, stalk about 3 cm long, bases joined across stem in a ridge, blade 1–10 cm long, 0.5–5 cm wide, egg-shaped, pale green, thick, succulent, 3- to 5-lobed to coarsely blunt-toothed, margin dark, especially notches between teeth. Reproduces vegetatively by growth of plantlets along leaf margins, which fall and take root. **Flowers** reddish brown to pinkish green, tubular, radially symmetrical, about 4 cm long, 1 cm wide, petals slightly longer than pale green calyx; blooms on and off most of the year. **Fruit** dry. **Habitat:** Escaped from cultivation, in part shade or open sites. Widely tolerant of soils and moisture. Altitude: Sea level to 1500 m. Conservation areas: CVC, LAC, LAP, OSA, PAC. **Range:** Native to Africa, India, Madagascar; now pantropical. **Notes:** Used for many medicinal purposes. There is one other species of *Kalanchoe* in Costa Rica, but it is very uncommon.

■ *Chamaesyce hirta* (golondrina)
Family Euphorbiaceae

Herb 10–40 cm tall, erect to kneeling, stems hairy, sap milky.
Leaves opposite, often marked with red, stalk about 0.3 cm
long, hairy; blade 0.7–3.5 cm long, 0.4–1.4 cm wide, egg-
shaped, tip pointed, base asymmetrical, usually rough above,
hairy below, veins palmate, margin toothed. **Flowers** pale

green to reddish green, minute, in compact clusters
to 1.8 cm long, 1.6 cm wide, in leaf axils axillary
on a stalk to 0.9 cm, mostly 1 per node; blooms all
year. **Fruit** dry, about 0.1 cm, hairy. **Habitat:** Wet to
seasonally dry regions. Often a street weed in open
sunny habitats. Altitude: Sea level to 1400 m, mostly
below 500 m. Conservation areas: CVC (common
in San José), GUA, ICO, LAC, OSA, PAC, TEM.
Range: S US–Arg, WI. Introduced in Old World
tropics, invasive in SE Asia and some Pacific islands.
Notes: There are 14 species of *Chamaesyce* in Costa
Rica.

■ *Chamaesyce lasiocarpa*
Family Euphorbiaceae

Slender to shrublike herb 0.3–1.5 m tall, stems erect to
0.8 cm thick, stem dark red, sparsely branched base woody,
sap milky, leafy stem often with thick nodes. **Leaves** opposite, stalkless; blade 1–3.7 cm long, 0.2–1.6 cm wide, oblong,
tip blunt, base asymmetric, whitish hairy on both sides, margin minutely toothed. **Flowers** pale yellow green to white
(photo) turning pink, small, petals about 0.1 cm; inflorescence rather diffuse, stems often red, flowers in leafy clusters. **Fruit** dry, to 0.2 cm long, 3-lobed, finely hairy. **Habitat:**
Moist to seasonally dry regions. In open sunny sites, roadside
weed. Altitude: Sea level to 1200 m. Conservation areas:
CVC, ICO, LAP, PAC, TEM. **Range:** FL, Mex–N S Amer,
WI. **Notes:** Larger than most other species of *Chamaesyce*.

■ *Manihot esculenta* (yuca cassava, manioc, ari)
   Family Euphorbiaceae
Shrublike herb to 5 m tall, sap milky, stems with prominent leaf scars; roots form elongate, edible tubers. **Leaves** alternate, stalk to 12 cm long, blade to 12 cm long, 3 cm wide, variable, deeply, palmately 5- to 7-lobed, lobes narrowly elliptic, pale waxy below; leaf and plant forms vary with cultivar. **Flowers** yellow green, small, inconspicuous, to 1 cm, in branched clusters to 15 cm long. **Fruit** dry, to 1.5 cm, exploding to release and disperse seeds. **Habitat:** Cultivated throughout the country, occasionally escaping into weedy, open sites. Altitude: Can be grown up to 2000 m but usually found at lower elevations. Conservation areas: OSA. **Range:** Native to the Neotropics but transported to Africa in the 1500s. **Notes:** The starchy roots are used for food throughout tropics. Yuca grows well in poor soil and is very resistant to drought. The edible roots vary from sweet to very bitter, depending on their cyanide content. Cyanide must be removed by cooking and washing repeatedly. Usually seen as a stand of feathery plants in garden plots. There are two other species of *Manihot* in Costa Rica.

■ *Plectranthus scutellarioides (Coleus blumei,*
   Solenostemon s.) (coleus)
   Family Lamiaceae
Herb sprawling to 70 cm long, young stems densely hairy. **Leaves** opposite, stalk 1–4 cm long, blade 2–15 cm long, 2–10 cm wide, tip pointed, base blunt, sparsely hairy, usually variegated with red or white, margin blunt-toothed. **Flowers** blue purple, to 1 cm, bilaterally symmetrical, tubular, 5-parted, petal tube curved, upper lip 2-lobed, lower lip entire, enlarged, boat-shaped, calyx to 0.2 cm, unevenly lobed and toothed. **Fruit** dry, small, 4 nutlets. **Habitat:** Cultivated in tropical and temperate regions. Altitude: Widely cultivated. **Range:** Native to SE Asia and New Guinea. Naturalized in the tropics worldwide, invasive in some places. **Notes:** This is the only species of *Plectranthus* in Costa Rica.

413

Inflorescence

■ *Dorstenia contrajerva* (contrayerba)
Family Moraceae

Low, stemless herb 20–40 cm tall, slightly succulent. **Leaves** all together at base of plant, stalks 8–26 cm, blade 7–26 cm long, 9–34 cm wide, very variable on different plants, 1–8 lobes or teeth per side, lobes very shallow to deep, tips pointed. **Flowers** green, minute, densely crowded and imbedded in a fleshy, rectangular to star-shaped inflorescence, 0.8–4.5 cm wide, on a long stalk 10–34 cm from base of plant; blooms and fruits Feb.–Nov., mostly June–Sept. **Fruit** developing inside the fleshy inflorescence and not appearing very different, seeds small. **Habitat:** Wet to seasonally dry forest understories and edges. Altitude: Sea level to 1800 m, mostly below 1000 m. Conservation areas: ARE, CVC, GUA, LAC, LAP, PAC, TEM. **Range:** Mex–Pr and Guy, WI. **Notes:** There are two other species of *Dorstenia* in Costa Rica, *D. choconiana* has leaves along its stem and is only found in very wet forests, *D. drakena* has a rounded inflorescence and is less common.

■ *Eulophia alta* (wild coco)
Family Orchidaceae

Terrestrial herb 0.7–1.7 m tall, from a short, thick underground stem (corm), flowering stem arising directly from corm, stout, waxy pale green, leafless, except for a bract. **Leaves** alternate, several, produced separately from flowering stem, stalk sheathlike, enclosing stem, blade 0.2–1.2 m long, 3–11 cm wide, narrowly elliptic to lance-shaped, pleated, whitish below. **Flowers** pinkish green and red maroon, 1.5–2.5 cm wide, sepals and lateral petal similar, pale green, sepals 3, gathered above central petal, about 1.3 cm long, 0.7 cm wide, lateral petals together in a hood over lower petal, lower petal (lip) greenish outside, red inside, lip rounded, shallowly 4-lobed, base inflated; inflorescence to 1.5 m, leafless, unbranched, with numerous, widely spaced flowers at the top; blooms Oct.–Nov. **Fruit** dry, 4–6 cm long, elliptical, 6-ribbed; seeds numerous, dustlike. **Habitat:** Wet and very wet regions in open, disturbed lowlands, roadsides. Altitude: Sea level to 650 m. Conservation areas: HNO, LAP, OSA. **Range:** Mex–Arg, WI, Africa. **Notes:** This is the only species of *Eulophia* in Costa Rica.

◾ *Stelis guatemalensis*
Family Orchidaceae

Small colonial epiphyte, stems 6–14 cm tall, clustered, not bulblike. **Leaves** 1 per stem, at base of inflorescence, stalk about 1 cm long, blade 5–9 cm long, about 1.5 cm wide, narrowly elliptical, fleshy, folded along midrib, other veins obscure. **Flowers** pale green, often pink-tinged, bilaterally symmetrical but appearing 3-parted, sepals 3, about 0.2–0.3 cm long, about 0.2 cm wide, side petals and lower petal (lip) inconspicuously short; inflorescence arising from base of the leaf, erect, unbranched, spikelike, 10–17 cm long, with numerous, tiny flowers along one side, all blooming at the same time; blooms Apr.–Nov. **Fruit** dry, seeds numerous, dustlike. **Habitat:** Very wet mountain forests. Altitude: Mostly 1200–1550. Conservation areas: CVC, LAP. **Range:** Mex, Gua, CR. **Notes:** There are 53 species of *Stelis* in Costa Rica. They are extremely difficult to identify to species even by experts; many are very similar to S. *guatemalensis*.

◾ *Peperomia galioides*
Family Piperaceae

Terrestrial or epiphytic herb, erect, 10–35 cm tall, branched, often with treelike form, single main axis with lateral branches. **Leaves** opposite or in whorls of 4, almost stalkless, blades 0.3–3 cm long, 0.2–0.7 cm wide, larger leaves (over 0.8 cm long) often just below inflorescence, narrowly oblong to widest above middle, tip rounded or slightly notched, base wedge-shaped, veins obscure. **Flowers** yellow green, minute, crowded on unbranched spikes 4–15 cm long, in clusters of 2–10, flowers often somewhat separated; blooms and fruits all year. **Fruit** fleshy, less than 0.1 cm wide, becoming blackish. **Habitat:** Moist forests, second growth, open sites at higher elevations. Altitude: 1000–3400 m, mostly above 2000 m. Conservation areas: CVC, LAC, LAP, PAC. **Range:** Throughout tropical Amer. **Notes:** Distinguished by their treelike form and high-elevation habitat.

415

■ *Rumex nepalensis*
Family Polygonaceae

Weedy herb 0.5–1.5 m tall, often in dense colonies, stems erect, finely ribbed, stipules membranous, pale tan, to 5 cm long sheathing stem. **Leaves** alternate, stalk 2–15 cm long, base clasping stem, basal leaves much larger than stem leaves, often in dense cluster, blade 4–25 cm long, 1–10 cm wide, narrowly arrow-shaped, surface puckered, tip pointed to blunt, base blunt to lobed, margins entire. **Flowers** greenish, not flowerlike, very small, 3-winged, the wing margins deeply fringed with numerous hooked spines, often reddish; inflorescence branched 10–50 cm long; probably blooms and fruits most of the year. **Fruit** dry, to 0.5 cm long, enclosed in a fringe of flower parts. **Habitat:** Street weed, curbs, vacant lots, roadsides. Altitude: 1100–1400. Conservation areas: CVC. **Range:** Native from SW Europe to E Asia. Introduced in CR. **Notes:** There are five species of *Rumex* in Costa Rica; *R. nepalensis* is distinctive because of its fringed flower/fruit.

■ *Typha domingensis* (enea, espadaña, tule, cattail)
Family Typhaceae

Large grasslike plant 2–4 m tall, colonial from thick, underground stems (rhizomes), often forming dense stands. **Leaves** alternate, about 2.5 m long, 0.6–2 cm wide, linear, thick, spongy, gray green. **Flowers** brown, minute, densely packed on a spike, male flowers on 7–22 cm of the upper inflorescence stalk, they fall off soon after shedding pollen, female flowers on the lower 10–46 cm with a gap of 2–4 cm between the sexes; blooms on and off, Aug.–Apr. **Fruit** dry, 1-seeded, white-plumed; wind dispersed as seeds detach from lower inflorescence spike in cottony tufts. **Habitat:** Shallow open water, mud, in lowland areas. Altitude: Sea level to 600 m, occasionally to 1200 m. Conservation areas: CVC, GUA, LAC, OSA, TEM. **Range:** US–Arg. **Notes:** The other species of *Typha, T. latifolia* is quite uncommon in Costa Rica. Young *Typha* inflorescences are often dried and used in floral arrangements.

Laportea aestuans
Family Urticaceae

Herb to 1.5 m tall, stems usually *covered with stinging hairs*, succulent, sometimes reddish, stipules to 1 cm, united at base, tips linear. **Leaves** alternate, spiraled, stalk to 12 cm, glandular hairy, blade 3–30 cm long, 2–22 cm wide, broadly egg- to heart-shaped, tip long-pointed, base blunt to slightly lobed, hairy on both sides, evenly, coarsely toothed (as if cut with pinking shears). **Flowers** pale green to pale pinkish white, tiny, about 0.1 cm; inflorescence to 20 cm, axillary, erect, branched; blooms all year. **Fruit** dry, 1-seeded, to 0.1 cm. **Habitat:** Very wet to seasonally dry lowlands (rainy season in dry areas), weedy open sites to partial shade. Altitude: Sea level to 700 m. Conservation areas: ICO, LAC, OSA, PAC, TEM. **Range:** Mex–Ven and Bol, WI, parts of Africa. **Notes:** This is the only species of *Laportea* in Costa Rica. It is found in many tropical parts of the world.

Pilea microphylla
Family Urticaceae

Herb 2–25 cm tall, small weed often forming dense mats, sometimes mosslike, much-branched, succulent. **Leaves** opposite, stalk to 0.8 cm, blade about 0.1–1 cm long, 0.1–0.5 cm wide, pair members at a node often very unequal, broadly elliptic to widest above middle, tip rounded to pointed, base tapered, margin entire. **Flowers** pale greenish, much less than 0.1 cm; inflorescences axillary, to 0.4 cm long, blooms most of the year, mostly from July–Jan. **Fruit** dry, much less than 0.1cm. **Habitat:** Wet to seasonally dry regions, rainy season in dry areas. An urban weed in gutters, cracks in walls and sidewalks. Altitude: Sea level to 1500. Conservation areas: ARE, CVC, LAC, PAC, TEM. **Range:** US NC–TX, Mex–Ven and Arg, WI. **Notes:** There are 28 species of *Pilea* in Costa Rica. Species in the genus *Pilea* are distinguished by opposite leaves with palmate veins like those in the family Melastomataceae. This is the largest genus of Urticaceae with 600 species worldwide. *Pilea microphylla* is distinguished by its small, opposite, unequal leaves and dense habit. Seen in San José.

417

GRASSES AND SEDGES

Cyperus ligularis
Cyperus luzulae
Cyperus niger
Cyperus odoratus
Eleocharis elegans
Kyllinga pumila
Rhynchospora nervosa
Scleria melaleuca
Uncinia hamata
Andropogon bicornis
Cenchrus brownii
Coix lacryma-jobi
Cymbopogon citratus
Digitaria costaricensis

Eleusine indica
Gynerium sagittatum
Hyparrhenia rufa
Lasiacis rhizophora
Oplismenus burmannii
Oryza sativa
Panicum maximum
Paspalum paniculatum
Paspalum saccharoides
Pennisetum purpureum
Rhynchelytrum repens
Rottboellia cochinchinensis
Saccharum officinarum

Sedges (Cyperaceae) and grasses (Poaceae) are known as graminoids (grass-like plants). Other herbs with grass-like leaves are not included with the graminoids. Graminoids stand out as a group, having slender stems and leaves and mostly inconspicuous flowers and fruit. They tend to make a natural botanical group that is easily recognizable. Rushes (Juncaeceae) are also included with the graminoids but we do not have any examples in this family, which is represented by only 9 species in 2 genera in Costa Rica.

■ *Cyperus ligularis* (navajala, razorgrass, sedge)
Family Cyperaceae

Sedge 0.3–1 m tall, tough, stiff, pale gray green, stems in tufts, rough-textured. **Leaves** alternate, 6–13, mostly basal, 0.3–1 m long, 0.5–1.5 cm wide, brown at base, folded along midrib, margins finely, sharply serrated. **Flowers** green to brownish, tiny, each covered by a small scale, densely clustered in spikes 1–3.5 cm long, about 1 cm wide; inflorescence large, brown at maturity, branched from top of stem, leaflike bracts just below inflorescence to 1 m long, 1.5 cm wide; blooms and fruits most of the year. **Fruit** dry, 1-seeded (achene), brown, sharply 3-sided, 0.1 cm long. **Habitat:** Seasonally dry to very wet regions, in open areas, sandy or rocky soil near river banks or beaches, wet roadsides, waste areas. Altitude: Sea level to 150 m. Conservation areas: GUA, LAC, OSA, TEM, TOR. **Range:** SE US, Mex–Brz, Jam, Bh, Africa, Pacific islands. **Notes:** There are 58 species of *Cyperus* in Costa Rica.

Cyperus niger (opposite)

Cyperus luzulae (cabezón, zacate de estrella, sedge)
Family Cyperaceae

Sedge 20–70 cm tall, dark green, shiny, stems in tufts, bluntly 3-sided, smooth but very tough. **Leaves** alternate, 3–10, from base or along lower stem, about as long as flowering stem, blade linear, 15–40 cm long, 0.3–0.7 cm wide, shiny. **Flowers** white or pale greenish, minute, eventually becoming brown, papery, in flat clusters 0.2–0.5 cm long of about 10 overlapping flowers, clusters arranged in dense, conical or rounded heads 1.5 cm long, about 1 cm wide, the central ones stalkless, the outer heads on short stalks, to about 2 cm long, all radiating from a central point above the bracts; bracts below inflorescence leaflike to 30 cm long, very narrow; blooms all year. **Fruit** dry, brown, 1-seeded, about 0.1 cm long. **Habitat:** Seasonally dry to very wet regions in moist forest clearings, pastures, wet ditches, roadsides. Altitude: Sea level to 1800 m, mostly below 200 m. Conservation areas: ARE, CVC, HNO, LAC, LAP, OSA, PAC, TOR. **Range:** S US, S Mex–Arg, Ant, Tr. **Notes:** *Cyperus luzulae* is distinguished by its whitish inflorescence.

Cyperus niger (black flatsedge)
Family Cyperaceae

Very slender sedge, 5–50 cm tall; stems blue green, in tufts. **Leaves** alternate, blade 3–20 cm long, 0.1–0.3 cm wide, blue green, much shorter than flowering stem. **Flowers** blackish or dark brown, scalelike, roughly 0.5 cm long, densely overlapping along both sides of a flower spike 0.3–0.9 cm long, about 0.2 cm wide, spikes solitary or in clusters, radiating from tops of short branches, above linear leaflike bracts directly below inflorescence; blooms and fruits all year. **Fruit** dry, 1-seeded. **Habitat:** Very wet mid- to high elevations in open wet areas, roadside ditches, pastures. Altitude: 600–3200 m. Conservation areas: ARE, CVC, HNO, LAP, PAC. **Range:** US–Ven and Chile, Arg, Africa.

■ *Cyperus odoratus* (coyolillo, pelo de chino, sedge) Family Cyperaceae

Sedge 0.3–1 m tall, stems solitary or a few together, bluntly triangular in cross section, base often swollen. **Leaves** alternate, 3–10, from base and to 1/2 way up stem, linear, 10–65 cm long, 0.5–1 cm wide. **Flowers** gold green, becoming brownish in fruit, each covered by a small papery scale, 0.3 cm long, scales overlapping along linear spikes 0.5–2.5 cm long, spikes radiating from along top of flowering branches, giving inflorescence a spiky appearance, flowering branches to 3–20 cm long, inflorescence above several leaflike linear bracts, 15–50 cm long, radiating from top of flowering stem, often longer than flowering branches; blooms and fruits all year. **Fruit** dark brown, dry, 1-seeded about 0.2 cm long. **Habitat:** Seasonally dry to very wet regions, in open sites, pasture edges, roadsides. Altitude: Sea level to 1000 m. Conservation areas: CVC, GUA, LAC, PAC, TEM, TOR. **Range:** Can and US–Arg, WI, Africa, SE Asia, Oceania. Introduced and invasive in the Galapagos. **Notes:** Distinctive for its gold green to gold brown, spiky appearing inflorescence.

■ *Eleocharis elegans* (junco, junquillo, tristura, tule, spike rush) Family Cyperaceae

Grasslike, unbranched herb 0.2–1.3 m tall, appearing leafless, colonial from underground stems, aboveground stems green, 0.3–1.0 cm diameter, cylindrical, hollow, internal partitions about every 1 cm, faintly visible up length of stem, bladeless leaf sheath on lower 10 cm of stem reddish brown. **Leaves** reduced to a basal sheath, without blade. **Flowers** minute, each covered by a small brownish scale, anthers white, inflorescence a single dense, cone-shaped cluster (spike) 1–3 cm long, at top of stem; blooms and fruits all year. **Fruit** dry, 1-seeded (achene). **Habitat:** Seasonally dry to very wet regions in shallow water, wet soil, open sun to part shade, disturbed sites, roadside ditches. Altitude: Sea level to 1300 m. Conservation areas: ARE, CVC, GUA, LAC, LAP, OSA, TEM, TOR. **Range:** S Mex–Arg, Tr, PtR. **Notes:** There are 19 species of *Eleocharis* in Costa Rica. *Eleocharis elegans* is the most common. Another common species is *E. retroflexa*, which is much smaller (about 5 cm tall), forming mats on wet soil.

▩ *Kyllinga pumila* (sedge)
Family Cyperaceae

Small sedge 7–30 cm tall; stems in tufts, often red-dish. **Leaves** alternate, blades linear, 0.1–0.3 cm wide, slightly rough-textured, much shorter than the flowering stems. **Flowers** tiny, white to greenish, anthers pale yellow; inflorescence of tiny scale-covered flattened flowers 0.3 cm long, tightly packed on short axis in 1–3 dense, rounded to egg-shaped heads 0.4–0.8 cm long, stalkless; inflorescence bracts just below inflorescence, 3–4, leaflike, linear, 3–10 cm long; blooms and fruits most of the year, except Apr.–June. **Fruit** dry, 1-seeded (achene), about 0.1 cm long, yellowish brown. **Habitat:** Seasonally dry to very wet regions in open, wet, marshy soil, seepage areas, garden and lawn weed in wet places. Altitude: Sea level to 1750 m. Conservation areas: ARE, CVC, LAP, OSA, PAC, TEM, TOR. **Range:** US–Arg, PtR, Africa. **Notes:** There are six species of *Kyllinga* in Costa Rica. Three are similar to *K. pumila*, the others are leafless (like *Eleocharis*) and found mostly along the coast.

▩ *Rhynchospora nervosa* (cuita de zoncho, cuitas, florecilla blanca, little star) Family Cyperaceae

Slender sedge 10–70 cm tall, stems in clumps, or colonial from underground stems. **Leaves** alternate, all at base of stem, grasslike, 10–45 cm long, 0.1–0.4 cm wide, much shorter than flowering stem. **Flowers** white, dry, scalelike, to about 1 cm long, in a dense head above 4–6 leaflike inflorescence bracts 1–15 cm long, bract bases white, making petal-like pattern below inflorescence; flowering most of the year. **Fruit** dry, 1-seeded, white to brownish. **Habitat:** Seasonally dry to very wet regions in open shade or part sun of old pastures, disturbed sites, vacant lots in San José, sometimes under taller herbs. Altitude: Sea level to 1750 m. Conservation areas: ARE, CVC, GUA, LAC, LAP, PAC, TEM. **Range:** Mex–S Brz and Arg, WI. **Notes:** There are 48 species of *Rhynchospora* in Costa Rica, *R. nervosa* is distinguished by its white flowerlike bract bases. It is found throughout tropical America.

■ *Scleria melaleuca* (navajuela, hojuela, sedge)
Family Cyperaceae
Sedge 0.3–1.2 m tall, stems 3-sided, with sharp edges, solitary or several together, leaf sheaths winged; plant colonial from underground stems (rhizomes). **Leaves** alternate, blade 0.4–1.5 cm wide, much shorter than flowering stem, drooping, bristly, margins raspy. **Flowers** becoming red brown or purplish, scalelike; inflorescence branched, elongate, to 10 cm long, 4 cm wide, above leaflike bracts. **Fruit** dry, 1-seeded, purplish to blackish, shiny. **Habitat:** Wet to very wet regions in open, disturbed areas, usually in wet soil, pastures, marshes, roadsides. Altitude: Sea level to 1400 m. Conservation areas: ARE, CVC, GUA, HNO, LAC, LAP, OSA, PAC, TEM, TOR. **Range:** S Mex–Arg, WI, Africa. **Notes:** There are 21 species of *Scleria* in Costa Rica; S. *melaleuca* is the most common. *Scleria* species are recognized by their once-branched inflorescences and very hard, purplish or white fruit (achenes)

■ *Uncinia hamata* (navajuela)
Family Cyperaceae
Terrestrial or epiphytic sedge 20–60 cm tall, stems 3-sided, leafy, growing in tufts. **Leaves** alternate, grasslike, linear, 30–50 cm long, 0.3–1 cm wide, slightly drooping. **Flowers** small, scalelike, at first pale greenish yellow, becoming reddish or brown; stamens and stigma white; inflorescence a linear spike 8–20 cm long, 0.2–0.5 cm wide; blooms and fruits all year. **Fruit** dry, 1-seeded, with hooks that cling to fur or clothing. **Habitat:** Very wet mountains in oak forests, cloud forests in open areas or part shade, trail and stream sides,

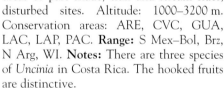

disturbed sites. Altitude: 1000–3200 m. Conservation areas: ARE, CVC, GUA, LAC, LAP, PAC. **Range:** S Mex–Bol, Brz, N Arg, WI. **Notes:** There are three species of *Uncinia* in Costa Rica. The hooked fruits are distinctive.

■ *Andropogon bicornis* (cola de venado, grass)
Family Poaceae

Grass 0.8–2 m tall, stiffly erect, in dense clumps, often many clumps together, stems often reddish, leafy, to 0.6 cm wide, hollow, branching freely, branches closely ascending together; leaf sheaths open, green with tufts of hair at top. **Leaves** alternate, blade 20–50 cm long, 0.2–0.6 cm wide, rough-textured, thick, waxy whitish below, sometimes slightly hairy, tip tapered to point. **Flowers** papery, 0.3 cm; clusters whitish-hairy, densely feathery, many-branched (broomlike), flowering branches 2–3 cm long, very hairy, in pairs; blooms and fruits most of the year, especially July–Oct. **Fruit** dry, 1-seeded (grain). **Habitat:** Wet and very wet regions in open areas, grasslands, rocky sites, roadsides. Altitude: Sea level to 1800 m. Conservation areas: ARE, CVC, LAP, OSA, PAC. **Range:** Mex–Arg, WI. **Notes:** There are 10 species of *Andropogon* in Costa Rica; *A. bicornis* is the most common.

■ *Cenchrus brownii* (mozote, sandbur)
Family Poaceae

Grass 0.25–1 m tall, stems in tufts, flattened, base usually bent, often rooting at nodes, leaf sheaths hairy along margins. **Leaves** alternate, blade to 9–34 cm long, 0.4–1 cm wide, often rough or hairy above. **Flowers** enclosed in hard, spiny burs, 0.5–0.8 cm wide (including spines); inflorescence spikes greenish to purplish, 3–10 cm long, *densely covered with burs* which hide the axis, ripe burs with seeds easily detach and cling to fur or clothing; blooms and fruits June–Nov., **Fruit** dry, 1-seeded grains enclosed in burs; burs persisting much of the year. **Habitat:** Wet to very wet lowlands, along open roadsides, beaches, weedy sites. Altitude: Sea level to 550 m, mostly below 100 m. Conservation areas: ICO, LAC, PAC, TEM, TOR. **Range:** SE US–Ec and Ven, WI. **Notes:** There are six species of *Cenchrus* in Costa Rica; they are recognized by their hard, spiny, burlike flowers.

425

■ *Coix lacryma-jobi* (lágrimas de San Pedro, cuentas de San Pedro, trigo adlai, Job's tears)
Family Poaceae

Grass 0.5–3 m tall, stems clustered, copiously branched, plant appearing cornlike but smaller. **Leaves** alternate, blade 10–50 cm long, 2–5 cm wide, tip tapered to a point, base blunt, clasping stem. **Flowers** with sexes separate, females enclosed in round, hard, gray white or blue gray, shiny, bead-like shell, 0.7–1.4 cm long, 0.5–0.9 cm wide; males with small, papery bracts (like most grasses); inflorescence of branched clusters in upper leaf axils; blooms and fruits all year. **Fruit** dry, 1-seeded, grain enclosed in beadlike shell. **Habitat:** Very wet regions in open sites, roadside ditches, second growth. Altitude: Sea level to 1450 m. Conservation areas: ARE, HNO, CVC, LAC, LAP, PAC, TEM, TOR. **Range:** Native to tropical Asia. Cultivated and naturalized throughout the tropics. Introduced and invasive in the Galapagos, Hawai'i, and other Pacific islands. **Notes:** This is the only species of *Coix* in Costa Rica. Often used to make necklaces and rosary beads. Some varieties have soft beads and are used as a grain called *trigo adlai*.

■ *Cymbopogon citratus* (zacate de limón, sontol, lemon grass) **Family Poaceae**

Stout grass 1–2 m tall (with leaves), waxy gray green, stems densely clustered, short, to 10 cm long, 1 cm wide, solid, woody, internodes very short, base of older plants somewhat flattened and fan-shaped; sheaths waxy white, closely overlapping, upper margin lobed. **Leaves** alternate, all at base of plant, blade 35–80 cm long, 0.9–1.8 cm wide, flat, lemon odor when crushed, blades thin, base tapered, tip long-pointed, drooping, margins thick, white, midrib white. **Flowers** papery; inflorescence branched, 35–65 cm long, rarely seen. **Fruit** dry 1-seeded, grain. **Habitat:** Cultivated, usually around houses. Altitude: Sea level to 1000 m or more, in gardens. Conservation areas: Cultivated in many parts of the country, not escaping. **Range:** Native to India. Cultivated worldwide in the tropics. **Notes:** This is the only species of *Cymbopogon* in Costa Rica; recognized by its lemon scent.

▓ *Digitaria costaricensis*
Family Poaceae

Coarse grass, stems 35–80 cm long, with numerous erect branches, stems clumped, colonial from lower stems lying along ground, rooting at nodes; leaf sheaths densely sticky-hairy, pale gray green, base often purple. **Leaves** alternate, blade 4–16 cm long, 0.4–0.8 cm wide, flat, soft, velvety-hairy, leaves of inflorescence smaller. **Flowers** grayish to tan, papery, 0.4 cm long, finely hairy on veins, narrow, tips pointed, in 2 rows along one side the spikelike branches; inflorescence a whorl of 4–9 spikes 5–14 cm long, on a cen-

tral short axis 2–3 cm long, at ends of stems, appearing more or less palmate; inflorescence stalk 6–15 cm long; blooms in Apr. and Oct. **Fruit** dry 1-seeded, grain. **Habitat:** Very wet regions, in open areas, roadsides, pastures. Altitude: 1300–1950 m. Conservation areas: CVC. Seen in pastures near Tapantí N.P. **Range:** Gua, El Salv, CR. **Notes:** There are 14 species of *Digitaria* in Costa Rica, some native, some from Africa or Asia. Of the 240 species worldwide, many are found in temperate regions. They are recognized by their very slender inflorescence branches and narrow, pointed flowers.

▓ *Eleusine indica* (goose grass)
Family Poaceae

Street weed, stems in tufts, flattened especially near base, 15–70 cm long, hollow between nodes, erect to spreading, often rooting at lower nodes, sheaths keeled, open, slightly hairy at top. **Leaves** alternate, blade 5–20 cm long, 0.2–0.5 cm wide, somewhat folded along midrib. **Flowers** papery, 0.4–0.8 cm long, flattened, in tightly overlapping clusters of 4–7 flowers (spikelets) 0.5 cm long, along one side of a flattened spike axis; inflorescence of 2–7 spikes, 2–16 cm long, mostly all clustered at the top of inflorescence stalk or with 1 additional spike lower on stalk; blooms all year. **Fruit** dry

1-seeded, grain. **Habitat:** Seasonally dry to very wet regions in open soil of vacant lots, sidewalk cracks, curbs, lawns. Altitude: Sea level to 1450 m. Conservation areas: ARE, CVC, ICO, LAC, LAP, OSA, PAC, TEM. **Range:** A native of S Asia and Africa, now a worldwide weed especially in urban areas. Invasive in the Galapagos, Hawai'i, other Pacific islands, and SE Asia. **Notes:** This is the only species of *Eleusine* in Costa Rica. The inflorescence looks much like *Digitaria* sp., but *Eleusine* is coarser and stems and flower spikes are broader and flattened.

427

■ *Gynerium sagittatum* (caña blanca, caña brava, caña de construcción) Family Poaceae

Grass to 6 m tall, colonial from underground stems, aerial stems woody in age, 2–5 cm wide, leaf sheath covering stem between nodes. **Leaves** alternate, in a fan-shaped cluster at top of the stem, blade 0.5–2.2 m long, 2–8 cm wide, midrib conspicuous, blade margins very rough. **Flowers** papery, sexes on different plants, colonies mostly either male or female, male flowers to 0.3 cm long, brownish, not plumed; female flowers to 1 cm long, base with long, white hairs; inflorescence plumelike, 0.8–1.6 m long, stalk about 1 m long; of one main axis with numerous fine, drooping branches covered by flowers; blooms and fruits Feb., June–Dec. **Fruit** dry 1-seeded, grain. **Habitat:** Wet to very wet regions in open areas, roadsides, river margins. Altitude: Sea level to 1600 m. Conservation areas: ARE, CVC, LAC, OSA, TEM, TOR.

Range: Mex–Arg, Tr, Ant, Bh. **Notes:** This is the only species of *Gynerium* in Costa Rica. It looks much like sugar-cane (*Saccharum officinarum*), but the inflorescence of *Gynerium* is much more fan-shaped and the sap is not sweet. It colonizes open soil and helps prevent erosion on slopes. Flower clusters sold as decorations.

■ *Hyparrhenia rufa* (jaraguá) Family Poaceae

Grass 1–2 m tall; stems light reddish brown, in large clumps with drooping leaves at base. **Leaves** alternate, narrow, basal blades 30–75 cm long, 0.4–0.8 cm wide, stem blades smaller. **Flowers** papery, 0.4–0.8 cm long, reddish-hairy, narrow, some with a long, bent, bristle; inflorescence 15–55 cm long, open, much-branched, branches 1–4 cm long, slender with a pair of flower spikes at tip, spikes bearing up to 8 pairs of flowers; blooms most of the year, but predominantly during Oct.–Jan. **Fruit** dry 1-seeded, grain. **Habitat:** A widespread pasture grass, mostly in seasonally dry lowlands, but occasionally in wet and very wet regions. Altitude: Sea level to 1700 m, mostly on the Pacific slope below 1000 m. Conservation areas: ARE, CVC, GUA (mostly), LAP, OSA, PAC, TEM. **Range:** Native to Africa but naturalized in the tropics worldwide. Invasive in Australia, Hawai'i, and some other Pacific islands. **Notes:** Dominant, invasive pasture grass in seasonally dry regions. Dry flower bristles sharp, irritating. There is one other species of *Hyparrhenia* in Costa Rica but it is quiet uncommon.

▓ *Lasiacis rhizophora* (carrizo)
Family Poaceae

Forest grass, like a small bamboo, stems slender, branching freely, creeping, colonial by rooting at nodes below leafy part of stem, roots often aerial, stiltlike; upper stems to 1 m tall, leaf sheaths finely hairy, upper margin conspicuously hairy. **Leaves** alternate, ranked along ends of stems, blade 7–15 cm long, 0.2–0.4 cm wide, elliptic, tip gradually tapered, long-pointed, base with sides unequal, one side lobed, clasping stem, surface dark green, glossy, hairy to smooth, often somewhat rippled. **Flowers** blackish, to 0.4 cm long, about 0.1 cm wide, solitary at tips of an inflorescence branch; inflorescence 10–24 cm long, at ends of stems, open, branching. **Fruit** dark red, becoming black, shiny, beadlike, floral parts enclosing fruit contain oil; fruit-eating birds consume fruits and disperse seeds in their droppings; blooms Aug.–Feb. **Habitat:** Very wet regions in open forest understories and edges. Altitude: 900–2000 m. Conservation areas: ARE (mostly), CVC, GUA, LAC, LAP. **Range:** Mex–Col and Ven. **Notes:** There are 13 species of *Lasiacis* in Costa Rica. All resemble small bamboos, have black, beadlike fruit, and are typically found along forest edges. The most common is *L. nigra*, to 12 m long, climbing on other vegetation.

▓ *Oplismenus burmannii* (zacate guácimo, zacate de ratón, panza de burro) Family Poaceae

Weedy grass, bright green, stems thin, wiry, 0.1 cm wide, lower stems creeping, rooting at nodes forming large colonies, leafy branches 10–30 cm long, erect, leaf sheaths short, hairy, margins overlapping. **Leaves** alternate, blade 1–5 cm long, 0.5–1.5 cm wide, short and wide, surface rough-textured to hairy, usually rippled perpendicular to midrib. **Flowers** papery, 0.3–0.4 cm long, whitish, hairy, each with 2 bristles (awns) to 0.5 cm long, anthers orange, stigmas red purple; inflorescence 3–6 cm long, bristly, with 3–7 compact, closely ascending branches each about 2 cm long; blooms Oct.–Mar. **Fruit** dry 1-seeded, grain. **Habitat:** Seasonally dry to very wet regions, in open forests, shady roadsides, coastal dunes, pastures, city vacant lots, often under taller weeds. Altitude: Sea level to 1800 m. Conservation areas: ARE, CVC, GUA, HNO, LAP, OSA, PAC, TEM. **Range:** Pantropical and subtropical. Native to Australia, SE Asia, C Amer. Introduced in Hawai'i and the Galapagos. **Notes:** *Oplismenus burmannii* appears similar to some smaller species of *Panicum*, but *Panicum* flowers are not bristly. There are three species of *Oplismenus* in Costa Rica.

429

■ *Oryza sativa* (arroz, rice)
Family Poaceae

Cultivated grain from less than 1 m to about 2 m tall, young plants bright green, becoming fairly stout and clumped, some cultivars remaining short. **Leaves** alternate, 23–63 cm long, 0.5–2 cm wide, variable with cultivar. **Flowers** dry, about 1 cm long, solitary, finely hairy, becoming tan, large, elliptic, beadlike, along inflorescence branches, sometimes with long bristles; inflorescence 9–30 cm long with many drooping branches; blooms and fruits mostly in the rainy season, occasionally into the dry season, Aug.–Feb. **Fruit** dry, 1-seeded grain. **Habitat:** Cultivated in the seasonally dry to very wet Pacific lowlands, occasionally escaping in open sites, along roadsides and river banks. Altitude: Sea level to 200 m. Conservation areas: GUA, LAP, OSA, TEM, TOR.

Range: Native to Asia. **Notes:** There are two other species of *Oryza* in Costa Rica. *Oryza latifolia,* is a native, wild plant to about 2 m tall with leaves to 55 cm long, 3.5 cm wide, much like *O. sativa,* found in wet soil in the Caribbean and Pacific lowlands. It is called *zacate zamora, arrozón, arroz pato* (duck rice). The third species, *O. rufipogon,* is nonnative and very uncommon.

Paspalum paniculatum

■ *Panicum maximum* (cebollana, guinea, zacate de guinea, pasto guinea) Family Poaceae

Large perennial grass 0.5–3.5 m tall, stems in clumps, erect, stout, to 0.8 cm wide, sparsely branched or not at all, nodes densely bearded with white hairs; leaf sheath hairy, especially near top. **Leaves** alternate, 20–95 cm long, 1–3.5 cm wide, midrib pale, blade rather stiff, margins minutely saw-toothed, base of blade bearded with long, white hairs. **Flowers** green or tan, solitary, beadlike, oval, about 0.3 cm long, with conspicuous parallel veins growing on secondary branches of inflorescence, on tiny individual stems; inflorescence 15–60 cm long, at tops of stems, broadly pyramid-shaped, lower primary branches whorled; flowers and fruits all year. **Fruit** dry, 1-seeded grain. **Habitat:** Seasonally dry to very wet regions; a pasture grass, often escaping along roadsides and open areas. Altitude: Sea level to 1350 m, mostly below 300 m. Conservation areas: CVC, GUA, ICO, LAC, LAP, OSA, PAC, TEM, TOR. **Range:** Native to Africa. Now pantropical and subtropical. Invasive in Australia, Hawai'i, the Galapagos, and other Pacific islands. **Notes:** There are 34 species of *Panicum* in Costa Rica. All have solitary, beadlike flowers without bristles.

■ *Paspalum paniculatum* (zacate cabezón) Family Poaceae

Coarse grass 0.45–1.6 m tall, stems in large clumps, branching, nodes large, bearded, leaf sheaths prickly-hairy, irritating to handle. **Leaves** alternate, blade 17–35 cm long, 1–2 cm wide, flat, base broad, rounded, midrib conspicuous, white, raised below, surface hairy on both sides. **Flowers** purple to brown, about 0.1 cm long, almost circular, flat on one side, finely hairy, arranged in 4 rows on one side of a bristly, spikelike inflorescence branch; inflorescence 5–32 cm long, a central axis with 18–70 flower spikes branching off it, base of each spike bearded, the lower spikes 4–11 cm long, smaller upward, dark purplish-red; blooms and fruits all year. **Fruit** dry, 1-seeded grain. **Habitat:** Seasonally dry to very wet regions in open, disturbed areas, city vacant lots and streets, roadsides, ditches, marshes. Altitude: Sea level to 1500 m. Conservation areas: ARE, CVC, LAC, LAP, OSA, PAC, TEM, TOR. **Range:** S Mex–Arg, WI, Galapagos. Introduced in US and Old World tropics. Invasive in Hawai'i and other Pacific islands. **Notes:** There are 48 species of *Paspalum* in Costa Rica. The flowers are much like those of *Panicum* but are very flat on one side and arranged in rows along one side of the spikelike inflorescence branches.

Paspalum paniculatum photo opposite

■ *Paspalum saccharoides*
Family Poaceae

Plumed grass 2 m tall; sprawling, drooping, hanging over embankments, rooting from lower nodes, lower stems to 0.8 cm thick, nodes swollen; leaf sheaths hairy, bearded at top. **Leaves** alternate, usually ranked in one plane along stem, blades 9–45 cm long, 0.5–1.4 cm wide, blades of upper and lower leaves much smaller, thick, hairy above. **Flowers** 0.2–0.3 cm long, bearded with long silky white hairs, overlapping in 2 rows along each inflorescence branch; inflorescence 10–34 cm long, whitish, plumelike, very silky-hairy, sometimes purplish, central axis to 7 cm long, with numerous long, slender, drooping branches to 25 cm long, extending well beyond central axis; blooms and fruits all year. **Fruit** dry, 1-seeded, grain. **Habitat:** Very wet regions, in open sites, road banks, bluffs, old landslides. Altitude: Sea level to 1800 m, usually above 400 m. Conservation areas: ARE, CVC, LAC, LAP, OSA, PAC, TOR. **Range:** Nic–Ven and Bol, Brz, WI. **Notes:** Flower structure unlike most other *Paspalum* species. Common along Ruta 32 through Braulio Carrillo N.P.

■ *Pennisetum purpureum* (pasto azul, pasto elefante, pasto gigante) **Family Poaceae**

Stout grass 1–3.5 m tall; stems in large clumps, often waxy pale green, to 2.5 cm wide, sometimes kneeling and rooting lower nodes. **Leaves** alternate, blade 0.25–1.3 m long, to 1–4 cm wide. **Flowers** 0.5–0.7 cm long, narrowly egg-shaped, in clusters of 1–5, amid hairs and yellow gold bristles; inflorescence a densely bristly-yellow, cylindrical spike 14–30 cm long, 1–2 cm wide, not including bristles; blooms and fruits all year. **Fruit** dry, 1-seeded grain. **Habitat:** Seasonally dry to very wet regions, a common pasture grass in open areas throughout Central Valley, roadsides, vacant lots in San José, many other places. Altitude: Sea level to 1800 m. Conservation areas: ARE, CVC, GUA, LAC, LAP, OSA, PAC, TOR. **Range:** Native to Africa. Naturalized worldwide in tropics and subtropics. Invasive in Australia, the Galapagos, Hawai'i, and many other Pacific islands. **Notes:** There are seven species of *Pennisetum* in Costa Rica.

Rhynchelytrum repens (zacate de seda, zacate ilusión) Family Poaceae

Weedy grass 0.3–1.1 m tall, stems in clumps, hairy, nodes bearded. **Leaves** alternate, blades 5–17 cm long, 0.2–0.6 cm wide, hairy, flat, upper leaves smaller, hairless. **Flowers** red pink to silvery, densely hairy, about 0.4–0.5 cm long; inflorescence 13–22 cm long, branched, more or less conical, delicate, appearing fluffy-pink from numerous, long-hairy flowers; blooms Jan., Feb., July–Sept. **Fruit** dry, 1-seeded grain. **Habitat:** Seasonally dry to very wet regions, in open, weedy sites, roadsides, coffee plantations, grasslands. Altitude: Sea level to 1300 m. Conservation areas: CVC, GUA, LAC, LAP, OSA, PAC, TEM, TOR. Very common along roadsides near San José. **Range:** Native to Africa. Naturalized in tropical and subtropical regions worldwide. FL, LA, Mex–Arg and Ven, WI. **Notes:** This is the only species of Rhynchelytrum in Costa Rica. Easily recognized by its pink, fluffy-looking inflorescence.

Rottboellia cochinchinensis (caminadora, zacate de fuego, zacate indio) Family Poaceae

Stout grass to 1–2 m tall, stems branched, prop roots sometimes at base, leaf sheaths very bristly, hairs irritating, base sometimes purplish. **Leaves** alternate, blades to 40 cm long, 2.5 cm wide with very white midrib especially in young leaves, margins minutely saw-toothed, blade rough above, tapered to base. **Flowers** in pairs, each to 0.5 cm long, narrowly egg-shaped, flattened and attached to sections of a linear, stiffly upright, jointed spike 7–15 cm long, to 0.3 cm wide, jointed sections stacked, each fitted into the one below, appearing out of leaf sheaths as they ripen, breaking into sections as flowers mature; blooms and fruits most of the year. **Fruit** dry, 1-seeded. **Habitat:** Wet, open areas, roadsides, pastures, stream banks. Altitude: Sea level to 1300 m, mostly in the Pacific lowlands. Conservation areas: CVC, GUA, LAP, OSA, PAC (mostly), TEM. **Range:** Native to Australia, Asia. Naturalized in the tropics worldwide. Invasive in the Galapagos and Pr. **Notes:** This is the only species of Rottboellia in Costa Rica.

433

■ *Saccharum officinarum* (caña de azúcar, sugarcane)
Family Poaceae

Stout grass 2–4 m tall, stems to 5 cm diameter, in clumps, sap sweet, stem solid, canelike with many nodes, older stem mostly yellowish to reddish brown, or waxy bluish; leaf sheaths cover upper stem. **Leaves** alternate, evenly distributed along stem, blade 1–2 m long, 2–6 cm wide, narrowed at base, midrib conspicuous, margin finely toothed, old leaves persistent on lower stem. **Flowers** 0.3–0.4 cm long, with long, silky hairs at base; inflorescence 25–50 cm long, more or less cone-shaped, silvery, plumelike, numerous fine, drooping branches, on a long stalk; blooms in Oct. **Fruit** dry, 1-seeded. **Habitat:** Cultivated in plantations, occasionally escaping. Altitude: Sea level to 1700 m, but mostly at lower elevations. Conservation areas: CVC, OSA. **Range:** Native to Papua New Guinea and other islands NE of Australia (Melanesia) but cultivated worldwide in tropical regions. **Notes:** Stems very juicy with a high concentration of sucrose. The only other species of *Saccharum* in Costa Rica is *S. spontaneum*, native to Africa and Asia; it is not very common.

FERNS AND OTHER SEEDLESS PLANTS

■ LICHENS

Dictyonema glabratum (Cora pavonia)
Sticta filicinella

■ MOSSES AND LIVERWORTS

Monoclea gottschei
Polytrichaceae

■ FERNS AND FERN ALLIES FERN ALLIES

Lycopodiella cernua
  (Lycopodium cernuum)
Lycopodium clavatum
Lycopodium thyoides
Selaginella anceps

Selaginella arthritica
Selaginella eurynota
Selaginella exaltata
Selaginella pallescens
Equisetum bogotense

■ FERNS

Asplenium rutaceum
Blechnum buchtienii
Blechnum falciforme
Blechnum occidentale
Salpichlaena volubilis
Alsophila polystichoides
Cyathea bicrenata
Cyathea multiflora
Cyathea mutica
  (Cnemidaria m.)
Sphaeropteris brunei
Pteridium arachnoideum
Dryopteris wallichiana
Dicranopteris pectinata
Gleichenia bifida
Gleichenia pallescens
  (Sticherus p.)
Micropolypodium taenifolium
Hymenophyllum
  consanguineum
Trichomanes elegans
Elaphoglossum eximium

Elaphoglossum lingua
Elaphoglossum peltatum
  (Peltapteris peltata)
Lophosoria quadripinnata
Nephrolepis biserrata
Dicranoglossum panamense
Microgramma reptans
Niphidium crassifolium
Phlebodium pseudoaureum
Polypodium fraxinifolium
Polypodium montigenum
Polypodium polypodioides
Acrostichum aureum
Adiantum concinnum
Eriosorus flexuosus
Pityrogramma calomelanos
Lygodium venustum
Thelypteris rudis
Antrophyum lineatum
Vittaria lineata
Diplazium palmense
Diplazium striatastrum

Ferns and other flowerless, seedless plants reproduce by spores.

A WORD ON LICHENS

Lichens belong to the kingdom Fungi rather than to the kingdom Plantae (mostly division Ascomycota; sac fungi). Many people tend to lump fungi in with plants, although their structure, ecology, and life cycles are very different. Fungi are built of threadlike mycelia, cannot make their own food, and have no roots, stems, or leaves. Fungi lack chlorophyll and other photosynthetic pigments and so cannot capture light energy to make sugars from carbon dioxide and water, as do plants.

Lichens are described most vividly as "fungi that have discovered agriculture" (Kershaw et al. 1998). They are recognized by their lack of leafy stems, their intricate forms, and variable colors (rarely including the bright green of "real" plants). They are able to incorporate algal cells (one-celled plants) into the fungal structure and live off the sugars produced by the photosynthetic activity of the algae. Many lichens appear as thin films of color on rocks and plant surfaces.

Dictyonema glabratum
(Cora pavonia)

■ *Dictyonema glabratum (Cora pavonia)*
Family Atheliaceae
This very conspicuous, white to pale gray lichen is abundant in open, disturbed sites at Tapantí N.P.

■ *Sticta filicinella*
Family Lobariaceae
This lichen is dark gray green and was seen at Monumento Guayabo. The brown dots are reproductive structures.

Sticta filicinella

A WORD ON MOSSES AND LIVERWORTS

Mosses and liverworts, on the other hand, are members in good standing of the kingdom Plantae (division Bryophyta). They all carry out photosynthesis and so make their own sugars and starches. However, unlike most plants, they are nonvascular, that is they have no system of tough, pipelike, "vascular" tissues (xylem and phloem) to conduct water and nutrients through their bodies or to hold them upright. Because of this, they must remain small in order for water and nutrients to diffuse to all their tissues. Most mosses, though small, have recognizable leaves. Many liverworts, on the other hand may look more like lichens, although they are usually bright green and all of them carry out photosynthesis. Their cells, structure, and reproductive cycles are also very similar to those of mosses. Other liverworts are conspicuously leafy and are difficult to tell from mosses. All of these plants reproduce by spores and lack seeds, flowers, and fruit, as well as vascular tissues.

■ *Monoclea gottschei*
Family Monocleaceae
A liverwort seen in Braulio Carrillo N.P.

■ Family Polytrichaceae
  The mosses in this family are quite large and look like tiny evergreen trees. The long-stalked capsule growing from the top of the moss plant produces spores that are dispersed by wind. This moss was seen growing on a rock at Tapantí N.P.

Polytrichaceae

FERNS AND FERN ALLIES

Ferns (Pteridophyta), horsetails (Equisetaceae), club mosses (Lycopodiaceae), and spike mosses (Selaginellaceae) are vascular, nonflowering plants that do not produce fruit or seed. These plants reproduce by dustlike spores produced on regular or specialized leaves in spore cases (sori). Unlike mosses and liverworts, however, vascular plants have tissues that are strong enough to hold the plant upright and conduct water up from the roots to distant leaves so that they can grow much taller than nonvascular plants. In fact, some ferns are tree-sized.

  All of these seedless, vascular plants have a life cycle separated into two stages. The large plant produces dustlike spores that are carried away by wind. If a spore settles down in a favorable place, it germinates and produces the second life cycle stage. This stage consists of either very small, flat, green, plantlets, in the case of most ferns and horsetails, or underground tuberlike plants closely associated with specific types of fungi, as in the case of many club mosses. These small plants produce sex cells (sperm and eggs). Sperm need water to swim to the eggs. The resulting fertilization produces another large plant.

  As is evident from the above, these plants produce neither flowers nor seeds. Spores are generally produced in specialized parts of the plant. Ferns may have spore cases on the undersides of some fronds, or fronds that specialize entirely in spore case production. Club mosses, spike mosses, and

437

horsetails often produce spore cases in conelike organs, usually at the tips of stems. Many of the important characteristics that differentiate families, genera, and species, such as details of scales, hairs, and internal vascular anatomy, are microscopic. All these seedless plants originated well before flowering plants, around 400 million years ago, but many are more modern. Although they are similar in reproducing by spores, these groups of plants are not closely related.

FERN ALLIES

■ *Lycopodiella cernua (Lycopodium cernuum)*
(nodding club moss)
Family Lycopodiaceae
Herb to 1 m long, much-branched, with the appearance of small, drooping fir trees, stems thin, stiff and appearing fuzzy, creeping, forking into 2 branches. **Leaves** scalelike, to 0.5 cm long, 0.2 cm wide, linear, in dense spirals along ends of stems. **Spore cones** yellow green, cylindrical, less than 1 cm long, 0.3 cm wide, at most stem ends. **Habitat:** Steep banks and roadsides in wet areas. Altitude: Sea level to 2700 m. Conservation areas: ARE, CVC, GUA, HNO, ICO, LAC, LAP, OSA, PAC, TOR. **Range:** SE US, Mex–Pan. **Notes:** There are six species of *Lycopodiella* in Costa Rica, *L. cernua* is the most common.

■ *Lycopodium clavatum* (stag horn club moss)
Family Lycopodiaceae
Herb with stems to 0.3 cm wide, forking into 2 branches, creeping ground cover, rooting at some nodes. **Leaves** scalelike, to 0.8 cm long, 0.1 cm wide, yellow green, numerous, spiraled around stem with erect, bristle tips, giving branches a narrowly bottle-brush appearance. **Spore cones** pale green to pale brown, erect, 1–4 per stem, to 0.9 cm long, 0.5 cm wide, at ends of almost leafless, erect branches. **Habitat:** High mountains, in open sites, along steep banks and roadsides. Altitude: 1150–3700 m. Conservation areas: ARE, CVC, LAC, LAP, PAC. **Range:** Nearly worldwide, in undisturbed sites, with a number of varieties. N N Amer, Mex–Brz, WI, N Europe, Asia, Pacific islands. **Notes:** There are five species of *Lycopodium* in Costa Rica. *Lycopodium clavatum* and *L. thyoides* are the most common.

■ *Lycopodium thyoides*
Family Lycopodiaceae

Creeping herb to 45 cm, stem forking into 2, branches flat, erect, growing from prostrate stems just below soil (rhizomes), branches green, those at ends of stems in an irregular, fan-shaped, lacy pattern. **Leaves** scalelike, bright green, needlelike, 0.2 cm long, in 4 ranks. **Spore cones** yellowish green, thin, on leafless stems longer than the leafy branches, in small clusters, like irregular candelabras. **Habitat:** Mountain areas in open habitats, roadside banks. Altitude: 1800–3800 m. Conservation areas: CVC, LAC, LAP, PAC. **Range:** Mex–Brz. **Notes:** There are also 35 species in the genus *Huperzia* in Costa Rica. All are very much like those of both *Lycopodiella* and *Lycopodium* and are often included in *Lycopodium*. The three genera are separated by technical details that are not readily visible.

■ *Selaginella anceps* (spikemoss)
Family Selaginellaceae

Terrestrial plant 15–75 cm tall, generally upright, roots fibrous, clinging to rock surface, no rhizomes seen, stem rough, frond 15 cm long, 8 cm wide, curved, drooping, overlapping other plants, fairly symmetrical from a central axis. **Leaves** scalelike, about 0.3 cm long, those of main stem and major branches appressed to stem. **Spore cones** small, at tips of stems. **Habitat:** Wet to moist forests, forest edges, often along streams. Altitude: Sea level to 1000 m. Conservation areas: ARE, CVC, GUA, HNO, LAC, OSA, PAC, TOR. **Range:** Pan–Bol, Ven. **Notes:** There are about 22 species of *Selaginella* in Costa Rica. They are similar in appearance to species of Lycopodiaceae, although Selaginellaceae species have a more open, widely branching, fernlike appearance. Their life cycles are quite different however.

Selaginella arthritica (above)

■ *Selaginella arthritica*
Family Selaginellaceae
Terrestrial or epiphytic herb, 15–40 cm tall, lower parts creeping, rooted, leafless, upper stems erect, larger stems swollen appearing jointed, few branches, sparsely leafy, erect, appearing fuzzy, fernlike shape. **Leaves** scalelike, fused to stem, flat, about 0.5 cm long, tips pointed to blunt. **Spore cones** green, about 1.5 cm long, 0.1 cm wide, sharply 4-sided, mostly solitary, at ends of top branches. **Habitat:** Wet forests. Altitude: Sea level to 1100 m. Conservation areas: CVC, GUA, LAC, LAP, OSA, TOR. **Range:** Nic–Pan.

■ *Selaginella eurynota*
Family Selaginellaceae
Terrestrial herb, stems erect, 0.1 cm diameter, appearing jointed, rooting at nodes near base. **Leaves** scalelike, in 4 ranks along stems, differing in form, 1 row of outward-pointing leaves along each side of stem, 2 rows of appressed, upward pointing leaves along midline of stem; side (lateral) leaves 0.4 cm long near stem tips, smaller near base, sides unequal, tip pointed, base blunt, margins wavy, finely fringed at base, middle leaves long-tipped, base unequal, lobed on one side, margin finely fringed, leaves in branch forks (axils) narrower, base lobed on both sides, upper part toothed. Spores not in cones, spore bearing leaves green, margins toothed. **Habitat:** Wet lowland forests. Altitude: Sea level to 700 m. Conservation areas: CVC, PAC, TOR. Abundant at La Selva Biological Station. **Range:** Gua–Pan.

Selaginella eurynota (below)

440

■ *Selaginella exaltata*
Family Selaginellaceae

Terrestrial herb to 1–2 m long, bright green, fern-like habit, stems erect to arching, often reddish, brittle, sending out long aerial roots; main stem appearing jointed, with few leaves, smaller stems not jointed, more densely leafy. **Leaves** scalelike, those of branches in 4 ranks, 1 along each side, 2 along center covering branch; median leaves asymmetrical, tip long-pointed, base extending down stem, lateral leaves oblong, 0.2–0.4 cm long, tips long-pointed, base attached to stem, leaves of main stems sparse, to 1 cm long, base lobed. **Spore cones** cylindrical, to nearly 4-sided, at tips of branches, 1–2 cm long. **Habitat:** Wet forests or roadsides in part shade. Altitude: Sea level to 950 m, mostly in the southern Pacific lowlands. Conservation areas: CVC, OSA (mostly). **Range:** CR–Pr. **Notes:** Conspicuous for its stiff, reddish stems and fernlike appearance.

■ *Selaginella pallescens*
Family Selaginellaceae

Stems tufted, to 25 cm long, forming a rosette of leafy branches, rooting at base, shiny, whitish when dry. **Leaves** scalelike, those of main stem all alike, pale tan when dry, tip abruptly pointed, base deeply lobed, margin fringed; leaves of branches in 4 ranks, lateral leaves egg-shaped, to 0.2 cm long, bristle-tipped, base rounded to slightly lobed, margin finely fringed, silvery below when dry; median leaves smaller, base asymmetrically lobed, margin bordered with white; leaves of branch axils narrow, smaller than lateral leaves, lance-shaped. **Spore cones** inconspicuous in axils of green leaves, in 4 ranks, all of one form, at the tips of branches. **Habitat:** Very variable, seasonally dry to wet regions on soil or rocks. Altitude: 100–2300 m, especially in GUA. Conservation areas: CVC, GUA, LAP, PAC, TEM. **Range:** Mex–Pan. **Notes:** A "resurrection plant" able to withstand drying.

■ *Equisetum bogotense* (cola de caballo, horsetail)
Family Equisetaceae

Herb 0.1–1.5 m tall, colonial from underground stems (rhizomes); aboveground stems delicate, slender, jointed, green; branches in whorls at nodes, of unequal lengths, often elongate, making stem difficult to see. **Leaves** reduced to a toothed sheath surrounding each node. **Spore cases** borne at top of stem in small cones about 2 cm long; produced on and off all year. **Habitat:** Wet regions, in weedy, open sites, roadside ditches, second growth, edges. Altitude: 400–2500 m, mostly above 900 m. Conservation areas: ARE, CVC, LAC, LAP, PAC. **Range:** CR–Col, Ven and W S Amer. **Notes:** There are three species of *Equisetum* in Costa Rica, *E. bogotense* is by far the most common.

FERNS

Costa Rica has about 800 species of ferns (called *helechos*) in 29 families.

■ *Asplenium rutaceum*
Family Aspleniaceae

Epiphytic or terrestrial fern from an erect, scaly stem, scales black. **Leaves** in tufts, stalk 1–3 cm long, reddish brown, smooth, finely winged, blade 15–35 cm long, 4–8 cm wide, 3 times pinnate, delicate, lacy, translucent, elongate, base tapered, tip with midrib extending far beyond blade tip, tendril-like and forming more branches, primary midrib red brown, margins narrowly winged, primary pinnae 10–24 pairs, stalkless, secondary pinnae very thin (membranous), ultimate segments to 0.4 cm long, widest above middle, tips barely pointed. **Spore cases** linear, along veins on undersides of ultimate leaf segments. **Habitat:** Wet mountain forests. Altitude: 1000–2300 m. Conservation areas: CVC, LAC, LAP. **Range:** S Mex–Col and Sur. **Notes:** There are at least 60 species of *Asplenium* in Costa Rica. A similar, more common species, is *A. maxonii*.

Equisetum bogotense (above)

Asplenium rutaceum (below)

442

■ *Blechnum buchtienii*
Family Blechnaceae

Small tree fern 1–2.5 m tall, palmlike appearance, trunk consisting of old leaf bases and black, cord-like roots, very hard scales 2–3 cm long, 0.2 cm wide. **Leaves** all at top of trunk, stalk 3–20 cm, yellow brown, with long, coarse hairy scales, blade once pinnate, to 0.45–1 m long, 7–25 cm wide, midrib (rachis) black, hairy, leaflets 40–60, smooth, 6–13 cm long, 0.4–0.8 cm wide, pointed at both ends, dark green, stiff, underside brown-scaly; leaflets of fertile leaves narrow, 5–9 cm long, 0.2–0.5 cm wide. **Spore cases** round, dotlike, along midrib and veins on undersides of leaflets of fertile leaves. **Habitat:** High in mountains in open, often boggy sites, in cloud forests. Altitude: 2400–3300 m. Conservation areas: LAC, LAP, PAC. Seen in the bog of Reserva Forestal Rio Macho, along Ruta 2 (Interamerican Highway). **Range:** CR–Ven and Bol. **Notes:** There are 23 species of *Blechnum* in Costa Rica.

■ *Blechnum falciforme*
Family Blechnaceae

Coarse fern to 1.5 m tall, from a woody, scaly stem, scales to 0.3 cm long, 0.1 cm wide. **Leaves** in a rosette, stalks 25–80 cm long (up to 1/2 length of leaf) pale green, densely coarsely scaly, blade once pinnate, 0.3–1 m long, 19–35 cm wide, leaflets thick, dark green, leathery, about 11–18 cm long, 2–3 cm wide, tip pointed, base rounded, slightly unequal, midrib dark, scaly-hairy, secondary veins numerous, at right angle to midrib, margin toothed; young fronds reddish; fronds in bud curled, covered with thick slime. **Spore cases** covering the undersides

of narrow, spore-bearing leaflets, which are 9–18 cm long, 0.3–0.6 cm wide. **Habitat:** Wet forest understories. Altitude: 800–3300 m. Conservation areas: CVC, GUA, LAC, LAP, PAC. **Range:** Mex–Ec. **Notes:** Very similar to *B. schiedeanum*, which has smooth leaf margins and is sparsely scaly on the leaflet midribs below.

■ *Blechnum occidentale*
Family Blechnaceae

Terrestrial fern; colonial from a creeping stem. **Leaves** in tufts, stalk 17–28 cm (as long as blade), straw-colored, smooth, with a few scales at base, blade 17–28 cm long, 10–20 cm wide, pinnate, tip merely lobed, axis (rachis) smooth, straw-colored, largest leaflet 5–12 cm long, to 1.8 cm wide, narrowly lance-shaped, slightly curved upward, base lobed, basal leaflets not becoming smaller, often short-stalked, midvein grooved below, secondary veins forked once, ends enlarged, margin minutely toothed, rather distant from one another toward base of blade; new leaves often reddish. **Spore cases** continuous as a pair of dark brown ridges, 1 along each side of midrib; leaflets of spore-bearing blades not narrowed. **Habitat:** Moist to wet forests, on old road banks, slopes. Altitude: Sea level to 2300 m. Conservation areas: ARE, CVC, GUA, HNO, ICO, LAC, LAP, OSA, PAC, TEM. **Range:** Gua–Pan. **Notes:** Very similar to *B. glandulosum,* which has a densely hairy leaf axis and smaller leaf blade.

■ *Salpichlaena volubilis*
Family Blechnaceae

Vinelike fern, climbing high in trees, stems twining, thin, green, tough, scaly, sometimes woody. **Leaves** twice pinnate, primary divisions alternate, to 15 m long, secondary divisions about 40 cm long, 30 cm wide, with about 9–11 leaflets, each about 15 cm long, 1–3 cm wide, margins smooth, secondary veins closely spaced, at right angles to midrib, tip pointed, base rounded, shiny, leathery, dark green, new leaves red to pinkish; fertile leaflets 1–2 cm wide, opposite or nearly so. **Spore cases** black in a thick continuous line on either side of the midrib. **Habitat:** Very wet to moist forests. Altitude: Sea level to 1700 m. Conservation areas: ARE, CVC, GUA, LAC, LAP, OSA, TOR. **Range:** Gua–Bry, LsAnt. **Notes:** The only other species of *Salpichlaena* in Costa Rica is *S. thalassica.*

■ *Alsophila polystichoides*
  (helechos arborescente, tree fern)
  Family Cyatheaceae

Tree fern, trunk to 6 m tall, to 12 cm diameter, dark, lower trunk with bulges, upper trunk with pale, flat, oval leaf scars, spines black, old fronds falling off of trunk. **Leaves** 3 times pinnate, stalks about 80 cm long, base about 2.5 cm wide, flat, remotely spiny, spines black, about 0.5 cm long, scaly at base, leaf blade 1.5–2.5 m long, primary pinnae to 80 cm long, 30 cm wide, stalks to 6 cm long; axis of secondary pinnae winged, rusty greenish, blade 16 cm long, 4 cm wide, leaflets about 2 cm long, 1 cm wide deeply lobed, pale below. **Spore cases** round, close to midrib of leaflet. **Habitat:** Wet forests. Altitude: 500–2000 m. Conservation areas: ARE, CVC, LAC, LAP. **Range:** CR, Pan. **Notes:** There are five species of *Alsophila* in Costa Rica.

■ *Cyathea bicrenata* (helechos
  arborescente, fabo de mico, tree fern)
  Family Cyatheaceae

Tree fern 5–15 m tall, trunk 4–6 cm wide, not spiny, but densely covered with wiry, black roots. **Leaves** all at top of trunk, stalk

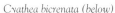

spiny, straw-colored to pale brown, to 4 m long including stalk, twice pinnate, primary pinnae about 30 cm long, 7 cm wide, midrib spiny, secondary pinnae 8–12 cm long, about 2 cm wide, deeply lobed or divided, leaflets 0.1–0.3 cm wide, margins toothed. **Spore cases** in rows of dots along either side of leaflet midrib. **Habitat:** Moist to wet forests. Altitude: 900–1600 m. Conservation areas: LAP, OSA, TEM. **Range:** Mex–Ec. **Notes:** There are 25 species of *Cyathea* in Costa Rica.

Alsophila polystichoides (above)

Cyathea bicrenata (below)

■ *Cyathea multiflora* (helechos arborescente, tree fern)
   Family Cyatheaceae

Tree fern, trunk to 3 m tall, to 8 cm diameter, spiny, old leaves sometimes persistent on trunk. **Leaves** to 2 m long, stalk with spines and scales, dark, base densely raggedy-scaly, scales to 2 cm long; blade twice pinnate, primary pinnae 30–50 cm long, 9–15 cm wide, stalk short, or none, leaflets to about 1.2 cm long, 0.4 cm wide, lobed, lobes and leaflets blunt-tipped, margins minutely toothed. **Spore cases** round, in a row of dots between midvein and margin of leaflets. **Habitat:** Wet forests. Altitude: Sea level to 2100 m. Conservation areas: ARE, CVC, GUA, HNO, LAC, LAP, OSA, PAC, TOR. **Range:** Gua–N Brz. **Notes:** One of the more common species of tree fern in Costa Rica.

■ *Cyathea mutica (Cnemidaria m.)*
   (helechos arborescente, tree fern)
   Family Cyatheaceae

Tree fern, usually without a trunk, or sometimes a trunk to 50 cm tall, 4–6 cm wide. **Leaves** all from top, 2–3 m long, 0.5–1.4 m wide, stalk and lower midrib about 3 cm diameter, brown to straw-colored, spiny, blade pinnate, leaflets deeply lobed nearly to leaflet axis (midrib), alternate on leaf axis, blades 30–70 cm long, 7–25 cm wide, lobes alternate, smooth, lowest pinnae slightly smaller than middle ones, scaly. **Spore cases** round in a line (sometimes 2 lines) between midrib and margin. **Habitat:** Wet forests in gaps, along streams. Distribution: 300–2100 m, mostly above 1200 m. Conservation areas: ARE, CVC, GUA, LAC, LAP. **Range:** CR–Col.

■ *Sphaeropteris brunei*
(helechos arborescente, tree fern)
Family Cyatheaceae

Spineless tree fern, trunk to 20 m tall, to 20 cm diameter, old leaves persistent, making trunk appear thicker. **Leaves** to 2–4.5 m long, stalk very shaggy, pale tan or brown, scales to 5 cm long, 0.3 cm wide; blade 2 times pinnate, primary pinnae 50–95 cm long, 20–30 cm wide, stalk to 7 cm; leaflets toothed to deeply lobed, somewhat finely hairy, whitish below. **Spore cases** round, in rows along midrib. **Habitat:** Wet forests, mostly in lower mountain areas. Altitude: 100–2200 m, usually above 1000 m. Conservation areas: CVC, GUA, LAC, LAP. **Range:** CR–N Col. **Notes:** There is only one species of *Sphaeropteris* in Costa Rica.

■ *Pteridium arachnoideum* (bracken, brake)
Family Dennstaedtiaceae

Tough, weedy fern 1–3 m tall, colonial from a creeping underground stem. **Leaves** stiff, upright, on stalks about 1 m tall, yellowish above, hairy-scaly toward base, blade triangular in outline, 3–4 times pinnate, divisions at base much larger than those above, often as large as entire upper part of frond, so fern appears branched in 3 parts; ultimate leaflets elongate, leathery, often deeply lobed, lower surface densely white-hairy or woolly. **Spore cases** continuous along underside of leaflet margins. **Habitat:** Usually in mountains open sites, pastures, roadsides. Altitude: 200–2500 m, mostly above 1500 m. Conservation areas: CVC, HNO, LAC, LAP, PAC. **Range:** Mex–N Arg, Ant, Tr. **Notes:** There are two other species of *Pteridium* in Costa Rica. Neither has a white-woolly lower leaflet surface.

■ *Dryopteris wallichiana*
Family Dryopteridaceae
Fronds from the top of a stout, underground stem (rhizome).
Leaves tufted, stalk 8–25 cm long, up to 1/4 of frond length,
straw-colored, densely scaly, scales to 2.5 cm long, 0.3 cm
wide, blade to 0.5–1 m long, 18–28 cm wide, pinnate, leaflets
narrow, stalkless, 5–15 cm long, smaller toward base of blade,
deeply lobed, dark green above, paler below, midrib densely
scaly, leaflet lobes oblong, tip truncate, asymmetrical, veins
dark. **Spore cases** round, in a line along each side of midrib of
each lobe. **Habitat:** Mountains, along roadsides, fern banks.
Altitude: 2200–3200 m. Conservation areas: CVC, LAC,
LAP, PAC. **Range:** Mex–Arg, His, Hawai'i, Africa, NE Asia.
Notes: There are seven species of *Dryopteris* in Costa Rica.
Dryopteris wallichiana stands out because of its once-pinnate
leaves and leaflets with squared-off lobes.

■ *Dicranopteris pectinata*
Family Gleicheniaceae
Vinelike colonial fern from a creeping underground stem,
aboveground stems are actually elongate leaves, branching repeatedly into 2 equal forks, stalk wiry, brittle, brown,
shiny. **Leaves** appear to be of forked pairs of pinnately lobed
divisions 10–25 cm long, 2–6 cm wide, stalkless, narrowly
oblong, lobes 0.3–0.6 cm wide, firm, yellow green above, pale
waxy whitish below, margins smooth; fertile leaflets with in-
rolled margins, veins 2- to 4-forked. **Spore cases** round, in 1
row down each side of midrib on the lower side of each lobe.
Habitat: Open sites on steep, open roadside banks, old landslides, often covering large areas of disturbed soil in dense,
mixed fern banks. Altitude: 150–1900 m. Conservation
areas: CVC, ICO, LAC, LAP, OSA, PAC, TEM. **Range:**
Mex–Pan. **Notes:** *Dicranopteris flexuosa* is the only other species of *Dicranopteris* in Costa Rica. It has opposite pairs of
leaflets and a pair of smaller leaflets at each branching point
of the leaf.

Dryopteris wallichiana (above)

Dicranopteris pectinata (below)

■ *Gleichenia bifida*
Family Gleicheniaceae

Vinelike colonial fern from a creeping underground stem, aboveground stems are actually elongate leaves, branching repeatedly into 2 equal forks, growing tip usually between 2 pinnately lobed leaflets, buds with a tuft of orange scales, stems wiry, brown scaly-hairy, branching into 2 equal forks. **Leaves** pinnate with distant pinnately lobed leaflets, 25–45 cm long, 2–8 cm wide, paired at frond tip, lobes about 2–4 cm long, 0.2–0.3 cm wide, midrib brown-scaly above, underside densely hairy-scaly, margins smooth. **Spore cases** round in 1 row along each side of midrib on underside of lobes. **Habitat:** Open sites, on steep, roadside banks, old landslides, often covering large areas of disturbed soil in dense, mixed fern banks. Altitude: 200–2000 m. Conservation areas: ARE, CVC, GUA, HNO, LAP, OSA, PAC. **Range:** Mex–Brz, WI, Tr. **Notes:** There are 14 species of Gleichenia in Costa Rica, G. *bifida* is the most common one.

■ *Gleichenia pallescens (Sticherus p.)*
Family Gleicheniaceae

Stiff, vinelike fern, forming dense colonies from creeping, much-branched, underground stems (rhizome), aboveground stems are scaly, and are actually elongate, repeatedly branching leaves. **Leaves** branching evenly in sets of 2 (forked), axis of branches with a scaly bud that sometimes grows new leaflets; ultimate leaflets in pairs, each pinnately lobed, about 12 cm long, segments narrow, in a comb-like arrangement, *white below*, margins smooth. **Spore cases** round, in a lines between the midrib and margin of each leaflet lobe. **Habitat:** Open, sunny banks in mountain regions, old landslides, often covering large areas of disturbed soil in dense, mixed fern banks. Altitude: 1700–2200 m. Conservation areas: LAC, LAP, TEM. **Range:** CR–Col and Ven. **Notes:** Not very common but conspicuous for its white leaflet undersides.

■ *Micropolypodium taenifolium*
Family Grammitidaceae

Small epiphytic fern, leaves in tufts, stem scales 0.2 cm long, brownish orange. **Leaves** linear, stalk mostly absent, blade 5–20 cm long, 0.4–1 cm wide, somewhat stiff, deeply pinnately lobed, midrib dark, wiry, lobes more or less oval, tips blunt. **Spore cases** solitary at the base of each lobe, round, brown, overlapping the primary midrib of the leaf. **Habitat:** Wet forests on tree trunks or logs. Altitude: 500–2500 m. Conservation areas: ARE, CVC, GUA, HNO, ICO, LAC, LAP, OSA, PAC. **Range:** S Mex–Ec and Guy. **Notes:** There are eight species of *Micropolypodium* in Costa Rica, most are very similar.

■ *Hymenophyllum consanguineum* (filmy fern)
Family Hymenophyllaceae

Epiphytic fern, fronds at intervals along very thin, wiry, climbing stem, clinging to tree surface. **Leaves** very thin, stalk 5–10 cm long, blade generally egg-shaped, 8–15 cm long, 6–10 cm wide, finely divided, midribs of leaflets winged, very dark green, translucent, very thin, flat. **Spore cases** dotted along leaflet lobes, small, paddle-shaped on margins of fronds, inconspicuous. **Habitat:** Wet forests, often low on tree trunks. Altitude: 500–2500 m, usually above 1000 m. Conservation areas: ARE, CVC, GUA, LAC, LAP. **Range:** CR, Pan, Ven. **Notes:** There are 39 species of *Hymenophyllum* in Costa Rica.

■ *Trichomanes elegans* (filmy fern)
   Family Hymenophyllaceae

Usually terrestrial fern to about 40 cm tall, stems creeping, elongate. **Leaves** in clusters on a short stem, leaf stalks about 0.1–0.2 cm wide, blade 3 times pinnate 15–30 cm long, triangular, midribs winged, wings to over 0.5 cm wide, leaflets deeply lobed, lobes toothed, teeth fine, color a vivid metallic blue green, stiff, appearing artificial. **Spore cases** appearing as small tubes inserted along lobe margins, often difficult to see. **Habitat:** Dark understories of wet forests. Altitude: Sea level to 1600 m, mostly 100–600 m. Conservation areas: CVC, GUA, HNO,

Courtesy of Margaret Gargiullo

ICO, LAC, TOR. **Range:** Bel–Brz, LsAnt, Tr. **Notes:** There are 49 species of *Trichomanes* in Costa Rica. *Trichomanes elegans* is not one of the most common but is very distinctive because of its dark blue green "plastic fern" appearance.

■ *Elaphoglossum eximium* (helecho
   lengua, hart's tongue)
   Family Lomariopsidaceae

Epiphyte, leaves forming a rosette, roots fibrous, stem short. **Leaves** simple, straplike, stalk short, base orange brown, scaly, blade 13–27 cm long, 1–2 cm wide, linear to elliptical, pointed at both ends, texture, leathery, secondary veins conspicuous, closely spaced, at about a 45 degree angle from the midrib, margins wavy. **Spore cases** in a solid line along margins of fertile leaves, leaf stalk longer than that of sterile fronds, blade lance-shaped to heart-shaped; arrow-shaped when young. **Habitat:** Wet mountain forests, often low on tree trunks. Altitude: 1000–2700 m. Conservation areas: ARE, CVC (mostly), GUA, HNO, LAC, LAP, PAC. **Range:** S Mex–Ven and Pr. **Notes:** There are about 98 species of *Elaphoglossum* in Costa Rica.

■ *Elaphoglossum lingua* (helecho lengua, hart's tongue)
Family Lomariopsidaceae

Terrestrial fern, colonial from a creeping horizontal stem. **Leaves** simple, arising 2–4 cm apart along stem, leaf stalks tan, scaly, becoming black with age, about 15 cm long, wiry, blade to about 38 cm long, 6 cm wide, undivided, oblong, pointed at both ends, erect, stiff, leathery, midrib pale. **Spore cases** cover underside of fertile leaves, these are longer than sterile leaves. **Habitat:** Wet mountains in forest understories, open areas, gaps. Altitude: 1000–2600 m. Conservation areas: ARE, CVC, HNO, LAC, LAP, PAC. **Range:** CR–Chile and Par, Ant.

■ *Elaphoglossum peltatum (Peltapteris peltata)*
Family Lomariopsidaceae

Very small epiphytic fern from very slender creeping horizontal stems. **Leaves** arising singly along stem, 3–15 cm long, to 5 cm wide, sterile fronds irregularly fan-shaped, finely divided 4–5 times, segments linear about 0.1 cm wide. **Spore cases** covering surface of very different, fertile fronds, blade rounded, undivided, 0.5–2 cm wide, usually 2-lobed. **Habitat:** Wet mountain forests, on mossy logs or low on tree trunks. Altitude: Mostly 1000–2400 m, occasionally to near sea level. Conservation areas: ARE, CVC, GUA, HNO, LAC, LAP, OSA (rarely), PAC. Very common in the Cordillera de Talamanca. **Range:** Mex–Guy and Ec.

■ *Lophosoria quadripinnata*
Family Lophosoriaceae

Tree fern with little or no trunk, stem creeping to sometimes erect, 4–8 cm wide, densely golden-hairy, hairs often over 1 cm long. **Leaves** forming large rosettes, 1–3 m long, stalk about 1.5 m long, dark brown, shiny, smooth, base yellowish-hairy, young stalks golden- to reddish-hairy, blade more or less triangular, about 1.5 m wide near base, 3–4 times pinnate with a very regular pattern of leaflets, leaflets waxy whitish below, midribs yellow-hairy; primary pinnae widest at base, tips pointed, secondary pinnae narrow, regularly spaced; old leaves persistent. **Spore cases** round, brown, at the base of each lobe of leaflets, between the midrib and upper lobe margin. **Habitat:** Wet mountain forests, often along roadside banks. Altitude: 1000–2900 m. Conservation areas: ARE, CVC, GUA, LAC, LAP, PAC. Most frequent in Cordillera de Talamanca. **Range:** Mex–Ven and Col–Chile, Ant, Tr. **Notes:** There is the one other species of *Lophosoria* in Costa Rica, *L. quesadae*. It is found only in Costa Rica from 2200–2900 m.

■ *Nephrolepis biserrata*
Family Oleandraceae

Epiphytic or terrestrial, roots fibrous, in dense clumps. **Leaves** very long, at first erect, then arching downward and hanging, stalk to 30 cm long, scaly, scales pale brown to orange, 0.5–0.7 cm long, blade 75 cm to 2 m long, 11–24 cm wide, once pinnate, midrib pale tan, densely scaly, scales fringed; leaflets short-stalked, blade 5–20 cm long, 1–2 cm wide, tips pointed, minutely scaly-hairy below, base unequal, lobed on upper side, margin toothed. **Spore cases** round to kidney-shaped, in lines along leaflet margins. **Habitat:** Wet lowlands. Epiphytic on oil palms in large plantations in the PAC lowlands. Altitude: Sea level to 400 m. Conservation areas: HNO, ICO, PAC, TEM, TOR (common). **Range:** Mex–Brz, Tr, WI, Old World tropics. **Notes:** There are eight species of *Nephrolepis* in Costa Rica. The Asian sword fern, *N. multiflora*, is nearly identical to *N. biserrata* but is found up to 1700 m. It has escaped from cultivation and is found along roadsides and open, weedy sites.

■ *Dicranoglossum panamense*
Family Polypodiaceae

Epiphytic fern, 10–40 cm tall, stem scaly, short, creeping.
Leaves in tufts, stalk very short, densely scaly near base, blade

simple, deeply few-lobed, lobes to 1 cm wide, elongate, irregular in size, margins entire but wavy. **Spore
cases** in continuous lines along leaf margins, mostly
near ends of lobes. **Habitat:** Wet to moist, mostly
lowland, forests. Altitude: Sea level to 1200 m, usually below 500 m. Conservation areas: CVC, GUA,
LAC, OSA, PAC, TOR. **Range:** Bel–Col. **Notes:**
This is the only species of *Dicranoglossum* in Costa
Rica. It is conspicuous because of its very distinctive
seaweedlike form.

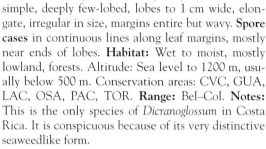

■ *Microgramma reptans*
Family Polypodiaceae

Small epiphytic vine, stems threadlike, creeping, scaly, rooting at nodes. **Leaves** of two types; sterile fronds lance-shaped
to elliptic, 1–5 cm long, about 1 cm wide, midrib dark; fertile fronds linear, about 5 cm long, 0.4 cm wide. **Spore cases**

round, red brown dots in a row on each side of midrib, about filling space from midrib to margin. **Habitat:** Wet to moist forests or disturbed sites, often on
low branches. Altitude: Sea level to 1000 m. Conservation areas: ARE, CVC, GUA, HNO, LAC,
OSA, PAC, TOR. **Range:** S Mex–N Brz, Cuba, To.
Notes: There are seven species of *Microgramma* in
Costa Rica. A few other species have different sterile
and fertile leaves.

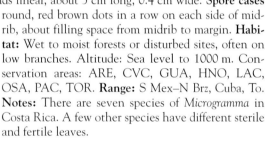

■ *Niphidium crassifolium*
Family Polypodiaceae

Large fern, terrestrial or epiphytic, leaves forming a vaselike rosette, scales of stem to 0.7 cm long, pale. **Leaves** simple, stalk to 30 cm long, blade 0.35–1.25 m long, 5–11 cm wide, lance-shaped, tip pointed, tapered to base, stiff, leathery, secondary veins prominent, arising from midrib, extending to margin of blade, making a conspicuous fish-bone pattern on blade underside. **Spore cases** on upper part of leaf underside (distal), round, tan, 0.3 cm wide, in conspicuous rows between secondary veins. **Habitat:** Wet forests. Altitude: Sea level to 2000 m. Conservation areas: ARE, CVC, GUA, HNO, LAC, LAP, OSA, PAC, TOR. **Range:** Mex–Brz, WI. **Notes:** There are three species of *Niphidium* in Costa Rica, this is the most common; *N. oblanceolatum* is very similar to *N. crassifolium* (photo: leaves and spore pattern).

■ *Phlebodium pseudoaureum*
Family Polypodiaceae

Epiphytic or sometimes terrestrial from a creeping stem, scales to 1 cm long, reddish brown, enlarged base attached to stem, margin toothed. **Leaves** clustered, stalk to 1/2 the length of leaf, blade once pinnately divided, to 90 cm long, 35 cm wide, often pale, waxy green, smooth, lobes 15 cm long, 2 cm wide, margins smooth. **Spore cases** round, dark tan, in 1 row on each side of leaflet midrib. **Habitat:** Wet forests and second growth. Altitude: Sea level to 2500 m. Conservation areas: ARE, CVC, GUA, HNO, ICO, LAC, LAP, PAC, TOR. **Range:** FL, Mex–Arg, Ant. **Notes:** There is one other species of *Phlebodium* in Costa Rica. It is very uncommon.

455

■ *Polypodium fraxinifolium*
Family Polypodiaceae
Epiphytic or (rarely) terrestrial fern, stem creeping, dark, scaly, usually bound tightly to a tree trunk. **Leaves** arising

one at a time along stem, stalk base green, smooth, blade once pinnate, 20–80 cm long, 12–30 cm wide, leaflets 4–19 nearly opposite, no stalk, blades about 10 cm long, 1–3 cm wide, linear to lance-shaped, tip tapered, base rounded, lowest leaflet the largest, veins in a fish-bone pattern, conspicuous above. **Spore cases** round, brown dots in a row between secondary veins. **Habitat:** Wet forests. Altitude: 400–3000 m, mostly 900–1700 m. Conservation areas: ARE, CVC, GUA, HNO, LAC, LAP, OSA, PAC. **Range:** S Mex–Brz. **Notes:** There are about 52 species of *Polypodium* in Costa Rica.

■ *Polypodium montigenum*
Family Polypodiaceae
Small fern, epiphytic or terrestrial; stem finely scaly, creeping, black, branched. **Leaves** arising singly along the stem, 16–30 cm long, stalk brown, mostly smooth, nearly as long as blade, blade broadly egg-shaped, pinnate-lobed, lobes deep, upper lobes 3–6 cm long, 0.4–0.8 cm wide, arching upward, lower lobes 5–12 cm long, narrowly lance-shaped, base fused to pale leaf axis, margins finely toothed. **Spore cases**

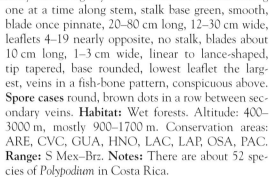

in rounded dots, yellow to brown, along each side of the lobe midvein, often appearing pale green above. **Habitat:** Wet mountain forests and disturbed sites, roadside banks. Altitude: 1700–3300 m. Conservation areas: CVC, LAC, LAP, PAC. **Range:** Mex–Pan. **Notes:** Often found along the Interamerican Highway (Ruta 2), at high elevations.

■ *Polypodium polypodioides*
Family Polypodiaceae

Small, colonial fern, from a creeping stem, attached to trees or rocks, scales 0.4 cm long, linear, overlapping. **Leaves** well spaced along stem, stalk much shorter than blade, blade to 3–25 cm long, 1–6 cm wide, pinnately divided almost to midrib, tip pointed, base truncate, lobes 6–13 pairs, about 0.2 cm wide, leathery, tips blunt, backside scaly, silvery when young, becoming densely reddish brown, scales with pale margins. **Spore cases** round, along lobe margins, sometimes lobes of fertile fronds have club-shaped tips. **Habitat:** Trees or rocks along pasture edges, roadsides. Altitude: 60–2400 m. Conservation areas: ARE, CVC, GUA, LAP, OSA, PAC, TEM. **Range:** Mex–CR.

■ *Acrostichum aureum* (helecho mangle, marsh fern)
Family Pteridaceae

Aquatic fern to 3 m tall, from a creeping, massive, branched, scaly stem (rhizome), fronds in large clusters, usually many clusters together. **Leaves** 1.5–3 m long, stalk stout, about 1/3 length of leaf, often short-spiny, blade once pinnate, 20–40 cm wide; leaflets 10–30 pairs, to 25 cm long, 4 cm wide, thick, leathery, margins smooth, bases overlapping. **Spore cases** brown, covering underside of upper 1–5 pairs leaflets on fertile leaves. **Habitat:** Lowland marshes and mangrove swamps, especially along the coasts. Altitude: Sea level to 30 m, to 300 m on ICO. Conservation areas: ICO, OSA (mostly), TEM. **Range:** Mex–Brz and Par, WI, Tr, Old World tropics. **Notes:** There is one other species of *Acrostichum* in Costa Rica, *A. danaeifolium*, usually found on the Caribbean slope, mostly in coastal marshes (ARE, HNO, LAC, TOR), occasionally in OSA or at elevations to 800 m. It has many more (40–60 pairs) of linear leaflets, leaves are either entirely sterile or all leaflets fertile (underside covered with spore cases). Both these ferns are conspicuous for their very large size.

■ *Adiantum concinnum*
Family Pteridaceae

Terrestrial fern from a short, creeping, scaly, stem. **Leaves** in tufts, 20–95 cm long, stalk to 1/3 length of leaf, red brown to dark purplish, smooth, few scales at base, overall blade 6–25 cm wide, 2–3 times pinnate, 10–15 pairs of primary pinnae; the leaflets minutely stalked, those at the base of the pinna overlapping the axis (rachis); leaflet blades to 1 cm long, irregularly fan-shaped, widest along upper margin, which is irregularly lobed, base wedge-shaped, veins running into notches between lobes. **Spore cases** usually pale, kidney-shaped, notched at apex, spaced along leaflet margins at lobe tips, spores tan. **Habitat:** Wet to seasonally dry forests, shady roadsides, second growth. Altitude: Sea level to 1900 m. Conservation areas: ARE, CVC, GUA, LAP, PAC, TEM. **Range:** Mex–Ven and Pr, WI, Tr. **Notes:** There are about 29 species of *Adiantum* in Costa Rica. Most are 1 to several times pinnate, often with irregularly shaped leaflets, leaflets are always stalked, with spore cases along leaflet margins.

■ *Eriosorus flexuosus*
Family Pteridaceae

Terrestrial fern from a slender, scaly, creeping stem. **Leaves** vinelike, to 3 m long, 15 cm wide, stalk red brown, 1/3 the length of frond or less; blade 4–5 times pinnate, finely divided, appearing lacey, ultimate segments forked, linear, tips notched. **Spore cases** elongate, along midrib of ultimate segments, dark brown. **Habitat:** Mountains, in open sites, often in large roadside fern banks on old landslides and other disturbances. Altitude: 1600–3400 m. Conservation areas: CVC, HNO, LAC, LAP, PAC. **Range:** Mex–CR, Col–Guy and Bol, His. **Notes:** Often with other vinelike, weedy ferns such as *Gleichenia* and *Dicranopteris*. There are five species of *Eriosorus* in Costa Rica.

■ *Pityrogramma calomelanos*
Family Pteridaceae

Terrestrial fern from a woody, scaly stem, scales to 0.5 cm, yellow brown. **Leaves** tufted, to 1.2 m long, 20 cm wide, stalk blackish, to 1/2 the length of leaf, smooth, with a few scales at base; blade 2–3 times pinnate, lance-shaped, dark green above, white-mealy below when sterile, ultimate segments narrow, wrinkled, margin toothed to deeply lobed. **Spore cases** very small, linear, along veins on white underside, turning it pale purplish brown. **Habitat:** Wet to seasonally dry regions in open or partly shady sites, roadsides, ditches. Altitude: Sea level to 1800 m. Conservation areas: ARE, CVC, GUA, HNO, ICO, LAP, OSA, PAC, TEM, TOR. **Range:** S FL, Mex–Brz and Arg, Ant. Naturalized in Old World tropics. **Notes:** Conspicuous for its white leaf underside, especially on young leaves. There are eight species of *Pityrogramma* in Costa Rica, this is by far the most common.

■ *Lygodium venustum*
Family Schizaeaceae

Vinelike fern from a short, very thin, creeping stem. **Leaves** with wiry, tan stem growing indefinitely long, twining around other vegetation; blade with 2 primary axes, paired on a short stalk, secondary leaflets alternate, 3- to 5-parted, often densely hairy, the terminal (central) lobe 3–10 cm long, 0.5–1.4 cm wide, much longer than the lateral ones, margins finely toothed. **Spore cases** numerous, small, fringe-like, outgrowths along margins of lobes, whitish-hairy. **Habitat:** Wet to seasonally very dry forest understories, second growth, edges. Altitude: Sea level to 800 m, mostly in the Pacific lowlands. Conservation areas: GUA, OSA, PAC, TEM. **Range:** Mex–Par, Ant, Tr. **Notes:** There are four species of *Lygodium* in Costa Rica. All have vinelike leaves and fringe-like spore cases along leaflet margins.

■ *Thelypteris rudis*
Family Thelypteridaceae

Terrestrial fern, from short, dark underground stems (rhizomes), often appears colonial. **Leaves** in clusters at ends of rhizome; stalk to about 25 cm long, dark gray green, hairy, base of stem black, finely brown scaly, often with warty outgrowths 2–3 cm long; blade pinnate, to 1 m long, 45 cm wide, including 5–12 pairs of rudimentary, budlike leaflets at base, like little tags of leaf tissue on the upper stalk, midrib dark, hairy; leaflets 5–25 cm long, 1–4 cm wide, deeply lobed, lobes becoming smaller at tip and base, lobes about 1 cm long, 0.4 cm wide, tips rounded, base broadly attached

to midrib of leaflet, margin slightly rolled-under. **Spore cases** of fertile fronds round, regularly spaced between midvein and margin of leaflet lobes. **Habitat:** Wet mountain regions, along shady roadsides, trails edges, disturbed forest understories. Altitude: 1200–2500 m. Conservation areas: CVC, HNO, LAC, LAP, PAC. **Range:** Mex–Pan, Ven–Bol, Ant. **Notes:** There are about 71 species of *Thelypteris* in Costa Rica. They have pinnate leaf blades with deeply lobed leaflets that become very small at the base of the blade, many have small outgrowths at the bases of the leaflets.

■ *Antrophyum lineatum*
Family Vittariaceae

Small epiphytic fern, from a short, creeping scaly stem. **Leaves** clustered, stalks winged, pale, blade simple, unlobed, linear, to about 20 cm long, 0.5–0.8 cm wide, leathery, veins and midrib obscure. **Spore cases** in 2–3 fine lines along each side of the midrib for the length of underside. **Habitat:** Wet forests, often growing low on tree trunks. Altitude: 850–2200 m. Conservation areas: ARE, CVC, LAC, LAP. **Range:** Mex–Pan, Ven–SW Brz, NW Arg, WI, Tr. **Notes:** There are six species of *Antrophyum* in Costa Rica. All are epiphytes and have simple, narrow, unlobed leaves and spore cases in lines along the leaf underside.

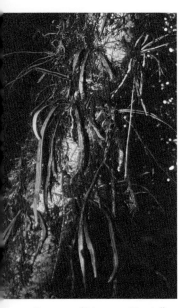

Courtesy of Margaret Gargiullo

■ *Vittaria lineata*
Family Vittariaceae

Epiphytic fern from a dense, scaly-hairy, fibrous stem. **Leaves** clustered, stalk very much like blade, blade 0.25–1 m long, 0.1–0.3 cm wide, linear, widest at base, grasslike in appearance, pendant leathery, flat with rolled-under margins, veins obscure. **Spore cases** very fine, in lines along in-rolled margins on lower leaf surface. **Habitat:** Wet forests, also seen

growing in large, grasslikelike clumps on oil palms in plantations. Altitude: Sea level to 1650 m. Conservation areas: ARE, CVC, GUA, HNO, LAC, OSA, TOR. **Range:** FL, Mex–Ur, Ant, Tr. **Notes:** There are eight species of *Vittaria* in Costa Rica. All have linear, undivided leaves in tufts, and spore cases in lines along leaf margins.

■ *Diplazium palmense*
Family Woodsiaceae

Terrestrial fern, stem to about 10 cm tall, 2 cm wide, becoming erect with age, black, wiry, scales to 1 cm long, 0.2 cm wide. **Leaves** in tufts, 50–90 cm long, stalk 20–50 cm long, black, smooth with scaly base, blade, 30–45 cm long, 20–30 cm wide, once pinnate, 3–7 leaflets, alternate to almost opposite, 8–20 cm long, 3–9 cm wide (terminal blade larger), egg-shaped to elliptical, tip pointed, base rounded, surface thick, stiff, shiny, very dark blue green above, lateral veins closely parallel at right angles to midrib, margins smooth. **Spore cases** elongate to 2.5 cm long, along secondary veins on leaflet undersides, forming a fish-bone pattern; fertile fronds longer than sterile fronds. **Habitat:** Wet forests, usually in mountains. Altitude: 700–2170 m, mostly above 1200 m. Conservation areas: CVC, LAC, LAP. **Range:** CR–N Col. **Notes:** There are about 55 species of *Diplazium* in Costa Rica. Most have typical fern leaves, once to twice pinnate, leaflets often toothed or lobed, spore cases mostly elongate, in fish-bone pattern along veins of leaflet undersides.

■ *Diplazium striatastrum*
  Family Woodsiaceae

Terrestrial fern, developing a slender trunklike stem of inter-woven black stems and roots to about 1.5 m tall, young ferns lack trunk. **Leaves** tufted at top of "trunk," stalk 20–50 cm long, blackish, scaly; blade 0.3–1 m long, 20–40 cm wide cm long, once pinnate, larger leaflets 7–14 cm long, 3 cm wide, deeply lobed, decreasing in size toward base of blade, lobes about 1 cm long, tips blunt, toothed, midrib dark dull green. **Spore cases** linear, in a fish-bone pattern along secondary veins of leaflet lobe undersides. **Habitat:** Wet forest under-stories. Altitude: 100–1400 m. Conservation areas: ARE, CVC, GUA, HNO, LAC, LAP. Common at La Selva Bio-logical Station. **Range:** S Mex–W Col, Ven, W Ec. **Notes:** Conspicuous for its upright, "trunk" like a small tree fern.

GLOSSARY

Achene: A dry, 1-seeded fruit with a tight fruit wall that does not split open but is not fused to the seed. (See **grain**)

Aerial roots: Roots growing out from the trunk above the ground, sometimes many meters long and reaching the ground. Developed by many epiphytic plants and vines and commonly seen in large numbers hanging from some trees. Other aerial roots help support the plant and in wet, oxygen-poor soil, they may help the plant "breath" by exchanging oxygen and carbon dioxide. Also known as prop roots.

Alternate: One leaf at each node along a stem. (Compare **opposite**)

Amazonia: Amazon River Basin, including northern Brazil, most of Columbia, southern Venezuela, and eastern Ecuador, Peru, and northeastern Bolivia.

Angiosperms: Flowering plants that produce flowers, and seeds within a fruit. Seeds develop within an ovary that becomes all or part of the fruit.

Anther: Pollen bearing part of a stamen, usually at the top of a slender stalk (filament). The male part of a flower. (See **flower**)

Aril: In flowering plants (angiosperms), a fleshy coat partly or completely surrounding a seed inside the fruit wall (not part of the fruit itself). Most often found in fruit that has an inedible outer wall that splits open to reveal the aril-covered seeds. In gymnosperms, seed plants that do not produce flowers or true fruit, arils are modified cone scales that form a fleshy coat around the seeds. Birds and other animals eat the fleshy coat and disperse the seed. Some small seeds of low-growing plants with arils are dispersed by ants.

Awn: An elongate, stiff bristle often attached to the flowers of grasses.

Axil: The angle between a leaf and stem.

Axillary: A structure in an axil, as in "axillary bud." (Compare **terminal**)

Axis: The central supporting structure of a compound or divided leaf. The main stem supporting branches or individual flowers of an inflorescence.

Basal: Leaves all grouped at the base of the plant. A radial arrangement of basal leaves is called a rosette.

Banner: The top-most petal in flowers of the family Fabaceae/Faboideae. (See **bean-flower-shaped**)

Bean-flower-shaped: Same as "pea-flower-shaped." Flowers of the family Fabaceae/Faboideae.

Bilaterally symmetrical: Two sides are mirror images of one another, like the two sides of a face.

Blade: The expanded (flat) portion of a leaf. (See **leaf**)

Brackish: Coastal tidal water that is somewhat salty, but not as salty as seawater.

Bract: A small to large leaflike structure, usually just below a flower or inflorescence. Bracts can range from very small, green, and inconspicuous, like those in the inflorescences of some Acanthaceae, to large and colorful, such as those of *Heliconia*. The lower bracts of some *Heliconia* species may develop a leaf blade at the tip.

Bulb: An underground storage organ, usually rounded, made up of leaflike layers, like an onion.

Buttress: Planklike supporting structure extending outward from the base of a tree trunk at the juncture of the roots and trunk. Some are relatively narrow but very tall (10 m [30 ft] or more) and extend high up on the tree trunk, others are fairly low but extend far outward from the base of the tree, merging with surface roots.

Calyx: Nonreproductive whorl of flower parts, below the petals. Collective term for sepals.

Capsule: A dry fruit that splits open to release seeds. (See **achene**)

Catkin: A pendant, lax, spikelike inflorescence, usually with many small bracts and inconspicuous flowers.

Centimeter (cm): 1 cm = 0.4 inch; 1 inch = 2.5 cm; 100 cm = 1 m = 3.3 ft.

Colonial: Plants with several, or numerous, separate stems arising from a common system of roots, underground stems (rhizomes), above-ground runners, bulb off-shoots, or other means of asexual (vegetative) reproduction.

Compound leaf: Leaf with more than one blade (leaflet) connected to a common stalk.

Deciduous: Falling off, not persistent, leaves, stipules, flower parts. Many trees in the seasonally dry forest drop their leaves during the dry season.

Dioecious: Plant species in which male and female flowers are on separate plants. In these species, fruit is produced only by female plants. In most flowering plants, male and female parts occur within the same flower. These flowers are referred to as hermaphroditic, bisexual, or perfect. (Compare **monoecious**)

Dispersal: Referring to seeds, this describes the removal of seeds from parent plant to a new location by wind, water, birds, or other animals. Many fruits are fleshy or have a fleshy coat around the seeds. This is attractive to animals, which eat the flesh and pass seeds in feces. Birds often regurgitate large seeds.

Elliptical: A structure (leaf, fruit, petal, etc.) that is widest in the center and pointed at both ends.

Endemic: A plant originating in and restricted to a certain region.

Entire: Leaves with smooth margins, without teeth or lobes.

Epiphytic: Plants growing on other plants. Many ferns, orchids, and bromeliads and even shrubs grow on tree branches. Not parasitic.

Family: A group of genera with similar characteristics; these genera are more closely related to each other than to other families.

Ferns: Vascular, nonflowering plants, which do not produce fruit or seed and instead reproduce by spores (see Chapter 8). (See **spore, spore case**)

Filament: The stalk of an anther; lower part of a stamen. (See **flower**)

Fleshy: Relatively soft, succulent; not dry or woody. Fleshy fruits are usually eaten by birds or other animals that disperse the seeds by discarding, regurgitating, or defecating them.

Flower: The parts of a flowering plant (angiosperm) that carry out sexual reproduction. Female flower parts include the stigma, style, and ovary, (which contains ovules that develop into seeds). Collectively, these parts are called the pistil. Male parts are the filament (anther stalk) and the anther (which contains pollen that produces sperm cells). Collectively, the male parts are termed the stamen. Petals and sepals are accessory structures, which may or may not be present. The top of the flower stalk is often expanded and may become part of the fruit. (Compare **gymnosperms, ferns**)

Free: Petals not fused to one another or flower parts not attached to one another (i.e., free stamens are not fused to petals). Tubular flowers have petals fused together for most of their length.

Fruit: The ovary and associated tissues bearing seeds of flowering plants. Fruit may consist of a single seed surrounded by the dried ovary wall (such as fruits of Asteraceae), may be dry and contain several seeds, or may be fleshy, with the ovary wall and associated tissues thickened. Fleshy fruit is usually adapted to be eaten by animals that then disperse the seeds away from the parent. In some cases a dry fruit may contain seeds that have a fleshy coat or attachment. (See **aril**)

Fused: Petals, sepals, or other parts attached to one another, forming a single, usually tubular, structure. Fruits are sometimes fused, as in *Rubus* and *Castilla* species.

Genus: A closely related group of species in one plant family. The genus name is a proper noun and is always capitalized, i.e., *Piper*. It is Latinized and usually written in italics or underlined.

Grain: A dry, 1-seeded fruit in which the fruit wall is fused to the seed (grasses).

Gymnosperms: Woody plants that produce seeds but no flowers and no true fruits. Developing seeds are produced on the scales of woody, occasionally fleshy, cones. Include cycads, pines (conifers), and cypresses. (Compare Angiosperm)

Herb/herbaceous: A plant that does not develop woody tissue. Some tropical herbs develop woody lower stems or become somewhat shrublike. There is no sharp division between woody and herbaceous plants, but herbaceous plants usually die back to the ground at the end of the growing season. Tropical herbs sometimes die back after fruiting and then resprout from the rootstock.

Inferior ovary: The ovary is positioned below the base of the flower parts. The old, remnant flower parts, or scar, will be located at the top of the fruit.

Inflorescence: The flowering parts of a plant, or the arrangement of flowers on a simple or branched axis.

Irregular: Plant parts that are asymmetrical.

Internode: Stem between nodes.

Invasive: According to the National Invasive Species Information Center: "An 'invasive species' is defined as a species that is (1) nonnative to the ecosystem under consideration and (2) whose introduction causes or is likely to cause economic or environmental harm or harm to human health. (Executive Order 13112).... Human actions are the primary means of invasive species introductions."

Keel/keeled: A plant part (sheath, bract) that has a single sharp edge, appearing folded, like the keel of a boat. The lowest petal of a bean-flower-shaped flower.

Kneeling stem: Lower part of a plant stem lying against ground while the top of the stem is growing upward. Also called reclining stem.

Leaf: The flattened parts of a plant that are specialized to carry out photosynthesis. Usually with an axillary bud at the base.

Leaflet: A division of a compound leaf with a narrow attachment to a common leaf axis (rachis), often with a small stalk. Leaflets lack an axillary bud at their base. (See **compound leaf**)

Liana: A woody vine.

Lip: A broad division at the tip of a tubular, bilaterally symmetrical flower.

Lobed: A leaf that is divided but not compound, the divisions are connected to one another along the leaf axis. The free, top part of a flower with fused petals (a tubular flower) or sepals. (See **lip**)

Loop connection: Leaf veins that do not reach the margin but connect one with another near the margin forming a series of partial loops.

Lowland: Sea level to 500 m elevation. (See **montane**)

Meter (m): 1 m = 100 cm; about 40 inches (slightly more than 1 yard).

Mangrove: Trees or shrubs tolerant of salt or brackish water and water-saturated soil, growing in sheltered sites along coastal areas, often with stilt roots or root structures that stick up through the mud. (See **pneumatophore**)

Marginal vein: Leaf vein that runs parallel to the edge of the leaf, around the margin of the blade. Often connecting other secondary veins in a looping pattern (loop-connected).

Midrib: Central, major vein in a leaf, bract, petal, or sepal.

Monoecious: Plants in which male and female flowers are separate but occur on the same plant. (Compare **dioecious**)

Montane: Referring to mountainous regions, including the following zones: premontane 500–1500 m elevation, montane 1500–3500 m elevation. This may be divided into lower montane 1500–2500 m elevation, upper montane 2500–3500 m elevation, and above tree level.

Nectar cup: Nectary. A small structure, flat to rounded or cuplike that secretes nectar, a sugary sap, as an attractant.

Neotropics: Tropical portion of the Western Hemisphere, from southern Mexico and Florida to just south of Paraguay, including all the Caribbean islands. (See map p. iv.)

Node: Point at which a leaf or leaves arise from a stem.

Opposite: Two leaves at one node, on opposite sides of the stem.

Ovary: the major part of a pistil (female parts of a flower). The ovary contains ovules (eggs) that develop into seeds. The ovary develops into the fruit surrounding the seeds. Sometimes the petals and sepals are attached to a cuplike floral base (hypanthium), as in Rosaceae. (See **flower, pistil**)

Palmate: Referring to either compound leaves with more than three parts, with leaflets, arising from one point, as fingers of a hand; or leaf veins arising from the base of the leaf blade in a fan-shaped arrangement. Veins may be palmate only at the base of the blade, becoming pinnate along the upper part of the midrib, or less commonly, all the major veins may arise at the base of the blade.

Páramo: Elevations above the tree line; cold, rainy, windy; dominated by shrubs, herbs.

Petal: A nonreproductive flower part, often leaflike, white, or colored, situated above the sepals. Petals may be separate (free) or fused in various ways forming a tube.

Pinnae: The primary axes of a twice pinnately compound leaf. Pinnae bear leaflets. In a triplely compound leaf the primary pinnae bear secondary pinnae, which bear the leaflets.

Pinnate: Referring to either a compound leaf with leaflets along opposite sides of the midrib (leaf axis), same form as a feather (when the bases of the leaf segments are borne on the main axis, without stalks, they are considered lobes rather than leaflets, and the leaf is pinnately divided, rather than pinnately compound); or secondary veins in a leaf that arise along opposite sides of the midrib.

Pioneer: Usually referring to fast growing, soft-wooded trees that are very intolerant of shade, such as *Cecropia*, *Ochroma*, and *Heliocarpus* species. These are early colonizers of open areas such as landslides, forest gaps, or abandoned pastures. Also used for herbs "pioneering" on newly exposed soils.

Pistil: Female reproductive structures with ovary, containing ovules that develop into seeds, and style, a stalk above the ovary bearing the stigma, which is the receptacle for pollen, which contains sperm.

Plume: Referring mostly to a tuft of long hairs or bristles at one end of a seed, used for dispersal by wind.

Pneumatophores: Aerial roots that protrude from the soil.

Prop roots: See **aerial roots**.

Raceme: An unbranched, spikelike inflorescence in which each flower has an individual stalk.

Rachis: The main stem (midrib, axis) of a compound leaf, the central axis of an inflorescence.

Radially symmetrical: Symmetry spreading from a common center, equal in all directions, like a wheel.

Reclining stem: See **kneeling stem**.

Regular: Flowers that are radially symmetrical.

Rhizome: Horizontal, underground stem, bears roots and leafy stems.

Rosette: A tight spiral of leaves. Form resembling the petals of a rose. (See **basal**)

Scale: A small, papery, bractlike structure. Flower parts of grasses are scalelike.

Seed: The reproductive unit of higher plants; gymnosperms (nonflowering plants) and angiosperms (flowering plants). Contains an embryo that grows into a new plant. This is usually surrounded by storage tissue, often in the form of "seed leaves," like the two halves of a bean or the grain of a corn seed. The outer layer of the seed is the protective seed coat.

Secondary veins: Smaller veins arising from the midrib (midvein), or from the major veins, of a leaf.

Sepal: A nonreproductive flower part directly below the petals, usually leaflike and green, sometimes petallike; collectively, sepals form the calyx.

Sheath: A tubular envelope extending downward from the base of a leaf blade or leaf stalk and covering the plant stem. A characteristic of all grasses and grasslike plants as well as many other plant families such as Heliconiaceae, Costaceae, Bromeliaceae, Apiaceae, and Marantaceae.

Simple: Leaves with a single blade, not compound. Simple leaves may be toothed, lobed, or divided, but the divisions are always connected to one another by tissue along the leaf axis (rachis).

Smooth: In reference to a leaf margin; not toothed or divided (entire).

Species: A group of organisms that can interbreed and produce fertile young. This applies better to animals than to plants, however, since plants hybridize rather easily if they are very closely related. The species name is an adjective modifying the genus name, it is always Latinized and in lower case, i.e., *Piper guanacastense* (Piper of Guanacaste).

Spike: An unbranched inflorescence in which the flowers are attached directly to the axis (stalk) and have no individual stems. (Compare **raceme**)

Spore: Single celled, reproductive structure produced by ferns and other plants that do not produce flowers, fruit, or seeds (ferns, club mosses, and spike mosses).

Spore case: Sorus (plural: sori). Clusters of sporangia, the structures containing spores, in non-seed-bearing plants. Sori are usually covered by a thin protective structure called an indusium. A hand lens is necessary to see these details.

Stamen: Male flower part, usually composed of a thin filament (stalk) holding up a thicker, pollen-bearing anther. Pollen contains the sperm nucleus (flowering plants do not have swimming sperm).

Stigma: Female flower part that receives pollen. Located above the ovary and connected to it by the stemlike style.

Stipule: A small, often leaflike appendage on the base of the leaf stalk, often paired, sometimes on the stem between leaf stalks of opposite leaves, as in Rubiaceae, or forming a tube around the stem, as in Polygonaceae. In some cases the stipule serves to cover the leaf bud and falls off as the leaf expands, often leaving a scar around the plant stem, as in Cecropiaceae.

Subspecies: A regional form of a species isolated from other populations. Usually abbreviated: subsp.

Succulent: Fleshy and juicy.

Superior ovary: An ovary positioned above the base of the petals and sepals. The flower remnants, except for the stigma, will be located at the base of the fruit.

Tendril: A slender outgrowth of a stem or leaf, usually coiled, that serves as an organ of support.

Terminal: At the end of a stem or branch. Usually referring to an inflorescence. (Compare **axillary**)

Toothed: A leaf or petal with a jagged or serrated margin.

Tuber: An enlarged, fleshy root, such as a potato. (Compare **rhizome**)

Vascular: A plant with tubelike tissues (xylem and phloem cells) that conduct water and nutrients to and from roots and throughout the plant. Mosses, liverworts, seaweeds (and other algae) are nonvascular plants.

Vein: Strands of tissue that carry water and nutrients and provide support. Collectively they constitute the vascular system of the plant.

Venation: Pattern of veins in a leaf.

Whorled: Three or more leaves, or other structures, in a circle at the same level (node) on the stem.

Winged: A thin expanse of tissue bordering or surrounding another structure, usually applied to seeds, or the axes of compound leaves.

REFERENCES

Almeda, F. 2000. A synopsis of the genus *Blakea* (Melastomataceae) in Mexico and Central America. Novon 10(4):299–319.

Anderson, T. 2005. *Satureja viminea.* Top Tropicals Botanical Center/ Retail and Wholesale Nursery/Davie and Fort Lauderdale, FL. http:// toptropicals.com/cgi-bin/garden_catalog/cat.cgi?uid = Satureja_viminea.

Anonymous. 2004. *Dioscorea bulbifera.* FEPPC Florida Exotic Pest Plant Council. www.fleppc.org/pdf/Dioscorea_bulbifera.pdf.

Anonymous. 2005. *Sphagneticola trilobata* (L.C. Rich.) Pruski. Invasive Species Specialist Group. www.issg.org/database/species/ ecology.asp?si = 44andfr = 1andsts.

Anonymous. 2004. *Tectona grandis* Linn. f. Verbenaceae. ASEAN's 100 most precious plants. ASEAN Regional Centre for Biodiversity Conservation (ARCBC). www.arcbc.org/arcbcweb/ ASEAN_Precious_plants/timber/Tectona_grandis_Linn.htm.

Armstrong, W. P. 2005. Wayne's word: An on-line textbook of natural history. http://waynesword.palomar.edu/fruits.htm≠u.

Baker, R., and W. Burger. 1983. Family #70 Caryophyllaceae. Flora Costaricensis. Fieldiana Botany, New Series 13:227–247.

Barlow, C. 2000. The Ghosts of Evolution. Basic Books, New York.

Berry, F., and W. J. Kress. 1991. *Heliconia*: An Identification Guide. Smithsonian Institution Press, Washington, DC.

Blake, S. F. 1919. *Schizolobium parahyba* (Vell.) Contributions from the U.S. National Herbarium 20(7):240. www.conabio.gob.mx/conocimiento/ info_especies/arboles/doctos/21-legum48m.pdf.

Börner, A. 2000. Classification of premontane tropical forests at the eastern slope of the Andes in the Río Avisado Watershed, Alto Mayo Region, northern Perú. Masters thesis. University of Bayreuth, Department of Biogeography. www.uni-bayreuth.de/obg/diplomarbeiten/ diplomarbeit_annett.pdf.

Brown, D. 1988. Aroids. Timber Press, Portland, OR.

Burger, W. 1971. Family #40, Casuarinaceae. Flora Costaricensis. Fieldiana Botany 35:3–4.

———. 1971. Family #41, Piperaceae. Flora Costaricensis. Fieldiana Botany 35:5–218.

———. 1977. Family #46, Myricaceae. Flora Costaricensis. Fieldiana Botany 40:21–27.

———. 1977. Family #50, Fagaceae. Flora Costaricensis. Fieldiana Botany 40:59–82.

———. 1977. Family #51, Ulmaceae. Flora Costaricensis. Fieldiana Botany 40:83–93.

———. 1977. Family #52, Moraceae. Flora Costaricensis. Fieldiana Botany 40:94–215.

———. 1977. Family #53, Urticaceae. Flora Costaricensis. Fieldiana Botany 40:218–283.

Burger, W. 1983. Family #56 Olacaceae. Flora Costaricensis. Fieldiana Botany, New Series 13:14–27.

————. 1983. Family #62 Polygonaceae. Flora Costaricensis. Fieldiana Botany, New Series 13:99–138.

————. 1983. Family #63 Chenopodiaceae. Flora Costaricensis. Fieldiana Botany, New Series 13:138–142.

————. 1983. Family #64 Amaranthaceae. Flora Costaricensis. Fieldiana Botany, New Series 13:142–180.

————. 1983. Family #65 Nyctaginaceae. Flora Costaricensis. Fieldiana Botany, New Series 13:180–199.

————. 1983. Family #66 Phytolaccaceae. Flora Costaricensis. Fieldiana Botany, New Series 13:199–213.

————. 1983. Family #98 Oxalidaceae. Flora Costaricensis. Fieldiana Botany, New Series 28:2–16.

————. 1983. Family #99 Geraniaceae. Flora Costaricensis. Fieldiana Botany, New Series 28:16–21.

————. 1991. Family #103 Zygophyllaceae. Flora Costaricensis. Fieldiana Botany, New Series 28:38–41.

Burger, W., and M. Huft. 1995. Flora Costaricensis. Family #113 Euphorbiaceae. Fieldiana Botany, New Series 36:1–163.

Burger, W., and C. M. Taylor. 1993. Family #202 Rubiaceae. Flora Costaricensis. Fieldiana Botany, New Series 33.

Burger, W., and J. Kuijt. 1983. Family #58 Loranthaceae. Flora Costaricensis. Fieldiana Botany, New series 13:29–79.

Burger, W., and H. van der Werff. 1990. Family #80 Lauraceae. Flora Costaricensis. Fieldiana Botany, New Series 23:1–129.

Cannon M. J., and J. F. M. Cannon. 1986. *Oreopanax nicaraguensis*. Annals of the Missouri Botanical Garden 73:482.

Center for Invasive Plant Management. 2006. Weed ID. Department of Land Resources and Environmental Sciences Montana State University, Bozeman. www.weedcenter.org/management/weed_id.html.

Christman, S. 2003. *Crocosmia X crocosmiiflora*. Plant profile. Floridata. www.floridata.com/ref/C/croc_xcr.cfm.

Cornejo, L. J., C. Rengifo, and P. Soriano. 2000. Foraging strategy of *Heliangelus spencei* (Trochilidae), on two Ericaceas, in a Venezuelan Andes cloud forest. www.geocities.com/lamucuy2000/helies.html.

Courtright, G. 1988. Tropicals. Timber Press, Portland, OR.

Croat, T. B. 1976. Family 108. Sapindaceae. Flora of Panama. Part VI. Annals of the Missouri Botanical Garden63(3):419–540.

Croat, T. B. 1978. The flora of Barro Colorado Island. Stanford University Press, Stanford, CA.

Croat, T. B. 1999. *Philodendron crassispathum* Croat and Grayum, sp. nov. A revision of *Philodendron* subgenus *Philodendron* (Araceae) of Central America. International Aroid Society. www.aroid.org/genera/Philodendron/Calostigma/Macrobelium/Ecordata/crassispathum.htm.

Croat, T. B. 1999. *Philodendron wendlandii* Schott. A revision of *Philodendron* subgenus *Philodendron* (Araceae) of Central America. International Aroid Society. www.aroid.org/genera/Philodendron/Calostigma/Glossophyllum/wendlandi.htm.

Croat, T. B. 2002. The Genus Anthurium. International Aroid Society. http://www.aroid.org/genera/Anthurium/anthwel.html.

Cronquist, A. 1981. An integrated system of classification of flowering plants. Columbia University Press, New York.

Cronquist, A. 1988. The evolution and classification of flowering plants. 2nd ed. The New York Botanical Garden, Bronx, New York.

Davidse, G., M. Sousa S., A. O. Chater, and C. J. Humphries (eds.). 1997. W³FM, Flora Mesoamerica. Missouri Botanical Garden, Instituto de Biología de la Universidad Nacional Autónoma de México, British Museum. www.mobot.org/mobot/fm/intro.html, http://mobot.mobot.org/W3T/Search/meso.html.

D'Arcy, W. G. 1973. Family 170. Solanaceae. Flora of Panama. Part IX. Annals of the Missouri Botanical Garden 60(3):573–780.

———. 1975. Family 184. Compositae. Flora of Panama. Part IX. Annals of the Missouri Botanical Garden 62(4):83–1321.

———. 1980. *Clusia croatii.* Annals of the Missouri Botanical Garden 67:979.

Dressler, R. L. 1990. The Orchids. Harvard University Press, Cambridge, MA.

———. 1993. Field Guide to the Orchids of Costa Rica and Panama. Comstock Publishing Associates, Ithaca, NY.

Dubs, B. 1998. Prodromus Florae Matogrossensis. Betrona Verlag, Küsnacht, Switzerland. www.systbot.unizh.ch/datenbanken/matogrosso/datenblattInclude.php?species = Allosidastrum%20pyramidatum.

Duke, J. A. 1983. *Cajanus cajan* (L.) Millsp. In: Handbook of Energy Crops (unpublished). Posted: Center for New Crops and Plants Products, Purdue University. www.hort.purdue.edu/newcrop/duke_energy/Cajanus_cajun.html.

Durkee, L. H. 1986. Family #200 Acanthaceae. Flora Costaricensis. Fieldiana Botany. New Series 18:1–87.

Dwyer, J. D. 1965. Family 83. Leguminosae, subfamily Papilionoideae (in part). Flora of Panama. Part V, Fascicle 4. Annals of the Missouri Botanical Garden 52(1):1–54.

Dwyer, J. D. and Collaborators. 1980. Family 83. Leguminosae, subfamily Papilionoideae (Conclusion). R. E. Woodson Jr., R. W. Schery, and Collaborators. Flora of Panama. Part V, Fascicle 5. Annals of the Missouri Botanical Garden 67(3).

Dwyer, J. D., and W. G. D'Arcy. 1980. Family 83. Leguminosae, subfamily Papilionoideae, Erythrina. Flora of Panama, Part V. Annals of the Missouri Botanical Garden 67(3).

Earle, C. J. 2004. *Cupressus lusitanica* Miller 1768. Gymnosperm Database. www.botanik.uni-bonn.de/conifers/cu/cup/lusitanica.htm.

Enquist, B. J., and J. J. Sullivan. 2001. Vegetative key and description of tree species of the tropical dry forests of upland Sector Santa ROSA, Area de Conservación GUA, Costa Rica. http://eeb37.biosci.arizona.edu/~brian/Enquist_Sullivan.pdf.

Farmer, C. 2002. Skye Flora: Elder. *Sambucus nigra.* www.plant-identification.co.uk/skye/caprifoliaceae/sambucus-nigra.htm.

Faust, J. L. 1973. *The New York Times* Book of House Plants. Quadrangle Books, New York.

Ferrari, A. R. L., J. C. Romero, A. Z. Hurtado, R. E. G. Cuspinero, and Z. C. Romero. 2005. *Licania arborea.* Especies con usos no maderables en bosques tropicales y subtropicales. Universidad Autónoma Metropolitana–Iztapalapa, Mexico. www.semarnat.gob.mx/pfnm2/indices/creditos.htm.

Fletcher, K., and D. Baylis. 2005. Wild side photography. www. wildsidephotography.ca/gallery/.

Flora of North America Editorial Committee (eds.). 1993+. *Crocosmia × crocosmiiflora* (Lemoine) N. E. Brown, Trans. Roy. Soc. South Africa. 20:264. 1932. Flora of North America North of Mexico. 7+ vols. Vol 26. New York: Flora of North America. http://flora.huh.harvard.edu:8080/ flora/browse.do?flora_id = 1andtaxon_id = 242102234andkey_no = 1.

Flora of North America Editorial Committee (eds.). 1993+. *Eulophia alta* (wild coco). Flora of North America North of Mexico. 7+ vols. Vol. 26. New York: Flora of North America. www.efloras.org/florataxon. aspx?flora_id = 1andtaxon_id = 242101610.

Flora of North America Editorial Committee (eds.). 1993+. *Laportea aestuans* (Linnaeus) Chew, Gard. Bull. Straits Settlem. 21:200. 1965. Flora of North America North of Mexico. 7+ vols. Vol. 3. New York: Flora of North America. www.efloras.org/florataxon.aspx?flora_id = 1andtaxon_id = 233500742.

Flora of North America Editorial Committee (eds.). 1993+. *Nothoscordum gracile* (Dryander) Stearn, Taxon. 35:335. 1986. In: Flora of North America North of Mexico. 7+ vols. Vol. 26. New York: Flora of North America. www.efloras.org/florataxon.aspx?flora_id = 1andtaxon_id = 242101808.

Fournier, L. A., and E. G. García. 1998. Nombres Vernaculares y Científicos de los Árboles de Costa Rica. Editorial Guayacán Centroamericana, S. A. San José, Costa Rica.

Francis, J. K. 2003. *Acnistus arborescens* (L.) Schlecht. Solanaceae. USDA, Forest Service, International Institute of Tropical Forestry, San Juan, Puerto Rico. www.fs.fed.us/global/iitf/pdf/shrubs/ Acnistus%20arborescens.pdf.

———. 2003. *Bocconia frutescens* L. Papaveraceae. USDA, Forest Service, International Institute of Tropical Forestry, San Juan, Puerto Rico. www.fs.fed.us/global/iitf/pdf/shrubs/Bocconia%20frutescens.pdf.

———. 2003. *Caesalpinia bonduc* (L.) Roxb. Fabaceae. USDA, Forest Service, International Institute of Tropical Forestry, San Juan, Puerto Rico. www.fs.fed.us/global/iitf/pdf/shrubs/Caesalpinia%20bonduc.pdf.

———. 2003. *Cajanus cajan* (L.) Millsp. Fabaceae. USDA, Forest Service, International Institute of Tropical Forestry, San Juan, Puerto Rico. www.fs.fed.us/global/iitf/pdf/shrubs/Cajanus%20cajan.pdf.

———. 2003. *Duranta erecta* (L.) Verbenaceae. USDA, Forest Service, International Institute of Tropical Forestry, San Juan, Puerto Rico. www.fs.fed.us/global/iitf/pdf/shrubs/Duranta%20erecta.pdf.

———. 2003. *Gossypium hirsutum* L. Malvaceae. USDA, Forest Service, International Institute of Tropical Forestry, San Juan, Puerto Rico. www.fs.fed.us/global/iitf/pdf/shrubs/Gossypium%20hirsutum.pdf.

———. 2003. *Ixora coccinea* L. Rubiaceae. USDA, Forest Service, International Institute of Tropical Forestry, San Juan, Puerto Rico. www.fs.fed.us/global/iitf/pdf/shrubs/Ixora%20coccinea.pdf.

———. 2003. *Lantana camara* L. Verbenaceae. USDA, Forest Service, International Institute of Tropical Forestry, San Juan, Puerto Rico. www.fs.fed.us/global/iitf/pdf/shrubs/Lantana%20camara.pdf.

———. 2003. *Ludwigia octovalvis* (Jacq.) Raven. Onagraceae. USDA, Forest Service, International Institute of Tropical Forestry, San Juan, Puerto Rico. www.fs.fed.us/global/iitf/pdf/shrubs/ Ludwigia%20octovalvis.pdf.

———. 2003. *Mimosa pudica* (L.). Fabaceae. USDA, Forest Service, International Institute of Tropical Forestry, San Juan, Puerto Rico. www.fs.fed.us/global/iitf/pdf/shrubs/MimOSA%20pudica.pdf.

———. 2003. *Passiflora edulis* Sims. Passifloraceae. USDA, Forest Service, International Institute of Tropical Forestry, San Juan, Puerto Rico. www.fs.fed.us/global/iitf/pdf/shrubs/Passiflora%20edulis.pdf.

———. 2003. *Waltheria indica* (L.) Sterculiaceae. USDA, Forest Service, International Institute of Tropical Forestry, San Juan, Puerto Rico. www.fs.fed.us/global/iitf/pdf/shrubs/Waltheria%20indica.pdf.

Fryxell, P. A. 1992. Fasciculo 68, Flora de Veracruz, Malvaceae. Instituto de Ecologica, A.C. Xalapa, Veracruz. University of California, Riverside.

Fryxell, P. A. n.d. *Malvaviscus concinnus* Kunth, en Humb., Bonpl. and Kunth. Nov. gen. sp. Quarto ed. 5:286, Folio ed. 5 222. 1822. (communication from B. Hammel).

Furlow, J. G. 1977. Family #44, Betulaceae. Flora Costaricensis. Fieldiana Botany 40:56–58.

Grandtner, M. M. 2005. World Dictionary of Trees. Wood and Forest Sciences Department Faculty of Forestry and Geomatics, Laval University, Quebec, Canada. www.wdt.qc.ca/.

Gentry, A. H. 1973. Family 172. Bignoniaceae. Flora of Panama. Part IX. Annals of the Missouri Botanical Garden 60(3):781–977.

Gentry, J. L. Jr., and P. C. Standley. 1974. Flora of Guatemala. Solanaceae. Fieldiana Botany 24(part 10, nos. 1–2):1–151.

Gilman, E. F. 1999. *Agave angustifolia*. Fact Sheet FPS-21. University of Florida Cooperative Extension Service, Institute of Food and Agricultural Services. http://hort.ufl.edu/shrubs/AGAANGA.PDF.

Gilman, E. F., and A. Meerow. 1999. *Pachystachys lutea*. Fact Sheet FPS-452. University of Florida Cooperative Extension Service, Institute of Food and Agricultural Services. http://edis.ifas.edu.

Gleason, H. A., and A. Cronquist. 1991. Manual of Vascular Plants of Northeastern United States and Adjacent Canada. The New York Botanical Garden, Bronx, New York.

Gomez, L. D. 1977. Family #44, Salicaceae. Flora Costaricensis. Fieldiana Botany 40:14–17.

González, R. R. 1996. A Field Guide to the Common Plants of the Caribbean Coast of Costa Rica. Tortuguero National Park.

Grayum, M. H. 2000. *Dieffenbachia, Dracontium, Homalomena, Monstera*. Araceae. Draft treatments for the Manual de Plantas de Costa Rica. Missouri Botanical Garden. www.mobot.org/MOBOT/research/treat/caladium.html#TOP.

Grayum, M. H. 2000. *Philodendron*. Araceae. Draft treatments for the Manual de Plantas de Costa Rica. Missouri Botanical Garden. www.mobot.org/MOBOT/research/treat/philodendron.shtml.

Grayum, M. H. 2000. *Spathiphyllum montanum* (R. A. Baker) Grayum, Phytologia 82:50. 1997. Araceae. Draft treatments for the Manual de Plantas de Costa Rica. Missouri Botanical Garden. www.mobot.org/MOBOT/research/treat/pistia.html.

Haber, W. A. 2001. Monteverde plants: *Solanum chrysotrichum*. www.cs.umb.edu/~whaber/Monte/Plant/Sola/Sol-chr.html.

Haber, W. A., W. Zuchowski, and E. Bello. 1996. An Introduction to Cloud Forest Trees: Monteverde, Costa Rica. Published by the Authors, Monteverde, Costa Rica.

Hammel, B. E. 1986. Systematic treatment of the Cyclanthaceae, Marantaceae, Cecropiaceae, Clusiaceae, Lauraceae and Moraceae for the flora of a wet, lowland tropical forest, Finca La Selva. Ph.D. dissertation. Duke University, Durham, North Carolina.

———. 2001. Plantas Ornamentales Nativas de Costa Rica. 2nd ed. Instituto Nacional de Bioversidad, Costa Rica.

Hammel, B. E., M. H. Grayum, C. Herrera, and N. Zamora (eds.). 2003. Manual de Plantas de Costa Rica. Vols. 1 and 2. Missouri Botanical Garden Press, St. Louis, MO.

Harmon, P. 2005. Trees of Costa Rica's Pacific Slope. National Biodiversity Institute, Costa Rica: Santo Domingo de Heredia. www.cds.ed.cr/teachers/harmon/page36.html.

Harrington, H. D., and L. W. Durrell. 1957. How to Identify Plants. The Swallow Press, Chicago.

Hauke, R. L. 1978. A taxonomic monograph of the genus *Equisetum* subgenus *Equisetum*. Nova Hedwigia 30:385. http://members.eunet.at/m.matus/Equisetum_bogotense.html.

Heiser, C. B. Jr. 1969. The Fascinating World of the Nightshades. Dover Publications, New York.

Henderson, A., G. Galeano, and R. Bernal. 1995. Field Guide to the Palms of the Americas. Princeton University Press, Princeton, New Jersey.

Henshel, J. 1990. A self guided tour to selected trees. Revised by M. M. Currier. 1992. Jardín Botánico Wilson, San Vito, Costa Rica.

Hernández, D., and J. Gómez. 1993. La flora acuatica del humidal de Palo Verde. Editorial de la Universidad Nacional, Heredia, Cost Rica.

Heywood, V. H. (Consult. ed.). 1978. Flowering Plants of the World. Oxford University Press, New York.

Holdridge, L. R., L. J. Poveda, and Q. Jiménez. 1997. Árboles de Costa Rica Vol. 1. 2nd ed. Centro Cientifico Tropical, San José, Costa Rica.

Howard, R. A. 1976. Family 106. Icacinaceae. Flora of Panama. Part VI. Annals of the Missouri Botanical Garden 63(3):399–417.

Hunter, G. E. 1965. Family 118. Dilleniaceae. Flora of Panama. Part VI. Annals of the Missouri Botanical Garden 52(4):579–598.

Instituto Nacional de Bioversidad (INBio). 2001. Herbarium database on-line. Costa Rica. www.inbio.ac.cr/bims/k03.htm.

International Aroid Society. 2005. International Aroid Society. www.aroid.org/genera/.

International Legume Database and Information Service (ILDIS). 2005. Legume Web. Centre for Plant Diversity and Systematics, School of Plant Sciences. The University of Reading, Reading, UK. www.ildis.org/LegumeWeb/.

Jackson, B. D. 1928. A Glossary of Botanical Terms. 4th ed. G. Duckworth and Co., New York.

Janick, J. (ed.) 2007. *Nephelium lappaceum*. NewCROP. Perdue University, West Lafayette, IN. Horticulture and Landscape Architecture. www. hort.purdue.edu/newcrop/morton/rambutan.html.

Janzen, D. H. 1983. Costa Rican Natural History. University of Chicago Press, Chicago.

Janzen, D. H., and P. S. Martin. 1982. Neotropical anachronisms: The fruits the gomphotheres ate. Science 215:19–27.

Jensen, W.A., and.B. Salisbury. 1984. Botany. 2nd ed. Wadsworth Publishing Co., Belmont, CA.

Johnson H., and Kimnach. 1963. *Weberocereus trichophorus.* Cact. Succ. J. (Los Angeles) 35:205.

Jøker. D., and R. Salazar. 2000. *Pentaclethra macroloba* (Willd.) Kuntz. Seed Leaflet No. 35. Danida Forest Seed Center. www.dfsc.dk/pdf/Seedleaflets/Pentaclethra%20macroloba_int.pdf.

Kershaw, L., A. MacKinnon, and J. Polar. 1998. Plants of the Rocky Mountains. Lone Pine Publishing, Auburn, WA.

Kingsbury, J. M. 1988. 200 Conspicuous, Unusual, or Economically Important Tropical Plants of the Caribbean. Bullbrier Press, Ithaca, NY.

Krempin, J. 1990. Palms and Cycads around the World. Horwitz Grahame Pty., Sydney, Australia.

Kricher, J. C. 1989. A Neotropical Companion. Princeton University Press, Princeton, NJ.

Lawrence, G. H. M. 1951. Taxonomy of Vascular plants. MacMillan Co., New York.

Lellinger, D. B. 1985. A Field Manual of the Ferns and Fern-Allies of the United States and Canada. Smithsonian Institution Press, Washington, DC.

———. 1989. The Ferns and Ferns-Allies of Costa Rica, Panama, and the Chocó. Part 1. Psilotaceae through Dicksoniaceae. *Pteridologia,* American Fern Society, Washington, DC.

Lonchamp, J. P. 2000. Nom scientifique: *Nothoscordum borbonicum* Kunth. HYPPA, Unité de Malherbologie and Agronomie INRA-Dijon. www.dijon.inra.fr/malherbo/hyppa/hyppa-f/notfr_fh.htm.

Lötschert, W., and G. Beese. 1983. Collins Photo Guide to Tropical Plants. Trans. C. King. Harper Collins, London.

Luteyn, J. L. 1995. Flora Neotropica. Monograph 35. Ericaceae. Part 1. Cavendishia. Organization for Flora Neotropica, New York Botanical Garden, New York.

Luteyn, J. L., and P. Pedraza. 2006. Neotropical blueberries, the family Ericaceae. Species descriptions. Bronx, NY: The New York Botanical Garden. www.nybg.org/bsci/res/lut2/.

Luteyn, J. L., and R. L. Wilbur. 1978. Family 149. Ericaceae. Flora of Panama. Part VIII. Annals of the Missouri Botanical Garden 65(1):27–143.

Maas, P. J. M., L. Y. Th. Westra, and A. Farjon. 1998. Neotropical Plant Families: A concise guide to families of vascular plants in the Neotropics. Koeltz Scientific Books, Champaign, IL.

Mabberly, D. J. 1997. The Plant Book. 2nd ed. Cambridge University Press, New York.

Mannetje, L. 2004. *Arachis glabrata* Benth. Food and Agriculture Organization of the United Nations. www.fao.org/ag/AGP/AGPC/doc/GBASE/data/Pf000007.HTM.

Manual de Plantas de Costa Rica. 2001. Herbarium data base on-line. Missouri Botanical Garden. www.mobot.org/manual.plantas/lista.html.

McDade, L. A., K. S. Bawa, H. A. Hespenheide, and G. S. Hartshorn. 1994. La Selva Ecology and Natural History of a Neotropical Rainforest. University of Chicago Press, Chicago.

McNeal, D. W. 2004. *Nothoscordum*, false garlic, *N. gracile* (Dryander) Stearn. Treatment from the Jepson Manual. 1993. University of California Press, Berkeley. http://ucjeps.berkeley.edu/cgi-bin/get_JM_treatment.pl?8352,8632,8633.

Mickel, J. T., and J. M. Beitel. 1988. Pteridophyte Flora of Oaxaca, Mexico. The New York Botanical Garden, Bronx, New York.

Miller, I. L., and G. C. Schultz. 2002. Hyptis or horehound (*Hyptis suaveolens*). Agnote 477 No. F25. Agdex No. 642. ISSN No. 0157–8243. Northern Territory of Australia. www.nt.gov.au/dbird/dpif/pubcat/ agnotes/weeds/477.pdf.

Molau, O. 1988. Flora Neotropica. Monograph 47. Scrophulariaceae. Part I. Calceolarieae. New York Botanical Garden, Bronx, New York.

Morales, J. F. 1998. Bromelias de Costa Rica. Instituto Nacional de Bioversidad, Santo Domingo de Heredia, Costa Rica.

———. 2001. Orquídeas, cactus y bromelias del bosque seco Costa Rica. Instituto Nacional de Bioversidad, Santo Domingo de Heredia, Costa Rica.

Morton, J. 1987. Sapote. In: Fruits of Warm Climates. Julia F. Morton, Miami, FL. www.hort.purdue.edu/newcrop/morton/sapote_ars.html# Origin%20and%20Distribution.

Nelson, G. 1994. The Trees of Florida. Pineapple Press, Sarasota, FL.

Newcomb, L. 1977. Newcomb's Wildflower Guide. Little Brown and Co., Boston.

Peterson, R. T, and M. McKenny. 1968. A Field Guide to Wildflowers of Northeastern and Central North America. Houghton Mifflin Co., Boston.

Pohl, R. W. 1980. Family #15, Graminae. Flora Costaricensis. W. Burger (ed.). Fieldiana Botany New Series No. 4. Field Museum of Natural History, Chicago.

Pounds, W. Z. 1987. Common Flowering Plants of the Monteverde Cloud Forest. Tropical Science Center, San José, Costa Rica.

Prance, G. T. 1976. Family 120. Caryocaraceae. Flora of Panama. Part VI. Annals of the Missouri Botanical Garden 63(3):541–546.

Quesada, F. J. Q., Q. Jiménez Madrigal, N. Zamora Villalobos, R. Aguilar Fernandez, and J. González Ramirez. 1997. Arboles de la Peninsula de OSA. Instituto Nacional de Biodiversidad, Heredia, Costa Rica.

Rachmawati, H., D. Iriantono, and C. P. Hansen. 2002. *Gmelina arborea* Roxb. Seed Leaflet No. 62. Danida Forest Seed Center, Humlebaek, Denmark. www.dfsc.dk/pdf/Seedleaflets/Gmelina%20arborea_int.pdf.

Rachmawati, H., D. Iriantono, and C. P. Hansen. 2002. *Tectona grandis* L. f. Seed Leaflet No. 61. Danida Forest Seed Center, Humlebaek, Denmark. www.dfsc.dk/pdf/Seedleaflets/Tectona%20grandis_61_int.pdf.

Ramey, V., and A. Murray. 2007. *Caesalpinia bonduc*, gray nicker. Aquatic, Wetland, and Invasive Plant. University of Florida, Center for Aquatic and Invasive Plants Center APIRS, Gainesville. http://aquat1.ifas.ufl. edu/caebon.html.

Robson, N. K. B. 1978. Family 123A. Hypericaceae. Flora of Panama. Part VI. Annals of the Missouri Botanical Garden 65(1):9–26.

Robyns, A. 1965. Family 115. Malvaceae. Flora of Panama. Part VI. Annals of the Missouri Botanical Garden 52(4):487–578.

Runesson, U. 2004. *Digitalis purpurea*. Foxglove. Scrophulariaceae (Figwort family). Faculty of Forestry and the Forest Environment, Lakehead University, Thunder Bay, ON. www.borealforest.org/world/herbs_shrubs/ foxglove.htm.

Salazar, R., and D. Jøker. 2000. *Pinus caribaea* Morelet. Seed Leaflet No. 40. Danida Forest Seed Center, Humlebaek, Denmark. www.dfsc.dk/pdf/ Seedleaflets/Pinus%20caribaea_int.pdf.

Sánchez-Vindas, P. E., and L. J. P. Álvarez1997. Claves Dendrológicas para la Identificación de los Principales Árboles y Palmas de la Zona Norte y Atlántica de Costa Rica. Overseas Development Association, San José, Costa Rica.

Schmidt, L., and D. Jøker. 2000. *Swietenia humilis* Zucc. Seed Leaflet No. 33. Danida Forest Seed Center, Humlebaek, Denmark. www.dfsc.dk/pdf/ Seedleaflets/Swietenia%20humilis_int.pdf.

Schubert, B. G. 1980. Flora of Panama. Part V. Family 83. Leguminosae, subfamily Papilionoideae, Desmodium. Annals of the Missouri Botanical Garden 67(3).

Skerman, P. J., D. G. Cameron, and F. Riveros. 1988. *Indigofera hirsuta* L. Tropical forage legumes. Food and Agriculture Organization of the United Nations. www.fao.org/ag/AGP/AGPC/doc/Gbase/DATA/ Pf000045.HTM.

Skerman, P. J., D. G. Cameron, and F. Riveros. 1988. *Pueraria phaseoloides* (Roxb.) Benth. Tropical Forage legumes. Food and Agriculture Organization of the United Nations. www.fao.org/ag/AGP/AGPC/doc/ Gbase/DATA/Pf000058.HTM.

Skog, L. E. 1978. Family 175. Gesneriaceae. Flora of Panama. Part IX. Annals of the Missouri Botanical Garden 65(3):783–996.

Smith, C. E. Jr. 1965. Family 92. Meliaceae. Flora of Panama. Part VI. Annals of the Missouri Botanical Garden 52(1):55–79.

Smith, J. H., J. T. Williams, D. L. Plucknett, and J. P. Talbot. 1992. Tropical Forests and Their Crops. Cornell University Press, Ithaca, NY.

Smith, L. B. 1944. Bromeliaceae. Flora of Panama. Part II, Fascicle 3. Annals of the Missouri Botanical Garden 31:73–137.

———. 1944. Commelinaceae. Flora of Panama. Part II, Fascicle 3. Annals of the Missouri Botanical Garden 31:138–151.

———. 1944. Pontederiaceae. Flora of Panama. Part II, Fascicle 3. Annals of the Missouri Botanical Garden 31:151–157.

Standley, P. C. 1937. *Clusia gracilis*. Publications of the Field Museum of Natural History and Botany Series 18:704.

———. 1944. Araceae. Flora of Panama. Part II, Fascicle 3. Annals of the Missouri Botanical Garden 31:1–60.

Standley, P. C., and J. A. Steyermark. 1946. Flora of Guatemala. Fieldiana: Botany. Vol. 24, Part V. Chicago Natural History Museum, Chicago.

———. 1949. Flora of Guatemala. Fieldiana: Botany Vol. 24, Part VI. Chicago Natural History Museum, Chicago.

Standley, P. C., and L. O. Williams. 1961. Flora of Guatemala. Fieldiana: Botany Vol. 24, Part VII, No. 1. Chicago Natural History Museum, Chicago.

———. 1961. Flora of Guatemala. Fieldiana: Botany Vol. 24, Part VII, No. 4. Chicago Natural History Museum, Chicago.

———. 1973. Flora of Guatemala. Fieldiana: Botany Vol. 24, Part IX, Nos. 3 and 4. Chicago Natural History Museum, Chicago.

Starr, F., K. Starr, and L. Loope. 2003. *Rubus glaucus*, Andean raspberry, Rosaceae. United States Geological Survey, Biological Resources Division, Haleakala Field Station, Maui, Hawai'i. www.hear.org/starr/ hiplants/reports/html/rubus_glaucus.htm.

Starr, F., K. Starr, and L. Loope. 2003. *Thunbergia grandiflora*, trumpet vine, Acanthaceae. Plants of Hawai'i Reports. USGS, Biological Resources

Division, Haleakala Field Station, Maui, Hawai'i. www.hear.org/starr/hiplants/reports/html/.

Stearn, W. T. 1995. Botanical Latin, 4th ed. Timber Press, Portland, OR.

Stevens, W. D., C. U. Ulloa, A. Pool, and O. M. Montiel (eds.). 1995. Flora de Nicaragua. Missouri Botanical Garden Press, St. Louis, MO. www.mobot.org/MOBOT/research/nicaragua/portada.shtml

Tan, R. 2001. Sea almond tree, *Terminalia catappa*. Mangrove and Wetland Wildlife at Sungei Buloh Wetlands Reserve. www.naturia.per.sg/buloh/.

Taylor, C. M. 1985. A revision of the Central American species of *Monnina* (Polygalaceae). Rhodora 78(850):159–188.

Taylor, P. 1976. Family 176. Lentibulariaceae. Flora of Panama. Part VI. Annals of the Missouri Botanical Garden 63(3):565–580.

Taylor, W. K. 1992. The Guide to Florida Wildflowers. Taylor Publishing Co., Dallas, TX.

Ting, E. P. 1982. Plant Physiology. Addison-Wesley Publishing Co., Reading, MA.

USDA Forest Service. 2006. Institute of Pacific Islands Forestry, Pacific Island Ecosystems at Risk (PIER). www.hear.org/pier/

Usher, G. 1966. A Dictionary of Botany. D. Van Nostrand Co., Princeton, NJ.

van Roosmalen, M. G. 1985. Fruits of the Guinean Flora. Institute of Systematic Botany, Utrect University, Netherlands.

Wagner, W. L., D. R. Herbst, and S. H. Sohmer. 1999. Manual of the Flowering Plants of Hawai'i. Rev. ed. University of Hawai'i Press, Honolulu.

Watson, L., and M. J. Dallwitz. 1999. *Rauvolfia tetraphylla*. Ecology and Evolutionary Biology Conservatory, University of Connecticut. http://florawww.eeb.uconn.edu/acc_num/198800150.html.

White, F. 1978. Family 155. Ebenaceae. Flora of Panama. Part VIII. Annals of the Missouri Botanical Garden 65(1):145–154.

White, M. E. 1990. The Flowering of Gondwana. Princeton University Press. Princeton, NJ.

Wilbur, R. L. 1976. Family 183. Campanulaceae. Flora of Panama. Part IX. Annals of the Missouri Botanical Garden 63(3):593–655.

Wilbur, R. L., and J. L. Luten. 1978. Ericaceae. Flora of Panama. Annals of the Missouri Botanical Garden 65:27–145.

Wikipedia: The Free Encyclopedia. 2006. *Monoclea*. Wikimedia Foundation. http://en.wikipedia.org/wiki/Monoclea.

Wunderlin, R. P. 1978. Family 182. Cucurbitaceae. Flora of Panama. Part IX. Annals of the Missouri Botanical Garden 65(1):285–366.

Young, A. M. Sarapiquí Chronicle A Naturalist in Costa Rica. Smithsonian Institution Press, Washington, DC.

Zamora, N. 1989. Flora Arborescente de Costa Rica. I Especies de Hojas Simples. Instituto Tecnológico de Costa Rica, Cartago, C.R.

Zamora, N., and T. D. Pennington. 2001. Guabas y cuajiniquiles de Costa Rica. Instituto Nacional de Biodiversidad, Heredia, Costa Rica.

Zhu, G. 2003. The genus *Dracontium*. International Aroid Society. www.aroid.org/genera/dracontium/dracwel.html.

INDEX

INDEX